THE AMERICAN NATION

LAKE WINNIPE
LAKE MANITOBA
LAKE OF THE WOODS
STRAIT OF JUAN DE FUCA
PUGET SOUND
Continental Divide
Red R. of the North
Columbia R.
CASCADE MTS.
Blue Mts.
Bitterroot Ra.
Yellowstone R.
Big Horn Mts.
Black Hills
Badlands
Snake R.
Teton Ra.
Wind River Ra.
Cape Mendocino
Sacramento R.
GREAT SALT LAKE
Wasatch Ra.
Wyoming
Basin
Medicine Bow Ra.
Laramie Ra.
Sand Hills
Green R.
Uinta Mts.
Great Salt Lake Desert
SIERRA NEVADA
San Francisco Bay
Monterey Bay
San Joaquin R.
Platte R.
Missouri R.
Front Ra.
Sawatch Ra.
High Plains
Kansas
Sangre de Cristo Ra.
PACIFIC OCEAN
Painted Desert
Colorado R.
Mojave Desert
Continental Divide
Canadian R.
Red R.
Quachita Mt
Gila R.
Staked Plains
Baja California
Brazos R.
Trinity R.
Rio Grande
Pecos R.
Nueces R.
Rio Grande
R O C K Y   M O U N T A I N S
Kauai I.
Niihau I.
Oahu I.
Molokai I.
Maui I.
Hawaii I.
PRINCIPAL ISLANDS OF HAWAII
0 100 200
MILES
Brooks Ra.
Seward Peninsula
Yukon R.
Alaska Ra.
BERING SEA
Coast Ranges
Kodiak I.
Alaska Peninsula
Aleutian Islands
ALASKA
0 200 400
MILES

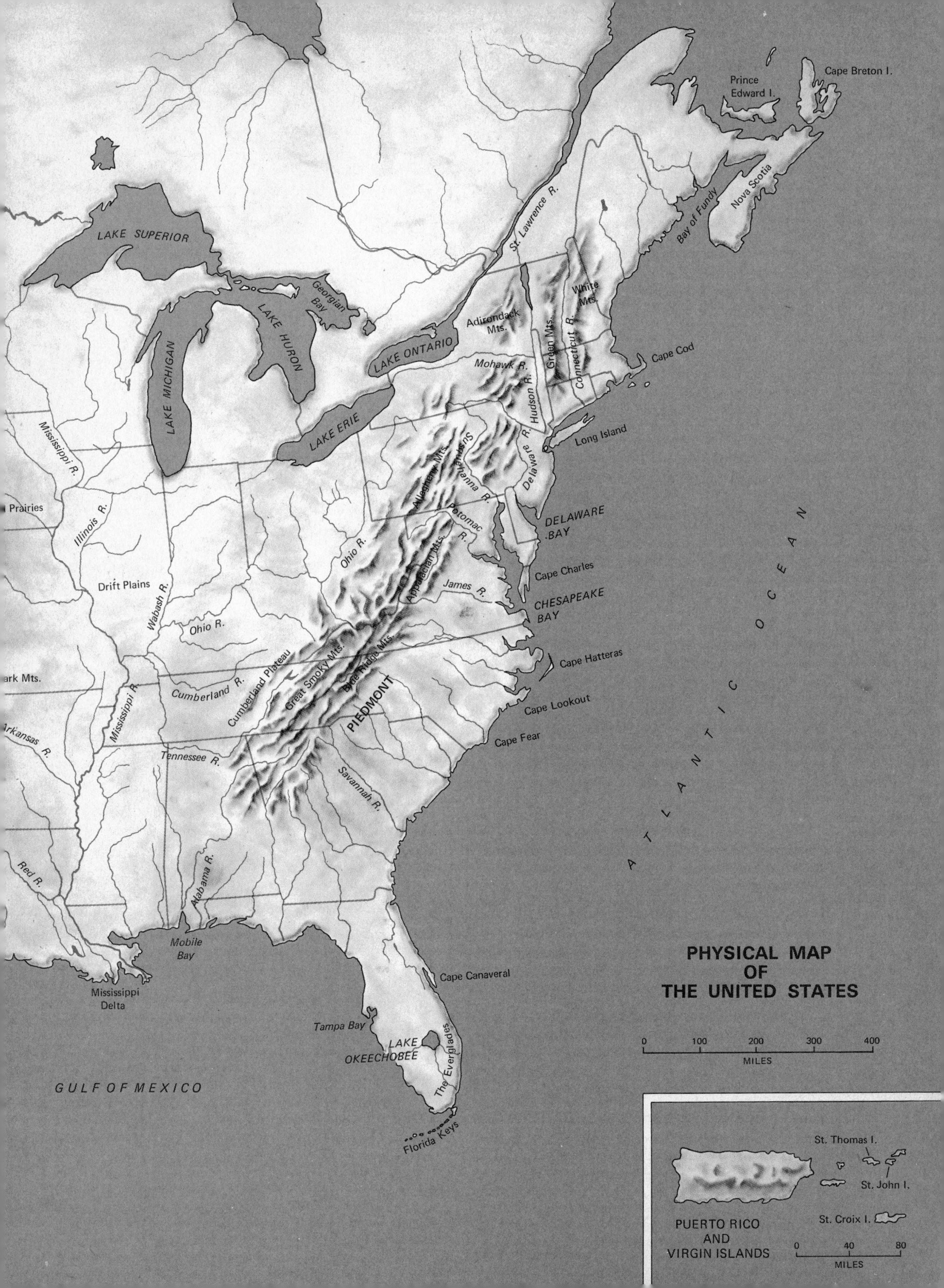
Cape Breton I.
Prince Edward I.
Nova Scotia
Bay of Fundy
St. Lawrence R.
LAKE SUPERIOR
Georgian Bay
LAKE HURON
LAKE MICHIGAN
LAKE ONTARIO
LAKE ERIE
Adirondack Mts.
White Mts.
Green Mts.
Connecticut R.
Mohawk R.
Hudson R.
Cape Cod
Long Island
Delaware R.
Susquehanna R.
Allegheny Mts.
Potomac R.
DELAWARE BAY
Appalachian Mts.
Ohio R.
Cape Charles
James R.
CHESAPEAKE BAY
Mississippi R.
Prairies
Illinois R.
Drift Plains
Wabash R.
Ohio R.
Cumberland Plateau
Great Smoky Mts.
Blue Ridge Mts.
Cape Hatteras
ark Mts.
Cumberland R.
PIEDMONT
Cape Lookout
Mississippi R.
Arkansas R.
Cape Fear
Tennessee R.
Savannah R.
ATLANTIC OCEAN
Red R.
Alabama R.
Mobile Bay
Mississippi Delta
Cape Canaveral
Tampa Bay
LAKE OKEECHOBEE
The Everglades
GULF OF MEXICO
Florida Keys
0
100
200
300
400
MILES
St. Thomas I.
St. John I.
St. Croix I.
PUERTO RICO AND VIRGIN ISLANDS
0
40
80
MILES
PHYSICAL MAP OF THE UNITED STATES

THE AMERICAN NATION

A History of the United States Since 1865

VOLUME TWO

Fifth Edition

John A. Garraty
COLUMBIA UNIVERSITY

1817

HARPER & ROW, PUBLISHERS, New York
Cambridge, Philadelphia, San Francisco,
London, Mexico City, São Paulo, Sydney

Sponsoring Editor: Jean Hurtado
Special Projects Editor: Mary Lou Mosher
Project Editor: Beena Kamlani
Designer: Robert Sugar
Production Manager: Willie Lane
Photo Researcher: Mira Schachne
Portfolio Five: Mary Barnett and Ben Kann
Portfolio Six: Text revision by Mamie Harmon
Compositor: Lehigh/Rocappi, Inc.
Printer and Binder: R. R. Donnelley & Sons, Co.
Art Studio: Vantage Art, Inc.

The author makes grateful acknowledgment to:

New Directions, New York; Faber & Faber, London; and A. V. Moore, Knebworth, Herts, England, for permission to quote from "Hugh Selwyn Mauberley" by Ezra Pound. From *Personae* by Ezra Pound. Copyright 1926 by Ezra Pound. Reprinted by permission of New Directions.

New Directions, New York, for permission to quote "The Great Figure" by William Carlos Williams, from *Collected Earlier Poems.* Copyright 1938 by New Directions Publishing Corporation. Reprinted by permission of New Directions.

Liveright Publishing Corporation for permission to quote "the first president to be loved by his . . ." Reprinted from *VIVA,* Poems by E. E. Cummings, by permission of Liveright Publishing Corporation. Copyright 1931, 1959 by E. E. Cummings. Copyright © 1973, 1979 by Nancy T. Andrews. Copyright © 1973, 1979 by George James Firmage.

Cover: Photograph of Tucson, Arizona, by Bishop. Courtesy, DPI photo agency.
Cover title letter forms: Ray Barber

THE AMERICAN NATION: **A History of the United States Since 1865**
Fifth Edition

Library of Congress Cataloging in Publication Data

Garraty, John Arthur, 1920–
The American Nation.

Includes indexes.
Contents: v. 1. A history of the United States to 1877—v. 2. A history of the United States since 1865.
1. United States—History. I. Title.
[E178.1.G24 1982] 973 82-15567
ISBN 0-06-042277-7 (v. 2)

For Kathy, Jack, and Sarah

Contents

Maps and Graphs

Maps

Graphs

Preface

Once again, in this fifth edition of *The American Nation* I have tried to present my personal view of American history, while at the same time paying proper attention to the most important books and articles on this immense subject that have come out during the past four years. I have taken a fresh look at each chapter and topic in this book, questioning each general statement and interpretation and seeking to satisfy myself that it fairly represents the best thinking of the profession today.

By far the most extensive changes involve the post World War II period. The passage of time since the book was first published in 1966 has altered my perspective considerably. Some of the events, laws, and people that seemed important then now appear less significant. Other matters that I dismissed (or was unaware of) have been proved by later developments to merit extensive discussion. I have integrated the treatment of domestic and foreign affairs that previously were described in separate chapters. In the process of these changes I have combined four chapters into three, while at the same time carrying the story through the first years of the Reagan administration. Some sections dealing with social and cultural developments have been moved forward to the interwar chapters. I believe these extensive alterations make the account of modern history clearer.

I have also made important changes in the treatment of the era of the American Revolution, changes which stress the effects of domestic events on the causes and course of that conflict. There is a new portfolio dealing with the various patterns of colonial family life. But there are changes of one kind or another on nearly every page. Although I have always been at pains to write as clearly and interestingly as I can, I continue to make small changes that I think improve the flow of the narrative.

However, I do not believe that my basic approach to my subject has changed. This edition has been constructed on the same principles as its predecessors. It assumes, to begin with, that American history is important for its own sake—an epic and unique tale of human experience in a vast land, almost uninhabited at the start, now teeming with more than 200 million people. Beyond this, our history provides an object lesson in how the past affects the present, or rather, how a series of pasts has changed a series of presents in an unending pattern of development. Thus, while historians have never been any better at foretelling the future than politicians, economists, or soothsayers, good ones have always been able to illuminate their own times, adding depth and perspective to their readers' understanding of how they got to be where they were at any particular point.

I have attempted to tell the story of the American past clearly and intelligibly, with adequate attention to its complexities and subtleties. Of course, it is not the final word—that will never be written. It is, however, up-to-date and as accurate and thoughtful and wide-ranging as I could make it. Though I reject the theory that a few great individuals, cut from larger cloth than the general run of human beings, have shaped the destiny of humankind, as a biographer, I think that history becomes more vivid and comprehensible when attention is paid to how the major figures on the historical stage have reacted to events and to one another. I have attempted to portray the leading actors in my account as distinct individuals and to explain how their personal qualities influenced the course of history.

I also believe that generalizations require concrete illustration if they are to be grasped fully. Readers will find many anecdotes and quotations in the following pages along with the facts and dates and statistics that every good history must contain. I am confident that most of this illustrative material is interesting, but I think that it is instructive too. Above all, I have sought to keep in mind the grandeur of my subject. One need not be an uncritical admirer of the American nation and its people to recognize that, as I have said, the history of the United States is a great epic. I have tried to treat this history with the dignity and respect that it deserves, believing, however, that a subject of such magnitude is not well served by foolish praise or by slighting or excusing its many dark and even discreditable aspects.

John A. Garraty

16/RECONSTRUCTION AND THE SOUTH

On April 5, 1865, Abraham Lincoln visited Richmond. The fallen capital lay in ruins, sections blackened by fire, but the president was able to walk the streets unmolested and almost unattended. The townspeople seemed to have accepted defeat without resentment. A few days later, in Washington, Lincoln delivered an important speech on Reconstruction, urging compassion and open-mindedness. On April 14 he held a Cabinet meeting at which postwar readjustment was considered at length. That evening, while Lincoln was watching a performance of the play *Our American Cousin* at Ford's Theater, a half-mad actor, John Wilkes Booth, slipped into his box and shot him in the back of the head with a small pistol. Early the next morning, without having regained consciousness, Lincoln died.

The murder was part of a complicated plot organized by die-hard prosoutherners. Seldom have fanatics displayed so little understanding of their own interests, for with Lincoln perished the South's best hope for a mild peace. After his body had been taken home to Illinois, the national mood hardened. It was not a question of avenging the beloved Emancipator; rather a feeling took possession of the public mind that the time of pain and suffering was not yet over, that the awesome drama was still unfolding, that retribution and a final humbling of the South were inevitable.

Presidential Reconstruction

Despite its bloodiness, the Civil War had caused less intersectional hatred than might have been expected. Although civilian property was often seized or destroyed, the invading armies treated the southern population with remarkable forbearance, both during the war and after Appomattox. While he was ensconced in Richmond behind Lee's army, northerners boasted that they would "hang Jeff Davis to a sour apple tree," and when he was captured in Georgia in May 1865, he was at once clapped into irons preparatory to being tried for treason and murder. But feeling against him subsided quickly. In 1867 the military turned him over to the civil courts, which released him on bail. He was never brought to trial. A few other Confederate officials spent short periods behind bars, but the only southerner executed for war crimes was Major Henry Wirz, the commandant of Andersonville military prison.

The legal questions related to bringing the defeated states back into the Union were extremely complex. Since southerners believed that secession was legal, logic should have compelled them to argue that they were out of the Union and would thus have to be formally readmitted. Northerners should have taken the contrary position, for they had fought to prove that secession was illegal. Yet the people of both sections did just the opposite. Senator Charles Sumner and Congressman Thaddeus Stevens, in 1861 uncompromising expounders of the theory that the Union was indissoluble, now insisted that the Confederate states had "committed suicide" and should be treated like "conquered provinces." Erstwhile states' rights southerners claimed that their states were still within the Union. Lincoln believed the issue a "pernicious abstraction" and tried to ignore it.

The process of readmission began in 1862, when Lincoln appointed provisional governors for those parts of the South that had been occupied by federal troops. On December 8, 1863, he issued a proclamation setting forth a general policy. With the exception of high Confederate officials and a few other special groups, all southerners could reinstate themselves as United States citizens by taking a simple loyalty oath. When, in any state, a number equal to ten percent of those voting in the 1860 election had taken this oath, they could set up a state government. Such governments had to be republican in form, must recognize the "permanent freedom" of the slaves, and must provide for black education. The plan, however, did not require that blacks be given the right to vote.

This "ten percent plan" reflected Lincoln's lack of vindictiveness and his political wisdom. He realized that any government based on such a small minority of the population would be, as he put it, merely "a tangible nucleus which the remainder . . . may rally around as fast as it can," a sort of puppet regime, like the paper government established in those sections of Virginia under federal control.* The regimes established under this plan in Tennessee, Louisiana, and Arkansas bore, in the president's mind, the same relation to finally reconstructed states that an egg bears to a chicken. "We shall sooner have the fowl by hatching it than by smashing it," he remarked. He knew that eventually representatives of the southern states would again be sitting in Congress, and he wished to lay the groundwork for a strong Republican party in the section. Yet he realized that Congress had no intention of seating representatives from the "ten percent" states at once.

The Radicals in Congress disliked the ten percent plan, partly because of its moderation and partly because it enabled Lincoln to determine Union policy toward the recaptured regions. In July 1864 they passed the Wade-Davis bill, which provided for constitutional conventions only after a *majority* of the voters in a southern state had

*By approving the separation of the western counties that had refused to secede, this government provided a legal pretext for the creation of West Virginia.

■ **Andrew Johnson, as recorded by Mathew Brady's camera in 1865. Johnson, Charles Dickens reported, radiated purposefulness but no "genial sunlight."**

taken a loyalty oath. Confederate officials and anyone who had "voluntarily borne arms against the United States" were barred from voting in the election or serving at the convention. Besides prohibiting slavery, the new state constitutions would have to repudiate Confederate debts. Lincoln disposed of the Wade-Davis bill with a pocket veto and thus managed to retain the initiative in Reconstruction for the remainder of the war. There matters stood when Andrew Johnson became president following the assassination.

Lincoln had picked Johnson for a running mate in 1864 because he was a border-state Unionist Democrat and something of a hero as a result of his courageous service as military governor of Tennessee. From origins even more lowly than Lincoln's, Johnson had risen to be congressman, governor of Tennessee, and United States senator. He was able and ambitious but fundamentally unsure of himself, as could be seen in his boastfulness and stubbornness. His political strength came from the poor whites and yeomen farmers of eastern Tennessee, and he was inordinately fond of extolling the common man and attacking "stuck-up aristocrats." Thaddeus Stevens called him a "rank demagogue" and a "damned scoundrel," and it is true that he was a masterful rabble-rouser. But few men of his generation labored so consistently in behalf of small farmers. Free homesteads, public education, absolute social equality—such were his objectives. The father of communism, Karl Marx, a close observer of American affairs at this time, wrote approvingly of Johnson's "deadly hatred of the oligarchy."

Johnson was a Democrat, but because of his record and his reassuring penchant for excoriating southern aristocrats, the Republicans in Congress were ready to cooperate with him. "Johnson, we have faith in you," said Radical Senator Ben Wade, author of the Wade–Davis bill, the day after Lincoln's death. "By the gods, there will be no trouble now in running the government!"

Johnson's reply, "Treason must be made infamous," delighted the Radicals, but the president proved temperamentally unable to work with them. As Eric L. McKitrick has shown in *Andrew Johnson and Reconstruction,* he was an "outsider," a "lone wolf" in every way. "The only role whose attributes he fully understood was that of the maverick," McKitrick writes. "For the full nourishment and maximum functioning of his mind, matters had to be so arranged that all the organized forces of society could in some sense, real or symbolic, be leagued against him." Like Randolph of Roanoke, his antithesis intellectually and socially, opposition was his specialty; he soon alienated every powerful Republican in Washington.

Radical Republicans listened to Johnson's diatribes against secessionists and the great planters and assumed that he was antisouthern. Nothing could have been further from the truth. He shared most of his poor white Tennessee constituents' prejudices against blacks. "Damn the negroes, I am fighting these traitorous aristocrats, their masters," he told a friend during the war. "I wish to God," he said on another occasion, "every head of a family in the United States had one slave to take the drudgery and menial service off his family."

The new president did not want to injure or humiliate the entire South. On May 29, 1865, he issued an amnesty proclamation only slightly

■ **Brady photographed two of the stalwart Radical Republicans, Thaddeus Stevens of Pennsylvania (top) and Benjamin Wade of Ohio (bottom). Stevens served in the House from 1859 until his death in 1868. During the Civil War, Senator "Bluff Ben" Wade chaired the Joint Committee on the Conduct of the War.**

more rigorous than Lincoln's. It assumed, correctly enough, that with the war over most southern voters would freely take the loyalty oath; thus it contained no ten percent clause. More classes of Confederates, including those who owned taxable property in excess of $20,000, were excluded from the general pardon. By the time Congress convened in December, all the southern states had organized governments, ratified the Thirteenth Amendment abolishing slavery, and elected senators and representatives. Johnson promptly recommended these new governments to the attention of Congress.

Republican Radicals

Peace found the Republicans in Congress no more united than they had been during the war. A small group of "ultra" Radicals were demanding immediate and absolute racial equality. Senator Sumner led this faction. A second group of Radicals, headed by Thaddeus Stevens in the House and Ben Wade in the Senate, agreed with the ultras' objectives but were prepared to accept half a loaf if necessary to win the support of less radical colleagues.* The moderate Republicans wanted to protect ex-slaves from exploitation and guarantee their basic rights but were unprepared to push for full political and social equality. A handful of Republicans sided with the Democrats in support of Johnson's approach, but all the rest insisted at least on the minimum demands of the moderates. Thus Johnsonian Reconstruction had no chance of winning congressional approval.

Johnson's proposal that Congress accept Reconstruction as completed and admit the new southern representatives was also doomed for reasons having little to do with black rights. The Thirteenth Amendment had the effect of increasing the representation of the southern states in Congress because it made the Three-fifths Compromise (see page 121) meaningless. Henceforth those who had been slaves would be counted as

*When Stevens died, he was buried in a black cemetery. Here is his epitaph, written by himself: "I repose in this quiet and secluded spot, not from any natural preference for solitude, but finding other cemeteries limited as to race, by charter rules, I have chosen this that I might illustrate in my death the principles which I advocated through a long life, equality of man before his Creator."

whole persons in apportioning seats in the House of Representatives. If Congress seated the southerners, the balance of power might swing to the Democrats. To expect the Republicans to surrender power in such a fashion was unrealistic. Former Copperheads gushing with extravagant praise for Johnson put them instantly on guard. And northerners remained suspicious of ex-Confederates. Although most of them were ready to reenter the Union, they were not overflowing with goodwill toward their conquerors.

Some of the new state governments were less than straightforward about accepting the most obvious results of the war. South Carolina, instead of repudiating secession, merely repealed its secession ordinance. A minority of southerners would have nothing to do with amnesties and pardons:

> Oh, I'm a good old rebel,
> Now that's just what I am;
> For the "fair land of freedom,"
> I do not care a dam.
> I'm glad I fit against it—
> I only wish we'd won
> And I don't want no pardon
> For anything I done.

Southern voters had further provoked northern resentment by their choice of congressmen. Georgia elected Alexander H. Stephens, vice-president of the Confederacy, to the Senate, though he was still in a federal prison awaiting trial for treason! Several dozen men who had served in the Confederate Congress had been elected to either the House or the Senate, together with four generals and many other high officials. The southern people understandably selected locally respected and experienced leaders, but it was equally reasonable that these choices would sit poorly with northerners.

Finally, the so-called Black Codes enacted by southern governments to control former slaves alarmed the North. These varied in severity from state to state. When seen in historical perspective, even the strictest codes represented a considerable improvement over slavery. Most permitted blacks to sue and to testify in court, at least in cases involving members of their own race. Blacks were allowed to own certain kinds of property; marriages were made legal; other rights were guaranteed. However, blacks could not bear arms, be employed in occupations other than farming and domestic service, or leave their jobs without forfeiting back pay. The Louisiana code required them to sign labor contracts for the year during the first ten days of January. In Mississippi any "vagrant" who could not pay the stiff fine assessed was to be "hired out . . . at public outcry" to the white person who would take him for the shortest period in return for paying his fine. Such laws, apparently designed to get around the Thirteenth Amendment, outraged even moderate northerners.

For all these reasons the Republicans in Congress rejected Johnsonian Reconstruction. Quickly they created a joint committee on Reconstruction, headed by Senator William P. Fessenden of Maine, a moderate, to study the question of readmitting the southern states.

The committee held extensive public hearings that produced much evidence of the mistreatment of blacks. Colonel George A. Custer, stationed in Texas, testified: "It is of weekly, if not of daily occurrence that Freedmen are murdered." The nurse Clara Barton told a gruesome tale about a pregnant woman who had been brutally whipped. Others described the intimidation of blacks by poor whites. The hearings played into the hands of the Radicals, who had been claiming all along that the South was perpetuating slavery under another name.

President Johnson's attitude speeded the swing toward the Radical position. While the hearings were in progress, Congress passed a bill expanding and extending the Freedmen's Bureau, which had been established in March 1865 to care for refugees. The bureau, a branch of the War Department, was already exercising considerable coercive and supervisory power in the South. Now Congress sought to add to its authority in order to protect the black population. The bill had wide support even among moderates. Nevertheless Johnson vetoed it, arguing that it was an unconstitutional extension of military authority in peacetime. Congress then passed a Civil Rights Act that, besides declaring that blacks were citizens of the United States, denied the states the power to restrict their rights to testify in court and to hold property.

Once again the president refused to go along, though his veto was sure to drive more moderates into the arms of the Radicals. On April 9, 1866, Congress repassed the Civil Rights Act by a two-thirds majority, the first time in American history that a major piece of legislation became law over the veto of a president. This event marked a revolution in the history of Reconstruction. Thereafter Congress, not President Johnson, had the upper hand, and it placed progressively stricter controls on the South.

In the clash between the president and Congress, Johnson was his own worst enemy. His language was often intemperate, his handling of men inept, his analysis of southern conditions incorrect. He had assumed that the small southern farmers who made up the majority in the Confederacy shared his prejudices against the planter class. They did not, as their choices in the postwar elections demonstrated. In fact, Johnson's hatred of the southern aristocracy may have been based more on jealousy than on principle. Under the Reconstruction plan, persons excluded from the blanket amnesty could apply individually for the restoration of their rights. When wealthy and socially prominent southerners flocked to Washington, hat in hand, he found their flattery and humility exhilarating. He issued pardons wholesale, saying: "I did not expect to keep out all who were excluded from the amnesty. . . . I intended they should sue for pardon, and so realize the enormity of their crime."

The president misread northern opinion. He believed that Congress had no right to pass laws affecting the South before southern representatives had been readmitted to Congress. However, in the light of the refusal of most southern whites to grant any real power or responsibility to the freedmen (an attitude that Johnson did not condemn) the public would not accept this point of view. Johnson placed his own judgment over that of the overwhelming majority of northern voters, and this was a great error, morally and tactically. By encouraging southerners to resist efforts to improve the lot of blacks, Johnson played into the hands of northern extremists.

The Radicals encountered grave problems in fighting for their program. Northerners might object to the Black Codes and to seating "rebels" in Congress, but few believed in racial equality. Between 1865 and 1868 Wisconsin, Minnesota, Connecticut, Nebraska, New Jersey, Ohio, Michigan, and Pennsylvania all rejected bills granting blacks the vote.

The Radicals were in effect demanding not merely equal rights for freedmen but *extra* rights: not merely the vote but special protection of that right against the pressure that southern whites would surely apply to undermine it. This idea flew in the face of conventional American beliefs in equality before the law and individual self-reliance. Such protection would involve interference by the federal government in local affairs, a concept at variance with American practice. Events were to show that the Radicals were correct—that what amounted to a political revolution in state-federal relations was essential if blacks were to achieve real equality. But in the climate of that day their proposals encountered bitter resistance, and not only from southerners.

Thus, while the Radicals sought partisan advantage in their battle with Johnson and sometimes played on war-bred passions in achieving their ends, they were taking large political risks in defense of genuinely held principles. One historian has aptly called them the "moral trustees" of the Civil War.

The Fourteenth Amendment

In June 1866 Congress submitted to the states a new amendment to the Constitution. The Fourteenth Amendment was a milestone along the road to the centralization of political power, for it significantly reduced the power of *all* the states. In this sense it confirmed the great change wrought by the Civil War: the growth of a more complex, more closely integrated social and economic structure requiring closer national supervision. Few people understood this aspect of the amendment at the time.

First the amendment supplied a broad definition of American citizenship: "All persons born or naturalized in the United States, and subject to the jurisdiction thereof, are citizens of the United States and of the State wherein they reside." Obviously this included blacks. Then it struck at discriminatory legislation like the Black Codes: "No State shall make or enforce any law which shall abridge the privileges or immunities of citizens of the United States; nor shall any State deprive any person of life, liberty, or property, without due process of law." The next section attempted to force the southern states to permit blacks to vote. If a state denied the vote to any class of its adult male citizens, its representation was to be reduced proportionately. Under another clause, former federal officials who had served the Confederacy were barred from holding either state or federal office unless specifically pardoned by a two-thirds vote of Congress. Finally, the Confederate debt was repudiated.

While the amendment did not specifically outlaw segregation or prevent a state from disfranchising blacks if it was willing to see its representation in Congress reduced, the southern states would have none of it. Without them the necessary three-fourths majority of the states could not be obtained. The governor of Mississippi denounced it as "an insulting outrage" to those "who have shed glory and lustre upon our section and our race." Women's rights groups in the North objected to the implication that black men were more fitted to vote than white women. Elizabeth Cady Stanton warned that the amendment would create "an antagonism between black men and all women."

President Johnson vowed to make the choice between the Fourteenth Amendment and his own policy the main issue of the 1866 congressional elections. He embarked on "a swing around the circle" to rally the public to his cause. He failed dismally. Northern opinion had hardened; a large majority was determined that blacks must have at least formal legal equality. The Republicans won better than two-thirds of the seats in both houses, together with control of all the northern state governments. Johnson emerged from the campaign discredited, the Radicals stronger and determined to have their way. The southern states, Congressman James A. Garfield of Ohio said in February 1867, have "flung back into our teeth the magnanimous offer of a generous nation. It is now our turn to act."

The Reconstruction Acts

Had the southern states been willing to accept the Fourteenth Amendment, coercive measures might have been avoided. Their recalcitrance and continuing indications that local authorities were persecuting blacks finally led to the passage, on March 2, 1867, of the First Reconstruction Act. This law divided the former Confederacy—exclusive of Tennessee, which had ratified the Fourteenth Amendment—into five military districts, each controlled by a major general. It gave these officers almost dictatorial power to protect the civil rights of "all persons," maintain order, and supervise the administration of justice. To rid themselves of military rule, the former states were required to adopt constitutions guaranteeing blacks the right to vote and disfranchising broad classes of ex-Confederates. If the new constitutions proved satisfactory to Congress, and if the new governments ratified the Fourteenth Amendment, their representatives would be admitted to Congress and military rule ended. Johnson's veto of the act was easily overridden.

Although drastic, the Reconstruction Act was so vague that it proved unworkable. Military control was easily established, for federal bayonets were already exerting considerable authority throughout the South. But in deference to moderate Republican views, the law had not spelled out the process by which the new constitutions were to be drawn up. Southern whites preferred the status quo, even under army control, to enfranchising blacks and retiring their own respected leaders. They made no effort to follow the steps laid down in the law. Congress therefore passed a second act, requiring the military authorities to register voters and supervise the election of delegates to constitutional conventions. A third act further clarified procedures.

Still white southerners resisted. The laws required that the constitutions be approved by a majority of the registered voters. Simply by staying away from the polls, whites prevented ratification in state after state. At last, in March 1868, a full year after the First Reconstruction Act, Congress changed the rules again. The constitutions were to be ratified by a majority of the *voters*. In June 1868 Arkansas, having fulfilled the requirements, was readmitted to the Union, and by July a sufficient number of states had ratified the Fourteenth Amendment to make it part of the Constitution. But it was not until July 1870 that the last southern state, Georgia, qualified to the satisfaction of Congress.

Congress versus the President

To carry out this program in the face of determined southern resistance required a degree of single-mindedness over a long period seldom demonstrated by an American legislature. The persistence resulted in part from the suffering and frustrations of the war years. The refusal of the South to accept the spirit of even the mild reconstruction designed by Johnson goaded the North to ever more overbearing efforts to bring the ex-Confederates to heel. President Johnson's stubbornness also influenced the mood of Congress; Republican leaders became obsessed with the need to defeat him. The unsettled times and the large Republican majorities, always threatened by the possibility of a Democratic resurgence if "unreconstructed" southern congressmen were readmitted, sustained their determination.

These considerations led Republicans to attempt a kind of grand revision of the federal government, one that almost destroyed the balance between judicial, executive, and legislative power established in 1789. A series of measures passed between 1866 and 1868 increased the authority of Congress over the army, over the process of amending the Constitution, and over Cabinet members and lesser appointive officers. Even the Supreme Court felt the force of the congressional drive for power; its size was reduced, as was the range of its jurisdiction over civil rights cases. Finally, in a showdown caused by emotion more than by practical considerations, the Republicans attempted to remove President Johnson from office.

Johnson was a poor president and out of touch with public opinion, but he had done nothing to merit ejection from office. While he had a low opinion of blacks, his opinion was so widely shared by whites that it is unhistorical to condemn him as a reactionary on this ground. Johnson believed that he was fighting to preserve constitutional government. He was honest and devoted to duty, and his record easily withstood the most searching examination. When Congress passed laws taking away powers granted him by the Constitution, he refused to submit.

The chief issue was the Tenure of Office Act of 1867, which prohibited the president from removing officials who had been appointed with the consent of the Senate without first obtaining Senate approval. In February 1868 Johnson "violated" this act by dismissing Secretary of War Edwin M. Stanton, who had been openly in sympathy with the Radicals for some time. The House, acting under the procedure set up in the Constitution for removing the president, promptly impeached him before the bar of the Senate, Chief Justice Salmon P. Chase presiding.

This "great act of ill-directed passion," as it has been characterized by one historian, was conducted in a partisan and vindictive manner. Johnson's lawyers easily established that he had removed Stanton only in an effort to prove the Tenure of Office Act unconstitutional. They demonstrated that the act did not protect Stanton to begin with, since it gave Cabinet members tenure "during the term of the President by whom they may have been appointed," and Stanton had been appointed by Lincoln! Nevertheless the Radicals pressed the charges (11 separate articles) relentlessly. To the argument that Johnson had committed no crime, the learned Senator Sumner retorted that the proceedings were "political in character" rather than judicial. Thaddeus Stevens, directing the attack on behalf of the House, warned the senators that although "no corrupt or wicked motive" could be attributed to Johnson, they would "be tortured on the gibbet of everlasting obloquy" if they did not convict him. Tremendous pressure was applied to the handful of Republican senators who were unwilling to disregard the evidence.

Seven of them resisted to the end, and the Senate failed by a single vote to convict Johnson. This was probably fortunate. Had he been forced from office on such flimsy grounds, the independence of the executive might have been permanently weakened. Then the legislative branch would have become supreme.

The Fifteenth Amendment

The failure of the impeachment did not affect the course of Reconstruction. The president was acquitted on May 16, 1868. A few days later the Republican National Convention nominated General Ulysses S. Grant for the presidency. At the Democratic convention Johnson had considerable support, but the delegates nominated Horatio Seymour, a former governor of New York. In November Grant won an easy victory in the electoral college, 214 to 80, but the popular vote was close: 3 million to 2.7 million. Although he would probably have carried the electoral college in any case,

■ **In honor of the Fifteenth Amendment, the black community of New York City held a parade in April, 1870. Many of the marchers represented social and political clubs, and carried identifying banners for these groups such as the "Grant and Colfax Club, No. 1" and the "2nd Ward Grant Club."**

Grant's margin in the popular vote was supplied by southern blacks enfranchised under the Reconstruction Acts, about 450,000 of whom supported him. A majority of white voters probably preferred Seymour. Since many citizens undoubtedly voted Republican because of personal admiration for General Grant, the election statistics suggest that a substantial white majority opposed the policies of the Radicals.

The ratification of the Fourteenth Amendment and the Reconstruction Acts achieved the purpose of enabling black southerners to vote. The Radicals, however, were not satisfied; despite the unpopularity of the idea in the North, they wished to guarantee the right of blacks to vote in every state. Another amendment seemed the only way to accomplish this objective, but passage of such an amendment appeared impossible. The Republican platform in the 1868 election had smugly distinguished between blacks voting in the South ("demanded by every consideration of public safety, of gratitude, and of justice") and in the North (where the question "properly belongs to the people").

However, after the election had demonstrated how crucial the votes of ex-slaves could be, Republican strategy shifted. Grant had carried Indiana by less than 10,000 votes and lost New York by a similar number. If blacks in these and other closely divided states had voted, Republican strength would have been greatly enhanced.

Suddenly Congress blossomed with suffrage amendments. After considerable bickering over details, the Fifteenth Amendment was sent to the states for ratification in February 1869. It forbade *all* the states to deny the vote to anyone "on account of race, color, or previous condition of servitude." Once again nothing was said about denial of the vote on the basis of sex.

Most southern states, still under federal pressure, ratified the amendment swiftly. The same was true in most of New England and in some western states. Bitter battles were waged in Connecticut, New York, Pennsylvania, and the states immediately north of the Ohio River, but by March 1870 most of them had ratified the amendment and it became part of the Constitution. The debates occasioned by these contests show that partisan advantage was not the only reason why voters approved black suffrage at last. The unfairness of a double standard of voting, North and South, the contribution of black soldiers during the war, and the hope that by passing the amendment the strife of Reconstruction could finally be ended all played a part.

When the Fifteenth Amendment went into effect, President Grant called it "the greatest civil change and . . . the most important event that has occurred since the nation came to life." The American Anti-Slavery Society formally dissolved itself, its work apparently completed. One prominent Radical Republican called this triumph over prejudice "hardly explicable on any other theory than that God willed it."

Many of the celebrants lived to see the amendment subverted in the South. That it could be evaded by literacy tests and other restrictions was apparent at the time and may even have influenced some persons who voted for it. But a stronger amendment—one, for instance, that positively granted the right to vote to all men and put the supervision of elections under national control—could not have been ratified.

"Black Republican" Reconstruction

The Radicals had at last succeeded in imposing their will upon the South. Throughout the region former slaves voted, held office, and exercised the "privileges" and enjoyed the "immunities" guaranteed them by the Fourteenth Amendment. Almost to a man they voted Republican.

The spectacle of blacks not five years removed from slavery in positions of power and responsibility attracted much attention at the time and has since been examined exhaustively by historians. The subject is controversial, but certain facts are beyond argument. Black officeholders were neither numerous nor inordinately influential. None was ever elected governor of a state; fewer than a dozen and a half during the entire period served in Congress; only one (in South Carolina) rose to be a justice of a state supreme court. Blacks held many minor offices and were influential in southern legislatures, though (except in South Carolina) they never made up the majority. Certainly they did not share the spoils of office in proportion to their numbers.

The real rulers of the "black Republican" governments were white: the "carpetbaggers"—northerners who went to the South as idealists eager to help the freedmen, as employees of the federal government, or more commonly as settlers hoping to improve their lot—and the "scalawags"—southerners willing to cooperate with the freedmen out of principle or to advance their own interests. A few scalawags were well-to-do planters and merchants who had been Whigs until the crises of the 1850s destroyed that party in the South, but most were former opponents of secession from sections that had small slave populations before the war.

That blacks should fail to dominate southern governments is certainly understandable. They lacked experience in politics and were mostly poor and uneducated. They were nearly everywhere a minority. Those blacks who held office during Reconstruction tended to be better educated and more prosperous. In his interesting analysis of South Carolina black politicians, Thomas Holt shows that a disproportionate number of them had been free before the war. Of those freed by the Thirteenth Amendment, a large percentage had been house servants or artisans, not field hands. Mulatto politicians were also disproportionately numerous and (as a group) more conservative and economically better off than other black leaders.

In South Carolina and elsewhere, black officeholders proved in the main able and conscientious public servants: able because the best tended to rise to the top in such a fluid situation and conscientious because most of those who achieved importance sought eagerly to demonstrate the capacity of their race for self-government. Extensive studies of states such as Mississippi show that even at the local level, where the quality of officials was usually poor, there was little difference

■ **South Carolina's House of Representatives in session during Reconstruction, from *Frank Leslie's Illustrated Newspaper.* Black voters were in the majority in South Carolina.**

in the degree of competence displayed by white and black officeholders. In power, the blacks were not vindictive; by and large they did not seek to restrict the rights of ex-Confederates.

Not all black legislators and administrators were paragons of virtue. In South Carolina, despite their control of the legislature, they broke up into factions repeatedly and failed to press for laws that would improve the lot of poor black farm workers. And waste and corruption were common among them. Legislators paid themselves large salaries and surrounded themselves with armies of useless, incompetent clerks. Half the budget of Louisiana in some years went for salaries and "mileage" for representatives and their staffs. In South Carolina the legislature ordered an expensive census in 1869, only one year before the regular federal census was to be taken. Large sums were appropriated for imposing state capitols and other less than essential buildings. As for corruption, in *The South During Reconstruction* Professor E. Merton Coulter described dozens of defalcations that occurred during these years. One Arkansas black took $9,000 from the state for repairing a bridge that had cost only $500 to build. A South Carolina legislator was voted an additional $1,000 in salary after he lost that sum on a horse race.

However, the corruption must be seen in perspective. The big thieves were nearly always white; blacks got mostly crumbs. Furthermore, graft and callous disregard of the public interest characterized government in every section and at every level during the decade after Appomattox. Big-city bosses in the North made off with sums that dwarfed the most brazen southern frauds. The New York City Tweed Ring probably made off with more money than all the southern thieves, black and white, combined. While the evidence does not justify the southern corruption, it suggests that the unique features of Reconstruction politics—black suffrage, military supervision, carpetbagger and scalawag influence—do not explain it.

The "black Republican" governments displayed qualities that grew directly from the ignorance and political immaturity of the former slaves. There was a tragicomic aspect to the South Carolina legislature during these years, its many black members—some dressed in old frock coats, others in rude farm clothes—rising to points of order and personal privilege without reason, discoursing ponderously on subjects they did not understand. "A wonder and a shame to modern civilization," one northern observer called this spectacle.

The country might have been better served if blacks had been enfranchised gradually, as Lincoln suggested. But those who complained about the ignorance and irresponsibility of blacks conveniently forgot that the tendency of 19th-century American democracy was away from educational, financial, or any other restrictions on the franchise. Thousands of white southerners were as illiterate and uncultured as the freedmen, yet no one suggested depriving them of the ballot.

Despite the corruption, confusion, and conflict, the Radical southern governments accomplished a great deal. They spent money freely but not entirely wastefully. Tax rates zoomed, but the money financed the repair and expansion of the South's dilapidated railroad network, rebuilt crumbling levees, and expanded social services. Before the Civil War, public education in the South had lagged far behind the rest of the country, and the education of blacks was illegal. During Reconstruction an enormous gap had to be filled, and it took a great deal of money to fill it. The Freedmen's Bureau made a start, and northern religious and philanthropic organizations did important work. Eventually, however, the state

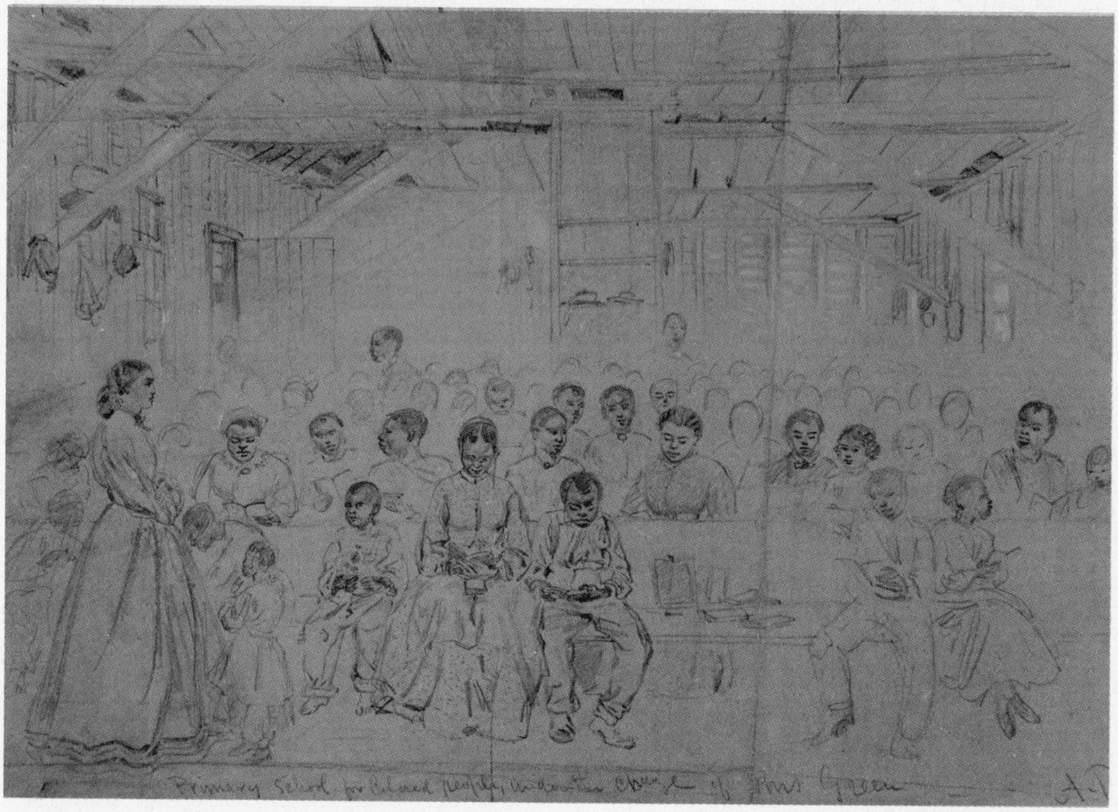

■ **The Freedmen's Bureau established 4,329 schools, attended by some 250,000 ex-slaves, in the South in the postwar period. *Harper's Weekly* artist Alfred Waud did this sketch of a Freedmen's Bureau school in Vicksburg, Mississippi, in 1866. Many of the teachers were northern white women.**

■ A Currier & Ives print honoring the first black senator—Hiram R. Revels of Mississippi, seated at the left—and representatives who served in the 41st and 42nd Congresses from 1869 to 1873.

governments established and supported systems of free public education that, while segregated, greatly benefited everyone, whites as well as blacks.

The former slaves grasped eagerly at the opportunity to learn. Nearly all appreciated the immense importance of knowing how to read and write; the sight of elderly men and women poring laboriously over elementary texts beside their grandchildren was common everywhere. Schools and other institutions were supported chiefly by property taxes, and these, of course, hit well-to-do white farmers hard. Hence much of the complaining about the "extravagance" of Reconstruction governments concealed selfish objections to paying for public projects. Eventually the benefits of expanded government services to the entire population became clear, and when white supremacy was reestablished, most of the new services, together with the corruption and inefficiency inherited from the carpetbagger governments, were retained.

Southern Economic Problems

The South's grave economic problems complicated the rebuilding of its political system. The section had never been as prosperous as the North, and wartime destruction left it desperately poor by any standard. In the long run the abolition of slavery released immeasurable quantities of human energy previously stifled, but the immediate effect was to create confusion. Understandably, many former slaves at first equated legal freedom with freedom from having to earn a living, a tendency reinforced for a time by the willingness of the Freedmen's Bureau to provide rations and other forms of relief in war-devastated areas. Freedom to move about without a pass, to "see the world," was one of the most cherished benefits of emancipation. "I's want to be free man, cum when I please, and nobody say nuffin to me, nor order me roun'," one Alabama black told a northern journalist after Appomattox. Thousands flocked to southern towns and cities where there was little they could do to earn a living.

Others expected that freedom would also mean free land, and the slogan "forty acres and a mule" achieved wide popularity in the South in 1865. This idea was forcefully supported by the relentless Congressman Thaddeus Stevens, whose hatred of the planter class was pathological. "The property of the chief rebels should be seized," he stated. If the lands of the richest "70,000 proud, bloated and defiant rebels" were confiscated, the federal government would obtain 394 million acres. Every adult male ex-slave could easily be supplied with 40 acres. The beauty of his scheme, Stevens insisted, was that "nine-tenths of the [southern] people would remain untouched." Dispossessing the great planters would make the South "a safe republic," its lands cultivated by "the free labor of intelligent citizens." If the plan drove the planters into exile, "all the better."

Although Stevens' figures were faulty, many Radicals agreed with him. "We must see that the freedmen are established on the soil," Senator Sumner declared. "The great plantations, which have been so many nurseries of the rebellion, must be broken up, and the freedmen must have the pieces." Stevens, Sumner, and others who wanted to give land to the freedmen weakened their case by associating it with the idea of punish-

■ **Among the few blacks to emigrate to the West and obtain land under the provisions of the Homestead Act was the Shores family. S.D. Butcher took this family portrait in Custer County, Nebraska, in the 1880s. Black homesteaders received limited aid from the Freedmen's Relief Association and eastern philanthropists.**

ing the former rebels; the average American had too much respect for property rights to support a policy of confiscation.

Aside from its vindictiveness, the extremists' view was simplistic. Land without tools, seed, and other necessities would have done the freedmen little good. Congress did throw open 46 million acres of poor-quality federal land in the South to blacks under the Homestead Act, but few settled upon it. Establishing former slaves on small farms with adequate financial aid would have been of incalculable benefit to them and to the nation. This would have been practicable, but it was not done.

The freedmen therefore had to work out their destiny within the established framework of southern agriculture. White planters predicted that the ex-slaves, being incapable of self-directed effort, would either starve to death or descend into barbarism. Of course the blacks did neither. True, the output of cotton and other southern staples declined precipitously after slavery was abolished. Observers soon came to the conclusion that a free black produced no more than half as much as a slave had produced, and modern econometric studies indicate that this estimate was not far off.

However, the decline in productivity was not caused by the *inability* of free blacks to work independently. What happened was that since they now held, in the pithy phrase of the economist Robert Higgs, "property rights over their own bodies," they chose no longer to work like slaves. They let their children play instead of forcing them into the fields. Mothers devoted more time to child care and housework, less to farm labor. Elderly blacks worked less.

Noting these changes, white critics spoke scornfully of black laziness and shiftlessness. "You cannot make the negro work without physical compulsion," was the common view. As the economic historians Roger Ransom and Richard Sutch have said, the perfectly reasonable desire of ex-slaves to devote more time to leisure was "taken as 'evidence' to support racist characterizations of blacks as lazy, incompetent, and unwilling to work." A leading southern magazine complained in 1866 that black women now expected their husbands "to support them in idleness" (it would never have made such a comment about white housewives). Ransom and Sutch also point out that, while working less, emancipated blacks were far better off materially than under slavery. Their earnings brought them almost 30 percent more than the value of the subsistence provided by their former masters.

In the beginning blacks usually worked for wages, but the wage system did not function well in the postwar South. Money was scarce, and banking capital, never adequate even before the collapse of the Confederacy, accumulated slowly. Interest rates were extremely high. This situation made it difficult for landowners to meet their labor bills. More important, blacks did not like working for wages because it kept them under the direction of whites. Since the voluntary withdrawal of so much black labor from the work force had produced a shortage, they had their way.

A new agricultural system known as sharecropping emerged. Instead of cultivating the land by gang labor as in antebellum times, planters broke up their estates into small units and established on each a black family. The planter provided housing, agricultural implements, draft animals, seed, and other supplies, and the family provided labor. The crop was divided between them, usually on a fifty-fifty basis. If the landlord supplied only land and housing, the laborer got a larger share. This was called share tenancy.

Sharecropping gave blacks at least the hope of earning enough to buy a small farm. But few achieved this ambition because whites resisted their efforts adamantly. As late as 1880 blacks owned less than 10 percent of the agricultural land in the South, though they made up more than half of the region's farm population. Mississippi actually prohibited the purchase of farmland by blacks.

The main cause of southern rural poverty for whites as well as blacks was the lack of enough capital to finance the sharecropping system. Like their colonial ancestors, the landowners had to borrow against October's harvest to pay for April's seed. Thus the crop-lien system developed, and to protect their investments, lenders tended to insist that the grower concentrate on readily marketable cash crops: tobacco, sugar, and especially cotton.

The system injured everyone. Diversified farming would have reduced the farmers' need for cash, preserved the fertility of the soil, and, by placing a premium on imagination and shrewd-

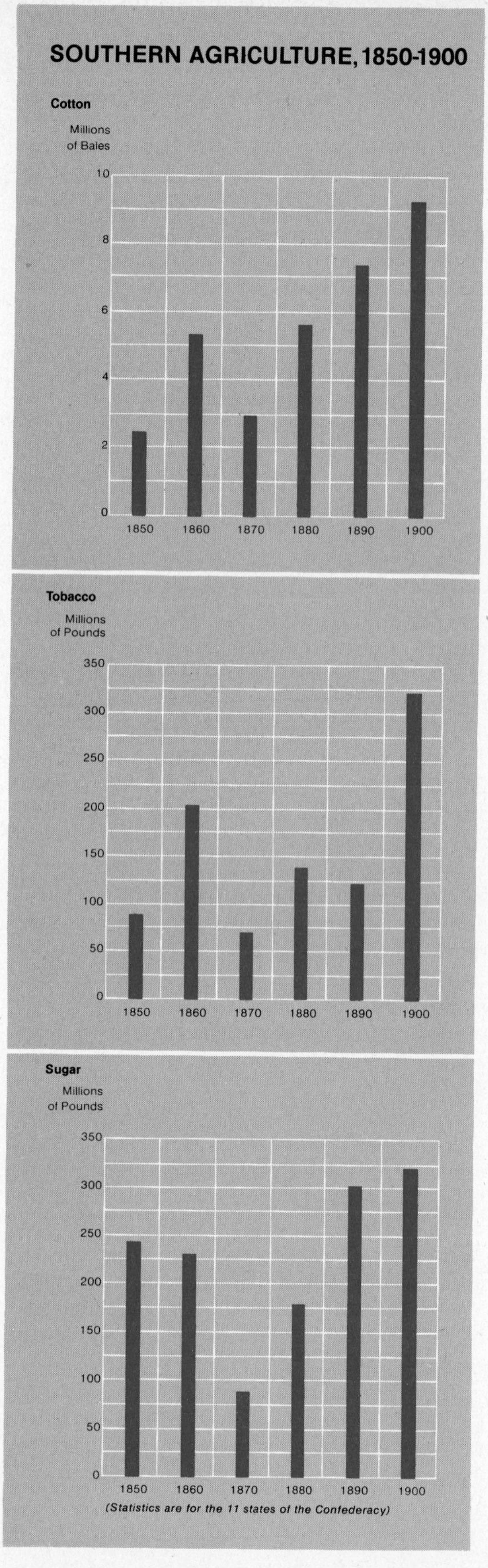

ness, aided the best of them to rise in the world. Under the crop-lien system, both landowner and sharecropper depended on credit supplied by local bankers, merchants, and storekeepers for everything from seed, tools, and fertilizer to overalls, coffee, and salt. Crossroads stores proliferated, and a new class of small merchants appeared. The prices of goods sold on credit were high, adding to the burden borne by the rural population. The small southern merchants were almost equally victimized by the system, for they also lacked capital, bought goods on credit, and had to pay high interest rates.

Seen in broad perspective, the situation is not difficult to understand. The South, drained of every resource by the war, was competing for funds with the North and West, both vigorous and expanding and therefore voracious consumers of capital. Reconstruction, in the literal sense of the word, was accomplished chiefly at the expense of the standard of living of the producing classes. The crop-lien system and the small storekeeper were only agents of an economic process dictated by national, perhaps even worldwide, conditions.

This does not mean that the South's economy was paralyzed by the shortage of capital or that recovery and growth did not take place. But compared with the rest of the country, progress was slow. Just before the Civil War cotton harvests averaged about 4 million bales. During the conflict, output fell to about half a million, and the former Confederate states did not enjoy a 4 million bale year again until 1870. Only after 1874 did the crop begin to top that figure consistently. In contrast, national wheat production in 1859 was 175 million bushels and in 1878, 449 million. About 7,000 miles of railroad were built in the South between 1865 and 1879; in the rest of the nation nearly 45,000 miles of track were laid.

In manufacturing the South made important gains after the war. The tobacco industry, stimulated by the sudden popularity of the cigarette, expanded rapidly. The town of Durham, North Carolina, home of the famous Bull Durham pipe

■ **Cotton production recovered to its prewar level by 1880, but tobacco and sugar production lagged. Not until 1900 did tobacco growers have a better year than they had in 1860.**

and cigarette tobacco, flourished. So did Virginia tobacco towns like Richmond, Lynchburg, and Petersburg. The exploitation of the coal and iron deposits of northeastern Alabama in the early 1870s made a boom town of Birmingham. The manufacture of cotton cloth increased, productive capacity nearly doubling between 1865 and 1880. Yet the mills of Massachusetts alone had eight times the capacity of the entire South in 1880. Despite the increases, the South's share of the national output of manufactured goods declined sharply during the Reconstruction era.

The White Counterrevolution

Radical southern governments could sustain themselves only so long as they had the support of a significant proportion of the white population, for except in South Carolina and Louisiana, the blacks were not numerous enough to win elections alone. The key to Radical survival lay in the hands of the wealthy merchants and planters, mostly former Whigs. People of this sort had nothing to fear from black economic competition. Taking a broad view, they could see that improving the lot of the former slaves would benefit all classes.

These southerners exercised a restraining influence on the rest of the white population. Poor white farmers, the most "unreconstructed" of all southerners, bitterly resented blacks, whose every forward step seemed to weaken their own precarious economic and social position. When the Republicans began to organize and manipulate the new voters in much the way big-city bosses were managing voters in the North, the poor whites seethed with resentment.

Southern Republicans used the Union League of America, a patriotic club founded during the war, to control the black vote. Employing secret rituals, exotic symbols, and other paraphernalia calculated to impress unsophisticated people, they enrolled the freedmen in droves, made them swear to support the League list of candidates at elections, and then marched them to the polls en masse.

Powerless to check the League by open methods, dissident southerners established a number of secret terrorist societies, bearing such names as the Ku Klux Klan, the Knights of the White Camelia, and the Pale Faces. The most notorious of these organizations was the Klan, which originated in Tennessee in 1866. At first it was purely a social club, but by 1868 it had been taken over by vigilante types dedicated to driving blacks out of politics, and it was spreading rapidly across the South. Sheet-clad nightriders roamed the countryside, frightening the impressionable and chastising the defiant. Klansmen, using a weird mumbo

■ **A graphic warning by the Alabama Klan to scalawags and carpetbaggers, "those great pests of Southern society"; from the Tuscaloosa *Independent Monitor* for September 1, 1868.**

jumbo and claiming to be the ghosts of Confederate soldiers, spread horrendous rumors and published broadsides designed to persuade the freedmen that it was unhealthy for them to participate in politics:

> Niggers and Leaguers, get out of the way,
> We're born of the night and we vanish by day.
> No rations have we, but the flesh of man—
> And love niggers best—the Ku Klux Klan;
> We catch 'em alive and roast 'em whole,
> Then hand 'em around with a sharpened pole.
> Whole Leagues have been eaten, not leaving a man,
> And went away hungry—the Ku Klux Klan. . . .

When intimidation failed, the Klansmen beat their victims and in hundreds of cases murdered them, often in the most gruesome manner. Congress struck at the Klan with three Force Acts (1870–1871), which placed elections under federal jurisdiction and imposed fines and prison sentences on persons convicted of interfering with any citizen's exercise of the franchise. Troops were dispatched to areas where the Klan was strong, and by 1872 the federal authorities had arrested enough Klansmen to break up the organization.

Nevertheless the Klan contributed substantially to the destruction of Radical regimes in the South. Its depredations weakened the will of white Republicans (few of whom really believed in racial equality), and it intimidated many blacks, who gave up trying to exercise their rights.

Gradually it became respectable to intimidate black voters. Beginning in Mississippi in 1874 a number of terrorist movements spread through the South. Instead of hiding behind masks and operating in the dark, these terrorists donned red shirts, organized into military companies, and paraded openly. The Mississippi red-shirts seized militant blacks and whipped them publicly. Killings were frequent. When blacks dared to fight back, the well-organized whites easily put them to rout. In other states similar organizations sprang up, and the same tragic results followed.

Terrorism fed on fear, fear on terrorism. White violence led to fear of black retaliation and thus to even more brutal attacks. The slightest sign of resistance came to be seen as the beginning of race war, and when the blacks suffered indignities and persecutions in silence, the awareness of how much they must resent the mistreatment made them appear more dangerous still. Thus self-hatred was displaced, guilt suppressed, aggression justified as self-defense, individual conscience submerged in the animality of the mob.

Before long the blacks learned to stay home on election day. One by one, "Conservative" parties—Democratic in national affairs—took over southern state governments. Angry northern Radicals attributed the Democratic victories entirely to intimidation, but intimidation was only a partial explanation. The increasing solidarity of whites, northern and southern, was equally significant.

Many northerners had supported the Radical policy only out of irritation with President Johnson. After his retirement their enthusiasm waned. The war was fading into the past and with it the worst of the bad feeling it had generated. Northern voters could still be stirred by references to the sacrifices Republicans had made to save the Union and by reminders that the Democratic party was the organization of rebels, Copperheads, and the Ku Klux Klan. Yet emotional appeals could not push legislation through Congress or convince northerners that it was still necessary to maintain a large army in the South. In 1869 the occupying forces were down to 11,000 men.

Nationalism was reasserting itself. Had not Washington and Jefferson been Virginians? Was not Andrew Jackson Carolina-born? Since most northerners had little real love or respect for blacks, their interest in racial equality flagged once they felt reasonably certain that blacks would not be reenslaved if left to their own devices in the South.

Another, much subtler force was also at work. The prewar Republican party had stressed the common interest of workers, manufacturers, and farmers in a free and mobile society, a land of equal opportunity where all could work in harmony. Southern whites had insisted that laborers must be disciplined if large enterprises were to be run efficiently. By the 1870s, as large industrial enterprises developed in the northern states, the thinking of business leaders changed—the southern argument began to make sense to them, and therefore they became more sympathetic to the southern demand for more control over "their" labor force.

Grant as President

Other matters occupied the attention of northern voters. The expansion of industry and the rapid development of the West, stimulated by a new wave of railroad building, loomed more important to many than the fortunes of ex-slaves. Beginning in 1873, when a stock market panic struck at public confidence, economic difficulties plagued the country for nearly a decade. Heated controversies arose over tariff policy, with western agricultural interests seeking to force reductions from the high levels established during the war, and over the handling of the wartime greenback paper money, with debtor groups and many manufacturers favoring further expansion of the supply of dollars and conservative merchants and bankers arguing for retiring the greenbacks in order to return to a "sound" currency. These controversies tended to divert attention from conditions in the South.

More damaging to the Republicans was the failure of Ulysses S. Grant to live up to expectations as president. Qualities that had made Grant a fine military leader for a democracy—his dislike of political maneuvering and his simple belief that the popular will could best be observed in the actions of Congress—made him a poor chief executive. When Congress failed to act on his suggestion that the quality of the civil service needed improvement, he announced meekly that if Congress did nothing, he would assume the country did not want anything done, and he dropped the subject. Grant was honest, but his honesty was of the naive type that made him the dupe of unscrupulous friends and schemers. In fact he disliked being president and avoided the responsibilities of the office whenever he could.

His most serious weakness as president was his failure to deal effectively with economic and social problems, but the one that injured him and the

■ **The cartoonist Thomas Nast was a staunch Grant man; in a *Harper's Weekly* drawing made during the 1872 campaign, Greeley (center) and Charles Sumner urge a black to "clasp hands" with a Klansman and a Tammany Hall instigator of Civil War draft riots.**

Republicans most was his inability to cope with government corruption. Grant did not cause the corruption, nor did he participate in the remotest way in the rush to "fatten at the public trough," as the reformers of the day might have put it. But he did nothing to prevent the scandals that disgraced his administration. Out of a misplaced belief in the sanctity of friendship, he protected some of the worst culprits and allowed calculating tricksters to use his good name and the prestige of his office to advance their own interests at the country's expense.

The worst of the scandals—such as the Whiskey Ring affair, which implicated Grant's private secretary, Orville E. Babcock, and cost the government millions in tax revenue, and the defalcations of Secretary of War William W. Belknap in the management of Indian affairs—did not become public knowledge during Grant's first term. However, in 1872 a reform group in the Republican party, alarmed by rumors of corruption and disappointed by Grant's failure to press for civil service reform, organized the Liberal Republican party and nominated Horace Greeley, the able but eccentric editor of the New York *Tribune,* for president. The Democrats also nominated Greeley, though he had devoted his political life to flailing the Democratic party in the *Tribune.* That surrender to expediency, together with Greeley's temperamental unsuitability for the presidency, made the campaign a fiasco for the reformers. Grant triumphed easily, with a popular majority of nearly 800,000.

Nevertheless the defection of the Liberal Republicans hurt the Republican party in Congress. In the 1874 elections, no longer hampered as in the presidential contest by Greeley's notoriety and Grant's fame, the Democrats carried the House of Representatives. It was clear that the days of military rule in the South were ending. By the end of 1875 only three southern states, South Carolina, Florida, and Louisiana, were still under Republican control. The Republican party in the South was "dead as a doornail," a reporter noted. He reflected the opinion of thousands when he added: "We ought to have a sound sensible republican . . . for the next President as a measure of safety; but only on the condition of absolute noninterference in Southern local affairs, for which there is no further need or excuse."

The Disputed Election of 1876

Against this background the presidential election of 1876 took place. Since corruption in government was the most widely discussed issue, the Republicans passed over their most attractive political personality, the dynamic James G. Blaine, Speaker of the House of Representatives, who had been connected with some chicanery involving railroad securities. Instead they nominated Governor Rutherford B. Hayes of Ohio, a former general with an unsmirched reputation. The Democrats picked Governor Samuel J. Tilden of New York, who had attracted national attention for his part in breaking up the Tweed Ring in New York City.

In November Tilden triumphed easily in all the southern states from which the Radical regimes had been ejected. He also carried New York, New Jersey, Connecticut, and Indiana. In the three "unredeemed" southern states, Florida, South Carolina, and Louisiana, he won apparent majorities. This seemed to give him 203 electoral votes to Hayes' 165, with a popular plurality in the neighborhood of 250,000 out of more than 8 million votes cast.

Republican leaders had anticipated the possible loss of Florida, South Carolina, and Louisiana and were prepared to use their control of the election machinery in those states to throw out sufficient Democratic ballots to alter the results if doing so would change the national outcome. Realizing that the 19 electoral votes of those states were exactly enough to elect their man, they telegraphed their henchmen on the scene, ordering them to go into action. The board of canvassers in each of the states invalidated Democratic ballots in wholesale lots and filed returns showing Hayes the winner. Naturally the local Democrats protested vigorously and filed their own returns.

The Constitution provides that presidential electors must meet in their respective states to vote and forward the results to "the Seat of the Government." There, it adds, "the President of the Senate shall, in the Presence of the Senate and House of Representatives, open all the Certificates, *and the Votes shall then be counted.*" But who was to do the counting? The House was Democratic, the Senate Republican; neither would agree to allow the other to do the job. On January 29,

1877, scarcely a month before inauguration day, Congress created an electoral commission to decide the disputed cases. The commission consisted of five senators (three Republicans and two Democrats), five representatives (three Democrats and two Republicans), and five justices of the Supreme Court (two Democrats, two Republicans, and one "independent" judge, David Davis). Since it was a foregone conclusion that the others would vote for their party no matter what the evidence, Davis would presumably swing the balance in the interest of fairness.

But before the commission met the Illinois legislature elected Davis senator! He had to resign from the Court and the commission. Since independents were rare even on the Supreme Court, no neutral was available to replace him. The vacancy went to Associate Justice Joseph P. Bradley of New Jersey, a Republican.

Evidence presented before the commission revealed a disgraceful picture of election shenanigans. On the one hand, in all three disputed states Democrats had clearly cast a majority of the votes; on the other, it was unquestionable that many blacks had been forcibly prevented from voting.

The sordid truth was that both sides had been shamefully corrupt. Lew Wallace, a northern politician later famous as the author of the novel *Ben Hur,* visited Louisiana and Florida shortly after the election. "It is terrible to see the extent to which all classes go in their determination to win," he wrote his wife from Florida. "Money and intimidation can obtain the oath of white men as well as black to any required statement. . . . If we win, our methods are subject to impeachment for possible fraud. If the enemy win, it is the same thing." The governor of Louisiana was reported willing to sell his state's electoral votes for $200,000. The Florida election board was supposed to have offered itself to Tilden for the same price. "That seems to be the standard figure," Tilden remarked ruefully.

Most modern authorities take the view that in a fair election the Republicans would have carried South Carolina and Louisiana but that Florida would have gone to Tilden, giving him the election, 188 electoral votes to 181. In the last analysis, this opinion has been arrived at simply by counting white and black noses: blacks were in the majority in South Carolina and Louisiana. Amid the tension and confusion of early 1877, however, even a Solomon would have been hard pressed to judge rightly amid the rumors, lies, and contradictory statements, and the electoral commission was not composed of Solomons. The Democrats had some hopes that Justice Bradley would be sympathetic to their case, for he was known to be opposed to harsh Reconstruction policies. On the eve of the commission's decision in the Florida controversy, he was apparently ready to vote in favor of Tilden. But the Republicans subjected him to tremendous political pressure. When he read his opinion on February 8, it was for Hayes. Thus, by a vote of 8 to 7, the commission awarded Florida's electoral votes to the Republicans.

The rest of the proceedings were routine. The atmosphere of judicial inquiry and deliberation was a façade. With the spitefulness common to rejected suitors, the Democrats assailed Bradley until, as the New York *Times* put it, he seemed like "a middle-aged St. Sebastian, stuck full of Democratic darts." Unlike Sebastian, however, Bradley was protected from the arrows by the armor of his Republican faith. The commission assigned all the disputed electoral votes (including one in Oregon, where the Democratic governor had seized on a technicality to replace a single Republican elector with a Democrat) to Hayes.

To such a level had the republic of Jefferson and John Adams descended. Democratic institutions, shaken by the South's refusal to go along with the majority in 1860 and by the suppression of civil rights during the rebellion, and further weakened by military intervention and the intimidation of blacks in the South during Reconstruction, seemed now a farce. According to Tilden's campaign manager, angry Democrats in 15 states, chiefly war veterans, were readying themselves to march on Washington to force the inauguration of Tilden. Tempers flared in Congress, where some spoke ominously of a filibuster that would prevent the recording of the electoral vote and leave the country, on March 4, with no president at all.

The Compromise of 1877

Fortunately, forces for compromise had been at work behind the scenes in Washington for some time. Although northern Democrats threatened to fight to the last ditch, many southern Democrats

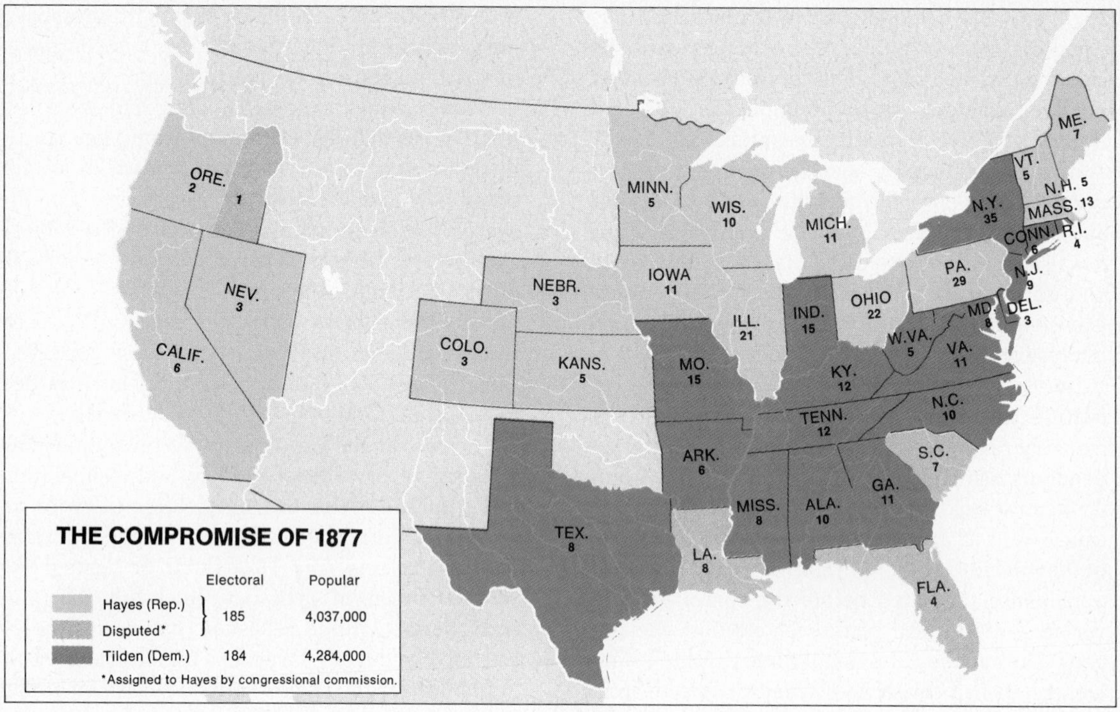

were willing to accept Hayes if they could gain something in exchange. If Hayes would promise to remove the troops and allow the southern states to manage their internal affairs by themselves, they would be sorely tempted to go along with his election. A more specialized but extremely important group consisted of the ex-Whig planters and merchants who had reluctantly abandoned the carpetbag governments and who were always uncomfortable in alliance with poor whites. If Hayes would agree to let the South alone and perhaps appoint a conservative southerner to his Cabinet, these men would support him willingly, hoping eventually to restore the two-party system that had been destroyed in the South during the 1850s.

Other southerners favored Republican policies because of their economic interests. The Texas and Pacific Railway Company, chartered to build a line from Marshall, Texas, to San Diego, had many southern backers, and supporters of Hayes were quick to point out that a Republican administration would be more likely to help the Texas and Pacific than a retrenchment-minded Democratic one. Ohio Congressman James A. Garfield urged Hayes to find "some discreet way" of showing these southerners that he favored "internal improvements." Hayes replied: "Your views are so nearly the same as mine that I need not say a word."

Tradition has it that a great compromise between the sections was worked out during a dramatic meeting at the Wormley Hotel in Washington on February 26. Actually, as C. Vann Woodward has demonstrated in his important book *Reunion and Reaction,* the negotiations were long-drawn-out and informal, and the Wormley conference was but one of many. With the tacit support of many Democrats, the electoral vote was counted by the president of the Senate on March 2, and Hayes was declared elected, 185 votes to 184.

Like all compromises, this agreement was not entirely satisfactory; like most, it was not honored in every detail. Hayes recalled the last troops from South Carolina and Louisiana in April. He appointed a former Confederate general, David M. Key of Tennessee, postmaster general and delegated to him the congenial task of finding southerners willing to serve their country as officials of a Republican administration. The new alliance of ex-Whigs and northern Republicans did not flourish, however, and the South remained solidly Democratic. The hoped-for federal aid for the Texas and Pacific did not materialize. The major significance of the compromise, one of the great intersectional political accommodations of American history, has been well summarized by Professor Woodward:

> The Compromise of 1877 marked the abandonment of principles and force and a return to the traditional ways of expediency and concession. The compromise laid the political foundation for reunion. It established a new sectional truce that proved more enduring than any previous one and provided a settlement for an issue that had troubled American politics for more than a generation. It wrote an end to Reconstruction and recognized a new regime in the South. More profoundly than Constitutional amendments and wordy statutes it shaped the future of four million freedmen and their progeny for generations to come.

For most of the former slaves, this future was to be bleak. Forgotten in the North, manipulated and then callously rejected by the South, rebuffed by the Supreme Court, voiceless in national affairs, they and their descendants were condemned in the interests of sectional harmony to lives of poverty, indignity, and little hope. Meanwhile, the rest of the United States continued its golden march toward wealth and power.

SUPPLEMENTARY READING

Titles marked with an asterisk have been published in paperback

J. G. Randall and David Donald, **The Civil War and Reconstruction** (1961), is as excellent on postwar readjustments as it is on the war years. K. M. Stampp, **The Era of Reconstruction*** (1964), and J. H. Franklin, **Reconstruction: After the Civil War*** (1961), are outstanding. E. M. Coulter, **The South During Reconstruction** (1947), presents a prosouthern point of view and is strong on economic developments. The older approach to the period, stressing the excesses of black-influenced governments and criticizing the Radicals, derives from the seminal work of W. A. Dunning, **Reconstruction, Political and Economic*** (1907). W. E. B. Du Bois, **Black Reconstruction in America*** (1935), militantly problack, was the pioneering counterattack against the Dunning view. See also Eric Foner, **Politics and Ideology in the Age of the Civil War** (1980).

Lincoln's ideas about Reconstruction are analyzed in W. B. Hesseltine, **Lincoln's Plan of Reconstruction*** (1960), and in many of the Lincoln volumes mentioned in earlier chapters. There is no satisfactory biography of Andrew Johnson; both G. F. Milton, **The Age of Hate: Andrew Johnson and the Radicals** (1930), and Milton Lomask, **Andrew Johnson: President on Trial** (1960), are far too sympathetic in approach. Of the special studies of Johnson's battle with the congressional Radicals, H. K. Beale, **The Critical Year** (1930), takes Johnson's side, but recent studies have been critical of the president. See H. L. Trefousse, **The Radical Republicans: Lincoln's Vanguard for Racial Justice*** (1969), E. L. McKitrick, **Andrew Johnson and Reconstruction*** (1960), and W. R. Brock, **An American Crisis: Congress and Reconstruction*** (1963), the last a particularly thoughtful analysis of the era.

A number of biographies provide information helpful in understanding the Radicals. These include B. P. Thomas and H. M. Hyman, **Stanton** (1962), F. M. Brodie, **Thaddeus Stevens*** (1959), R. N. Current, **Old Thad Stevens** (1942), and H. L. Trefousse, **Benjamin Franklin Wade** (1963); J. M. McPherson, **The Struggle for Equality: Abolitionists and the Negro in the Civil War and Reconstruction*** (1964), is also valuable. On the Fourteenth Amendment, see Joseph James, **The Framing of the Fourteenth Amendment*** (1956); on the Fifteenth Amendment, see William Gillette, **The Right to Vote: Politics and the Passage of the Fifteenth Amendment*** (1965).

Conditions in the South during Reconstruction are discussed in all the works cited in the first paragraph. Of state studies, see V. L. Wharton, **The Negro in Mississippi*** (1947), C. E. Wynes, **Race Relations in Virginia** (1961), W. L. Rose, **Rehearsal for Reconstruction: The Port Royal Experiment*** (1964), Thomas Holt, **Black over White: Negro Political Leadership in South Carolina** (1977), and Joel Williamson, **After Slavery: The Negro in South Carolina During Reconstruction*** (1965). G. R. Bentley, **A History of the Freedmen's Bureau** (1955), discusses the work of that important organization, but see also W. S. McFeely, **Yankee Stepfather: General O. O. Howard and the Freedmen*** (1968). On the Ku Klux Klan, see A. W. Trelease, **White Terror: The Ku Klux Klan Conspiracy and Southern Reconstruction** (1971).

On the economic and social effects of Reconstruction, see R. L. Ransom and Richard Sutch, **One Kind of Freedom: The Economic Consequences of Emancipation*** (1977), Robert Higgs, **Competition and Coercion: Blacks in the American Economy, 1865–1914** (1977), and C. F. Oubre, **Forty Acres and a Mule** (1978). F. A. Shannon, **The Farmer's Last Frontier*** (1945), is also useful on southern agriculture. For the growth of industry, see Broadus Mitchell, **The Rise of Cotton Mills in the South** (1921), and J. F. Stover, **The Railroads of the South** (1955).

On Grant's presidency, see W. S. McFeely, **Grant** (1981), but Allan Nevins, **Hamilton Fish: The Inner History of the Grant Administration** (1936), and Matthew Josephson, **The Politicos*** (1938), contain much additional information. On the election of 1868, see C. H. Coleman, **The Election of 1868** (1933), and Stewart Mitchell, **Horatio Seymour** (1938); on the reform movement of the period within the Republican party, see J. G. Sproat, **"The Best Men": Liberal Reformers in the Gilded Age*** (1968), and M. B. Duberman, **Charles Francis Adams*** (1961). For the disputed election of 1876 and the compromise following it, consult C. V. Woodward, **Reunion and Reaction*** (1951), Harry Barnard, **Rutherford B. Hayes and His America** (1954), K. I. Polakoff, **The Politics of Inertia: The Election of 1876 and the End of Reconstruction** (1973), and Allan Nevins, **Abram S. Hewitt** (1935). P. H. Buck, **The Road to Reunion*** (1937), traces the gradual reconciliation of North and South after 1865. William Gillette, **Retreat from Reconstruction** (1980), is an important recent study.

Portfolio Four

THE PLAINS INDIANS

The history of the plains Indians, those undying if often-killed favorites of American entertainment, is testimony that the truth is stranger and more interesting than the fiction. For about a century, from roughly 1780 to 1880, the plains tribes maintained a unique and colorful existence in the midst of an immense grassland, feeding on the numberless buffalo and living mobile and free on their fleet ponies. Much of the vitality of this culture, however, was a direct result of the Indians' adoption of such elements of white civilization as horses, guns, and metal tools. And in the end the white culture's lust for land, its diseases, and the deadly efficiency of its mechanical genius devastated the plains civilization.

At the height of this cultural flowering in the middle decades of the 19th century, artists such as George Catlin, Karl Bodmer, Paul Kane, Friedrich Kurz, and Alfred Jacob Miller, as well as the Indians themselves, created a vivid, accurate pictorial record of plains life. Bodmer's 1832 portrait above of the Mandan chief Mato-Tope (Four Bears) is both a skillful work of art and a finely detailed reproduction of war paint patterns—even to the yellow hand painted over Mato-Tope's heart, which was meant to protect him during hand-to-hand combat.

Horse Indians

In 1834 the western painter George Catlin wrote, "A Comanche on his feet is out of his element . . . almost as awkward as a monkey on the ground, without a limb or a branch to cling to; but the moment he lays his hand upon his horse, his face even becomes handsome, and he gracefully flies away like a different being." Before the coming of the horse, the plains were populated by a few scattered tribes who found hunting buffalo on foot a risky business at best. For almost a century and a half after Coronado's trek from Mexico into the plains in the 1540s, the Spaniards were largely successful in keeping their horses out of Indian hands. But after a bloody revolt by the Pueblos in 1680 loosened Spain's grip on the Southwest, the horse spread northward rapidly. By 1780 the plains tribes were making full use of this highly efficient means of pursuing the buffalo, and the population of the region had tripled to an estimated 150,000.

■ George Catlin's painting at left, ca. 1835, shows a Crow chieftain and his horse in full battle array. It is evident from Catlin's portrait why historian Walter Prescott Webb spoke of plains warriors as "The Red Knights of the Prairie."

■ The elkskin painting above of a buffalo hunt, the work of a Crow artist, dates from about 1895. Three cowboys (upper left) suggest that by this time Indians no longer hunted alone.

■ At right is an 1862 sketch of a Cree saddle made of buffalo skin and stitched with buffalo sinew. Women's saddles had both a pommel and a cantle.

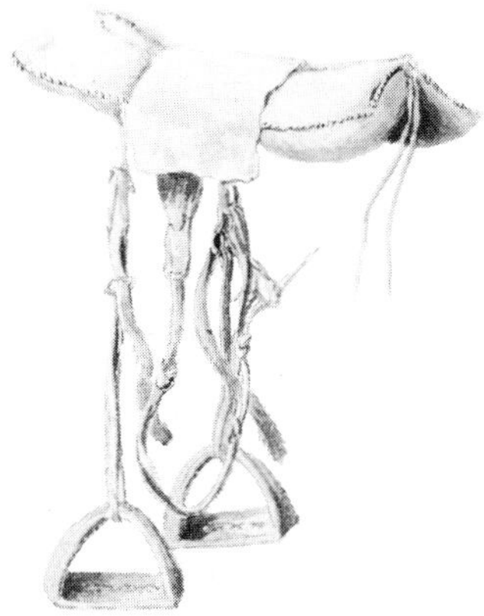

Sioux Camp

This remarkable photograph by J. H. C. Grabill shows a large Sioux encampment near the Pine Ridge Reservation in South Dakota. It was probably taken in March 1891 after the "battle" of Wounded Knee, in which some 150 Hunkpapa Sioux, including 44 women and 18 children, were massacred by the Seventh Cavalry. An encampment as extensive as this was

rare until the plains tribes became wards of the government and were confined on reservations. Except for special occasions—a tribal festival, a full-scale buffalo hunt, a war council—food was too scarce to permit an entire tribe to camp in one spot. The making, moving, and caring for the tepee was woman's work. In camp the men did little but feast, attend tribal councils and meetings of warrior societies, and decorate their tepees with figures and symbols based on highly valued dreams and visions and on hunting and martial exploits.

The Nomadic Life

The plains Indians were best known as wanderers who traveled by horse to follow the buffalo. They were indeed nomads, but it should not be forgotten that the horse was a latecomer to the plains and that for thousands of years a few tribes had been farming the more fertile parts of the region as well as hunting buffalo. In the 18th and 19th centuries this pattern persisted. Along the upper Missouri in present-day North Dakota, for example, the Hidatsas and the Mandans continued to live in permanent earthen lodges, to farm, and to hunt buffalo only part time, even after acquiring the horse.

For most plains Indians farther west, such as the Arapahos, Crow, Comanches, Cheyenne, Apaches, Blackfeet, Sioux, and Kiowas, life was truly nomadic, spent ever on the move. They might pursue the roaming buffalo for hundreds of miles, taking food, clothing, and shelter with them packed on their travois. While traveling they subsisted on pemmican, a smelly but nourishing concoction of dried meat, berries, bone marrow, and melted fat. The hunting grounds of the various tribes were only vaguely defined and intertribal contact was frequent, especially for trading purposes. On these occasions the nomads would barter their buffalo pelts and meat for corn and other agricultural products raised by the more sedentary peoples who made their homes on the fringes of the plains.

■ As Alfred Jacob Miller's *Migration of the Pawnees* (above) shows, nomadic life imposed a grueling routine. With the travois, dogs could drag 40-pound loads 5 or 6 miles a day.

■ Friedrich Kurz drew these Hidatsas (at left) portaging their bullboats on the upper Missouri in 1851. The bullboat was made of buffalo hide stretched over a willow framework.

■ A Mandan woman carrying a pack (at right) leads a loaded dog sled on which her child rides across the frozen Missouri in what is now North Dakota. A Bodmer watercolor, 1834.

K. Bodmer

The Buffalo

"Again and again that morning rang out the same welcome cry of *buffalo, buffalo!* . . . At noon the plain before us was alive with thousands of buffalo—bulls, cows, and calves—all moving rapidly as we drew near. . . . In a moment I was in the midst of a cloud, half suffocated by the dust and stunned by the trampling of the flying herd; but I was drunk with the chase and cared for nothing but the buffalo." That was how historian Francis Parkman was affected by a buffalo hunt in 1846, the year before H. G. Hines painted the scene below. For Parkman the hunt was an exhilarating experience; for the plains Indian it was the central act of life, combining necessity, passion, and sport. Alfred Jacob Miller's *Yell of Triumph* (right) captures something of this feeling.

Once killed and butchered, there was little the buffalo did not provide. From the carcass came fresh meat for feasting and dried meat for lean times. The skin provided blankets, moccasins, mittens, shirts, leggings, dresses, underclothes—and a "canvas" for the artist. Sinew was turned into thread and bowstrings; bones into farming tools; horns into cups, ladles, and spoons; the stomach into a water bottle. Even vanity was served: the rough side of a buffalo tongue was used as a hairbrush and the oily fat became a plains hair tonic.

Religion and the Hunt

In common with many primitive peoples, the plains Indians drew no clear distinction between the natural and the supernatural. They paid as much attention to the one as to the other, believing that all things had spirits and that these spirits controlled the natural world. No aspect of plains life reflects this harmonious fusion of natural and supernatural better than the buffalo hunt.

A hunt was as carefully organized and as skillfully managed as a modern military operation. In early spring the various bands of the tribe would gather at a predetermined place. There the chiefs and the elders convened a council and deliberated their strategy and tactics. To insure that plans were followed precisely, one of the warrior societies policed the hunt while scouts kept tabs on the movements of the herd. Once the "battle" was joined, the animals were slaughtered until all needs were met. Little seemed left to chance.

However effective and well organized the hunters were, they believed that without the assistance of the spirits the herds would not come within range, the hunters would lack courage and skill at the crucial moment, and ultimately the harmonious relationship between the shaggy "four-leggeds" and the "two-leggeds" would be destroyed. To insure the overall success of the hunt, the tribesmen therefore devoted as much attention to religious ceremonies and "medicine signs" as they did to planning, discipline, and the perfection of their hunting skills.

■ Devices for luring the buffalo varied from tribe to tribe. Karl Bodmer's watercolor of Assiniboin "magic" (lower left) was painted in 1834.

■ Of grimmer composition is the Mandan "medicine sign" for attracting the herds (right).

■ For centuries before the plains Indians obtained the horse, a favorite method of buffalo hunting was impounding, illustrated below by Canadian artist Paul Kane in 1845.

■ Bodmer's painting of a Mandan Bull Society dance, held periodically to draw the herds close to the village, reflects the plains Indians' intense feelings toward the buffalo.

After the Hunt

Plains life was not all buffalo hunting. There were days to be spent around the domestic hearth, children to be raised, ceremonies to be performed, games to be played. Work, other than hunting and making war, was generally for women. Education was in the school of experience—a boy learned his role by riding alongside his father, while a girl's mother was her tutor in the arts of the tepee. Elaborate rituals at the onset of puberty were rare, though in most tribes young men went off on a lonely vigil in search of a vision to guide them. A young man could marry when he possessed the requisite number of horses to give to the girl's family as tokens of his esteem. Courtship largely consisted of the lover's playing a flute to his sequestered sweetheart. There was no elaborate marriage ceremony in the modern sense, though custom demanded certain ceremonial observances. The bride, while very much the servant of her husband, was not considered an inferior being.

Hunting and war were in part sport, but they did not exhaust the plains Indians' delight in recreation. Horse racing and dice gave free rein to their love of chance; lacrosse and foot races provided tests of their athletic skills; storytelling presented the central myths of their culture; and clowning gave vent to a Rabelaisian wit.

■ Not all horse-riding, buffalo-hunting plains Indians lived in tepees. The earthen lodges of the Mandans (at left, by Miller, and opposite, by Bodmer) each housed several families, a few favorite horses, a number of dogs, and a wide range of equipment for cooking, hunting, and ceremonial observances. The plains tribes enjoyed rough stick and ball games such as lacrosse (sketches on this page) and shinny, an early rugged form of field hockey favored by plains women. As Paul Kane's painting (below) of a Blackfoot horse race suggests, equestrian games took the spotlight. Since Indians loved a sporting bet, games were carefully refereed to insure fair play.

The Road to Glory

War was the greatest game of all; it was the plains Indian's career, hobby, and the touchstone of honor and prestige. Indians were told from childhood, as a Blackfoot litany put it, that "It is bad to live to be old. Better to die young fighting bravely in battle." Young boys listened to the elaborate recountings of the valor of a successful war party or to the derisive mocking directed at a man unlucky enough to be accounted a coward as though they were hearing sermons on heaven and hell. They longed for the day when they could join a warrior society and embrace its Spartan discipline. In their teens they fasted alone in the hope of seeing a vision of the spirit of their adoptive father (usually an animal or an impressive natural phenomenon). This spirit would confirm the warrior's identity and give instructions for the "medicine bundle" that was to protect him in battle.

On occasion tribal war had an economic motive, as in the defense of hunting grounds, but its usual objective was glory and its trappings. Honor was quantified by the system of counting coups, which were won not just by mere slaughter but by such feats as stealing an enemy's favorite horse or touching an armed foe with the hand or with nothing more wounding than a decorated coup stick.

■ About 1832 Karl Bodmer did a facsimile (above) of an earlier Indian painting of a hand-to-hand fight with a trapper, a combat rating the highest coup.

■ George Catlin's 1850 drawing (at left) shows the virtuoso horsemanship of a Comanche who, hanging only by his heel, unleashes a rapid-fire volley of arrows.

■ Among the artifacts in Bodmer's print (facing page) is a coup stick, complete with feathers for the number of coups, above the arrow at right. The edged weapon at right is a type of tomahawk; at lower center is a war shield decorated with "medicine."

■ This Apache skin painting shows a blending of plains and southwestern cultural elements. The ceremony in progress is a girls' puberty rite, rare in the northern plains but much observed in the Southwest. The rest of the tribe watches from in front of their tepees (a plains element) while the girls, paired with older women who are their guardians and accompanied by posturing medicine men (wearing southwestern-style headdresses), perform a dance around the purifying fire.

■ Alfred Jacob Miller's painting above, *Snake Indian Council* (ca. 1840), pictures a tribal powwow as a dignified, ceremonious affair.

Lovers of Ceremony

Few people have been as self-sufficient as the plains Indians while at the same time professing to be so dependent on forces outside themselves. The plains resembled the ocean (a metaphor repeatedly appearing in the accounts of white explorers)—vast and mysterious, inspiring both humility and a feeling of what might be called "cosmic togetherness." Far from seeing themselves as masters of the environment, Indians felt adrift on a great sea of whispering prairie grass, endlessly searching for the life-giving buffalo that symbolized the miraculous world of nature.

Under such circumstances it is hardly surprising that the plains Indians believed themselves to be dwelling within a web of supernatural powers. Survival depended on maintaining contact with these powers; thus the Indian became a seeker of visions and a practicer of rituals, devoted to ceremonies that would bring partnership with the cosmos. The primacy of this relationship helps explain the general lack of scientific curiosity in the plains cultures, and it accounts for an estimable sense of humility and awe.

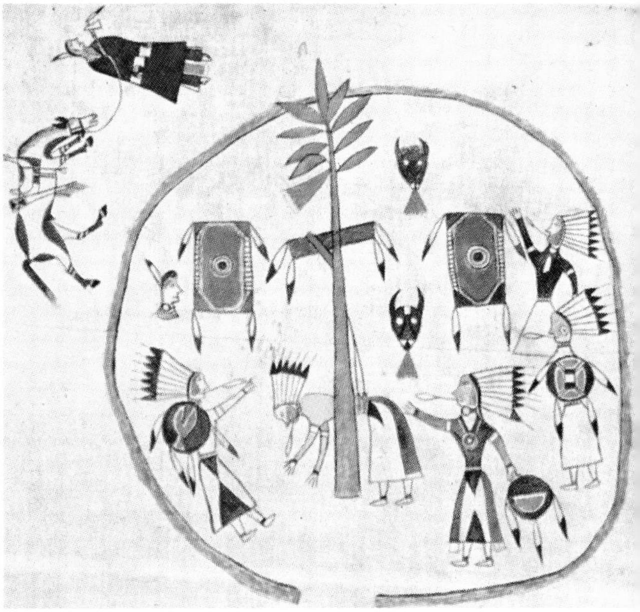

■ A Shoshoni skin painting that dates from the 1880s portrays in careful detail a ritualistic sun dance as seen from above a tepee.

An Indian Horse Dance.

Art and Artifacts

The artifacts of the plains Indian, like so much else in the culture, combined art with utility. Textiles were poorly developed, pottery limited, and wood carving and stone sculpture almost absent, all for good reasons—cotton was unknown, pottery easily broken in transit, trees few and far between, and stone too heavy to transport. But when it came to making clothes and utensils decorated with quills, beads, paint, feathers, and the fur from that all-purpose beast the buffalo, the plains artisans were in their element. The women dressed and prepared buffalo hides and then, from beaded moccasin to feathered headdress, made the tribe's clothing, such as the girl's dress at the right. They cut, fitted, and sewed buffalo hides to make the covering for the tepee, but it was the man's prerogative to decorate the tepee's exterior with his paintings. The painting reproduced opposite, by Kills Two, an Oglala Sioux, is a striking demonstration of the skill and technical virtuosity of the plains artists.

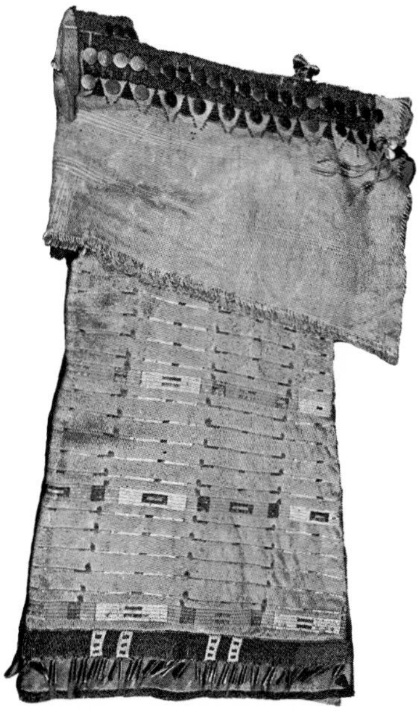

■ The examples below of porcupine quillwork include an Arapaho disk used as a tepee ornament, a Sioux knife sheath, a quill pouch made from an elk bladder, and a decorated tobacco pouch.

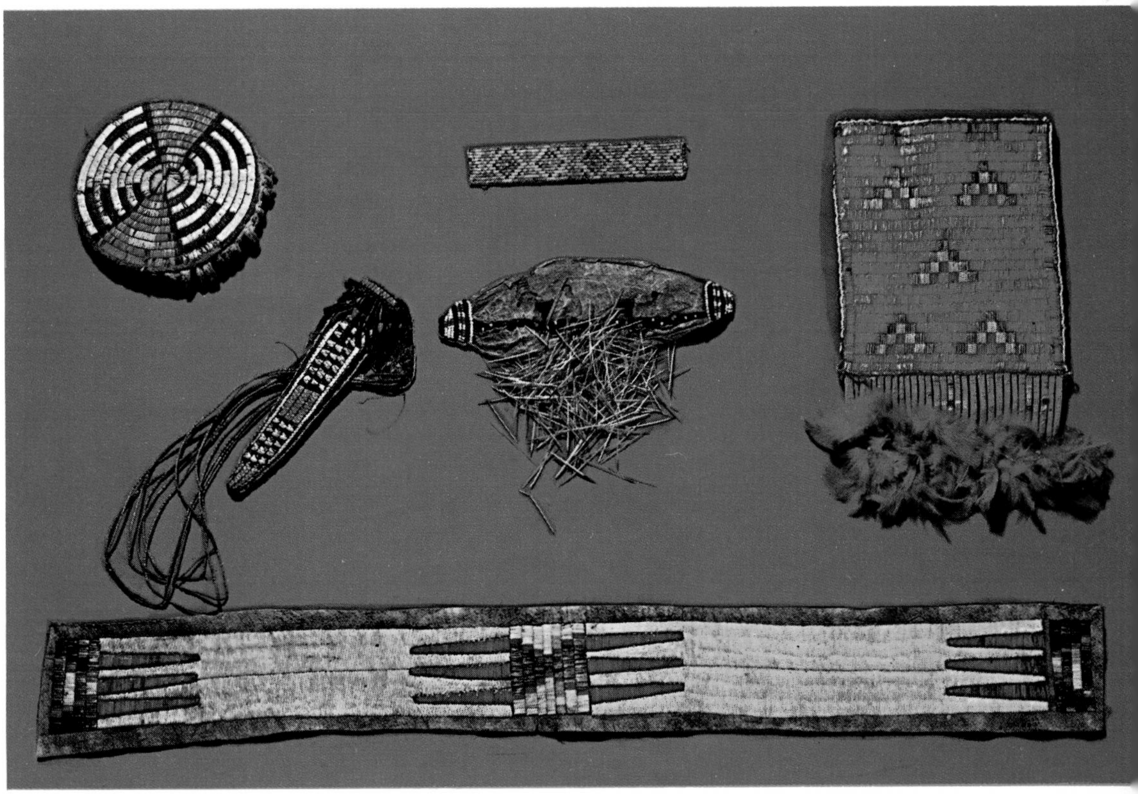

Changing Ways

In just about 50 years, from 1840 to 1890, the plains civilization reached its peak and then plunged to the verge of extinction. In his 1885 painting *Caught in the Act,* Charles Russell, the "cowboy artist," depicted a starving Indian family reduced to stealing ranchers' cattle. By this time the plains tribes had suffered the ravages of white diseases, the debasing

effects of whiskey, the harassment of the army, and the grim hardship resulting from the senseless slaughter of the buffalo. Having smashed the Indians' way of life beyond repair, the government confined them to the reservation. Just before committing suicide, Satanta, a Kiowa chief, spoke for all the plains tribes when he said, "I don't want to settle. I love to roam the prairie. . . . These soldiers cut down my timber, they kill my buffalo, and when I see that, it feels as if my heart would burst with sorrow."

■ Reproduced above, in a detail, is a heroic Sioux version of the Battle of the Little Big Horn, in which Crazy Horse (center) leads the slaughter of Custer's men. L. A. Huffman's portrait of the Cheyenne scout Red Panther (opposite) offers testimony to the true nobility of the "noble red man."

The Legacy

Although by the end of the 19th century the civilization of the plains tribesmen was "fast traveling to the shades of their fathers, towards the setting sun," the very conquerors who had been unable to live in peace with the Indians surrounded their memory with romance and myth. In defeat the Indian became the "noble savage"; Custer's Last Stand will be remembered as long as Gettysburg or Pearl Harbor. Yet the real importance of the plains Indians stems from their attitude toward life, not merely from their courage and their war skills.

In 1947 John Collier, former commissioner of Indian affairs, spoke out for another interpretation of Indian culture. "They had what the world has lost," Collier wrote, ". . . the ancient, lost reverence and passion for human personality, joined with the ancient, lost reverence and passion for the earth and its web of life. . . . They had . . . this power for living . . . as world-view and self-view, as tradition and institution, as practical philosophy dominating their societies, and as an art supreme. . . ."

17/AN AGE OF EXPLOITATION

When Americans turned from fighting and making weapons to more constructive occupations, they transformed their agriculture, trade, manufacturing, mining, and means of communication. Immigration increased rapidly. Cities grew in size and number, exerting on every aspect of life an influence at least as pervasive as that exercised on earlier generations by the frontier. More and more Americans were flocking to the towns and cities, supporting themselves by laboring at machines or by scratching accounts in ledgers. Yet such was the expansive force of the time that farm production rose to new heights, invigorated by new marketing methods and the increased use of machinery. Railroad construction stimulated and unified the economy, helping to make possible still larger and more efficient industrial and agricultural enterprises. The flow of gold and silver from western mines excited people's imaginations and their avarice, while petroleum, the "black gold" discovered in Pennsylvania shortly before the war, gave rise to a new industry soon to become one of the most important in the nation. These developments amounted to more than a mere change of scale; they altered the structure of society.

"Root, Hog, or Die"

After Appomattox, boom conditions existed everywhere outside the South. Americans seemed to have abandoned all restraint in a mad race for personal gain. The immense resources of the United States, combined with certain aspects of the American character, such as the high value assigned to work and achievement, made the people strongly materialistic. From colonial times they had assumed that prosperity was the natural state of things, and they had shown an inordinate respect for wealth. The Civil War further encouraged the glorification of material values. The North's capacity to produce the tools of war had helped preserve the Union; the role of businessmen and manufacturers in winning the struggle was clear to every soldier from General Grant to the lowliest private.

During the emotional letdown that followed the war, Americans seemed even more enamored of material values. They were tired of sacrifice, eager to act for themselves. Except in their attitude toward the South, still psychologically "outside" the United States, they professed to believe strongly in a government policy of noninterference, or laissez faire. "'Things regulate themselves' . . . means, of course, that God regulates them by his general laws," Professor Francis Bowen of Harvard wrote in his *American Political Economy* (1870). "The progress of the country," another economist said, "is independent of legislation."

Impressed by such logic and never especially noted for their sophistication, taste, or interest in preserving the resources of the country, the people now tolerated the grossest kind of waste and seemed to care little about corruption in high places, so long as no one interfered with their personal pursuit of profit. The writer Mark Twain, raised in an earlier era, called this a Gilded Age, dazzling on the surface, base metal below. A later writer named the period the Great Barbecue, a time when everyone rushed to gobble up the national inheritance like hungry picnickers crowding around the savory roast at one of the big political outings common in those years. Twain and other critics took too dark a view of the era. Never, perhaps, did Americans display more vigor, more imagination, or greater confidence in themselves and the future of the country. In his novel *The Gilded Age,* written with Charles Dudley Warner, Twain portrayed this aspect of the period along with its cheapness and corruption.

Certain intellectual currents encouraged the exploitative drives of the people. Charles Darwin's *Origin of Species* was published in 1859, and by the seventies his theory of evolution was beginning to influence opinion in the United States. That nature had ordained a kind of inevitable progress, governed by the natural selection of those individual organisms best adapted to survive in a particular environment, seemed eminently reasonable to most Americans, for it fitted well with their own experiences. "Let the buyer beware; that covers the whole business," the sugar magnate Henry O. Havemeyer explained to an investigating committee. "You cannot wet-nurse people from the time they are born until the time they die. They have to wade in and get stuck, and that is the way men are educated."

This reasoning was similar to that of the classical economists and was thus at least as old as Adam Smith's *Wealth of Nations* (1776). But it appeared to supply a hard scientific substitute for Smith's somewhat vague "invisible hand" as an explanation of why free competition advanced the common good. Yale professor William Graham Sumner, an ardent advocate of laissez faire economics in the 1870s, sometimes used the survival-of-the-fittest analogy in teaching undergraduates. "Professor," one student asked Sumner, "don't you believe in any government aid to industries?" "No!" Sumner replied, "it's root, hog, or die." The student persisted: "Suppose some professor of political science came along and took your job away from you. Wouldn't you be sore?" "Any other professor is welcome to try," Sumner answered promptly. "If he gets my job, it is my fault. My business is to teach the subject so well that no one can take the job away from me."

Few men of practical affairs were directly influenced by Darwin's ideas. Most eagerly accepted any aid they could get from the government, many were active in philanthropy, some felt a deep sense of social responsibility. Nevertheless, most were sincere individualists. They believed in competition, being convinced that the nation would best prosper if all people were free to seek their personal fortunes by their own methods. With such ideas ascendant, exploitation and complacency became the hallmarks of the postwar decades.

The Plains Indians

For 250 years the Indians had been driven back steadily, yet on the eve of the Civil War they still inhabited roughly half the United States. By the time of Hayes' inauguration, however, the Indians had been shattered as an independent people, and in another decade the survivors were penned up on reservations, the government committed to a policy of extinguishing their way of life.

In 1860 the survivors of most of the eastern tribes were living peacefully in what is now Oklahoma. In California the forty-niners had made short work of the local tribes. Elsewhere in the West—in the deserts of the Great Basin between the Sierras and the Rockies, in the mountains themselves, and on the semiarid, grass-covered plains between the Rockies and the edge of white civilization in eastern Kansas and Nebraska—nearly a quarter of a million Indians dominated the land.

By far the most important lived on the High Plains. From the Blackfeet of southwestern Canada and the Sioux of Minnesota and the Dakotas to the Cheyenne of Colorado and Wyoming and the Comanche of northern Texas, the tribes possessed a generally uniform culture. All lived by hunting the hulking American bison, or buffalo, which ranged over the plains by the million. The buffalo provided the Indians with food, clothing, even shelter, for the famous Indian tepee was covered with hides. On the treeless plains, dried buffalo dung was used for fuel. The buffalo was also an important symbol in Indian religion.

Although they seemed the epitome of freedom, pride, and self-reliance, the plains Indians had begun to fall under the sway of white power. They eagerly adopted the products of the more technically advanced culture—cloth, metal tools, weapons, cheap decorations—but the most important thing the whites gave them was the horse.

The geological record shows that the genus *Equus* was native to America, but it had become extinct in the Western Hemisphere long before Cortés brought the first modern horses to America in the 16th century. Multiplying rapidly thereafter, the animals soon roamed wild from Texas to the Argentine. By the 18th century the Indians of the plains had made them a vital part of their culture. Horses thrived on the plains and so did their masters. Mounted Indians could run down buffalo instead of stalking them on foot. They could move more easily over the country and fight more effectively too. They could acquire and transport more possessions and increase the size of their tepees, for horses could drag heavy loads heaped on A-shaped frames (called *travois* by the French), where earlier Indians had only dogs to depend on as pack animals. The frames of the *travois*, when disassembled, served as poles for tepees. The Indians also adopted modern weapons, the cavalry sword, which they particularly admired, and the rifle. Both added to their effectiveness as hunters and fighters. However, like the whites' liquor and diseases, to which Indians quickly succumbed, horses and guns caused problems. The buffalo herds began to diminish, and warfare became bloodier and more frequent.

In a familiar and tragic pattern, the majority of the western tribes greeted the first whites to enter their domains in a friendly fashion. As late as the 1830s, white hunters and trappers ranged freely over most of the West, trading with the Indians and often marrying Indian women. Settlers pushing cross country toward Oregon in the 1840s met with relatively little trouble, though at times bands of braves on the warpath molested small groups or indulged in petty thievery that the migrants found annoying.

After the start of the gold rush the need to link the East with California meant that the tribes were pushed aside. Deliberately the government in Washington prepared the way. In 1851 Thomas Fitzpatrick, an experienced mountain man, a founder of the Rocky Mountain Fur Company, scout for the first large group of settlers to Oregon in 1841 and for American soldiers in California during the Mexican War, and now an Indian agent, summoned a great "council" of the tribes. About 10,000 Indians, representing nearly all the plains tribes, gathered that September at Horse Creek, 37 miles east of Fort Laramie, in what is now Wyoming. Fitzpatrick was an intelligent and sensible man whom the Indians respected. He had recently married a woman who was half Indian. At Horse Creek he persuaded each tribe to accept definite limits to its hunting grounds. For example, the Sioux nations were to keep north of the Platte River, and the Cheyenne and Arapaho were to confine themselves to the Colorado foothills. In return the Indians were promised gifts and annual payments. This policy, known as "concentration," was designed to cut down on intertribal warfare and—far more important—to enable the government to negotiate separately with each tribe. It was the classic strategy of divide and conquer.

Although it made a mockery of diplomacy to treat with Indian tribes as though they were European powers, the United States maintained that each tribe was a sovereign nation, to be dealt with as an equal in solemn treaties. Both sides knew that this was not the case. When Indians agreed to meet in council, they were tacitly admitting defeat. They seldom drove hard bargains or broke off negotiations. Moreover, tribal chiefs had only limited power; young braves frequently refused to respect agreements made by their elders.

Indian Wars

The government showed little interest in honoring agreements with Indians. "Treaties," the historian Wilcomb E. Washburn writes, "were often made, often modified, often ignored, and often broken." No sooner had the Kansas-Nebraska bill become law than the Kansa, Omaha, Pawnee, and Yankton Sioux tribes began to feel pressure for further concessions of territory. By 1860 most of Kansas and Nebraska had been cleared; the Indians had lost all but 1.5 million of their 19-odd million acres. A gold rush into Colorado in 1859 sent thousands of greedy prospectors across the plains to drive the Cheyenne and Arapaho from land guaranteed them in 1851. Other trouble developed in the Sioux country. Thus it happened that in 1862, after federal troops had been pulled out of the West for service against the Confederacy, most of the plains Indians rose up against the whites. For five years intermittent but bloody clashes kept the entire area in a state of alarm.

This was guerrilla warfare, with all its horror and treachery. In 1864 a party of Colorado militia fell upon an unsuspecting Cheyenne community at Sand Creek and killed an estimated 450. "Kill and scalp all, big and little," Colonel J. M. Chivington, a minister in private life, told his men. "Nits make lice." A white observer described the scene: "They were scalped, their brains knocked out; the men used their knives, ripped open women, clubbed little children, knocked them in the head with their guns, beat their brains out, mutilated their bodies in every sense of the word." General Nelson A. Miles called this "Chivington Massacre" the "foulest and most unjustifiable crime in the annals of America," but it was no worse than many incidents in earlier conflicts with Indians, no worse than what was later to occur in guerrilla wars involving American troops in the Philippines and (more recently) in Vietnam.

In turn the Indians slaughtered dozens of isolated white families, ambushed small parties, and fought many successful skirmishes against troops and militia. They achieved their most notable triumph in December 1866, when the Oglala Sioux, under their great chief Red Cloud, wiped out a party of 82 soldiers under Captain W. J. Fetterman. Red Cloud fought ruthlessly, but only when goaded by the construction of the Bozeman Trail, a road through the heart of the Sioux hunting grounds in southern Montana.

In 1867 the government tried a new strategy. The "concentration" policy had evidently not gone far enough. All the plains Indians would be confined to two small reservations, one in the Black Hills of Dakota Territory, the other in Oklahoma, and forced to become farmers. At two great conclaves held in 1867 and 1868 at Medicine Lodge Creek and Fort Laramie, the principal chiefs yielded to the government's demands.

Many Indians refused to abide by these agreements. With their whole way of life at stake, they raged across the plains like a prairie fire—and were almost as destructive. General Philip Sheridan, Grant's cavalry commander, explained the situation accurately: "We took away their country and their means of support, broke up their mode of living, their habits of life, introduced disease and decay among them, and it was for this and against this that they made war. Could anyone expect less?"

That a relative handful of "savages," without

■ **General Sherman and the United States commissioners in council with the Sioux chiefs at Fort Laramie in 1868.**

central leadership or plan, could hold off the cream of the army, battle-hardened in the Civil War, can be explained by the character of the vast, trackless country and the ineptness of most American military commanders. Indian leadership was also poor in that few chiefs were capable of organizing a campaign or following up an advantage. But the Indians made superb guerrillas. Every observer called them the best cavalry soldiers in the world. Armed with stubby, powerful bows capable of driving an arrow clear through a bull buffalo, they were a fair match for troops equipped with carbines and Colt revolvers. Expertly they led pursuers into traps, swept down on unsuspecting supply details, stole up on small parties the way a mountain lion stalks a grazing lamb. They could sometimes be rounded up, as Sheridan herded the tribes of the Southwest into Indian Territory in 1869, but once the troops withdrew, braves began to melt away into the emptiness of the surrounding grasslands. The distinction between "treaty" Indians, who had agreed to live on the new reservations, and the "nontreaty" variety shifted almost from day to day. Trouble flared here one week, next week somewhere else, perhaps 500 miles away. No less an authority than General William Tecumseh Sherman testified that a mere 50 Indians could often "checkmate" 3,000 soldiers.

If one concedes that no one could reverse the direction of history or stop the invasion of Indian lands, then some version of the "small reservation" policy would probably have been best for the Indians. Had they been given a reasonable amount of land and adequate subsidies and allowed to maintain their way of life, they might have accepted the situation and ceased to harry the whites.

Whatever chance that policy had was greatly weakened by the government's maladministration of Indian affairs. In dealing with Indians, 19th-century Americans displayed a grave lack of talent for administration. After 1849 the Department of the Interior supposedly had charge of tribal affairs. Most of its agents systematically cheated the Indians. One, heavily involved in mining operations on the side, diverted goods intended for his charges to his private ventures. When an inspector looked into his records, he sold him shares in a mine. That worthy in turn protected himself by sharing some of the loot with the son of the commissioner of Indian affairs. Army officers squabbled frequently with Indian agents over policy, while an "Indian Ring" in the Department of the Interior systematically stole funds and supplies intended for the reservation Indians. "No branch of the national government is so spotted with fraud, so tainted with corruption, so utterly unworthy of a free and enlightened government, as this Indian Bureau," Republican Congressman James A. Garfield charged in 1869.

At about this time a Yale paleontologist, Professor Othniel C. Marsh, who wished to dig for fossils on the Sioux reservation, asked Red Cloud for permission to enter his domain. The chief agreed on condition that Marsh, whom the Indians called Big Bone Chief, take back with him samples of the moldy flour and beef that government agents were supplying to his people. Appalled by what he saw on the reservation, Marsh took the rotten supplies directly to President Grant and prepared a list of charges against the agents. General Sherman, in overall command of the Indian country, claimed in 1875: "We could settle Indian troubles in an hour, but Congress wants the patronage of the Indian bureau, and the bureau wants the appropriations without any of the trouble of the Indians themselves."

Grant wished to place the reservations under army control, but even the Indians opposed this. In areas around army camps Indians fared no better than on the reservations. A quartermaster in the Apache country in New Mexico made off with 12,000 pounds of corn from the meager supplies set aside for Indian relief. According to one late 19th-century historian, "officers at those camps where the Indians were fed habitually used their official position to break the chastity of Indian women."

In 1869 Congress created a nonpolitical Board of Indian Commissioners to oversee Indian affairs, but the bureaucrats in Washington stymied the commissioners at every turn. "Their recommendations were ignored . . . gross breaking of the law was winked at, and . . . many matters were not submitted to them at all," the biographer of one commissioner has written. "They decided that their task was as useless as it was irritating."

In time the Indians might have submitted had they been allowed to hold the lands granted them under the "small reservation" policy, for they knew they could never eject the whites from their country. This was not to be. Gold was discovered in the Black Hills in 1874. By the next winter thousands of miners had invaded the reserved area. Already alarmed by the approach of crews building the Northern Pacific Railroad, the Sioux once again went on the warpath. Joining with nontreaty tribes to the west, they concentrated in the region of the Bighorn River, in southern Montana Territory.

The summer of 1876 saw three columns of troops in the field against them. The commander of one column, General Alfred H. Terry, sent ahead a small detachment of the Seventh Cavalry under Colonel George A. Custer with orders to locate the Indians' camp and then block their escape route into the inaccessible Bighorn Mountains. Custer was vain and rash, and vanity and rashness were grave handicaps in Indian fighting. Grossly underestimating the number of the Indians, he decided to attack directly with his tiny force of 264 men. At the Little Bighorn late in June he found himself surrounded by 2,500 Sioux under Rain-in-the-Face, Crazy Horse, and Sitting Bull. He and his men fought bravely, but every one of them died on the field.

Because it was so one-sided, "Custer's Last Stand" was not a typical battle, though it may be taken as symbolic of the Indian warfare of the period in the sense that it was characterized by bravery, foolhardiness, and a tragic waste of life. The battle greatly heartened the Indians, but it did not gain them their cause. That autumn, short of rations and hard pressed by overwhelming numbers of soldiers, they surrendered and returned to the reservation.

Destruction of Tribal Life

Thereafter, the plains fighting slackened. For this the building of transcontinental railroads and the destruction of the buffalo were chiefly responsible. An estimated 13 to 15 million head had roamed the plains in the mid sixties. Then the slaughter began. Thousands were butchered to feed the gangs of laborers engaged in building the Union Pacific Railroad. Thousands more fell before the guns of sportsmen. Buffalo hunting became a fad, and a brisk demand developed for buffalo rugs and mounted buffalo heads. Railroads ran excursion trains for hunters; even the shameful practice of gunning down the beasts directly from the cars was allowed. In 1871–1872 the Grand Duke Alexis of Russia headed a gigantic hunt, supported by "Buffalo Bill" Cody, most famous of the professional buffalo killers, by the Seventh United States Cavalry under General Sheridan, and by hundreds of Indians.

The discovery in 1871 of a way to make commercial use of buffalo hides completed the tragedy. In the next three years about 9 million head were killed; after another decade the animals were almost extinct. No more efficient way could have been found for destroying the plains Indians. The disappearance of the bison left them starving, homeless, purposeless.

In 1887 Congress passed the Dawes Severalty Act, designed to put an end to tribal life and convert the Indians to the white way of living. Tribal lands were split up into small units, each head of a family being given a quarter section (160 acres). In order to keep speculators from wresting it from the Indians during the period of adjustment, this land could not be disposed of for 25 years. Indians who accepted allotments, took up residence "separate and apart from any tribe," and "adopted the habits of civilized life" were granted United States citizenship. (Those who did not were finally made citizens in 1924.)

The government also set aside funds for educating and training the Indians. Now that the Indians' power to resist had been destroyed, many persons became interested in helping them, stimulated by such books as Helen Hunt Jackson's *A Century of Dishonor* (1881), a somewhat romantic but essentially just denunciation of past policy.

Although intended as a humane reform, the Dawes Act had disastrous results. Devised in an age that knew almost nothing about anthropology or social structure, it assumed that Indians could be transformed into small agricultural capitalists by an act of Congress. It shattered what was left of the Indians' culture without enabling them to adapt to white ways. Moreover, unscrupulous white men systematically tricked many Indians into leasing their allotments for a pittance, and local authorities often taxed Indian lands at excessive rates. In 1934, after about 86 million of the 138 million acres assigned under the Dawes Act had passed into white hands, the government returned to a policy of encouraging tribal ownership of Indian lands.

By 1887 the tribes of the mountains and deserts beyond the plains had also given up the fight. Typical of the heartlessness of the government's treatment of these peoples was that afforded the Nez Percé of Oregon and Idaho, who were led by the remarkable Chief Joseph. After outwitting federal troops in a campaign across more than a thousand miles of rough country, Joseph finally surrendered in October 1877. The Nez Percé were then settled on "the malarial bottoms of the Indian Territory" in far-off Oklahoma. The last Indians to abandon the unequal battle were the bitter, relentless Apaches of the Southwest, who finally yielded upon the capture of their fanatical leader, Geronimo, in 1886.

Victims of Prejudice

Americans shunted the Indians aside merely because they stood in their way. Other minorities were treated with equal callousness and contempt in the postwar decades. That the South would deal harshly with the former slaves once federal control was relaxed probably should have been expected. Men like Governor Wade Hampton of South Carolina had piously promised to respect black civil rights. "We . . . will secure to every citizen, the lowest as well as the highest, black as well as white, full and equal protection in the enjoyment of all his rights under the Constitution," Hampton said in 1877. This pledge was not kept.

President Hayes had urged blacks to trust the southern whites. A new Era of Good Feelings had dawned, he announced after making a goodwill tour of the South shortly after his inauguration. By December 1877 he had been sadly disillusioned.

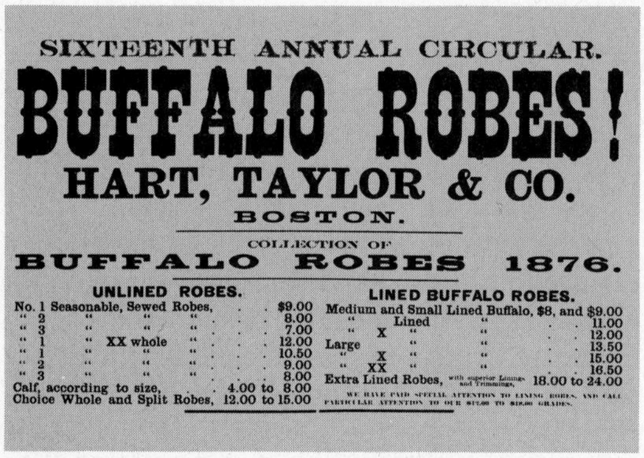

■ **Buffalo robes for carriages and sleighs were enormously popular in the eastern states, as were buffalo overcoats, which sold for less than $20. Strips of the tough hides were widely used as belts on power-driven machinery.**

■ **After his surrender in 1886, the celebrated Chiricahua Apache Geronimo (right) posed with a fellow chief, Natiche, at an army post in Arizona Territory. Geronimo and the Chiricahuas were eventually settled in Oklahoma.**

"By state legislation, by frauds, by intimidation, and by violence of the most atrocious character, colored citizens have been deprived of the right of suffrage," he wrote in his diary. However, though he had written earlier, "My task was to wipe out the color line," he did nothing to remedy the situation except, as his biographer Harry Barnard says, "to scold the South and threaten action." Frederick Douglass called Hayes' policy "sickly conciliation."

Hayes' successors in the 1880s did no better. "Time is the only cure," President Garfield said, thereby confessing that he had no policy at all. President Arthur gave federal patronage to anti-black groups in an effort to split the Democratic South. In President Cleveland's day blacks had scarcely a friend in high places, North or South. In 1887 Cleveland explained to a correspondent why he opposed "mixed schools." Expert opinion, the president said, believed "that separate schools were of much more benefit for the colored people." Hayes, Garfield, and Arthur were Republicans, Cleveland a Democrat; party made little difference. Both parties subscribed to hypocritical statements about equality and constitutional rights, and neither did anything to implement them.

For a time blacks were not totally disfranchised in the South. Rival white factions tried to manipulate them, and corruption flourished as widely as in the machine-dominated wards of the northern cities. In the 1890s, however, the southern states, led by Mississippi, began to deprive blacks of the vote despite the Fifteenth Amendment. Poll taxes, often cumulative, raised a formidable economic barrier, one that also disfranchised many poor whites. Literacy tests completed the work; a number of states provided a loophole for illiterate whites by including an "understanding" clause whereby an illiterate person could qualify by demonstrating an ability to explain the meaning of a section of the state constitution when an election official read it to him. Blacks who attempted to take the test were uniformly declared to have failed it.

In Louisiana, 130,000 blacks voted in the election of 1896. Then the law was changed. In 1900 only 5,000 votes were cast by blacks. With unctuous hypocrisy, white southerners insisted that they loved "their" blacks dearly and wished only to protect them from "the machinations of those who would use them only to further their own base ends." "We take away the Negroes' votes," a Louisiana politician explained, "to protect them just as we would protect a little child and prevent it from injuring itself with sharp-edged tools."

Practically every Supreme Court decision after 1877 that affected blacks somehow "nullified or curtailed" their rights, Professor Rayford W. Logan writes. In *Hall* v. *De Cuir* (1878) the Court even threw out a state law *forbidding* segregation on river boats, arguing that it was an unjustifiable interference with interstate commerce. The *Civil Rights Cases* (1883) declared unconstitutional the Civil Rights Act of 1875, which had barred segregation in public facilities. Blacks who were refused equal accommodations or privileges by hotels, theaters, and other privately owned facilities had no recourse at law, the Court announced. The Fourteenth Amendment guaranteed their civil rights against invasion by the states, not by individuals.

Finally, in *Plessy* v. *Ferguson* (1896), the Court ruled that even in places of public accommodation, such as railroads and, by implication, schools, segregation was legal so long as "separate but equal" facilities were provided. "If one race be inferior to the other socially, the Constitution of the United States cannot put them upon the same plane." In a noble dissent in the Plessy case, Justice John Marshall Harlan protested this line of argument. "Our Constitution is color-blind," he said. "The arbitrary separation of citizens, on the basis of race . . . is a badge of servitude wholly inconsistent with civil freedom and the equality before the law established by the Constitution." Alas, more than half a century was to pass before the Court came around to Harlan's reasoning and reversed the Plessy decision. Meanwhile, total segregation was imposed throughout the South. Separate schools, prisons, hospitals, recreational facilities, and even cemeteries were provided for blacks, and these were almost never equal to those available to whites.

Most northerners supported the government and the Court. "The Negro's day is over," the tough-minded William Graham Sumner explained. "He is out of fashion." Nearly all the newspapers commented favorably on the decision in the *Civil Rights Cases.* In news stories, papers presented a stereotyped, derogatory picture of blacks, no matter what the circumstances. Northern magazines, even high-quality publications such as *Harper's, Scribner's,* and the *Century,* repeatedly made blacks the butt of crude jokes.

Since nearly all contemporary biologists, physicians, and other supposed experts on race were convinced that blacks were inferior beings, educated northerners could hardly avoid accepting black inferiority as fact. James Bryce, an Englishman whose study of the United States at this time, *The American Commonwealth,* has become a classic, saw much of Americans of this type and often absorbed their point of view. Negroes, Bryce wrote, were docile, pliable, submissive, lustful, childish, impressionable, emotional, heedless, and "unthrifty." They had "no capacity for abstract thinking, for scientific inquiry, or for any kind of invention." Being "unspeakably inferior," they were "unfit to cope with a superior race."

Like Bryce, most Americans did not especially wish blacks ill; they simply refused to consider them quite human and consigned them complacently to oblivion, along with the Indians. A vicious circle was established. By denying blacks decent educational opportunities and good jobs, the dominant race could use the blacks' resultant ignorance and poverty to justify the inferior facilities offered them.

Southern blacks reacted to this deplorable situation in a variety of ways. Some sought redress in racial pride and what would later be called black nationalism. Such persons founded a number of all-black communities in Oklahoma Territory and led the great "exodus" of 1879, when, to the consternation of southern whites, thousands of blacks suddenly migrated to Kansas.* Some became so disaffected with American life that they tried to revive the African colonization movement. "Africa is our home," insisted Bishop Henry M. Turner, a huge, plain-spoken man who had served as an army chaplain during the war and as a member of the Georgia legislature during Reconstruction. "Every man that has the sense of an animal must see there is no future in this country for the Negro." Another militant, T. Thomas Fortune, editor of the New York *Age* and founder of the Afro-American League (1887), called on blacks to demand full civil rights, better schools, and fair wages and to fight against discrimination of every sort. "Let us stand up like men in our own organization," he urged. "If others use . . . violence to

*When a congressman asked Henry Adams, a leader of the exodus, why he and his followers had left the South, Adams replied: "We seed there was no way on earth . . . that we could better our condition there. . . . The white people . . . treat our people so bad in many respects that it is impossible for them to stand it."

■ **Booker T. Washington about 1901, when his autobiography, *Up From Slavery*, was published. He wrote his memoirs in the hope of gaining aid for Tuskegee.**

combat our peaceful arguments, it is not for us to run away from violence."

Militancy and black separatism won few adherents among southern blacks. For one thing, life was better than it had been under slavery. According to the most conservative estimates, the living standard of the average southern black more than doubled between 1865 and 1900. On the other hand, the forces of repression were extremely powerful. The late 19th century saw more lynchings in the South than any other period of American history. This helps explain the tactics of Booker T. Washington, one of the most extraordinary Americans of that generation.

Washington had been born a slave in Virginia in 1856. Laboriously he obtained an education, supporting himself while a student by working as a janitor. In 1881, with the financial help of northern philanthropists, he founded Tuskegee Institute in Alabama, which specialized in vocational training. His experiences convinced Washington that blacks must lift themselves by their own bootstraps but that they must also accommodate themselves to white prejudices. A persuasive speaker and a brilliant fund raiser, he soon developed a national reputation as a "reasonable" champion of his race. (In 1891 Harvard awarded him an honorary degree.)

Washington's greatest fame and influence followed his speech to a mixed white and black audience in Atlanta in 1895. To the blacks he said: "Cast down your bucket where you are," by which he meant stop fighting segregation and second-class citizenship and concentrate on learning useful skills. "Dignify and glorify common labor," he urged. "Agitation of questions of racial equality is the extremest folly." Progress up the social and economic ladder would come not from "artificial forcing" but from self-improvement. "There is as much dignity in tilling a field as in writing a poem."

Washington asked the whites of what he called "our beloved South" to lend the blacks a hand in their efforts to advance themselves. If you will do so, he promised, you will be "surrounded by the most patient, faithful, law-abiding, and unresentful people that the world has seen."

This "Atlanta Compromise" delighted white southerners and won Washington financial support in every section of the country. He became one of the most powerful men in the United States, consulted by presidents, in close touch with business and philanthropic leaders, and capable of influencing in countless unobtrusive ways the fate of millions of blacks.

Blacks responded to the Compromise with mixed feelings. Accepting Washington's approach would relieve them of many burdens and dangers and bring them considerable material assistance. After all, being obsequious seemed, like discretion, the better part of valor. But the cost was high in surrendered personal dignity and lost hopes of obtaining real justice.

Washington's career illustrates the terrible dilemma that American blacks have always faced: the choice between confrontation and accommodation. This choice was particularly difficult in the late 19th century.

Washington chose accommodation. It is easy to condemn him as a toady but difficult to see how, at that time, a more aggressive policy could have succeeded. One can even interpret the Atlanta Compromise as a subtle form of black nationalism; in a way, Washington was urging his people not to *accept* inferiority and racial slurs but to *ignore* them. His own behavior lends force to this view, for his method of operating was indeed subtle, even devious. In his public speeches he minimized the importance of civil and political rights and accepted separate but equal facilities—if they were truly equal. Behind the scenes he lobbied against restrictive measures, marshaled large sums of money to fight test cases in the courts, and worked hard in northern states to organize the black vote and make sure that black political leaders got a share of the spoils of office. As one black militant put it, Washington knew the virtue of "sagacious silence." He was perhaps not personally an admirable man, but he was a useful one. His defects point up more the unlovely aspects of the age than those of his own character.

Other disadvantaged groups also suffered during this period. Beginning in the mid 1850s a steady flow of Chinese migrated to the United States, most of them finding work in the California gold fields. About four or five thousand a year came until the negotiation of the Burlingame Treaty of 1868, the purpose of which was to provide cheap labor to fill out the construction crews building the Central Pacific Railroad. Thereafter the annual influx more than doubled, though before 1882 it exceeded 20,000 only twice. When the railroads were completed and the Chinese began to compete with native workers, a great cry of resentment went up on the West Coast. Riots broke out in San Francisco in 1877. Chinese workers were called "groveling worms," "more slavish and brutish than the beasts that roam the fields." When the migration suddenly increased in 1882 to nearly 40,000,* the protests reached such a peak that Congress passed a law prohibiting all Chinese immigration for ten years. Later legislation extended the ban indefinitely.

Chinese immigrants created genuine social problems. Most did not intend to remain in the United States and therefore made little effort to accommodate themselves to American ways. Their attachment to gambling, opium, and prostitutes—over 90 percent of the Chinese in America in the 1880s were males—alarmed respectable citizens. But the attitudes of westerners toward the Chinese differed only in degree from their attitude toward the Mexicans who flocked into the Southwest to work as farm laborers and to help build the railroads of the region, or from that of the rest of the country toward the European immigrants who were flooding into the country in the 1880s. While industrialists wished to keep the gates wide open in order to obtain plentiful supplies of cheap labor, organized workers and many middle-class Americans were beginning to display antiforeign attitudes reminiscent of the 1850s, when Know-Nothingism was at its height. During economic depressions and in periods of social unrest, the underlying intolerance of the majority burst forth. The Chicago Haymarket bombing of 1886, supposedly the work of foreign anarchists, produced a wave of denunciations of "long-haired, wild-eyed, bad-smelling, atheistic, reckless foreign wretches."

Women also felt the sting of discrimination in these years. Their efforts to win the vote through the Fifteenth Amendment failed, as did similar attempts in the states, seven of which rejected female suffrage proposals between 1867 and 1877. In *Minor* v. *Happersett* (1875) the Supreme Court unanimously rejected the argument that women could vote because they were citizens. Although Congress passed a law allowing women lawyers to practice in federal courts, some states barred them from the profession and the Supreme Court upheld such laws. "The natural and proper timidity and delicacy which belongs to the female sex," one justice proclaimed, "unfits it for many . . . occupations." Women, he added, should stick to "the noble and benign offices of wife and mother." Thus women too received short shrift in post-Civil War America.

Exploiting Mineral Wealth in the West

The inanimate resources of the nation were exploited in these decades even more ruthlessly and thoughtlessly than were its human resources. Americans had long regarded the West as a limitless treasure to be grasped as rapidly as possible, and after 1865 they engrossed its riches still faster and in a wider variety of ways. Miners had invaded the western mountains long before the Civil War. From the mid fifties to the mid seventies

*This was still only about 5 percent of the total immigration of that year. From Germany alone, in 1882, over 250,000 people came to the United States.

thousands of gold-crazed prospectors fanned out through the Rockies, panning every stream and hacking furiously at every likely outcropping from the Fraser River country of British Columbia to Tucson in southern Arizona, from the eastern slopes of the Sierras to the Great Plains.

Gold and silver were scattered throughout the area, though usually too thinly to make mining profitable. Whenever anyone made a "strike," prospectors flocked to the site, drawn by rumors of stream beds gleaming with auriferous gravel and of nuggets the size of men's fists. For a few months the area teemed with activity. Towns of 5,000 or more sprang up overnight; improvised roads were crowded with men and supply wagons. Claims were staked out along every stream and gully. Then, usually, expectations faded in the light of reality: high prices, low yields, hardship, violence, and deception. The boom collapsed and the towns died as quickly as they had risen. A few would have found wealth, the rest only backbreaking labor and disappointment—until tales of another strike sent them scurrying feverishly across the land on another golden chase.

In the spring of 1858 it was upon the Fraser River in Canada that the horde descended, 30,000 Californians in the van. The following spring, Pikes Peak in Colorado attracted the pack, experienced California prospectors ("yonder siders") mixing with "greenhorns" from every corner of the globe. In June 1859 came the finds in Nevada, where the famous Comstock Lode yielded ores worth nearly $4,000 a ton. In 1861, while men in the settled areas were laying down their tools to take up arms, the miners were racing to the Idaho panhandle, hoping to become millionaires overnight. The next year the rush was to the Snake River valley, then in 1863 and 1864 to Montana. In 1874–1876 the Black Hills in the heart of the Sioux lands were inundated.

In a sense the Denvers, Aurarias, Virginia Cities, Orofinos, and Gold Creeks of the West during the war years were harbingers of the point of view that flourished in the East in the age of President Grant and his immediate successors. The miners enthusiastically adopted the get-rich-quick philosophy, willingly enduring privations and laboring hard, always with the object of striking it rich. The idea of reserving any part of the West for future generations never entered their heads.

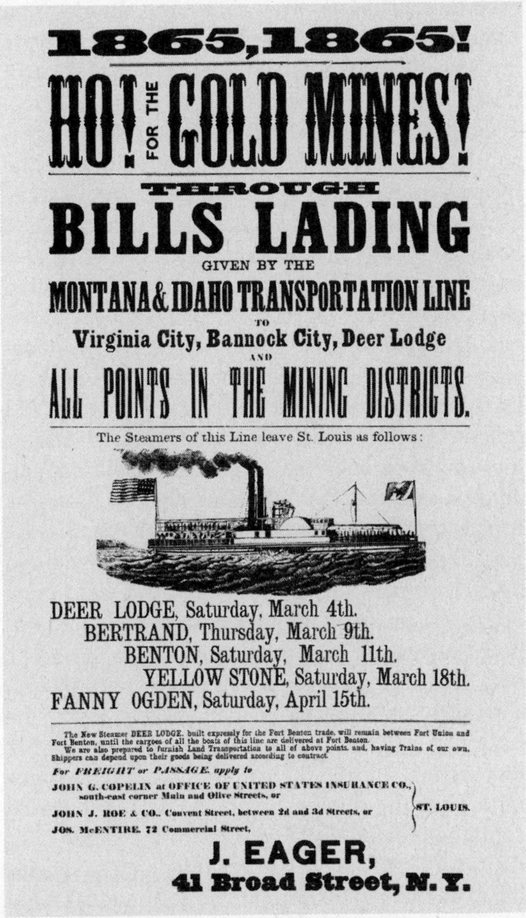
1865, 1865!

HO! FOR THE GOLD MINES!

THROUGH

BILLS LADING

GIVEN BY THE

MONTANA & IDAHO TRANSPORTATION LINE

TO

Virginia City, Bannock City, Deer Lodge

AND

ALL POINTS IN THE MINING DISTRICTS.

The Steamers of this Line leave St. Louis as follows:

DEER LODGE, Saturday, March 4th.
BERTRAND, Thursday, March 9th.
BENTON, Saturday, March 11th.
YELLOW STONE, Saturday, March 18th.
FANNY OGDEN, Saturday, April 15th.

The New Steamer DEER LODGE, built expressly for the Fort Benton trade, will remain between Fort Union and Fort Benton, until the cargoes of all the boats of this line are delivered at Fort Benton.

We are also prepared to furnish Land Transportation to all of above points, and, having Trains of our own, Shippers can depend upon their goods being delivered according to contract.

For FREIGHT or PASSAGE, apply to

JOHN G. COPELIN at OFFICE OF UNITED STATES INSURANCE CO., south-east corner Main and Olive Streets, or
JOHN J. ROE & CO., Convent Street, between 2d and 3d Streets, or
JOS. McENTIRE, 72 Commercial Street,
ST. LOUIS.

J. EAGER,
41 Broad Street, N. Y.

■ **A broadside offering transportation to the Montana gold strikes. It took a steamboat as long as two months to reach Fort Benton on the upper Missouri from St. Louis.**

The sudden prosperity of the mining towns attracted every kind of shady character. The mines, one forty-niner wrote, were "loaded to the muzzle" with "rascals from Oregon, pickpockets from New York, accomplished gentlemen from Europe, interlopers from Lima and Chile, Mexican thieves, gamblers from no particular spot, and assassins manufactured in Hell." Gambling dens, dance halls, saloons, and brothels mushroomed wherever precious metal was found. Law enforcement was a constant problem, but sooner or later the "better element" in every mining community formed a "vigilance committee" and by a few summary hangings drove the outlaws out of town. Much of the difficulty lay in the antisocial attitudes of the miners themselves. "They were hardened individualists who paid little attention to community affairs unless their own interests were threatened," Ray Allen Billington, a historian of the frontier, has written.

Gold and silver dominated people's thoughts and dreams, and few paid much attention to the means employed in accumulating this wealth. Storekeepers charged outrageous prices, claim holders "salted" worthless properties with nuggets in order to swindle gullible investors. Ostentation characterized the successful, braggadocio those who failed. During the administration of President Grant, Virginia City, Nevada, was at the peak of its vulgar prosperity, producing an average of $12 million a year in ore. Built upon the richness of the Comstock Lode ($306 million in gold and silver was extracted from the Comstock in 20 years), it had 25 saloons before it had 4,000 people. By the seventies its mountainside site was disfigured by ugly, ornate mansions where successful mine operators ate from fine china and swilled champagne as though it were water.

In 1873, after the discovery of the Big Bonanza, a seam of rich ore more than 50 feet thick, the future of Virginia City seemed boundless. Other discoveries shortly thereafter indicated to optimists that the mining boom in the West would continue indefinitely. The finds in the Black Hills district in 1875 and 1876, heralding deposits yielding eventually $100 million, led to the mushroom growth of Deadwood, home of Wild Bill Hickok, Deadwood Dick, Calamity Jane, and such lesser-known characters as California Jack and Poker Alice. In Deadwood, according to Professor Billington, "the faro games were wilder, the hurdy-gurdy dance halls noisier, the street brawls more common, than in any other western town." New strikes in Colorado in 1876 and 1877 caused the town of Leadville to boom; in 1880 there were 30,000 people in the area. However, this was the last important flurry to ruffle the mining frontier. The West continued to yield much gold and silver, especially silver, but big corporations produced nearly all of it. The mines around Deadwood were soon controlled by one large company, Homestake Mining.

This is the culminating irony of the history of the mining frontier: Shoestring prospectors, independent and enterprising, made the key discoveries. They established local institutions and supplied the West with much of its color and folklore. But the stockholders of large corporations, many of whom had never seen a mine, made off with the lion's share of the wealth. Those whose worship of gold was direct and incessant, the prospectors who peopled the mining towns and gave the frontier its character, mostly died poor, still seeking a prize as elusive if not as illusory as the pot of gold at the end of the rainbow.

For the mining of gold and silver is essentially like that of coal and iron. To operate profitably, large capital investments, heavy machinery, railroads, and hundreds of hired hands are required. Henry Comstock, the prospector who gave his name to the Comstock Lode, was luckier than most, but he sold his claims to the lode for a pittance, disposing of what became one valuable mine for $40 and receiving only $10,000 for his share of the fabulous Ophir, the richest concentration of gold and silver ever found. His greatest financial gain from the Comstock came some years later when the owners of the Ophir paid him well to testify in their corporation's behalf in an important lawsuit. More typical of the successful mine owner was George Hearst, senator from California and father of the newspaper tycoon William Randolph Hearst, who, by shrewd speculations, obtained large blocks of stock in mining properties scattered from Montana to Mexico.

Though marked by violence, fraud, greed, and lost hopes, the gold rushes had valuable results. The most obvious was the new metal itself, which bolstered the financial position of the United States during and after the Civil War. Quantities of European goods needed for the war effort and for postwar economic development were paid for with the yield of the new mines. Gold and silver also caused a great increase of interest in the West. A valuable literature appeared, part imaginative, part reportorial, describing the mining camps and the life of the prospectors. These works fascinated contemporaries (as they have continued to fascinate succeeding generations when adapted to the motion picture and to television). Mark Twain's *Roughing It* (1872), based in part on his experiences in the Nevada mining country, is the most famous example of this literature.

Each new strike and rush, no matter how ephemeral, brought permanent settlers along with the prospectors: farmers, cattlemen, storekeepers, teamsters, lawyers, and ministers. Some saw from the start that a better living could be made supplying the needs of the gold seekers than looking for the elusive metal. Others, failing to find mineral wealth, took up whatever occupation they could rather than starve or return home empty-handed. In every mining town—along with the saloons and brothels—schools, churches, and newspaper offices sprang up.

The mines also speeded the political organization of the West. Colorado and Nevada became territories in 1861, Arizona and Idaho in 1863, Montana in 1864. Although Nevada was admitted before it had 60,000 residents in 1864 to ratify the Thirteenth Amendment and help reelect Lincoln, most of these territories did not become states for decades. But because of the miners, the framework for future development was early established.

The Land Bonanza

While the miners were engrossing the mineral wealth of the West, other interests were snapping up the region's choice farmland. Presumably the Homestead Act of 1862 had ended the reign of the speculator and the large landholder. An early amendment to the act even prevented husbands

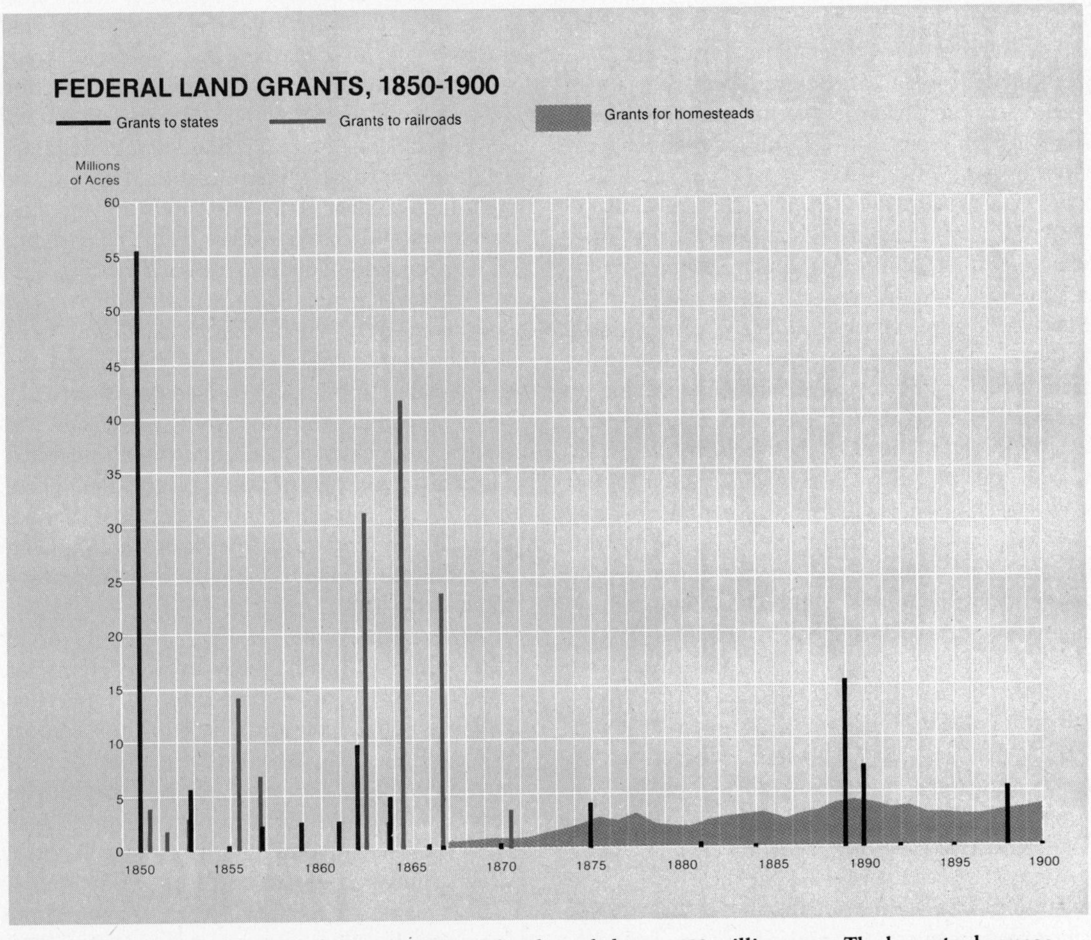

■ **Between 1850 and 1871, grants of federal land to railroads totaled some 130 million acres. The homestead acreage shown indicates land to which homesteaders took title after fulfilling the necessary conditions.**

and wives from filing separate claims. The West, land reformers had assumed, would soon be dotted with 160-acre family farms.

They were doomed to disappointment. Most landless Americans were too poor to become farmers even when they could obtain land without cost. The expense of moving a family to the ever receding frontier exceeded the means of many, and the costs of hoes and scythes, harvesting machines, fencing, and housing, presented a formidable barrier. As for the industrial workers for whom the free land was supposed to provide a "safety valve," they had neither the skills nor the inclination to become farmers. Homesteaders usually came from districts not far removed from frontier conditions. And despite the intent of the law, speculators often managed to obtain large tracts. They hired men to stake out claims, falsely swear that they had fulfilled the conditions laid down in the law for obtaining legal title, and then deed the land over to their employers.

Furthermore, 160 acres was not enough for raising livestock or for the kind of commercial agriculture that was developing west of the Mississippi. Congress made a feeble attempt to make larger holdings available to homesteaders by passing the Timber Culture Act of 1873, which permitted individuals to claim an additional 160 acres if they would agree to plant a quarter of it in trees within 10 years. This law proved helpful to some farmers in the tier of states from North Dakota to Kansas. Nevertheless, fewer than 25 percent of the 245,000 who took up land under it obtained final title to the property. Raising large numbers of seedling trees on the plains was a difficult task.

While futilely attempting to make a forest of parts of the treeless plains, the government permitted private interests to gobble up and destroy many of the great forests that clothed the slopes of the Rockies and the Sierras. The Timber and Stone Act of 1878 allowed anyone to claim a quarter section of forest land for $2.50 an acre if it was "unfit for civilization." This laxly drawn measure enabled lumber companies to obtain thousands of acres by hiring dummy entrymen, whom they marched in gangs to the land offices, paying them a few dollars for their time after they had signed over their claims. "In many instances whole townships have been entered under this law in the interest of one person or firm, to whom the lands have been conveyed as soon as receipts for the purchase price were issued," the commissioner of the General Land Office complained in 1901.

Had the land laws been better drafted and more honestly enforced, it is still unlikely that the policy of granting free land to small homesteaders would have succeeded. Aside from the built-in difficulties faced by small-scale agriculturalists in the West, too many people in every section were eager to exploit the nation's land for their own profit, without regard for the general interest. Immediately after the war, for example, Congress reserved 47.7 million acres of public land in the South for homesteaders, stopping all cash sales in the region. But in 1876 this policy was reversed and the land thrown open. Speculators flocked to the feast in such numbers that the Illinois Central Railroad ran special trains from Chicago to Mississippi and Louisiana. Between 1877 and 1888 over 5.6 million acres were sold, much of them covered with valuable pine and cypress.

However they attained their acres, frontier farmers of the 1870s and 1880s grappled with novel problems as they pushed across the grasslands of Kansas, Nebraska, and the Dakotas with their families. The first settlers took up land along the rivers and creeks, where they found enough timber for home building, fuel, and fencing. Later arrivals had to build houses of the tough prairie sod and depend on hay, dried sunflower stalks, even buffalo dung for fuel. The soil was rich, but the climate, especially in the semiarid regions beyond the 98th meridian of longitude, made agriculture frequently difficult and often impossible. Blizzards, floods, grasshopper plagues, and prairie fires caused repeated heartaches, but periodic drought and searing summer heat were the worst hazards, destroying the hopes and fortunes of thousands.

At the same time, the flat immensity of the land, combined with newly available farm machinery and the development of rail connections with the East, encouraged the growth of corporation-controlled "bonanza" farms, some of them, tens of thousands of acres in size. One such organization was the railroad-owned empire managed by Oliver Dalrymple in Dakota Territory, which cultivated 25,000 acres of wheat in 1880. Dalrymple employed 200 pairs of harrows to prepare his soil, 125 seeders to sow his seed, and 155 binders to harvest his crop. Bonanza farmers could buy supplies wholesale and obtain conces-

■ **The crews of five combines stopped during the wheat harvest on a bonanza farm in eastern Washington in 1890 to have their picture taken. Combines such as these reaped, threshed, cleaned, and bagged grain in a single operation.**

sions from railroads and processors, which added to their profits.

Even the biggest organizations could not cope with prolonged drought, however, and most of the bonanza outfits failed in the dry years of the late eighties. Those wise farmers who diversified their crops and cultivated their land intensively fared better in the long run, though even they could not hope to earn a profit in really dry years.

Despite the hazards of plains agriculture, the region became the breadbasket of America in the decades following the Civil War. By 1889 Minnesota topped the nation in wheat production, and 10 years later four of the five leading wheat states lay west of the Mississippi. The plains also accounted for heavy percentages of the nation's other cereal crops, together with immense quantities of beef, pork, and mutton.

Like other exploiters of the nation's resources, farmers took whatever they could from the soil with little heed for preserving its fertility and preventing erosion. The consequent national loss was less apparent because it was diffuse and slow to assume drastic proportions, but it was very real.

Western Railroad Building

Further exploitation of land resources by private interests resulted from the government's policy of subsidizing western railroads. Here was a clear illustration of the conflict between the idea of the West as a national heritage to be disposed of to deserving citizens and the concept of the region as a cornucopia pouring forth riches to be gathered up and carted off by anyone powerful and determined enough to take them. When it came to a choice between giving a particular tract to railroads or to homesteaders, the homesteaders nearly always lost out. To serve the valuable national purpose of the linking of the sections by rail, the land of the West was dispensed wholesale as a substitute for cash subsidies.

Federal land grants to railroads began in 1850 with those allotted the Illinois Central. Over the next two decades about 49 million acres were given to various lines indirectly in the form of grants to the states, but the most lavish gifts of the public domain were those made directly to builders of intersectional trunk lines. These roads received more than 155 million acres in this fashion, although about 25 million acres reverted to the government when certain companies failed to construct the required miles of track. About 75 percent of this went to aid the construction of four transcontinental railroads: the Union Pacific-Central Pacific line, running from Nebraska to San Francisco, completed in 1869; the Atchison, Topeka and Santa Fe, running from Kansas City to Los Angeles by way of Santa Fe and Albuquerque, completed in 1883; the Southern Pacific line, running from San Francisco to New Orleans by way of Yuma and El Paso, completed in 1883; and the Northern Pacific, running from Duluth, Minnesota, to Portland, Oregon, completed in 1883.

Unless the government had been willing to build the transcontinental lines itself—and this was unthinkable in an age dominated by belief in individual exploitation—some system of subsidy was essential. For private investors would not hazard the huge sums needed to lay tracks across hundreds of miles of rugged, empty country when traffic over the road could not possibly produce profits for many years. Grants of land seemed a sensible way of financing construction. The method avoided direct outlays of public funds, for the companies could pledge the land as security for bond issues or sell it directly for cash. Moreover, land and railroad values were intimately linked in contemporary thinking. "The occupation of new land and the building of new mileage go hand in hand," the *Commercial and Financial Chronicle* explained in 1886.

> There could be no great or continuous opening up of new territory without the necessary facilities in the way of railroads. On the other hand, most new mileage on the borders of our Western territory is prosecuted with the idea and expectation that it is to pave the way for an accession of new settlers and an extension of the area of land devoted to their uses.

In many cases the value of the land granted might be recovered by the government when it sold other lands in the vicinity, for such properties would certainly be worth more after transportation facilities to eastern markets had been constructed. "Why," the governor of one eastern state asked in 1867, "should private individuals be called upon to make a useless sacrifice of their means, when railroads can be constructed by the unity of public and private interests, and made profitable to all?"

The Pacific Railway Act of 1862 established the pattern for these grants. It gave the builders of the Union Pacific and Central Pacific railroads 5 square miles of public land on each side of their right of way for each mile of track laid. The land was allotted in alternate sections, forming a pattern like a checkerboard, the squares of one color representing railroad property, the other government property. Presumably this arrangement benefited the entire nation since half the land close to the railroad remained in public hands.

However, whenever grants were made to railroads, the adjacent government lands were not opened to homesteaders—on the theory that free land in the immediate vicinity of a line would prevent the road from disposing of its properties at good prices. Since, in addition to the land granted the railroads, a wide zone of "indemnity" lands was reserved to allow the roads to choose alternative sites to make up for lands that settlers had already taken up within the checkerboard, homesteading was in fact prohibited near land-grant railroads. Grants per mile of track ranged from five alternate sections on each side of the track to the Union and Central Pacific to 40 sections to the Northern Pacific, authorized in 1864. In the latter case, when the indemnity zone was included, homesteaders were barred from an area 100 miles wide, all the way from Lake Superior to the Pacific. More than 20 years after receiving its immense grant, the Northern Pacific was still attempting to keep homesteaders from filing in the indemnity zone. President Cleveland finally put a stop to this in 1887, saying that he could find "no evidence" that "this vast tract is necessary for the fulfillment of the grant."

Historians have argued at length about the fairness of the land-grant system. No railroad corporation waxed fat directly from the sale of its lands, which were sold at prices averaging between $2 and $5 an acre. Collectively the roads have taken in between $400 million and $500 million from this source, but only over the course of a century. Land-grant lines did a great deal to encourage the growth of the West by advertising their property widely and providing cheap transportation for prospective settlers and efficient shipping services for farmers. They were required by law to carry troops and handle government business free or at reduced rates, which saved the government many millions over the years. At the same time, the system imposed no effective restraints on how the railroads used the funds raised with federal aid. Building their lines largely with money obtained from land grants, the operators tended to be extravagant and often downright corrupt.

The Union Pacific was built by a construction company, the Crédit Mobilier, which was owned by the promoters. These men awarded themselves contracts at prices that assured the Crédit Mobilier exorbitant profits. When Congress threatened to investigate the Union Pacific in 1868, Oakes Ames, a stockholder in both companies who was also a member of Congress, sold key congressmen and government officials over 300 shares of Crédit Mobilier stock at a price far below its real value. The shares were placed "where they will do the most good," Ames said. "I have found," he also said, "there is no difficulty in inducing men to look after their own property."

When these transactions were exposed, the House of Representatives censured Ames, but such was the temper of the times that neither he nor most of his associates believed he had done anything immoral. According to the president of one western railroad, congressmen frequently tried to use their influence to get railroad land at bargain prices. "Isn't there a discount?" they

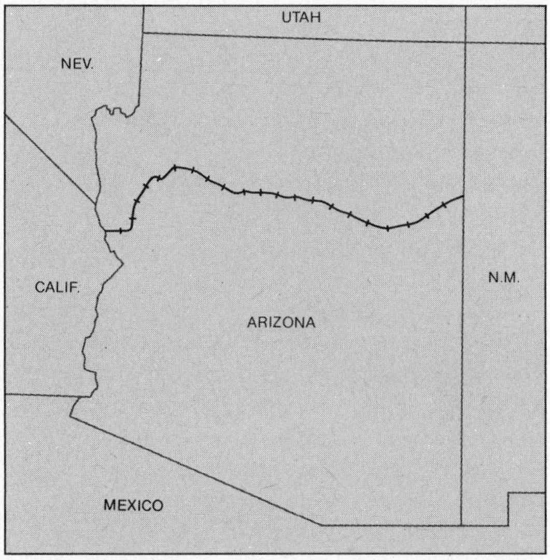

■ **On the contemporary map below the Atlantic and Pacific Railroad land grant in Arizona appears as shaded squares on a checkerboard. The grant cut a 100-mile-wide swath across the entire territory (above).**

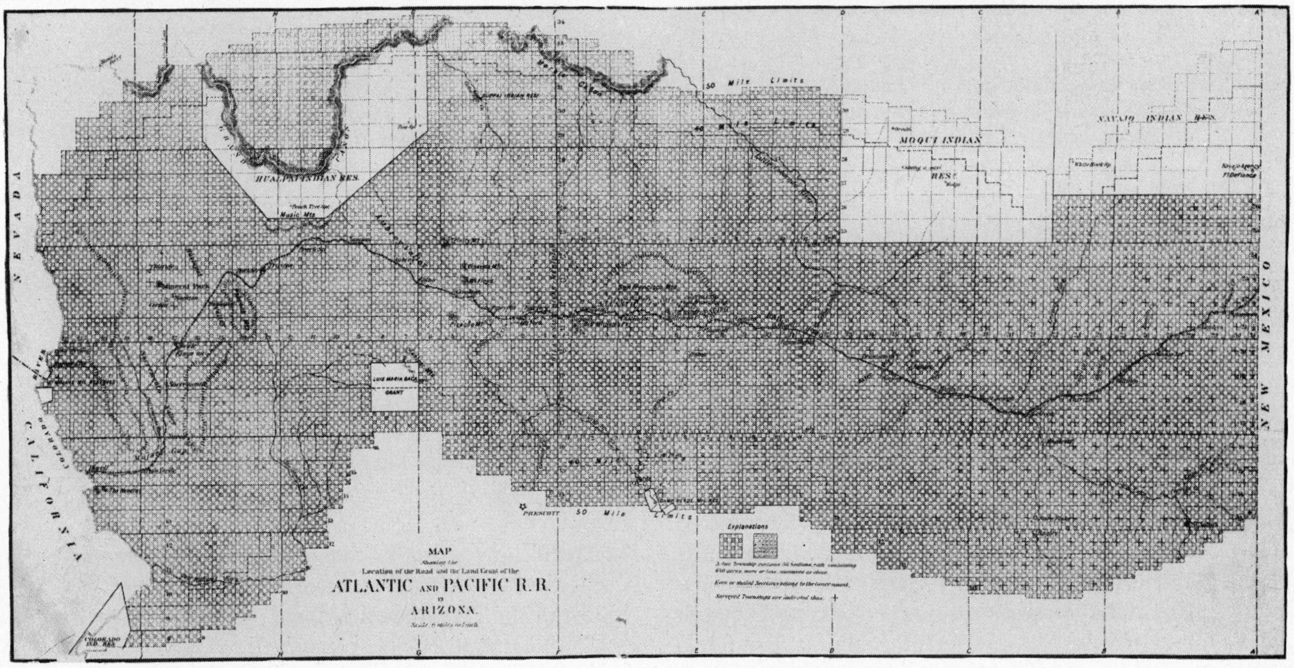

■ **The meeting of the rails at Promontory, Utah, May 10, 1869. Andrew J. Russell took this picture from atop the Central Pacific's engine Jupiter as it moved slowly toward the Union Pacific's No. 119. Dignitaries gathered for the ceremonial driving of the golden spike by rail magnate Leland Stanford. Stanford swung and missed.**

would ask. "Surely you can give the land cheaper to a friend. . . ." The railroads seldom resisted this type of pressure.

The construction of the Central Pacific in the 1860s illustrates how the system encouraged extravagance. In addition to land grants, the Central Pacific and the Union Pacific were given loans in the form of government bonds—from $16,000 to $48,000 for each mile of track laid, depending on the difficulty of the terrain. The two competed with each other for the subsidies, the Central Pacific building eastward from Sacramento, the Union Pacific westward from Nebraska. They put huge crews to work grading and laying track, bringing up supplies over the already completed road. The Union Pacific employed Civil War veterans and Irish immigrants, the Central Chinese immigrants.

This plan favored the Union Pacific. While the Central Pacific was inching upward through the gorges and granite of the mighty Sierras, the Union Pacific was racing across the level plains. Once beyond the Sierras, the Central Pacific would have easy going across the Nevada-Utah plateau country, but by then it might be too late to prevent the Union Pacific from making off with most of the government aid.

The Central Pacific construction crews were

managed by Charles Crocker, a hulking, relentless driver of men who had come to California during the gold rush and made a small fortune as a merchant in Sacramento. Crocker wasted huge sums by working through the winter in the High Sierras. Often the men labored in tunnels dug through 40-foot snowdrifts to get at the frozen ground. To speed construction of the Summit Tunnel, Crocker had a shaft cut down from above so that crews could work out from the middle as well as in from each end. In 1866, over the most difficult terrain, he laid 28 miles of track—at a cost of more than $280,000 a mile. Experts later estimated that 70 percent of this sum could have been saved had speed not been a factor. Such prodigality made economic sense to the "Big Four" (Collis P. Huntington, Leland Stanford, Mark Hopkins, and Crocker) who controlled the Central Pacific because of the fat profits they were making through its construction company and because of the gains they could count on once they reached the flat country beyond the Sierras, where construction costs would amount to only half the federal aid.

Crocker's herculean efforts paid off. The mountains were conquered, and then the crews raced across the Great Basin to Salt Lake City and beyond. The meeting of the rails—the occasion of a national celebration—took place at Promontory, north of Ogden, Utah, on May 10, 1869. Leland Stanford drove the final ceremonial golden spike with a silver hammer.* The Union Pacific had built 1,086 miles of track, the Central 689 miles.

In the long run the wasteful way in which the Central Pacific was built hurt the road severely. It was ill constructed, over grades too steep and around curves too sharp, and burdened with debts that were too heavy. Such was the fate of nearly all the railroads constructed with the help of government subsidies. The only transcontinental built without land grants was the Great Northern, running from St. Paul, Minnesota, to the Pacific. Spending private capital, its guiding genius, James J. Hill, was compelled to build economically and to plan carefully. As a result, his was the only transcontinental line to weather the depression of the 1890s without going into bankruptcy.

*A mysterious "San Francisco jeweler" passed among the onlookers, taking orders for souvenir watch chains that he proposed to make from the spike at $5 each.

The Cattle Kingdom

While miners were digging out the mineral wealth of the West and railroaders were taking possession of much of its land, another group was avidly acquiring its endless acres of grass. For 20 years after the Civil War cattlemen and sheep raisers dominated huge areas of the High Plains, making millions of dollars by grazing their herds on lands they did not own.

Columbus brought the first cattle to the New World in 1493, on his second voyage, and later *conquistadores* took them to every corner of Spain's American empire. Mexico proved to be so well suited to cattle raising that many were allowed to roam loose. They multiplied rapidly, and by the late 18th century what is now southern Texas harbored enormous herds. The beasts interbred with nondescript "English" cattle, brought into the area by American settlers, to produce the Texas longhorn. Hardy, wiry, ill-tempered, and fleet, with horns often attaining a spread of 6 feet, these animals were far from ideal as beef cattle and almost as hard to capture as wild horses, but they existed in southern Texas by the million, most of them unowned.

The lack of markets and transportation explains why Texas cattle were so lightly regarded. But conditions were changing. Industrial growth in the East was causing an increase in the urban population and a consequent rise in the demand for food. At the same time, the expansion of the railroad network made it possible to move cattle cheaply over long distances. As the iron rails inched across the plains, astute cattlemen began to do some elementary figuring. Longhorns could be had locally for $3 or $4 a head. In the northern cities they would bring ten times that much, perhaps even more. Why not round them up and herd them northward to the railroads, allowing them to feed along the way on the abundant grasses of the plains?

In 1866 a number of Texans drove large herds northward toward Sedalia, Missouri, railhead of the Missouri Pacific. This route took the herds through wooded and settled country and across Indian reservations, which provoked many difficulties. The next year the drovers, inspired by a clever young Illinois cattle dealer named Joseph G. McCoy and other entrepreneurs, led their herds

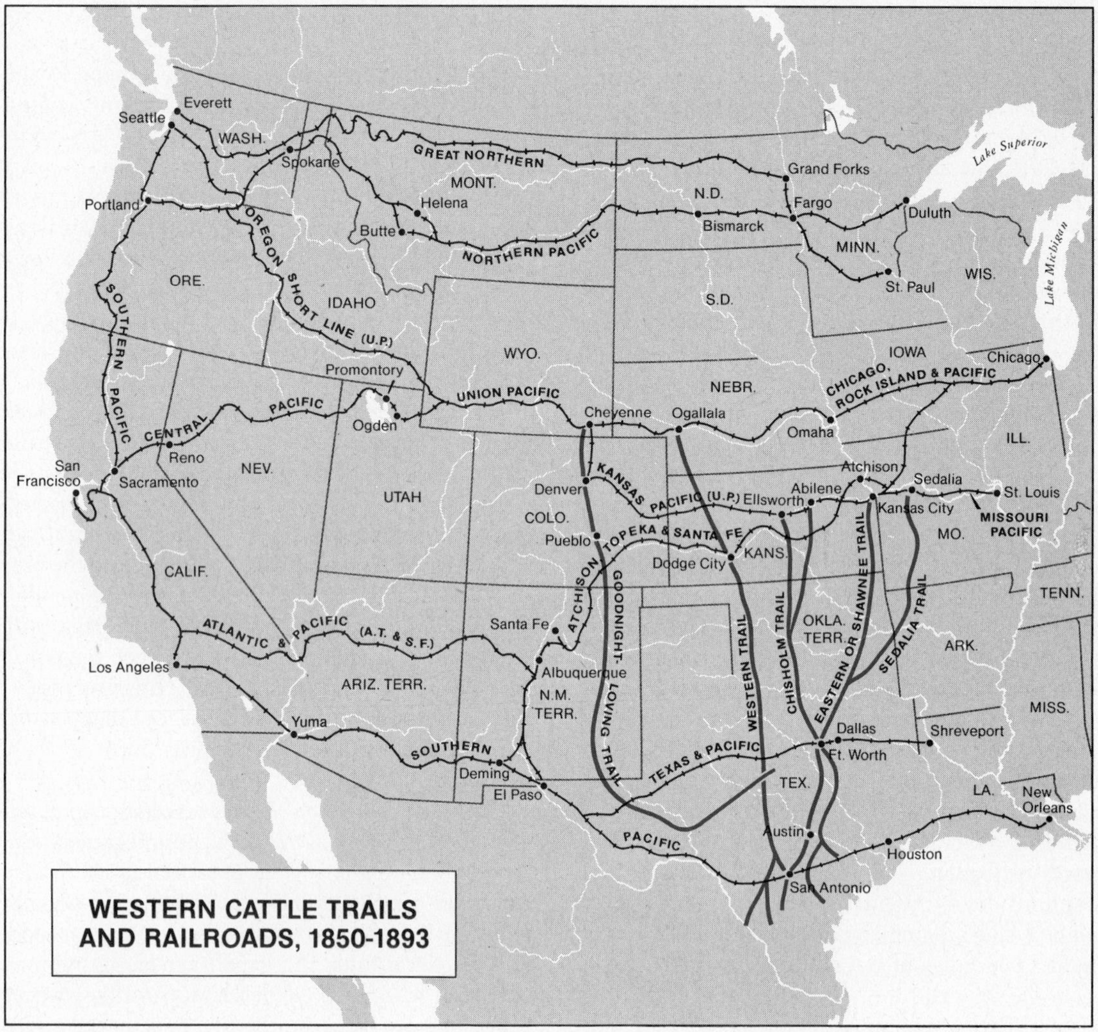

north by a more westerly route, across unsettled grasslands, to Abilene, Kansas, on the Kansas Pacific line. They earned excellent profits, and during the next five years about 1.5 million head made the "long drive" over the Chisholm Trail to Abilene, where they were sold to ranchers, feedlot operators, and the agents of eastern meat packers. Other shipping points sprang up as the railroads pushed westward.

The technique of the long drive, which involved guiding herds of two or three thousand cattle slowly across as much as a thousand miles of country, produced the American cowboy, renowned in song, story, and on film. Half a dozen of these men could control several thousand steers. Mounted on wiry ponies, they would range alongside the herd, keeping the animals on the move but preventing stampedes, allowing them time to rest yet steadily pressing them toward the yards of Abilene.

Although the cowboy's life was far more prosaic than it appears in modern legend, consisting mainly of endless hours on the trail surrounded by thousands of bellowing beasts, he was indeed an interesting type, perfectly adapted to his environment. Cowboys virtually lived on horseback, for their work kept them far from human habitation for months on end. Most, accustomed to solitude, were indeed "strong, silent men." They were courageous—and expert marksmen, too, for they lived amid many dangers and had to know how to protect themselves. Few grew rich, yet like the miners they were true representatives of their time—determinedly individualistic, contemptuous of authority, crude, devoted to coarse pleasures.

The major "cattle towns," Abilene, Wichita, Ellsworth, Dodge City, and Caldwell, had their full share of saloons, gambling dens, and "dance houses" patronized by cowboys and other transients bent on having a good time. Most were young, male, and single; a good deal of violence punctuated their activities. The violence, however, has been greatly exaggerated. Stories of individual desperadoes and gangs of outlaws "shooting up" towns and terrorizing honest citizens are fictitious. Police forces were well organized. Indeed, the "respectable" town residents tended to urge leniency for lawbreakers because of the money they and their fellows brought to the towns. A careful check of the records by the historian Robert Dykstra revealed that between 1870 and 1885 there were only 45 homicides in these five towns, and some of them had nothing to do with the cattle trade.

Open-Range Ranching

Soon cattlemen discovered that the hardy Texas stock could survive the winters of the northern plains. Attracted by the apparently limitless forage, they began to bring up herds to stock the vast regions where the buffalo had so recently roamed. Introducing pedigreed Hereford bulls, they improved the stock without weakening its resistance to harsh conditions. By 1880 some 4.5 million head had spread across the sea of grass that ran from Kansas to Montana and west to the Rockies.

The prairie grasses offered cattlemen a bonanza almost as valuable as the gold mines. Open-range ranching required actual ownership of no more than a few acres along some watercourse. In this semiarid region, control of water enabled a rancher to dominate all the surrounding area back to the divide separating his range from the next stream without investing a cent in the purchase of land. His cattle, wandering freely on the public domain, fattened on grass owned by all the people, to be turned into beefsteak and leather for the profit of the rancher. Theoretically, anyone could pasture stock on the open range, but without access to water it was impossible to do so. "I have 2 miles of running water," a cattleman said in testifying before the Public Land Commission. "That accounts for my ranch being where it is. The next water from me in one direction is 23 miles; now no man can have a ranch between these two places. I have control of the grass, the same as though I owned it." By having his cowhands take out homestead claims along watercourses in his region, a rancher could greatly expand the area he dominated. In the late 1870s one Colorado cattle baron controlled an area roughly the size of Connecticut and Rhode Island even though he owned only 105 small parcels that totaled about 15,500 acres.

Generally a group of ranchers acted together, obtaining legal title to the lands along the bank of a stream and grazing their cattle over the area drained by it. The herds became thoroughly intermixed, each owner's being identified by his individual brand mark. Every spring and fall the ranchers staged a great roundup, driving in all the cattle to a central place, separating them by brand marks, culling steers for shipment to market, and branding new calves.

With the demand for meat rising and transportation cheap, a princely fortune could be made in a few years with a relatively small investment. Capitalists from the East and from Europe began to pour funds into the business. Attracted by what one writer called the "Beef Bonanza"—in a book subtitled *How to Get Rich on the Plains*—Eastern "dudes" like Theodore Roosevelt, a young New York assemblyman who sank over $50,000 in his Elkhorn Ranch in Dakota Territory in 1883, bought up cattle as a sort of profitable hobby. Soon large outfits such as the Prairie Cattle Company and the Nebraska Land and Cattle Company, controlled by British investors, and the Union Cattle Company of Wyoming, a $3 million corporation, dominated the business, just as large companies had taken over most of the important gold and silver mines.

Unlike other exploiters of the West's resources, the ranchers did not at first injure or reduce any public resource. Grass eaten by their stock annually renewed itself, the soil enriched by the droppings of the animals. Furthermore, ranchers poached on the public domain because there was no reasonable way for them to obtain legal possession of the large areas necessary to raise cattle

■ **In 1885 masked Nebraskans seeking access to water posed for photographer S.D. Butcher, who captioned the picture, "Settlers taking the law in their own hands: cutting 15 miles of the Brighton Ranch fence."**

on the plains. Federal land laws made no allowance for the special conditions of the semiarid West. "Title to the public lands [of the West] cannot be honestly acquired under the homestead laws," S. E. Burdett, commissioner of the General Land Office, reported in 1875. "That cultivation and improvement which are required . . . in the place of price, are impossible. . . . A system of sale should be authorized in accordance with the necessities of the situation."

Such a system was soon devised by Major John Wesley Powell, later the director of the United States Geological Survey. His *Report on the Lands of the Arid Region of the United States* (1879) suggested that western lands be divided into three classes: irrigable lands, timber lands, and "pasturage" lands. On the pasturage lands the "farm unit" ought to be at least 2,560 acres (four sections), Powell urged. Groups of these units should be organized into "pasturage districts" in which the ranchers "should have the right to make their own regulations for the division of lands, the use of the water . . . and for the pasturage of lands in common or in severalty."

Congress refused to change the land laws in any basic way, and this had two harmful effects. First, it encouraged fraud: those who could not get title to enough land honestly turned to subterfuge. The Desert Land Act (1877) allowed anyone to obtain 640 acres in the arid states for $1.25 an acre provided the owner irrigated part of it within three years. Since the original claimant could transfer the holding, the ranchers set their cowboys and other hands to filing claims, which were then signed over to them. Over 2.6 million acres were taken up under the act, and according to the best estimate, about 95 percent of the claims were fraudulent—no sincere effort was made to irrigate the land.

Second, overcrowding became a problem that led to serious conflicts, even to shooting, because no one had uncontestable title to the land. The leading ranchers banded together in cattlemen's associations to deal with overcrowding and with such problems as quarantine regulations, water rights, and thievery. In most cases these associations devised effective and sensible rules, but their functions would better have been performed by the government, as such matters usually are.

To keep other ranchers' cattle from those sections of the public domain they considered their own, the associations, and many individuals, began to fence huge areas. This was possible only because of the invention in 1874 of barbed wire by Joseph F. Glidden, an Illinois farmer. By the 1880s thousands of miles of the new fencing had been strung across the plains, often across roads and in a few cases around entire communities. "Barbed-wire wars" resulted, fought by rancher against rancher, cattleman against sheepman, herder against farmer. The associations tried to police their fences and to punish anyone who cut their wire. Signs posted along lonely stretches gave dire warnings to trespassers. "The Son of a Bitch who opens this fence had better look out for his scalp," one such sign announced, a perfect statement of the philosophy of the age.

By installing fences the cattlemen were unwittingly destroying their own way of doing business. On a truly open range, cattle could fend for themselves, instinctively finding water during droughts, drifting safely downwind before blizzards. Barbed wire prevented their free movement. During winter storms these slender strands became as lethal as high-tension wires: the drifting cattle piled up against them and died by the thousands. "The advent of barbed wire," Walter Prescott Webb wrote in his classic study *The Great Plains* (1931), "brought about the disappearance of the open, free range and converted the range country into the big-pasture country."

The boom times were ending. Overproduction was driving down the price of beef; expenses were on the rise; many sections of the range were badly overgrazed. The dry summer of 1886 left the stock in such poor condition as winter approached that the *Rocky Mountain Husbandman* urged its readers to sell their cattle despite the prevailing low prices rather than "endanger the whole herd by having the range overstocked."

Some ranchers took this advice; those who did not made a fatal error. Winter that year arrived early and with unparalleled fury. Blizzards raged and temperatures plummeted far below zero. Cattle crowded into low places only to be engulfed in giant snowdrifts; barbed wire took a fearful toll. When spring finally came, the streams were choked with rotting carcasses. Between 80 and 90 percent of all cattle on the range were dead. "We have had a perfect smashup all through the cattle country," Theodore Roosevelt wrote sadly in April 1887 from Elkhorn Ranch.

After that cruel winter, open-range cattle raising was finished. The large companies were bankrupt; many independent operators, like Roosevelt, became discouraged and sold out. When the industry revived, it was on a smaller, more efficiently organized scale. The fencing movement continued, but now each stockman enclosed land he actually owned. It then became possible to bring in pedigreed bulls to improve the breed. Cattle raising, like mining before it, ceased to be an adventure in rollicking individualism and reckless greed and became a business.

By the late 1880s the bonanza days of the West were over. No previous frontier had caught the imagination of Americans so completely as the Great West, with its wealth, its heroic size, its awesome emptiness, its massive, sculptured beauty. Now the frontier was no more. Most of what Professor Webb called the "primary windfalls" of the region—the furs, the precious metals, the forests, the cattle, and the grass—had been snatched up by first-comers and by individuals already wealthy. Big companies were taking over all the West's resources. The nation was becoming more powerful, richer, larger, and its economic structure more complex and diversified as the West yielded its treasures. But the East, and especially eastern industrialists and financiers, were increasingly dominating the economy of the entire nation.

SUPPLEMENTARY READING

Titles marked with an asterisk have been published in paperback

The economic, political, and legal ideas current in this period are covered in Sidney Fine, **Laissez Faire and the General Welfare State*** (1956), and J. W. Hurst, **Law and the Conditions of Freedom in the Nineteenth-Century United States*** (1956). C. D. Warner and Mark Twain, **The Gilded Age*** (1873), is a useful and entertaining contemporary impression. On Social Darwinism, Richard Hofstadter's **Social Darwinism in Ameri-**

can Thought* (1945) should be supplemented by R. C. Bannister, **Social Darwinism** (1979). On the views of businessmen, see E. C. Kirkland, **Dream and Thought in the Business Community*** (1956), Kirkland's edition of Andrew Carnegie's writings, **The Gospel of Wealth** (1962), R. G. McCloskey, **American Conservatism in the Age of Enterprise*** (1951), T. C. Cochran, **Railroad Leaders** (1953), and J. D. Rockefeller, **Random Reminiscences of Men and Events** (1909).

R. A. Billington, **Westward Expansion** (1967), is the best introduction to the history of the exploitation of the West. On the Indians, general works include W. E. Washburn, **The Indian in America*** (1975), and W. T. Hagan, **American Indians*** (1961). Of more specialized books, the following are useful: F. G. Roe, **The Indian and the Horse** (1955), R. W. Mardock, **The Reformers and the American Indian** (1971), R. M. Utley, **Frontier Regulars: The United States Army and the Indian*** (1973), L. R. Hafen and W. J. Ghent, **Broken Hand: The Life Story of Thomas Fitzpatrick** (1931), and R. G. Athearn, **William Tecumseh Sherman and the Settlement of the West** (1956). The destruction of the buffalo is described in vivid if highly imaginative terms in Mari Sandoz, **The Buffalo Hunters*** (1954). H. H. Jackson, **A Century of Dishonor*** (1881), is a powerful contemporary indictment of United States Indian policy.

For the fate of other minority groups, see J. H. Franklin, **From Slavery to Freedom*** (1956), R. W. Logan, **The Negro in American Life and Thought: The Nadir*** (1954), J. M. Kousser, **The Shaping of Southern Politics: Suffrage Restriction and the Establishment of the One-Party South** (1974), L. R. Harlan, **Booker T. Washington*** (1972), S. P. Hirshson, **Farewell to the Bloody Shirt*** (1962), V. P. De Santis, **Republicans Face the Southern Question** (1959), C. V. Woodward, **The Strange Career of Jim Crow*** (1966), J. A. Garraty (ed.), **Quarrels That Have Shaped the Constitution*** (1964), Gunther Barth, **Bitter Strength: A History of the Chinese in the United States** (1964), R. A. Billington, **The Protestant Crusade*** (1938), and John Higham, **Strangers in the Land*** (1955).

For the mining frontier, consult R. W. Paul, **Mining Frontiers of the Far West*** (1963), W. T. Jackson, **Treasure Hill: Portrait of a Silver Mining Camp*** (1963), D. A. Smith, **Rocky Mountain Mining Camps: The Urban Frontier*** (1967), and W. J. Trimble, **The Mining Advance into the Inland Empire** (1914). Mark Twain, **Roughing It*** (1872), is a classic contemporary account, and W. H. Goetzmann, **Exploration and Empire** (1966), throws much light on all aspects of western development. For federal land policy, see R. M. Robbins, **Our Landed Heritage*** (1942), P. W. Gates, **Fifty Million Acres*** (1954), and F. A. Shannon, **The Farmer's Last Frontier*** (1945), which is excellent on all questions relating to post-Civil War agriculture. Everett Dick, **The Sod-House Frontier** (1937), presents a graphic picture of farm life on the treeless plains. Bonanza farming is described in H. M. Drache, **The Day of the Bonanza** (1964).

The development of transcontinental railroads is discussed in R. E. Riegel, **The Story of the Western Railroads*** (1926), Julius Grodinsky, **Transcontinental Railway Strategy** (1962), O. O. Winther, **The Transportation Frontier*** (1964), and G. R. Taylor and I. D. Neu, **The American Railroad Network** (1956). For a sampling of the literature on specific roads, see Oscar Lewis, **The Big Four** (1938), J. B. Hedges, **Henry Villard and the Railroads of the Northwest** (1930), Albro Martin, **James J. Hill and the Opening of the Northwest** (1976), R. G. Athearn, **Union Pacific Country*** (1971), and L. L. Waters, **Steel Rails to Santa Fe** (1950). Matthew Josephson, **The Robber Barons*** (1934), discusses the chicanery connected with railroad construction at length.

On cattle ranching on the plains, a good account is Lewis Atherton, **The Cattle Kings*** (1961), but see also Don Worcester, **The Chisholm Trail** (1980), E. S. Osgood, **The Day of the Cattleman*** (1929), and Louis Pelzer, **The Cattlemen's Frontier** (1936). For the cowboy and his life, see J. B. Frantz and J. E. Choate, **The American Cowboy: The Myth and Reality** (1955), and R. R. Dykstra, **The Cattle Towns*** (1968). W. P. Webb, **The Great Plains*** (1931), is a fascinating analysis of the development of a unique civilization on the plains.

18/AN INDUSTRIAL GIANT

When the Civil War began, the country's industrial output, while important and increasing, did not approach that of major European powers. By the end of the century it had become far and away the colossus among world manufacturers, dwarfing the production of Great Britain and Germany. The world had never seen such a remarkable example of rapid economic growth. The value of American manufactured products rose from $1.8 billion in 1859 to over $13 billion in 1899. Modern economists estimate that the output of goods and services in the country (the gross national product, or GNP) increased by 44 percent between 1874 and 1883 and continued to expand in succeeding years.

Industrial Growth: An Overview

American manufacturing flourished for many reasons. New natural resources were discovered and exploited steadily, thereby increasing opportunities and attracting the brightest and most energetic of a vigorous and expanding population. The growth of the country added constantly to the size of the national market, and protective tariffs shielded that market from foreign competition. Yet foreign capital entered the market freely, in part because tariffs kept out so many foreign goods. The dominant spirit of the time encouraged businessmen to maximum effort by emphasizing progress, glorifying material wealth, and justifying aggressiveness. European immigrants provided the additional labor needed by expanding industry; 2.5 million arrived in the 1870s, twice that number in the eighties.

It was a period of rapid advance in basic science, and technicians created a bountiful harvest of new machines, processes, and power sources that increased productivity in many industries and created new industries as well. In agriculture there were what one contemporary expert called "an endless variety of cultivators," better harvesters and binding machines, and combines capable of threshing and bagging 450 pounds of grain a minute. An 1886 report of the Illinois Bureau of Labor Statistics claimed that "new machinery has displaced fully 50 percent of the muscular labor formerly required to do a given amount of work in the manufacture of agricultural implements." As a result of improvements in the milling of grain, packaged cereals appeared on the American breakfast table. The commercial canning of food, spurred by the "automatic line" canning factory, expanded so rapidly that by 1887 a writer in *Good Housekeeping* magazine could say: "Housekeeping is getting to be ready made, as well as clothing." The Bonsack cigarette-rolling machine created a new industry that changed the habits of millions. George B. Eastman created still another with his development of mass-produced roll photographic film and the simple but efficient Kodak camera.

■ **Links in the nation's increasingly complex and interdependent transportation network can be glimpsed in this 1878 painting by a primitive artist, Herman Decker. The scene is the bustling Lonsdale Wharf in Providence, Rhode Island.**

The perfection of the typewriter by the Remington company in the 1880s revolutionized the way office work was performed.

The Railroad Network

In 1866, returning from his honeymoon in Europe, 30-year-old Charles Francis Adams, Jr., grandson and great-grandson of presidents, full of ambition and ready, as he put it, to confront the world "face to face," looked about in search of a career. "Surveying the whole field," he later explained, "I fixed on the railroad system as the most developing force and the largest field of the day, and determined to attach myself to it." Adams' judgment was acute: for the next 25 years the railroads were probably the most significant element in American economic development, railroad executives the most powerful people in the country.

Railroads were important first as an industry in themselves. Less than 35,000 miles of track existed when Lee laid down his sword at Appomattox. In 1875 railroad mileage exceeded 74,000 and the skeleton of the network was complete. Over the next two decades the skeleton was fleshed out. In 1890 the mature but still growing system took in over $1 billion in passenger and freight revenues. (The federal government's income in 1890 was only $403 million.) The value of railroad properties and equipment was more than $8.7 billion. The national *railroad* debt of $5.1 billion was almost five times the national debt of $1.1 billion! By 1900 the nation had 193,000 miles of track.

The emphasis in railroad construction after 1865 was on organizing integrated systems. The lines had high fixed costs: taxes, interest on their bonds, maintenance of track and rolling stock, salaries of office personnel. A short train with half-empty cars required almost as many workers and as much fuel to operate as a long one jammed with freight or passengers. In order to earn profits the railroads had to carry as much traffic as possible. They therefore spread out feeder lines to draw business to their main lines the way the root network of a tree draws water into its trunk.

Before the Civil War, as we have seen, passengers and freight could travel by rail from beyond Chicago and St. Louis to the Atlantic Coast, but only after the war did true trunk lines appear. In 1861, for example, the New York Central ran from Albany to Buffalo. One could proceed from Buffalo to Chicago, but on a different company's trains. In 1867 the Central passed into the hands of "Commodore" Cornelius Vanderbilt, who had made a large fortune in the shipping business. Vanderbilt already controlled lines running from Albany to New York City; now he merged these properties with the Central. In 1873 he integrated the Lake Shore and Michigan Southern into his empire and two years later the Michigan Central. The Commodore spent large sums improving his properties and buying feeder lines. At his death in 1877 the Central operated a network of over 4,500 miles of track between New York City and most of the principal cities of the Middle West.

While Vanderbilt was putting together the New York Central complex, Thomas A. Scott was fusing roads to Cincinnati, Indianapolis, St. Louis, and Chicago to his Pennsylvania Railroad, which linked Pittsburgh and Philadelphia. In 1871 the Pennsylvania obtained access to New York; soon it reached Baltimore and Washington. By 1869 another important system, the Erie, controlled by a triumvirate of railroad freebooters, Daniel Drew, Jay Gould, and Jim Fisk, had extended itself from New York to Cleveland, Cincinnati, and St. Louis. Soon thereafter it too tapped the markets of Chicago and other principal cities. In 1874 the Baltimore and Ohio also obtained access to Chicago.

The transcontinentals were trunk lines from the start; the emptiness of the western country would have made short lines unprofitable, and builders quickly grasped the need for direct connections to eastern markets and thorough integration of feeder lines.

The dominant system builder of the Southwest was Jay Gould, a soft-spoken, unostentatious man who looked, according to one witness, "like an insignificant pigmy." Gould was in fact ruthless, cynical, and aggressive. His mere appearance in Wall Street, one Texas newspaper reported in 1890, made "millionaires tremble like innocent sparrows . . . when a hungry hawk swoops down upon them." (A railroad president used a better image when he called Gould a "perfect eel.") With millions acquired in shady railroad and stock market ventures, Gould invaded the West in the 1870s, buying 370,000 shares of Union Pacific stock. He took over the Kansas Pacific, running

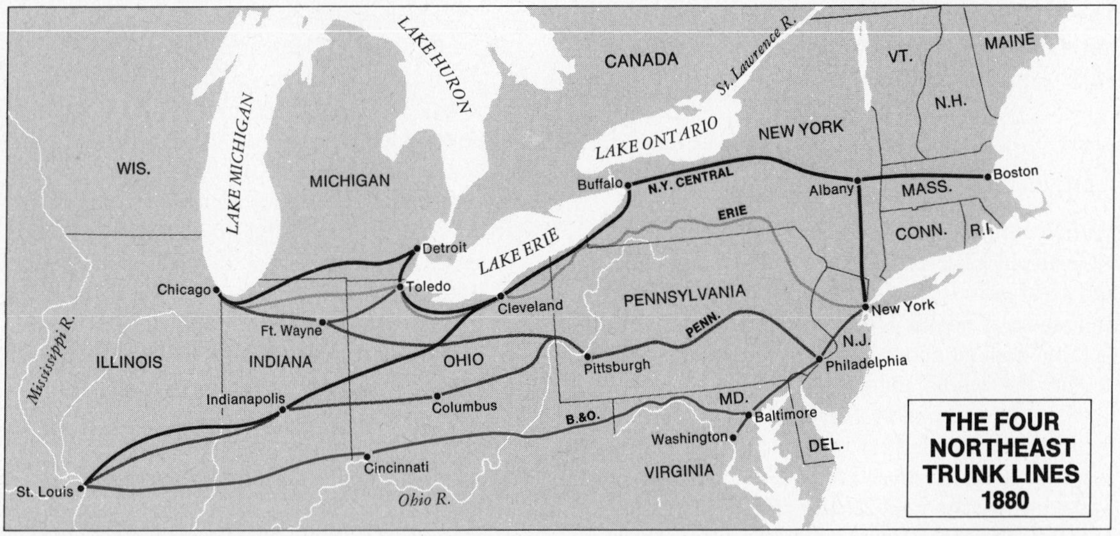

■ **Trunk lines are generally defined as systems handling long-distance through traffic. These northeast trunk lines also linked up with the western railroads through Chicago and St. Louis; look back at the map on Western Cattle Trails and Railroads (page 438).**

from Denver to Kansas City, which he consolidated with the Union Pacific, and the Missouri Pacific, a line from Kansas City to St. Louis, which he expanded through mergers and purchases into a 5,300-mile system. Often Gould put together such properties merely to unload them on other railroads at a profit, but his grasp of the importance of integration was sound.

In the Northwest, Henry Villard, a German-born ex-newspaperman, constructed another great complex based on his control of the Northern Pacific and properties in Oregon and California. James J. Hill's expansion of the St. Paul and Pacific Railroad into the Great Northern system, absorbing a number of other lines in addition to laying track all the way to Seattle, produced still another western network.

The Civil War had highlighted the need for through railroad connections in the South. Shortly after the conflict, northern capital began to flow into southern railroad construction. The Chesapeake and Ohio, organized in 1868, opened a direct line from Norfolk, Virginia, to Cincinnati. The Richmond and Danville absorbed some 26 lines after the war, forming a system that ran from Washington to the Mississippi. It in turn became part of the Richmond and West Point Terminal Company, which by the late eighties controlled an 8,558-mile network. Like other southern trunk lines such as the Louisville and Nashville and the Atlantic Coast Line, this system was largely controlled by northern capitalists.

The trunk lines interconnected and thus had to standardize many of their activities. The present system of time zones was developed in 1883 by the roads. The standard track gauge (4 feet $8\frac{1}{2}$ inches) was established in 1886. Standardized car coupling and braking mechanisms, standard signal systems, even standard methods of accounting were essential to the effective functioning of the network.

The lines sought to work out fixed rates for carrying different types of freight, charging more for valuable manufactured goods than for bulky products like coal or wheat, and they agreed to permit rate concessions to shippers when necessary to avoid hauling empty cars. In other words, they charged what the traffic would bear, but they also tried to cooperate with one another to avoid "senseless" competition. To enforce cooperation they founded regional organizations such as the Eastern Trunk Line Association and the Western Traffic Association.

The railroads stimulated the economy indirectly. Like foreign commerce and the textile industry in earlier times, they were a "multiplier" speeding development. In 1869 they bought $41.6 million worth of cars and locomotives, in 1889 $90.8 million. The roads in 1881 used about 94 percent of all the rolled steel manufactured in the United States. Such purchases created thousands of jobs and led to countless technological advances.

Because of their voracious appetite for traffic, railroads in sparsely settled regions and in areas with undeveloped resources devoted much money and effort to stimulating local economic growth. The Louisville and Nashville, for instance, was a prime mover in the expansion of the iron industry in Alabama in the 1880s. The state's output of iron increased tenfold between 1880 and 1889, in considerable part because of the railroad's activities in building spur lines to mines and furnaces and attracting capital into the industry.

To speed the settlement of new regions, the land-grant railroads sold land cheaply and on easy terms, for sales meant future business as well as current income. Roads like the Northern Pacific offered reduced rates to travelers interested in buying farms, and they entertained potential customers with a free hand. Land-grant lines set up "bureaus of immigration" that distributed elaborate brochures describing the wonders of the new country. Their agents greeted immigrants at the great eastern ports and tried to steer them to railroad property. They sent agents who were usually themselves immigrants—often ministers—all over Europe to recruit prospective settlers, many of whom could be expected to buy railroad land. Occasionally entire colonies migrated to America under railroad auspices, such as the 1,900 Mennonites who came to Kansas from Russia in 1874 to settle on the land of the Atchison, Topeka and Santa Fe.

Technological advances in railroading accelerated economic development in complex ways. In 1869 George Westinghouse invented the air brake. By enabling an engineer to apply the brakes to all cars simultaneously (formerly each car had to be braked separately by its own conductor or brakeman) this invention made possible revolutionary increases in the size of trains and the speed at which they could safely operate. The sleeping car, invented in 1864 by George Pullman, now came into its own.

To pull the heavier trains, more powerful locomotives were needed. They in turn produced a

■ **A Northern Pacific poster offers its land as the "best and cheapest" available. By 1917 this railroad had realized $136 million on its land grants.**

call for stronger and more durable rails to bear the additional weight. Steel, itself reduced in cost because of technological developments, supplied the answer, for steel rails outlasted iron many times despite the use of much heavier equipment. "Steel rails," one expert said in the eighties, "form the very 'cornerstone' of the great improvements which have taken place in railroad efficiency." In 1880 only 50 percent of the nation's rails were of steel; by 1890 less than 1 percent were not.

A close tie developed between the railroads and the nation's telegraph network, dominated by the Western Union Company. Commonly the roads allowed Western Union to string wires along their rights of way, and they transported telegraphers and their equipment without charge. In return they received free telegraphic service, important for efficiency and safety. It is no coincidence that the early 1880s, a period of booming railroad construction, saw a fantastic expansion of Western Union. By 1883 the company was transmitting 40 million messages a year over 400,000 miles of wire. The two industries, as Jay Gould put it, went "hand in hand, . . . integral parts" of American civilization.

Iron, Oil, and Electricity

The transformation of iron manufacturing affected the nation almost as much as railroad development. Output rose from 920,000 tons in 1860 to 10.3 million tons in 1900, but the big change came in the development of ways to mass produce steel. In its pure form (wrought iron) the metal is tough but relatively soft. Ordinary cast iron, which contains large amounts of carbon and other impurities, is hard but brittle. Steel, which contains 1 or 2 percent carbon, combines the hardness of cast iron with the toughness of wrought iron. For nearly every purpose—structural girders for bridges and buildings, railroad track, machine tools, boiler plate, barbed wire—steel is immensely superior to other kinds of iron.

But steel was so expensive to manufacture that it could not be used for bulky products until the invention in the 1850s of the Bessemer process, perfected independently by Henry Bessemer, an Englishman, and William Kelly of Kentucky. Bessemer and Kelly discovered that a stream of air directed into a mass of molten iron caused the carbon and other impurities to combine with oxygen and burn off. When measured amounts of carbon, silicon, and manganese were then added, the brew became steel. What had been a rare metal could now be produced by the hundreds and thousands of tons. The Bessemer process and the open-hearth method, a slower but more precise technique that enabled producers to sample the molten mass and thus control quality closely, were introduced commercially in the 1860s. In 1870, 77,000 tons of steel were manufactured, less than 4 percent of the volume of pig iron. By 1880, however, 1.39 million tons were pouring annually from the converters, and by 1900 nearly 11.4 million tons.

Such growth would have been impossible but for the huge supplies of iron ore in the United States and the coal necessary to fire the furnaces that refined it. In the 1870s the great iron fields rimming Lake Superior began to yield their treasures. The Menominee range in Michigan began production in 1877, followed in 1884 by the Gogebic range, on the Michigan-Wisconsin border. In each case the completion of rail connections to the fields had been necessary before large-scale mining could take place—another illustration of the importance of railroads in the economic history of the era. The Vermilion range, in the northeast corner of Minnesota, was opened up at about the same time, and somewhat later the magnificent Mesabi region, where the enormous iron concentrations made a compass needle spin like a top. Mesabi ores could be mined with steam shovels, almost like gravel.

Pittsburgh, surrounded by vast coal deposits, became the iron and steel capital of the country, the Minnesota ores reaching it by way of steamers on the Great Lakes and rail lines from Cleveland. Other cities in Pennsylvania and Ohio were important producers, and a separate complex, centering on Birmingham, Alabama, developed to exploit local iron and coal fields.

The petroleum industry expanded even more spectacularly than iron and steel. Edwin L. Drake drilled the first successful well in Pennsylvania in 1859. During the Civil War, production ranged between 2 million and 3 million barrels a year. In 1873 almost 10 million barrels were produced, and in the early eighties annual output averaged over 20 million barrels. A decade later the figure had leaped to about 50 million barrels.

Before the invention of the gasoline engine and the automobile, the most important petroleum product was kerosene, which was burned in lamps. In the early years in Pennsylvania hundreds of tiny refineries, often reminiscent of the ramshackle stills of nearby moonshiners, were engaged in making kerosene. The refiners heated crude oil in large kettles and, after the volatile elements had escaped, condensed the kerosene in coils cooled by water. The heavier petroleum tars were discarded.

Technological advances came rapidly. By the early 1870s, refiners had learned how to "crack" petroleum by applying high temperatures to the crude in order to rearrange its molecular structure, thereby increasing the percentage of kerosene yielded. By-products such as naphtha, gasoline (used in vaporized form as an illuminating gas),

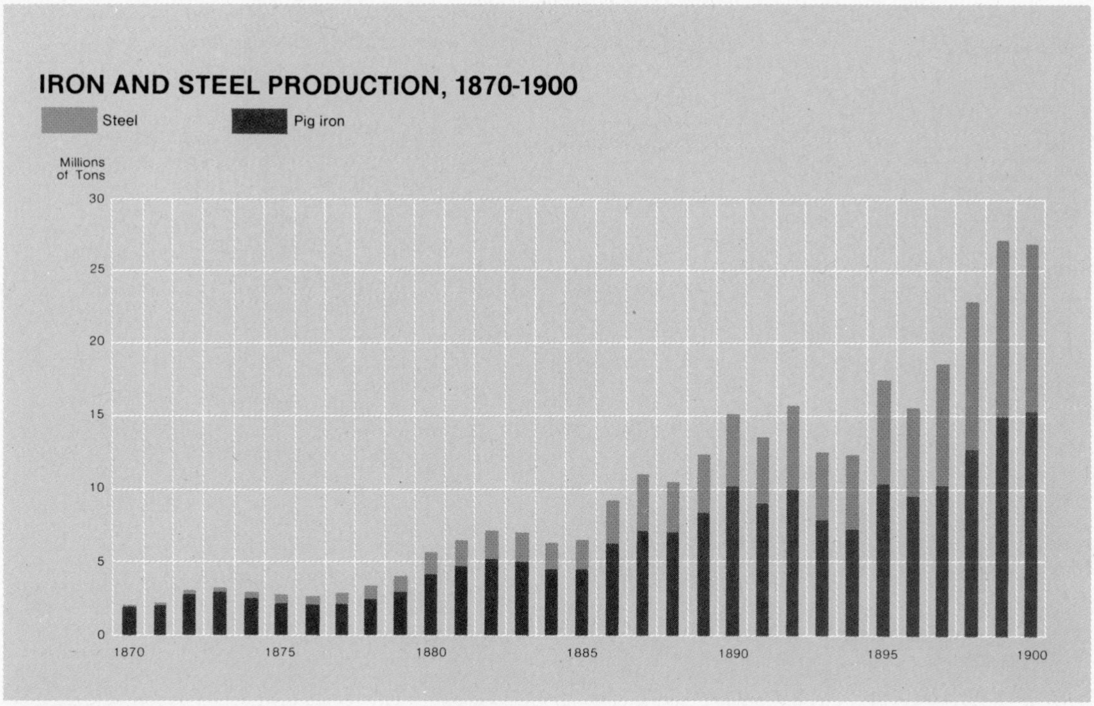

■ **Minnesota's Mesabi Range (below, shown in 1899) was developed largely with Rockefeller money. It shipped 4,000 tons of iron ore in 1892 and within a decade tripled that amount—an increase reflected in the graph above.**

■ **A scene on the Oil Creek Railroad in western Pennsylvania in the early 1860s. Initially, crude oil was shipped to refineries in barrels by barge or on railroad flatcars, as shown here. The familiar "boiler-shaped" tank car was invented in 1869, and by the 1870s a network of pipelines was laid to handle the growing oil output.**

rhigolene (a local anesthetic), cymogene (a coolant for refrigerating machines), and many lubricants and waxes began to appear on the market. At the same time a great increase in the supply of crude oil—especially after the chemist Herman Frosch perfected a method for removing sulfur from low-quality petroleum—drove prices down.

These circumstances put a premium on refining efficiency. Larger plants utilizing expensive machinery and employing skilled technicians became more important. In the mid sixties only three refineries in the country could process 2,000 barrels of crude a week; a decade later plants capable of handling 1,000 barrels a day were common.

Two other important new industries were the telephone and electric light businesses. Both were typical of the period, being products of technical advances and intimately related to the growth of a high-speed, urban civilization that put great stress on communication. The telephone was invented in 1876 by Alexander Graham Bell, who had been led to the study of acoustics through his interest in the education of the deaf. Bell's work with a device for transcribing tone vibrations electrically to help deaf-mutes learn to speak encouraged him to experiment with a "speaking telegraph" that used electrified metal disks, acting like the drum of the human ear, to convert sound waves into electrical impulses and electrical impulses back into sound waves.

Although considered little more than a clever gadget at first—the Western Union Company passed up an opportunity to buy the invention for $100,000, its president calling the telephone an "electrical toy"—Bell's invention soon proved its practical value. By 1880, 85 towns and cities had local telephone networks. In 1895 there were more than 300,000 phones in the country, in 1900 almost 800,000, twice the total for all Europe. By that date the American Telephone and Telegraph Company, a consolidation of over 100 local systems, dominated the business.

When Western Union realized the importance of the telephone, it tried for a time to compete with Bell by developing a machine of its own. The man it commissioned to devise this machine was Thomas A. Edison. Bell's patents proved unassailable, however, and Western Union abandoned the effort to maintain a competing system, but Edison vastly improved telephonic transmission. Not yet 30 when he turned to the telephone problem, Edison had already made a number of contributions toward solving what he called the "mysteries of electrical force," including a multiplex telegraph capable of sending four messages over a single wire at the same time. At Menlo Park, New Jersey, he built the prototype of the modern research laboratory, where specific problems could be attacked on a mass scale by a team of trained specialists. During his lifetime he took out more than a thousand patents, dealing with machines as varied as the phonograph, the motion-picture projector, the storage battery, and the mimeograph. He also contributed substantially to the development of the electric dynamo, ore-separating machinery, and railroad signal equipment.

Edison's most significant achievement was unquestionably his perfection of the incandescent lamp, or electric light bulb. Others before Edison had experimented with the idea of producing light by passing electricity through a filament in a vacuum. Always, however, the filaments quickly burned out. Edison tried hundreds of fibers before producing, in 1879, a carbonized filament that would glow brightly in a vacuum tube for as long as 170 hours without crumbling. At Christmastime he decorated the grounds about his laboratory with a few dozen of the new lights. People flocked by the thousands to see this miracle of the "Wizard of Menlo Park." To the admirers of his "bright, beautiful light, like the mellow sunset of an Italian autumn," the inventor boasted that soon he would be able to illuminate entire towns, even great cities like New York.

He was true to his promise. In 1882 his Edison Illuminating Company opened a power station in New York and began to supply current for lighting to 85 consumers, including the New York *Times* and the banking house of J. P. Morgan and Company. Soon central stations were springing up everywhere until, by 1898, there were about 3,000 in the country. Edison's manufacturing subsidiaries flourished equally: in 1885 they turned out 139,000 incandescent lamps, by the end of the decade nearly a million a year.

■ **Edison patented the phonograph in 1878, budgeting $18 for its invention. He was photographed in his laboratory in 1888 working on a wax-cylinder model.**

The Edison system employed direct current at low voltages, which limited the distance that power could be transmitted to about 2 miles. Technicians soon demonstrated that by using alternating current, stepped up to high voltages by transformers, power could be transported over great distances economically and then reduced to safe levels for use by consumers. This encouraged George Westinghouse, inventor of the air brake, to found the Westinghouse Electric Company in 1886.

Edison stubbornly refused to accept the superiority of high-voltage alternating current. "Just as certain as death Westinghouse will kill a customer within 6 months," he predicted. For a time the language was graced with the term "to Westinghouse," meaning to electrocute. But the Westinghouse system quickly proved itself safe as well as efficient, and alternating current became standard.

The substitution of electric for steam power in factories was as liberating as that of steam for waterpower before the Civil War. Small, safe electric

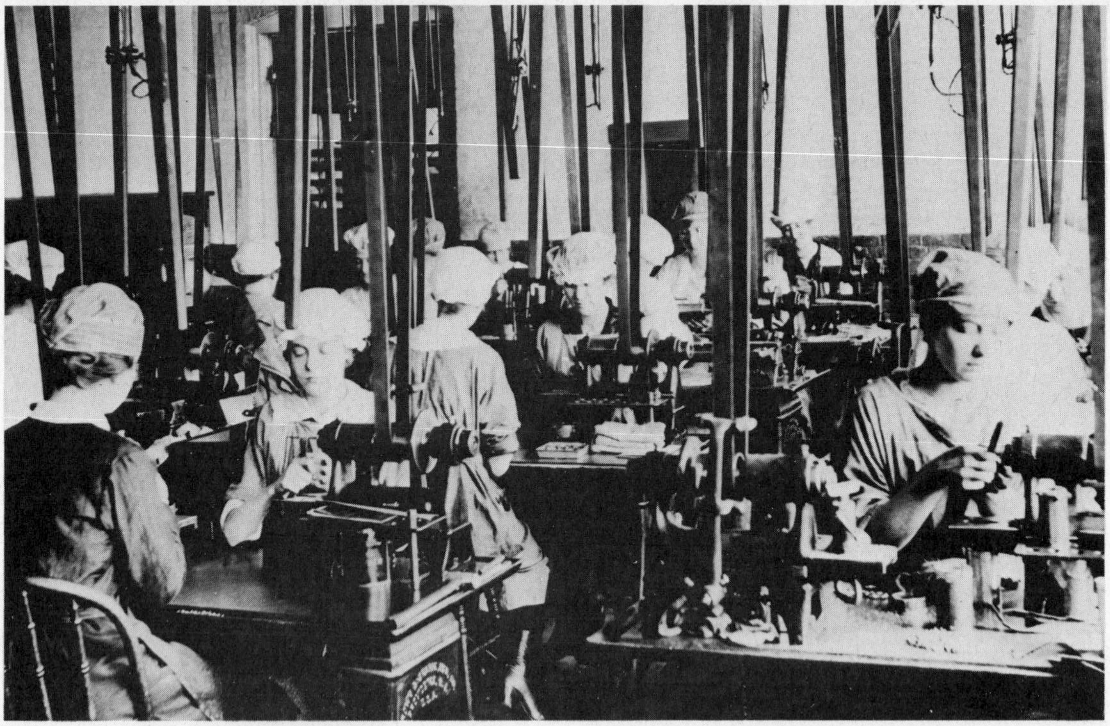

■ **These women operated power machines driven by overhead moving belts. Sometimes the belts were made of buffalo hide; often such systems were steam powered. Most factory equipment was not designed with safety considerations in mind. In this case the women wore caps to keep their hair out of the moving belts and wheels.**

motors replaced dangerous and cumbersome mazes of belts and wheels. The electric power industry expanded rapidly. By the early years of the 20th century almost 6 billion kilowatt-hours of electricity were being produced annually. Yet this was only the beginning.

Competition and Monopoly: The Railroads

During the post-Civil War era, expansion in industry went hand in hand with concentration. With each passing decade, fewer and larger firms controlled an increasing share of the business. The principal cause of this trend, aside from the obvious economies resulting from large-scale production and the growing importance of expensive machinery, was the downward trend of prices after 1873. The deflation, which resulted mainly from the failure of the money supply to keep pace with the rapid increase in the volume of goods produced, affected agricultural goods as well as manufactures, and it lasted until 1896 or 1897.

Contemporaries believed they were living through a "great depression." That label is misleading, for output expanded almost continuously, and at a rapid rate, until 1893, when a true depression struck the country. Falling prices, however, kept a steady pressure on profit margins, and this led to increased production and thus to intense competition for markets. Rival concerns battled for business, the strongest, most efficient, and most unscrupulous destroying or absorbing their foes. If no clear victor emerged, the exhausted contenders frequently ended the warfare by combining voluntarily. For a time the government did little about laying down rules for the fighting or preventing the consolidations that seemed to result from it.

According to the classical economists (see page 500), competition advanced the public interest by keeping prices low and assuring the most efficient producer the largest profit. Up to a point it accomplished these purposes in the years after 1865, but it also fathered side effects that injured both the economy and society as a whole. Railroad managers, for instance, found it impossible to enforce "official" rate schedules and maintain their regional associations once competitive pressures

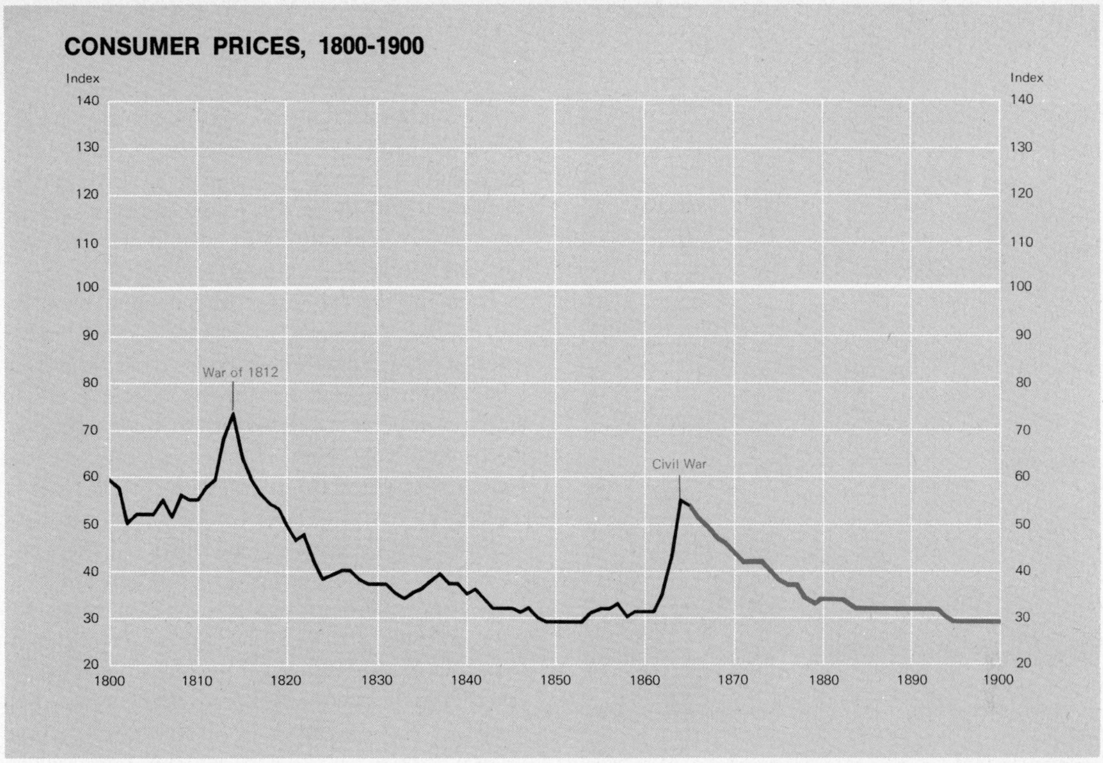

■ **This chart shows consumer prices from 1800 to 1900. The portion of the line in color shows the post-Civil War period. Based on information supplied by the Bureau of Labor Statistics, the "index" is very rough for this period—especially before the Civil War. The base line is 100. It represents the consumer price index, averaged, for the years 1957–1959.**

mounted. In 1865 it had cost from 96 cents to $2.15 per 100 pounds, depending on the class of freight, to ship goods from New York to Chicago. In 1888 rates ranged from 35 cents to 75 cents. A decade later the cost of shipping 100 pounds of wheat from Chicago to New York had dropped to 20 cents.

Competition cut deeply into railroad profits, causing the lines to seek desperately to increase volume. They did so chiefly by reducing rates still more, on a selective basis. They gave rebates (secret reductions below the published rates) to large shippers in order to capture their business. The granting of discounts to those who shipped in volume made economic sense: it was easier to handle freight in carload lots than in smaller units. So intense was the battle for business, however, that the roads often made concessions to big customers far beyond what the economies of bulk shipment justified. In the 1870s the New York Central regularly reduced the rates charged important shippers by 50 to 80 percent. One large Utica dry-goods merchant received a rate of 9 cents while others paid 33 cents. Two big New York City grain merchants paid so little that they soon controlled the grain business of the entire city.

Railroad officials disliked rebating but found no way to avoid the practice. "Notwithstanding my horror of rebates," the president of a New England trunk line told one of his executives in discussing the case of a brick manufacturer, "bill at the usual rate, and rebate Mr. Cole 25 cents a thousand." In extreme cases the railroads even gave large shippers drawbacks, which were rebates on the business of the shippers' competitors!

Besides rebating, railroads issued passes to favored shippers, built sidings at the plants of important companies without charge, and gave freely of their landholdings to attract businesses to their territory. Railroads also battled directly with one another in ways damaging both to themselves and to the public. Unscrupulous operators like Jay Gould often threw together roundabout, inefficient trunk lines merely to blackmail established roads, forcing them to buy up the essentially useless properties at inflated prices. Others tried to win control of competing lines in the stock market. Between 1866 and 1868 Vanderbilt of the

■ **Edward Steichen's memorable photograph of J. Pierpont Morgan, taken in 1903. Looking the formidable Morgan in the eye, Steichen said, was like facing the headlights of an onrushing express train.**

New York Central waged a futile campaign to win control of the Erie. The raffish Erie directors fought back by issuing themselves thousands of shares of new stock without paying for them, thereby grossly inflating the capitalization of the line. Both roads stooped to bribery in an effort to obtain favorable action in the New York legislature, and there were pitched battles between the hirelings of each side.

"The force of competition," a railroad man explained, "is one that no carrying corporation can withstand and before which the managing officers of a corporation are helpless." James F. Joy of the Chicago, Burlington, and Quincy made the same point more bluntly: "Unless you prepare to defend yourselves," he advised the president of the Michigan Central, "you will be boarded by pirates in all quarters." Railroad executives are "hardly better than a race of horse-jockeys," Charles Francis Adams, Jr., wrote in *Railroads: Their Origin and Problems* (1879). A person trying to run a railroad honestly, Adams also said, would be like Don Quixote tilting at a windmill.

To make up for losses forced upon them by competitive pressures, railroads charged higher rates at way points along their tracks where no competition existed. Frequently it cost more to ship a product a short distance than a longer one. Rochester, New York, was served only by the New York Central. In the 1870s it cost 30 cents to transport a barrel of flour from Rochester to New York City, a distance of 350 miles. At the same time flour could be shipped from Minneapolis to New York, a distance of well over 1,000 miles, for only 20 cents a barrel. One Rochester businessman told a state investigating committee that he could save 18 cents a hundredweight by sending goods to St. Louis by way of New York, where several carriers competed for the traffic, even though, in fact, the goods might come back through Rochester over the same tracks on the way to St. Louis!

Although cheap transportation stimulated the economy, few people benefited from cutthroat competition. Small shippers—and all businessmen in cities and towns with limited rail outlets—suffered heavily; railroad discrimination speeded the concentration of industry in large corporations located in major centers. The instability of rates even troubled interests like the middle-western flour millers who benefited from the competitive situation, for it hampered planning. Nor could manufacturers who received rebates be entirely happy, since few could be sure that some other producer was not getting a larger reduction.

Probably the worst sufferers were the roads themselves. The loss of revenue resulting from rate cutting, combined with inflated debts, put most of them in grave difficulty when faced with a downturn in the business cycle. In 1876 two-fifths of all railroad bonds were in default; three years later 65 lines were bankrupt. Since the public would not countenance bankrupt railroads going out of business, these companies were placed in the hands of court-appointed receivers. The receivers, however, seldom provided efficient management and had no funds at their disposal for new equipment.

During the 1880s the major roads responded to these pressures by building or buying lines in order to create interregional systems. These were the first giant corporations, capitalized in the hundreds of millions of dollars. The enormous cost of these systems led to another wave of bankruptcies when a true depression struck in the 1890s.

The consequent reorganizations brought most of the big systems under the control of financiers, notably J. Pierpont Morgan, head of a powerful firm of New York bankers, and such other private bankers as Kuhn, Loeb of New York and Lee, Higginson of Boston. The economic historian A. D. Noyes described in 1904 what the bankers did:

> Bondholders were requested to scale down interest charges, receiving new stock in compensation, while the shareholders were invited to pay a cash assessment, thus providing a working fund. [The bankers] combined to guarantee that the requisite money should be raised. They too were paid in new stock. . . . Though the total capital issues were increased, fixed charges were diminished and a sufficient fund for road improvement and new equipment was provided.

The reorganizations—critics called them Morganizations—put the bankrupt trunk lines back on their feet. Representatives of the bankers sat on the board of every line they saved. While they generally took no part in the everyday affairs of the roads, their influence was predominant. They consistently opposed rate wars, rebating, and other competitive practices. In effect, control of the railroad network became centralized, even though the companies maintained their separate existences and operated in a seemingly independent manner. When Morgan died in 1913, "Morgan men" dominated the boards of the New York Central, the Erie, the New York, New Haven and Hartford, the Southern, the Pere Marquette, the Atchison, Topeka and Santa Fe, and many other lines.

■ Andrew Carnegie at the age of 61. His phenomenal rags-to-riches career was one of the real-life models for Horatio Alger's dime novels on "poor boy makes good."

The Steel Industry: Carnegie

The iron and steel industry was also intensely competitive. Despite the trend toward higher production, demand varied erratically from year to year, even from month to month. In good times producers built new facilities, only to suffer heavy losses when demand declined and much of their capacity lay idle. The forward rush of technology put a tremendous emphasis on efficiency; expensive plants quickly became obsolete. Improved transportation facilities allowed manufacturers in widely separated places to compete with one another; despite the importance of the Pittsburgh region, in the early 1890s multimillion-dollar mills existed in Alabama, Colorado, Illinois, and elsewhere.

The kingpin of the industry was Andrew Carnegie. Carnegie was born in Dunfermline, Scotland, and came to the United States in 1848 at the age of 12. His first job as a bobbin boy in a cotton mill brought him $1.20 a week, but his talents perfectly fitted the times, and he rose rapidly: to Western Union messenger boy, to telegrapher, to private secretary, to railroad manager. He saved his money, made some shrewd investments, and by 1868 had an income of $50,000 a year.

At about this time he decided to specialize in

the iron business, saying, in an oft-quoted remark, that he believed in putting all his eggs in one basket and then watching the basket. Carnegie possessed great talent as a salesman, boundless faith in the future of the country, an uncanny knack of choosing topflight subordinates, and enough ruthlessness to survive in the iron and steel jungle. Where other steelmen built new plants in good times, he preferred to expand in bad times, when it cost far less to do so. During the 1870s, he later recalled, "many of my friends needed money. . . . I . . . bought out five or six of them. That is what gave me my leading interest in this steel business."

Carnegie grasped the importance of technological improvements in his industry. Slightly skeptical of the Bessemer process at first, once he became convinced of its practicality he adopted it enthusiastically. In 1875 he built the J. Edgar Thomson Steel Works, named after a president of the Pennsylvania Railroad, his biggest customer. He employed chemists and other specialists and was soon making steel from iron oxides that other manufacturers had discarded as waste. He was a merciless competitor. When a plant manager announced: "We broke all records for making steel last week," Carnegie replied: "Congratulations! *Why not do it every week?*" Carnegie sold rails by paying "commissions" to railroad purchasing agents, and he was not above reneging on a contract if he thought it profitable and safe to do so.

By 1890 the Carnegie Steel Company dominated the industry, and its output increased nearly tenfold during the next decade. Profits mounted from $3 million in 1893 to $6 million in 1896 and then soared to $40 million in 1900. Alarmed by his increasing control of the industry, the makers of finished steel products such as barbed wire and tubing began to combine and to consider entering the primary field. Carnegie, his competitive temper aroused, threatened to turn to finished products himself. A colossal steel war seemed imminent.

However, Carnegie longed to retire in order to devote himself to philanthropic work. He believed that great wealth entailed social responsibilities and that it was a disgrace to die rich. When J. P. Morgan approached him through an intermediary with an offer to buy him out, he assented readily. In 1901 Morgan put together United States Steel, the "world's first billion-dollar corporation." This combination included all the Carnegie properties, the Federal Steel Company (Carnegie's largest competitor), and such important fabricators of finished products as the American Steel and Wire Company, the American Tin Plate Company, and the National Tube Company. Vast reserves of Minnesota iron ore and a fleet of Great Lakes ore steamers were also included. U. S. Steel was capitalized at $1.4 billion, about twice the value of its component properties but not necessarily an overestimation of its profit-earning capacity. The owners of Carnegie Steel received $492 million, of which $250 million went to Carnegie himself.

The Standard Oil Trust

The pattern of fierce competition leading to combination and monopoly is well illustrated by the history of the petroleum industry. Irresistible pressures pushed the refiners into a brutal struggle to dominate the business. Production of crude oil, subject to the uncertainties of prospecting and drilling, fluctuated constantly and without regard for need. In general, output surged ahead far in excess of demand.

By the 1870s the chief oil-refining centers were Cleveland, Pittsburgh, Baltimore, and the New York City area. Of these Cleveland was the fastest growing, chiefly because the New York Central and Erie railroads competed fiercely for its oil trade and the Erie Canal offered an alternative route. Pittsburgh depended entirely on the Pennsylvania Railroad, and New York and Baltimore suffered from being far removed from the oil fields.

The Standard Oil Company of Cleveland, whose president was a merchant named John D. Rockefeller, emerged as the giant among the refiners. Rockefeller exploited every possible technical advance and employed fair means and foul to persuade competitors first in the Cleveland area and then elsewhere either to sell out or to join forces. By 1879 he controlled 90 percent of the nation's oil-refining capacity along with a network of oil pipelines and large reserves of petroleum in the ground. The existence of this monopoly, together with the remarkable expansion of the entire industry, caused Standard Oil to attract far more attention than its importance warranted in the late 19th century. The period of its greatest growth and economic influence did not come until later.

Standard Oil emerged victorious from the competitive wars because Rockefeller and his associates were the toughest and most imaginative fighters as well as the most efficient refiners in the business. In addition to obtaining from the railroads a 10 percent rebate and drawbacks on its competitors' shipments, Standard Oil cut prices locally to force small independents to sell out or face ruin. One Massachusetts refiner testified that Standard drove down the price of kerosene in his district from 9¼ cents to 5¼ cents simply to destroy his business. Since kerosene was sold in grocery stores, Standard supplied its own outlets with meat, sugar, and other products at artificially low prices to help crush the stores that handled other brands of kerosene. The company employed spies to track down the customers of independents and offer them oil at bargain prices. Bribery was also a Standard practice; the reformer Henry Demarest Lloyd quipped that the company had done everything to the Pennsylvania legislature except refine it. Rockefeller's sympathetic biographer, Allan Nevins, admitted that Standard Oil "committed acts against competitors which could not be defended."

Although a bold planner and a daring taker of necessary risks, Rockefeller was far too orderly and astute to enjoy the free-swinging battles that plagued his industry. Born in an upstate New York village in 1839, he settled in Cleveland in 1855 and became a produce merchant. During the Civil War he invested in a local refinery and by 1865 was engaged full time in the oil business.

Like Carnegie, Rockefeller was an organizer; he knew little about the technology of petroleum. He sought efficiency, order, and stability. His forte was meticulous attention to detail: stories are told of his ordering the number of drops of solder used to seal oil cans reduced from 40 to 39 and of his insisting that the manager of one of his refineries account for 750 missing barrel bungs. Not miserliness but a profound grasp of the economies of large-scale production explain this behavior. By reducing the cost of refining a gallon of crude oil by a mere .082 cents, Standard Oil increased its annual profit by about $600,000.

Rockefeller competed ruthlessly not primarily to crush other refiners but to persuade them to join with him, to share the business peaceably and rationally so that all could profit. Competition was obsolescent, he argued, though no more effective competitor than he ever lived. In truth most of the independent refiners that Standard Oil destroyed by unfair competition had previously turned down offers to merge or sell out on terms that modern students consider generous.

■ John D. Rockefeller carried his passion for perfection onto the golf course, hiring a boy to do nothing but intone "keep your head down" on each shot.

Having achieved his monopoly, Rockefeller stabilized and structured it by creating a new type of business organization, the trust. Standard Oil was an Ohio corporation, prohibited by local law from owning plants in other states or holding stock in out-of-state corporations. As Rockefeller and his associates took over dozens of companies with facilities scattered across the country, serious legal and managerial difficulties arose. How could these many organizations be integrated with Standard Oil of Ohio?

A rotund, genial little Pennsylvania lawyer named Samuel C. T. Dodd came up with an answer to this question in 1879.* The stock of Stan-

*The trust formula was not "perfected" until 1882.

dard of Ohio and of all the other companies that the Rockefeller interests had swallowed up was turned over to nine trustees, who were empowered to "exercise general supervision" over all the properties. Stockholders received in exchange trust certificates, on which dividends were paid. Thus order came to the petroleum business. Competition almost disappeared; prices steadied; profits skyrocketed. By 1892 John D. Rockefeller was worth over $800 million.

The Standard Oil Trust was not a corporation. It had no charter, indeed no legal existence at all. For many years few people outside the organization knew that it existed. The form they chose persuaded Rockefeller and other Standard Oil officials that without violating their consciences, they could deny under oath that Standard Oil of Ohio owned or controlled other corporations "directly or indirectly through its officers or agents." The *trustees* controlled these organizations—and Standard of Ohio too!

After Standard Oil's secret was revealed during a New York investigation in 1888, the word *trust,* formerly signifying a fiduciary arrangement for the protection of the interests of individuals incompetent or unwilling to guard them themselves, immediately became a synonym for monopoly. Standard Oil became the most hated and feared company in the United States. However, from the company's point of view, monopoly was not the purpose of the trust—that had been achieved before the device was invented. Centralization of the management of diverse and far-flung operations in the interest of efficiency was its chief function. Standard Oil headquarters in New York became the brain of a complex network where information from salaried managers in the field was collected and digested, where top managerial decisions were made, and whence orders went out to armies of drillers, refiners, scientists, and salesmen.

Public Utilities and Retailing

That public utilities such as the telephone and electric lighting industries tended to form monopolies is not difficult to explain, for in such fields competition involved costly duplication of equipment and, particularly in the case of the telephone, loss of service efficiency. However, competitive pressures were strong in the early stages of their development. Since these industries depended on patents, Bell and Edison had to fight mighty battles in the courts with rivals seeking to infringe upon their rights. Few quibbled over means when so much money hung in the balance. After Western Union employed Edison to invent a device that would enable it to circumvent Bell's rights, the Bell interests challenged Edison's improved telephone transmitter, claiming that it infringed on patents issued to one Emile Berliner, which they had bought up. Western Union was the victor in this particular battle, but in the end the telegraph company became convinced that the courts would uphold Bell's claims and abandoned the field.

Much of Edison's own time was taken up with legal battles to protect his many patents. When he first announced his electric light, capitalists, engineers, and inventors flocked to Menlo Park. Edison proudly revealed to them the secrets of his marvelous lamp. Many hurried away to turn this information to their own advantage, thinking the "Wizard" a naive fool. When they invaded the field, the law provided Edison with far less protection than he had expected. He had to fight a "Seven Years' War" with Westinghouse over the carbon-filament incandescent lamp. Although he won, his legal fees exceeded $2 million, and when the courts finally decided in his favor, only two years remained before the patent expired. "My electric light inventions have brought me no profits, only forty years of litigation," Edison later complained. A patent, he said bitterly, was "simply an invitation to a lawsuit."

The attitude of businessmen toward the rights of inventors and industrial pioneers is illustrated by an early advertisement of the Westinghouse Company:

> We regard it as fortunate that we have deferred entering the electrical field until the present moment. Having thus profited by the public experience of others, we enter ourselves for competition, hampered by a minimum of expense for experimental outlay. . . . In short, our organization is free, in large measure, of the load with which [other] electrical enterprises seem to be encumbered. The fruit of this . . . we propose to share with the customer.

Competition in the electric lighting business

■ **Marshall Field's notions department sales staff stands for a group portrait in the late 1800s. Linen handkerchiefs were selling for 35¢ apiece. The partly obscured sign over the counter on the left reads: Kid Glove Cleaning Department. (Credit: Marshall Field's.)**

raged for some years between Edison, Westinghouse, and another corporation, the Thomson-Houston Electric Company, which was operating 870 central lighting stations by 1890. In 1892 the Edison and Thomson-Houston companies merged, forming General Electric, a $35 million corporation. Thereafter, General Electric and Westinghouse maintained their dominance in the manufacture of bulbs and electrical equipment as well as in the distribution of electrical power.

The pattern of competition leading to dominance by a few great companies was repeated in many businesses. In life insurance an immense expansion took place after the Civil War, stimulated by the development of a new type of group policy, the "tontine," by Henry B. Hyde of the Equitable Life Company.* High-pressure salesmanship prevailed; agents gave rebates to customers by shaving their own commissions; companies stole crack agents from their rivals and raided new territories. They sometimes invested as much as 96 percent of the first year's premiums in obtaining new business. By 1900, after three decades of fierce competition, three giants dominated the industry, Equitable, New York Life, and Mutual Life, each with approximately $1 billion of insurance in force.

In retailing, the period saw the growth of huge urban department stores. In 1862 Alexander T. Stewart had built an eight-story emporium in New York City that covered an entire block and employed 2,000 persons. John Wanamaker in Philadelphia and Marshall Field in Chicago headed similar establishments by the 1880s, and there were others. These department stores did not depend on machines, but they were run like factories. Although small shops where salesmen bargained with customers over price and often did the purchasing as well did not disappear, they were not as efficient as the new giants. Here is how one of Field's biographers described his methods:

> His was a one-price store, with the price plainly marked on the merchandise. Goods were not misrepresented, and a reputation for quality merchandise and for fair and honest dealing was built up. . . . Courtesy toward customers was an unfailing rule. Stocks of goods were bought at wholesale for cash in anticipation of consumer demand and then a demand for them was created.

*A tontine policy paid no dividends for a stated period of years. If a policyholder died, his heirs received the face value but no dividends. At the end of the tontine period, survivors collected not only their own dividends but those of the unfortunates who had died or permitted their policies to lapse. This was psychologically appealing, since it stressed living rather than dying and added an element of gambling to insurance.

Americans React to Big Business

The expansion of industry and its concentration in fewer and fewer hands changed the way many people felt about the role of government in economic and social affairs. The fact that Americans disliked powerful governments in general and strict regulation of the economy in particular had never meant that they objected to *all* government activity in the economic sphere. Banking laws, tariffs, internal-improvement legislation, and the granting of public land to railroads are only the most obvious of the economic regulations enforced in the 19th century by both the federal government and the states. Americans saw no contradiction between government activities of this type and the free enterprise philosophy, for such laws were intended to release human energy and thus *increase* the area in which freedom could operate. Tariffs stimulated industry and created new jobs, railroad grants opened up new regions for development, and so on. As J. W. Hurst has written in a thought-provoking study, *Law and the Conditions of Freedom in the Nineteenth-Century United States,* the people "resort[ed] to law to enlarge the options open to private individual and group energy."

The growth of huge industrial and financial organizations and the increasing complexity of economic relations frightened people yet made them at the same time greedy for more of the goods and services the new society was turning out. To many, the great new corporations and trusts resembled Frankenstein's monster—marvelous and powerful but a grave threat to society. The astute James Bryce described the changes clearly in *The American Commonwealth* (1888):

> New causes are at work. . . . Modern civilization . . . has become more exacting. It discerns more benefits which the organized power of government can secure, and grows more anxious to attain them. Men live fast, and are impatient of the slow working of natural laws. . . . There are benefits which the law of supply and demand do not procure. Unlimited competition seems to press too hard on the weak. The power of groups of men organized by incorporation as joint-stock companies, or of small knots of rich men acting in combination, has developed with unexpected strength in unexpected ways, overshadowing individuals and even communities, and showing that the very freedom of association which men sought to secure by law . . . may, under the shelter of the law, ripen into a new form of tyranny.

To some extent public fear of the industrial giants reflected concern about monopoly. If Standard Oil dominated oil refining, it might raise prices inordinately at vast cost to consumers. Charles Francis Adams, Jr., expressed this feeling in the 1870s: "In the minds of the great majority, and not without reason, the idea of any industrial combination is closely connected with that of monopoly, and monopoly with extortion."

Although in isolated cases monopolists did raise prices unreasonably, generally they did not. On the contrary, prices tended to fall until by the 1890s a veritable "consumer's millennium" had arrived. Far more important in causing resentment was the fear that the monopolists were destroying economic opportunity and threatening democratic institutions. It was not the *wealth* of tycoons like Carnegie and Rockefeller and Morgan so much as their *influence* that worried people. In the face of the growing disparity between rich and poor, could republican institutions survive? Was the avalanche of cheap new products worth the sacrifice of the American way of life? "We must place . . . ethics above economics," one foe of monopoly insisted at a turn-of-the-century conference on trusts, and his audience gave him an ovation.

Some observers believed either autocracy or a form of revolutionary socialism to be almost inevitable. In 1890 former president Hayes pondered "the wrong and evils of the money-piling tendency of our country, which is changing laws, government, and morals and giving all power to the rich" and decided that he was going to become a "nihilist." Campaigning for the governorship of Texas in 1890, James S. Hogg, a staunch conservative, said: "Within a few years, unless something is done, most of the wealth and talent of our country will be on one side, while arrayed on the other will be the great mass of the people, composing the bone and sinew of this government." John Boyle O'Reilly, a liberal Catholic journalist, wrote in 1886: "There is something worse than Anarchy, bad as that is; and it is irresponsible power in the hands of mere wealth." William Cook, a New York lawyer, warned in *The Corporation Problem* (1891) that "colossal aggregations of capital" were "dangerous to the republic."

These were typical reactions of responsible citizens to the rise of industrial combinations. Less thoughtful Americans sometimes went much further in their hatred of entrenched wealth. In 1900 Eddie Cudahy, son of a prominent member of the Beef Trust, was kidnaped. His captor, Pat Crowe, received $25,000 ransom but was apprehended. Crowe's guilt was clear: "I want to start right by confessing in plain English that I was guilty of the kidnapping," he wrote. Yet a jury acquitted him, presumably on the theory that it was all right to rob a member of the Beef Trust.

As criticism mounted, business leaders rose to their own defense. Rockefeller described in graphic terms the chaotic conditions that plagued the oil industry before the rise of Standard Oil: "It seemed absolutely necessary to extend the market for oil . . . and also greatly improve the process of refining so that oil could be made and sold cheaply, yet with a profit. We proceeded to buy the largest and best refining concerns and centralized the administration of them with a view to securing greater economy and efficiency." Carnegie, in an essay published in 1889, insisted that the concentration of wealth was necessary if humanity was to progress, softening this "Gospel of Wealth" by insisting that the rich must use their money "in the manner which . . . is best calculated to produce the most beneficial results for the community." The rich man was merely a trustee for his "poorer brethren," Carnegie said, "bringing to their service his superior wisdom, experience, and ability to administer." Lesser tycoons echoed these arguments.

The voices of the critics were louder if not necessarily more influential. Many clergymen denounced unrestrained competition, which they considered un-Christian. The new class of professional economists (the American Economic Association was founded in 1885) tended to repudiate laissez faire. State aid, Richard T. Ely of Johns Hopkins University wrote, "is an indispensable condition of human progress."

The Radical Reformers

The popularity of a number of radical theorists reflects public feeling in the period. In 1879 Henry George, a California newspaperman, published *Progress and Poverty,* a forthright attack on the maldistribution of wealth in the United States. George argued that labor was the true and only source of capital. Observing the speculative fever of the West, which enabled landowners to reap profits merely by holding property while population increased, George proposed a property tax that would confiscate this "unearned increment." The value of land depended on society and should belong to society; allowing individuals to keep this wealth was the major cause of the growing disparity between rich and poor, George believed.

George's "Single Tax," as others called it, would bring in so much money that no other taxes would be necessary, and the government would have plenty of funds to establish new schools, museums, theaters, and other badly needed social and cultural services. While the Single Tax was never adopted, George's ideas attracted enthusiastic attention. Single Tax clubs sprang up throughout the nation, and *Progress and Poverty* became a best seller.

Even more spectacular was the reception afforded *Looking Backward, 2000–1887,* a utopian novel written in 1888 by Edward Bellamy. This book, which sold over a million copies in its first few years, described a future America that was completely socialized, all economic activity carefully planned. Bellamy compared 19th-century society to a lumbering stagecoach upon which the favored few rode in comfort while the mass of the people hauled them along life's route. Occasionally one of the toilers managed to fight his way onto the coach; whenever a rider fell from it, he had to join the multitude dragging it along.

Such, Bellamy wrote, was the working of the vaunted American competitive system. He suggested that the ideal socialist state, in which all citizens shared equally, would arrive without revolution or violence. The trend toward consolidation would continue, he predicted, until one monster trust controlled *all* economic activity. At this point everyone would realize that nationalization was essential.

A third influential attack on monopoly was that of Henry Demarest Lloyd, whose *Wealth Against Commonwealth* appeared in 1894. Lloyd, a journalist of independent means, devoted years to preparing a denunciation of the Standard Oil Company. Marshaling masses of facts and vivid examples of Standard's evildoing, he assaulted the trust at every point. Although in his zeal Lloyd sometimes distorted and exaggerated the evidence to make his indictment more effective—"Every important man in the oil, coal and many other trusts ought to-day to be in some one of our penitentiaries," he wrote in a typical overstatement—as a polemic his book was peerless. His forceful but uncomplicated arguments and his copious references to official documents made *Wealth Against Commonwealth* utterly convincing to thousands. The book was more than an attack on Standard Oil. Lloyd denounced the application of Darwin's concept of survival of the fittest to economic and social affairs, and he condemned laissez faire policies as leading directly to monopoly.

The popularity of these books indicates that the trend toward monopoly in the United States worried many people. But despite the drastic changes suggested in their pages, none of these writers questioned the underlying values of the middle-class majority. They rejected Marxian ideas, abjured the use of force to achieve their goals, and assumed that people were basically altruistic and reasonable. They insisted that reform could be accomplished without serious inconvenience to any individual or class. In *Looking Backward* Bellamy pictured the socialists of the future gathered around a radiolike gadget in a well-furnished parlor listening to a minister delivering an inspiring sermon.

Nor did most of their millions of readers seriously consider trying to apply the reformers' ideas. Henry George ran for mayor of New York City in 1886 and lost narrowly to Abram S. Hewitt, a wealthy iron manufacturer, but even if he had won, he would have been powerless to apply the Single Tax to metropolitan property. The national discontent was apparently not as profound as the popularity of these works might suggest. If John D. Rockefeller became the bogeyman of American industry because of Lloyd's attack, no one prevented him from also becoming the richest man in the United States.

Railroad Regulation

Political action came first on the state level and dealt chiefly with the regulation of railroads. Even before the Civil War a number of New England states established railroad commissions to supervise lines within their borders; by the end of the century, 28 states had such boards. The New England type held mere advisory powers; those set up in the Middle West were true regulatory bodies with authority to fix rates and control other railroad activities.

Strict regulation was largely the result of agitation by western farm groups, principally the National Grange of the Patrons of Husbandry. The Grange, founded in 1867 by Oliver H. Kelley, was created to provide social and cultural benefits for isolated rural communities. As it spread and grew in influence—14 states had Granges by 1872 and membership reached 800,000 in 1874—the movement became political too. "Granger" candidates, often not themselves farmers (many local businessmen resented such railroad practices as rebating), won control of a number of state legislatures in the West and South. Railroad regulation invariably followed, for while farmers were eager for internal improvements, they tended to become disillusioned after the lines were built. Intense competition might reduce rates between major centers like Chicago and the East, but most western farm districts were served by only one railroad. In 1877, for example, the freight charges of the Burlington road were almost four times as high west of the Missouri as they were east of the river. It cost less to ship wheat from Chicago to Liverpool, England, than from some parts of the Dakotas to Minneapolis.

Granger-controlled legislatures tried to eliminate this kind of discrimination. The Illinois Granger laws were typical. The revised state constitution of 1870 declared railroads to be public highways and authorized the legislature to "pass laws establishing reasonable maximum rates" and to "prevent unjust discrimination." The legislature did so and set up a commission to enforce the laws and punish violators. The railroads protested, insisting that they were being deprived of property without due process of law. In *Munn* v. *Illinois* (1877), one of the most important decisions in its long history, the Supreme Court upheld the constitutionality of this kind of act in very broad terms.* Any business that served a public interest, such as a railroad or a grain warehouse, was sub-

*The Munn case involved a grain elevator whose owner had refused to comply with a state warehouse act. It was heard along with seven railroad cases dealing with violations of Illinois regulatory legislation.

ject to state control, the justices ruled. Legislatures might fix maximum charges; if the charges seemed unreasonable to the parties concerned, they should direct their complaints to the legislatures or to the voters, not to the courts.

Regulation of the railroad network by the individual states was inefficient, and in some cases the commissions were incompetent and even corrupt. When the Supreme Court, in the Wabash case (1886), declared unconstitutional an Illinois regulation outlawing the long-and-short-haul evil, federal action became necessary. The Wabash, St. Louis and Pacific Railroad had charged 25 cents a 100 pounds for shipping goods from Gilman, Illinois, to New York City and only 15 cents from Peoria, which was 86 miles farther from New York. Illinois judges had held this to be illegal, but the Supreme Court decided that Illinois could not regulate interstate shipments.

Congress had been considering federal railroad regulation for years, so the legislators were prepared to fill the gap created by the Wabash decision. In February 1887 the Interstate Commerce Act was passed. All charges made by railroads "shall be reasonable and just," the act stated. Rebates, drawbacks, the long-and-short-haul evil, and other competitive practices were declared unlawful, and so were their monopolistic counterparts—pools and traffic-sharing agreements. Railroads were required to publish schedules of rates and forbidden to change them without due public notice. Most important, the law established an Interstate Commerce Commission (ICC), the first federal regulatory board, to supervise the affairs of railroads, investigate complaints, and issue "cease and desist" orders when the roads acted illegally.

The Interstate Commerce Act broke new ground, yet it was neither a radical nor a particularly effective measure. Its terms contradicted one another, some being designed to stimulate, others to penalize competition. The chairman of the commission soon characterized the law as an "anomaly." It sought, he said, to "enforce competition" at the same time that it outlawed "the acts and inducements by which competition is ordinarily effected." The commission had less power than the law seemed to give it. It could not fix rates, only bring the roads to court when it considered rates unreasonably high. Such cases could be extremely complicated; applying the law "was like cutting a path through a jungle." With the truth so hard to determine and the burden of proof on the commission, the courts in nearly every instance decided in favor of the railroads. "This commission," the ICC reported in 1903, "has no power to determine what rate is reasonable, and such orders as it can make have no binding effect."

■ **Thomas Nast's "The Senatorial Round-House," drawn for *Harper's Weekly* in 1896, predicted that any federal legislation passed to regulate railroads would be toothless.**

State regulatory commissions fared poorly in the Supreme Court in the last years of the century. Overruling part of their decision in *Munn* v. *Illinois,* the justices declared in *Chicago, Milwaukee and St. Paul Railroad Company* v. *Minnesota* (1890) that the reasonableness of rates was "eminently a question for *judicial* investigation." In a Texas case, *Reagan* v. *Farmers' Loan and Trust Company* (1894), the Court held that it had the "power and duty" to decide if rates were "unjust and unreasonable" even when the state legislature itself had established them. Nevertheless, by describing so clearly the right of Congress to regulate private corporations engaged in interstate commerce, the Interstate Commerce Act challenged the philosophy of laissez faire. Later legislation made the commission more effective. The commission also served as the prototype of a host of similar federal administrative authorities, such as the Federal Communications Commission (1934).

Sherman Antitrust Act

As with railroad legislation, the first antitrust laws originated in the states, but they were southern and western states with relatively little industry, and most of the statutes were vaguely worded and ill enforced. Federal action came in 1890 with the passage of the Sherman Antitrust Act. Any combination "in the form of trust or otherwise" that was "in restraint of trade or commerce among the several states, or with foreign nations," was declared illegal. Persons forming such combinations were subject to fines of $5,000 and a year in jail. Individuals and businesses suffering losses because of actions that violated the law were authorized to sue in the federal courts for triple damages.

Where the Interstate Commerce Act sought to outlaw the excesses of competition, the Sherman Act was supposed to restore competition. If businessmen joined together to "restrain" (monopolize) trade in a particular field, they should be punished and their deeds undone. Monopoly was already illegal under the common law, but as Senator George Frisbie Hoar of Massachusetts pointed out during the antitrust debates, no *federal* common law existed.

"The great thing this bill does," Senator Hoar explained, "is to extend the common-law principle . . . to international and interstate commerce." This was important because the states ran into legal difficulties when they tried to use the common law to restrict corporations engaged in interstate activities. The Sherman Act was rather loosely worded—Thurman Arnold, a modern authority, once said that it made it "a crime to violate a vaguely stated economic policy." Critics have argued that the congressmen were more interested in quieting the public clamor for action against the trusts than in actually breaking up any of the new combinations. Quieting the clamor was certainly one of their objectives. No politician likes having to cope with indignant voters, especially in an election year. Yet Congress was trying to solve a new problem and was not sure how to proceed. A law with teeth too sharp might do more harm than good. Most Americans assumed that the courts would deal with the details, as they always had in common-law matters.

In fact the Supreme Court quickly emasculated the Sherman Act. In *United States* v. *E. C. Knight Company* (1895) it held that the American Sugar Refining Company had not violated the law by taking over a number of important competitors. Although the Sugar Trust now controlled about 98 percent of all sugar refining in the United States, it was not restraining *trade.* "Doubtless the power to control the manufacture of a given thing involves in a certain sense the control of its disposition," the Court said in one of the greatest feats of judicial understatement of all time. "Although the exercise of that power may result in bringing the operation of commerce into play, it does not control it, and affects it only incidentally and indirectly."

If the creation of the Sugar Trust did not violate the Sherman Act, it seemed unlikely that any other combination of manufacturers could be convicted under the law. In *The History of the Last Quarter-Century in the United States* (1896), E. Benjamin Andrews, president of Brown University, delivered a strong indictment of trusts. "The crimes to which some of them resorted to crush out competition were unworthy of civilization," he wrote. Yet he referred only obliquely to the Sherman Act, dismissing it as "obviously ineffectual" and "of little avail."

But in a series of cases in 1898 and 1899 the Supreme Court ruled that agreements to fix prices or divide markets violated the Sherman Act. These decisions precipitated a wave of outright mergers in which a handful of large companies swallowed up hundreds of smaller ones. Presumably mergers were not illegal. When, some years after his retirement, Andrew Carnegie was asked by a committee of the House of Representatives to explain how he had dared participate in the formation of the U.S. Steel Corporation, he replied: "Nobody ever mentioned the Sherman Act to me, that I remember."

American industry was flourishing, but each year more of it seemed to fall into fewer hands. As with the railroads, other industries were coming to be strongly influenced, if not completely dominated by bankers—the Money Trust seemed fated to become the ultimate monopoly. The firm of J. P. Morgan and Company controlled many railroads, the largest steel, electrical, agricultural machinery, rubber, and shipping companies in the nation, two life insurance companies, and a number of banks. By 1913 Morgan and the Rockefeller-National City Bank group between them could name 341 directors to 112 corporations worth over $22.2 billion.

Centralization unquestionably increased efficiency, at least in industries that used a great deal of expensive machinery to turn out goods for the mass market, and in those where close coordination of output, distribution, and sales was important. The public benefited immensely from the productive efficiency and the rapid growth of the new empires. Living standards rose. But the trend toward giantism raised doubts. With ownership falling into fewer hands, what would be the ultimate effect of big business on American democracy?

SUPPLEMENTARY READING

Titles marked with an asterisk have been published in paperback

Of works dealing with industrial growth, E. C. Kirkland, **Industry Comes of Age*** (1961), is the best general introduction, but see also V. S. Clark's detailed **History of Manufactures in the United States** (1929), Allan Nevins, **The Emergence of Modern America*** (1927), I. M. Tarbell, **Nationalizing Big Business*** (1936), and T. C. Cochran and William Miller, **The Age of Enterprise*** (1942). Matthew Josephson, **The Robber Barons*** (1934), is highly critical but provocative. Rendigs Fels, **American Business Cycles** (1959), is technical but valuable. A. D. Chandler, Jr., **The Visible Hand** (1977), covers the way businesses were organized and managed. On technological developments, see H. J. Habakkuk, **American and British Technology in the Nineteenth Century*** (1962), W. P. Strassmann, **Risk and Technological Innovation: American Manufacturing Methods During the Nineteenth Century** (1959), and Lewis Mumford, **Technics and Civilization*** (1934).

For the railroad industry, consult G. R. Taylor and I. D. Neu, **The American Railroad Network** (1956), J. F. Stover, **American Railroads*** (1961), T. C. Cochran, **Railroad Leaders** (1953), Julius Grodinsky, **Transcontinental Railway Strategy** (1962) and **Jay Gould** (1957). C. F. Adams, Jr., **Railroads: Their Origin and Problems** (1879), is a valuable contemporary analysis.

The iron and steel business is discussed in detail in J. F. Wall, **Andrew Carnegie** (1970), Peter Temin, **Iron and Steel in Nineteenth-Century America** (1964), an economic analysis, J. H. Bridge, **The Inside History of the Carnegie Steel Company** (1903), and in Carnegie's **Autobiography** (1920); there is no solid scholarly history of the industry. For the oil industry, however, a number of excellent volumes exist. See Carl Solberg, **Oil Power*** (1976), a good survey, H. F. Williamson and A. R. Daum, **The American Petroleum Industry: Age of Illumination** (1959), Allan Nevins, **Study in Power: John D. Rockefeller** (1953), and R. W. and M. E. Hidy, **Pioneering in Big Business** (1955), the first volume of their **History of Standard Oil Company (New Jersey)** (1955–1956).

The electrical industry is discussed in an excellent study, H. C. Passer, **The Electrical Manufacturers** (1953), and in an equally good biography, Matthew Josephson, **Edison*** (1959). H. G. Prout, **A Life of George Westinghouse** (1921), is also useful. On the telephone, see John Brooks, **Telephone: The First Hundred Years** (1976), and R. V. Bruce, **Alexander Graham Bell and the Conquest of Solitude** (1973).

Many of these volumes deal with the problems of competition and monopoly. See also, however, E. G. Campbell, **The Reorganization of the American Railroad System** (1938), Gabriel Kolko, **Railroads and Regulation*** (1965), which is critical of both railroad leaders and of government policy, J. D. Rockefeller, **Random Reminiscences of Men and Events** (1909), H. D. Lloyd, **Wealth Against Commonwealth** (1894), Lewis Corey, **The House of Morgan** (1930), H. W. Laidler, **Concentration of Control in American Industry** (1931), and J. W. Jenks, **The Trust Problem** (1905).

For contemporary discussions of the monopoly problem, see Lloyd's **Wealth Against Commonwealth,** Henry George, **Progress and Poverty*** (1879), and Edward Bellamy, **Looking Backward*** (1888). The background of government regulation of industry is treated in Sidney Fine, **Laissez Faire and the General-Welfare State*** (1956), J. W. Hurst, **Law and the Conditions of Freedom in the Nineteenth-Century United States*** (1956), J. A. Garraty, **The New Commonwealth*** (1968), and Lee Benson, **Merchants, Farmers, and Railroads** (1955). Other useful volumes include Ari and Olive Hoogenboom, **A History of the ICC*** (1976), H. B. Thorelli, **The Federal Antitrust Policy** (1954), S. J. Buck, **The Granger Movement*** (1913), and G. W. Miller, **Railroads and the Granger Laws** (1971).

19/THE RESPONSE TO INDUSTRIALISM

The industrialization that followed the Civil War profoundly affected every aspect of American life. New machines, improvements in transportation and communication, the appearance of the great corporation with its uncertain implications for the future—all made deep impressions on the economy and on the social and cultural development of the nation. Indeed, the history of the period may be treated, historian Samuel P. Hays suggests, as a "response to industrialism," the "story of the impact of industrialism on every phase of human life."

The American Worker

Wage earners felt the full force of the tide, being affected in countless ways—some beneficial, others unfortunate. As industry became more important, the number of industrial workers multiplied rapidly: from 885,000 in 1860 to more than 3.2 million in 1890. While workers lacked much sense of solidarity, they exerted a far larger influence on society at the turn of the century than they had in the years before the Civil War. More efficient methods of production enabled them to increase their output, making possible a rise in their standard of living. Yet an unskilled worker still could not maintain a family decently by his own efforts. And the evidence indicates that industrial workers did not receive a fair share of the fruits of economic growth.

Industrialization also created problems for those who toiled in the mines, mills, and shops. When machines took the place of human skills, jobs became monotonous. Mechanization undermined both the artisans' pride and their bargaining power vis-à-vis their employers. As expensive machinery became more important, the worker seemed of necessity less important. Machines more than workers controlled the pace of work and its duration. The time clock regulated the labor force more rigidly than the most exacting foreman. As businesses grew larger, personal contact between employer and hired hand tended to disappear. Relations between them became less human, more businesslike and ruthless.

The trend toward bigness seemed to make it more difficult for workers to rise from the ranks of labor to become themselves manufacturers, as Andrew Carnegie, for example, had done during the Civil War era. Moreover, industrialization tended to accentuate swings of the business cycle. On the upswing something approaching full employment existed, but in periods of depression unemployment became a problem that affected workers without regard for their individual abilities. It is significant that the word *unemployment* (though not, of course, the condition itself) was a late 19th-century invention.

By and large, skilled workers, always better off than the unskilled, improved their positions relatively, despite the increased use of machinery. Women and children continued to supply a significant percentage of the industrial working force, always receiving lower wages than adult male workers. But now many more women were working outside their homes; the factory had almost completely replaced the household as the seat of manufacturing.

Women found new types of work in these years. They made up the overwhelming majority of salespersons and cashiers in the new department stores. Managers considered women more polite, easier to control, and more honest than male workers, all qualities especially valuable in the huge emporiums. Women also replaced men in business offices. They operated the new typewriters, mastery of which demanded a sound knowledge of spelling and grammar. Most men with these skills had better opportunities and were uninterested in office work, so women high school graduates, of whom there was an increasing number, filled the gap. Both department store clerks and "typewriters" (as they were called) earned more money than unskilled factory workers, and working conditions were more pleasant. Opportunities for promotion, however, were rare; managerial posts in these fields remained almost exclusively in the hands of men.

Early social workers who visited the homes of industrial laborers in this period reported enormous differences in the standard of living of people engaged in the same line of work, differences related to such variables as the wife's ability as a homemaker and the degree of the family's commitment to middle-class values. Some families spent most of their income on food, others saved substantial sums even when earning no more than $400 or $500 a year. Family incomes varied greatly among workers who received similar hourly wages, depending on the steadiness of employment and on the number of family members holding jobs.

For most laborers the working day still tended to approximate the hours of daylight, but it was shortening perceptibly by the 1880s. In 1860 the average was 11 hours; by 1880 only one worker in four labored more than 10 hours, and radicals were beginning to talk about 8 hours as a fair day's work. To some extent the exhausting pace of the new factories made longer hours uneconomical, but employers realized this only slowly, and until they did, many workers suffered.

Despite the improvement in living standards, there was a great deal of dissatisfaction among industrial workers. Writing in 1885, the labor leader Terence V. Powderly reported that "a deep-rooted feeling of discontent pervades the masses." A few years later a Connecticut official conducted an informal survey of labor opinion in the state and found a "feeling of bitterness" and "distrust of employers" endemic.

The discontent had many causes. For some, poverty was still the chief problem, but for others, rising aspirations triggered discontent. Workers were confused about their destiny; the tradition that no one of ability need remain a hired hand died hard. They wanted to believe their bosses and the politicians when those worthies voiced the old slogans about a classless society and the community of interest of capital and labor. "Our men," William Vanderbilt of the New York Central said in 1877, "feel that, although I . . . may have my millions and they the rewards of their daily toil, still we are about equal in the end. If they suffer, I suffer, and if I suffer, they cannot escape." "The poor," another conservative spokesman said a decade later, "are not poor because the rich are rich." Instead "the service of capital" softened their lot and gave them many benefits.

Statements such as these, though self-serving, were essentially correct. The rich were growing richer and more people were growing rich, but ordinary workers were better off too. However, the gap between the very rich and the ordinary citizen was widening. "The tendency . . . is toward centralization and aggregation," the Illinois Bureau of Labor Statistics reported in 1886. "This involves a separation of the people into classes, and the permanently subordinate status of large numbers of them."

To study social and economic mobility in a large industrial country is extraordinarily difficult. Americans in the late 19th century believed their society offered great opportunities for individual advancement, and to prove it they pointed to men like Andrew Carnegie and to other poor boys who accumulated large fortunes. How general was the rise from rags to riches (or even to modest comfort) is another question.

Fascinating studies of census records, the most important being those of Stephan Thernstrom, show that there was considerable geographical mobility in urban areas throughout the last half of the 19th century and into the 20th. Most investigations reveal that only about half the people recorded in one census were still in the same place ten years later; as Thernstrom puts it, "transiency was part of the American way of life. . . . The country had an enormous reservoir of footloose men, who could be lured to new destinations when opportunity beckoned."

In most of the cities studied, mobility was accompanied by substantial economic and social improvement. On the average, about a quarter of the manual laborers traced rose to middle-class status during their lifetimes, and the sons of manual laborers were still more likely to improve their place in society. In New York City about a third of the Italian and Jewish immigrants of the 1890s had risen from unskilled to skilled jobs a decade later. Even in Newburyport, Massachusetts, a town that was something of an economic backwater, most laborers made some progress, though far fewer rose to skilled or white-collar positions than in more prosperous cities.

There is no evidence, however, that progress from rags to real riches was common. The Carnegies, clearly, were rare exceptions. The dashing of unrealistic hopes inspired by such cases more than the absence of real opportunity probably explains why so many workers were dissatisfied. Any conclusion must be tentative, but this one offers a plausible explanation for the coexistence of discontent and rising living standards. In any case, most workers, even when expressing dissatisfaction with life as it was, continued to subscribe to such middle-class values as hard work and thrift—that is, they continued to hope. Thernstrom notes that hundreds of poor families in Newburyport, by practicing what he calls "ruthless underconsumption," gradually accumulated enough money to buy their own homes and provide for themselves in their old age.

Growth of Labor Organizations

Discontent and class consciousness led some workers to join unions, but only a small percentage of the work force was organized, and most of this consisted of cigarmakers, printers, carpenters, and other skilled workers rather than factory hands. Aside from ironworkers, railroad workers, and miners, few industrial laborers belonged to unions. Nevertheless the union was the worker's response to the big corporation: a combination designed to eliminate competition for jobs and to provide efficient organization for labor.

After 1865 the growth of national craft unions similar to those of the iron molders, the printers, and the cigarmakers, which had been organized in the fifties, quickened perceptibly. By the early 1870s about 300,000 workers belonged to such organizations, and many new trades, notably in railroading, had been unionized. A federation of such unions, the National Labor Union, was created in 1866, but it remained chiefly a paper organization. Most of its leaders were visionaries who were out of touch with the practical needs and aspirations of workers. They opposed the wage system, strikes, and anything that increased the laborers' sense of being members of the working class. A major objective was the formation of worker-owned cooperatives.

Far more remarkable was the Knights of Labor, a curious organization founded in 1869 by a group of Philadelphia garment workers headed by Uriah S. Stephens. Like so many labor organizers of the period, Stephens was a reformer of wide interests rather than a man dedicated to the specific problems of industrial workers. He, his successor Terence V. Powderly, and many other leaders of the Knights would have been thoroughly at home in the labor organizations of the Jacksonian era. Like the Jacksonians, they supported political objectives that had no direct connection with working conditions, such as currency reform and the curbing of land speculation. They rejected the idea that workers must resign themselves to remaining wage earners. By pooling their resources, workingmen could advance up the economic ladder and enter the capitalist class. "There is no good reason," Powderly wrote in his autobiography, *The Path I Trod,* "why labor cannot, through cooperation, own and operate mines, factories, and railroads." The leading Knights saw no contradiction between their denunciation of "soulless" monopolies and "drones" like bankers and lawyers and their talk of "combining all branches of trade in one common brotherhood." Such muddled thinking led the Knights to attack the wage system and to frown on strikes as "acts of private warfare."

If the Knights had one foot in the past, they also had one foot in the future. They supported some startlingly advanced ideas. Rejecting the traditional grouping of workers by crafts, they developed a concept closely resembling modern industrial unionism. They welcomed blacks (though mostly in segregated locals), women, and immigrants, and they accepted unskilled workers as well as craftsmen. The 8-hour day was one of their basic demands, their argument being that increased leisure would give workers time to develop more cultivated tastes and higher aspirations. Higher pay would inevitably follow.

■ **A black delegate introduces Terence V. Powderly at a Knights of Labor Convention held in Richmond. At one point the union had some 60,000 black members.**

The growth of the union, however, had little to do with ideology. Stephens had made the Knights a secret organization with an elaborate ritual. Under his leadership, as late as 1879 it had fewer than 10,000 members. Under Powderly, secrecy was discarded. Between 1882 and 1886 successful strikes by local "assemblies" against western railroads, including one against the hated Jay Gould's Missouri Pacific, brought recruits by the thousands. The membership passed 42,000 in 1882, 110,000 in 1885, and in 1886 it soared beyond the 700,000 mark. Alas, sudden prosperity was too much for the Knights. Its national leadership was unable to control local groups. A number of

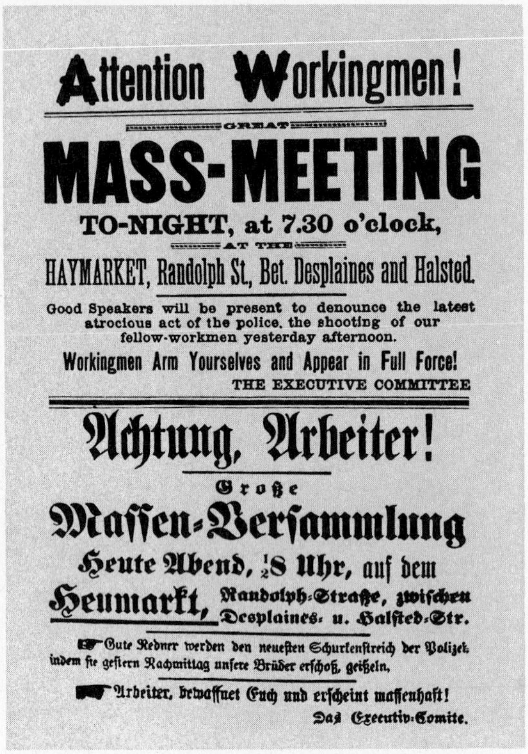

■ An anarchist group printed and distributed 20,000 of these bilingual handbills on the day of the Haymarket Square bombing in Chicago in 1886.

poorly planned strikes failed dismally, and the public was alienated by sporadic acts of violence and intimidation. Disillusioned recruits began to drift away.

Circumstances largely fortuitous caused the collapse of the organization. By 1886 the movement for the 8-hour day had gained wide support among workers. Several hundred thousand (estimates vary) were on strike in various parts of the country by May of that year. In Chicago, a center of the 8-hour movement, about 80,000 workers were involved, and a small group of anarchists was trying to take advantage of the excitement to win support.

When a striker was killed in a fracas at the McCormick Harvesting Machine Company, the anarchists called a protest meeting on May 4, at Haymarket Square. Police intervened to break up the meeting, and someone—his identity was never established—hurled a bomb into their ranks. Seven policemen were killed and many others injured.

While the anarchists were the immediate victims of the resulting public indignation and hysteria—seven were condemned to death and four eventually executed—organized labor, especially the Knights, suffered heavily. No tie between the Knights and the bombing could be established, but the union had been closely connected with the 8-hour agitation, and the public tended to associate it with violence and radicalism. Its membership declined as suddenly as it had risen, and soon it ceased to exist as a force in the labor movement.

The Knights' place was taken by the American Federation of Labor, a combination of national craft unions established in 1886. In a sense the AFL was a reactionary organization. Its principal leaders, Adolph Strasser and Samuel Gompers of the Cigarmakers Union, were, like the founders of the Knights of Labor, originally interested in utopian social reforms. They even toyed with the idea of forming a workingmen's political party. Experience, however, soon led them to concentrate on organizing skilled workers and fighting for "bread-and-butter" issues such as higher wages and shorter hours. "Our organization does not consist of idealists," Strasser explained to a congressional committee. "We do not control the production of the world. That is controlled by the employers. . . . I look first to cigars."

The AFL was modern in its attitude toward industrial trends. It accepted the fact that most workers would remain wage earners all their lives and tried to develop in them a sense of common purpose and pride in their skills and station. Strasser and Gompers paid great attention to building a strong organization of dues-paying members committed to unionism as a way of improving their lot.

The chief weapon of the federation was the strike, which it used to win concessions from employers and to attract recruits. Gompers, president of the AFL almost continuously from 1886 until his death in 1924, encouraged workers to make "an intelligent use of the ballot" in order to advance their own interests. The federation adopted a "legislative platform" that demanded such things as 8-hour, employers' liability, and mine-safety laws, but it avoided direct involvement in politics. "I have my own philosophy and my own dreams," Gompers once told a left-wing French politician, "but first and foremost I want to increase the workingman's welfare year by year. . . .

The French workers waste their economic force by their political divisions." Gompers' approach to labor problems produced solid, if unspectacular, growth for the AFL. Unions with a total of about 150,000 members formed the federation in 1886. By 1892 the membership had reached 250,000, and in 1901 it passed the million mark.

Labor Unrest

The stress of the AFL on the strike weapon reflected rather than caused the increasing militancy of labor. Workers felt themselves threatened from all sides: the growing size and power of their corporate employers, the substitution of machines for human skills, the invasion of foreign workers willing to accept substandard wages. At the same time they had tasted some of the material benefits of industrialization and had learned the advantages of concerted action.

The average employer behaved like a tyrant when dealing with his workers. He discharged them arbitrarily when they tried to organize unions; he hired scabs to break strikes; he frequently failed to provide the most rudimentary protections against injury on the job. Some employers professed to approve of unions, but almost none would bargain with labor collectively. To do so, they argued, would be to deprive the individual worker of his freedom to contract for his own labor in any way he saw fit.

The industrialists of the period were not all ogres; they were as alarmed by the rapid changes of the times as their workers, and since they had more at stake materially, they were probably more frightened by the uncertainties. Deflation, technological change, and intense competition kept even the most successful under constant pressure.

The thinking of most employers was remarkably confused. They considered workers who joined unions "disloyal," and at the same time they treated labor as a commodity to be purchased as cheaply as possible. "If I wanted boiler iron," Henry B. Stone, a railroad official, explained, "I would go out on the market and buy it where I could get it cheapest, and if I wanted to employ men, I would do the same." Yet Stone was furious when the men he had "bought" joined a union. When labor was scarce, employers resisted demands for higher wages by arguing that the price of labor was controlled by its productivity; when it was plentiful, they justified reducing wages by referring to the law of supply and demand.

Thus capital and labor were often spoiling for a fight, frequently without fully understanding why. When labor troubles developed, they tended to be bitter, even violent. In 1877 a great railroad strike convulsed much of the nation. It began on the Baltimore and Ohio system in response to a wage cut and spread to other eastern lines and then throughout the West until about two-thirds of the railroad mileage of the country had been shut down. Violence broke out, rail yards were put to the torch, dismayed and frightened businessmen formed militia companies to patrol the streets of Chicago and other cities. Eventually President Hayes sent federal troops to the trouble spots to restore order, and the strike collapsed. There had been no real danger of revolution, but the violence and destruction of the strike had been without precedent in America.

The disturbances of 1877 were a response to a business slump, those of the next decade a response to good times. Twice as many strikes occurred in 1886 as in any previous year. Even before the Haymarket bombing centered the country's attention on labor problems, the situation had become so disturbing that President Cleveland, in the first presidential message devoted to labor problems, had urged Congress to create a voluntary arbitration board to aid in settling labor disputes—a remarkable suggestion for a man of Cleveland's conservative, laissez faire approach to economic issues.

In 1892 a violent strike broke out among silver miners at Coeur d'Alene, Idaho, and a far more important clash shook Andrew Carnegie's Homestead steel plant near Pittsburgh when strikers attacked 300 private guards brought in to protect strikebreakers. Seven guards were killed and the rest forced to "surrender" and march off ignominiously. The Homestead affair was part of a harsh struggle between capital and labor in the steel industry. The steel men insisted that the workers were holding back progress by resisting technological advances, while the workers believed that the company was refusing to share the fruits of more efficient operation fairly. The strike was precipitated by the decision of company officials to

■ **A newspaper artist's dramatic version of an episode during the 1894 Pullman strike, in which national guard troops, using railroad work cars as a barricade, fired into a mob of strikers.**

crush the union at all costs. The final defeat, after a 5-month walkout, of the 24,000-member Amalgamated Association of Iron and Steel Workers, one of the most important elements in the AFL, destroyed unionism as an effective force in the steel industry and set back the progress of organized labor all over the country.

As in the case of the Haymarket bombing, the activities of radicals on the fringe of the dispute turned the public against the steelworkers. The boss of Homestead was Henry Clay Frick, a tough-minded foe of unions who was determined to "teach our employees a lesson." Frick made the decision to bring in strikebreakers and to employ Pinkerton detectives to protect them. During the course of the strike, Alexander Berkman, an anarchist, burst into Frick's office and attempted to assassinate him. Frick was only slightly wounded, but the attack brought him much sympathy and unjustly discredited the strikers.

The most important strike of the period took place in 1894. It began when the workers at George Pullman's Palace Car factory outside Chicago walked out in protest against wage cuts. (While reducing wages, Pullman insisted on holding the line on rents in the company town of Pullman; when a delegation called on him to remonstrate, he refused to give in and had three of the leaders fired.) Some Pullman workers belonged to the American Railway Union, headed by Eugene V. Debs. After the strike had dragged along for weeks, the union voted to refuse to handle trains with Pullman cars. The resulting railroad strike tied up trunk lines running in and out of Chicago.

Bypassing Governor John Peter Altgeld of Illinois because of his prolabor views, the railroad owners appealed to President Cleveland to send troops to preserve order. On the pretext that the soldiers were needed to ensure the movement of the mails, Cleveland agreed.* When Debs defied a

*The union was perfectly willing to handle mail trains. The owners, however, refused to run trains unless they were made up of a full complement of cars. When Pullman cars were added to mail trains, the workers refused to move them.

■ After the collapse of his American Railway Union in 1897, Eugene V. Debs (shown here addressing a Socialist party gathering) devoted himself to politics.

federal injunction, he was jailed for contempt and the strike was broken.

The crushing of the Pullman strike demonstrated the power of the courts to break strikes by issuing injunctions. Even more ominous for organized labor was the fact that the government based its request for the injunction on the Sherman Antitrust Act, arguing that the American Railway Union was a combination in restraint of trade. Another result of the strike was that Eugene V. Debs became a national figure. While serving his sentence for contempt, he was visited by a number of prominent socialists who sought to convert him to their cause. One gave him a copy of Karl Marx's *Capital,* which he found too dull to finish, but he did read *Looking Backward* and *Wealth Against Commonwealth.* In 1897 he became a socialist. Later he ran for president five times on the Socialist party ticket.

The "New" Immigration

Industrial expansion increased the need for labor, and this in turn powerfully stimulated immigration. Between 1866 and 1915 about 25 million foreigners entered the United States. Industrial growth alone does not explain the influx. The Atlantic crossing, once so hazardous and uncomfortable, became safe and speedy with the perfection of the steamship. Competition between the great packet lines such as Cunard, North German Lloyd, and Holland-America drove down the cost of the passage, and advertising by the lines further stimulated traffic. Improved transportation wrought changes in the economies of many European countries that caused an increase in the flow of people to America. Cheap wheat from the United States, Russia, and other parts of the world could now be imported into western Europe, bringing disaster to farmers in England, Germany, and the Scandinavian countries. The spreading industrial revolution led to the collapse of the peasant economy of central and southern Europe. For rural inhabitants this meant the loss of self-sufficiency, the fragmentation of landholdings, poverty, and for many the decision to make a new start in the New World. Political and religious persecutions pushed still others into the migrating stream. However, the main reason for immigration remained the desire for economic betterment. "In America," a British immigrant said, "you get pies and puddings."

While immigrants continued to people the farms of America, industry absorbed an ever increasing number of them. In 1870 one industrial worker in three was foreign-born. When congressional investigators examined 21 major industries early in the new century, they discovered that 57.9 percent of the labor force was foreign-born.

Most of the new millions came into the United States by way of New York City. A Serbian immigrant, Michael Pupin, later a distinguished physicist at Columbia University, has left a moving description of what it was like to enter. He arrived in 1874 on the Hamburg-American liner *Westphalia* amid a horde of newcomers. Disembarking at Hoboken, he was taken by tug to the immigration reception center at Castle Garden on the southern tip of Manhattan. He confessed to the authorities that he had only 5 cents to his name and knew no Americans except—by reputation—Franklin, Lincoln, and Harriet Beecher Stowe. But he explained in eloquent phrases why he wanted to live in the land of liberty rather than in the Austro-Hungarian empire. The officials conferred briefly, then admitted him. After a good breakfast, supplied by the immigration authorities, the Castle Garden Labor Bureau offered him a job as a farmhand in Delaware. Within 24 hours of his arrival he had reached his destination, ready to work.

Before 1882, when—in addition to the Chinese—criminals, idiots, lunatics, and persons liable to become public charges were excluded, entry into the United States was almost unrestricted. Indeed, until 1891 the Atlantic Coast states, not the federal government, exercised whatever controls were imposed on newcomers. Private agencies, philanthropic and commercial, served as a link between the new arrivals and employers looking for labor. Until the Foran Act of 1885 outlawed the practice, a few companies brought in skilled workers under contract, advancing them passage money and collecting it in installments from their paychecks. Numerous nationality groups assisted (and sometimes exploited) their compatriots by organizing "immigrant banks" that recruited labor in the old country, arranged transportation, and then housed the newcomers in boardinghouses in the United States while finding them jobs. The *padrone* system of the Italians and Greeks was typical. The *padrone*, a sort of contractor who agreed to supply gangs of unskilled workers to companies for a lump sum, usually signed on immigrants unfamiliar with American wage levels at rates that assured him a fat profit.

Beginning in the 1880s, the spreading effects of industrialization in Europe caused a shift in the sources of American immigration from northern and western to southern and eastern sections of the Continent. In 1882, when 789,000 immigrants entered the United States, more than 350,000 of them came from Great Britain and Germany, only 32,000 from Italy, and less than 17,000 from Russia. In 1907—the all-time peak year, with 1,285,000 immigrants—Great Britain and Germany supplied only 116,000, while 285,000 Italians and 258,000 Russians entered.*

The "new" immigrants, like the Irish of the 1840s and 1850s, were mostly poor and uneducated. They also seemed more than ordinarily clannish; southern Italians typically called all people outside their families *forestieri*, foreigners. Old-stock Americans thought them harder to assimilate, and in fact many were. Some Italian immigrants, for example, were unmarried men who had come to the United States to earn enough money to buy a farm back home. Such people made hard and willing workers but were not much concerned with rising in an American community.

The "birds of passage" were a substantial minority, but the single immigrant who saved in order to bring his wife and children or his younger brothers and sisters to America was more typical. In addition, thousands of immigrants came as family groups and intended to remain. Some, like the eastern European Jewish migrants, were refugees who could not have returned to the land of their birth if they wanted to. They were almost desperately eager to become Americans, though of course they retained and nurtured much of their traditional culture.

Cultural differences among immigrants were often large and had important effects on their relations with native-born Americans and with other immigrant groups. Italians who settled in the city of Buffalo, the historian Virginia Yans-McLaughlin has shown, adjusted relatively smoothly to urban industrial life because of their close family and kinship ties. Poverty, unemployment, female job holding outside the home, and other trauma that might have been expected to disrupt family relationships apparently had little effect. Polish immigrants in Buffalo, having different traditions, found adjustment more difficult. German-American and Irish-American Catholics had different attitudes that caused them to clash over such matters as the policies of the Catholic University in Washington. Although (or perhaps because) the Haymarket anarchists were German-born, in 1887 one prominent German-American denounced the Knights of Labor as a hotbed of radicalism—and was said to have claimed that it was dominated by "Irish ignoramuses." Controversies erupted between Catholic and Protestant German-Americans, between Greek-American groups supporting various political factions in their homeland, and so on.

Confused by such differences and conflicts, many "older" Americans concluded, wrongly but understandably, that the new immigrants were incapable of becoming good citizens and should be kept out. During the 1880s large numbers of social

*Up to 1880, only about 200,000 southern and eastern Europeans had migrated to America. Between 1880 and 1910, approximately 8.4 million arrived.

workers, economists, and church leaders, worried by the social problems that arose when so many poor immigrants flocked into cities already bursting at the seams, began to believe that some restriction should be placed on the incoming human tide. The directors of charitable organizations, which bore the burden of aiding the most unfortunate immigrants, complained that their resources were being exhausted by the needs of the flood.

Pseudoscientific thinkers obsessed with ideas about "racial purity" also found the new immigration alarming. Misunderstanding the findings of the new science of genetics, they attributed the social problems associated with mass immigration to supposed physiological characteristics of the newcomers. Forgetting that earlier Americans had accused pre-Civil War Irish and German immigrants of similar deficiencies, they decided that the peoples of southern and eastern Europe were racially (and therefore permanently) inferior to "Nordic" and "Anglo-Saxon" types and ought to be kept out.

■ **Contemporary magazine cartoonists reflected the "new nativist" attitudes toward unrestricted immigration. Part of the caption under this drawing says, "A possible curiosity of the twentieth century, the last Yankee."**

Organized labor, fearing the competition of workers with low living standards and no bargaining power, spoke out against the "enticing of penniless and unapprised immigrants . . . to undermine our wages and social welfare." Some corporations, especially in fields like mining, which employed large numbers of unskilled workers, made use of immigrants as strikebreakers, and this particularly angered union members. "The Poles, Slavs, Huns and Italians," a labor paper editorialized in 1909, "come over without any ambition to live as Americans live and . . . accept work at any wages at all, thereby lowering the tone of American labor as a whole." David Brody, historian of the steelworkers, describes an "unbridgeable gulf" in the steel industry between native and foreign laborers.

Employers were not disturbed by the influx of people with strong backs willing to work hard for low wages. Nevertheless, by the late 1880s many of them were alarmed about the supposed radicalism of the immigrants. The Haymarket bombing focused attention on the handful of foreign-born extremists in the country and loosed a flood of unjustified charges that "anarchists and communists" were dominating the labor movement. Nativism, which had waxed in the 1850s under the Know-Nothing banner and waned during the Civil War, now flared up again. Denunciations of "long-haired, wild-eyed, bad-smelling, atheistic, reckless foreign wretches," of "Europe's human and inhuman rubbish," of the "cutthroats of Beelzebub from the Rhine, the Danube, the Vistula and the Elbe" crowded the pages of the nation's press. The Grand Army of the Republic, an organization of Civil War veterans, grumbled about foreign-born radicals.

The nativists denounced Catholics and other minority groups more than immigrants as such. The largest nativist organization of the period, the American Protective Association, founded in 1887, existed primarily to resist what its members called "the Catholic menace." But nowhere in America did prejudice lead to interference with religious freedom in the narrow sense. The Protestant majority treated "new" immigrants as underlings, tried to keep them out of the best jobs, and discouraged their efforts to climb the social ladder. This prejudice functioned only at the so-

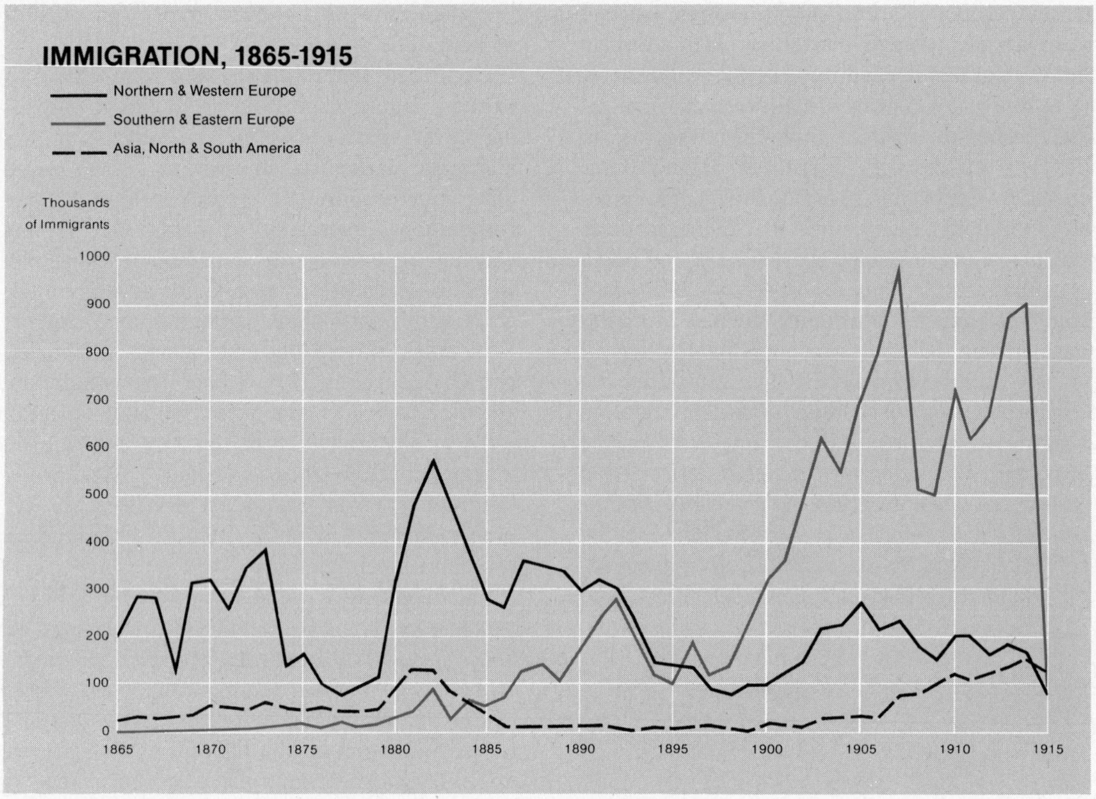

■ **Note the tide of "new" immigration from Southern and Eastern Europe in the early 1900s.**

cial and economic level. And neither labor leaders nor important industrialists, despite their misgivings about immigration, took a broadly antiforeign position.

After the Exclusion Act of 1882 and the almost meaningless 1885 ban on importing contract labor, no further restrictions were imposed on immigration until the 20th century. Strong support for a literacy test for admission developed in the 1890s, pushed by a new organization, the Immigration Restriction League. Since there was much more illiteracy in the southeastern quarter of Europe than in the northwestern, such a test would discriminate without seeming to do so on national or racial grounds. A literacy test bill passed both houses of Congress in 1897, but President Cleveland vetoed it. Such a "radical departure" from the "generous and free-handed policy" of the past, Cleveland said, was unjustified. He added, perhaps with tongue in cheek, that a literacy requirement would not keep out "unruly agitators," who were only too adept at reading and writing.

The Expanding City and Its Problems

Americans who favored restricting immigration made much of the fact that so many of the newcomers crowded into the cities, aggravating problems of housing, public health, crime, and immorality. Immigrants concentrated in the cities because the jobs created by expanding industry were located there. So, of course, did native Americans; the proportion of urban dwellers had been steadily increasing since about 1820.

It is important to keep in mind that population density is not necessarily related to the existence of large cities. In the late 19th century there were areas in Asia as large as the United States that were as densely populated as Belgium and England yet were overwhelmingly rural. The United States by any standard was sparsely populated, but well before the Civil War it had become one of the most urban nations in the world. Industrialization does not entirely explain the growth of

19th-century cities. All the large American cities began as commercial centers, and the development of huge metropolises like New York and Chicago would have been impossible without the national transportation network. But by the final decades of the century, the expansion of industry had become the chief cause of city growth. Thus the urban concentration continued; in 1890 one person in three lived in a city, by 1910 nearly one in two.

A steadily increasing proportion of the urban population was made up of immigrants. In 1890 the foreign-born population of Chicago almost equaled the *total* population of Chicago in 1880; a third of all Bostonians and a quarter of all Philadelphians were immigrants; and four out of five residents of New York City were either foreign-born or the children of immigrants.

After 1890 the immigrant concentration became even more dense. The "new" migrants from eastern and southern Europe lacked the resources to travel to the agriculturally developing regions (to say nothing of the sums necessary to acquire land and farm equipment). As the concentration progressed it fed upon itself, for all the eastern cities developed many ethnic neighborhoods, in each of which immigrants of one nationality congregated. Lonely, confused, often unable to speak English, the Italians, the Greeks, the Polish and Russian Jews, and other immigrants tended to settle where their predecessors had settled. Eager to maintain their traditional culture, they supported "national" churches and schools. Newspapers in their native languages flourished, as did social organizations of all sorts. Each great American city became a Europe in microcosm where it sometimes seemed that every language in the world but English could be heard. New York, the great entrepôt, had a Little Italy, Polish, Greek, Jewish, and Bohemian quarters, even a Chinatown.

Although "ethnic" neighborhoods were crowded, unhealthy, and crime-ridden and many of the residents were desperately poor, they were not ghettos in the European sense, for those who lived there were not compelled by law to remain. Thousands "escaped" yearly to better districts. The ghettos were places where hopes and ambitions were fulfilled, where people worked hard and endured hardships in order to improve their own and their children's lot.

Observing the immigrants' attachment to "foreign" values and institutions, numbers of "natives" accused the newcomers of resisting Americanization and blamed them for urban problems. The immigrants were involved in these problems, but the rapidity of urban expansion explains the troubles associated with city life far more fully than the high percentage of foreigners. The cities were suffering from growing pains. Sewer and water facilities frequently could not keep pace with skyrocketing needs. By the nineties the tremendous growth of Chicago had put such a strain on its sanitation system that the Chicago River had become virtually an open sewer, and the city's drinking water contained such a high concentration of germ-killing chemicals that it tasted like creosote. In the eighties all the sewers of Baltimore emptied into the sluggish Back Basin, and, according to the journalist H. L. Mencken, every summer the city smelled "like a billion polecats."

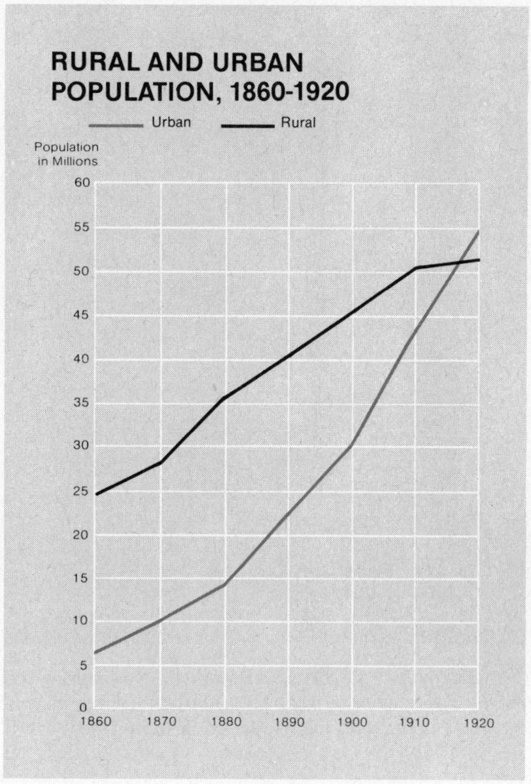

Fire protection became increasingly inadequate, garbage piled up in the streets faster than it could be carted away, and the streets themselves crumbled beneath the pounding of heavy traffic. Urban

■ **An alley known as "Bandit's Roost," on New York's Lower East Side, photographed for the New York *Sun* in 1887 or 1888 by police reporter Jacob Riis, himself an immigrant. "What sort of an answer, think you, would come from these tenements to the question 'Is life worth living?' Riis asked in his *How the Other Half Lives.***

growth proceeded with such speed that new streets were laid out more rapidly than they could be paved. Chicago had more than 1,400 miles of dirt streets in 1890.

People poured into the great cities faster than housing could be built to accommodate them. The influx into areas already densely packed in the 1840s became unbearable as rising property values and the absence of zoning laws conspired to make builders utilize every possible foot of space, squeezing out light and air ruthlessly in order to wedge in a few additional family units. Substandard living quarters aggravated other evils such as disease and the disintegration of family life with its attendant mental anguish, crime, and juvenile delinquency. The bloody New York riots of 1863, though sparked by dislike of the Civil War draft and blacks, reflected the bitterness and frustration of thousands jammed together amid filth and threatened by disease. A citizens' committee seeking to discover the causes of the riots expressed its amazement after visiting the slums "that so much misery, disease, and wretchedness can be huddled together and hidden . . . unvisited and unthought of, so near our own abodes."

New York City created a Metropolitan Health Board in 1866, and a state tenement house law the following year made a feeble beginning at regulating city housing. Another law in 1879 placed a limit on the percentage of lot space that could be covered by *new* construction and established minimal standards of plumbing and ventilation. The magazine *Plumber and Sanitary Engineer* sponsored a contest to pick the best design for a tenement that met these specifications. The winner of the competition was James E. Ware, whose plan for a "dumbbell" apartment house managed to crowd from 24 to 32 four-room apartments on a plot of ground only 25 by 100 feet.

> The feat was accomplished [writes Oscar Handlin in *The Uprooted*] by narrowing the building at its middle so that it took on the shape of a dumbbell. The indentation was only two-and-a-half feet wide and varied in length from five to fifty feet; but, added to the similar indentations on the adjoining houses, it cre-

> ated on each side an air-shaft five feet wide. . . . The stairs, halls, and common water closets were cramped into the narrow center of the building so that almost the whole of its surface was available for living quarters.

Despite these efforts at reform, in 1890 more than 1.4 million persons were living on Manhattan Island, and in some sections the population density exceeded 900 persons per acre. Jacob Riis, a reporter, captured the horror of the crowded warrens in his classic study of life in the slums, *How the Other Half Lives* (1890):

> Be a little careful, please! The hall is dark and you might stumble. . . . Here where the hall turns and dives into utter darkness is . . . a flight of stairs. You can feel your way, if you cannot see it. Close? Yes! What would you have? All the fresh air that enters these stairs comes from the hall-door that is forever slamming. . . . The sinks are in the hallway, that all the tenants may have access—and all be poisoned alike by their summer stenches. . . . Here is a door. Listen! That short, hacking cough, that tiny, helpless wail—what do they mean? . . . The child is dying of measles. With half a chance it might have lived; but it had none. That dark bedroom killed it.

The unhealthiness of the tenements was notorious; one noxious corner of New York became known as the "lung block" because of the prevalence of tuberculosis among its inhabitants. In 1900 three out of five babies born in one poor district of Chicago died before their first birthday. Equally frightening was the impact of overcrowding on the morals of the tenement dweller. The number of prison inmates in the United States increased by 50 percent in the eighties, and the homicide rate nearly tripled, most of the rise occurring in cities. Driven into the streets by the squalor of their homes, slum youths formed gangs bearing names like Alley Gang, Rock Gang, and Hell's Kitchen Gang. From petty thievery and shoplifting they graduated to housebreaking, bank robbery, and murder. According to Jacob Riis, when the leader of the infamous Whyo Gang, convicted of murder, confessed his sins to a prison chaplain, "his father confessor turned pale . . . though many years of labor as chaplain of the Tombs had hardened him to such rehearsals."

Slums bred criminals—the wonder was that they bred so few. They also drove well-to-do residents into exclusive sections and to the suburbs. From Boston's Beacon Hill and Back Bay to San Francisco's Nob Hill, the rich retired into great cluttered mansions and ignored conditions in the poorer parts of town.

City Government

The big-city political bosses, with their corrupt yet useful "machines," filled the vacuum created by upper-class abdication of responsibility. The immigrants, largely of peasant stock, had no experience with representative government, and the tendency of urban workers to move frequently lessened the likelihood that they would develop political influence independently. Furthermore, the difficulties of life in the slums bewildered and often overwhelmed newcomers, both native and foreign-born. Hopeful, passive, naive, they could hardly be expected to take a broad view of social problems when so harassed by personal ones. Shrewd urban politicians, most of them of Irish origin—the Irish being the first-comers among the migrants and less likely to move about, according to the mobility studies—took command of the city masses and marched them in obedient phalanxes to the polls.

Most city machines were loose-knit neighborhood organizations headed by ward bosses, not tightly geared hierarchical bureaucracies ruled by a single leader. "Big Tim" Sullivan of New York's lower east side and "Hinky Dink" Kenna of Chicago were typical of the breed. They found jobs for new arrivals and distributed food and other help to all in bad times. Anyone in trouble with the law could obtain at least a hearing from the ward boss, and often, if the crime was venial or due to ignorance, the difficulty was quietly "fixed" and the culprit sent off with a word of caution. Sullivan provided turkey dinners for 5,000 or more derelicts each Christmas, distributed new shoes to the poor children of his district on his birthday, arranged summer boat rides and picnics for young and old alike. At any time of year the victim of some sudden disaster could turn to the local clubhouse for help. Informally, probably without consciously intending to do so, the bosses educated the immigrants in the complexities of

■ **Thomas Nast's devastating assaults on the Tweed ring, printed in *Harper's Weekly*, helped bring about its demise. Tweed and his fellow vultures cower under the storm raised against them. Tweed offered Nast a $500,000 bribe to stop the cartoons.**

American civilization, helping them to leap the gulf between the almost medieval society of their origins and the modern industrial world.

The price of such aid—the bosses were no altruists—was unquestioning political support, which the bosses converted into cash. In New York Sullivan levied tribute on gambling, had a hand in the liquor business, and controlled the issuance of peddlers' licenses. When he died in 1913, he was reputedly worth a million dollars. Yet he and others like him were immensely popular; 25,000 grieving constituents followed Big Tim's coffin to the grave.

While he served a useful social function, the typical boss was not a reformer. Surveying the role of the Irish in New York City politics, Daniel P. Moynihan notes that despite their successes, "they did not know what to do with power. . . . They never thought of politics as an instrument of social change." The more visible and better-known "city" bosses played even less socially justifiable roles than the ward bosses. Their principal technique for extracting money from the public till was the "kickback." In order to get city contracts, suppliers were made to pad their bills and turn over the excess to the politicians. Similarly, operators of streetcar lines, gas and electricity companies, and other public utilities were compelled to pay huge bribes to obtain favorable franchises.

The most notorious—and probably the most despicable—of the major 19th-century city bosses was William Marcy Tweed, whose "Ring" extracted tens of millions of dollars from New York City during the brief period 1869–1871. Tweed was swiftly lodged in jail. More typical of the city bosses was Richard Croker, who ruled New York's Tammany Hall organization from the mid 1880s to the end of the century. Croker held a number of local offices, but his power rested on his position as chairman of the Tammany Hall finance committee. Although more concerned than Tweed with the social and economic services that machines provided, Croker was primarily a corrupt political manipulator; he accumulated a large fortune, owned a $200,000 mansion and a stable of racehorses, one of which was good enough to win the English Derby.

Despite their welfare work and their popularity, most bosses were essentially thieves. Efforts to romanticize them as the Robin Hoods of industrial society grossly distort the facts. However, the system developed and survived because too many middle-class city dwellers were indifferent to the fate of the poor. Except during occasional "reform waves," few tried to check the rapaciousness of the politicos. Many substantial citizens shared at least indirectly in the corruption. The owners of tenements were interested in crowding as many rent payers as possible into their buildings. Utility companies seeking franchises preferred a system that enabled them to buy favors. Honest citizens who had no selfish stake in the system and who were repelled by the sordidness of city government were seldom sufficiently concerned to do anything about it. When young Theodore Roosevelt decided to seek a political career in 1880, his New York socialite friends laughed in his face. "[They] told me," Roosevelt wrote in his autobiography, "that politics were 'low'; that the organizations were not controlled by 'gentlemen'; that I would find them run by saloon-keepers, horse-car conductors, and the like."

Many so-called urban reformers resented the boss system mainly because it gave political power to those who were not "gentlemen," or as one reformer put it, to a "proletarian mob" of "illiterate peasants, freshly raked from Irish bogs, or Bohemian mines, or Italian robber nests." A British visitor in Chicago struck at the root of the urban problem of the era. "Everybody is fighting to be rich," he said, "and nobody can attend to making the city fit to live in."

Urban Improvement

As American cities grew larger and more crowded, thereby aggravating a host of social problems, practical forces operated to bring about improvements. Once the relationship between polluted water and disease was fully understood, everyone saw the need for decent water and sewage systems. While some businessmen profited from corrupt dealings with the city machines, more of them wanted efficient and honest government in order to reduce their tax bills. City dwellers of all classes resented dirt, noise, and ugliness, and in many communities public-spirited groups formed societies to plant trees, clean up littered areas, and develop recreational facilities. When one city undertook improvements, others tended to follow suit, spurred on by local pride and the booster spirit.

Gradually the basic facilities of urban living were improved. Streets were paved, first with cobblestones and wood blocks and then with smoother, quieter asphalt. Gaslight, then electric arc lights, and finally Edison's incandescent lamps brightened the cities after dark, making law enforcement easier, stimulating night life, and permitting factories and shops to operate after sunset.

Urban transportation advanced phenomenally. Elevated steam railways helped reduce congestion, but the cheaper, quieter, and less unsightly electric trolley car soon became the principal means of municipal transportation. A retired naval officer, Frank J. Sprague, pioneered in this field, installing his first practical line in Richmond, Virginia, in 1887–1888. At once other cities seized upon the trolley; by 1895 some 850 lines were busily hauling city dwellers over 10,000 miles of track, and mileage more than doubled in the following decade. As with other new enterprises, control of street railways quickly became centralized until a few big operators controlled the trolleys of more than a hundred eastern cities and towns.

Streetcars changed the character of big-city life.

■ **A turn-of-the-century view of lower Broadway in New York City gives clear evidence of how important the trolley had become to urban life.**

Before their introduction urban communities were limited by the distances people could conveniently walk to work. The "walking city" could not easily extend more than $2\frac{1}{2}$ miles from its center. Streetcars increased this radius to 6 miles or more, which meant that the *area* of the city expanded enormously. Dramatic population shifts resulted as the better-off moved away from the center in search of air and space, abandoning the crumbling, jam-packed older neighborhoods to the poor. Thus economic segregation speeded the growth of ghettos. Older peripheral towns that had maintained some of the self-contained qualities of village life were swallowed up, becoming part of a vast urban sprawl. As time passed, each new area, originally peopled by rising economic groups, tended to become crowded and then to deteriorate. The middle class pushed steadily outward—which helps to explain why this group abandoned its interest in city government. On the other hand, by extending their tracks *beyond* the city limits, the streetcars enabled poorer residents to escape into the countryside on holidays.

Advances in bridge design, notably the perfection of the steel-cable suspension bridge by John A. Roebling, aided the ebb and flow of metropolitan populations. The Brooklyn Bridge—"a weird metallic Apparition under a metallic sky, out of proportion with the winged lightness of its arch, traced for the conjunction of worlds . . . the cables, like divine messages from above . . . cutting and dividing into innumerable musical spaces the nude immensity of the sky"—was Roebling's triumph. Completed in 1883 at a cost of $15 million, it was soon carrying more than 33 million passengers a year over the East River between Manhattan and Brooklyn.

Even the high cost of urban real estate, which fathered the tenement, produced some beneficial results in the long run. Instead of crowding squat structures cheek by jowl on 25-foot lots, architects began to build upward. The introduction of the iron-skeleton type of construction, which freed the walls from bearing the immense weight of a tall building, was the work of a group of Chicago architects who had been attracted to the metropolis of the Midwest by opportunities to be found amid the ashes of the great fire of 1871. The group included William Le Baron Jenney, John A. Holabird, Martin Roche, John W. Root, and Louis H. Sullivan. Jenney's Home Insurance Building, completed in 1885, was the first metal-frame edifice. Height alone, however, did not satisfy these innovators; they sought a form that would reflect the structure and purpose of their buildings.

Their leader was Louis Sullivan. Builders must discard "books, rules, precedents, or any such educational impedimenta" and design functional buildings, he argued. A tall building "must be every inch a proud and soaring thing, rising in sheer exultation . . . from bottom to top . . . a unit without a single dissenting line." Sullivan's Wainwright Building in St. Louis and his Prudential Building in Buffalo, both completed in the early nineties, combined beauty, modest construction costs, and efficient use of space in pathbreaking ways. Soon a "race to the skies" was on in the great cities of America, and the words "skyscraper" and "skyline" entered the language.

Efforts to redesign American cities, stimulated by the remarkable "White City" built for the Chicago World's Fair of 1893 by Daniel H. Burnham, with its broad vistas and acres of open space, resulted in a "City Beautiful" movement, the most lasting result of which was the development of many public parks. The landscape architect Frederick Law Olmsted, designer of New York's Central Park, was a leading figure in the movement.

Efforts to relieve the congestion in slum districts made little headway. In Brooklyn Alfred T. White established Home Buildings, a 40-family model tenement, in 1877; eventually he expanded the experiment to include 267 apartments. Each unit had plenty of light and air and contained its own sink and toilet. Ellen Collins developed a smaller project in Manhattan's Fourth Ward in the nineties. These model tenements were self-sustaining, but of necessity they yielded only modest returns. The landlords were essentially philanthropists; their work had no significant impact on urban housing in the 19th century.

Religion Responds to Industrialism

The modernization of the great cities was not solving most of the social problems of the slums. As this fact became clear, a number of urban religious leaders began to take a hard look at the situation. Traditionally, American churchmen had insisted that where sin was concerned there were no extenuating circumstances. To the well-to-do they preached the virtues of thrift and hard work; to the poor they extended the possibility of a better existence in the next world; to all they stressed one's responsibility for one's own behavior—and thus for one's own salvation. Such a point of view brought meager comfort to residents of slums. Consequently the churches lost influence in the poorer sections. Furthermore, as better-off citizens followed the streetcar lines out from the city centers, their church leaders followed them.

In New York, 17 Protestant congregations abandoned the depressed areas of Lower Manhattan between 1868 and 1888. Catering thereafter almost entirely to middle-class and upper-class worshipers, the pastors tended to become even more conservative. No more strident defender of reactionary ideas existed than Henry Ward Beecher, pastor of Brooklyn's fashionable Plymouth Congregational Church. Beecher attributed poverty to the improvidence of laborers who, he claimed, squandered their wages on liquor and tobacco. "No man in this land suffers from poverty," he said, "unless it be more than his fault—unless it be his *sin*." The best check on labor unrest was a plentiful supply of cheap immigrant labor, he told President Hayes. Unions were "the worst form of despotism and tyranny in the history of Christendom."

An increasing proportion of the residents of the blighted districts were Catholics, and the Roman church devoted much effort to distributing alms, maintaining homes for orphans and old people, and other forms of social welfare. But church leaders seemed unconcerned with the social causes of the blight; they were deeply committed to the idea that sin and vice were personal, poverty an act of God. They deplored the rising tide of crime, disease, and destitution among their coreligionists, yet they failed to see the connection between these evils and the squalor of the slums. "Intemperance is the great evil we have to overcome," wrote the president of the leading Catholic charitable organization, the Society of St. Vincent de Paul. "It is the source of the misery for at least three-fourths of the families we are called upon to visit and relieve." The Church, according to the historian Aaron I. Abell, "seemed oblivious to the bearing of civil legislation on the course of moral and social reform." Instead it invested much money and energy in chimerical attempts to colonize poor city dwellers in the West.

Like conservative Protestant clergymen, the Catholic hierarchy tended to be at best neutral toward organized labor. Cardinal James Gibbons spoke favorably of the Knights of Labor in 1886 after the Haymarket bombing, but even he took a dim view of strikes. The clergy's attitude changed somewhat after Pope Leo XIII issued his encyclical *Rerum novarum* (1891). This statement criticized the excesses of capitalism, including the "greed of unchecked competition," defended the right of labor to form unions, and stressed the duty of government to care for the poor. Workers were entitled to wages that would guarantee their families a reasonable and frugal comfort, Leo declared, and they committed no sin by seeking government aid to get it. Concrete action by American Catholics, however, was slow in coming. One leading authority notes "the isolation of Catholics from the reform movements of the 19th century," which he attributes to the conservatism of the clergy and the parochial concerns of lay leaders.

The conservatism of most Protestant and Catholic clergymen did not prevent some earnest preachers from working directly to improve the lot of the city poor. Some followed the path blazed by Dwight L. Moody, who became famous throughout America and Great Britain as a lay evangelist. A gargantuan figure weighing nearly 300 pounds, Moody conducted a vigorous campaign to persuade the denizens of the slums to cast aside their sinful ways. He went among them full of enthusiasm and God's love and made an impact no less powerful than that of George Whitefield during the Great Awakening of the 18th century. The evangelists founded mission schools in the slums and tried to provide spiritual and recreational facilities for the unfortunate. They were prominent in the establishment of American branches of the Young Men's Christian Association (1851) and the Salvation Army (1880).

However, the evangelists paid little heed to the causes of urban poverty and vice, believing that faith in God would enable the poor to transcend the material difficulties of life. For a number of Protestant clergymen who had become familiar with the slums, a different approach seemed called for. Slum conditions caused the sins and crimes of the cities; the wretched human beings who committed them could not be blamed, these ministers argued. They began to preach a "Social Gospel" that focused on improving living conditions rather than on saving souls. If people were to lead pure lives, they must have enough to eat, decent homes, and opportunities to develop their talents. Social Gospelers advocated civil service reform to break the power of the machines, child labor legislation, the regulation of big corporations, and heavy taxes on incomes and inheritances.

The most influential preacher of the Social Gospel was probably Washington Gladden. At first Gladden, who was raised on a Massachusetts farm, had opposed all government interference in social and economic affairs, but his experiences as a minister in Springfield, Massachusetts, and Columbus, Ohio, exposed him to the realities of life in industrial cities, and his views changed. In *Applied Christianity* (1886) and in other works he defended labor's right to organize and strike and denounced the idea that supply and demand should control wage rates. He favored factory inspection laws, strict regulation of public utilities, and other reforms.

Gladden never questioned the basic values of capitalism. By the nineties a number of ministers had gone all the way to socialism. The Reverend William D. P. Bliss of Boston, for example, believed in the kind of welfare state envisioned by Edward Bellamy in *Looking Backward.* He founded the Society of Christian Socialists (1889) and edited a radical journal, *The Dawn.* In addition to nationalizing industry, Bliss and other Christian Socialists advocated government unemployment relief programs, public housing and slum clearance projects, and other measures designed to aid the city poor.

Nothing so well reveals the receptivity of the public to the Social Gospel as the popularity of Charles M. Sheldon's novel *In His Steps* (1896), one of America's all-time best sellers. Sheldon, a minister in Topeka, Kansas, described what happened in the mythical city of Raymond when a group of leading citizens decided to live truly Christian lives, asking themselves "What would Jesus do?" before adopting any course of action. Naturally the tone of Raymond's society was immensely improved, but basic social reforms followed quickly. The "Rectangle," a terrible slum area, "too dirty, too coarse, too sinful, too awful for close contact," became the center of a great reform effort. One of Raymond's "leading society heiresses" undertook a slum clearance project, and a concerted attack was made on drunkenness and immorality. The moral regeneration of the entire community was soon accomplished.

The Settlement Houses

Although millions read *In His Steps,* its effect, and that of other Social Gospel literature, was merely inspirational. On the practical level, a number of earnest souls began to grapple with slum problems by organizing what were known as settlement houses. These were community centers located in poor districts which provided guidance and services to all who would use them. The settlement workers, most of them idealistic, well-to-do young people, lived in the houses and were active in neighborhood affairs.

The prototype of the settlement house was London's Toynbee Hall, founded in the early eighties; the first American example was the Neighborhood Guild, opened on the lower east side of New York in 1886 by Dr. Stanton Coit. By the turn of the century a hundred had been established, the most famous being Jane Addams' Hull House in Chicago (1889), Robert A. Woods' South End House in Boston (1892), and Lillian Wald's Henry Street Settlement in New York (1893).

While a number of men were active in the movement, a large percentage of the most important settlement house workers were women fresh from college—the first generation of young women to experience the trauma of having developed their capacities only to find that society offered them few opportunities to use them (see pages 497–498). The settlements provided an outlet for their hopes and energies, and they seized upon it avidly. An English social reformer who visited Hull House around the turn of the century described the residents as "strong-minded energetic women, bustling about their various enterprises" and "earnest-faced self-subordinating and mild-mannered men who slide from room to room apologetically."

The settlement workers tried to interpret American ways to the new immigrants and to create a community spirit in order to teach, in the words of one of them, "right living through social relations." Unlike most charity workers, who acted out of a sense of upper-class responsibility toward the unfortunate, they expected to benefit morally and intellectually themselves by experiencing a way of life far different from their own and by obtaining "the first-hand knowledge the college classroom cannot give." Lillian Wald, a nurse by training, explained the concept succinctly in *The House on Henry Street* (1915): "We were to live in the neighborhood . . . identify ourselves with it socially, and, in brief, contribute to it our citizenship."

Lillian Wald and other leaders soon discovered that practical problems occupied most of their energies. They agitated for tenement house laws, the regulation of the labor of women and children, and better schools. They employed private resources to establish playgrounds in the slums, along with libraries, classes in arts and crafts, social clubs, and day nurseries. In Boston Robert A. Woods organized clubs to get the youngsters of the South End off the streets, helped establish a restaurant where a meal could be had for 5 cents, acted as an arbitrator in labor disputes, and lobbied for laws tightening up the franchises of public utility companies. In Chicago Jane Addams developed an outstanding cultural program that included classes in music and art and an excellent "little theater" group. Hull House soon boasted a gymnasium, a day nursery, and several social clubs. Addams also worked tirelessly and effectively for improved public services and for social legislation of all kinds. She even got herself appointed garbage inspector in her ward and

■ **Jane Addams in a striking full-length portrait taken at about the time she was establishing Hull House.**

hounded local landlords and the garbage contractor until something approaching decent service was established.

A few critics considered the settlement houses mere devices to socialize the unruly poor by teaching them the "punctilios of upper-class propriety," but almost everyone appreciated their virtues. By the end of the century even the Catholics, laggard in entering the arena of practical social reform, were joining the movement, partly because they were losing many communicants to socially minded Protestant churches. The first Catholic-run settlement house was founded in 1898 in an Italian district of New York. Two years later Brownson House in Los Angeles, catering chiefly to Mexican immigrants, threw open its doors.

With all their accomplishments, the settlement houses seemed to be fighting a losing battle. "Private beneficence," Jane Addams wrote of Hull House, "is totally inadequate to deal with the vast numbers of the city's disinherited." As a tropical forest grows faster than a handful of men armed with machetes can cut it down, so the slums, fed by an annual influx of hundreds of thousands, blighted new areas more rapidly than the intrepid settlement house workers could clean up old ones. It became increasingly apparent that the wealth and authority of the state must be brought to bear in order to keep abreast of the problem.

Social Legislation

The first state laws aimed at the social problems resulting from industrialism and urbanization date from before the Civil War, but the early ones were either so imprecise as to be unenforceable or—like the Georgia law "limiting" textile workers to 11 hours a day—so weak as to be ineffective. As time passed, however, a scattering of workable laws was enacted. In 1874 Massachusetts restricted the working hours of women and children to 10 per day, and by the 1890s many other states, mostly in the East and Middle West, had followed suit. Illinois passed an 8-hour law for women workers in 1893. A New York law of 1882 struck at the sweatshops of the slums by prohibiting the manufacture of cigars on premises "occupied as a house or residence."

As part of this trend, some states established special rules for workers in hazardous industries. In the 1890s Ohio and several other states began to regulate the hours of railroad workers on the ground that fatigue sometimes caused railroad accidents. New York set a 10-hour-per-day limit for brickyard workers (1893) and bakers (1897). Utah restricted miners to 8 hours in 1896. California in 1881 made it illegal for women to work as waitresses in saloons. In 1901 New York finally enacted an effective tenement house law, greatly increasing the area of open space on building lots and requiring toilets for each apartment, better ventilation systems, and more adequate fireproofing. Many other states soon passed laws modeled on acts of these types.

The collective impact of such legislation was not impressive. Powerful interests, such as manufacturers and landlords, threw their weight against many kinds of social legislation and often succeeded in defeating the bills or rendering them innocuous. Many of the early laws limiting hours, for example, were made to apply only "in the absence of agreements" to work longer hours.

The federal system itself complicated the task of obtaining effective legislation. Throughout the 19th century few authorities contested the right of government to protect society and individuals from anything that threatened the general welfare, but these authorities assumed that such problems would be dealt with by the states, not the national government.* As a rule, this "police power" of the states was broadly interpreted; the courts even upheld laws prohibiting the manufacture and sale of liquor on the ground that drunkenness was a social as well as an individual problem, affecting nonimbibers as well as drinkers.

The development of a truly national economy after the Civil War complicated the problem of coping with social and industrial problems at the state level. Once producers throughout the country could compete effectively with one another, it became difficult, for example, to persuade legislators in one state to prohibit child labor when others refused to do so. If they did, they would injure their own manufacturers by giving firms in other states an unfair advantage. Yet a federal child la-

*Congress enacted an 8-hour-law for government workers in 1892.

bor law seemed out of the question on constitutional grounds.

The enemies of state social legislation discovered still another weapon: the Fourteenth Amendment to the Constitution. Although enacted to protect the civil rights of blacks, the amendment imposed a revolutionary restriction on state power, for it forbade the states to "deprive any person of life, liberty, or property without due process of law." Since state tenement house laws, child labor laws, and other social legislation represented new uses of police power that conservative judges considered dangerous and unwise, the Fourteenth Amendment gave them an excuse to overturn the laws on the ground that they deprived someone of liberty or property. Both state and federal courts began to draw lines beyond which the states could not go in this area.

Some measures seemed unexceptionable; the courts did not interfere with laws requiring fire escapes on tall buildings, though these regulations certainly deprived builders of property (by increasing their costs) and of the liberty to erect any kind of structure they pleased. Laws regulating the hours and conditions of labor, however, met mixed fates, depending on the wording of the acts and the prejudices of particular judges.

Where women and children were concerned, and in dangerous and unhealthy occupations like mining, the new legislation fared better than where it involved the laboring population as a whole. But it is difficult to generalize. The pioneering Massachusetts 10-hour law of 1874, restricting the working day of women and children, was upheld as a valid exercise of the police power by the Massachusetts courts. The Illinois law of 1893 limiting the hours of women employed in manufacturing to 8 per day was declared unconstitutional. "The mere fact of sex will not justify the legislature in putting forth the police power," the Illinois court declared in *Ritchie* v. *People.* "There is no reasonable ground . . . for fixing upon eight hours in one day as the limit within which woman can work without injury to her physique." The New York Court of Appeals threw out the sweatshop law of 1882 on similar grounds. "It cannot be perceived," Justice Earl wrote in a decision so unrealistic that it appears preposterous to anyone who knows even a little about slum conditions in the 1880s, "how the cigar maker is to be improved in his health or his morals by forcing him from his home with its hallowed associations and beneficient influences, to ply his trade elsewhere."

As stricter and more far-reaching laws were enacted, conservative judges, sensing what they took to be a trend toward socialism and regimentation, adopted an increasingly narrow interpretation of state police power. The United States Supreme Court upheld the Utah mining law of 1896 (*Holden* v. *Hardy,* 1898), but in 1905 it declared a piece of state social legislation unconstitutional for the first time. New York's 10-hour act for bakers, the Court declared in *Lochner* v. *New York,* deprived bakers of the liberty of working as long as they wished and thus violated the Fourteenth Amendment. Justice Oliver Wendell Holmes, Jr., wrote a famous dissenting opinion in this case. If the people of New York believed that the public health was endangered by bakers working long hours, he reasoned, it was not the Court's job to overrule them. "A constitution is not intended to embody a particular economic theory, whether of paternalism . . . or of *laissez faire,*" Holmes said. "The word 'liberty,' in the Fourteenth Amendment, is perverted when it is held to prevent the natural outcome of a dominant opinion." Of course Holmes' dissent did not alter the decision, which was deplored by all those who hoped to limit the hours of labor through legislation.

Civilization and Its Discontents

As the 19th century died, the majority of the American people, especially those comfortably well off, the residents of small towns, the shopkeepers, many farmers, some skilled workers, remained confirmed optimists and uncritical admirers of their civilization. However, blacks, immigrants, and others who failed to share equitably in the good things of life, along with a growing number of humanitarian reformers, found little to cheer about and much to lament in their increasingly industrialized society. Giant monopolies flourished despite federal restrictions. The gap between rich and poor appeared to be widening, while the slum spread its poison and the materially successful made a god of their success. Human values seemed in grave danger of being crushed by impersonal forces typified by the great corporations.

In 1871 Walt Whitman, usually so full of extravagant praise for the American way of life, called his fellow countrymen the "most materialistic and money-making people ever known":

> I say we had best look our times and lands searchingly in the face, like a physician diagnosing some deep disease. Never was there, perhaps, more hollowness of heart than at present, and here in the United States.

By the late eighties a well-known journalist could write to a friend: "The wheel of progress is to be run over the whole human race and smash us all." Others noted an alarming jump in the national divorce rate and an increasing taste for all kinds of luxury. "People are made slaves by a desperate struggle to keep up appearances," a Massachusetts commentator declared, and the economist David A. Wells expressed concern over statistics showing that heart disease and mental illness were on the rise. These "diseases of civilization," Wells explained, were "one result of the continuous mental and nervous activity which modern high-tension methods of business have necessitated."

Wells was a prominent liberal, but pessimism was no monopoly of liberals. A little later, Senator Henry Cabot Lodge of Massachusetts, himself a millionaire, complained of the "lawlessness" of "the modern and recent plutocrat" and his "disregard of the rights of others." Lodge spoke of "the enormous contrast between the sanguine mental attitude prevalent in my youth and that, perhaps wiser, but certainly darker view, so general today."

Of course intellectuals often tend to be critical of the world they live in, whatever its nature; Thoreau denounced materialism and the worship of progress in the 1840s as vigorously as any late 19th-century prophet of gloom. But the voices of the dissatisfied were rising. Despite the many benefits that industrialization had made possible, it was by no means clear around 1900 that the American people were really better off under the new dispensation.

SUPPLEMENTARY READING

Titles marked with an asterisk have been published in paperback

The idea of interpreting social and economic history in the post-Civil War decades as a broad reaction to the growth of industry is presented in S. P. Hays, **The Response to Industrialism*** (1957). Other general treatments of the period include R. H. Wiebe, **The Search for Order*** (1968), and Ray Ginger, **The Age of Excess*** (1965). J. A. Garraty, **The New Commonwealth*** (1968), treats all the subjects covered in this chapter; A. M. Schlesinger, **The Rise of the City*** (1933), stresses the importance of urban developments and provides a wealth of information about social trends. Both H. U. Faulkner, **Politics, Reform, and Expansion*** (1959), and Blake McKelvey, **The Urbanization of America** (1962), contain useful information. Henry Adams, **The Education of Henry Adams*** (1918), is a fascinating if highly personal view of the period. James Bryce, **The American Commonwealth*** (1888), while primarily a political analysis, contains a great deal of information about social conditions, as does D. A. Wells, **Recent Economic Changes** (1889).

On industrial workers, see David Montgomery, **Beyond Equality*** (1967), N. J. Ware, **The Labor Movement in the United States*** (1929), and H. G. Gutman, **Work, Culture, and Society in Industrializing America*** (1977). J. A. Garraty (ed.), **Labor and Capital in the Gilded Age*** (1968), provides a convenient selection of testimony from the great 1883 Senate investigation of that subject, while David Brody, **Steelworkers in America*** (1960), and Stephan Thernstrom, **Poverty and Progress: Social Mobility in a Nineteenth-Century City*** (1964), throw much light on the lives of workingmen. S. M. Rothman, **Woman's Proper Place** (1978), discusses the new job opportunities for women. Thernstrom's **The Other Bostonians: Poverty and Progress in the American Metropolis*** (1973), is a brilliant analysis of social and geographical mobility and an excellent summary of work on these important topics. Businessmen's attitudes are covered in T. C. Cochran, **Railroad Leaders** (1953), and E. C. Kirkland, **Dream and Thought in the Business Community*** (1956). On the growth of unions, see Montgomery's **Beyond Equality,** Philip Taft, **The A.F. of L. in the Time of Gompers** (1957), G. N. Grob, **Workers and Utopia*** (1961), Samuel Gompers, **Seventy Years of Life and Labor** (1925), and T. V. Powderly, **Thirty Years of Labor** (1889). The important strikes and labor violence of the period are described in R. V. Bruce, **1877: Year of Violence*** (1959), Henry David, **History of the Haymarket Affair*** (1936), Leon

Wolff, **Lockout** (1965), Almont Lindsey, **The Pullman Strike*** (1942), and W. G. Broehl, Jr., **The Molly Maguires*** (1964).

On immigration, see M. A. Jones, **American Immigration*** (1960), John Higham, **Send These to Me*** (1975), M. L. Hansen, **The Immigrant in American History*** (1940), and I. S. Hourwich, **Immigration and Labor** (1923). Oscar Handlin, **The Uprooted*** (1951), describes the life of the new immigrants somewhat romantically but with sensitivity, while John Higham, **Strangers in the Land*** (1955), and B. M. Solomon, **Ancestors and Immigrants*** (1956), stress the reactions of native Americans to successive waves of immigration. Moses Rischin, **The Promised City: New York's Jews*** (1962), Thomas Kessner, **The Golden Door: Italian and Jewish Immigrant Mobility** (1977), Humbert Nelli, **The Italians of Chicago*** (1970), Virginia Yans-McLaughlin, **Family and Community: Italian Immigrants in Buffalo** (1977), T. N. Brown, **Irish-American Nationalism*** (1966), Charlotte Erickson, **American Industry and the European Immigrant** (1957), and R. T. Berthoff, **British Immigrants in Industrial America: 1790–1950** (1953), are important monographs.

A brief interpretive history of urban development is C. N. Glaab and A. T. Brown, **A History of Urban America*** (1967). For the growing pains of American cities, consult the volumes by Schlesinger and McKelvey mentioned above, and also R. H. Bremner, **From the Depths*** (1956), Jacob Riis, **How the Other Half Lives*** (1890), Gordon Atkins, **Health, Housing, and Poverty in New York City** (1947), and R. Lubove, **The Progressives and the Slums: Tenement House Reform in New York City** (1962). For urban government, see the classic criticisms in Bryce's **American Commonwealth,** and also F. W. Patton, **The Battle for Municipal Reform: Mobilization and Attack** (1940). Urban architecture is discussed in O. W. Larkin, **Art and Life in America** (1949), Lewis Mumford, **The Brown Decades*** (1931), and J. E. Burchard and Albert Bush-Brown, **The Architecture of America*** (1961). S. B. Warner, Jr., **Streetcar Suburbs*** (1962), is an interesting study of Boston's development that is full of suggestive ideas about late 19th-century growth.

The response of religion to industrialism is discussed in H. F. May, **Protestant Churches and Industrial America*** (1949), in two books by A. I. Abell, **The Urban Impact on American Protestantism** (1943) and **American Catholicism and Social Action*** (1960), Arthur Mann, **Yankee Reformers in the Urban Age*** (1954), and C. H. Hopkins, **The Rise of the Social Gospel in American Protestantism*** (1940). See also Washington Gladden, **Applied Christianity** (1886), and R. T. Ely, **Social Aspects of Christianity** (1889). For the settlement house movement, see A. F. Davis, **Spearheads for Reform*** (1967), Davis' life of Jane Addams, **American Heroine*** (1973), and two classic personal accounts, Jane Addams, **Twenty Years at Hull House*** (1910), and Lillian Wald, **The House on Henry Street*** (1915).

Sidney Fine, **Laissez Faire and the General-Welfare State*** (1956), deals with both social and economic thought and with state and federal social legislation, but see also C. G. Groat, **Attitude of American Courts in Labor Cases** (1911), A. M. Paul, **Conservative Crisis and the Rule of Law: Attitudes of Bar and Bench*** (1960), and R. G. McCloskey, **American Conservatism in the Age of Enterprise*** (1951).

20/INTELLECTUAL AND CULTURAL TRENDS

Industrialization altered the way Americans thought at the same time that it transformed their ways of making a living. Technological advances revolutionized the communication of ideas more drastically than they did the transportation of goods or the manufacture of steel. The materialism that permeated American attitudes toward business also affected contemporary education and literature, while Charles Darwin's theory of evolution influenced American philosophers, lawyers, and historians profoundly. At the same time, the older ideologies of romantic individualism and faith in democracy continued to affect American thinking. No dominant pattern emerged; the American mind, like the people themselves, was too diverse—one might say confused, even incoherent—to be neatly delimited.

Public Education

The history of American education after about 1870 reflects the impact of many social and economic forces. While Horace Mann, Henry Barnard, and others had laid the foundations for state-supported school systems in the Age of Jackson, these systems became compulsory only after the Civil War, when the growth of cities provided the concentrated populations necessary for economical mass education. Only then did the spurt of human productivity resulting from industrialization produce the huge sums that universal education required. In the 1860s about half the children in the country received some formal education, but this did not mean that half the children were attending school at any one time. Sessions were short, and many students dropped out after only two or three years of classes; as late as 1870 the average American had received only four years of schooling.

Thereafter, steady growth and improvement took place. Attendance in the public schools increased from 6.8 million in 1870 to 15.5 million in 1900, a remarkable expansion even when allowance is made for the growth of the population. Public expenditures for education rose from $63 million in 1870 to $234 million in 1902. The national rate of illiteracy declined from 20 percent in 1870 to 10.7 percent in 1900.* Nearly all the states outside the South had compulsory education laws by 1900, and over the years the laws were gradually extended to cover broader age groups and longer school sessions. The number of high schools jumped from perhaps 100 in 1860 to 6,000 at the end of the century. At the other extreme, the kindergarten, developed in Germany in the 1830s by Friedrich Froebel, caught on rapidly. The first public kindergarten was opened in St. Louis in 1873, and by the 1890s most systems of any size had adopted the idea.

Southern schools lagged behind the rest of the nation, in part because the section was poor and still predominantly rural. The restoration of white rule abruptly halted the progress in public education for blacks that the reconstruction governments had made. Church groups and private foundations such as the Peabody Fund and the Slater Fund, financed chiefly by northern philanthropists, supported black schools after 1877, among them two important experiments in vocational training, Hampton Institute (1868) and Booker T. Washington's Tuskegee Institute (1881).

These schools had to overcome considerable resistance and suspicion in the white community; they survived only because they taught a docile, essentially subservient philosophy, preparing students to accept second-class citizenship and become farmers and craftsmen. Since proficiency in academic subjects might have given the lie to the southern belief that blacks were intellectually inferior to whites, such subjects were avoided. The southern insistence on segregating the public schools, buttressed by the "separate but equal" decision of the Supreme Court in *Plessy* v. *Ferguson,* imposed a crushing financial burden on sparsely settled communities, and the dominant opinion that blacks were not really educable did not encourage communities to make special efforts in their behalf.

An industrial society created demands for vocational and technical training. Science courses appeared in the new high schools. In 1880 Calvin M. Woodward opened his Manual Training School in St. Louis, and soon a number of institutions were offering courses in carpentry, metalwork, sewing, and other crafts. By 1890, 36 American cities had public vocational high schools. Woodward thought of vocational training as part of a broad general education rather than as preparation for a specific occupation, but manual training attracted the backing of industrialists with more practical objectives. Their support in turn made organized labor suspicious of the new trend. One union leader called the trade schools "breeding schools for scabs and rats." Fortunately, the usefulness of such training soon became evident to the unions; by 1910 the AFL was lobbying side by side with the National Association of Manufacturers for more trade schools.

Foreign influences also caused a revolution in teaching methods. Traditionally, American teachers had emphasized the three Rs and relied on strict discipline and rote learning. Typical of the pedagogues of the period was the Chicago teacher, described by a reformer in the 1890s, who told her students firmly: "Don't stop to think, tell me what you know!" Yet the ideas of early 19th-century

*At present the rate is about 2 percent.

■ **Tuskegee, Booker T. Washington said, began as "a broken down shanty and an old hen house." As seen here, students built many of the school's buildings, learning a trade and earning their board as they did so.**

German educators, notably Johann Friedrich Herbart, were attracting attention in the United States. According to Herbart, teachers could best arouse the interest of their students by relating new information to what they already knew; good teaching called for professional training, psychological insight, enthusiasm, and imagination, not merely facts and a birch rod. At the same time, evolutionists were pressing for a kind of education that would help children to "survive" by adapting to the demands of their environment.

Forward-looking educators seized upon these ideas because dynamic social changes were making the old system increasingly inadequate. Settlement house workers discovered that slum children needed training in handicrafts, good citizenship, and personal hygiene as much as in reading and writing. They were appalled by the local schools, which suffered from the same diseases—filth, overcrowding, rickety construction—that plagued the tenements, and by the school systems, most of which were controlled by machine politicians who doled out teaching positions to party hacks and other untrained persons. They recognized the value of school playgrounds, kindergartens, adult education programs, and extracurricular clubs. Gradually they came to regard educational reform as central to the problem of improving society. "We are impatient with the schools which lay all stress on reading and writing," Jane Addams declared. This type of education "fails to give the child any clew to the life about him."

The philosopher who summarized and gave direction to these forces was John Dewey, a professor at the University of Chicago. Dewey was concerned with the implications of evolution—indeed, of all science—for education. Essentially his approach was ethical. Was the nation's youth being properly prepared for the tasks it faced in the modern world? He became interested in Francis W. Parker's remarkable experimental school in Chicago, which was organized as "a model home, a complete community and embryonic democracy." In 1896, together with his wife, Dewey founded the Laboratory School to put his educational ideas to the test. Three years later he published *The School and Society,* describing and defending his theories.

"Education," Dewey insisted, was "the fundamental method of social progress and reform." To seek to improve conditions merely by passing laws was "futile." Moreover, in an industrial society the family no longer performed many of the educational functions it had carried out in an agrarian society. Farm children learn about nature, about work, about human character in countless ways denied to children in cities. The school can fill the gap by becoming "an embryonic community . . . with types of occupations that reflect the life of the larger society." At the same time, education should center on the child, and new information should be related to what the child already knows. Children's imagination, energy, and curiosity are tools for broadening their outlook and increasing their store of information. Finally, the school should become an instrument for social reform, "saturating [the child] with the spirit of service" and helping to produce a "society which is worthy, lovely, and harmonious." Education, in other words, ought to build character and teach good citizenship as well as transmit knowledge.

The School and Society created a stir, and Dewey immediately assumed leadership of what in the next generation was called "progressive education." Although the gains made in public education before 1900 were more quantitative than qualitative and the philosophy dominant in most schools was not very different at the end of the century from that prevailing in Horace Mann's day, change was in the air. The best educators of the period were full of optimism, convinced that the future was theirs.

Keeping the People Informed

The inadequacy of so much of their schooling left many Americans with a hunger for knowledge. Nothing so well illustrates the mass desire for information as the rise of the Chautauqua movement, founded by John H. Vincent, a Methodist minister, and Lewis Miller, an Ohio manufacturer of farm machinery. Vincent had charge of Sunday schools for the Methodist church. In 1874 he and Miller organized a two-week summer course for Sunday school teachers on the shores of Lake Chautauqua in New York. Besides instruction, they offered good meals, evening songfests around the campfire, and a relaxing atmosphere—all for $6 for the two weeks.

The 40 young teachers who attended were delighted with the program, and soon the leafy shore of Lake Chautauqua became a city of tents each summer as thousands poured into the region from all over the country. The founders expanded their offerings to include instruction in literature, science, government, and economics. Famous authorities, including, over the years, six presidents of the United States, came to lecture to open-air audiences on every subject imaginable. Eventually Chautauqua supplied speakers to Reading Circles throughout the country; it even offered correspondence courses leading over a four-year period to a diploma, the program designed, in Vincent's words, to give "the college outlook" to persons who had not had the opportunity to obtain a higher education. Books were written specifically for the program and a monthly magazine, the *Chautauquan,* was published.

Such success provoked imitation, and by 1900 there were about 200 Chautauqua-type organizations. Intellectual standards in these programs varied greatly; in general they were very low. Entertainment was as important an objective as enlightenment. Musicians (good and bad), homespun humorists, inspirational lecturers, and assorted quacks shared the platform with prominent divines and scholars. Moneymaking undoubtedly motivated many of the entrepreneurs who operated the centers, all of which, including the original Chautauqua, reflected the prevailing tastes of the American people—diverse, enthusiastic, uncritical, and shallow. Nevertheless the movement provided opportunities for thousands seeking stimulation and intellectual improvement.

Still larger numbers profited from the proliferation of public libraries. By the end of the century nearly all the states supported libraries. Private donors, led by the ironmaster Andrew Carnegie, contributed millions to the cause. In 1900 over 1,700 libraries in the United States had collections of more than 5,000 volumes.

Newspapers and magazines were important means for disseminating information and educating the masses. Here new technology supplied the major incentive for change. The development by Richard Hoe and Stephen Tucker of the web press (1871), which printed simultaneously on both sides of paper fed into it from large rolls, and Ottmar Mergenthaler's linotype machine (1886), which cast rows of type as needed directly from molten metal, cut printing costs dramatically. Machines for making paper out of wood pulp reduced the cost of newsprint to a quarter of what it had been in the 1860s. By 1895 machines were printing, cutting, and folding 24,000 32-page newspapers an hour.

The telegraph and transoceanic cables wrought

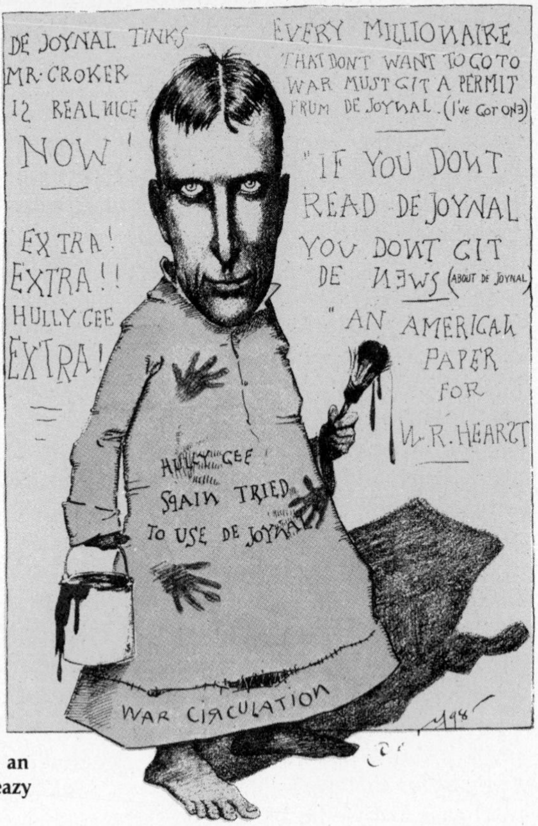

■ Left, John Singer Sargent's portrait of Joseph Pulitzer. Right, an opposition paper's caricature of Hearst as the Yellow Kid, a sleazy comic strip character and inspiration for the phrase "yellow journalism."

a similar transformation in the gathering of news. Press associations, led by the New York Associated Press, flourished; the syndicated article appeared; and a few publishers—Edward W. Scripps was the first—began to acquire chains of newspapers.

Population growth and better education created an ever larger demand for printed matter. At the same time, the integration of the economy enabled manufacturers to sell their goods all over the country. Advertising became important, and sellers soon learned that newspapers and magazines were excellent means of placing their products before millions of eyes. Advertising revenues soared just when new machines and general expansion were making publishing an expensive business. The day of the journeyman printer-editor ended; magazine publishing and newspaper publishing were becoming big business. Rich men such as the railroad magnates Jay Gould, Henry Villard, and Tom Scott and the mining tycoon George Hearst invested heavily in important newspapers in the postwar decades. These publishers tended to be conservative, a tendency increased by the prejudices of their businessmen-advertisers. On the other hand, reaching the masses meant lowering intellectual and cultural standards, appealing to emotions, and adopting popular, sometimes radical, causes.

Cheap, mass-circulation papers had first appeared in the 1830s and 1840s, the most successful being the *Sun*, the *Herald*, and the *Tribune* in New York, the Philadelphia *Public Ledger*, and the Baltimore *Sun* (see page 266). None of them much exceeded a circulation of 50,000 before the Civil War. The first publisher to reach a truly massive audience was Joseph Pulitzer, a Hungarian-born immigrant who made a first-rate paper of the St. Louis *Post-Dispatch*. In 1883 Pulitzer bought the New York *World*, a sheet with a circulation of perhaps 20,000. Within a year he was selling 100,000 copies daily, and by the late nineties the *World*'s circulation regularly exceeded 1 million.

Pulitzer achieved this brilliant success by casting a wide net. To the masses he offered bold, black headlines devoted to crime (ANOTHER MURDERER TO HANG), scandal (VICE ADMIRAL'S SON IN JAIL), catastrophe (TWENTY-FOUR MINERS KILLED), society and the theater (LILY LANGTRY'S NEW ADMIRER), together with feature stories, political cartoons, comics, and pictures. For the educated and affluent he provided better political and financial coverage than the most respectable New York journals. Pulitzer made the *World* a crusader for civic improvement by attacking political corruption, monopoly, and slum problems. His energetic reporters literally made news, masquerading as criminals and poor workers in order to write graphic accounts of conditions in New York's jails and sweatshops.

"The *World* is the people's newspaper," Pulitzer boasted, and in the sense that it interested men and women of every sort, he was correct. Pulitzer's methods were quickly copied by competitors, especially William Randolph Hearst, who purchased the New York *Journal* in 1895 and soon outdid the *World* in sensationalism. But no other newspaperman of the era approached Pulitzer in originality, boldness, and the knack of reaching the masses without abandoning seriousness of purpose and basic integrity.

Growth and ferment also characterized the magazine world. In 1865 there were about 700 magazines in the country, by the turn of the century more than 5,000. Until the mid eighties, few of the new magazines were in any way unusual. A handful of serious periodicals, such as the *Atlantic Monthly, Harper's,* and the *Century* among the monthlies and the *Nation* among the weeklies, dominated the field. They were staid in tone and conservative in political caste. Articles on current affairs, a good deal of fiction and poetry, historical and biographical studies, and similar material filled their pages, and many of them justly prided themselves on the quality of their illustrations. Although they had great influence, none approached a mass circulation because of the limited size of the upper-middle-class audience they aimed at. The *Century* touched a peak in the 1880s of about 250,000 when it published a series of articles on Civil War battles by famous commanders, but it could not sustain that level. A circulation of 100,000 was considered good for such magazines; the *Nation,* though extremely influential, seldom sold more than 8,000 copies.

Magazines directed at the average citizen were of low quality. The leading publisher of this type in the sixties and seventies was Frank Leslie, whose periodicals bore such titles as *Frank Leslie's Chimney Corner, Frank Leslie's Illustrated Newspaper,* and *Frank Leslie's Jolly Joker.* Leslie specialized in illustrations of current events (he put as many as 34 engravers to work on a single picture in order to bring it out quickly) and on providing what he frankly admitted was "mental pabulum"—a combination of cheap romantic fiction, old-fashioned poetry, jokes, and advice columns. Some of his magazines sold as many as 300,000 copies per issue.

After about 1885 vast changes began to take place. New magazines such as the *Forum* (1886) and the *Arena* (1889) emphasized hard-hitting articles on controversial subjects by leading experts. The weekly *Literary Digest* (1890) offered summaries of press opinion on current events, and the *Review of Reviews* (1891) provided monthly commentary on the news. Even more startling changes revolutionized the mass-circulation field. Between 1883 and 1893 the *Ladies' Home Journal, Cosmopolitan, Munsey's,* and *McClure's* appeared on the scene. Although superficially similar to the Frank Leslie type, these magazines maintained a far higher intellectual level.

In 1889 Edward W. Bok became editor of the *Ladies' Home Journal.* Besides advice columns ("Ruth Ashmore's Side Talks with Girls"), he offered articles on child care, gardening, and interior decorating, published fine contemporary novelists, and commissioned public figures, such as presidents Grover Cleveland and Benjamin Harrison, to discuss important questions. He printed colored reproductions of art masterpieces—the invention of cheap photoengraving was of enormous significance in the success of mass-circulation magazines—and crusaded for women's suffrage, conservation, and other reforms. Bok did more than cater to public tastes, he created new tastes. He even refused to accept patent medicine advertising, a major source of revenue for many popular magazines.

Samuel S. McClure and Frank A. Munsey were also masters of popular journalism. *McClure's* specialized in first-class fiction, serious historical studies, and articles attacking political corruption, monopoly, and other social evils. *Munsey's* adopted the same formula but pitched its appeal somewhat lower.

Bok, McClure, Munsey, and a number of their competitors reached millions of readers. Like Pulitzer in the newspaper field, they found ways of interesting rich and poor, the cultivated and the ignorant. Utilizing the new printing technology to cut costs and drawing heavily on advertising revenues, they sold their magazines for 10 or 15 cents a copy and still made fortunes. Under Bok the *Journal* reached a circulation of 2 million. Between 1894 and 1907, Munsey cleared over $7.8 million from his numerous publications. All had an acute sensitivity to the shifting interests of the masses. "I want to know if you enjoy a story," McClure once told his star reporter, Lincoln Steffens. "If you do, then I know that, say, ten thousand readers will like it. . . . But I go most by myself. For if I like a thing, then I know that millions will like it. My mind and my taste are so common that I'm the best editor."*

Colleges and Universities

Improvements in public education and the needs of an increasingly complex society for every type of intellectual skill led to advances in higher education and professional training. The number of colleges rose from about 350 to 500 between 1878 and 1898, and the student body roughly tripled. Less than 2 percent of the population attended college, but the aspirations of the nation's youth were rising, and more and more parents had the financial means necessary for fulfilling them.

More significant than the expansion of the colleges were the alterations in their curricula and in the atmosphere permeating the average campus. In 1870 most colleges were much as they had been in the 1830s: small, limited in their offerings, intellectually stagnant. The ill-paid professors were seldom scholars of stature. Thereafter, change came like a flood tide. State universities proliferated; the federal government's land-grant program in support of training in "agriculture and the mechanic arts," established under the Morrill Act of 1862, came into its own; wealthy philanthropists poured fortunes into old institutions and founded new ones; educators introduced new courses and adopted new teaching methods; professional schools of law, medicine, education, business, journalism, and other specialties increased in number.

In the forefront of reform was Harvard, the oldest and most prestigious college in the country. In the 1860s it possessed an excellent faculty, but teaching methods were antiquated and the curriculum had remained almost unchanged since the colonial period. In 1869, however, a dynamic president, the chemist Charles W. Eliot, undertook a transformation of the college. Eliot introduced the elective system, gradually eliminating required courses and expanding offerings in such areas as modern languages, economics, and the laboratory sciences. He encouraged the faculty to experiment with new teaching methods, and he brought in professors with original minds and new ideas. One was Henry Adams, grandson of John Quincy Adams, who made the study of medieval history a true intellectual experience. "Mr. Adams roused the spirit of inquiry and controversy in me," one student later wrote. Another, the historian Edward Channing, called Adams "the greatest teacher that I ever encountered."

Under Eliot's guidance the standards of the medical school were raised and the case method was introduced in the law school. For the first time, students were allowed to borrow books from the library! In some respects Eliot went too far—the elective system encouraged superficiality and laxness in many students—but on balance he transformed Harvard from a college, "a place to which a young man *is sent*," to a university, a place "to which he *goes*."

An even more important development in higher education was the founding of Johns Hopkins in 1876. This university was one of many established in the period by wealthy industrialists; its benefactor, the Baltimore merchant Johns Hopkins, had made his fortune in the Baltimore and Ohio Railroad. Its distinctiveness, however, was due to the vision of Daniel Coit Gilman, its first president. Gilman modeled Johns Hopkins on the German universities, where meticulous research and absolute freedom of inquiry were the guiding principles. In staffing the institution, he sought scholars of the highest reputation, scouring Europe as well as America in his search for talent and offering outstanding men high salaries for that time—up to $5,000 for a professor. At the same time, he employed a number of relatively unknown but brilliant younger scholars, such as the physicist Henry A. Rowland and Herbert Baxter Adams, whom he made an associate in history on the strength of his excellent doctoral dissertation at the University of Heidelberg. Gilman promised his teachers good students and ample

*McClure added ruefully: "There's only one better editor than I am, and that's Frank Munsey. If *he* likes a thing, then *everybody* will like it."

opportunity to pursue their own research (which explains why so many Hopkins professors repeatedly turned down attractive offers from other universities).

Johns Hopkins specialized in graduate education. In the generation after its founding, it turned out a remarkable percentage of the most important scholars in the nation, including Woodrow Wilson in political science, John Dewey in philosophy, Frederick Jackson Turner in history, and John R. Commons in economics. The seminar conducted by Herbert Baxter Adams was particularly productive: the Adams-edited *Johns Hopkins Studies in Historical and Political Science,* consisting of the doctoral dissertations of his students, was both voluminous and influential—"the mother of similar studies in every part of the United States." At Johns Hopkins, the reformer Frederick C. Howe recalled, "my life really began. . . . I felt a sense of responsibility to the world. I wanted to change things."

The success of Johns Hopkins did not stop the migration of American scholars to Europe; more than 2,000 matriculated at German universities during the 1880s. But as Hopkins graduates took up professorships at other institutions and as scholars trained elsewhere adopted the Hopkins methods, true graduate education became possible in most sections of the country.

The example of Johns Hopkins encouraged other wealthy individuals to endow universities offering advanced work. Clark University in Worcester, Massachusetts, founded by Jonas Clark, a merchant and real estate speculator, opened its doors in 1889. Its president, G. Stanley Hall, had been a professor of psychology at Hopkins, and he built the new university in that institution's image. More important was John D. Rockefeller's creation, the University of Chicago (1892). The president of Chicago, William Rainey Harper, was a brilliant biblical scholar—he received his Ph.D. from Yale at the age of 18—and an energetic and imaginative administrator. The new university, he told Rockefeller, should be designed "with the example of Johns Hopkins before our eyes."

Like Daniel Coit Gilman, Harper sought top-flight scholars for his faculty. He offered such high salaries that he was besieged with over a thousand applications. Armed with Rockefeller dollars, he "raided" the best institutions in the nation. He decimated the faculty of the new Clark University—"an act of wreckage," the indignant President Hall complained, "comparable to anything that the worst trust ever attempted against its competitors." Chicago offered first-class graduate and undergraduate education. During its first year there were 120 instructors for fewer than 600 students, and despite fears that the mighty tycoon Rockefeller would enforce his social and economic views on the institution, academic freedom was the rule.

State and federal aid to higher education expanded rapidly. The Morrill Act, granting land to each state at a rate of 30,000 acres for each senator and representative, provided the endowments that gave many important modern universities, such as Illinois, Michigan State, and Ohio State, their start. While the federal assistance was earmarked for specific subjects, the land-grant colleges offered a full range of courses, and all received additional state funds. Other state institutions benefited, for the public was displaying an increasing willingness to support their activities.

The land-grant universities adopted new ideas quickly. They were coeducational from the start, and most developed professional schools and experimented with extension work and summer programs. Typical of the better state institutions was the University of Michigan, which reached the top rank among the nation's universities during the presidency of James B. Angell (1871–1909). Like Eliot at Harvard, Angell expanded the undergraduate curriculum and strengthened the law and medical schools. He encouraged graduate studies, seeking to make Michigan "part of the great world of scholars," and sought ways in which the university could serve the general community.

Important advances were made in women's education. Beginning with Vassar College, which opened its doors to 300 women students in 1865, the opportunity for young women to pursue serious academic work gradually expanded. Wellesley and Smith, both founded in 1875, completed the so-called Big Three women's colleges. Together with the already established Mount Holyoke, and with Bryn Mawr (1885), Barnard (1889), and Radcliffe (1893), they became known as the Seven Sisters.

Opportunities for women graduates were severely limited. The only career easily available to them was teaching; of the first 815 graduates of

■ **A geology field trip in the 1880s sets out from the administration building of Smith College. Along with their picks and hammers, the young women carry baskets which look as though they contain lunch.**

Vassar, all but 10 taught at some time in their lives. Nevertheless, the remarkable women that these institutions trained were conscious of their uniqueness and determined to demonstrate their capabilities. "Sending a daughter to college," the historian William H. Chafe writes, was "like letting the genie out of the bottle."

Not all the changes in higher education were beneficial. The election system led to superficiality; students gained a smattering of knowledge of many subjects and mastered none. Intensive graduate work often produced narrowness of outlook and research monographs on trivial subjects. Attempts to apply the scientific method in fields such as history and economics often enticed students into making smug claims to objectivity and definitiveness which from the nature of the subjects they could not even approach in their work.

The gifts of rich industrialists sometimes came with strings, and college boards of trustees tended to be dominated by businessmen who sometimes attempted to impose their own social and economic beliefs on faculty members. While few professors lost their positions because their views offended trustees, at many institutions trustees exerted constant nagging pressures that limited academic freedom and scholarly objectivity. At state colleges politicians often interfered in academic affairs, even treating professorships as part of the patronage system.

Thorstein Veblen pointed out in his caustic study of *The Higher Learning in America* (1918) that "the intrusion of businesslike ideals, aims and methods" harmed the universities in countless subtle ways. Size alone—the verbose Veblen called it "an executive weakness for spectacular magnitude"—became an end in itself, and the practical values of education were exalted over the humanistic. When universities grew bigger, administration became more complicated and the prestige of administrators rose inordinately. At many institutions professors came to be regarded as mere employees of the governing boards. In 1893 the members of the faculty of Stanford University were officially classified as personal servants of Mrs. Leland Stanford, widow of the founder. This was done in a good cause—the Stanford estate was tied up in probate court and the ruling made it possible to pay professors out of Mrs. Stanford's allowance for household expenses—but that such a procedure was even conceivable must have appalled the scholarly world.

As the number of college graduates increased, and as colleges ceased being primarily training institutions for clergymen, the influence of alumni on educational policies began to make itself felt, not always happily. Campus social activities became more important. Fraternities proliferated. Interest in organized sports first appeared as a laudable outgrowth of the general expansion of the curriculum, but soon athletic contests were playing a role all out of proportion to their significance. Football evolved as the leading intercollegiate sport, especially after Walter Camp, coach of the Yale team, began selecting "All America" squads in 1889. By the early nineties important games were attracting huge crowds (over 50,000 attended the Yale-Princeton game in 1893). Football became a source of revenue that many colleges dared not neglect. Since students, alumni, and the public demanded winning teams, college administrators stooped to subsidizing student athletes, in extreme cases employing players who were not students at all. One exasperated college president quipped that the B.A. degree was coming to mean Bachelor of Athletics.

Thus higher education reflected American values, with all their strengths and weaknesses. A complex society required a more professional and specialized education for its youth; the coarseness and the rampant materialism and competitiveness of the era inevitably found expression in the colleges and universities.

Scientific Advances

Much has been made of the crassness of late 19th-century American life, yet the period produced intellectual achievements of the highest quality. If the business mentality dominated society, and if the great barons of industry, exalting practicality over theory, tended to look down on the life of the mind, intellectuals, quietly pondering the problems of their generation, nonetheless created works that affected the country as profoundly as the achievements of industrial organizers like Rockefeller and Carnegie and technicians like Edison and Bell.

In pure science America produced a number of outstanding figures in these years. The giant among them, whose contributions some experts rank with those of Newton, Darwin, and Einstein, was Josiah Willard Gibbs, professor of mathematical physics at Yale from 1871 to 1903. Gibbs created an entirely new science, physical chemistry, and made possible the study of how complex substances respond to changes in temperature and pressure. Purely theoretical at the time, Gibbs' ideas led to vital advances in metallurgy and in the manufacture of plastics, drugs, and other products. Gibbs is often used to illustrate the supposed indifference of the age to its great minds, but this is hardly fair; he was a shy, self-effacing man who cared little for the spotlight or for collecting disciples. He published his major papers in the obscure *Transactions of the Connecticut Academy of Arts and Sciences.* Furthermore, he was so far ahead of his time that only a handful of specialists had a glimmering of the importance of his work. The editors of *Transactions* admitted that they did not understand his papers.

Of lesser but still major significance was the work of Henry A. Rowland, the first professor of physics at Johns Hopkins University. President Gilman, with characteristic insight, had plucked the youthful Rowland from the faculty of Rensselaer Polytechnic Institute, where his brilliance was not fully appreciated. Rowland conducted research in spectrum analysis and contributed to the development of electron theory. His work led to the improvement of transformers and dynamos and laid the basis for the modern electric power industry. Still another important American physicist was Albert A. Michelson of the University of Chicago, who made the first accurate measurements of the speed of light. Michelson's researches in the 1870s and 1880s helped prepare the way for Einstein's theory of relativity; in 1907 he became the first American scientist to win a Nobel prize.

Many scientists of the period deserve mention: the astronomer Edward C. Pickering, director of the Harvard Observatory, a pioneer in the field of astrophysics; Samuel P. Langley of the Smithsonian Institution, an expert on solar radiation who contributed to the development of the airplane; the paleontologist Othniel C. Marsh, whose study of fossil horses provided a convincing demonstration of evolution; John Wesley Powell, director of the U. S. Geological Survey, noted for his studies of the Grand Canyon and for his work on the uses of water in arid regions (see page 440). These and others of only slightly lesser stature give the lie to the myth that late 19th-century Americans were interested only in applied science.

The New Social Sciences

In the social sciences a close connection existed between the practical issues of the age and the achievements of the leading thinkers. The application of the theory of evolution to every aspect of human relations, the impact of industrialization on society—such topics were of intense concern to American economists, sociologists, and historians. An understanding of Darwin increased the already strong interest in studying the *development* of institutions and their interactions one with another. Controversies over trusts, slum conditions, and other problems drew scholars out of their towers and into practical affairs. Social scientists were impressed by the progress being made in the physical and biological sciences. They eagerly applied the scientific method to their own specialties, hoping thereby to arrive at objective truths in fields that by nature were essentially subjective.

Among the economists something approaching a revolution took place in the 1880s. The classical school, which maintained that immutable natural laws governed all human behavior, and which used the insights of Darwin only to justify unrestrained competition and laissez faire, was challenged by a group of young economists who argued that as times changed, economic theories and laws must be modified in order to remain relevant. Richard T. Ely, another of the scholars who made Johns Hopkins a font of new ideas in the eighties, summarized the thinking of this group in 1885. "The state [is] an educational and ethical agency whose positive aid is an indispensable condition of human progress," Ely proclaimed. Laissez faire was outmoded and dangerous. Economic problems were basically moral problems; their solution required "the united efforts of Church, state and science." The proper way to study these problems was by analyzing actual conditions, not by applying abstract laws or principles.

This approach led Henry Carter Adams (Ph.D., Johns Hopkins, 1878) to analyze the circumstances under which the government might regulate competition and even, in certain industries, establish monopolies under public control. Simon Patten of the University of Pennsylvania offered a theory justifying state economic planning. Such ideas gave birth to the so-called institutionalist school of economics, whose members made detailed, on-the-spot investigations of sweatshops, factories, and mines, studied the history of the labor movement, and conducted similar research activities of a concrete nature. The study of institutions would lead both to theoretical insights and to practical social reform, they believed. John R. Commons, one of Ely's students at Johns Hopkins and later professor of economics at the University of Wisconsin, was the outstanding member of this school. His 10-volume *Documentary History of American Industrial Society* (1910–1911) reveals the institutionalist approach at its best.

A similar revolution struck sociology in the mid eighties. Prevailing opinion up to that time rejected the idea of government interference with the organization of society. The influence of the Englishman Herbert Spencer, who objected even to public schools and the postal system, was immense. Spencer and his American disciples, among them Edward L. Youmans, editor of *Popular Science Monthly,* twisted the ideas of Darwin to mean that society could be changed only by the force of evolution, which moved with cosmic slowness. "You and I can do nothing at all," Youmans told the reformer Henry George. "It's all a matter of evolution. Perhaps in four or five thousand years evolution may have carried men beyond this state of things."

Such a point of view made little sense in America, where society was changing rapidly and the range of government social and economic activity was expanding. It was first challenged by an obscure scholar employed by the U. S. Geological Survey, Lester Frank Ward, whose *Dynamic Sociology* was published in 1883. Ward assailed the Spencerians for ignoring the possibility of "the improvement of society by cold calculation." In *The Psychic Factors of Civilization* (1893) he blasted the "law of competition." Human progress, he argued, consisted of "triumphing little by little over this law,"—for example, by interfering with biological processes through the use of medicines to kill harmful bacteria. Government regulation of the economy offered another illustration of how people could control the environment. "Nothing is more obvious today," Ward wrote in the *Forum* in 1895, "than the signal inability of capital and private enterprise to take care of themselves unaided by the state." Society must indeed evolve, but it would evolve through careful social planning.

Like the new economists, Ward emphasized the practical and ethical sides of his subject. Sociologists should seek "the betterment of society," he said. "Dynamic Sociology aims at the organization of happiness." He had little direct influence because his writings were highly technical. In six years only 500-odd copies of *Dynamic Sociology* were sold. However, a handful of specialists, including the economist Ely, President Andrew D. White of Cornell, the Social Gospel preacher Washington Gladden, and the sociologists Albion W. Small and Edward A. Ross—two more products of Johns Hopkins—carried his ideas to a wider audience. Their arguments yielded few concrete results before 1900, but they effectively demolished the Spencerians and laid the theoretical basis for the modern welfare state.

Similar currents of thought influenced other social sciences. In *Systems of Consanguinity* (1871) the pioneer anthropologist Lewis Henry Morgan developed a theory of social evolution and showed how kinship relationships reflected and affected tribal institutions. Morgan's *Ancient Society* (1877–1878) stressed the mutability of social and cultural patterns and the need to adjust these patterns to meet altered conditions. Applying his knowledge of primitive societies to modern life, he warned against overemphasizing the importance of property. "Since the advent of civilization, the outgrowth of property has been so immense . . . that it has become, on the part of the people, an unmanageable power," he wrote. "The time will come, nevertheless, when human intelligence will rise to the mastery over property, and define the relations of the state to the property it protects."

The new political scientists were also evolutionists and institutionalists. The Founding Fathers, living in a world dominated by Newton's concept of the universe as an immense, orderly machine, had conceived of the political system as an impersonal set of institutions and principles—a government of laws rather than of men. Nineteenth-century thinkers (John C. Calhoun is the best example) concerned themselves with abstractions, such as states' rights, and ignored the extralegal aspects of politics, such as parties and pressure groups. In the 1880s political scientists began to employ a different approach. In his doctoral dissertation at Johns Hopkins, *Congressional Government* (1885), Woodrow Wilson analyzed the American political system. He concluded that the real locus of authority lay in the committees of Congress, which had no constitutional basis at all. Wilson was by no means a radical—he idolized the great English conservative Edmund Burke. Nevertheless, he viewed politics as a dynamic process and offered no theoretical objection to the expansion of state power. In *The State* (1889) he distinguished between essential functions of government, such as the protection of property and the punishment of crime, and "ministrant" functions, such as education, the regulation of corporations, and social welfare legislation. The desirability of any particular state action of the latter type was simply a matter of expediency. "Every means," he wrote, "by which society may be perfected through the instrumentality of government . . . ought certainly to be diligently sought."

Law and History

Even jurisprudence, by its nature conservative and rooted in tradition, felt the pressure of evolutionary thought and the new emphasis on studying institutions as they actually are. In 1881 Oliver Wendell Holmes, Jr., published *The Common Law.* Rejecting the ideas that judges should limit themselves to the mechanical explication of statutes and that law consisted only of what was written in lawbooks, Holmes argued that "the felt necessities of the time" rather than precedent should determine the rules by which people are governed. "The life of the law has not been logic; it has been experience," he wrote. "It is revolting," he added on another occasion, "to have no better reason for a rule of law than that so it was laid down in the time of Henry IV."

Holmes went on to a long and brilliant judicial career, during which he repeatedly stressed the right of the people, through their elected representatives, to deal with contemporary problems in any reasonable way, unfettered by outmoded conceptions of the proper limits of government authority. Like the societies they regulated, laws should evolve as times and conditions changed, he said.

This way of reasoning caused no sudden reversal of judicial practice. Holmes' most notable opinions as a judge tended, as in the Lochner bakeshop case (see page 487), to be dissenting opinions. But his philosophy reflected the advanced thinking of the late 19th century, and his influence grew with every decade of the 20th.

The new approach to knowledge did not always advance the cause of liberal reform. Historians in the graduate schools became intensely interested in studying the origins and evolution of political institutions. They concluded, after much "scientific" study of old charters and law codes, that the roots of democracy were to be found in the customs of the ancient tribes of northern Europe. This theory of the "Teutonic origins" of democracy, which has since been thoroughly discredited, fitted well with the prejudices of people of British stock, and it provided ammunition for those who favored restricting immigration and for those who argued that blacks were inferior beings.

Out of this work came the frontier thesis of Frederick Jackson Turner, still another scholar trained at Johns Hopkins. Turner's essay "The Significance of the Frontier in American History" (1893) argued that the frontier experience, through which every section of the country had passed, had affected the thinking of the people and the shape of American institutions. The isolation of the frontier and the need during each successive westward advance to create civilization anew account, Turner wrote, for the individualism of Americans and the democratic character of their society. Nearly everything unique in our culture could be traced to the existence of the frontier, he claimed.

Turner, and still more his many disciples, made too much of his basic insights. Life on the frontier was not as democratic as Turner believed, and it certainly does not "explain" American development as completely as he said it did. Nevertheless, his work showed how important it was to investigate the evolution of institutions, and it encouraged historians to study social and economic, as well as purely political, subjects. If the claims of the new historians to objectivity and definitiveness were absurdly overstated, their emphasis on thoroughness, exactitude, and impartiality did much to raise standards in the profession. Perhaps the finest product of the new scientific school, a happy combination of meticulous scholarship and literary artistry, was Henry Adams' nine-volume *History of the United States During the Administrations of Jefferson and Madison.*

Realism in Literature

When what Mark Twain called the Gilded Age began, American literature was dominated by the romantic mood. All the important writers of the 1840s and 1850s except Hawthorne, Thoreau, and Poe were still living. Longfellow stood at the height of his fame, and the lachrymose Susan Warner—"tears on almost every page"—continued to turn out stories in the style of her popular *The Wide, Wide World.* Romanticism, however, had lost its creative force; most writing in the decade after 1865 was sentimental trash pandering to the preconceptions of middle-class readers. Magazines like the *Atlantic Monthly* overflowed with stories about fair ladies worshiped from afar by stainless heroes, women coping selflessly with drunken husbands, and poor but honest youths rising through various combinations of virtue and assiduity to positions of wealth and influence. Most writers of fiction tended to ignore the eternal conflicts inherent in human nature and the social problems of the age; polite entertainment and pious moralizing appeared to be their only objectives.

The patent unreality, even dishonesty of contemporary fiction eventually caused a reaction. In the mid sixties, Thomas Wentworth Higginson, essayist, historian, abolitionist, Civil War commander of a black regiment, attacked the sentimentality of American literature and urged writers to concern themselves with "real human life." New antiromantic foreign influences—Emile Zola's first novels appeared in the sixties—began to affect American interests and tastes. But the most important forces giving rise to the Age of Realism were those that were transforming every other aspect of American life: industrialism, with its associated complexities and social problems; the theory of evolution, which made people more aware of the force of the environment and the basic conflicts of existence; the new science, which taught dispassionate, empirical observation.

The 1870s saw a gradual shift in styles; by the 1880s realism was beginning to flower. Novelists undertook the examination of social problems such as slum life, the conflict between capital and labor, and political corruption. They created multidimensional characters, depicted persons of every social class, used dialect and slang to capture the flavor of particular types, and fashioned painstaking descriptions of the surroundings into which they placed their subjects.*

One early sign of the new realism was the "local color" school, for writers seeking to describe real situations turned to the regions they knew best for material. In 1880 Joel Chandler Harris began to publish his Uncle Remus stories, faithfully reproducing the dialect of Georgia blacks and incidentally creating a remarkably realistic literary character. The novels of Edward Eggleston, from *The Hoosier Schoolmaster* (1871) to *The Graysons* (1888), drew vivid pictures of middle-western life. Sarah Orne Jewett's carefully constructed tales of life in Maine, first published in the *Atlantic Monthly* in the mid seventies, caught the spirit of that region. Most local colorists could not rise above the conventional sentimentality of the era. By concentrating, as most did, on depicting rural life, they were retreating from current reality. Yet their concern for precise description and their fascination with local types reflected a growing interest in realism.

Mark Twain

While it was easy to romanticize the West, that region also lent itself to the realistic approach. Almost of necessity, novelists writing about the West employed dialect, described coarse characters from the lower levels of society, and dealt with crime and violence. It would have been difficult indeed to write a genteel romance about a mining camp. The outstanding figure of western literature, the first great American realist, was Mark Twain. Born Samuel L. Clemens in 1835, he grew up in Hannibal, Missouri, on the banks of the Mississippi. After having mastered the printer's trade and worked as a riverboat pilot, he went west to Nevada in 1861. The wild, rough life of Virginia City fascinated him, but prospecting got him nowhere, and he became a reporter for the *Territorial Enterprise.* Soon he was publishing humorous stories about the local life under the *nom de plume* Mark Twain. In 1865, while working in California, he wrote "The Celebrated Jumping Frog of Calaveras County," a story that brought him national recognition. A tour of Europe and the Holy Land in 1867–1868 led to the writing of *The Innocents Abroad* (1869), which made him famous.

Twain's greatness stemmed from his acute reportorial eye and ear, his eagerness to live life to the full, his marvelous sense of humor, his ability to be at once "in" society and outside it, to love humanity yet be repelled by human vanity and perversity. He epitomized the zest and adaptability of his age and also its materialism. No contemporary pursued the almighty dollar more assiduously. An inveterate speculator, he made a fortune with his pen and lost it in foolish business ventures. He wrote tirelessly and endlessly about America and Europe, his own times and the feudal past, about tourists, slaves, tycoons, cracker-barrel philosophers—and human destiny. He was equally at home and equally successful on the Great River of his childhood, in the mining camps, and in the eastern bourgeois society of his mature years. But every prize slipped through his fingers. Twain died a dark pessimist, surrounded by adulation yet alone, an alien and a stranger in the land he loved and knew so well.

Twain excelled every contemporary in the portrayal of character. In his biting satire *The Gilded Age* (1873) he created that magnificent mountebank Colonel Beriah Sellers, purveyor of eyewash ("the Infallible Imperial Oriental Optic Liniment") and false hopes, ridiculous, unscrupulous, but lovable. In *Huckleberry Finn* (1884), his masterpiece, his portrait of the slave Jim, loyal, patient, naive, yet withal a man, is unforgettable. When Huck takes advantage of Jim's credulity merely for his own amusement, the slave turns from him coldly and says: "Dat truck dah is *trash;* en trash is what people is dat puts dirt on de head er dey fren's en makes 'em ashamed." And there is Huck Finn himself, one of the great figures of literature, full of deviltry, romantic, amoral—up to a point—and

*The romantic novel did not disappear. General Lew Wallace's *Ben Hur* (1880) and Frances Hodgson Burnett's *Little Lord Fauntleroy* (1886) were best sellers. Francis Marion Crawford's shamelessly romantic tales, published in wholesale lots between 1883 and his death in 1909, were very popular. In the nineties a spate of historical romances made the realists fume.

■ Mark Twain in the limelight. An affectionate caricature by Keppler of the beloved author shows a smiling audience as his books—*Huckleberry Finn, Innocents Abroad*—take wing.

at bottom the complete realist. When Miss Watson tells him he can get anything he wants by praying for it, he makes the effort, is disillusioned, and concludes: "If a body can get anything they pray for, why don't Deacon Winn get back the money he lost on pork? . . . Why can't Miss Watson fat up? No, I says to myself, there ain't nothing in it."

Whether directly, as in *The Innocents Abroad* and in his fascinating account of the world of the river pilot, *Life on the Mississippi* (1883), or when transformed by his imagination in works of fiction such as *Tom Sawyer* (1876) and *A Connecticut Yankee in King Arthur's Court* (1889), Mark Twain always put much of his own experience and feeling into his work. "The truth is," he wrote in 1886, "my books are mainly autobiographies." A story, he told a fellow author, "must be written with the blood out of a man's heart." His innermost confusions, the clash between his recognition of the pretentiousness and meanness of human beings and his wish to be accepted by society, added depths and overtones to his writing that together with his comic genius give it lasting appeal. He could not rise above the sentimentality and prudery of his generation entirely, for these qualities were part of his nature. He never dealt effectively with sexual love, for example, and often—even in *Huckleberry Finn*—he contrived to end his tales on absurdly optimistic notes that ring false after so many brilliant pages portraying life as it is. On balance Twain's achievement was magnificent. Rough and uneven like the man himself, his works catch more of the spirit of the age he named than those of any other writer.

William Dean Howells

Mark Twain's realism was far less self-conscious than that of his longtime friend William Dean Howells. Like Twain, Howells, who was born in Ohio in 1837, had little formal education. He learned the printer's trade from his father and became a reporter for the *Ohio State Journal.* In 1860 he wrote a campaign biography of Lincoln and was rewarded with an appointment as consul in Venice. His sketches in *Venetian Life* (1866) were a product of this experience. After the Civil War he worked briefly for the *Nation* in New York and then moved to Boston, where he became editor of the *Atlantic Monthly.* In 1886 he returned to New York as editor of *Harper's.*

A long series of novels and much literary criticism poured from Howells' pen over the next 34 years. While he insisted on treating his material honestly, he was not at first a critic of society, being content to write about what he called "the smiling aspects" of life. Realism to Howells meant concern for the complexities of individual personalities and faithful description of the genteel, middle-class world he knew best. Nevertheless, he did not hesitate to discuss what prudish critics called "sordid" and "revolting" subjects, such as the unhappy marriage of respectable people, which he treated sensitively in *A Modern Instance* (1882).

Besides a sharp eye and an open mind, Howells had a real social conscience. Gradually he became aware of the problems that industrialization had created. In 1885, in *The Rise of Silas Lapham,* he dealt with some of the ethical conflicts faced by businessmen in a competitive society. The harsh public reaction to the Haymarket bombing in 1886

■ **An 1897 drawing from the comic weekly *Life*, titled "Our Popular but Over-advertised Authors," features (from left) William Dean Howells, George W. Cable, John K. Bangs, James Whitcomb Riley, Mark Twain, Mary Freeman, Richard Harding Davis, F. Marion Crawford, Frances Burnett, and Joel Chandler Harris.**

stirred him, and he threw himself into a futile campaign to prevent the execution of the anarchist suspects. Thereafter he moved rapidly toward the left; soon he was calling himself a socialist. "After fifty years of optimistic content with 'civilization' . . . I now abhor it, and feel that it is coming out all wrong in the end, unless it bases itself anew on a real equality," he wrote.* *A Hazard of New Fortunes* (1890), in which Howells put his own ideas in the mouth of a magazine editor, Basil March, contained a broad criticism of industrial America—of the slums, of the callous treatment of workers, of the false values of the promoter and the new-rich tycoon.

Howells was more than a reformer, more than an inventor of utopias like Edward Bellamy, though he admired Bellamy and wrote a utopian novel of his own, *A Traveller from Altruria* (1894). *A Hazard of New Fortunes* attempted to portray the whole range of metropolitan life, its plot weaving the destinies of a dozen interesting personalities from diverse sections and social classes. The book represents a triumph of realism in its careful descriptions of various sections of New York and the ways of life of rich and poor, in the intricacy of its characters, and in its rejection of sentimentality and romantic love. "A man knows that he can love and wholly cease to love, not once merely, but several times," the narrator says, "but in regard to women he cherishes the superstition of the romances that love is once for all, and forever." Basil March, himself happily married, tells his wife: "Why shouldn't we rejoice as much at a nonmarriage as a marriage? . . . In reality, marriage is dog cheap, and anyone can have it for the asking—if he keeps asking enough people."

Aside from his own works, which were widely read, Howells was the most influential critic of his time. He helped bring the best contemporary foreign writers, including Tolstoy, Dostoevsky, Ibsen, and Zola, to the attention of readers in the United States, and he encouraged many important young American novelists, among them Stephen Crane, Theodore Dreiser, Frank Norris, and Hamlin Garland.

Some of these writers went far beyond Howells'

*With remarkable self-insight he added immediately: "Meanwhile I wear a fur-lined overcoat, and live in all the luxury my money can buy." Like nearly all American reformers of the era, he was not really very radical.

realism to what they called naturalism. Many, like Twain and Howells, began as newspaper reporters. Working for a big-city daily in the 1890s was sure to teach anyone a great deal about the dark side of life. Naturalist writers believed that the human being was essentially an animal, a helpless creature whose fate was determined by environment. Their world was Darwin's world—mindless, without mercy or justice. They wrote chiefly about the most primitive emotions—lust, hate, greed. In *Maggie, A Girl of the Streets* (1893) Stephen Crane described the seduction, degradation, and eventual suicide of a young woman, all set against the background of a sordid slum; in *The Red Badge of Courage* (1895) he captured the pain and humor of war. In *McTeague* (1899) Frank Norris told the story of a brutal, dull-witted dentist who murdered his greed-crazed wife with his bare fists.

Such stuff was too strong for Howells, yet he recognized its importance and befriended the younger writers in many ways. He found a publisher for *Maggie* after it had been rejected many times, and he wrote appreciative reviews of the work of Garland and Norris. Even Theodore Dreiser, who was contemptuous of Howells' writings and considered him hopelessly middle-class in point of view, appreciated his aid and praised his influence on American literature. Dreiser's first novel, *Sister Carrie* (1900), treated sex so forthrightly that it was withdrawn after publication.

Henry James

Henry James was very different in spirit and background from the tempestuous naturalists. Born to wealth, reared in a cosmopolitan atmosphere, twisted in some strange way while still a child and unable to achieve satisfactory relationships with women, James spent most of his mature life in Europe, writing novels, short stories, plays, and volumes of criticism. Although far removed from the world of practical affairs, he was preeminently a realist, determined, as he once said, "to leave a multitude of pictures of my time" for the future to contemplate. He admired the European realists and denounced the "floods of tepid soap and water which under the name of novels are being vomited forth" by the romancers. "All life belongs to you," he told his fellow novelists. "There is no impression of life, no manner of seeing it and feeling it, to which the plan of the novelist may not offer a place."

While he preferred living in the cultivated surroundings of London high society, James yearned for the recognition of his fellow Americans almost as avidly as Mark Twain. However, he was incapable of modifying his rarefied, overly subtle manner of writing. Most serious writers of the time admired his books, and he received many honors, but he never achieved widespread popularity. His major theme was the clash of American and European cultures, his primary interest the close-up examination of wealthy, sensitive, yet often corrupt persons in a cultivated but far from polite society.

James dealt with social issues such as feminism and the difficulties faced by artists in the modern world, but he subordinated them to his interest in his subjects as individuals. *The American* (1877) told the story of the love of a wealthy American in Paris for a French noblewoman who rejected him because her family disapproved of his "commercial" background. *The Portrait of a Lady* (1881) described the disillusionment of an intelligent woman married to a charming but morally bankrupt man and her eventual decision to remain with him nonetheless. *The Bostonians* (1886) was a complicated and psychologically sensitive study of the varieties of female behavior in a seemingly uniform social situation.

James' reputation, greater today than in his lifetime, rests more on his highly refined accounts of the interactions of individuals and their environment and his masterful commentaries on the novel as a literary form than on his ability as a storyteller. Few major writers have been more long-winded, more prone to circumlocution. Yet few have been so dedicated to their art, possessed of such psychological penetration, or so successful in producing a large body of important work.

Realism in Art

American painters responded to the times as writers did, but with this difference: despite the new concern for realism, the romantic tradition retained its vitality. Preeminent among the realists was Thomas Eakins, who was born in Philadelphia in 1844. Eakins studied in Europe in the late sixties and was influenced by the great realists of the 17th century, Velásquez and Rembrandt. Returning to America in 1870, he passed the remainder of his life teaching and painting in Philadelphia.

The scientific spirit of the age suited Eakins perfectly. He mastered human anatomy; some of his finest paintings, such as *The Gross Clinic* (1875), are graphic illustrations of surgical operations. He was an early experimenter with motion pictures, using the camera to capture exactly the attitudes of human beings and animals in action. Like his friend Walt Whitman, whose portrait is one of his greatest achievements, Eakins gloried in the ordinary. But he had none of Whitman's weakness for sham and self-delusion. His portraits are monuments to his integrity and craftsmanship: never would he touch up or soften a likeness to please his sitter. When the Union League of Philadelphia commissioned a canvas of Rutherford B. Hayes, Eakins showed the president working in his shirt sleeves, which scandalized the club fathers. His work was no mere mirror reflecting surface values. His study of six men bathing *(The Swimming Hole)* is a stark portrayal of nakedness; his surgical scenes catch the tenseness of a situation without descending into sensationalism.

Winslow Homer, a Boston-born painter best known for his brilliant watercolors, was also influenced by realist ideas. Homer was a lithographer as well as a master of the watercolor medium, yet he had had almost no formal training. Indeed, he had contempt for academicians and refused to go abroad to study. Aesthetics seemed not to concern him at all; he liked to shock people by referring to his profession as "the picture line." His concern for accuracy was so intense that in preparation for painting *The Life Line* (1884) he made a trip to Atlantic City to observe the handling of a breeches buoy. "When I have selected [a subject]," he said, "I paint it exactly as it appears."

During the Civil War, Homer worked as an artist-reporter for *Harper's Weekly*, and he continued to do magazine illustrations for some years thereafter. He roamed America, painting scenes of southern farm life, Adirondack campers, and after about 1880, magnificent seascapes and studies of fishermen and sailors. For years he made his home in a cottage at Prout's Neck, in Maine, though he traveled extensively in the Caribbean region, where some of his best watercolors were executed.

In some ways Homer resembled the local colorists of American literature. Like the work of many members of that group, Homer's work contains romantic elements. His *Gulf Stream* (1899), showing a sailor on a small, broken boat menaced by an approaching waterspout and a school of sharks, and his *Fox Hunt* (1893), in which huge, ominous crows hover over a fox at bay, express his interest in the violence and drama of raw nature, a distinctly romantic theme. However, his approach, even in these works, was utterly prosaic. When some silly women complained about the fate of the black sailor in *Gulf Stream*, Homer wrote his dealer sarcastically: "Tell these ladies that the unfortunate Negro . . . will be rescued and returned to his friends and home, and live happily ever after."

The outstanding romantic painter of the period was Albert Pinkham Ryder, a strange, neurotic genius haunted by the mystery and poetry of the sea. Ryder was born in New Bedford, Massachusetts, in 1847, during that city's heyday as a whaling port, and spent most of his mature years in New York City, living and working in a dirty, cluttered attic studio. He typified the solitary romantic—brooding, eccentric, otherworldly, mystical. His heavily glazed paintings of dark seas and small boats "bathed in an atmosphere of golden luminosity" beneath a pale moon, and weird canvases like *The Race Track (Death on a Pale Horse)*, which shows a specter carrying a scythe riding on an empty track under an ominous sky, radiate a strange magic. Yet they are masterpieces of design.

The careers of Eakins, Homer, and Ryder show that the late 19th-century American environment was not uncongenial to first-rate artists. Nevertheless, at least two major American painters abandoned native shores for Europe. One was James A. McNeill Whistler, whose portrait of his mother, which he called *Arrangement in Grey and Black*, is probably the most famous canvas ever painted by an American. Whistler left the United States in 1855 when he was 21 and spent most of his life in Paris and London. "I shall come to America," he announced grandly, "when the duty on works of art is abolished!" Whistler made a profession of eccentricity, but he was a remarkably talented and versatile artist. Some of his portraits are triumphs of realism, while his misty studies of the London waterfront—which the critic

■ **Thomas Eakins' interest in science was as great as his interest in art. In the early 1880s he collaborated with the photographer Eadweard Muybridge in serial-action photographic experiments and later devised a special camera for his anatomical studies; one of his pictures is reproduced above. The impact of these studies can be seen in *The Swimming Hole* (page 509), painted by Eakins in 1883. He was then director of the Pennsylvania Academy's art school.**

John Ruskin characterized as pots of paint flung in the face of the beholder, and which Whistler conceived as visual expressions of poetry—are thoroughly romantic in conception. Paintings such as "Whistler's Mother" represent still another expression of his talent. Spare and muted in tone, they are more interesting as precise arrangements of color and space than as images of particular objects; they had a tremendous influence on the course of modern art.

The second important expatriate artist was Mary Cassatt, daughter of a wealthy Pittsburgh banker and sister of Alexander J. Cassatt, who was president of the Pennsylvania Railroad around the turn of the century. She went to Paris as a tourist and dabbled in art like many conventional young socialites, then was caught up in the impressionist movement and decided to become a serious painter. Her work is more French than American and was little appreciated in the United States before the First World War. When once she returned to America for a visit, the Philadelphia *Public Ledger* reported: "Mary Cassatt, sister of Mr. Cassatt, president of the Pennsylvania Railroad, returned from Europe yesterday. She has been studying painting in Paris, and owns the smallest Pekinese dog in the world."

If Mary Cassatt was unappreciated and if Whistler had reasons for considering Americans uncultured, it remains true that interest in art was considerable. Museums and art schools increased in number and settlement house workers put on exhibitions that attracted enthusiastic crowds. Wealthy patrons gave countless commissions to portrait painters, the most fashionable of whom, a fine craftsman if not a great artist, was John Singer Sargent. Millionaires poured fortunes into collecting, and if some were interested only in display and others had execrable taste, some were discriminating collectors. Martin A. Ryerson, with a fortune made in lumber, bought the works of the French impressionists when few Americans understood their importance. Charles L. Freer of the American Car and Foundry Company, a friend and admirer of Whistler, was a specialist in oriental art. John G. Johnson, a successful corporation lawyer, covered the walls of his Philadelphia mansion with a carefully chosen collection of Italian

primitives, accumulated before anyone else appreciated them.

Other enthusiasts, notably the banker J. P. Morgan, employed experts to help them put together their collections. Nor were the advanced painters of the day rejected by all wealthy patrons. Only a handful of his contemporaries recognized the talent of the weird, avant-garde Ryder. But while Eakins' work was undervalued, he received many important commissions. Some of Homer's canvases commanded thousands of dollars, and so did those of the radical Whistler.

The Pragmatic Approach

It would have been remarkable indeed if the intellectual ferment of the late 19th century had not affected contemporary ideas about the meaning of life, the truth of revealed religion, moral values, and similar fundamental problems. In particular the theory of evolution, so important in altering contemporary views of science, history, and social relations, produced significant changes in American thinking about religious and philosophical questions.

Evolution posed an immediate challenge to religion: if Darwin was correct, the Biblical account of the creation was obviously untrue and the idea that man had been formed in God's image was highly unlikely. A bitter controversy erupted, described by president Andrew D. White of Cornell in *The Warfare of Science with Theology in Christendom* (1896). While millions continued to believe in the literal truth of the Bible, among intellectuals, lay and clerical, victory went to the evolutionists because in addition to the arguments of the geologists and the biologists, scholars were throwing light on the historical origins of the Bible, showing it to be of human rather than divine inspiration.

Evolution did not undermine the faith of any large percentage of the population. If the account of the creation in Genesis could not be taken literally, the Bible remained a repository of wisdom and inspiration. Such books as John Fiske's *The Outlines of Cosmic Philosophy* (1874) provided religious persons with the comforting thesis that evolution, while true, was merely God's way of order-

■ **William James (with the beard) and his novelist brother Henry James in a warm photographic portrait taken around 1900.**

ing the universe—as the liberal preacher Washington Gladden put it, "a most impressive demonstration of the presence of God in the world."

The effects of Darwinism on philosophy were less dramatic but in the end more significant. Fixed systems and eternal verities were difficult to justify in a world that was constantly evolving. By the early 1870s a few philosophers had begun to reason that ideas and theories mattered little except when applied to specifics. "Nothing justifies the development of abstract principles but their utility in enlarging our concrete knowledge of nature," wrote Chauncey Wright, secretary of the American Academy of Arts and Sciences. In "How to Make Our Ideas Clear" (1878), Wright's friend Charles S. Peirce, an amazingly versatile and talented albeit obscure thinker, argued that concepts could be fairly understood only in terms of their practical effects. Once the mind accepted the truth of evolution, Peirce believed, logic required that it accept the impermanence even of scientific laws. There was, he wrote, "an element of indeterminacy, spontaneity, or absolute chance in nature."

This startling philosophy, which Peirce called pragmatism, was presented in more understandable language by William James, brother of the novelist. James was one of the most remarkable persons of his generation. Educated in London, Paris, Bonn, and Geneva—as well as at Harvard—he studied painting, participated in a zoological expedition to South America, took a medical degree, and was professor at Harvard successively of comparative anatomy, psychology, and finally philosophy. His *Principles of Psychology* (1890) may be said to have established that discipline as a modern science. His *Varieties of Religious Experience* (1902), which treated the subject from both psychological and philosophical points of view, helped thousands of readers to reconcile their religious faith with their increasing knowledge of psychology and the physical universe.

Although less rigorous a logician than Peirce, James' wide range and his verve and imagination as a writer made him by far the most influential philosopher of his times. He rejected the deterministic interpretation of Darwinism and all other one-idea explanations of existence. Belief in free will was one of his axioms; environment might influence survival, but so did the *desire* to survive, which existed independently of surrounding circumstances. Even truth was relative; it did not exist in the abstract; it *happened* under particular circumstances. What a person thought helped to make what he thought occur, or come true. The mind, James wrote in a typically vivid phrase, has "a vote" in determining truth. Religion was true, for example, because people were religious.

The pragmatic approach inspired much of the reform spirit of the late 19th century and even more of that of the early 20th. James' hammer blows shattered the laissez faire extremism of Herbert Spencer. In "Great Men and Their Environment" (1880) he argued that social changes were brought about by the actions of geniuses whom society had selected and raised to positions of power, rather than by the impersonal force of the environment. Such reasoning fitted the preconceptions of rugged individualists yet encouraged those dissatisfied with society to work for change. Educational reformers like John Dewey, the institutionalist school of economists, settlement house workers, and other reformers adopted pragmatism eagerly. James' philosophy did much to revive the buoyant optimism that had characterized the pre-Civil War reform movement.

Yet pragmatism brought Americans face to face with somber problems. While relativism made them optimistic, it bred insecurity, for there could be no certainty, no comforting reliance on any eternal value in the absence of absolute truth. Pragmatism also seemed to suggest that the end justified the means, that what worked was more important than what ought to be. At the time of James' death in 1910, the *Commercial and Financial Chronicle* pointed out that the pragmatic philosophy was helpful to businessmen in making decisions. By emphasizing practice at the expense of theory, the new philosophy encouraged materialism, anti-intellectualism, and other unlovely aspects of the American character. And what place had conventional morality in such a system? Perhaps pragmatism placed too much reliance on the free will of human beings, ignoring their capacity for selfishness and self-delusion.

The people of the new century found pragmatism a heady wine. They would quaff it freely and enthusiastically—down to the bitter dregs.

SUPPLEMENTARY READING

Titles marked with an asterisk have been published in paperback

All the surveys of American intellectual history deal extensively with this period. See, for example, Merle Curti, **The Growth of American Thought** (1943), Louis Hartz, **The Liberal Tradition in America*** (1955), and Clinton Rossiter, **Conservatism in America: The Thankless Persuasion*** (1962). P. A. Carter, **The Spiritual Crisis of the Gilded Age** (1971), H. S. Commager, **The American Mind*** (1950), and A. M. Schlesinger, **The Rise of the City*** (1933), contain much interesting information, and there are useful essays on some aspects of the subject in H. W. Morgan (ed.), **The Gilded Age: A Reappraisal*** (1970). Ray Ginger, **The Age of Excess*** (1965), is also stimulating.

L. A. Cremin, **The Transformation of the School: Progressivism in American Education*** (1961), is an excellent introduction to the subject. On education in the South, see C. W. Dabney, **Universal Education in the South** (1936). For the work of Dewey, consult Sidney Hook, **John Dewey** (1939). The best treatment of the Chautauqua movement is Victoria and R. O. Case, **We Called It Culture** (1948). Trends in the history of journalism are discussed in J. M. Lee, **History of American Journalism** (1923), B. A. Weisberger, **The American Newspaperman** (1961), and F. L. Mott, **A History of American Magazines** (1938–1957). George Juergens, **Joseph Pulitzer and the New York World** (1966), W. A. Swanberg, **Citizen Hearst*** (1961), and Peter Lyon, **Success Story: The Life and Times of S. S. McClure** (1963), are useful biographies.

On higher education, see L. R. Veysey, **The Emergence of the American University*** (1965), Richard Hofstadter and W. P. Metzger, **The Development of Academic Freedom in the United States*** (1955), and E. A. Green, **Mary Lyon and Mount Holyoke** (1979). Of the many histories of particular universities, S. E. Morison, **Three Centuries of Harvard** (1936), and Hugh Hawkins, **Pioneer: A History of the Johns Hopkins University** (1960), are particularly important for this period. E. D. Ross, **Democracy's College** (1942), deals with the land-grant institutions. Hugh Hawkins, **Between Harvard and America: The Educational Leadership of Charles W. Eliot** (1972), and Allan Nevins, **John D. Rockefeller: The Heroic Age of American Enterprise** (1940), also contain valuable information. Thorstein Veblen, **The Higher Learning in America*** (1918), is full of stimulating opinions.

For developments in American science, see the excellent essay by P. F. Boller, Jr., in H. W. Morgan (ed.), **The**

Gilded Age* (1970), and Bernard Jaffe, **Men of Science in America** (1944). Muriel Rukeyser, **Willard Gibbs*** (1942), is a good biography. A good general introduction to the work of the social scientists is Sidney Fine, **Laissez Faire and the General-Welfare State*** (1957), but H. S. Commager's **American Mind** is also useful, as are Richard Hofstadter, **Social Darwinism in American Thought*** (1944), and Jurgen Herbst, **The German Historical School in American Scholarship** (1965). Biographies of prominent figures include P. G. Rader, **The Academic Mind and Reform: The Influence of Richard T. Ely in American Life** (1967), H. W. Bragdon, **Woodrow Wilson: The Academic Years** (1967), Samuel Chugerman, **Lester F. Ward: The American Aristotle** (1939), Carl Resek, **Lewis Henry Morgan*** (1960), M. DeW. Howe, **Justice Oliver Wendell Holmes: The Proving Years** (1963), and W. H. Jordy, **Henry Adams: Scientific Historian*** (1952).

The great literary figures of the age are discussed in Everett Carter, **Howells and the Age of Realism** (1954), Alfred Kazin, **On Native Grounds*** (1942), Larzer Ziff, **The American 1890s*** (1966), and Van Wyck Brooks, **New England: Indian Summer, 1865–1915*** (1940) and **The Confident Years: 1885–1915** (1952). See also, on Twain, Bernard De Voto, **Mark Twain's America*** (1932), and Justin Kaplan, **Mr. Clemens and Mark Twain*** (1966); on Howells, E. H. Cady, **The Realist at War** (1958); on James, Leon Edel, **Henry James*** (1953–1962).

American painting is discussed in O. W. Larkin, **Art and Life in America** (1949). Biographies of leading artists include Lloyd Goodrich, **Thomas Eakins** (1933) and **Winslow Homer*** (1944), F. N. Price, **Ryder** (1932), and E. R. and Joseph Pennell, **The Life of James McNeill Whistler** (1911).

On pragmatism, see Hofstadter's **Social Darwinism***, Commager's **American Mind***, R. B. Perry, **The Thought and Character of William James*** (1935), and Bruce Kuklick, **The Rise of American Philosophy** (1977).

21/NATIONAL POLITICS 1877–1896

Most students of the subject have concluded that the political history of the United States in the last quarter of the 19th century was singularly divorced from the meaningful issues of that day. On the rare occasions that important, supposedly controversial measures such as the Sherman Antitrust Act, the Interstate Commerce Act, the Pendleton Civil Service Act, and the Dawes Severalty Act were debated, they excited far less argument than they merited.

A graduated income tax, the greatest instrument for orderly economic and social change that a democratic society has devised, was enacted during the Civil War, repealed after that conflict, reenacted in 1894 as part of the maneuvering over tariff reform, and then declared unconstitutional in 1895 without causing much more than a ripple in the world of partisan politics. Proponents of the tax argued only that it offered a fairer way of distributing the costs of government, its foes that it penalized efficiency and encouraged government extravagance. Almost no one saw it as a means of redistributing wealth. This was typical; as the English observer James Bryce noted in the late eighties, the politicians were "clinging too long to outworn issues" and "neglecting to discover and work out new principles capable of solving the problems which now perplex the country." Congress, another critic wrote, "does not solve the problems, the solution of which is demanded by the life of the nation."

Yet the public remained intensely interested in politics. Huge crowds gathered to hear orators mouth hackneyed slogans and meaningless generalities. Most elections were closely contested; millions of voters turned out enthusiastically to choose, essentially, between Tweedledum and Tweedledee.

The American Commonwealth

A succession of weak presidents presided over the White House. Although the impeachment proceedings against Andrew Johnson had failed, Congress dominated the government. "There has not been a single presidential candidate since Abraham Lincoln," Bryce wrote in 1888, "of whom his friends could say that he had done anything to command the gratitude of the nation."

Within Congress, the Senate generally overshadowed the House of Representatives. In his novel *Democracy* (1880), the cynical Henry Adams wrote that the United States had a "government of the people, by the people, for the benefit of Senators." Critics called the Senate a "rich man's club," and it did contain many millionaires, among them Leland Stanford, founder of the Central Pacific Railroad, James G. "Bonanza" Fair of Nevada, who extracted a fortune of $30 million from the Comstock Lode, Philetus Sawyer, a self-made Wisconsin lumberman, and Nelson Aldrich of Rhode Island, whose wealth derived from banking and a host of corporate connections. However, the true sources of the Senate's influence lay in the long tenure of many of its members (which enabled them to master the craft of politics), in the fact that it was small enough to encourage real debate, and in its long-established reputation for wisdom, intelligence, and statesmanship.

The House of Representatives, on the other hand, was one of the most disorderly and inefficient legislative bodies in the world. "As I make my notes," a reporter wrote in 1882 while sitting in the House gallery, "I see a dozen men reading newspapers with their feet on their desks. . . . 'Pig-Iron' Kelley of Pennsylvania has dropped his newspaper and is paring his fingernails. . . . The vile odor of . . . tobacco . . . rises from the two-for-five-cents cigars in the mouths of the so-called gentlemen below. . . . They chew, too! Every desk has a spittoon of pink and gold china beside it to catch the filth from the statesman's mouth."

An infernal din rose from the crowded chamber. Desks slammed, members held private conversations, hailed pages, shuffled from place to place, clamored for the attention of the Speaker—and all the while some poor orator tried to discuss the question of the moment. Speaking in the House, one writer said, was like trying to address the crowd on a passing Broadway bus from the curb in front of the Astor House in New York. On one occasion in 1878 the adjournment of the House was held up for more than 12 hours because most of the members of an important committee were too drunk to prepare a vital appropriations bill for final passage. President Hayes was furious. *"It should be investigated,"* he wrote in his diary.

The great political parties professed undying enmity to each other, but they seldom took clearly opposing positions on the questions of the day. Democrats were separated from Republicans more by accidents of geography, religious affiliation, ethnic background, and emotion than by economic issues. Questions of state and local importance, unrelated to national politics, often determined the outcome of congressional elections and thus who controlled the federal government.

The fundamental division between Democrats and Republicans was sectional, a result of the Civil War. The South, after the political rights of blacks had been drastically circumscribed, became heavily Democratic. Most of New England was solidly Republican. Elsewhere the two parties stood in fair balance, though the Republicans tended to have the advantage. A preponderance of the well-to-do, cultured northerners was Republican. Perhaps in reaction to this concentration, immigrants,

■ **Joseph Keppler's 1890 *Puck* cartoon, "None but millionaires need apply; the coming style of Presidential election," comments acidly on the low status of the presidency. The tag "eight pieces with this set" on the chief executive's chair refers to the Cabinet. As the examples in this chapter show, the late 19th century was a heyday for political cartoonists.**

Catholics, and—except for blacks—other minority groups tended to vote Democratic. But there were so many exceptions that these generalizations are of little practical importance. German and Scandinavian immigrants usually voted Republican; many powerful business leaders supported the Democrats.

The personalities of political leaders often dictated the voting patterns of individuals and groups. In 1884 J. P. Morgan voted Democratic because he admired Grover Cleveland, while Irish-Americans, traditionally Democrats, cast thousands of ballots for Republican James G. Blaine. In 1892, when Cleveland defeated Benjamin Harrison, a prominent steel manufacturer wrote to Andrew Carnegie: "I am very sorry for President Harrison, but I cannot see that our interests are going to be affected one way or the other." And Carnegie replied: "We have nothing to fear. . . . Cleveland is [a] pretty good fellow. Off for Venice tomorrow."

The bulk of the people—farmers, laborers, shopkeepers, white-collar workers—distributed their ballots fairly evenly between the two parties in most elections; the balance of political power after 1876 was almost perfect—"the most spectacular degree of equilibrium in American history." Between 1856 and 1912 the Democrats elected a president only twice (1884 and 1892), but most contests were extremely close. Majorities in both the Senate and the House fluctuated continually. Between 1876 and 1896, the "dominant" Republican party controlled both houses of Congress and the presidency at the same time for only one two-year period.

Issues of the Gilded Age

Four questions obsessed politicians in these years. One was the "bloody shirt." The term, which became part of the language after a Massachusetts congressman dramatically displayed to his colleagues in the House the bloodstained shirt of an Ohio carpetbagger who had been flogged by terrorists in Mississippi, referred to the tactic of reminding the electorate of the northern states that the men who had taken the South out of the Union and precipitated the Civil War had been Democrats and that they and their descendants were still Democrats. Should their party regain power, former rebels would run the government and undo all the work accomplished at such sacrifice during the war. "Every man that endeavored to tear down the old flag," a Republican orator proclaimed in 1876, "was a Democrat. Every man that tried to destroy this nation was a Democrat. . . . The man that assassinated Abraham Lincoln was a Democrat. . . . Soldiers, every scar you have on your heroic bodies was given you by a Democrat."

Every scoundrel or incompetent who sought office under the Republican banner waved the bloody shirt in order to divert the attention of northern voters from his own shortcomings, and the technique worked so well that many decent candidates could not resist the temptation to employ it in close races. Nothing, of course, so effectively obscured the real issues of the day.

Waving the bloody shirt was related intimately to the issue of the rights of blacks. Throughout this period Republicans vacillated between trying to build up their organization in the South by appealing to black voters—which required them to make sure that blacks in the South could vote—and trying to win conservative white support by stressing economic issues such as the tariff. When the former strategy seemed wise, they waved the bloody shirt with vigor; in the latter case they piously announced that the blacks' future was "as safe in the hands of one party as it is in the other."

The question of veterans' pensions also bore a close relationship to the bloody shirt. Following the Civil War, Union soldiers founded the Grand Army of the Republic. By 1890 the organization had a membership of 409,000. The GAR put immense pressure on Congress, first for aid to veterans with service-connected disabilities, then for those with *any* disability, and eventually for all former Union soldiers. Republican politicians played on the emotions of the ex-soldiers by waving the bloody shirt, but the tough-minded leaders of the GAR demanded that they prove their sincerity by treating in openhanded fashion the warriors whose blood had stained the shirt.

The tariff was another perennial issue in post-Civil War politics. Despite considerable loose talk about free trade, almost no one in the United States except for a handful of professional economists, most of them college professors, believed in eliminating duties on imports. Manufacturers desired protective tariffs to keep out competing products, and a majority of their workers were convinced that wage levels would fall if goods produced by cheap foreign labor entered the United States untaxed. Many farmers supported protection, though almost no competing agricultural products were being imported. Congressman William McKinley of Ohio, who reputedly could make a tariff schedule sound like poetry, stated the majority opinion in the clearest terms: high tariffs foster the growth of industry and thus create jobs. "Reduce the tariff and labor is the first to suffer," he said. Whatever the professors may say about the virtues of free trade, "the school of experience" teaches that protection is necessary if America is to prosper.

Voters found this reasoning irrefutable. Duties had been raised during the Civil War to an average of about 50 percent ad valorem. Some slight reductions were made in the seventies and eighties, but in 1890 the McKinley tariff restored these cuts. This law even granted protection to a nonexistent industry, the manufacture of tin plate, and to agricultural products, such as eggs and potatoes, that would not have been imported under free trade. When the legislators decided to remove the duty on raw sugar in order to get rid of an embarrassing revenue surplus, they compensated domestic sugar raisers by awarding them a subsidy of 2 cents a pound on their product.

The tariff could have been a real political issue because American technology was advancing so rapidly that many industries no longer required protection from foreign competitors. A powerful argument could have been made for scientific rate making that would adjust duties to actual conditions and avoid overprotection. The Democrats professed to believe in moderation, yet whenever party leaders tried to revise the tariff downward, Democratic congressmen from industrial states like Pennsylvania and New York sided with the Republicans. Many Republicans endorsed tariff reform in principle, but when particular schedules came up for discussion, most of them demanded the highest rates for industries in their own districts and traded votes shamelessly with colleagues representing other interests in order to get what they wanted. Every new tariff bill became an occasion for logrolling, lobbying, and outrageous politicking rather than for sane discussion and careful evaluation of the public interest.

■ **Uncle Sam walks the floor with a fretful "Infant Industries," and says: "I guess he won't stop howling until I give him enough Protection Soothing Syrup to burst him!" An 1896 *Puck* cartoon.**

A third political question in this period was currency reform. During the Civil War, it will be recalled, the government, faced with obligations it could not meet by taxing or borrowing, suspended specie payments and issued about $450 million in paper money. The greenbacks did not command the full confidence of a people accustomed to money readily convertible into gold or silver. Greenbacks seemed to threaten inflation, for how could one trust the government not to issue them in wholesale lots to avoid passing unpopular tax laws? Thus, when the war ended, strong sentiment developed for withdrawing the greenbacks from circulation and returning to a bullion standard. "By a law resting on the concurring judgment . . . of mankind in all ages and countries, the precious metals have been the measure of value," one politician wrote. "That law can no more be repealed by act of Congress than the law of gravitation."

At the same time, the nation's burgeoning population and the rapid expansion of every kind of economic activity increased the need for currency. In fact, prices declined sharply after Appomattox. The deflation increased the real income of bondholders and other creditors but injured debtors. Farmers were particularly hard hit, for many of them had borrowed heavily during the wartime boom to finance expansion.

Here was a question of great significance. Many groups supported some kind of currency inflation. A National Greenback party nominated Peter Cooper, an iron manufacturer, for president in 1876. Cooper received only 81,000 votes, but a new Greenback Labor party polled over a million in 1878, electing 14 congressmen. However, the major parties refused to confront each other over the currency question. While Republicans professed to be the party of sound money, most western Republicans favored expansion of the currency. And while one wing of the Democrats flirted with the Greenbackers, the conservative, or "Bourbon" Democrats favored deflation as much as Republicans did.

In 1874 a bill to increase the supply of greenbacks was defeated in a Republican-dominated Congress only by the veto of President Grant. The next year Congress voted to resume specie payments, but in order to avoid a party split on the question, the Republicans agreed to allow $300 million in greenbacks to remain in circulation and to postpone actual resumption of specie payments until 1879.

Spurred on by the silver miners and by those advocating any measure that would increase the volume of money in circulation, numbers of congressmen introduced proposals to coin large amounts of silver. Neither party took a clear-cut stand on silver. Under various administrations steps were taken to increase or decrease the amount of money in circulation, but the net effect on the economy was not significant. Few politicians before 1890 considered fiscal policy as a device for influencing economic development. The effect of all the controversy, in the words of the economist Joseph Schumpeter, was "so light as to justify exclusion from the general analysis of the determining factors of the economic process."

The final major political issue of these years was civil service reform. That the federal bureaucracy needed overhauling nearly everyone agreed. As American society grew larger and more complex in an industrial age, the government necessarily took on more functions. The need for professional administration increased. The number of federal employees rose from 53,000 in 1871 to

256,000 at the end of the century. Corruption flourished; waste and inefficiency were the normal state of affairs. The collection of tariff duties offered perhaps the greatest opportunity for venality. The New York Custom House, one observer wrote in 1872, teemed with "corrupting merchants and their clerks and runners, who think that all men can be bought, and . . . corrupt swarms [of clerks], who shamelessly seek their price."

With a succession of relatively ineffective presidents and a Congress that squandered its energies on private bills, pork-barrel projects, and other trivia, the administration of the government was monumentally inefficient. "The federal system from Grant through McKinley was generally undistinguished," the historian Leonard D. White concluded after an exhaustive study of the period. "Nobody, whether in Congress or in the executive departments, seemed able to rise much above the handicraft office methods that were cumbersome even in the simpler days of the Jacksonians."

Every honest observer could see the need for reform, but the politicians refused to surrender the power of dispensing government jobs to their lieutenants without regard for their qualifications. They argued that patronage was the lifeblood of politics, that parties could not function without armies of loyal political workers, and that the workers expected and deserved the rewards of office when their efforts were crowned with victory at the polls. Typical was the attitude of the New York assemblyman who, according to Theodore Roosevelt, had "the same idea about Public Life and the Civil Service that a vulture has of a dead sheep." When reformers suggested establishing the most modest kind of professional, nonpartisan civil service, politicians of both parties subjected them to every kind of insult and ridicule even though both the Democratic and Republican parties regularly wrote civil service reform planks into their platforms.

Political Strategy and Tactics

The major American parties have nearly always avoided clear-cut stands on controversial questions in order to appeal to as wide a segment of the electorate as possible, but in the last quarter of the 19th century their equivocations assumed abnormal proportions. This was due in part to the precarious balance of power between them: neither dared declare itself too clearly on any question lest it drive away more voters than it attracted. The rapid pace of social and economic change also militated against political decisiveness. No one in or out of politics had as yet devised effective solutions for many current problems. When party leaders tried to deal with the money question, they discovered that the bankers and the professional economists were as confused as the public at large. "We dabble in theories of our own and clutch convulsively at the doctrines of others," a Philadelphia banker confessed. "From the vast tract of mire by which the subject is surrounded, overlaid, and besmeared, it is almost impossible to arrive at anything like a fair estimate of its real nature." How could mere politicians act rationally or consistently in such circumstances?

The parties stumbled badly when they confronted the tariff problem because tariffs in a complex industrial economy are not susceptible to determination by counting noses. Modern experience has shown that they are better arrived at by impartial boards of experts, once broad policies have been laid down by Congress, but in the 19th century specialists had not yet arrived at this conclusion. Reformers could thunder self-righteously against the spoils system, but how could political parties exist without it? They could denounce laissez faire, but who had devised instruments for social and economic control that could be centrally administered with intelligence and efficiency? The embryonic social sciences had not devised the techniques or even collected the statistical information necessary for efficient social management.

If the politicians steered clear of the "real" issues, they did so as much out of a healthy respect for their own ignorance as out of any desire to avoid controversy. Unable to provide answers to the meaningful questions, they turned to simpler issues that they and their constituents could understand in order to provide the political system with a semblance of purposefulness. Meanwhile, society blindly but steadily accumulated the experience and skills required for dealing with the results of the industrial revolution.

With the Democrats invincible in the South and the Republicans predominant in New England and most of the states beyond the Mississippi, the outcome of presidential elections was usually determined in a handful of populous states: New York (together with its satellites, New Jersey and Connecticut), Ohio, Indiana, and Illinois. The fact that opinion in these states on important questions such as the tariff and monetary policy was divided goes far to explain why the parties hesitated to commit themselves on issues. In every presidential election Democrats and Republicans concentrated their heaviest guns on these states.

Campaigns were conducted in a carnival atmosphere, entertainment being substituted for serious debate. Large sums were spent on brass bands, barbecues, uniforms, and banners. Speakers of national reputation were imported to attract crowds, and spellbinders noted for their leather lungs—this was before the day of the loudspeaker—and their ability to rouse popular emotions were brought in to address mass meetings. With so much depending on so few, the level of political morality was abysmal. Mudslinging, character assassination, and plain lying were standard practice, bribery routine. Drifters and other dissolute citizens were paid in cash—or more often in free drinks—to vote the party ticket. The names of persons long dead were solemnly inscribed in voting registers, their suffrages exercised by impostors. Since both parties indulged in these tactics, their efforts often canceled one another, yet in some instances presidents were made and unmade in this sordid fashion.

The Men in the White House

The leading statesmen of the period showed as little interest in important contemporary questions as the party hacks who made up the rank and file of their organizations. Consider the presidents.

Rutherford B. Hayes, president from 1877 to 1881, came to office with a distinguished record. Born in Delaware, Ohio, in 1822, he attended Kenyon College and the Harvard Law School before settling down to practice in Cincinnati. Although he had a family to support, he volunteered for service within weeks after the first shell fell on Fort Sumter. "This [is] a just and necessary war," he wrote in his diary. "I would prefer to go into it if I knew I was to die . . . than to live through and after it without taking any part."

Hayes fought bravely, even recklessly, through nearly four years of war. He was wounded at South Mountain on the eve of Antietam, and later he served under Sheridan in the Shenandoah Valley campaign of 1864. Entering the army as a major, he emerged a major general. In 1864 he was elected to Congress; four years later he became governor of Ohio, serving three terms altogether. The Republicans nominated him for president in 1876 because of his reputation for honesty and moderation, and his election, made possible by the Compromise of 1877, seemed to presage an era of sectional harmony and political probity.

Hayes was a long-faced man with deep-set blue eyes, a large nose, a broad, smooth forehead, and a full beard. Outwardly he had a sunny disposition, inwardly, in his own words, he was sometimes "nervous to the point of disaster." Despite his geniality, he was utterly without political glamour. Politically temperate and cautious, he had never been a vigorous waver of the bloody shirt, though in the heat of a hard campaign he was not above urging others to stress the dangers of "rebel rule" should the Democrats win. He played down the tariff issue whenever possible, favoring protection in principle but refusing to become a mere spokesman for local interests. On the money question he was conservative. He cheerfully approved the resumption of gold payments in 1879 and vetoed bills to expand the currency by coining silver. He accounted himself a civil service reformer, appointing Carl Schurz, a leader of the movement, to his Cabinet. He opposed the collection of political contributions from federal officeholders and issued an order forbidding them "to take part in the management of political organizations, caucuses, conventions, or election campaigns."

Hayes was a president in the Whig tradition. He saw himself more as a caretaker than a leader and believed that Congress should assume the main responsibility for solving national problems. According to a recent biographer, "he had no intention of . . . trying to be a President in the heroic mold," and another historian writes that he showed "no capacity for such large-minded leadership as might have tamed the political hordes and aroused the enthusiasm, or at least the interest, of the public."

Hayes hated having to make decisions on controversial questions. He complained about the South's failure to treat blacks decently after the withdrawal of federal troops, but he took no ac-

■ **In one of Keppler's more original—and outrageous—*Puck* cartoons, done for the 1880 campaign, "bride" Garfield is reminded of a shady past. "But it was such a little one!" the bride murmurs (Garfield's alleged link with Crédit Mobilier netted him only $329). GOP notables Carl Schurz and Whitelaw Reid are the bridesmaids.**

tion. He worked harder for civil service reform yet failed to achieve the "thorough, rapid and complete" change he had promised. In this as in most other matters, he was content to "let the record show that he had made the requests."

In the eyes of contemporaries the Hayes administration was a failure. Neither he nor they seriously considered him for a second term. "I am not liked as President," he confessed to his diary, and the Republican minority leader of the House admitted that the president was "almost without a friend" in Congress.

Hayes' successor, James A. Garfield, was cut down by an assassin's bullet four months after his inauguration. Even in that short time, however, his ineffectiveness had been demonstrated. Garfield grew up in poverty on an Ohio farm. He was only 29 when the Civil War broke out, but he helped organize a volunteer regiment and soon proved himself a fine disciplinarian and an excellent battlefield commander. He fought at Shiloh and later at Chickamauga, where he was General William S. Rosecrans' chief of staff. He rose in two years from lieutenant colonel to major general. In 1863 he won a seat in Congress, where his oratorical and managerial skills brought him to prominence in the affairs of the Republican party.

Garfield was a big, broad-shouldered man, balding, with sharp eyes, an aquiline nose, and a full beard. Studious, industrious, with a wide-ranging, well-stocked mind, he was called by one friend "the ideal self-made man." His great weakness was indecisiveness—what another of his admirers described as a "want of certainty" and a "deference for other men's opinions." As President Hayes put it, Garfield "could not face a frowning world. . . . His course at various times when trouble came betrayed weakness."

Like many ex-soldiers, including Hayes and even General Ulysses S. Grant, Garfield did not enjoy waving the bloody shirt, but when hard pressed politically—as when his name was linked with the Crédit Mobilier railroad scandal—he would lash out at the South in an effort to distract the voters. In theory he was inclined toward low tariffs. "The scholarship of modern times," he said in 1870, "is . . . leading in the direction of what is called free trade." Nevertheless, he would not sacrifice the interests of Ohio manufacturers for a mere principle. "I shall not admit to a considerable reduction of a few leading articles in which my constituents are deeply interested when many others of a similar character are left untouched," he declared. Similarly, though eager to improve the efficiency of the government and resentful of the "intellectual dissipation" resulting from time wasted listening to the countless appeals of office seekers, he often wilted under pressure from the spoilsmen. Only on fiscal policy did he take a firm stand: he opposed categorically all inflationary schemes.

Political patronage proved to be Garfield's undoing. The Republican party in 1880 was split into two factions, the "Stalwarts" and the "Half-Breeds." The Stalwarts, led by the New York politico Senator Roscoe Conkling, believed in the blatant pursuit of the spoils of office. The Half-Breeds did not disagree but behaved more circumspectly, hoping to attract the support of independents. Competition for office was the main reason for their rivalry.

Garfield had been a compromise choice at the 1880 Republican convention. His election precipitated a great battle over patronage, the new president standing in a sort of no-man's-land between the factions. "I am considering all day whether A or B shall be appointed to this or that office," he moaned. "Once or twice I felt like crying out in the agony of my soul against the greed for office and its consumption of my time." Soon he was complaining to his secretary of state: "My God! What is there in this place that a man should ever want to get into it?"

Garfield did stand up to the most grasping politicians, resisting in particular the demands of Senator Conkling. By backing the investigation of a post office scandal, and by appointing a Half-Breed collector of the Port of New York, he infuriated the Stalwarts. In July 1881 an unbalanced Stalwart lawyer named Charles J. Guiteau, who had been haunting Washington offices in search of a consulship or some other post, shot Garfield in the Washington railroad station. After lingering for weeks, the president died on September 19.

The assassination of Garfield elevated Chester A. Arthur to the presidency. Arthur was born in Vermont in 1829. After graduating from Union College, he studied law and settled in New York City. An abolitionist, he became an early convert to the Republican party and rose rapidly in its local councils. In 1871 Grant gave him the juiciest political plum in the country, the collectorship of the Port of New York, which he held until removed by Hayes in 1878 for refusing to keep his hands out of party politics.

The only elective position that Arthur had ever held was the vice-presidency. Before Garfield's death he had paid little attention to questions like the tariff and monetary policy, being content to take in fees ranging upward of $50,000 a year as collector of the port and to oversee the operations of the New York customs office, with its hordes of clerks and laborers. (During Arthur's tenure, the novelist Herman Melville was employed as an "outdoor inspector" by the Custom House.) Of course Arthur was an unblushing defender of the spoils system, though in fairness it must be said that he was personally honest and an excellent administrator.

The tragic circumstances of his elevation to the presidency sobered Arthur considerably. Although he was a genial, convivial man, perhaps overly fond of good food and flashy clothes, he comported himself with great dignity as president. He did not cut his ties with the Stalwart faction, but he handled patronage matters with restraint. He continued the investigation of the post office scandals over the objections of important Republican politicians who were involved in them, and he gave at least nominal support to the movement for civil service reform, which had been strengthened by the public indignation following the assassination of Garfield. In 1883 Congress passed the Pendleton Act, "classifying" about 10 percent of all government jobs and creating a bipartisan Civil Service Commission to prepare and administer competitive examinations for these positions. The law made it illegal to force officeholders to make political contributions and empowered the president to expand the list of classified positions at his discretion.

While many politicians resented the new system—one senator denounced it as "un-American"—the Pendleton Act opened a new era in government administration. The results have been summed up by the historian Ari Hoogenboom: "An unprofessional civil service became more professionalized. Better educated civil servants were recruited and society accorded them a higher place . . . . Local political considerations gave way in civil servants' minds to the national concerns of a federal office. Business influence and ideals replaced those of the politician."

Arthur also took a moderate position on the tariff. He urged the appointment of a nonpartisan commission to study existing rates and to suggest rational reductions; when such a commission was created, he urged Congress to adopt its recommendations. He came out for federal regulation of railroads several years before the passage of the Interstate Commerce Act. "Congress should protect the people . . . against acts of injustice which the State governments are powerless to prevent," he said. He vetoed pork-barrel legislation and pushed for the much-needed construction of a modern navy. As an administrator he was systematic, thoughtful, businesslike, and at the same time cheerful and considerate. Just the same, he too was a political failure. He made no real attempt to push his program through Congress, instead devoting most of his energies to a futile effort to build up his personal following in the Republican party by distributing favors. But the Stalwarts would not forgive his "desertion," and the reform element could not forget his past. At the 1884 convention the politicos shunted him aside.

The election of 1884 brought the Democrat Grover Cleveland to the White House. Born in New Jersey in 1837, Cleveland grew up in western New York. After studying law, he settled in Buffalo. While somewhat lacking in the social graces and in intellectual pretensions, he had a basic integrity that everyone recognized; when a group of reformers sought a candidate for mayor in 1881, he was a natural choice. His success in Buffalo led to his election as governor of New York in 1882. In the governor's chair his no-nonsense attitude toward public administration endeared him to civil service reformers at the same time that his basic conservatism pleased businessmen. When he vetoed a popular bill to force a reduction of the fares charged by the New York City elevated railway on the ground that it was an unconstitutional violation of the company's franchise, his stock soared. Here was a man who cared more for principle than the adulation of the multitude, a man of

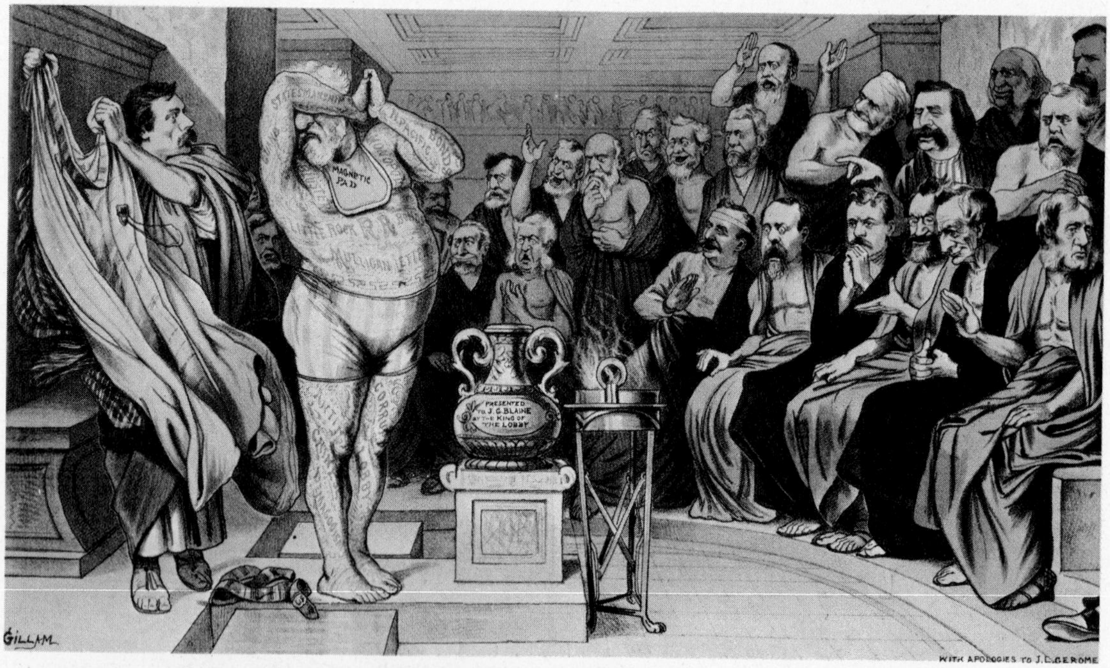

■ **Parodying a popular painting of the day of a beautiful Greek courtesan being unveiled before Athenian statesmen, *Puck*'s Bernhard Gillam drew James G. Blaine revealed to Republican leaders in 1884. The "Mulligan letters" receive prominent display among the tattoos, and Blaine's renowned personal magnetism is labeled as a fraud.**

courage, honest, hardworking, and eminently sound. The Democrats nominated him for president in 1884.

The election revolved around personal issues, for the platforms of the parties were almost identical. The Republican candidate, the dynamic James G. Blaine, had an immense following, but his reputation had been soiled by the publication of the "Mulligan letters," which connected him with the corrupt granting of congressional favors to the Little Rock and Fort Smith Railroad. On the other hand, it came out during the campaign that Cleveland, a bachelor, had fathered an illegitimate child. Instead of debating public issues, the Republicans chanted the ditty

> Ma! Ma! Where's my pa?
> Gone to the White House,
> *Ha! Ha! Ha!*

to which the Democrats countered

> Blaine, Blaine, James G. Blaine,
> The continental liar from the State of Maine.

Blaine lost more heavily in the mudslinging than Cleveland, whose quiet courage in saying "Tell the truth" when his past was brought to light contrasted favorably with Blaine's glib and unconvincing denials. A significant group of distinguished eastern Republicans, known as Mugwumps, campaigned for the Democrats.* However, Blaine ran a strong race against a general pro-Democratic trend; Cleveland won the election by fewer than 25,000 votes. The change of 600 ballots in New York would have given that state, and the presidency, to his opponent.

As a Democrat, Cleveland had no stomach for refighting the Civil War in every campaign. He did not overly favor the South when in office, thereby quieting Republican fears that a Democratic administration would fill Washington with unreconstructed rebels. Civil service reformers overestimated his commitment to their cause, for he believed in rotation in office, being as convinced as Andrew Jackson that anyone of "reasonable intelligence" could handle most government jobs. He would not summarily dismiss Republicans, but he thought that when they had served four years, they "should as a rule give way to good men of our party." He did, however, insist on honesty and efficiency regardless of party. As a result, he made few poor appointments.

Probably no president could have handled patronage problems much better, considering the times. The Democrats had been out of the White House since before the Civil War. They clamored for the spoils of victory. The Mugwumps, who had contributed considerably to Cleveland's election, were dead set against politicking with government jobs. Steering a middle course, Cleveland failed to satisfy either group.

Cleveland had little imagination and too narrow a conception of his powers and duties to be a successful president. His appearance perfectly reflected his character: a squat, burly man weighing well over 200 pounds, he could defend a position against heavy odds, yet his mind lacked flexibility and he provided little effective leadership. He took a fairly broad view of the powers of the federal government—he supported the Interstate Commerce Act and agricultural research, and he even came out for federal arbitration of labor disputes—but he thought it unseemly to put pressure on Congress, believing in "the entire independence of the executive and legislative branches."

As a mayor and a governor, Cleveland had been best known for his vetoes. Little wonder that he found being president a burdensome duty. Scarcely a year after his inauguration he was complaining of the "cursed constant grind." Later he grumbled about "the want of rest" and "the terrible nagging" he had to submit to. One of his biographers says that he "approached the presidency as though he were a martyr."

Toward the end of his term, Cleveland bestirred himself and tried to provide constructive leadership on the tariff question. The government was embarrassed by a large surplus revenue, which Cleveland hoped to reduce by cutting the duties on necessities and on raw materials used in manufacturing. He devoted his entire annual message of December 1887 to the tariff, thereby focusing public attention on the subject. When worried Democrats reminded him that an election was coming up and that the tariff might cause a rift in

*The Mugwumps considered themselves reformers, but on social and economic questions nearly all of them were very conservative. They were sound-money proponents and advocates of laissez faire. Reform to them consisted almost entirely of doing away with corruption and making the government more efficient.

■ **Even in an age when the well-fed look was the trademark of most politicians, Grover Cleveland's rotund form was exceptional.**

the organization, he replied simply: "What is the use of being elected or re-elected, unless you stand for something?"

The House of Representatives, dominated by southern Democrats, passed a bill reducing many duties, but the measure, known as the Mills bill, was flagrantly partisan: it slashed the rates on iron products, glass, wool, and other items made in the North and left those on southern goods almost untouched. The Republican-controlled Senate rejected the Mills bill, and the issue was left to be settled by the voters at the 1888 election. However, in a fashion typical of the period, it did not work out this way. The Democrats hedged by nominating a protectionist, 75-year-old Allen G. Thurman, for vice-president and putting another high-tariff man at the head of the Democratic National Committee. Cleveland toned down his attacks on the important protected industries.

Other issues attracted attention. In the "Murchison letter," Sir Lionel Sackville-West, the British minister at Washington, was tricked into expressing the opinion that the reelection of Cleveland would best advance the interests of Great Britain. This undoubtedly cost the Democrats the votes of many Irish-Americans, who were rabidly anti-British. Corruption was perhaps more flagrant than in any other presidential election. Cleveland obtained a plurality of the popular vote, but his opponent, Benjamin Harrison, grandson of President William Henry Harrison, carried most of the key northeastern industrial states by narrow margins, thereby obtaining a comfortable majority in the electoral college, 233 to 168.

The new president was a short, rather rotund but erect man with a full, graying beard, narrow blue eyes, and a broad forehead. Although intelligent and able, he was too reserved to make a good politician. He did not suffer fools gladly and kept even his most important advisers at arm's length. One observer called him a "human iceberg." Nevertheless, his career, like his ancestry, had been distinguished. After graduating from Miami University in 1852 at the age of 18, he studied law. He settled in Indiana, where for a number of years he was Indiana Supreme Court reporter, editing five volumes of *Reports* with considerable skill. During the Civil War he rose to command a brigade. He fought under Sherman at Atlanta and won a reputation as a stern, effective disciplinarian. In 1876 he ran unsuccessfully for governor of Indiana, but in 1881 he was elected to the Senate.

Harrison believed ardently in the principle of protection, stating firmly if illogically that he was against "cheaper coats" because cheaper coats seemed "necessarily to involve a cheaper man and woman under the coat." His approach to fiscal policy was conservative, though he was freehanded in the matter of veterans' pensions. He would not use "an apothecary's scale," he said, "to weigh the rewards of men who saved the country." No more flamboyant waver of the bloody shirt existed. "I would a thousand times rather march under the bloody shirt, stained with the lifeblood of a Union soldier," he said in 1883, "than to march under the black flag of treason or the white flag of cowardly compromise."

Harrison professed to favor civil service reform, but his biographer, Father Harry J. Sievers, admits that he fashioned a "singularly unimpressive" record on the question. He objected to the law forbidding the solicitation of campaign funds from officeholders. He appointed the vigorous young reformer Theodore Roosevelt to the Civil Service Commission and then proceeded to undercut him systematically. Before long the frustrated Roosevelt was calling the president a "cold blooded, narrow minded, prejudiced, obstinate, timid old psalm singing Indianapolis politician."

Under Harrison, Congress distinguished itself by expending, for the first time in a period of peace, more than $1 billion in a single session. It raised the tariff to an all-time high. The Sherman Antitrust Act was passed; so was a Silver Purchase Act authorizing the government to coin large amounts of that metal, a measure much desired by mining interests and those favoring inflation. A Federal Elections, or "Force" bill, providing for federal control of elections as a means of protecting the right of southern blacks to vote, a right increasingly under attack, passed the House only to be filibustered to death in the Senate.

Harrison had little to do with the fate of any of these measures. By and large he failed, as one historian has said, to give the people "magnetic and responsive leadership." The Republicans lost control of Congress in 1890, and two years later Grover Cleveland swept back into power, defeating Harrison by more than 350,000 votes.

Congressional Leaders

Among the lesser politicians of the period, the most outstanding was unquestionably James G. Blaine of Maine, who served in Congress from 1863 to 1881, first in the House and then in the Senate. Blaine had many of the qualities that mark a great leader: personal dynamism, imagination, political intuition, oratorical ability, and a broad view of the national interest. President Lincoln spotted him when he was a freshman congressman, calling him "one of the brightest men in the House" and "one of the coming men of the country."

Blaine was essentially a reasonable man. He favored sound money without opposing inflexibly every suggestion for increasing the volume of the currency. He supported the protective system yet advocated reciprocity agreements to increase trade. He adopted a moderate and tolerant attitude toward the South. Almost alone among the men of his generation, he was deeply interested in foreign affairs. His personal warmth captivated thousands. He never forgot a name. His handshake—he would grasp a visitor's hand firmly at a reception and often hold it throughout a brief conversation with unaffected, open friendliness—won him hundreds of adherents. This was perhaps calculated, yet he was capable of impulsive acts of generosity and kindness too.

That Blaine, though perennially an aspirant, never became president was in part a reflection of his very abilities and his participation in so many controversial affairs. Naturally, he aroused jealousies and made many enemies. But some inexplicable flaw marred his character. He had a streak of recklessness entirely out of keeping with his reasonable position on most issues. He waved the bloody shirt with cynical vigor, heedless of the effect on the nation as a whole. He showered contempt on civil service reformers, characterizing them as "noisy but not numerous . . . ambitious but not wise, pretentious but not powerful." The scandal of the Mulligan letters made a dark blot on his record, and there is reason to doubt his general honesty, for, as one historian has pointed out, he "became wealthy without visible means of support." Sometimes he seemed almost deliberately to injure himself by needlessly antagonizing powerful colleagues. Blaine moved through history amid cheers and won a host of spectacular if petty triumphs, yet his career was barren, essentially tragic.

Roscoe Conkling's was another remarkable but empty career. Handsome, colorful, companionable, and dignified, Conkling served in Congress almost continually from 1859 to 1881 and was a great power, dominating the complex politics of New York for many years. Such was his prestige that two presidents offered him a seat on the Supreme Court. Yet no measure of importance was attached to his name; he squandered his energies in acrimonious personal quarrels, caring only for partisan advantage. While he wanted very much to be president, he had no conception of what a president must be, and in the end even his own hack followers deserted him.

Dozens of other figures might be mentioned; the following are representative types.

Congressman William McKinley of Ohio was the most personally attractive. He was a man of simple honesty, nobility of character, quiet warmth—and a politician to the core. The tariff was McKinley's special competence, the principle of protection his guiding star. The peak of his career still lay in the future in the early 1890s.

Another Ohioan, John Sherman, brother of the famous Civil War general, accomplished the remarkable feat of holding national office continuously for nearly half a century, from 1855 to 1898. Three times a prominent candidate for the Republican presidential nomination, he had a deserved reputation for expertise in financial matters. However, he was colorless and stiff—he was called the Ohio Icicle—and altogether too willing to compromise his beliefs for political advantage. He admired Andrew Johnson and sympathized with his attitude toward reconstructing the South, yet he voted to convict him at the impeachment trial. Repeatedly he made concessions to the inflationists despite his belief in sound money. Sherman gave his name (and not much else) to the Antitrust Act of 1890 and to other important legislation, but in retrospect he left little mark on the history of the country despite his long service.

Thomas B. Reed, Republican congressman from Maine, was a witty, widely read man but ultraconservative and cursed with a sharp tongue that he could never curb. Reed coined the famous definition of a statesman: "a politician who is dead." When one pompous politico said in his presence that he would rather be right than president, Reed advised him not to worry, since he would never be either. In 1890 Reed was elected Speaker of the House and quickly won the nickname Czar because of his autocratic way of expediting business. Since the Republicans had only a paper-thin majority, the Democrats attempted to block action on partisan measures by refusing to answer to their names on quorum calls. Reed coolly ordered the clerk to record them as present and proceeded to carry on the business of the House. His control became so absolute that Washington jokesters said that representatives dared not breathe without his permission. Reed had large ambitions and the courage of his convictions, but his vindictiveness kept him from exercising a constructive influence on his times.

One of the most attractive Democratic politicians of the era was Richard P. "Silver Dick" Bland of Missouri, congressman from 1873 until the late nineties. While a young man Bland had spent ten years as a prospector and miner, and he devoted most of his energies in politics to fighting for the free coinage of silver. Although almost fanatical on this question, he was no mere mouthpiece for special interests; he fought monopolies and consistently opposed the protective tariff. He lived simply and was immune to the temptations that led so many colleagues to use their political influence to line their pockets. Yet he never became a truly national leader.

More colorful yet utterly sterile was the career of Benjamin F. Butler of Massachusetts. Butler was a political chameleon. A states' rights Democrat before the Civil War, he supported Jefferson Davis for the Democratic presidential nomination in 1860. During the conflict he served as a Union general, during reconstruction as a Radical Republican congressman. In 1878 he came out for currency inflation and won a seat in Congress as a Greenbacker. In 1882 he was elected governor of Massachusetts, this time as a Democrat! Butler had a sharp wit, a vivid imagination, a real feeling for the interests of industrial workers. He detested sham and pretense. He was also a brutal, corrupt demagogue, almost universally hated by persons of culture and public spirit. By no means a typical politician, Butler typified many aspects of the age—its shaky morality, its extremism, its intense interest in meaningless political controversy.

Agricultural Discontent

The vacuity of American politics may well have stemmed from the complacency of the middle-class majority. The country was growing; no foreign enemy threatened it; the poor were mostly recent immigrants, blacks, and others with little influence, who were easily ignored by those in comfortable circumstances. However, one important group in society suffered increasingly as the years rolled by: the farmers. Out of their travail came the force that finally, in the 1890s, brought American politics face to face with the problems of the age.

Long the backbone of American society, the farmer was rapidly being left behind in the race for wealth and status. The number of farmers and the volume of agricultural production continued to rise, but agriculture's relative place in the national economy was declining. Between 1860 and 1890 the number of farms rose from 2 million to 4.5 million, wheat output leaped from 173 million bushels to 449 million, cotton from 5.3 million bales to 8.5 million. The rural population increased from 25 million to 40.8 million. Yet industry was expanding far faster, and the urban population, quadrupling in the period, would soon overtake and pass that of the countryside. Immediately after the Civil War wheat sold at nearly $1.50 a bushel, and in the early 1870s it was still worth well over a dollar. By the mid 1890s the average price stood in the neighborhood of 60 cents. Cotton, the great southern staple, which sold for more than 30 cents a pound in 1866 and 15 cents in the early 1870s, at times in the nineties fell below 6 cents.

The tariff on manufactured goods appeared to aggravate the farmers' predicament, and so did the domestic marketing system, which enabled a multitude of middlemen to gobble up a large share of the profits of agriculture. The shortage of credit, particularly in the South, was an additional burden. Furthermore, the improvements in transportation that made it practicable for farmers in Australia, Canada, Russia, and Argentina to sell their produce in western European markets increased the competition faced by Americans seeking to dispose of surplus produce abroad.

Along with declining income, farmers suffered a decline in status. Compared to city dwellers, they seemed provincial and behind the times. Rural educational standards did not keep pace, modern concepts such as evolution were either ignored or rejected, and religious fundamentalism, cast aside by eastern sophisticates, maintained its hold in the countryside. People in the cities began to refer to farmers as "rubes," "hicks," and "hayseeds" and to view them with amused tolerance or even contempt.

This combination of circumstances angered and frustrated farmers. Waves of radicalism swept the agricultural regions, giving rise to demands for social and economic experiments that played a major role in breaking down rural laissez faire prejudices. As we have seen, in the 1870s pressure from the Patrons of Husbandry produced legislation regulating railroads and warehouses. This Granger movement also led to many cooperative experiments in the marketing of farm products and in the purchase of machinery, fertilizers, and other goods.

Farmers were not all affected by economic developments in the same way. Because of the steady decline of the price level, those in newly settled regions were usually worse off than those in older areas, since they had to borrow money to get started and were therefore burdened with fixed interest charges that became harder to meet each year. In the 1870s farmers in Illinois and Iowa suffered most—which accounts for the strength of the Granger movement in that region. Except as a purely social organization, the Grange had little importance in eastern states where farmers were relatively prosperous. However, by the late 1880s farmers in the old Middle West had become better established. When prices dipped and a general depression gripped the country, they were able to weather the bad times nicely, as Allan G. Bogue has shown. Illinois farmers took advantage of the new technology to increase output, shifting from wheat to the production of corn, oats, hogs, and cattle, which did not decline so drastically in price.

On the agricultural frontier from Texas to the Dakotas, and through the states of the old Confederacy, farmers were less fortunate. The burdens of the crop-lien system (see pages 407–408) kept thousands of southern farmers in penury. On the plains life was a succession of hardships—the backbreaking labor, the hazards of storm, drought, and insect plagues, and isolation and loneliness. Hamlin Garland, a writer of the naturalist school who grew up in the region, described conditions in graphic and moving terms in his autobiography, *A Son of the Middle Border* (1890), and in *Main-Travelled Roads* (1891). Life was particularly hard for farm women, who in addition to endless heavy chores were forced to endure drab, cheerless surroundings without the companionship of neighbors or the respites and stimulations of social life. After Garland's mother read the grim discussions of women's lot in *Main-Travelled Roads,* she wrote him: "You might have said more, but I'm glad you didn't. Farmers' wives have enough to bear as it is."

Throughout the middle eighties farmers on the

plains experienced boom conditions. Adequate rainfall produced bountiful harvests, credit was available, and property values rose rapidly. In the 1880s the population of Kansas increased by 43 percent, that of Nebraska by 134 percent, that of the Dakotas by 278 percent. This agricultural expansion contributed to the destruction of open-range cattle raising and changed the economy of cattle towns like Dodge City, which became more dependent for business on farmers than on cowboys and ranchers.

Speculative booms occur periodically in every frontier district; like all others, this one collapsed when settlers and investors took a more realistic look at the prospects of the region. In this case special circumstances turned the slump into a catastrophe. A succession of dry years shattered the hopes of the farmers. Then the downward swing of the business cycle in the early 1890s completed the devastation. Settlers who had paid more for their lands than they were worth and borrowed money at high interest rates to do so found themselves squeezed relentlessly. Thousands lost their farms and returned eastward, penniless and dispirited. The population of Nebraska increased by fewer than 4,000 persons in the entire decade of the nineties.

The Populist Movement

The agricultural depression triggered a new outburst of farm radicalism, the Alliance movement. Alliances were organizations of farmers' clubs, most of which had sprung up during the bad times of the late seventies. The first "Knights of Reliance" was founded in 1877 in Lampasas County, Texas. Under the name The Farmers Alliance this organization gradually expanded in northeastern Texas, and after 1885 it spread rapidly throughout the cotton states. Alliance leaders stressed cooperation. Their co-ops bought fertilizer and other

■ The western land boom reached a climax on April 22, 1889, when parts of Oklahoma were opened to settlers. Within a few hours nearly 2 million acres were claimed by hordes of "boomers." This photograph by an unknown photographer was taken a few weeks later in the boom town of Guthrie, whose sign painter was working overtime.

supplies in bulk and sold them at fair prices to members. They sought to market their crops cooperatively but could not raise the necessary capital from banks—with the result that some of them began to question the workings of the American financial and monetary system. They became economic and social radicals in the process. In the northern regions a similar though less influential alliance movement developed.

The alliances adopted somewhat differing policies, but all agreed that agricultural prices were too low, that transportation costs were too high, and that something was radically wrong with the nation's financial system. "There are three great crops raised in Nebraska," an angry rural editor proclaimed in 1890. "One is a crop of corn, one is a crop of freight rates, and one a crop of interest. One is produced by farmers who by sweat and toil farm the land. The other two are produced by men who sit in their offices and behind their bank counters and farm the farmers." All agreed on the need for political action if the lot of the agriculturalist was to be improved.

Although the state alliances of the Dakotas and Kansas joined the Southern Alliance in 1889, for a time local prejudices and conflicting interests prevented the formation of a single national organization. Northern farmers mostly voted Republican, southerners Democratic, and resentments created during the Civil War lingered in all sections. Cotton-producing southerners opposed the protective tariff; most northerners, fearing the competition of foreign grain producers, favored it. Railroad regulation and federal land policy seemed vital questions to northerners, financial reform loomed most important in southern eyes. Northerners were receptive to the idea of forming a third party, while southerners, wedded to the one-party system, preferred working to capture local Democratic machines.

The farm groups entered local politics in the 1890 elections. Convinced of the righteousness of their cause, they campaigned with tremendous fervor. The results were encouraging. In the South, Alliance-sponsored gubernatorial candidates won in Georgia, Tennessee, South Carolina, and Texas; 8 southern legislatures fell under Alliance control; 44 congressmen and 3 senators committed to Alliance objectives were sent to Washington. In the West, Alliance candidates swept Kansas and captured a majority in the Nebraska legislature and enough seats in Minnesota and South Dakota to hold the balance of power between the major parties.

Such success, coupled with the reluctance of the Republicans and Democrats to make concessions to their demands, encouraged Alliance leaders to create a new national party. By uniting southern and western farmers, they succeeded in breaking the sectional barrier erected by the Civil War. If they could recruit industrial workers, perhaps a real political revolution could be accomplished. In February 1892, farm leaders, representatives of the Knights of Labor, and various professional reformers, some 800 in all, met at St. Louis, organized the People's, or Populist party, and issued a call for a national convention to meet at Omaha in July.

That convention nominated General James B. Weaver of Iowa for president (with a one-legged Confederate veteran as his running mate) and drafted a platform that called for a graduated income tax and national ownership of railroads and the telegraph and telephone systems. A "subtreasury" plan that would permit farmers to hold nonperishable crops off the market when prices were low was also advocated. Under this proposal the government would make loans in the form of greenbacks to farmers, secured by crops held in storage in federal warehouses. When prices rose, the farmers could sell their crops and repay the loans. To further combat deflation, the platform demanded the unlimited coinage of silver and an increase in the money supply "to no less than $50 per capita." To make the government more responsive to public opinion, it urged the adoption of the initiative and referendum procedures and the election of United States senators by popular vote. To win the support of industrial workers the platform denounced the use of Pinkerton detectives in labor disputes and backed the 8-hour day and the restriction of "undesirable" immigration.

The Populists created, in the phrase of the historian Lawrence Goodwyn, "a multi-sectional institution of reform." They were not, however, revolutionaries. They saw themselves not as a persecuted minority but as a victimized majority betrayed by what would now be called the establishment. They were at most ambivalent about the

■ **Mary Elizabeth Lease, whose signature under this picture includes "Famous spellbinder," was a prominent Populist noted for her rallying cry to "raise less corn and more hell."**

free enterprise system, and they tended to attribute social and economic injustices not to built-in inequities in the system but to nefarious conspiracies organized by selfish interests in order to subvert the system.

The appearance of the new party was the most exciting and significant aspect of the presidential campaign of 1892, which saw Harrison and Cleveland refighting the election of 1888. The Populists put forth a host of colorful spellbinders: Tom Watson, a Georgia congressman whose temper was such that on one occasion he administered a beating to a local planter with the man's own riding crop; William A. Peffer, a senator from Kansas whose long beard and grave demeanor gave him the look of a Hebrew prophet; "Sockless Jerry" Simpson of Kansas, unlettered but full of grassroots shrewdness and wit, a former Greenbacker and an admirer of the Single Tax doctrine of Henry George; Ignatius Donnelly, "the Minnesota Sage," who claimed to be an authority on science, Shakespeare (he believed that Francis Bacon wrote the plays), and economics, and whose widely read novel, *Caesar's Column* (1891), pictured an America of the future wherein a handful of plutocrats tyrannized masses of downtrodden workers and serfs.

In the one-party South, Populist strategists sought to wean black farmers away from the ruling Democratic organization. Their competition forced the "subsidies" paid for black votes up to as much as a dollar—two days' wages. Southern black farmers had their own Colored Alliance, and even before 1892 their leaders had worked closely with the white alliances. Nearly a hundred black delegates had attended the Populist convention at St. Louis. Of course the blacks would be useless if they could not vote; therefore white Populist leaders opposed the southern trend toward disfranchising blacks and called for full civil rights for all.

In the Northwest the Populists assailed the "bankers' conspiracy" in unbridled terms. Ignatius Donnelly, running for governor of Minnesota, wrote another futuristic political novel, *The Golden Bottle,* made 150 speeches, and talked personally with 10,000 voters, vowing to make the campaign "the liveliest ever seen" in the state.

The results proved disappointing. Tom Watson lost his seat in Congress, and Donnelly ran a poor third in the Minnesota gubernatorial race. The Populists did sweep Kansas. They elected numbers of local officials in other western states and cast over a million votes for Weaver. But the effort to unite white and black farmers in the South failed miserably. Conservative Democrats, while continuing with considerable success to attract black voters, played on racial fears cruelly, insisting that the Populists sought to undermine white supremacy. Since most white Populists saw the alliance with blacks as at most a marriage of convenience—they did not really believe in racial equality or propose to do anything for black sharecroppers—this argument had a deadly effect. Elsewhere, even in the old centers of the Granger movement, the party made no significant impression. Urban workers remained aloof.

By standing firmly for conservative financial policies, Cleveland attracted considerable Republican support and won a solid victory over Harrison in the electoral college, 277 to 145. Weaver's electoral vote was 22.

Showdown on Silver

One conclusion that politicians reached on analyzing the 1892 returns was that the money question, particularly the controversy over the coinage of silver, was of paramount interest to the voters. Despite the wide-ranging appeal of the Populist platform, most of Weaver's strength came from the silver-mining states. On the other hand, Cleveland's strong stand for gold proved popular in the Northeast.

In truth, the issue of gold versus silver was superficial; the important question was what, if anything, should be done to check the deflationary spiral. The declining price level benefited bondholders and others with fixed incomes, and injured debtors. Industrial workers profited from deflation except during periods of depression, when unemployment rose—which helps explain why the Populists made little headway among them. Southern farmers, prisoners of the crop-lien system, and farmers in the plains states were hit hard by the downward trend.

By the early 1890s, discussion of federal monetary policy revolved around the coinage of silver. Traditionally the United States had been on a bimetallic standard. Both gold and silver were coined, the number of grains of each in the dollar being adjusted periodically to reflect the commercial value of the two metals. An act of 1792 established a 15:1 ratio—371.25 grains of silver and 24.75 grains of gold were each worth one dollar at the Mint. In 1834 the ratio was changed to 16:1, and in 1853 to 14.8:1, the latter reduction in the value of gold reflecting the new discoveries in California. This ratio slightly undervalued silver. In 1861, for example, the amount of silver bullion in a dollar was worth $1.03 in the open market, so no one took silver to the Mint for coinage. However, an avalanche of silver from the mines of Nevada and Colorado gradually depressed the price until, around 1874, it again became profitable for miners to coin their bullion. Alas, when they tried to do so, they discovered that the Coinage Act of 1873, taking account of the fact that no silver had been presented to the Mint in years, had demonetized the metal.

The silver miners denounced this "Crime of 1873," and inflationists, who wanted more money put into circulation regardless of its base, joined them in demanding a return to bimetallism. Conservatives, still fighting the battle against greenback paper money, resisted strongly. The result was a series of compromises. In 1878 the Bland-Allison Act authorized the purchase of $2 million to $4 million of silver a month at the market price, but this had little inflationary effect because the government consistently purchased the minimum amount. The commercial price of silver continued to fall; in 1890 its ratio to gold was 20:1. In that year the Sherman Silver Purchase Act required the government to buy 4.5 million *ounces* of silver monthly, but in the face of increasing supplies the price of silver fell still further. The ratio reached 26:1 in 1893 and 32:1 in 1894.

The compromises satisfied no one. Silver miners grumbled because their bullion brought in only half what it had in the early seventies. Debtors noted angrily that because of the general decline of prices, the dollars they used to meet their obligations were worth more than twice as much as in 1865. Advocates of the gold standard feared that unlimited silver coinage would be authorized, "destroying the value of the dollar." When a financial panic brought on by the collapse of the London banking house of Baring Brothers ushered in a severe industrial depression, the confidence of both silverites and "gold bugs" was further eroded.

President Cleveland believed that the controversy over silver had caused the depression by shaking the confidence of the business community and that all would be well if the country returned to a single gold standard. He summoned a special session of Congress, and by exerting immense political pressure obtained the repeal of the Sherman Silver Purchase Act in October 1893. All that this accomplished was to split the Democratic party, its southern and western wings deserting him almost to a man.

During 1894 and 1895, while the nation floundered in the worst depression it had ever experienced, a series of events further undermined public confidence. In the spring of 1894 an "army" of unemployed led by Jacob S. Coxey, an eccentric Ohio businessman, marched on Washington to demand relief. Coxey wanted the government to undertake a program of federal public works and to authorize local communities to exchange noninterest-bearing bonds with the Treasury for $500 million in paper money, the funds to be used to hire unemployed workers to build roads. The

■ **Mutiny aboard the good ship *Democracy*, as seen by W.A. Rogers of *Harper's Weekly*, 1894. Civil Service and tariff reform (along with one of its advocates) are about to be thrown overboard, the Tammany tiger gorges himself, and, at the stern, Captain Cleveland cuts loose mutineers promoting a silver-purchase bill.**

scheme, Coxey claimed, would pump money into the economy, provide work for the jobless, and benefit the entire nation by improving transportation facilities. When Coxey's group of demonstrators, perhaps 500 in all, reached Washington, he and two other leaders were arrested for trespassing on the grounds of the Capitol. Their followers were dispersed by club-wielding policemen. This callous treatment convinced many Americans that the government had little interest in the suffering of the people, an opinion strengthened when Cleveland, in July 1894, used federal troops to crush the Pullman strike.

The next year the Supreme Court handed down several reactionary decisions. In *United States* v. *E. C. Knight Company* it refused to employ the Sherman Antitrust Act to break up the Sugar Trust. In *Pollock* v. *Farmers' Loan and Trust Company* it invalidated a federal income tax law despite the fact that a similar measure levied during the Civil War had been upheld by the Court in *Springer* v. *United States* (1881). Finally, the Court denied a writ of habeas corpus to Eugene V. Debs of the American Railway Union, who had been imprisoned for disobeying a federal injunction during the Pullman strike.

On top of these indications of official conservatism came a desperate financial crisis. Throughout 1894 the Treasury's supply of gold dwindled as worried citizens exchanged greenbacks (now convertible into gold) for hard money and foreign investors cashed in large amounts of American securities. The government tried to sell bonds for gold to bolster the reserve, but since most investors purchased the bonds with gold-backed paper money, in effect withdrawing gold from the Treasury and then returning it for the bonds, the gold reserve continued to melt away. Early in 1895 it touched a lowpoint of $41 million. At this juncture a syndicate of bankers headed by J. P. Morgan turned the tide by underwriting a $62 million bond issue, guaranteeing that half the gold would come from Europe. This caused a great public outcry; the spectacle of the nation being saved from bankruptcy by a private banker infuriated millions.

These events, together with the continuing depression, discredited the Cleveland administration. "I haven't got words to say what I think of that old bag of beef," Governor "Pitchfork Ben" Tillman of South Carolina, who had resolutely resisted the Populists in 1892, told a local audience two years later. "If you send me to the Senate, I promise I won't be bulldozed by him."

As the presidential election of 1896 approached, with the Populists demanding unlimited coinage of silver at a ratio of 16:1, the major parties found it impossible to continue straddling the money question. The Populist vote had increased by 42 percent in the 1894 congressional elections. Southern and western Democratic leaders feared that they would lose their entire following unless Cleveland was repudiated. Western Republicans, led by Senator Henry M. Teller of Colorado, were threatening to bolt to the Populists unless their party came out for silver coinage. After a generation of political equivocation, the major parties had to face an important issue squarely.

The Republicans, meeting to choose a candidate at St. Louis in June 1896, announced for the gold standard. "We are unalterably opposed to every measure calculated to debase our currency or impair the credit of our country," the platform declared. "We are therefore opposed to the free coinage of silver. . . . The existing gold standard must be maintained." The party then nominated Ohio's William McKinley for president. McKinley, best known for his staunch advocacy of the protective tariff yet highly regarded by labor, was expected to run strongly in the Middle West and East.

The Democratic convention met in July at Chicago. The pro-gold Cleveland element made a hard fight, but the silverites swept them aside. The highpoint came when a youthful Nebraskan named William Jennings Bryan spoke for silver against gold, for western farmers against the industrial East. Bryan's every sentence provoked ear-shattering applause.

> We have petitioned [he said] and our petitions have been scorned; we have entreated, and our entreaties have been disregarded; we have begged, and they have mocked when our calamity came. We beg no longer; we entreat no more; we petition no more. *We defy them!*

The crowd responded like a great choir to Bryan's oratorical cues. "Burn down your cities and leave our farms," he said, "and your cities will spring up again as if by magic; but destroy our farms and the grass will grow in the streets of every city in the country." He ended with a marvelous figure of speech that set the tone for the coming campaign. "You shall not press down upon the brow of labor this crown of thorns," he warned, bringing his hands down suggestively to his temples. "You shall not crucify mankind upon a cross of gold!" Dramatically, he extended his arms to the side, the very figure of the crucified Christ.

The convention promptly adopted a platform calling for "the free and unlimited coinage of both silver and gold at the present legal ratio of 16 to 1" and went on to nominate Bryan, who was barely 36, for president.

This action put tremendous pressure on the Populists. If they supported Bryan, they risked losing their party identity; if they nominated another man, they would insure McKinley's election. Those more concerned with immediate political advantage, especially holders of and seekers after office, took the former position. Those (mostly old Alliance members raised in the cooperative movement) who considered free silver a minor issue and a poor substitute for the subtreasury plan as an approach to the deflation problem, rejected "fusion" with the Democrats. "The Democratic idea of fusion," Tom Watson complained, is "that we play Jonah while they play whale." In part because the delegates could not find a person of stature willing to become a candidate against him, the Populist convention nominated Bryan, seeking to preserve the party identity by substituting Watson for the Democratic vice-presidential nominee, Arthur Sewall of Maine.

Election of 1896

Never did a presidential campaign raise such intense emotions or produce such drastic political realignments. The Republicans from the silver-mining states swung solidly behind Bryan. The gold Democrats refused to accept the decision of the Chicago convention. Cleveland professed to be "so dazed by the political situation that I am in no condition for speech or thought on the subject." Many others adopted the policy of Governor David B. Hill of New York, who said, "I am a Democrat still—very still." The extreme gold bugs, calling themselves National Democrats, nominated their own candidate, 79-year-old Senator John M. Palmer of Illinois. Palmer ran only to injure Bryan. "Fellow Democrats," he announced, "I will not consider it any great fault if you decide to cast your vote for William McKinley."

At the start the Republicans seemed to have everything in their favor. Bryan's youth and relative lack of political experience—two terms in the House—contrasted unfavorably with McKinley's distinguished war record, his long service in Congress and as governor of Ohio, and his reputation for honesty and good judgment. The severe depression operated in favor of the party out of power, although by repudiating Cleveland, the Democrats escaped much of the burden of explaining away his errors. The newspapers came out almost unanimously for the Republicans. Important Democratic papers such as the New York *World,* the Boston *Herald,* the Baltimore *Sun,* the Chicago *Chronicle,* and the Richmond *Times* supported McKinley editorially and even slanted news stories against the Democrats. The New York *Times* accused Bryan of being insane, his affliction being variously classified as "paranoia querulenta," "graphomania," and "oratorical monomania." The Democrats had very little money and few well-known speakers to fight the campaign.

But Bryan proved a formidable opponent. Casting aside tradition, he took to the stump personally, traveling 18,000 miles and making over 600 speeches. He was one of the greatest of orators. A big, handsome man with a voice capable of carrying without strain to the far corners of a great hall yet equally effective before a cluster of auditors at a rural crossroads, he projected an image of absolute sincerity without appearing fanatical or argumentative. At every major stop on his tour, huge crowds assembled. In Minnesota he packed the 10,000-seat St. Paul Auditorium, while thousands more milled in the streets outside. His energy was amazing, his charm and good humor unfailing. At one whistle stop, while he was shaving in his compartment, a small group outside the train began

■ **These oval portrait heads appeared on 1896 campaign posters. The Bryan poster included the full text of his Cross of Gold speech, and McKinley's poster contained pro-tariff, anti-free trade propaganda.**

clamoring for a glimpse of him. Flinging open the window and beaming through the lather, he shook hands cheerfully with each of the admirers. Everywhere he hammered away at the money question. Yet he did not totally neglect other issues. He was defending, he said, "all the people who suffer from the operations of trusts, syndicates, and combines."

McKinley's campaign was managed by a new type of politician, Marcus Alonzo Hanna, an Ohio businessman. In a sense Hanna was a product of the Pendleton Civil Service Act. When deprived of the contributions of officeholders, the parties turned to business for funds, and Hanna was one of the first leaders with a foot in both camps. Politics fascinated him, and despite his wealth and wide interests he was willing to labor endlessly at the routine work of political organization.

Hanna aspired to be a kingmaker and early fastened upon McKinley, whose charm he found irresistible, as the vehicle for satisfying his ambition. He spent about $100,000 of his own money on the preconvention campaign. His attitude toward the candidate, one mutual friend observed, was "that of a big, bashful boy toward the girl he loves."

Before most Republicans realized how effective Bryan was on the stump, Hanna perceived the danger and sprang into action. Since the late 1880s the character of political organization had been changing. The Civil Service Act was also cutting down on the number of jobs available to reward campaign workers. At the same time, the new mass-circulation newspapers and the nationwide press associations were increasing the pressure on candidates to speak openly and often on national issues. This trend put a premium on party organization and consistency—the old political trick of speaking out of one side of the mouth to one audience, out the other to another, no longer worked very well. The old military metaphors of political discourse, the terms "campaign" and "spoils" and "standard bearer," remained, but others more businesslike became popular: "boss," "machine," "lobbyist."

As the federal government became more involved in economic issues, business interests found more reason to be concerned about national elections and were more willing to spend money in behalf of candidates whose views they approved. In the campaign of 1888 the Republicans had set up a businessmen's "advisory board" to raise money and stir up enthusiasm for Benjamin Harrison.

Hanna understood what was happening to politics. Certain that money was the key to political power, he raised an enormous campaign fund. When businessmen hesitated to contribute, he pried open their purses by a combination of persuasiveness and intimidation. Banks and insurance companies were "assessed" a percentage of their assets, big corporations a share of their receipts, until some $3.5 million had been collected. Hanna disbursed these funds with efficiency and imagination. He sent 1,500 speakers into the doubtful districts and blanketed the land with 250 million pieces of campaign literature, printed in a dozen languages. "He has advertised McKinley as if he were a patent medicine," Theodore Roosevelt exclaimed.

Incapable of competing with Bryan as a swayer of mass audiences, McKinley conducted a "front-porch campaign." This technique dated from the first Harrison-Cleveland election, when Harrison regularly delivered off-the-cuff speeches to groups of visitors representing special interests or regions in his home town of Indianapolis. The system conserved the candidate's energies and enabled him to avoid the appearance of seeking the presidency too openly—which was still considered bad form—and at the same time allowed him to make headlines throughout the country.

Guided by the masterful Hanna, McKinley brought the front-porch method to perfection. Superficially the proceedings were delightfully informal. From every corner of the land, groups representing various regions, occupations, and interests descended on McKinley's unpretentious frame house in Canton, Ohio. Gathering on the lawn—the grass was soon reduced to mud, the fence stripped of pickets by souvenir hunters—the visitors paid their compliments to the candidate and heard him deliver a brief speech, while beside him on the porch his aged mother and adoring invalid wife listened with rapt attention. Then there was a small reception, during which the delegates were given an opportunity to shake their host's hand.

Despite the air of informality, these performances were carefully staged. The delegations arrived on a tightly coordinated schedule worked out by McKinley's staff and the railroads, which operated cut-rate excursion trains to Canton from

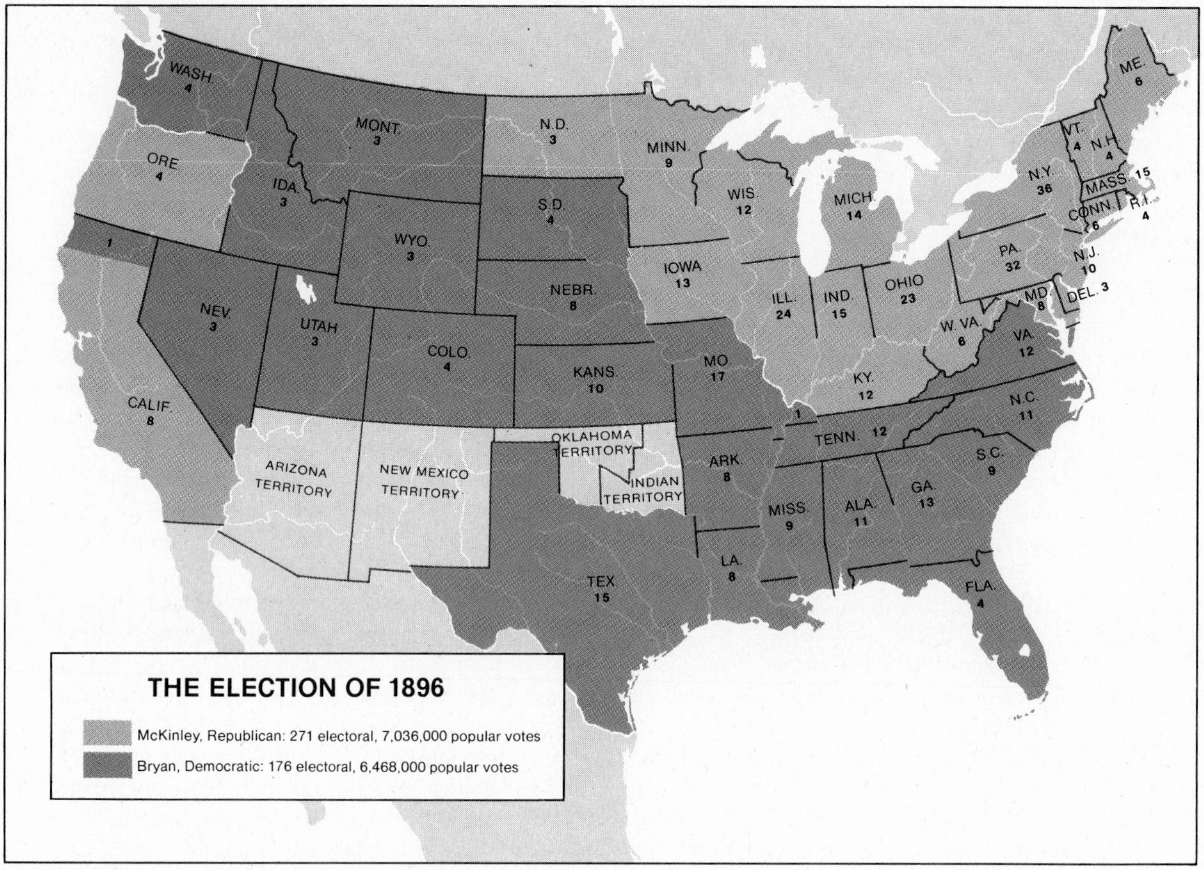

all over the nation. McKinley was fully briefed on the special interests and attitudes of each group, and the speeches of delegation leaders were submitted in advance. Often his secretary amended these remarks, and on occasion McKinley wrote the visitors' speeches himself. His own talks were carefully prepared in advance, each calculated to make a particular point. All were reported fully in the newspapers. Thus, without moving from his doorstep, McKinley met thousands of people from every section.

These tactics worked admirably. On election day McKinley carried the East, the Middle West, including even Iowa, Minnesota, and North Dakota, and the Pacific Coast states of Oregon and California. Bryan won in the South, the plains states, and the Rocky Mountain region. McKinley collected 271 electoral votes to Bryan's 176, the popular vote being 7,036,000 to 6,468,000.

The sharp sectional division marked the failure of the Populist effort to unite northern and southern farmers and also the triumph of the industrial part of the country over the agricultural. Business and financial interests voted solidly for the Republicans, fearing that a Democratic victory would bring economic chaos. When a Nebraska landowner tried to float a mortgage during the campaign, a loan company official wrote him: "If McKinley is elected, we think we will be in the market, but we do not care to make any investments while there is an uncertainty as to what kind of money a person will be paid back in."

Other social and economic interests were far from being united. Many thousands of farmers voted for McKinley, as his success in states such as North Dakota, Iowa, and Minnesota proved. In the East and in the states bordering the Great Lakes, the agricultural depression was not severe and farm radicalism was almost nonexistent.

A preponderance of the labor vote went to the Republicans. In part this resulted from the tremendous pressures that many industrialists applied to their workers. "Men," one manufacturer announced, "vote as you please, but if Bryan is elected . . . the whistle will not blow Wednesday morning." Some companies placed orders for materials subject to cancellation if the Democrats won. Yet coercion was not a major factor, for McKinley was highly regarded in labor circles. While governor of Ohio, he had advocated the arbitration of industrial disputes and backed a law fining employers who refused to permit workers to join unions. During the Pullman strike he had sent his brother to try to persuade George Pullman to deal fairly with the strikers. He had invariably based his advocacy of high tariffs on the argument that American wage levels would be depressed if foreign goods could enter the country untaxed. Mark Hanna too had the reputation of always giving his employees a square deal. The Republicans carried nearly all the large cities, and in critical states such as Illinois and Ohio this made the difference between victory and defeat.

During the campaign, some frightened Republicans had laid plans for fleeing the country if Bryan were elected, and belligerent ones, such as Theodore Roosevelt, then police commissioner of New York City, readied themselves to meet the "social revolutionaries" on the battlefield. Victory sent such people into transports of joy. Most conservatives concluded that the way of life they so fervently admired had been saved for all time.

However heartfelt, such sentiments were not founded on fact. With workers standing beside capitalists and with the farmers divided, it cannot be said that the election divided the nation class against class or that McKinley's victory saved the country from revolution.

Far from representing a triumph for the status quo, the election marked the coming of age of modern America. The battle between gold and silver, which everyone had considered so vital, had little real significance. The inflationists seemed to have been beaten, but new gold discoveries in Alaska and South Africa and improved methods of extracting gold from low-grade ores soon led to a great expansion of the money supply. In any case, within two decades the system of basing the volume of currency on bullion had been abandoned. Bryan and the "political" Populists who supported him, supposedly the advance agents of revolution, were oriented more toward the past than the future; their ideal was the rural America of Jefferson and Jackson.

McKinley, for all his innate conservatism, was capable of looking ahead toward the new century. His approach was national where Bryan's was basically parochial. While never daring and seldom imaginative, he was able to deal pragmatically with current problems. Before long, as the United States became increasingly an exporter of manufactures, he would even modify his position on the tariff. And no one better reflected the spirit of the age than Mark Hanna, the outstanding political realist of his generation. Far from preventing change, the outcome of the election of 1896 made possible still greater changes as the United States moved into the 20th century.

SUPPLEMENTARY READING

Titles marked with an asterisk have been published in paperback

The political history of this period is covered in lively and controversial fashion by Matthew Josephson, **The Politicos*** (1938), in briefer but equally controversial style by Ray Ginger, **Age of Excess*** (1965), and more solidly and sympathetically in H. W. Morgan, **From Hayes to McKinley** (1969). Both H. U. Faulkner, **Politics, Reform, and Expansion*** (1959), and J. R. Hollingsworth, **The Whirligig of Politics** (1963), treat the politics of the nineties in some detail, while H. S. Merrill, **Bourbon Democracy of the Middle West*** (1953), Samuel McSeveney, **The Politics of Depression: Political Behavior in the Northeast** (1972), and C. V. Woodward, **Origins of the New South*** (1951), are important regional studies. J. A. Garraty, **The New Commonwealth*** (1968), attempts to trace the changing character of the political system after 1877. See also R. D. Marcus, **Grand Old Party: Political Structure in the Gilded Age** (1971).

There are three superb analyses of the political system of the period written by men who studied it firsthand: James Bryce, **The American Commonwealth*** (1888), Woodrow Wilson, **Congressional Government*** (1886), and Moisei Ostrogorski, **Democracy and the Organization of Political Parties*** (1902). Morton Keller, **Affairs of State** (1977), is an interesting analysis of "public life" in the period. L. D. White, **The Republican**

Era* (1958), is an excellent study of the government in that period. D. J. Rothman, **Politics and Power: The United States Senate, 1869–1901*** (1966), analyzes the shifting structure of the upper house. R. J. Jensen, **The Winning of the Midwest** (1971), and Paul Kleppner, **The Cross of Culture: A Social Analysis of Midwestern Politics** (1970), are important studies based on modern computer techniques.

The issues of postreconstruction politics are discussed in P. H. Buck, **The Road to Reunion*** (1937), S. P. Hirshson, **Farewell to the Bloody Shirt*** (1962), J. W. Oliver, **History of the Civil War Military Pensions** (1917), F. W. Taussig, **The Tariff History of the United States*** (1914), D. R. Dewey, **Financial History of the United States** (1918), Allen Weinstein, **Prelude to Populism: Origins of the Silver Issue** (1970), Irwin Unger, **The Greenback Era*** (1964), Milton Friedman and A. J. Schwartz, **A Monetary History of the United States*** (1963), W. T. K. Nugent, **Money and American Society** (1968), Geoffrey Blodgett, **The Gentle Reformers: Massachusetts Democracy in the Cleveland Era** (1966), J. G. Sproat, **"The Best Men": Liberal Reformers in the Gilded Age** (1968), Ari Hoogenboom, **Outlawing the Spoils** (1961), and in several essays in H. W. Morgan (ed.), **The Gilded Age*** (1970).

Among biographies of political leaders, the following are especially worth consulting: Harry Barnard, **Rutherford B. Hayes and His America** (1954), R. G. Caldwell, **James A. Garfield** (1931), G. F. Howe, **Chester A. Arthur** (1934), Allan Nevins, **Grover Cleveland** (1932), H. S. Merrill, **Bourbon Leader: Grover Cleveland and the Democratic Party*** (1957), H. J. Sievers, **Benjamin Harrison** (1952–1968), H. W. Morgan, **William McKinley and His America** (1963), D. S. Muzzey, **James G. Blaine** (1934), and D. M. Jordan, **Roscoe Conkling** (1971).

For the farmers' problems, see F. A. Shannon, **The Farmer's Last Frontier*** (1945), S. J. Buck, **The Granger Movement*** (1913), J. D. Hicks, **The Populist Revolt*** (1931), and Theodore Saloutos, **Farmer Movements in the South*** (1960). Populism has been the subject in recent years of intensive reexamination. Richard Hofstadter, **The Age of Reform*** (1955), takes a dim view of Populism as a reform movement, while Norman Pollack, **The Populist Response to Industrial America*** (1962), pictures it as a radical one. W. T. K. Nugent, **The Tolerant Populists** (1963), leans in Pollack's direction but is more restrained. Lawrence Goodwyn, **Democratic Promise: The Populist Movement in America** (1976), rejects both positions, calling it "a people's movement of mass democratic aspiration." Both it and R. W. Cherny, **Populism, Progressivism, and the Transformation of Nebraska Politics** (1981), treat the differences between populism and early 20th-century reform. Sheldon Hackney's **Populism to Progressivism in Alabama** (1969) is more than a merely local study. C. V. Woodward, **Tom Watson: Agrarian Rebel*** (1938), and Martin Ridge, **Ignatius Donnelly: Portrait of a Politician** (1962), are excellent biographies of Populist leaders. F. E. Haynes, **James Baird Weaver** (1919), is also useful.

On the depression of the 1890s, consult Rendigs Fels, **American Business Cycles** (1959). The political and social disturbances connected with the depression are discussed in G. H. Knoles, **The Presidential Campaign and Election of 1892** (1942), Allan Nevins, **Grover Cleveland,** D. L. McMurry, **Coxey's Army** (1929), Almont Lindsey, **The Pullman Strike*** (1942), Ray Ginger, **The Bending Cross: Eugene V. Debs*** (1949) and **Altgeld's America*** (1958), and F. L. Allen, **The Great Pierpont Morgan*** (1949).

For the election of 1896, in addition to the books on Populism, see S. L. Jones, **The Presidential Election of 1896** (1964), R. F. Durden, **The Climax of Populism: The Election of 1896*** (1965), and P. W. Glad, **McKinley, Bryan, and the People*** (1964). On Bryan, consult Glad's **The Trumpet Soundeth*** (1960), and P. E. Coletta, **William Jennings Bryan** (1964); on McKinley, consult L. L. Gould, **The Presidency of William McKinley** (1980), and Herbert Croly, **Marcus Alonzo Hanna** (1912), the best life of Hanna.

22/FROM ISOLATION TO EMPIRE

Americans have always been somewhat ambivalent in their attitudes toward other nations, and at no time was this more clearly the case than in the decades following the Civil War. Occupied with exploiting the West and building their great industrial machine, they gave little thought to foreign affairs. Benjamin Harrison reflected a widely held belief when he said during the 1888 presidential campaign that the United States was "an apart nation" and so it should remain. James Bryce made the same point in *The American Commonwealth.* "Happy America," he wrote, stood "apart in a world of her own . . . safe even from menace."

The historian David W. Pletcher has called the period "the awkward age" of American diplomacy, a time when the foreign service was "amateurish" and "spoils-ridden," when policy was either nonexistent or poorly planned, when treaties were clumsily drafted and state secrets ill kept. "The general idea of the diplomatic service," one reporter commented at this time, "is that it is a soft berth for wealthy young men who enjoy court society." An important New York newspaper, the *Sun*, suggested in the 1880s that the State Department had "outgrown its usefulness" and ought to be abolished.

America's Divided View of the World

Late 19th-century Americans never ignored world affairs entirely. They had little direct concern for what went on in Europe, but their interest in Latin America was great and growing, in the Far East only somewhat less so. Economic developments, especially shifts in foreign commerce resulting from industrialization, strengthened this interest with every passing year. Whether one sees isolation or expansion as the hallmark of American foreign policy after 1865 depends on what part of the world one looks at.

The disdain of the people of the United States for Europe rested on several historical foundations. Faith in the unique character of American civilization—and the converse of that belief, suspicion of Europe's supposedly aristocratic and decadent society—formed the chief basis of this isolation. Bitter memories of indignities suffered during the Revolution and the Napoleonic wars and anger at the hostile attitude of the great powers toward the United States during the Civil War strengthened it, as did the dislike of Americans for the pomp and punctilio of European monarchies. Also important was the undeniable truth that the United States was practically invulnerable to European attack and at the same time incapable of mounting an offensive against any European power. In turning their backs on Europe, Americans were taking no risk and passing up few opportunities—hence their indifference.

When occasional conflicts with one or another of the great powers erupted, the United States pressed its claims hard. It insisted, for example, that Great Britain pay for the loss of some 100,000 tons of American shipping sunk by Confederate cruisers that had been built in British yards during the rebellion. Some politicians even demanded that the British pay for the entire cost of the war after the Battle of Gettysburg—some $2 billion—on the ground that without British backing the Confederacy would have collapsed at about that point. However, the controversy never became critical, and in 1871 the two nations signed the Treaty of Washington, agreeing to arbitrate the so-called *Alabama* claims. The next year the judges awarded the United States $15.5 million for the ships and cargoes that had been destroyed.

In the 1880s a squabble developed with Germany, France, and a number of other countries over their banning of American pork products, ostensibly because some uninspected American pork was discovered to be diseased. The affair produced a great deal of windy oratory denouncing European autocracy and led to threats of economic retaliation. Congress eventually provided for the inspection of meat destined for export, and in 1891 the European nations lifted the ban. Similarly, there were repeated alarms and outbursts of anti-British feeling in the United States in connection with Great Britain's treatment of Ireland—all motivated chiefly by the desire of politicians to appeal to Irish-American voters. None of the incidents amounted to much.

The nation's interests elsewhere in the world gradually increased. During the Civil War France had established a protectorate over Mexico, installing the Archduke Maximilian of Austria as emperor. In 1866 Secretary of State William H. Seward demanded that the French withdraw, and the government moved 50,000 soldiers to the Rio Grande. While fear of American intervention was only one of many reasons for their action, the French pulled their troops out of Mexico during the winter of 1866–1867. Nationalist rebels promptly seized and executed Maximilian. In 1867, at the instigation of Seward, the United States purchased Alaska from Russia for $7.2 million, thereby ridding the continent of another foreign power.

In 1867 the aggressive Seward acquired the Midway Islands in the western Pacific, which had been discovered in 1859 by an American naval officer, N. C. Brooks. Steward also made overtures toward annexing the Hawaiian Islands, and he looked longingly at Cuba. In 1870 President Grant submitted to the Senate a treaty annexing the Dominican Republic. He applied tremendous pressure in an effort to obtain ratification, thus forcing

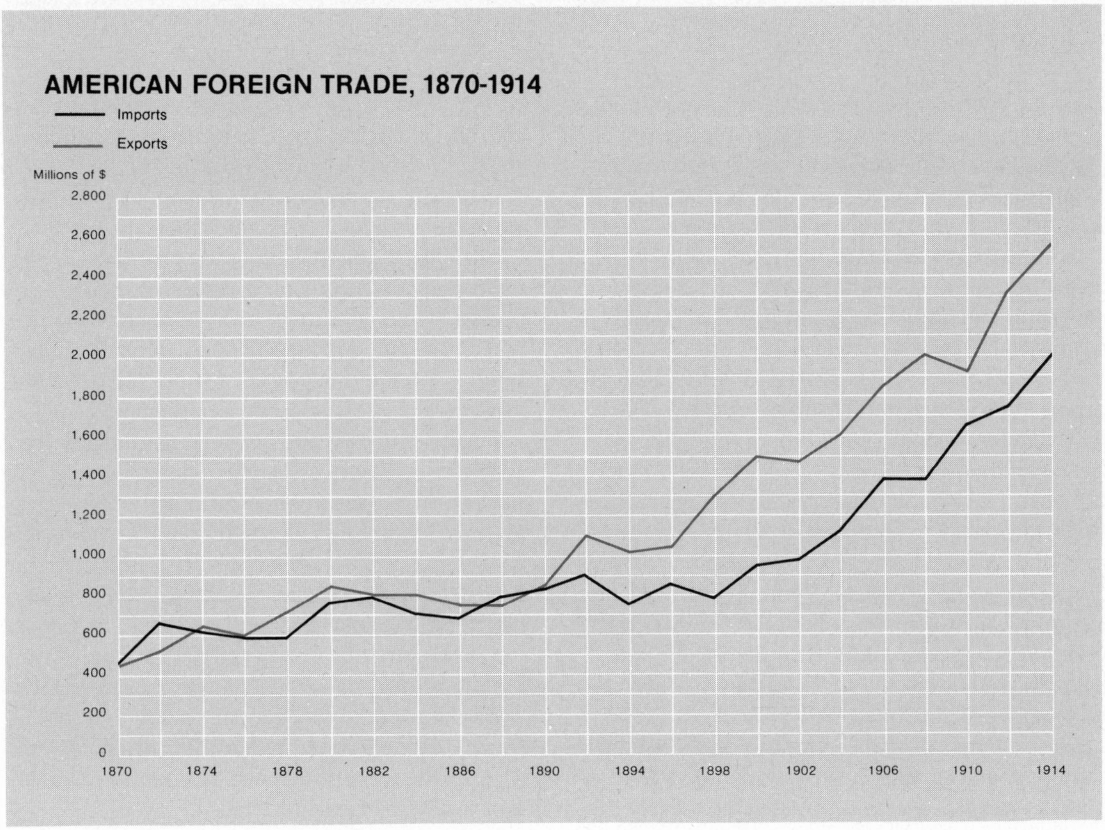

a "great debate" on extracontinental expansion. Expansionists stressed the wealth and resources of the country, the markets it would provide, even its "salubrious climate." But the arguments of the opposition proved more persuasive. The distance of the Dominican Republic from the continent, its crowded, dark-skinned population of what one congressman called "semi-civilized, semi-barbarous men who cannot speak our language," made annexation appear unattractive. The treaty was rejected. Seward had to admit that there was no significant support in the country for his expansionist plans. Prevailing opinion was well summarized by a Philadelphia newspaper: "The true interests of the American people will be better served . . . by a thorough and complete development of the immense resources of our existing territory than by any rash attempts to increase it."

The internal growth that preoccupied Americans eventually led them to look outward. By the late 1880s the country was exporting a steadily increasing share of its agricultural and industrial output. Exports, only $450 million in 1870, passed the billion-dollar mark early in the 1890s. Imports increased at a rate only slightly less spectacular.

The character of foreign trade was also changing: manufactures loomed ever more important among exports until in 1898 the country shipped abroad more manufactured goods than it imported. By this time American steelmakers could compete with British producers anywhere in the world. In 1900 one American firm received a large order for steel plates from a Glasgow shipbuilder, and another won contracts for structural steel to be used in constructing bridges for the Uganda Railroad in British East Africa. When a member of Parliament questioned the colonial secretary about the latter deal, the secretary replied: "Tenders [bids] were invited in the United Kingdom . . . [but] one of the American tenders was found to be considerably the lowest in every respect and was therefore accepted." When American industrialists became conscious of their ability to compete with Europeans in far-off markets, they took more interest in world affairs, particularly during periods of depression, when domestic consumption fell.

Shifting intellectual currents further altered the attitudes of Americans. Darwin's theories, applicable by analogy to international relations, gave the concept of manifest destiny a new plausibility. Darwinists like the historian John Fiske argued that the American democratic system of government was so clearly the world's "fittest" that it was destined to spread peacefully over "every land on the earth's surface." In *Our Country* Josiah Strong found racist and religious justifications for American expansionism, again based on the theory of evolution. The Anglo-Saxon race, centered now in the United States, possessed "an instinct or genius for colonization," Strong claimed. "God, with infinite wisdom and skill is training the Anglo-Saxon race for . . . *the final competition of races.*" Christianity, he added, had developed "aggressive traits calculated to impress its institutions upon mankind." Soon American civilization would "move down upon" Mexico and all Latin America, and "out upon the islands of the sea, over upon Africa and beyond." "Can anyone doubt," Strong asked, "that the result of this . . . will be 'the survival of the fittest'?"*

The completion of the conquest of the American West encouraged Americans to consider expansion beyond the seas. "For nearly 300 years the dominant fact in American life has been expansion," declared Frederick Jackson Turner, propounder of the frontier thesis. "That these energies of expansion will no longer operate would be a rash prediction." Turner and writers who advanced other expansionist arguments were much influenced by foreign thinking. European liberals had tended to disapprove of colonial ventures, but in the 1870s and 1880s many of them were changing their minds. English liberals in particular began to talk and write about the "superiority" of English culture, to describe the virtues of the "Anglo-Saxon race," to stress a "duty" to spread Christianity among the heathen, and to advance economic arguments for overseas expansion.

European ideas were reinforced for Americans by their observations of the imperialist activities of the European powers in what would today be called underdeveloped areas. By swallowing up most of Africa and biting off bits and pieces of the crumbling empire of China, the French, British, Germans, and other colonizers inspired some patriots in the United States to advocate joining the feast before all the choice morsels had been digested. "While the great powers of Europe are steadily enlarging their colonial domination in Asia and Africa," James G. Blaine said in 1884, "it is the especial province of this country to improve and expand its trade with the nations of America." While Blaine emphasized commerce, the excitement and adventure of overseas enterprises appealed to many people even more than the economic possibilities or any sense of obligation to fulfill a supposed national, religious, or racial destiny.

Finally, military and strategic arguments were advanced to justify adopting a "large" policy. The powerful Union army had been demobilized rapidly after Appomattox; in the 1880s only about 25,000 men were under arms, their chief occupation fighting Indians in the West. Half the navy had been scrapped after the war, and the remaining ships were obsolete. While other nations were building steam-powered iron warships, the United States depended on wooden sailing vessels. In 1867 a British naval publication accurately described the American fleet as "hapless, broken-down, tattered [and] forlorn."

Although no foreign power menaced the country, the decrepit state of the navy vexed many of its officers and led one of them, Captain Alfred Thayer Mahan, to develop a startling theory about the importance of sea power. He explained his theory in two important books, *The Influence of Sea Power upon History* (1890) and *The Influence of Sea Power upon the French Revolution and Empire* (1892). According to Mahan, history proved that a nation with a powerful navy and the overseas bases necessary to maintain it would be invulnerable in war and prosperous in time of peace. Applied to the current American situation, this meant that in addition to building a modern fleet, the United States should obtain a string of coaling stations and bases in the Caribbean, annex the Hawaiian Islands, and cut a canal across Central America. A more extensive colonial empire might follow, but these bases and the canal they would protect were essential first steps to insure America's future as a great power.

Writing at a time when the imperialist-minded European nations showed signs of extending their influence in South America and the Pacific islands, Mahan attracted many influential disciples. One was Congressman Henry Cabot Lodge of Massachusetts, a prominent member of the Naval Af-

*In later writings Strong insisted that by "fittest" he meant "social efficiency," not "mere strength."

fairs Committee. Lodge had married into a navy family and was intimate with the head of the new Naval War College, Commodore Stephen B. Luce. He helped push through Congress in 1883 an act authorizing the building of three steel warships, and he consistently advocated expanding and modernizing the fleet. Elevated to the Senate in 1893, Lodge pressed for expansionist policies, basing his arguments on the strategic concepts of Mahan. "Sea power," he proclaimed, "is essential to the greatness of every splendid people."

Another important follower of Mahan was Benjamin F. Tracy, President Harrison's secretary of the navy, who improved the administration of his department and helped persuade Congress to increase naval appropriations. Lodge's friend Theodore Roosevelt was another ardent supporter of the "large" policy, but he had little influence until McKinley appointed him assistant secretary of the navy in 1897.

The Course of Empire

The interest of the United States in the Pacific and the Far East began in the late 18th century, when the first American merchant ship dropped anchor in Canton harbor. After the Treaty of Wanghia (1844), American merchants in China enjoyed many privileges and trade expanded rapidly. Missionaries began to flock into the country—in the late eighties, over 500 were living there.

The Hawaiian Islands were an important way station on the route to China, and by 1820 merchants and missionaries were making contacts there. As early as 1854 a movement to annex the islands existed, though it foundered because Hawaii insisted on being admitted to the Union as a state. Commodore Perry's expedition to Japan led to the signing of a commercial treaty (1858) that opened several Japanese ports to American traders.

The United States pursued a policy of cooperating with the European powers in expanding commercial opportunities in the Far East. In Hawaii the tendency was to claim a special position but to accept the fact that Europeans also had interests in the islands. This state of affairs did not change radically following the Civil War. Despite Chinese protests over the exclusion of their nationals from the United States after 1882, American commercial privileges in China were not disturbed. American influence in Hawaii increased; the descendants of missionary families, most of them engaged in raising sugar, dominated the Hawaiian monarchy. In 1875 a reciprocity treaty admitted Hawaiian sugar to the United States free of duty in return for a promise to yield no territory to a foreign power. When this treaty was renewed in 1887, the United States obtained the right to establish a naval base at Pearl Harbor. In addition to occupying Midway, America obtained a foothold in the Samoan Islands in the South Pacific.

During the 1890s American interest in the Pacific area steadily intensified. Conditions in Hawaii had much to do with this. The McKinley Tariff Act of 1890, discontinuing the duty on raw sugar and compensating American producers of cane and beet sugar by granting them a bounty of 2 cents a pound, struck Hawaiian sugar growers hard, for it destroyed the advantage they had gained in the reciprocity treaty. The following year the death of the complaisant King Kalakaua brought Queen Liliuokalani, a determined nationalist, to the throne. Placing herself at the head of a "Hawaii for the Hawaiians" movement, she abolished the existing constitution under which the white minority had pretty much controlled the islands and attempted to rule as an absolute monarch. The resident Americans then staged a coup. In January 1893, with the connivance of the United States minister, John L. Stevens, who ordered 150 marines from the cruiser *Boston* into Honolulu, they deposed Queen Liliuokalani and set up a provisional government. Stevens recognized their regime at once, and the new government sent a delegation to Washington to seek a treaty of annexation.

In the closing days of the Harrison administration such a treaty was negotiated and sent to the Senate, but when Cleveland took office in March, he withdrew it. The new president disapproved of the way American troops had been used to overthrow the monarchy. He sent a special commissioner, James H. Blount, to Hawaii to investigate. When Blount reported that the Hawaiians opposed annexation, the president dismissed Stevens and attempted to restore Queen Liliuokalani. Since the provisional government was by that time firmly entrenched, this could not be accomplished peacefully. Because Cleveland was unwilling to use force against the Americans in the islands, however much he objected to their actions, he found himself unable to do anything. The revolutionary government of Hawaii remained in power, independent yet eager to be annexed.

The Hawaiian debate continued sporadically over the next four years. It provided a thorough airing of the question of overseas expansion. Fears that another power—Great Britain or perhaps Japan—might step into the void created by Cleveland's refusal to act alarmed those who favored annexation. When the Republicans returned to power in 1897, a new annexation treaty was negotiated, but domestic sugar producers now threw their weight against it, and the McKinley administration could not obtain the necessary two-thirds majority in the Senate. Finally, in July 1898, after the outbreak of the Spanish-American War, Congress annexed the islands by joint resolution, a procedure requiring only a simple majority vote.

Most of the arguments for extending American influence in the Pacific applied more strongly to Central and South America, where the United States had much larger economic interests and where the strategic importance of the region was clear. Furthermore, the Monroe Doctrine had long conditioned the American people to the idea of acting to protect national interests in the Western Hemisphere.

As early as 1869 President Grant had come out for an American-owned canal across the Isthmus of Panama, in spite of the fact that the United States had agreed in the Clayton-Bulwer Treaty with Great Britain (1850) that neither nation would "obtain or maintain for itself any exclusive control" over an interoceanic canal. In 1880, when the French engineer Ferdinand de Lesseps organized a company to build a canal across the isthmus, President Hayes announced that the United States would not permit a European power to control such a waterway. "The policy of the country is a canal under American control," he announced, another blithe disregard of the Clayton-Bulwer agreement.

In 1889 a Pan-American Conference met in Washington to discuss hemisphere problems. Secretary of State James G. Blaine hoped to use this meeting to obtain a reciprocity agreement with the Latin American countries, for the United States was importing about three times as much from them as they were purchasing in America. However, the delegates accomplished nothing beyond the establishment of an International Bureau—later known as the Pan-American Union—to promote commercial and cultural exchange. The conference was nevertheless significant, for it marked the first effort by the United States to assume the leadership of the nations of the hemisphere.

At the Washington meeting the United States posed as a friend of peace; Blaine's proposals included a general arbitration treaty to settle hemisphere disputes. A minor disagreement with the Republic of Chile in 1891 soon demonstrated that the country could quickly be brought to the verge of war with one of its southern neighbors. Anti-*Yanqui* feeling was high in Chile, chiefly because the United States had refused to sell arms to the current government during the revolution that had brought it to power. In October a group of sailors from the U.S.S. *Baltimore* on shore leave in Valparaiso were set upon by a mob. Two of the sailors were killed and more than a dozen injured. President Harrison, furious at what he called an "insult . . . to the uniform of the United States sailors," demanded "prompt and full reparation." When the Chilean authorities delayed in supplying an appropriate apology and issued a statement that "imputed untruth and insincerity" on Harrison's part, the president sent to Congress a special message virtually inviting it to declare war. Faced with this threat, Chile backed down, offering the required apology and agreeing to pay damages to the sailors. Chile's humiliation destroyed much of the goodwill engendered by the Pan-American Conference.

When Cleveland returned to power in 1893, the possibility of trouble in Latin America seemed remote, for he had always opposed imperialistic ventures. The Latin American diplomatic colony in Washington greeted him warmly after its experience with Harrison. Yet scarcely two years later the United States was again on the verge of war in South America as a result of a crisis in Venezuela, and before this issue was settled Cleveland had made the most powerful claim to American hegemony in the hemisphere ever uttered.

The tangled borderland between Venezuela and British Guiana had long been in dispute, Venezuela demanding more of the region than it was entitled to and Great Britain submitting exaggerated claims and imperiously refusing to submit the question to arbitration. What made a crisis of the controversy was the political situation in the

■ **This engraving from *Harper's Weekly*, portraying major units of the United States fleet, appeared in January 1892, at the height of the Chilean "crisis." The cruiser *Baltimore* later fought under Admiral Dewey in the Battle of Manila Bay in 1898. At center foreground is the ill-fated battleship *Maine*.**

United States. A minor incident in Nicaragua, where the British had temporarily occupied the port of Corinto to force compensation for injuries done British subjects in that country, had alarmed American supporters of the Monroe Doctrine. Cleveland had avoided involvement, and along with his refusal to take Hawaii, the incident had angered expansionists. With his party rapidly deserting him because of his stand on the silver question, and with the election of 1896 approaching, the president desperately needed a popular issue.

There was considerable latent anti-British feeling in the United States. By taking the Venezuelan side in the boundary dispute, Cleveland would be defending a weak neighbor against a great power, a position certain to evoke a popular response. "Turn this Venezuela question up or down, North, South, East or West, and it is a 'winner,'" one Democrat advised the president.

Since he believed that Venezuela's cause was just, Cleveland did not resist the temptation to intervene. In July 1895 he ordered Secretary of State Richard Olney to send a near-ultimatum to the British. By occupying the disputed territory, Olney insisted, Great Britain was invading Venezuela and violating the Monroe Doctrine. Quite gratuitously, he went on to boast: "To-day the United States is practically sovereign on this continent, and its fiat is law upon the subjects to which it confines its interposition." Unless Great Britain responded promptly by agreeing to arbitration, the president would call the question to the attention of Congress.

The note threatened war, but the British ignored it for months. They did not take the United States seriously as a world power, and with reason, for the American navy, although expanding, could not hope to stand up against the British, who had 50 battleships, 25 armored cruisers, and many smaller vessels. When Lord Salisbury, the prime minister and foreign secretary, finally re-

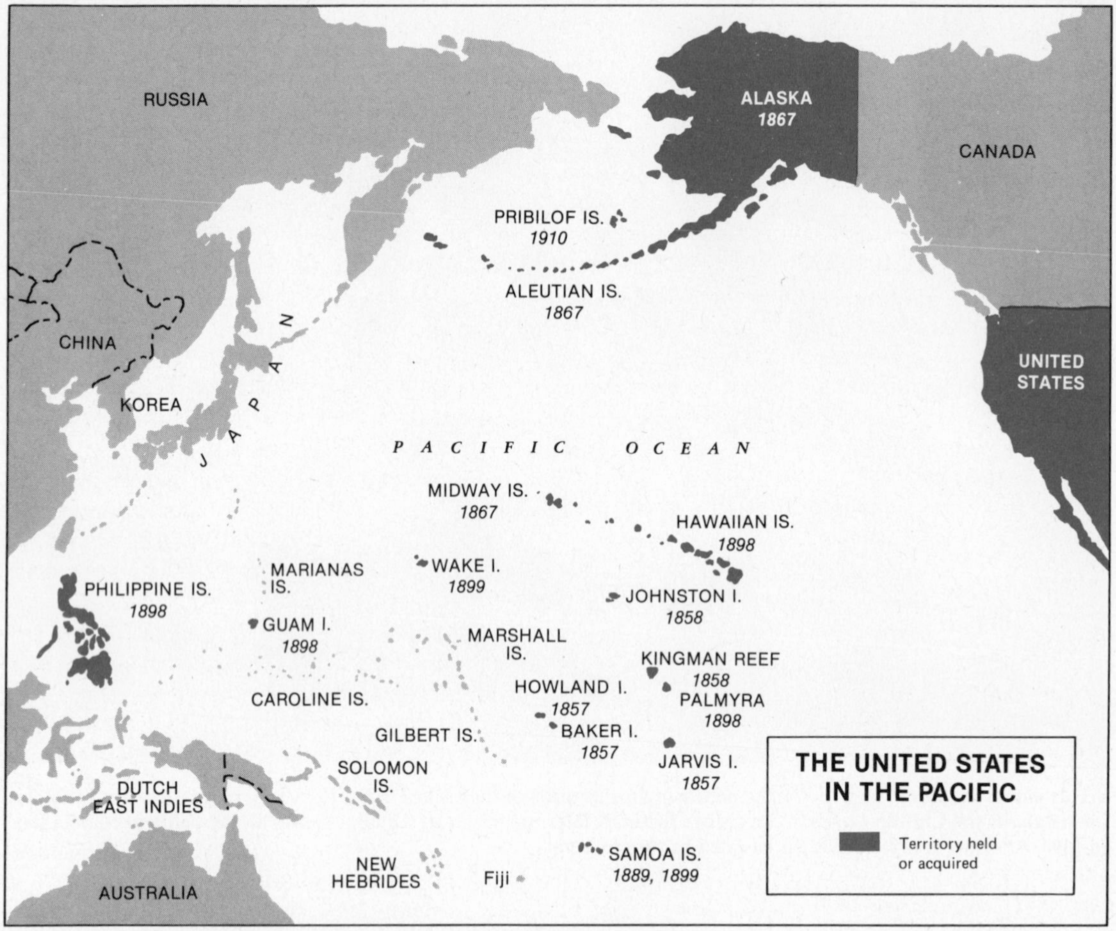

■ **The two dates given following the name of the Samoan Islands at the bottom of this map indicate a special situation. In 1889 these islands were put under a tripartite protectorate of the United States, Germany, and Great Britain. Later, in 1899, they were divided between the United States and Germany.**

plied, he rejected outright the argument that the Monroe Doctrine had any status under international law and refused to arbitrate what he called the "exaggerated pretentions" of the Venezuelans.

If Olney's note had been belligerent, this reply was supercilious and sharp to the point of asperity. Cleveland was furious. On December 17, 1895, he asked Congress for authority to appoint an American commission to determine the correct line between British Guiana and Venezuela. When that had been done, he added, the United States should "resist by every means in its power" the appropriation by Great Britain of any territory "we have determined of right belongs to Venezuela." Congress responded at once, and unanimously, appropriating $100,000 for the boundary commission. Popular enthusiasm was almost universal.

In Great Britain government and people suddenly awoke to the seriousness of the situation. No one wanted a war with the United States over a remote patch of tropical real estate. In Europe, Britain was concerned about German economic competition and the increased military power of that nation. In addition Canada would be terribly vulnerable to American attack in the event of war. The immense *potential* strength of the United States could no longer be ignored. Why make an enemy of a nation of 70 million, already the richest industrial power in the world? To fight with the United States, the British colonial secretary realized, "would be an absurdity as well as a crime."

Great Britain agreed to arbitrate the boundary. The war scare subsided; soon Olney was talking about "our inborn and instinctive English sympathies" and offering "to stand side by side and shoulder to shoulder with England in . . . the defence of human rights." When the boundary tribunal awarded nearly all the disputed region to Great Britain, whatever ill feeling the surrender may have occasioned in that country faded away. Instead of leading to war, the affair marked the beginning of an era of Anglo-American friendship. It had the unfortunate effect, however, of adding to the long-held American conviction that the nation could get what it wanted in international affairs by threat and bluster—a dangerous illusion.

Cuba and the War with Spain

On February 10, 1896, scarcely a week after Venezuela and Great Britain had signed the treaty ending their dispute, General Valeriano Weyler arrived in Havana from Spain to take up his duties as governor of Cuba. His assignment to this post was occasioned by the guerrilla warfare that Cuban nationalist rebels had been waging for almost a year. Weyler, a tough and ruthless soldier, set out to administer Cuba with "a salutary rigor." He began herding the rural population into wretched "reconcentration" camps in order to deprive the rebels of food and recruits. Resistance in Cuba hardened. The conflict, already bitter, became a cruel, bloody struggle that could not help affecting the American people.

The United States had been interested in Cuba since the time of John Quincy Adams and, were it not for northern opposition to adding more slave territory, might well have obtained the island one way or another before 1860. When the Cubans revolted against Spain in 1868, considerable support for intervening on their behalf developed. Hamilton Fish, Grant's secretary of state, resisted this sentiment, and Spain managed to pacify the rebels in 1878 by promising reforms. But change was slow in coming—slavery was not abolished until 1886. The worldwide depression of the 1890s hit the Cuban economy hard, and when an American tariff act in 1894 jacked up the rate on Cuban sugar by 40 percent, thus cutting off Cuban growers from the American market, the resulting distress precipitated another revolt.

Public sympathy in the United States went to the Cubans, who seemed to be fighting for liberty and democracy against an autocratic Old World power. Most American newspapers supported the Cubans; labor unions, veterans' organizations, many Protestant clergymen, and important politicians in both major parties demanded that the United States aid the rebel cause. Rapidly increasing American investments in Cuban sugar plantations, now approaching $50 million, were endangered by the fighting and by the social chaos sweeping across the island. Cuban propagandists in the United States played on American sentiments cleverly. When reports, often exaggerated, of the cruelty of "Butcher" Weyler and the horrors of his reconcentration camps filtered into America, the cry for action intensified. In April 1896 Congress adopted a resolution suggesting that the revolutionaries be granted the rights of belligerents. Since this would have been akin to formal recognition, Cleveland would not go that far, but he did exert diplomatic pressure on Spain to remove the causes of the rebels' complaints, and he offered the services of his government as mediator. The Spanish rejected the suggestion.

For a time the issue subsided. The election of 1896 deflected American attention from Cuba, and then McKinley refused to take any action that might disturb Spanish-American relations. Business interests—except those with holdings in Cuba—backed McKinley, for they feared that a crisis would upset the economy, which was just beginning to pick up after the depression. In Cuba General Weyler made some progress toward stifling rebel resistance.

American expansionists, however, continued to demand intervention, and the press, especially Joseph Pulitzer's New York *World* and William Randolph Hearst's New York *Journal*, competing fiercely to increase circulation, kept resentment alive with tales of Spanish atrocities. McKinley remained adamant. Although he warned Spain that Cuba must be pacified, and soon, his tone was friendly and he issued no ultimatum. A new government in Spain relieved the situation by recalling Weyler and promising partial self-government

■ **This cartoon appeared in *The Bee* after Dewey's Manila Bay victory but before the destruction of Spain's Caribbean squadron (the *New York* was one of the vessels blockading Santiago); thus its label, a "prophescopic-scoopagraph," is appropriate if improbable. The rowboat is a swipe at editor Hearst's reporting from Cuba.**

to the Cubans. In a message to Congress in December 1897, McKinley urged that Spain be given "a reasonable chance to realize her expectations" in the island. McKinley was not insensible to Cuba's plight—while far from being a rich man, he made an anonymous contribution of $5,000 to the Red Cross Cuban relief fund—but he genuinely desired to avoid intervention.

His hopes were doomed, primarily because Spain failed to "realize her expectations." The fighting in Cuba continued. When riots broke out in Havana in January 1898, McKinley ordered the battleship *Maine* to Havana harbor to protect American citizens.

Shortly thereafter Hearst's New York *Journal* printed a letter written to a friend in Cuba by the Spanish minister in Washington, Depuy de Lôme. The letter had been stolen by a spy. De Lôme, an experienced but arrogant diplomat, failed to appreciate McKinley's efforts to avoid intervening in Cuba. In the letter he characterized the president as a *politicastro,* or "small-time politician," which was a gross error, and a "bidder for the admiration of the crowd," which was equally insulting though somewhat closer to the truth. Americans were outraged, and De Lôme's hasty resignation did little to soothe their feelings.

Then, on February 15, the *Maine* exploded and sank in Havana harbor, 260 of her crew perishing in the disaster. Interventionists in the United States accused Spain of having destroyed the ship and clamored for war. The willingness of Americans to blame Spain indicates the extent of anti-Spanish opinion in the United States by 1898. No one has ever discovered what actually happened. A naval court of inquiry decided that the vessel had been sunk by a submarine mine, but it now seems more likely that an internal explosion destroyed the *Maine.* The Spanish government would never have been foolish enough to commit an act that would probably bring American troops into Cuba.

With admirable courage, McKinley refused to panic; but he could not resist the wishes of millions of citizens that something be done to stop the fighting and allow the Cubans to determine their own fate. Spanish pride and Cuban patriotism had taken the issue of peace or war out of the president's hands. Spain could not put down the rebellion, and it would not yield to the nationalists' increasingly extreme demands. To have granted independence to Cuba might have caused the Madrid government to fall, might even have led to the collapse of the monarchy, for the Spanish public was in no mood to surrender. The Cubans, sensing that the continuing bloodshed aided their cause, refused to give the Spanish regime room to maneuver. After the *Maine* disaster, Spain might have agreed to an armistice had the rebels asked for one, and in the resulting negotiations it might well have given up the island. The rebels refused to make the first move. The fighting continued, bringing the United States every day closer to intervention.

The president faced a dilemma. Most of the business interests of the country, to which he was particularly sensitive, opposed intervention. His personal feelings were equally firm. "I have been through one war," he told a friend. "I have seen the dead piled up, and I do not want to see another." Congress, however, seemed determined to act. When he submitted a restrained report on the sinking of the *Maine*, the Democrats in Congress, even most of those who had supported Cleveland's policies, gleefully accused him of timidity. Vice-President Garret A. Hobart warned him that the Senate could not be held in check for long; should Congress declare war on its own, the administration would be discredited. McKinley spent a succession of sleepless nights; sedatives brought him no repose. Finally, early in April, the president drafted a message asking for authority to use the armed forces "to secure a full and final termination of hostilities" in Cuba.

At the last moment the Spanish government seemed to yield; it ordered its troops in Cuba to cease hostilities. McKinley passed this information on to Congress along with his war message, but he gave it no emphasis and did not try to check the march toward war. To seek further delay would have been courageous but not necessarily wiser. Merely to stop fighting was not enough. The Cuban nationalists now insisted on full independence, and the Spanish politicians were unprepared to abandon the last remnant of their once great American empire. If the United States took Cuba by force, the Spanish leaders might save their political skins; if they meekly surrendered the island, they were done for.

On April 20 Congress, by joint resolution, recognized the independence of Cuba and authorized the use of the armed forces to drive out the Spanish. An amendment proposed by Senator Henry M. Teller disclaiming any intention of adding Cuban territory to the United States passed without opposition. Four days later Spain declared war on the United States.

The Spanish-American War was fought to free Cuba, but the first action took place on the other side of the globe, in the Philippine Islands. Weeks earlier, Assistant Secretary of the Navy Theodore Roosevelt, had alerted Commodore George Dewey, who was in command of the United States Asiatic Squadron located at Hong Kong, to move against the Spanish base at Manila if war came. Dewey had acted promptly, drilling his gun crews, taking on supplies, giving his gleaming white ships a coat of battle-gray paint, and establishing secret contacts with the Filipino nationalist leader, Emilio Aguinaldo. When word of the declaration of war reached him, he steamed from Hong Kong across the South China Sea with four cruisers and two gunboats. On the night of April 30 he entered Manila Bay, and at daybreak he opened fire on the Spanish fleet at 5,000 yards. His squadron made five passes, each time reducing the range; when the smoke had cleared, all ten of Admiral Montojo's ships had been destroyed. Not a single American was killed in the engagement.

Dewey immediately asked for troops to take and hold Manila, for now that war had been declared, he could not return to Hong Kong or put in at any other neutral port. McKinley took the fateful step of dispatching some 11,000 soldiers and additional naval support. On August 13 these forces, assisted by Filipino irregulars under Aguinaldo, captured Manila.

Meanwhile, in the main theater of operations, the United States had won a swift and total victory, though more because of the feebleness of the Spanish than because of the power or efficiency of American arms. When the war began, the regular

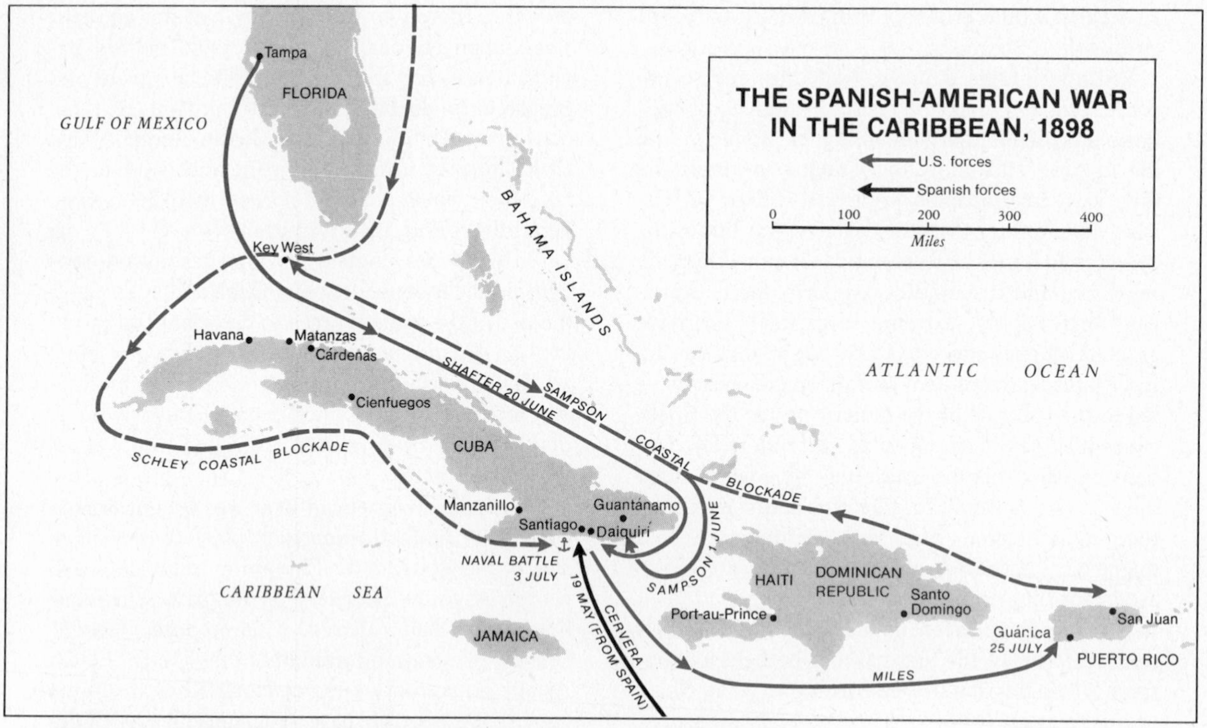

■ Spanish admiral Cervera evaded the American naval blockade to reach Santiago (map above). At the left is the grim aftermath of the storming of San Juan Hill, recorded by William Glackens, a painter who later became famous as a pioneer of American realism.

army consisted of about 28,000 men. This tiny force was bolstered by 200,000 hastily enlisted volunteers. In May an expeditionary force gathered at Tampa, Florida. That hamlet was inundated by the masses of men and supplies that descended upon it. Entire regiments sat without uniforms or weapons while hundreds of freight cars jammed with equipment lay forgotten on sidings. Army management was abominable, rivalry between commanders a serious problem. Aggressive units like the regiment of "Rough Riders" raised by Theodore Roosevelt, now a lieutenant colonel of volunteers, scrambled for space and supplies, shouldering aside other units to get what they needed. "No words could describe . . . the confusion and lack of system and the general mismanagement of affairs here," the angry Roosevelt complained.

Since a Spanish fleet under Admiral Pascual Cervera was known to be in Caribbean waters, no invading army could safely embark until the fleet could be located. On May 29 American ships found Cervera at Santiago harbor, on the eastern end of Cuba, and established a blockade. In June a 17,000-man expeditionary force commanded by General William Shafter landed at Daiquiri, east of Santiago, and pressed quickly toward the city, handicapped more by its own bad staff work than by the enemy, though the Spanish troops resisted bravely. The Americans sweated through Cuba's torrid summer in heavy wool winter uniforms, ate "embalmed beef" out of cans, and fought mostly with old-fashioned rifles using black powder cartridges that marked the position of each soldier with a puff of smoke whenever he pulled the trigger. On July 1 they broke through undermanned Spanish defenses and stormed San Juan Hill, the intrepid Roosevelt in the van. ("Are you afraid to stand up while I am on horseback?" Roosevelt demanded of one soldier.)

With Santiago harbor in range of American artillery, Admiral Cervera had to run the blockade. On July 3 his black-hulled ships, flags proudly flying, steamed forth from the harbor and fled westward along the coast. Like hounds after rabbits, five American battleships and two cruisers, commanded by Rear Admiral William T. Sampson and Commodore Winfield Scott Schley, ran them down. In four hours the entire Spanish force was destroyed by a hail of 8-inch and 13-inch projectiles. Damage to the American ships was superficial; only one seaman lost his life in the engagement.

The end then came abruptly. Santiago surrendered on July 17. A few days later, other United States troops completed the occupation of Puerto Rico. On August 12, one day before the fall of Manila, Spain agreed to get out of Cuba and to cede Puerto Rico and an island in the Marianas (Guam) to the United States. The future of the Philippines was to be settled at a formal peace conference, convening in Paris on October 1.

Developing a Colonial Policy

Although the Spanish resisted surrendering the Philippines at Paris, they had been so thoroughly defeated that they had no choice. The decision hung rather upon the outcome of a conflict over policy within the United States. The war, won at so little cost militarily, produced problems far larger than those it solved.* The nation had become a great power in the world's eyes. As a French diplomat wrote a few years later, "[The United States] is seated at the table where the great game is played, and it cannot leave it." European leaders had been impressed by the forcefulness of Cleveland's diplomacy in the Venezuela boundary dispute and by the efficiency displayed by the navy in the war. The annexation of Hawaii and other overseas bases intensified their conviction that the United States was determined to become a major force in international affairs.

But were the American *people* determined to exercise that force? The debate over taking the Philippine Islands throws much light on their attitudes. The imagination of Americans had been captured by the *trappings* of empire, not by its essence. It was titillating to think of a world map liberally sprinkled with American flags and of the economic benefits that colonies might bring, but most citizens were not prepared to join in a worldwide struggle for power and influence. They entered blithely upon adventures in far-off regions without facing the implications of their decision.

Since the United States (in the Teller Amendment) had abjured any claim to Cuba, even

*More than 5,000 Americans died as a result of the conflict, but fewer than 400 fell in combat. The others were mostly victims of yellow fever, typhoid, and other diseases.

though the island had long been desired by expansionists, logic dictated that a similar policy be applied to the Philippines, a remote land few Americans had ever thought about before 1898. But expansionists were eager to annex the entire archipelago. Even before he had learned to spell the name, Senator Lodge was saying that "the Phillipines mean a vast future trade and wealth and power," offering the nation a greater opportunity "than anything that has happened . . . since the annexation of Louisiana." President McKinley adopted a more cautious stance, but he too favored "the general principle of holding on to what we can get." A speaking tour of the Middle West in October 1898, during which he experimented with varying degrees of commitment to expansionism, convinced him that the public wanted the islands. Business opinion had shifted dramatically during the war. Business leaders were now calling the Philippines the gateway to the markets of the Far East.

An important minority objected strongly to the United States' acquiring overseas possessions. Persons as different in interest and philosophy as the tycoon Andrew Carnegie and the labor leader Samuel Gompers, as the venerable Republican Senator George Frisbie Hoar of Massachusetts and "Pitchfork Ben" Tillman, the southern Democratic firebrand, together with the writers Mark Twain and William Dean Howells, the reformers Lincoln Steffens and Jane Addams, and the educators Charles W. Eliot of Harvard and David Starr Jordan of Stanford united in opposing the annexation of the Philippines. These anti-imperialists insisted that since no one would even consider statehood for the Philippines, it would be unconstitutional to annex them. It was a violation of the spirit of the Declaration of Independence to govern a foreign territory without the consent of its inhabitants, Senator Hoar argued; by taking over "vassal states" in "barbarous archipelagoes" the United States was "trampling . . . on our own great Charter, which recognizes alike the liberty and the dignity of individual manhood."

McKinley was not insensitive to this appeal to idealism and tradition, but he rejected it for several reasons. Many people who opposed Philippine annexation were neither idealists nor constitutional purists. Partisanship led numbers of Democrats to object. Other anti-imperialists were governed by racial and ethnic prejudices, as Senator Hoar's statement indicates. They opposed not expansion as such—Carnegie, for example, was eager to have Canada added to the Union—but expansion that brought under the American flag people whom they believed unfit for American citizenship. Labor leaders particularly feared the competition of "the Chinese, the Negritos, and the Malays" who presumably would flood into the United States if the Philippines were taken.

More compelling to McKinley was the absence of any practical alternative to annexation. Public opinion would not sanction restoring Spanish authority in the Philippines or allowing some other power to have them. That the Filipinos were sufficiently advanced and united socially to form a stable government if granted independence seemed unlikely. Senator Hoar believed that "for years and for generations, and perhaps for centuries, there would have been turbulence, disorder and revolution" in the islands if they were left to their own devices. Strangely—for he was a kind and gentle man—Hoar faced this possibility with equanimity. McKinley was unable to do so. The president searched the depths of his soul and could find no solution but annexation. Of course the state of public feeling made the decision easier. And he probably found the idea of presiding over an empire appealing. Certainly the commercial possibilities did not escape him. In the end it was with a heavy sense of responsibility that he ordered the American peace commissioners to insist on acquiring the Philippines. To salve the feelings of the Spanish, the United States agreed to pay $20 million for the archipelago, but it was a forced sale, accepted by Spain under duress.

The peace treaty faced a hard battle in the United States Senate, where a combination of partisan politics and anticolonialism made it difficult to amass the two-thirds majority necessary for ratification. McKinley had shrewdly appointed three senators, including one Democrat, to the peace commission. This predisposed many members of the upper house to approve the treaty, but the vote was close. William Jennings Bryan, titular head of the Democratic party, could probably have prevented ratification had he urged his supporters to vote nay. Although he was opposed to taking the Philippines, he did not do so. To reject the treaty would leave the United States technically at war with Spain and the fate of the Philippines undetermined; better to accept the islands

■ **A photograph taken in 1899 shows guerilla troops captured during the Philippine Insurrection. Although the guerilla leader, Emilio Aguinaldo, was seized in March 1901, fighting in the islands did not end until mid-1902.**

and then grant them independence. The question should be decided, Bryan said, "not by a *minority* of the Senate but by a *majority* of the people" at the next presidential election. Perplexed by Bryan's stand, a number of Democrats allowed themselves to be persuaded by the expansionists' arguments and by McKinley's judicious use of patronage; the treaty was ratified in February 1899 by a vote of 57 to 27.

The national referendum that Bryan had hoped for never materialized. Bryan himself confused the issue in 1900 by making free silver a major plank in his platform, thereby driving conservative anti-imperialists into McKinley's arms. Moreover, early in 1899 the Filipino nationalists under Aguinaldo, furious because the United States would not withdraw, rose in rebellion. A savage guerrilla war resulted, one that cost far more in lives and money than the "splendid little" Spanish-American conflict.

Like all conflicts waged in tangled country chiefly by small, isolated units surrounded by a hostile civilian population that had little regard for the "rules" of war, this one produced many atrocities. Goaded by sneak attacks and instances of cruelty to captives, American soldiers, most of whom had little respect for Filipinos to begin with, responded in kind. Horrible tales of rape, arson, and murder by United States troops filtered into the country, providing ammunition for the anti-imperialists. "You seem to have about finished your work of civilizing the Filipinos," Andrew Carnegie wrote angrily to one of the American peace commissioners. "About 8,000 of them have been completely civilized and sent to Heaven. I hope you like it."

So long as the fighting continued it was politically impossible for the United States to withdraw from the islands. A commission appointed by McKinley in 1899 attributed the revolt to the ambitions of the nationalist leaders and recommended that the Philippines be granted independence at an indefinite future date. This seems to have been the wish of most Americans.

The reelection of McKinley in 1900 settled the Philippine question, though it took the efforts of 70,000 American soldiers and three years of guerrilla warfare before peace was restored. Meanwhile, McKinley sent a second commission, headed by William Howard Taft, an Ohio judge, to establish civil government in the islands. Taft, a warmhearted, affable man, took an instant liking to the Filipinos, and his policy of encouraging them to participate in the territorial government attracted many converts. In July 1901 he became the first civilian governor of the Philippines.

Anti-imperialists claimed that it was unconstitutional to take over territories without the consent of the local population. Their reasoning, while certainly not specious, was unhistorical. No American government had seriously considered the wishes of the American Indians, or those of the French and Spanish settlers in Louisiana, or those of the Eskimos of Alaska when it had seemed in the national interest to annex new lands.

Cuba and the Caribbean

Grave constitutional questions arose as a result of the acquisitions that followed the Spanish-American War. McKinley acted with remarkable independence in handling the problems involved in expansion. He set up military governments in Cuba, Puerto Rico, and the Philippines without specific congressional authority. Eventually both Congress and the Supreme Court took a hand in shaping colonial policy. In 1900 Congress passed the Foraker Act, establishing a civil government for Puerto Rico. It did not give the Puerto Ricans either American citizenship or full local self-government, and it placed a tariff on Puerto Rican products imported into the United States.

The tariff provision was promptly challenged in the courts on the ground that Puerto Rico was part of the United States, but in *Downes* v. *Bidwell* (1901) the Supreme Court upheld the legality of the duties. In this and other "insular cases" the reasoning of the judges was more than ordinarily difficult to follow. ("We suggest, without intending to decide, that there may be a distinction between certain natural rights enforced in the Constitution . . . and what may be termed artificial or remedial rights," the *Downes* opinion held.) The effect, however, was clear: the Constitution did not follow the flag; Congress could act toward the colonies almost as it pleased. A colony, one dissenting justice said, could be kept "like a disembodied shade, in an indeterminate state of ambiguous existence for an indefinite period."

While the most heated arguments raged over Philippine policy, the most difficult colonial problems concerned the relationship between the United States and Cuba, for there idealism and self-interest clashed painfully. Despite the desire of most Americans to free Cuba, an independent government could not easily be created. Order and prosperity did not automatically appear when the red and gold ensigns of Spain were hauled down from the flagstaffs of Havana and Santiago. The insurgent government was feeble, corrupt, and oligarchic, the Cuban economy in a state of collapse, life chaotic. The first Americans entering Havana found the streets littered with garbage and the corpses of horses and dogs. All public services were at a standstill; it seemed essential for the United States, as McKinley said, to give "aid and direction" until "tranquillity" could be restored.

As soon as American troops landed in Cuba, trouble broke out between them and the populace. Most American soldiers viewed the ragged, half-starved insurgents as "thieving dagoes" and displayed an unfortunate race prejudice against their dark-skinned allies. The novelist Stephen Crane, who covered the war for Pulitzer's *World*, reported: "Both officers and privates have the most lively contempt for the Cubans. They despise them." General Shafter did not help matters. He believed the Cubans "no more fit for self-government than gun-powder is for hell," and he used the insurgents chiefly as labor troops. After the fall of Santiago, he refused to let rebel leaders participate in the formal surrender of the city. This infuriated the proud and idealistic Cuban commander, General Calixto García. When McKinley established a military government for Cuba late in 1898, it was soon embroiled with local leaders. Then an eager horde of American promoters descended on Cuba in search of profitable franchises and concessions. Congress put a stop to this exploitation by forbidding all such grants as long as the occupation continued.

The problems were indeed knotty, for no strong local leader capable of uniting Cuba appeared. Even Senator Teller, father of the Teller Amendment, expressed concern lest "unstable and unsafe" elements gain control of the country. European leaders expected that the United States would eventually annex Cuba, and many Ameri-

cans, including General Leonard Wood, who became military governor in December 1899, considered this the best solution. The desperate state of the people, the heavy economic stake of Americans in the region, and its strategic importance militated against withdrawal.

In the end the United States did withdraw, after doing a great deal to modernize sugar production, improve sanitary conditions, establish schools, and restore orderly administration. In November 1900 a Cuban constitutional convention met at Havana and proceeded without substantial American interference or direction to draft a frame of government. The chief restrictions imposed by this document on Cuba's freedom concerned foreign relations; at the insistence of the United States, it authorized American intervention whenever necessary "for the preservation of Cuban independence" and "the maintenance of a government adequate for the protection of life, property, and individual liberty." Cuba had to promise to make no treaty with a foreign power compromising its independence and to grant naval bases on its soil to the United States.

This arrangement, known as the Platt Amendment, was accepted, after some grumbling, by the Cubans. It had the support of most American opponents of imperialism. The amendment was a true compromise; as David F. Healy, a leading student of Cuban-American relations, has said, "it promised to give the Cubans real internal self government . . . and at the same time to safeguard American interests." In May 1902 the United States turned over the reins of government to the new republic. The next year the two countries signed a reciprocity treaty tightening the economic bonds between them.

True friendship did not result. Although American troops occupied Cuba only once, in 1906, and then at the specific request of Cuban authorities, the United States repeatedly used the threat of intervention to coerce the Cuban government. American economic penetration proceeded rapidly and without regard for the well-being of the Cuban peasants, many of whom lived in a state of peonage on great sugar plantations. Nor did their good intentions make up for the tendency of Americans to consider themselves innately superior to the Cubans and to overlook the fact that Cubans did not always wish to adopt American customs and culture. The reform program instituted during the occupation was marred by attempts to apply American standards at every step. The new schools used American textbooks that had been translated into Spanish without adapting the material to the experience of Cuban children. General Wood considered the Cubans "inert" because they showed little interest in his plans to grant a large measure of self-government to municipal authorities. He failed to understand that the people were accustomed to a centralized system with decision making concentrated in Havana. Wood complained that the Cubans were mired in "old ruts," yet the same charge might well have been leveled at him, though he was an efficient and energetic administrator.

If the purpose of the Spanish-American War had been to bring peace and order to Cuba, the Platt Amendment was a logical step. The same purpose soon necessitated a further extension of the principle, for once the United States accepted the role of protector and stabilizer in part of the Caribbean, it seemed desirable, for the same economic, strategic, and humanitarian reasons, to supervise the entire region.

The Caribbean countries were economically underdeveloped, socially backward, politically unstable, and desperately poor. Everywhere a few families owned most of the land and dominated social and political life. The mass of the people were uneducated peasants, many of them little better off than slaves. Rival cliques of wealthy families struggled for power, force being the usual method of effecting a change in government. Most of the meager income of the average Caribbean state was swallowed up by the military or diverted into the pockets of the current rulers.

Cynicism and fraud poisoned the relations of most of these nations with the great powers. European merchants and bankers systematically cheated their Latin American customers, who in turn frequently refused to honor their obligations. Foreign bankers floated Caribbean bond issues on outrageous terms, while revolutionary Caribbean governments annulled concessions and repudiated debts with equal disdain for honest business dealing.

Because these countries were weak, the powers tended to intervene whenever their nationals were cheated or when chaotic conditions endangered the lives and property of foreigners. In one notorious instance Germany sent two warships to Portau-Prince, Haiti, and by threatening to bombard the town compelled the Haitian government to pay $30,000 in damages to a German citizen who had been arrested and fined for allegedly assaulting a local policeman. Such actions as this aroused the concern of the United States government.

In 1902, shortly after the United States had pulled out of Cuba, trouble erupted in Venezuela, where a dictator, Cipriano Castro, was refusing to honor debts owed the citizens of European nations. To force Castro to pay up, Germany and Great Britain established a blockade of Venezuelan ports and destroyed a number of Venezuelan gunboats and harbor defenses. Under American pressure the Europeans agreed to arbitrate the dispute. At last the great powers were coming to accept the broad implications of the Monroe Doctrine. The British prime minister, Arthur Balfour, went so far as to state publicly that "it would be a great gain to civilization if the United States were more actively to interest themselves in making arrangements by which these constantly recurring difficulties . . . could be avoided."

By this time Theodore Roosevelt had become president of the United States, and he quickly capitalized on the new European attitude. In 1903 the Dominican Republic defaulted on bonds totaling some $40 million. When European investors urged their governments to intervene, Roosevelt announced that under the Monroe Doctrine the United States could not permit foreign nations to intervene in Latin America. But, he added, Latin American nations should not be allowed to escape their obligations. "If we intend to say 'Hands off' . . . sooner or later we must keep order ourselves," he told Secretary of War Elihu Root.

The president did not want to make a colony of the Dominican Republic. "I have about the same

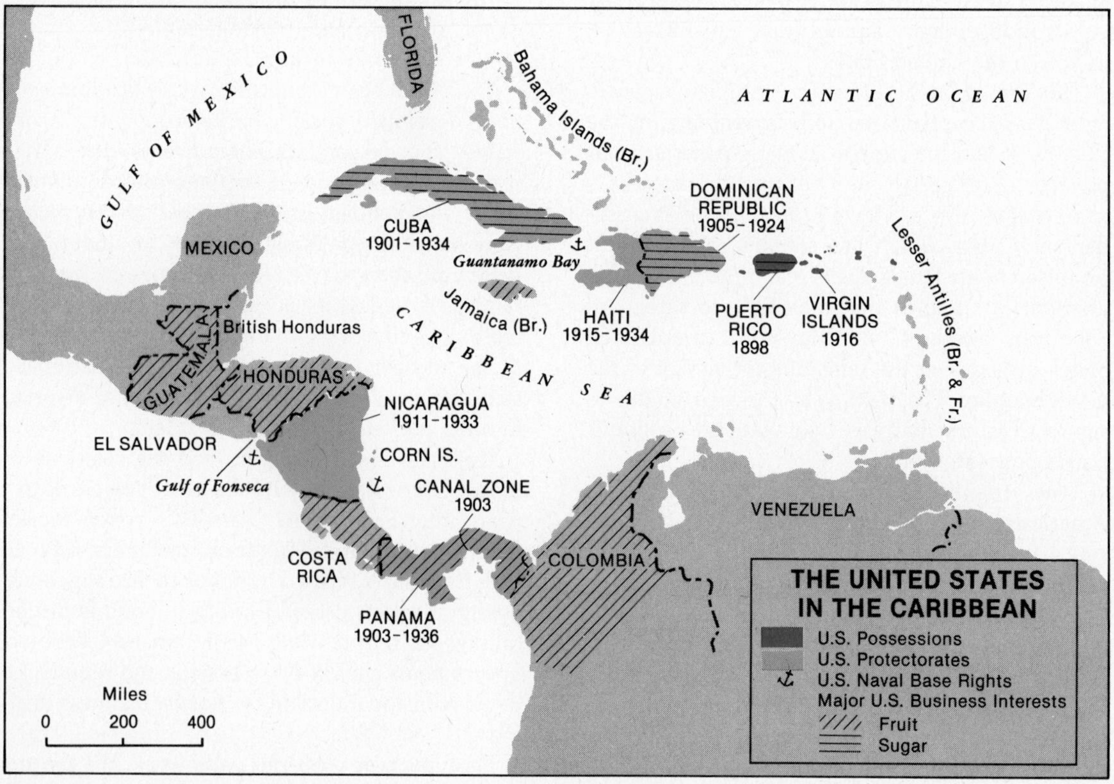

■ **Puerto Rico was ceded by Spain after the Spanish-American War; the Virgin Islands were bought from Denmark; and the Canal Zone was leased from Panama. The ranges of dates following Cuba, Dominican Republic, Haiti, Nicaragua, and Panama cover those years during which the United States either had troops in occupation or in some other way (such as financial) had a protectorate relationship with that country.**

■ **As the Monroe Doctrine became more significant around the turn of the century, chauvinistic cartoonists used it to taunt European powers. In this example, from a 1901 issue of *Puck*, the European chickens complain, "You're not the only rooster in South America!" to which Uncle Sam retorts, "I was aware of that when I cooped you up!"**

desire to annex it as a gorged boa constrictor might have to swallow a porcupine wrong-end-to," he said. He therefore arranged for the United States to take charge of the Dominican customs service—the one reliable source of revenue in that poverty-stricken country. Fifty-five percent of the customs duties would be devoted to debt payment, the remainder turned over to the Dominican government to care for its internal needs.

Roosevelt defined his policy, known as the Roosevelt Corollary to the Monroe Doctrine, in a message to Congress in December 1904. "Chronic wrongdoing" in Latin America, he stated with his typical disregard for the subtleties of complex affairs, might require outside intervention. Since, under the Monroe Doctrine, no other nation could step in, the United States must "exercise . . . an international police power."

In the short run this policy worked admirably. Dominican customs were honestly collected for the first time and the country's finances put in order. The presence of American warships in the area discouraged revolutionary elements (most of whom were cynical spoilsmen rather than social reformers), providing a needed measure of political stability. In the long run, however, the Roosevelt Corollary caused a great deal of resentment in Latin America, for it added to nationalist fears that the United States wished to exploit the region for its own benefit.

The Open Door Policy

The insular cases, the Platt Amendment, and the Roosevelt Corollary established the framework for American policy both in Latin America and in the Far East. Coincidental with the Cuban rebellion of the nineties, a far greater upheaval had convulsed the ancient empire of China. In 1894–1895 Japan easily defeated China in a war over Korea. Alarmed by Japan's aggressiveness, the European powers hastened to carve out for themselves new spheres of influence along China's coast. After the annexation of the Philippines, McKinley's secretary of state, John Hay, urged on by businessmen fearful of losing out in the scramble to exploit the Chinese market, tried to prevent the further absorption of China by the great pow-

■ In August 1900 the siege of Peking was broken by an international expeditionary force that included American, British, French, German, Russian, and Japanese troops.

ers. For the United States to join in the dismemberment of China was politically impossible because of anti-imperialist feeling, so Hay sought to protect American interests by clever diplomacy. In a series of "Open Door" notes (1899) he asked the powers to agree to respect the trading rights of all countries and to impose no discriminatory duties within their spheres of influence. Chinese tariffs should continue to be collected in these areas and by Chinese officials.

The replies to the Open Door notes were at best noncommittal, yet Hay blandly announced in March 1900 that the powers had "accepted" his suggestions! Thus he could claim to have prevented the breakup of the empire and protected the right of Americans to do business freely in its territories. In reality nothing had been accomplished; the imperialist nations did not extend their political control of China only because they feared that by doing so they might precipitate a major war among themselves. Nevertheless, Hay's action marked a revolutionary departure from the traditional American policy of isolation, a bold advance into the complicated and dangerous world of international power politics.

Within a few months of Hay's announcement

the Open Door policy was put to the test. Chinese nationalists, angered by the spreading influence of foreign governments, launched the so-called Boxer Rebellion. They swarmed into Peking and drove foreigners within the walls of their legations, which were placed under siege. For weeks, until an international rescue expedition (which included 2,500 American soldiers) broke through to free them, the fate of the foreigners was unknown. Fearing that the Europeans would use the rebellion as a pretext for further expropriations, Hay sent off another round of Open Door notes announcing that the United States believed in the preservation of "Chinese territorial and administrative entity" and in "the principle of equal and impartial trade with all parts of the Chinese Empire." This broadened the Open Door policy to include all China, not merely the European spheres of influence.

Hay's diplomacy was superficially successful. While the United States maintained no important military force in the Far East, American business and commercial interests there were free to develop and to compete with Europeans. But once again European jealousies and fears rather than American cleverness were responsible. When the Japanese, mistrusting Russian intentions in Manchuria, asked Hay how he intended to implement his policy, he replied meekly that the United States was "not prepared . . . to enforce these views on the east by any demonstration which could present a character of hostility to any other power." The United States was being caught up in the power struggle in the Far East without having faced the implications of its actions.

In time the country would pay a heavy price for this unrealistic attitude, but in the decade following 1900 its policy of diplomatic meddling unbacked by bayonets worked fairly well. Japan attacked Russia in a quarrel over Manchuria, smashing the Russian fleet in 1905 and winning a series of battles on the mainland. Japan was not prepared for a long war, however, and suggested to President Roosevelt that an American offer to mediate would be favorably received.

Eager to preserve the nice balance in the Far East, which enabled the United States to exert influence without any significant commitment of force, Roosevelt accepted the hint. In June 1905 he invited the belligerents to a conference at Portsmouth, New Hampshire. At the conference the Japanese won title to Russia's sphere around Port Arthur and a free hand in Korea, but when they demanded Sakhalin Island and a large money indemnity, the Russians balked. Unwilling to resume the war, the Japanese settled for half of Sakhalin and no money.

The Treaty of Portsmouth was unpopular in Japan, and the government managed to place the blame on Roosevelt, who had supported the compromise. Ill feeling against Americans increased in 1906 when the San Francisco school board, responding to local opposition to the influx of cheap labor from Japan, instituted a policy of segregating oriental children in a special school. Japan protested, and President Roosevelt persuaded the San Franciscans to abandon segregation in exchange for his pledge to cut off further Japanese immigration. He accomplished this through a "Gentlemen's Agreement" (1907) in which the Japanese promised not to issue passports to laborers seeking to come to America. Discriminatory legislation based specifically on race was thus avoided. However, the atmosphere between the two countries remained charged. Japanese resentment at American race prejudice was great; many Americans talked fearfully of the "yellow peril."

Theodore Roosevelt was preeminently a realist in foreign relations. "Don't bluster," he once said. "Don't flourish a revolver, and never draw unless you intend to shoot." In the Far East he failed to follow his own advice. He considered the situation in that part of the world fraught with peril. The Philippines, he said, were "our heel of Achilles," indefensible in case of a Japanese attack. He suggested privately that the United States ought to "be prepared for giving the islands independence . . . much sooner than I think advisable from their own standpoint." Yet he did not increase appreciably American naval and military strength in the Orient, he did not stop trying to influence the course of events in the area, and he took no step toward withdrawing from the Philippines. He sent the fleet on a world cruise to demonstrate its might to Japan but knew well that this was mere bluff. "The 'Open Door' policy," he warned his successor, "completely disappears as soon as a powerful nation determines to disregard it." Nevertheless he allowed the belief to persist in the United States that the nation could influence the course of Far Eastern history without risk or real involvement.

Caribbean Diplomacy

In the Caribbean region American policy centered on building an interoceanic canal across Central America. Expanding interests in Latin America and the Far East made a canal necessary, a truth pointed up during the war with Spain by the two-month voyage of the U.S.S. *Oregon* around South America from California waters to participate in the action against Admiral Cervera's fleet at Santiago. The first step was to get rid of the old Clayton-Bulwer Treaty with Great Britain, which barred the United States from building a canal on its own. In 1901 Lord Pauncefote, the British ambassador, and Secretary of State John Hay negotiated an agreement abrogating the Clayton-Bulwer pact and giving America the right to build, and by implication fortify, a transisthmian waterway. The United States agreed in turn to maintain any such canal "free and open to the vessels of commerce and of war of all nations."

One possible canal route lay across the Colombian province of Panama, where the French-controlled New Panama Canal Company had taken over the franchise of the old De Lesseps company (see page 544). Only 50 miles separated the oceans in Panama. The terrain, however, was rugged and unhealthy. While the French company had sunk much money into the project, it had little to show for its efforts aside from some rough excavations. A second possible route ran across Nicaragua. This route was about 200 miles long but was relatively easy, since much of it traversed Lake Nicaragua and other natural waterways.

President McKinley appointed a commission to study the alternatives. It reported that the Panamanian route was technically superior but recommended building in Nicaragua because the New Panama Canal Company was asking $109 million for its assets, which the commission valued at only $40 million. Lacking another potential purchaser, the French company lowered its price to $40 million, and after a great deal of clever propagandizing by Philippe Bunau-Varilla, a French engineer with heavy investments in the company, President Roosevelt settled on the Panamanian route.

In January 1903 Secretary of State Hay negotiated a treaty with Tomás Herrán, the Colombian chargé in Washington. In return for a 99-year lease on a zone across Panama 6 miles wide, the United States agreed to pay Colombia $10 million and an annual rent of $250,000. The Colombian senate, however, unanimously rejected this treaty, in part because it did not adequately protect Colombian sovereignty over Panama and in part because it hardly seemed fair that the New Panama Canal Company should receive $40 million for its frozen assets and Colombia only $10 million. The government demanded $15 million directly from the United States, plus $10 million of the company's share.

A little more patience might have produced a mutually satisfactory settlement, but Roosevelt looked upon the Colombians as highwaymen who were "mad to get hold of the $40,000,000 of the Frenchmen." ("You could no more make an agreement with the Colombian rulers," Roosevelt later remarked, "than you could nail currant jelly to a wall.") When Panamanians, egged on by the French company, staged a revolution in November 1903, he ordered the cruiser *Nashville* to Panama. Colombian government forces found themselves looking down the barrels of the guns of the *Nashville* and shortly thereafter eight other American warships. The revolution succeeded.

Roosevelt instantly recognized the new Republic of Panama. Secretary Hay and the new Panamanian minister, Bunau-Varilla, then negotiated a treaty granting the United States a zone *10* miles wide *in perpetuity*, on the same terms as those rejected by Colombia. Within the Canal Zone the United States could act as "the sovereign of the territory . . . to the entire exclusion of . . . the Republic of Panama." The United States guaranteed the independence of the republic. The New Panama Canal Company then received its $40 million.

Historians have condemned Roosevelt for his actions in this shabby affair, and with good reason. It was not that he fomented the revolution, for he did not. Separated from the government at Bogotá by an impenetrable jungle, the people of Panama province had long wanted to be free of Colombian rule. Since an American-built canal would bring a flood of dollars and jobs to the area, they were prepared to take any necessary steps to avoid having the United States shift to the Nicaraguan route. Nor was it that Roosevelt prevented Colombia from suppressing the revolution. He sinned, rather, in his disregard of Latin American sensibilities. He referred to the Colombians as

■ **A New York *Times* cartoonist did not approve of Roosevelt's handling of the Panamanian affair. When Bunau-Varilla asked the president to send a warship to Panama "to protect American lives and interests," he got no answer. "But his look was enough for me," Bunau-Varilla recalled.**

"dagoes" and insisted smugly that he was defending "the interests of collective civilization" when he overrode their opposition to his plans. "They cut their own throats," he said. "They tried to hold us up; and too late they have discovered their criminal error."

If uncharitable, Roosevelt's analysis was not entirely inaccurate, yet it did not justify his haste in taking Panama under his wing. "Have I defended myself?" Roosevelt asked Secretary of War Elihu Root. "You certainly have, Mr. President," Root retorted. "You were accused of seduction and you have conclusively proved that you were guilty of rape." Throughout Latin America, especially as nationalist sentiments grew stronger, Roosevelt's intolerance and aggressiveness in the canal incident bred resentment and fear.

In 1921 the United States made amends by giving Colombia $25 million. Colombia in turn recognized the independence of the Republic of Panama.* Meanwhile, the first vessels passed through the canal in 1914—and American hegemony in the Caribbean expanded. Yet even in that strategically vital area there was more show than substance to American strength. The navy ruled Caribbean waters largely by default, for it lacked adequate bases in the region. In 1903, as authorized by the Cuban constitution, the United States obtained an excellent site for a base at Guantanamo Bay, but before 1914 Congress appropriated only $89,000 to develop it.

The tendency was to try to influence outlying areas without actually controlling them. Roosevelt's successor, William Howard Taft, called this policy dollar diplomacy, his reasoning being that economic penetration would bring stability to underdeveloped areas and power and profit to the United States without the government's having to commit troops or spend public funds.

Under Taft the State Department won a place for American bankers in an international syndicate engaged in financing railroads in Manchuria. When Nicaragua defaulted on its foreign debt in 1911, the department arranged for American bankers to reorganize Nicaraguan finances and manage the customs service. Although the government truthfully insisted that it did not "covet an inch of territory south of the Rio Grande," dollar diplomacy provoked further apprehension in Latin America. Efforts to establish similar arrangements in Honduras, Costa Rica, and Guatemala all failed. In Nicaragua orderly administration of the finances did not bring internal peace. In 1912, 2,500 American marines and sailors had to be landed to put down a revolution.

*Panama was independent only in name because of American control of the canal. In 1978 the United States and Panama agreed to a treaty turning the entire Canal Zone over to Panama in the year 2000 (see page 787).

Economic penetration proceeded briskly. American investments in Cuba reached $500 million by 1920, and smaller but significant investments were made in the Dominican Republic and in Haiti. In Central America the United Fruit Company accumulated large holdings in banana plantations, railroads, and other ventures. Other firms plunged heavily in Mexico's rich mineral resources.

"Non-colonial Imperial Expansion"

The United States deserves fair marks for effort in its foreign relations following the Spanish-American War, barely passable marks for performance, and failing marks for results. If one defines imperialism narrowly as a policy of occupying and governing foreign lands, American imperialism lasted for an extremely short time. With trivial exceptions, all the American colonies—Hawaii, the Philippines, Guam, Puerto Rico, the Guantanamo base, and the Canal Zone—were obtained between 1898 and 1903. In retrospect it seems clear that the urge to own colonies was only fleeting; the legitimate questions raised by the anti-imperialists and the headaches connected with the management of overseas possessions soon produced a change of policy.

The objections of protectionists to the lowering of tariff barriers, the shock of the Philippine insurrection, and a growing conviction that the costs of colonial administration outweighed the profits affected American thinking. Hay's Open Door notes (which anti-imperialists praised highly) marked the beginning of the retreat from imperialism as thus defined, while the Roosevelt Corollary and dollar diplomacy signaled the consolidation of a new policy. Elihu Root summarized this policy as it applied to the Caribbean nations (and by implication to the rest of the underdeveloped world) in 1905: "We do not want to take them for ourselves. We do not want any foreign nations to take them for themselves. We want to help them."

Yet imperialism can be given a broader definition. The historian William Appleman Williams, a sharp critic, has described 20th-century American foreign policy as one of "non-colonial imperial expansion." Its object was to obtain profitable American economic penetration of underdeveloped areas without the trouble of owning and controlling them. Its subsidiary aim was to encourage these countries to "modernize," that is, to remake themselves in the image of the United States. The Open Door policy, in Williams' view, was not unrealistic and by no means a failure—indeed, it was *too* successful. He criticizes American policy not because it did not work or because it led to trouble with the powers but because of its harmful effects on underdeveloped countries.

Examined from this perspective, the Open Door policy, the Roosevelt Corollary, and dollar diplomacy make a single pattern of exploitation, "tragic" rather than evil, according to Williams, because its creators were not evil but only of limited vision. They did not recognize the contradictions in their ideas and values. They saw American expansion as beneficial to all concerned—and not exclusively in materialistic terms. They genuinely believed that they were exporting democracy along with capitalism and industrialization.

Williams probably goes too far in arguing that American statesmen consciously planned their foreign policy in these terms. American economic interests in foreign nations expanded enormously in the 20th century, but diplomacy had relatively little to do with this. Western industrial society (not merely American) was engulfing the rest of the world, as it continues to engulf it. Yet he is correct in pointing out that western economic penetration has had many unfortunate results for the nonindustrial nations. It is also true that Americans were particularly, though not uniquely, unimpressed by the different social and cultural patterns of people in far-off lands and insensitive to the wishes of such people to develop in their own way.

Both the United States government and American businessmen showed little interest in finding out what the people of Cuba wanted from life. They assumed that it was what *everybody* (read "Americans") wanted and, if by some strange chance this was not the case, that it was best to give it to them anyway. Dollar diplomacy had as its objectives the avoidance of violence and the economic development of Latin America; it paid small heed to how peace was maintained and how the fruits of development were distributed. The policy was self-defeating, for in the long run stability depended on the support of the people, and this was seldom forthcoming.

By the eve of World War I the United States had become a world power and had assumed what it saw as a duty to guide the development of many countries with traditions far different from its own. The American people, however, did not understand what these changes involved. While they stood ready to extend their influence into distant lands, they did so blithely, with little awareness of the implications of their behavior for themselves or for other peoples. The national psychology, if such a term has any meaning, remained fundamentally isolationist. Americans understood that their wealth and numbers made their nation strong and that geography made it practically invulnerable. Thus they proceeded to do what they wanted to do in foreign affairs, limited more by their humanly flexible consciences than by any rational analysis of the probable consequences. This policy seemed safe enough—in 1914.

SUPPLEMENTARY READING

Titles marked with an asterisk have been published in paperback

Among the many general diplomatic histories, Alexander De Conde, **A History of American Foreign Policy*** (1963), is the most detailed, and R. W. Leopold, **The Growth of American Foreign Policy** (1962), is the most thoughtful and interpretative. Milton Plesur, **America's Outward Thrust*** (1971), offers fuller detail, while J. A. S. Grenville and G. B. Young, **Politics, Strategy, and American Diplomacy: Studies in Foreign Policy** (1966), throws new light on many aspects of the period. Post-Civil War expansionism is treated in Dexter Perkins, **The Monroe Doctrine: 1867–1907*** (1937), and Allan Nevins, **Hamilton Fish** (1936). W. LaFeber, **The New Empire** (1963), presents a forceful but somewhat overstated argument on the extent of expansionist sentiment, especially on the part of American businessmen.

The new expansionism is also discussed in A. K. Weinberg, **Manifest Destiny*** (1935), J. W. Pratt, **Expansionists of 1898*** (1936), and Harold and Margaret Sprout, **The Rise of American Naval Power*** (1939). Contemporary attitudes are reflected in Josiah Strong, **Our Country** (1885), while A. T. Mahan, **The Influence of Sea Power upon History: 1660–1783*** (1890), provides the clearest presentation of Mahan's thesis. W. D. Puleston, **Mahan** (1939), is a good biography.

D. W. Pletcher, **The Awkward Years: American Foreign Relations Under Garfield and Arthur** (1962), is definitive. Other useful studies include A. F. Tyler, **The Foreign Policy of James G. Blaine** (1927), S. K. Stevens, **American Expansion in Hawaii** (1945), Allan Nevins, **Grover Cleveland** (1932) and **Henry White** (1930), L. M. Gelber, **The Rise of Anglo-American Friendship** (1938), and Henry James, **Richard Olney** (1923).

On the Spanish-American War, a good brief summary is H. W. Morgan, **America's Road to Empire*** (1965). For greater detail, consult E. R. May, **Imperial Democracy*** (1961), L. L. Gould, **The Presidency of William McKinley** (1980), and Orestes Ferrara, **The Last Spanish War** (1937).

On imperialism, see David Healy, **U. S. Expansionism: The Imperialist Urge in the 1890's** (1970), E. R. May, **American Imperialism: A Speculative Essay** (1968), and W. A. Williams, **The Tragedy of American Diplomacy*** (1962). R. L. Beisner, **Twelve Against Empire: The Anti-Imperialists*** (1968), contains lively and thoughtful sketches of leading foes of expansion. See also E. B. Thompkins, **Anti-Imperialism in the United States** (1970). For colonial problems, see Leon Wolff, **Little Brown Brother** (1961); on the Philippines, D. F. Healy, **The United States in Cuba: 1898–1902** (1963), and D. G. Munro, **Intervention and Dollar Diplomacy in the Caribbean: 1900–1921** (1964). S. F. Bemis, **The Latin American Policy of the United States*** (1943), is an excellent general account of the subject. Other useful volumes include D. C. Miner, **The Fight for the Panama Route** (1940), David McCullough, **The Path Between the Seas** (1977), H. K. Beale, **Theodore Roosevelt and the Rise of America to World Power*** (1956), A. W. Griswold, **The Far Eastern Policy of the United States*** (1938), Tyler Dennett, **John Hay** (1938), C. S. Campbell, Jr., **Special Business Interests and the Open Door Policy** (1951), Thomas McCormick, **China Market*** (1967), and H. C. Hill, **Roosevelt and the Caribbean** (1927). R. E. Osgood, **Ideals and Self-Interest in America's Foreign Relations*** (1953), and G. F. Kennan, **American Diplomacy: 1900–1950*** (1951), are important interpretations of early 20th-century United States policy, more general in scope than May's **American Imperialism** and Williams' **Tragedy of American Diplomacy.***

23/THE PROGRESSIVE ERA

The period bounded roughly by the end of the Spanish-American War and American entry into World War I is usually called the Progressive Era. Like all such generalizations about complex subjects, this title involves a great simplification. Whether *progressive* is taken to mean "tending toward change," or "improvement," or is merely used to suggest an attitude of mind, it was neither a unique nor a universal characteristic of the early years of the 20th century. Progressive elements had existed in earlier periods and did not disappear when the first American soldiers took ship for France. In important ways the progressivism of the time was a continuation of the response to industrialism that began after the Civil War, a response which has not ended. Historians have scoured the sources trying to define and explain the

Progressive Era without devising an interpretation of the period satisfactory to all. Nevertheless the term *progressive* provides a useful description of this exciting and significant period of American history.

Roots of Progressivism

The progressives were never a single group seeking a single objective. The movement sprang from many sources. One was the fight against corruption and inefficiency in government, which dated at least to the Grant era. The struggle for civil service reform was only the first skirmish in this battle; the continuing power of corrupt political machines and the growing influence of large corporations and their lobbyists on municipal and state governments outraged thousands of citizens and led them to seek ways of purifying politics and making the machinery of government responsive to the majority rather than to special-interest groups.

Progressivism also had roots in the effort to regulate and control big business, which characterized the Granger and Populist agitation of the 1870s and 1890s. The failure of the Interstate Commerce Act to end railroad abuses and of the Sherman Antitrust Act to check the growth of monopolies became increasingly apparent after 1900. The return of prosperity after the depression of the 1890s aggravated these problems by strengthening the big corporations. It encouraged the opposition by removing the inhibiting fear, so influential in the 1896 presidential campaign, that an assault on the industrial giants might lead to the collapse of the economy.

Between 1897 and 1904 the trend toward concentration in industry accelerated. Such new giants as Amalgamated Copper (1899), U. S. Steel (1901), and International Harvester (1902) attracted most of the attention, but even more alarming were the overall statistics. In a single year (1899) more than 1,200 firms were absorbed in mergers, the resulting combinations being capitalized at $2.2 billion. By 1904 there were 318 industrial combinations with an aggregate capital of $7.5 billion in the country. Those who considered bigness inherently evil demanded that the huge new "trusts" be broken up or at least strictly controlled.

Settlement house workers and other reformers concerned about the welfare of the urban poor made up a third battalion in the progressive army. The working and living conditions of slum dwellers remained abominable. The child labor problem was particularly acute; in 1900 about 1.7 million children under the age of 16 were working full time—more than the membership of the American Federation of Labor. Laws regulating the hours and working conditions of women in industry were far from adequate, and almost nothing had been done, despite the increased use of dangerous machinery in the factories, to enforce safety rules or to provide compensation or insurance for workers injured on the job. As the number of professionally competent social workers grew, the movement for social welfare legislation gained momentum.

All these tendencies may be summed up in Robert H. Wiebe's phrase, "the search for order." America was becoming more urban, more industrial, more mechanized, more centralized—in short, more complex. This trend put a premium on efficiency and cooperation. It seemed obvious to the progressives that people must become more socially minded, the economy more carefully organized.

By attracting additional thousands of sympathizers to the general cause of reform, the return of prosperity after 1896 produced the progressive movement. Good times made the average person tolerant and generous. So long as his own profits were on the rise, the average businessman did not object if labor improved its position too. Middle-class Americans who had been prepared to go to the barricades in the event of a Bryan victory in 1896 became conscience-stricken when they compared their own comfortable circumstances with those of the "huddled masses" of immigrants and native poor. Nonmaterialistic, humanitarian motives governed their behavior; they were reformers more "of the heart and the head than of the stomach."

Giant industrial and commercial corporations threatened not so much the economic well-being as the ambitions and sense of importance of the middle class. What owner of a small mill or shop could now hope to rise to the heights attained by Carnegie or merchants like John Wanamaker and Marshall Field? The growth of large labor organizations worried such types. Union membership

■ **The impact of *The Silent War*, a 1906 novel by J. Ames Mitchell that dealt with the growing class struggle in America, was enhanced by William Balfour Ker's graphic illustration, *From the Depths*.**

tripled between 1896 and 1910; bargaining became a clash of organized interests; individual relationships between employer and worker no longer counted for much. In general, character and moral values seemed less influential; organizations—cold, impersonal, heartless—were coming to control business, politics, and too many other aspects of life.

The historian Richard Hofstadter suggested still another explanation of the progressive movement. Numbers of moderately prosperous businessmen, together with members of the professions and other educated people, felt threatened by the increasing power and status of the new tycoons, many of them coarse, domineering, fond of vulgar display, and by machine politicians, who made a mockery of the traditions of duty, service, and patriotism associated with statesmanship. Comfortably well-off, middle-level businessmen lived in what seemed like genteel poverty compared to a Rockefeller or a Morgan, and they often found that the influence in the community that they considered their birthright had been usurped by a cynical local boss.

Protestant pastors accustomed to the respect and deference of their flocks found their moral leadership challenged by materialistic vestrymen who did not even pay them decent salaries. College professors watched their institutions fall under the sway of wealthy trustees who had little interest in or respect for learning. Lawyers had been "the aristocracy of the United States," James Bryce recalled in 1905; they were now merely "a part of the great organized system of industrial and financial enterprise."

Such people could support reform measures without feeling that they were being very radical because the intellectual currents of the time harmonized with their ideas of social improvement and the welfare state. The new doctrines of the social scientists, the Social Gospel religious leaders, and the philosophers of pragmatism provided a salubrious climate for progressivism. Many of the thinkers who formulated these doctrines in the 1880s and 1890s turned to the task of putting them into practice in the new century. Their number included the economist Richard T. Ely, the philosopher John Dewey, and the Baptist clergyman Walter Rauschenbusch, who, in addition to his many books extolling the Social Gospel, was active in civic reform movements in Rochester, New York.

The Muckrakers

As the diffuse progressive army gradually formed its battalions, a new journalistic fad brought the movement into focus. For many years the magazines *Forum, Arena, McClure's,* and even the staid *Atlantic Monthly* had been publishing articles discussing current political, social, and economic problems. Henry Demarest Lloyd's first blast at the Standard Oil monopoly appeared in the *Atlantic Monthly* in 1881; the radicals Henry George and Eugene V. Debs discussed a variety of problems in the pages of *Arena* in the early 1890s; Josiah Flynt exposed the corrupt relationship between criminals and the New York police for *McClure's* in 1900.

Over the years the tempo and forcefulness of this type of literature increased. Then, in the fall of 1902, *McClure's* began two particularly hard-hitting series of articles, one on Standard Oil by Ida Tarbell, the other on big-city political machines by Lincoln Steffens. These articles evoked much comment. When S. S. McClure decided to include in the January 1903 issue an attack on labor gangsterism in the coalfields along with installments of the Tarbell and Steffens series, he called attention to the circumstance in a striking editorial. Something was radically wrong with the "American character," he wrote. These articles showed that large numbers of American employers, workers, and politicians were fundamentally immoral. Lawyers were becoming tools of big business, judges were permitting evildoers to escape justice, the churches were materialistic, the colleges were incapable of understanding what was happening. "There is no one left; none but all of us," McClure concluded. "We have to pay in the end."

McClure's editorial, one of the most influential ever published in an American magazine, loosed a chain reaction. The issue sold out quickly. Thousands of readers found their own vague apprehensions brought into focus, some becoming active in progressive movements, more lending passive support.

Other editors jumped to adopt the McClure formula. A small army of professional writers soon flooded the periodical press with denunciations of the insurance business, the drug business, college athletics, prostitution, sweatshop labor, political corruption, and dozens of other subjects. The intellectual level and the essential honesty of their work varied greatly. Much of it was lurid, distorted, designed to titillate and scandalize rather than to inform. This type of article inspired Theodore Roosevelt, with his gift for vivid language, to compare the journalists to "the Man with the Muck-Rake" in Bunyan's *Pilgrim's Progress*, whose attention was so fixed on the filth

■ **"The smile that won't come off": a caricature of muckraker Ida M. Tarbell, the nemesis of Standard Oil, reproduced in the New York *Telegram* in 1906.**

at his feet that he could not notice the "celestial crown" that was offered him in exchange. Roosevelt's characterization grossly misrepresented the more worthy literature of exposure, but the label *muckraking* was thereafter permanently affixed to the type. Despite the connotations, *muckraker* became a term of honor.

The Progressive Mind

Progressives were essentially middle-class moralists seeking to arouse the conscience of "the people" in order to purify American life. They were convinced that human beings were by nature decent, well-intentioned, and kind. (After all, the words "human" and "humane" have the same root.) More deeply than earlier reformers they believed that the source of society's evils lay in the structure of its institutions, not in the weaknesses or sinfulness of individuals.

Therefore the solution to social problems lay in changing faulty institutions. Local, state, and national government must be made more responsive to the will of decent citizens who stood for the traditional virtues. Then the government (once purified) must *act.* Whatever its virtues, laissez faire was obsolete. Businessmen, especially big businessmen, must be compelled to behave fairly, their acquisitive drives curbed in the interests of justice and equal opportunity for all. The weaker elements in society—women, children, the poor, the infirm—must be protected against unscrupulous power. The people, by which (whether they realized it or not) most progressives meant the middle class, must assume new responsibilities toward the unfortunate.

Despite its fervor and democratic rhetoric, progressivism was paternalistic, moderate, and somewhat softheaded. Typical reformers of the period oversimplified complicated issues and treated their personal values as absolute standards of truth and morality. Thus progressives often acted at cross-purposes; at times some were even at war with themselves. This accounts for the diffuseness of the movement. Cutthroat business practices were criticized by great tycoons seeking to preserve their own positions and by small operators trying to protect themselves against the tycoons. But the former wanted federal regulation of big business and the latter strict enforcement of the antitrust laws. Political reforms like the direct primary election appealed to rural progressives but found few adherents among progressive businessmen.

Many progressives who desired to improve the living standards of industrial workers rejected the proposition that workers could best help themselves by organizing powerful national unions. They found it difficult to cooperate with actual working people, who seemed to them unrefined and narrow-minded. Union leaders favored government action to outlaw child labor and restrict immigration but adopted a laissez faire attitude toward wages-and-hours legislation; they preferred to win these objectives through collective bargaining, thereby justifying their own existence. Many who favored "municipal socialism" (public ownership of streetcar lines, waterworks, and other local utilities) adamantly opposed the national ownership of railroads. Progressives stressed individual freedom yet gave strong backing to the drive to deprive the public of its right to drink alcoholic beverages. Few progressives worked more assiduously than Congressman George W. Norris of rural Nebraska for reforms that would increase the power of the ordinary voter, such as the direct primary and popular election of senators, yet Norris characterized the mass of urban voters as "the mob."

The progressives never challenged the fundamental principles of capitalism, nor did they attempt a basic reorganization of society. They would have little to do with the socialist brand of reform. Wisconsin was the most progressive of states, but its leaders never cooperated with the Socialist party of Milwaukee. When socialists threatened to win control of Los Angeles in 1911, California progressives made common cause with reactionary groups in order to defeat them. Many progressives were anti-immigrant and only a handful had anything to offer blacks, surely the most exploited class in American society.

A good example of the relatively limited radicalism of progressives is offered by the experiences of progressive artists. Early in the century a number of painters, including Robert Henri, John Sloan, and George Luks, tried to develop a distinctively American style. They turned to city streets and the people of the slums for their models, depended more on inspiration and inner conviction than careful craftsmanship to achieve their effects. These "ashcan" artists were individualists, yet they supported social reform and were caught up in the progressive movement. Their idols were socially conscious painters such as Hogarth, Goya, and Daumier; they thought of themselves as rebels.

In 1912 they formed the Association of American Painters and Sculptors. The following year they organized a big showing of their work in New York's 69th Regiment Armory. Almost incidentally they decided to include a sampling of recent and current European art to add another dimension to the exhibition.

Artistically the ashcan painters were not very advanced, being uninfluenced by (if not ignorant of) the outburst of post-impressionist activity then taking place in Europe. The Europeans stole the show. For the first time Americans—well over 250,000 of them—were offered a comprehensive view of "modern" art, from Manet and Cézanne to Matisse and Picasso. Most found the dazzling color and weird distortions of the European "madmen" shocking but fascinating. A relatively unimportant cubist painting, Marcel Duchamp's *Nude Descending a Staircase,* became the focal point of the exhibition, attracting the scorn of conservative critics and the snickers of unschooled observers. One critic proposed renaming it "Explosion in a Shingle Factory"; another wit suggested "Rush Hour at the Subway"; Theodore Roosevelt, reviewing the exhibition for *Outlook,* compared it unfavorably with a Navaho rug in his bathroom.

Amid the furor the work of the Americans was virtually ignored. As a means of demonstrating their daring and originality, the show was an almost total failure. Even Roosevelt, who praised the ashcan painters while laughing off the cubist "Knights of the Isosceles Triangle" and other members of the "lunatic fringe," believed that the association had arranged the Armory Show "primarily . . . to give the public a chance to see what has recently been going on abroad." Most of the ashcan painters were confused and disheartened by their show; their hopes for creating a new American style died.

Neither the confusions nor the limitations of the progressives should obscure their accomplishments. They elevated the tone of politics, raised the aspirations of the American people, and fashioned many valuable practical reforms.

Reforming the Political System

To most progressives, political corruption and inefficiency lay at the root of the evils plaguing American society. As the cities grew, their antiquated and boss-ridden administrations became more and more disgraceful. Consider the example of San Francisco. After 1901, a shrewd lawyer named Abe Ruef ruled one of the most powerful and dissolute political machines in the nation. Only one kind of paving material was used on San Francisco's streets, and Ruef was the lawyer for the company that supplied it. When the gas company asked for a rate increase of 10 cents per 100 cubic feet, Ruef, who was already collecting $1,000 a month from the company as a "retainer," demanded and got an outright bribe of $20,000. A streetcar company needed city authorization to install overhead trolley wires; Ruef's approval cost the company $85,000. Prostitution flourished, with Ruef and his henchmen sharing in the profits. There was a brisk illegal trade in liquor licenses and other favors.

Similar conditions existed in dozens of communities. For his famous muckraking series for *McClure's* Lincoln Steffens visited St. Louis, Minneapolis, Pittsburgh, New York, Chicago, and Philadelphia and found them all riddled with corruption.

Beginning in the late 1890s progressives mounted a massive assault on dishonest and inefficient urban governments. In San Francisco a group headed by the newspaperman Fremont Older and Rudolph Spreckels, a wealthy sugar manufacturer, broke the machine and lodged Ruef in jail. In Toledo, Ohio, Samuel M. "Golden Rule" Jones won election as mayor in 1897 and succeeded in arousing the citizenry against the corruptionists. The signs that Jones placed on the lawns of Toledo's parks reflected the spirit of his administration. Instead of "Keep Off the Grass," they read: "Citizens, Protect Your Property." Other important progressive mayors were Tom L. Johnson of Cleveland, whose administration Lincoln Steffens called the best in the United States, Seth Low and later John P. Mitchell of New York, and Hazen S. Pingree of Detroit. In St. Louis the prosecutor Joseph W. Folk led a major reform drive.

City reformers could seldom destroy the machines without changing urban political institutions. Some cities obtained "home rule" charters that gave them greater freedom from state control in dealing with local matters. Many created research bureaus that investigated government problems in a scientific and nonpartisan manner. A number of middle-sized communities (Galveston, Texas, was the prototype) experimented with a system that integrated executive and legislative powers in the hands of a small elected commission, thereby concentrating responsibility and making it easier to coordinate complex activities. Out of this experiment came the city manager system under which the commissioners appointed a professional manager to administer city affairs on a nonpartisan basis. Dayton, Ohio, which adopted the plan after the town was devastated by a flood in 1913, offers the best illustration of the city manager system in the Progressive Era.

To carry out this kind of change required the support of state legislatures, since all municipal government depends on the authority of a sovereign state. Such approval was often difficult to obtain—local bosses were usually entrenched in powerful state machines, and most legislatures were controlled by rural majorities insensitive to urban needs. Therefore the progressives had to strike at inefficiency and corruption at the state level too.

During the first decade of the new century, Wisconsin, the progressive state par excellence, was transformed by Robert M. La Follette, one of the most remarkable figures of the age. La Follette was born in Primrose, Wisconsin, in 1855. He had served three terms as a Republican congressman (1885–1891) and developed a reputation as an uncompromising foe of corruption before being elected governor in 1900. That the people would do the right thing in any situation if properly informed and inspired was the fundamental article of his political faith. "Machine control is based upon misrepresentation and ignorance," La Follette said. "Democracy is based upon knowledge. . . . The only way to beat the boss and ring rule [is] to keep the people thoroughly informed." His own career seemed to prove his point, for in his repeated clashes with the conservative Wisconsin Republican machine, he won battle after battle by vigorous grassroots campaigning.

■ **Robert M. La Follette speaking to Wisconsin farmers in 1897. After six years as governor of the state, he won election to the Senate, serving four terms.**

La Follette overhauled the political structure of Wisconsin. Over the opposition of conservative Republicans subservient to railroad and lumbering interests, he obtained a direct primary system for nominating candidates, a corrupt practices act, and laws limiting campaign expenditures and lobbying activities. In power he became something of a boss himself. He made ruthless use of patronage, demanded absolute loyalty of his subordinates, and often stretched, or at least oversimplified, the truth when presenting complex issues to the voters.

La Follette was a consummate showman who never rose entirely above rural prejudices. He was prone to scent a nefarious "conspiracy" organized by "the interests" behind even the mildest opposition to his proposals. But he was devoted to the cause of honest government. Realizing that some state functions called for specialized technical knowledge, he used commissions and agencies to handle such matters as railroad regulation, tax assessment, conservation, and highway construction. Wisconsin established a legislative reference library to assist lawmakers in drafting bills. For work of this kind, La Follette called on the faculty of the University of Wisconsin, enticing such scholars as the economist Balthasar H. Meyer and the political scientist Thomas S. Adams into the public service and drawing freely on the advice of such outstanding social scientists as Richard T. Ely, John R. Commons, and E. A. Ross.

The success of what became known as the Wisconsin Idea led other states to adopt similar programs. Reform administrations swept into office in Iowa and Arkansas (1901), Oregon (1902), Minnesota, Kansas, and Mississippi (1904), New York and Georgia (1906), Nebraska (1909), New Jersey and Colorado (1910). In some cases the reformers were Republicans, in others Democrats, but in all these states and in many others, the example of Wisconsin was influential. By 1910, 15 states had established legislative reference services, most of them staffed by personnel trained in Wisconsin.

The direct primary system became almost universal.

Some states went beyond Wisconsin in striving to make their governments responsive to the popular will. In 1902 Oregon began to experiment with the initiative, a system by which a bill could be forced on the attention of the legislature by popular petition, and the referendum, a method for allowing the electorate to approve measures rejected by their representatives and to repeal measures that the legislature had passed. Eleven states, most of them in the West, had legalized these devices by 1914.

National Political Reforms

On the national level the Progressive Era saw the culmination of the struggle for women's suffrage. The shock occasioned by the failure of the Thirteenth and Fourteenth Amendments to give women the vote resulted in a split among feminists. One group, the American Women's Suffrage Association, focused on the vote question alone. The more radical National Women's Suffrage Association, led by Elizabeth Cady Stanton and Susan B. Anthony, concerned itself with many issues of importance to women as well as the suffrage. The NWSA took an exceedingly partisan stance, placing the immediate interests of women ahead of everything else. It was deeply involved in efforts to unionize women workers, yet it did not hesitate to urge women to be strikebreakers if they could get better jobs by doing so.

Aside from the weaknesses resulting from their lack of unity, feminists were handicapped in the late 19th century by Victorian sexual inhibitions, which most of their leaders shared. Dislike of male-dominated society was hard enough to separate from dislike of men under the best of circumstances. At a time when sex was an unmentionable topic in polite society and sexual feelings were often deeply repressed, some of the most militant advocates of women's rights probably did not understand their own feelings. Most feminists, for example, opposed contraception, insisting that birth control by any means other than continence would encourage what they called masculine lust. The Victorian idealization of female "purity" and the popular image of women as the revered guardians of home and family further confused many reformers. And the trend of 19th-century scientific thinking, influenced by the Darwinian concept of biological adaptation, led to the conclusion that the female personality was fundamentally different from the male and that the differences were inherent, not culturally determined.

These ideas and prejudices enticed feminists into a logical trap. If women were morally superior to men—a tempting conclusion—they could advance a practical argument for giving women the suffrage: it would improve the character of the electorate. Society would benefit in dozens of ways—politics would become less corrupt, war would become a thing of the past, and so on. "City housekeeping has failed," said Jane Addams of Hull House in arguing for the reform of municipal government, "partly because women, the traditional housekeepers, have not been consulted."

The trouble with this argument (aside from the fact that opponents could easily demonstrate that in states where women did vote, governments were no better or worse than elsewhere) was that it surrendered the principle of equality. In the long run this was to have serious consequences for the women's movement, though the immediate effect of the "purity" argument probably was to advance the suffragists' cause.

By the early 20th century there were signs of progress. In 1890 the two major women's groups combined as the National American Women's Suffrage Association. While Stanton and Anthony were the first two presidents of the association, new leaders were emerging, the most notable being Carrie Chapman Catt, a woman who combined superb organizing abilities and political skills with commitment to broad social reform. The NAWSA made winning the right to vote its main objective and concentrated on a state-by-state approach.

In the 1890s it won some minor victories; by 1896 Wyoming, Utah, Colorado, and Idaho had been conquered. The burgeoning of the progressive movement helped as middle-class recruits of both sexes adopted the cause. California voted for women's suffrage in 1911 after having defeated the proposal some years earlier, and several other states fell in line. For the first time, large numbers of working-class women began to agitate for the vote.

The suffragists then shifted the campaign back to the national level, the lead taken by a new or-

NEW YORK STATE DENIES
the VOTE To CRIMINALS
LUNATICS, IDIOTS & WOMEN

■ **A banner in a 1911 women's suffrage parade carries one of the longest-standing arguments in favor of women getting the vote.**

ganization, the Congressional Union, headed by Alice Paul. After some hesitation the NAWSA began to campaign for a constitutional amendment, which won congressional approval in 1918. By 1920 the necessary three-quarters of the states had approved the Nineteenth Amendment; the long fight was over.

The progressive drive for political democracy also found expression in the Seventeenth Amendment to the Constitution, ratified in 1913, which required the popular election of senators. And a group of "insurgent" congressmen managed to reform the House of Representatives by limiting the power of the Speaker. During the early years of the century, operating under the system established in the 1890s by "Czar" Thomas B. Reed, Speaker Joseph G. Cannon exercised tyrannical authority, appointing the members of all committees and controlling the course of legislation. Representatives could seldom obtain the floor without first explaining their purpose to Cannon and obtaining the Speaker's consent. In 1910 the insurgents, led by George W. Norris of Nebraska, stripped Cannon of his control over the House Rules Committee. Thereafter, appointments to committees were determined by the entire membership, acting through party caucuses. This change was thoroughly progressive. "We want the House to be representative of the people and each individual member to have his ideas presented and passed on," Norris explained.

No other important alterations of the national political system were made during the Progressive Era. Although some 20 states passed presidential primary laws, no change in the cumbersome and undemocratic method of electing presidents was accomplished. An attempt to improve the efficiency of the federal bureaucracy led Congress to create a Commission on Efficiency and Economy in 1911, but it did not act on the commission's recommendations. Congress did pass a law in 1911 requiring its members to file statements of their campaign expenses.

Social and Economic Reform

Political reform was only a means to an end; once the system had been made responsive to the desires of the people, the progressives hoped to use it to improve society itself. Many cities experimented with "gas and water socialism," taking over public utility companies and operating them as departments of the municipal government. Under "Golden Rule" Jones, Toledo established a minimum wage for city employees, built playgrounds and golf courses, and moderated its harsh penal code. Seth Low improved New York's public transportation system and obtained the passage of the tenement house law of 1901. Tom Johnson forced a fare cut to 3 cents on the Cleveland street railways.

At the state level progressives continued to battle for legislation based on the police power, despite restrictions imposed by the courts under the Fourteenth Amendment. Women played a particularly important part in these struggles; their campaign for the right to vote was part of a larger commitment to reform.

Industrial workers improved their position mainly because good times kept unemployment down. Real wages rose only slightly in spite of the rapid increase in labor productivity, and the length of the work week declined slowly. However, government action forced a significant decline in the employment of children. Sparked by the National Child Labor Committee, organized in 1904, reformers over the next ten years obtained laws in nearly every state banning the employment of young children (the minimum age varied from 12 to 16). Many states also limited the hours of older children to eight or ten per day and outlawed night work and labor in dangerous occupations by minors. These laws fixed no uniform standards and many were poorly enforced, yet when Congress passed a federal child labor law in 1916, the Supreme Court, in *Hammer* v. *Dagenhart* (1918), declared it unconstitutional.*

By 1917 nearly all the states had placed limitations on the hours of women industrial workers, and about ten states had set minimum wage standards for women. Once again federal action that would have extended such regulation to the entire country did not materialize. Even a ten-hour law for women workers in the District of Columbia was thrown out by the Court in *Adkins* v. *Children's Hospital* (1923).

Laws protecting workers against on-the-job accidents were enacted by many states. Disasters like the 1911 Triangle fire in New York City, in which nearly 150 women perished because the Triangle shirtwaist factory had no fire escapes, led to the passage of stricter municipal building codes and many state factory inspection acts. By 1910 most states had modified the common-law principle that a worker accepted the risk of accident as a condition of employment and was not entitled to compensation if injured unless it could be proved that the employer had been negligent. Gradually the states adopted accident insurance plans, and some began to grant pensions to widows with small children. Most manufacturers favored such measures, if for no other reason than that they regularized procedures and avoided costly lawsuits.

The passage of so much state social legislation sent conservatives scurrying to the Supreme Court for redress. Such persons believed, quite sincerely in most instances, that *no* government had the power to deprive either workers or employers of the right to negotiate any kind of labor contract they wished. The decision of the Supreme Court in the Lochner bakeshop case (1905) seemed to indicate that the justices would adopt this point of view. But when an Oregon law limiting women laundry workers to ten hours a day was challenged in *Muller* v. *Oregon* (1908), Florence Kelley and Josephine Goldmark of the Consumers' League persuaded Louis D. Brandeis to defend the statute before the Court.

The Consumers' League, whose slogan was "in-

*A second child labor law, passed in 1919, was also thrown out by the Court, and a child labor amendment, submitted in 1924, failed to achieve ratification by the necessary three-quarters of the states.

vestigate, agitate, legislate," was probably the most effective women's organization of the period. With the aid of League researchers Brandeis prepared a remarkable brief stuffed with economic and sociological evidence indicating that *in fact* long hours damaged both the health of individual women and the health of society. This nonlegal evidence greatly impressed the judges. "It may not be amiss," they declared, "to notice . . . expressions of opinion from other than judicial sources" in determining the constitutionality of such laws. "Woman's physical structure, and the functions she performs in consequence thereof, justify special legislation," they concluded. "The limitations which this statute places upon her contractual powers . . . are not imposed solely for her benefit, but also largely for the benefit of all."

The fact that the Oregon law applied only to women reduced the importance of the Muller decision. In some later cases the Court threw out labor laws based on the police power. Nevertheless, after 1908 the right of states to protect the weaker members of society by special legislation was widely accepted. The use of the "Brandeis brief" technique to demonstrate the need for such legislation became standard practice.

Progressives also launched a massive if ill-coordinated attack on problems related to monopoly and business influence on government. The variety of regulatory legislation passed by the states between 1900 and 1917 was almost infinite. In Wisconsin the progressives created a powerful railroad commission staffed with nonpartisan experts; they enacted a graduated income tax and strengthened the state tax commission, which then proceeded to force corporations to bear a larger share of the cost of government; they overhauled the laws regulating insurance companies and set up a small state-owned life insurance company to serve as a yardstick for evaluating the rates of private companies. In 1911, besides creating an industrial commission to enforce the state's labor and factory legislation, they established a conservation commission, headed by Charles R. Van Hise, president of the University of Wisconsin.

A similar spate of legislation characterized the brief reign of Woodrow Wilson as governor of New Jersey (1911–1913). Urged on by the relentless Wilson, the legislature created a strong public utility commission with authority to evaluate the properties of railroad, gas, electric, telephone, and express companies and to fix rates and set standards for these corporations. The legislature enacted storage and food inspection laws, and in 1913, after Wilson had moved on to the presidency, it passed seven bills (the "Seven Sisters" laws) tightening the state's loose controls over corporations, which had won New Jersey the unenviable reputation of being "the mother of trusts."

Economic reforms in other states were less spectacular but impressive in the mass. In New York an investigation of the big life insurance companies led to comprehensive changes in the insurance laws and put Charles Evans Hughes, who had conducted the investigation, in the governor's chair, where he achieved other progressive reforms. In Iowa stiff laws regulating railroads were passed in 1906. In Nebraska the legislature created a system of bank deposit insurance in 1909. Minnesota levied an inheritance tax and built a harvesting machine factory to compete with the harvester trust. Georgia raised the taxes on corporations.

These are examples plucked almost at random from among hundreds of laws passed by states in every part of the nation. However, as in the area of social legislation, piecemeal state regulation failed to solve the problems of an economy growing yearly more integrated and complex. It was on the national level that the most significant battles for economic reform were fought.

Theodore Roosevelt

On September 6, 1901, an anarchist named Leon Czolgosz shot President McKinley during a public reception at the Pan-American Exposition at Buffalo, New York. Eight days later McKinley died and Theodore Roosevelt became president of the United States. The new president hastened to assure the country that he intended to carry on in his predecessor's footsteps, but his ascension to the presidency marked the beginning of a new era in national politics.

Although only 42, by far the youngest president in the nation's history up to that time, Roosevelt brought solid qualifications to his high office. Son of a well-to-do New York merchant of Dutch ancestry, he had graduated from Harvard in 1880 and studied law briefly at Columbia, though he did not complete his degree. In addition to political experience that included three terms in the New York assembly, six years on the United States Civil Service Commission, two years as police commissioner of New York City, another as assistant secretary of the navy, and a term as governor of New York, he had been a rancher in Dakota Territory and a soldier in the Spanish-American War. He was also a well-known historian: his *Naval War of 1812* (1882), begun during his undergraduate days at Harvard, and his four-volume *Winning of the West* (1889–1896) were valuable works of scholarship, and he had written two popular biographies and other books as well. Politically, he had always been a loyal Republican. He rejected the Mugwump heresy in 1884, despite his distaste for Blaine, and during the tempestuous nineties he vigorously denounced Populism, Bryanism, and "labor agitators."

Nevertheless Roosevelt's elevation to the presidency alarmed many conservatives, and not without reason. He did not fit their conception, based on a composite image of the chief executives from Hayes to McKinley, of what a president should be like. He seemed too undignified, too energetic, too outspoken, too unconventional. It was one thing to have operated a cattle ranch, another to have captured a gang of rustlers at gunpoint; one thing to have run a metropolitan police force, another to have roamed New York slums in the small hours in order to catch patrolmen fraternizing with thieves and prostitutes; one thing to have commanded a regiment, another to have killed a Spaniard personally.

Roosevelt had been a weak and sickly child, plagued by asthma and poor eyesight, and he seems to have spent much of his adult life compensating for the sense of inadequacy that these troubles bred in him. He repeatedly carried his displays of physical stamina and personal courage, and his love of athletics and big-game hunting, to preternatural lengths. Mark Twain called him "the Tom Sawyer of the political world . . . always hunting for a chance to show off." Once, while fox hunting, he fell from his horse, cutting his face severely and breaking his left arm. Instead of waiting for help or struggling to some nearby house to summon a doctor, Roosevelt clambered back on his horse and resumed the chase. "I was in at the death," he wrote next day. "I looked pretty gay, with one arm dangling, and my face and clothes like the walls of a slaughter house."

■ **Teddy Roosevelt on the stump in the days before microphones and television cameras. The row of straw hats in the foreground belongs to newspaper reporters, eagerly taking notes.**

That evening, after his arm had been set and put in splints, he attended a dinner party.

Roosevelt worshiped aggressiveness and was extremely sensitive to any threat to his honor as a gentleman. When another young man showed some slight interest in Roosevelt's fiancée, he sent for a set of French dueling pistols. His teachers found him an interesting student, for he was intelligent and imaginative if rather annoyingly argumentative. "Now look here, Roosevelt," one Harvard professor finally said to him, "let me talk. I'm running this course."

Few individuals have rationalized or sublimated their feelings of inferiority as effectively as Roosevelt and to such good purpose. And few have been more genuinely warmhearted, more full of spontaneity, more committed to the ideals of public service and national greatness. As a political leader he was energetic and hard-driving. Conservatives and timid souls, sensing his aggressiveness even when he held it in check, distrusted Roosevelt's judgment, fearing he might go off half-cocked in some crisis. In fact his judgment was nearly always sound; responsibility usually tempered his aggressiveness.

Above all Roosevelt believed in action. When he was first mentioned as a running mate for McKinley in 1900, he wrote: "The Vice Presidency is a most honorable office, but for a young man there is not much to do." It would have been unthinkable for him to preside over a caretaker administration devoted to maintaining the status quo. However, the reigning Republican politicos, basking in the sunshine of the prosperity that had contributed so much to their victory in 1900, distrusted anything suggestive of change. Mark Hanna reflected the mood of most of his fellow senators when he urged the country to "stand pat and continue Republican prosperity." The same sentiment pervaded the House, where Speaker Cannon said that his philosophy could be summed up in the phrase "Stand by the status."

Had Roosevelt been the impetuous hothead that conservatives feared, he would have plunged ahead without regard for their feelings and influence. Instead he moved slowly and often got what he wanted by using his executive power rather than by persuading Congress to pass new laws. His domestic program, ill defined at first, included some measure of control of big corporations, more power for the Interstate Commerce Commission, and the conservation of natural resources. By consulting congressional leaders and following their advice not to bring up controversial matters like the tariff and currency reform, with which he was not deeply concerned in any case, he obtained a modest budget of new laws.

The Newlands Act (1902) funneled the proceeds from land sales in the West into federal irrigation projects. The Expedition Act (1903) speeded the handling of antitrust suits in the courts. Another 1903 law created a Department of Commerce and Labor, which was to include a Bureau of Corporations with authority to investigate industrial combines and issue reports. The Elkins Railroad Act of 1903 strengthened the Interstate Commerce Commission's hand against the railroads by making the receiving as well as the granting of rebates illegal and by forbidding the roads to deviate in any way from their published rates.

Roosevelt and Big Business

Roosevelt soon became known as a trustbuster, and in the sense that he considered the monopoly problem the most pressing issue of the times, the term has some meaning. But he did not believe in breaking up big corporations indiscriminately. "Much of the legislation . . . enacted against trusts," he said in 1900 while governor of New York, "is not one whit more intelligent than the mediaeval bull against the comet, and has not been one particle more effective." Regulation, rather than disruption, seemed the best way to deal with the big corporations because industrial giantism "could not be eliminated unless we were willing to turn back the wheels of modern progress."

With Congress unwilling to pass a stiff regulatory law—even the bill creating the relatively innocuous Bureau of Corporations ran into much opposition—Roosevelt resorted to the Sherman Act to get at the problem. Although the Supreme Court decision in the Sugar Trust case seemed to have emasculated that law, in 1902 he ordered the Justice Department to bring suit against the Northern Securities Company.

He chose his target wisely. The Northern Securities Company controlled the Great Northern, the Northern Pacific, and the Chicago, Burlington and Quincy railroads. It had been created in 1901 after a titanic battle on the New York Stock Exchange between the forces of J. P. Morgan and James J. Hill and those of E. H. Harriman, who was associated with the Rockefeller interests. In their efforts to obtain control of the Northern Pacific, the rivals had forced its stock up to $1,000 a share, ruining many speculators and threatening to cause a panic. Neither side could win a clear-cut victory, so they decided to put the stock of all three railroads in a holding company owned by the two groups. Since Harriman already controlled the Union Pacific and the Southern Pacific, a virtual monopoly of western railroads was effected. The public had been alarmed, for the merger seemed to typify the rapaciousness of the tycoons. Few big corporations had more enemies; thus Roosevelt's attack won wide support.

The announcement of the suit caused consternation in the business world. Morgan rushed to the White House. "If we have done anything wrong," he said to the president, "send your man to my man and they can fix it up." Roosevelt was not fundamentally opposed to this sort of agreement, but it was too late to compromise in this instance. Attorney General Philander C. Knox pressed the case vigorously, and in 1904 the Court ordered the dissolution of the Northern Securities Company. The decision served notice on the great corporations that they could no longer ignore the Sherman Act. Roosevelt ordered suits against the meat packers, the Standard Oil Trust, and the American Tobacco Company. His stock among progressives rose, yet he had not embarrassed the conservatives in Congress by demanding new antitrust legislation.

The president went out of his way to assure *cooperative* corporation magnates that he had no intention of attacking them. He saw no basic conflict between capital and labor and was not against size per se. "In our industrial and social system," he explained, "the interests of all men are so closely intertwined that in the immense majority of cases a straight-dealing man who by his efficiency, by his ingenuity and industry, benefits himself must also benefit others." His Bureau of Corporations followed a policy of "obtaining hearty co-operation rather than arousing [the] antagonism of business and industrial interests." At a White House conference in 1905, Roosevelt and Elbert H. Gary, chairman of the board of U. S. Steel, reached a "gentlemen's agreement" whereby Gary promised "to co-operate with the Government in every possible way." The Bureau of Corporations would conduct an investigation of U. S. Steel, Gary allowing it full access to company records. Roosevelt in turn promised that if the investigation revealed any corporate malpractices, he would allow Gary to set matters right voluntarily, thereby avoiding an antitrust suit. He reached a similar agreement with the International Harvester Company two years later.

There were limits to the effectiveness of such arrangements. Standard Oil agreed to a similar détente and then reneged, refusing to turn over vital records to the bureau. The Justice Department brought suit against the company under the Sherman Act of 1890, and eventually it was broken up at the order of the Supreme Court. Roosevelt would have preferred a more binding kind of regulation, but when he asked for laws giving the government supervisory authority over big combinations, Congress refused to act. Given this situation, gentlemen's agreements seemed the best alternative. Trusts that conformed to Roosevelt's somewhat subjective standards could remain as they were; others must take their chances with the Supreme Court.

Roosevelt made remarkable use of his executive power during the anthracite coal strike of 1902. In June the United Mine Workers, led by John Mitchell, laid down their picks and demanded higher wages, an eight-hour day, and recognition of the union. Most of the anthracite mines were owned by railroads. Two years earlier the miners had won a 10 percent wage increase in a similar strike, chiefly because the owners feared that labor unrest might endanger the election of McKinley. Now the coal companies were dead set against further concessions; when the men walked out, they shut down their properties and prepared to starve the strikers into submission.

The strike dragged on through summer and early fall. The miners conducted themselves with great restraint, avoiding violence and offering to submit their claims to arbitration. As the price of anthracite soared with the approach of winter, sentiment in their behalf mounted. The fact that railroad corporations allied with Wall Street controlled most of the mines and that the operators refused even to negotiate with the union predisposed the public in the workers' favor.

The owners' spokesman, George F. Baer of the Reading Railroad, proved particularly inept at public relations. Baer stated categorically that God was on the side of management, but when someone suggested asking an important Roman Catholic prelate to arbitrate the dispute, he replied icily: "Anthracite mining is a business and not a religious, sentimental or academic proposition."

Roosevelt shared the public's sympathy for the miners, and the threat of a coal famine alarmed him. For months he could think of no legal way to intervene. Early in October he summoned both sides to a conference in Washington. He urged them as patriotic Americans to sacrifice "personal consideration[s]" for the "general good." His action enraged the coal operators, for they believed he was trying to force them to recognize the union. They refused even to speak to the UMW representatives at the conference and demanded that Roosevelt end the strike by force and bring suit against the union under the Sherman Act. Mitchell, aware of the immense prestige that Roosevelt had conferred on the union by calling the conference, cooperated fully with the president.

The attitude of management strengthened public support for the miners. Even former president Grover Cleveland, who had used federal troops to break the Pullman strike, said that he was "disturbed and vexed by the tone and substance of the operators' deliverances." Encouraged by this state of affairs, Roosevelt took a bold step: he announced that unless a settlement was reached promptly, he would order federal troops into the anthracite regions, not to break the strike but to seize and operate the mines.

The threat of government intervention brought the owners to terms. A Cabinet member, Elihu Root, worked out the details with J. P. Morgan, whose firm had major interests in the Reading and other railroads, while cruising the Hudson River on Morgan's yacht. The miners would return to the pits and all issues between them and the coal companies would be submitted for settlement to a commission appointed by Roosevelt. After a last-minute crisis over the inclusion of a union representative on the commission—solved by Roosevelt's appointing the president of one of the railroad brotherhoods but classifying him as an "eminent sociologist" to save the faces of the owners—both sides accepted the arrangement and the men went back to work. In March 1903 the commission granted the miners a 10 percent wage increase and a 9-hour day.

To the public the incident seemed a perfect illustration of the progressive spirit—in Roosevelt's words, everyone had received a "square deal." In fact the results were by no means so clear-cut. The miners gained relatively little and the companies lost still less, for they were not required to recognize the United Mine Workers and the commission also recommended a 10 percent increase in the price of coal, ample compensation for the increased wage costs. The president was the main winner. The public acclaimed him as a fearless, imaginative, public-spirited leader.

Construing the powers of his office broadly, Roosevelt had interjected the federal government into a labor dispute, forced both sides to accept his leadership, and established an extralegal committee of neutrals representing the national interest to arbitrate the questions at issue. Without calling on Congress for support, he had expanded his own authority and hence that of the federal government in order to protect the public interest. His action marked a major forward step in the evolution of the modern presidency.

Roosevelt's Second Term

By reviving the Sherman Act, settling the coal strike, and pushing moderate reforms through Congress, Roosevelt insured that he would be elected president in 1904 in his own right. Progressives were pleased by his performance if not yet captivated. Conservative Republicans offered no serious objection to his renomination and supported him during the campaign. Sensing that Roosevelt had won over the liberals, the Democrats nominated a conservative, Judge Alton B. Parker of New York, and bid for the support of eastern industrialists.

This strategy failed, for businessmen continued to eye the party of Bryan with intense suspicion. They preferred, as the New York *Sun* put it, "the impulsive candidate of the party of conservatism to the conservative candidate of the party which the business interests regard as permanently and dangerously impulsive." Despite his resentment at Roosevelt's attack on the Northern Securities Company, J. P. Morgan contributed $150,000 to the Republican campaign. Other tycoons gave with equal generosity. Roosevelt swept the country, carrying even the normally Democratic border states Maryland and Missouri. According to one wit, "Parker ran for the presidency against Theodore Roosevelt and was defeated by acclamation."

Encouraged by the landslide and the increasing militancy of progressives, Roosevelt pressed for more reform legislation. His most imaginative proposal was a plan to make the District of Columbia a model progressive community. He suggested child labor and factory inspection laws and a slum clearance program, but Congress refused to act. Likewise, his request for a minimum wage for railroad workers was rejected.

He had greater success when he proposed still another increase in the power of the Interstate Commerce Commission. The Elkins Railroad Act had proved a disappointment, for the courts continued to favor the railroads in most cases. Rebating remained a serious problem. With progressive state governors demanding federal action and with farmers and manufacturers, especially in the Middle West, clamoring for relief against discriminatory rates, Roosevelt was ready by 1905 to make railroad legislation his major objective. The ICC should be empowered to fix rates, not merely to challenge unreasonable ones. It should have the right to inspect the private records of the railroads, since fair rates could not be determined unless the true financial condition of the roads was known.

Because these proposals struck at rights that businessmen considered sacrosanct, many congressmen balked. But Roosevelt applied presidential pressure, and that, combined with broad public support for stiffer regulation, caused a majority to fall in line.

In June 1906 the Hepburn bill became law. It gave the commission the power to inspect the books of railroad companies, to set maximum rates (once a complaint had been filed by a shipper), and to control sleeping car companies, owners of oil pipelines, and other firms engaged in transportation. Railroads could no longer issue passes freely—an important check on their political influence. In all, the Hepburn Act made the ICC a more powerful and more active body. While it did not outlaw judicial review of ICC decisions, thereafter those decisions were seldom overturned by the courts. The staff of the commission grew from fewer than 200 in 1905 to more than 500 in 1909. The number of complaints filed by shippers jumped from 65 to 1,097 in the same years.

How the commission exercised its power was another question. According to recent students of the subject, it adopted an "archaic" view of the public interest (one based on conditions in the railroad business that were long out of date) and became "a standpat body that ignored inflation and refused rate increases" almost automatically. With their costs rising, the railroads were soon again in financial difficulties. Profits slumped and capital investment declined.

Congress also passed meat inspection and pure food and drug legislation in 1906. The question of federal regulation of slaughterhouses dated to the "pork controversy" with the European powers in the 1880s. Feelings about meat inspection in the business world were mixed. The major packers tended to favor inspection because of their interest in the export market; most local packers objected. Other businessmen were divided, some objecting in principle to any extension of government regulation. In 1906 the president of the National Association of Manufacturers opposed regulating the packers, but the NAM board of directors voted not to campaign against inspection.

The publication in 1906 of Upton Sinclair's novel *The Jungle,* a devastating exposé of the filthy conditions in the Chicago slaughterhouses, focused attention on the issue. Sinclair was more interested in writing a socialist tract than he was in meat inspection, but his book, a best seller, raised a storm against the packers. After Roosevelt read *The Jungle* he sent two officials to Chicago to investigate. Their report was so shocking, he said, that its publication would "be well-nigh ruinous to our export trade in meat." He threatened to release the report, however, unless Congress acted. After a hot fight, the meat inspection bill passed. A Pure Food and Drug Act, forbidding the manufacture and sale of adulterated and fraudulently labeled products, rode through Congress on the coattails of this measure.

Roosevelt has probably received more credit than he deserves for these laws. He had never been deeply interested in pure food legislation, and he considered Dr. Harvey W. Wiley, chief chemist of the Department of Agriculture and the leader of the fight for this reform, something of a crank. He compromised with opponents of meat inspection cheerfully, despite his loud denunciations of the evils under attack. "As now carried on the [meat-packing] business is both a menace to health and an outrage on decency," he said. "No legislation that is not drastic and thoroughgoing will be of avail." Yet he went along with the packers' demand that the government pay the costs of inspection, though he believed that "the only way to secure efficiency is by the imposition upon the packers of a fee." Nevertheless the end results were positive and in line with his conception of the public good.

To advanced liberals Roosevelt's achievements seemed limited when placed beside his professed objectives and his smug evaluations of what he had done. How could he be a reformer and a defender of established interests at the same time? Roosevelt found no difficulty in holding such a position. As one historian has said, "he stood close to the center and bared his teeth at the conservatives of the right and the liberals of the extreme left."

As the progressive movement advanced, Roosevelt advanced with it. He never accepted all the ideas of what he called its "lunatic fringe," but he took steadily more liberal positions. He always insisted that he was not hostile to business interests, but when those interests sought to exploit the national domain, they had no more implacable foe. He placed some 150 million acres of forest lands in federal reserves, and he strictly enforced the laws governing grazing, mining, and lumbering. When his opponents attached to an important appropriations bill a rider prohibiting the creation of further reserves without the approval of Congress, Roosevelt, in a typical example of his broad use of executive power, transferred an additional 17 million acres to the reserve before signing the bill. In 1908 he organized a National Conservation Conference, attended by 44 governors and 500 others, to discuss conservation matters. As a result of this meeting, most states created conservation commissions.

As Roosevelt became more liberal, conservative Republicans began to balk at following his lead. The sudden panic that struck the financial world in October 1907 speeded the trend. Government policies had no direct bearing on the panic, which began with a run on several important New York trust companies and spread to the Stock Exchange when speculators found themselves unable to borrow money to meet their obligations. In the emergency Roosevelt authorized the deposit of large amounts of government cash in New York banks. He informally agreed to the acquisition of the Tennessee Coal and Iron Company by U. S. Steel when the bankers told him that the purchase was necessary to end the panic. In spite of his efforts, conservatives insisted on referring to the financial collapse as "Roosevelt's Panic," and they blamed the president for the depression that followed on its heels.

Roosevelt, however, turned left rather than right. In 1908 he came out for federal income and inheritance taxes, for stricter regulation of interstate corporations, and for reforms designed to help industrial workers. He denounced "the speculative folly and the flagrant dishonesty" of "malefactors of great wealth," further alienating conservative, or Old Guard Republicans, who believed that economic reform had gone far enough and that political reforms like the direct primary were undermining their power. They resented the attacks on their integrity implicit in many of Roosevelt's statements. When the president began criticizing the courts, the last bastion of conservatism, he lost all chance of obtaining further reform legislation. As he said himself, during his last months in office "the period of stagnation continued to rage with uninterrupted violence."

William Howard Taft

Roosevelt remained popular and politically powerful; before his term ended, he chose William Howard Taft, his secretary of war, to succeed him and easily obtained his nomination. William Jennings Bryan was again the Democratic candidate. Campaigning on Roosevelt's record, Taft carried the country by well over a million votes, defeating Bryan 321 to 162 in the electoral college.

Taft was intelligent, experienced, and public-spirited; he seemed ideally suited to carry out Roosevelt's policies. Born in Cincinnati in 1857, educated at Yale, he had served as an Ohio judge, as solicitor general of the United States under Harrison, and then as a federal circuit court judge before accepting McKinley's assignment to head the Philippine Commission in 1900. His success as civil governor of the Philippines led Roosevelt to make him secretary of war in 1904. He supported the "Square Deal" loyally. This, together with his mentor's ardent endorsement, won him the backing of most progressive Republicans. Yet the Old Guard liked him too; although outgoing, he had none of the Roosevelt impetuosity and aggressiveness. His antilabor opinions voiced while on the bench raised his status among conservatives. His genial personality and his obvious desire to avoid conflict appealed to moderates.

However, Taft lacked the physical and mental stamina required of a modern chief executive. While he was not lazy, he weighed over 300 pounds and needed to rest this vast bulk more than the job allowed. He liked to eat in leisurely fashion, to idle away mornings on the golf course, to take an afternoon nap. Campaigning bored him, speechmaking seemed a needless chore. The judicial life was his real love; intense partisanship dismayed and confused him. He was too reasonable to control a coalition and not ambitious

■ **Taft was the first presidential golfer, playing enthusiastically despite his bulk. He ended his career happily as chief justice of the United States.**

enough to impose his will on others. He found extremists irritating, persistent people (such as his wife) difficult to resist. He supported many progressive measures, but he never absorbed the progressive spirit.

Taft honestly desired to carry out most of Roosevelt's policies. He enforced the Sherman Act vigorously and continued to add land to the national forest reserves. He signed the Mann-Elkins Act of 1910, which empowered the Interstate Commerce Commission to suspend rate increases without waiting for a shipper to complain and established a Commerce Court to speed the settlement of railroad rate cases. An 8-hour day for all persons engaged in work on government contracts, mine safety legislation, and several other reform measures received his approval. He even summoned Congress into special session specifically to reduce tariff duties—something Roosevelt had not dared to attempt.

But Taft had been disturbed by Roosevelt's sweeping use of executive power. "We have got to work out our problems on the basis of law," he insisted. Where Roosevelt had excelled at maneuvering around congressional opposition and in finding ways to accomplish his objectives without waiting for Congress to act, Taft adamantly refused to use such tactics. His restraint was in many ways admirable, but it reduced his effectiveness.

In case after case Taft's lack of vigor and his political ineptness led to trouble. He had an uncanny ability to alienate politicians with views substantially like his own. In the matter of the tariff, he favored downward revision. When the special session met in 1909, the House promptly passed a bill that was in line with his desires. But Senate protectionists restored the high rates of the Act of 1897 on most items. A group of insurgent senators, led by Robert La Follette of Wisconsin, Jonathan Dolliver of Iowa, and Albert J. Beveridge of Indiana, fought these changes desperately, producing masses of statistics to show that the proposed schedules on cotton goods, woolens, and other products were unreasonably high. They were fighting the president's battle, yet Taft did little to help them. He signed the final Payne-Aldrich measure and called it "the best [tariff] bill that the Republican party ever passed." He had some justification for this faint praise, since the act did make important reductions in the duties on cotton goods, hides, shoes, and iron ore. But his attitude dumbfounded the progressives.

In 1910 Taft got into difficulty with the conservationists. While he believed in husbanding natural resources carefully, he did not like the way Roosevelt had circumvented Congress in adding to the forest reserves. He demanded, and eventually obtained, specific legislation to accomplish this purpose. The issue that roused the conservationists concerned the integrity of his secretary of the interior, Richard A. Ballinger. A less than ardent conservationist, Ballinger returned to the public domain certain waterpower sites that his predecessor in the Roosevelt administration had withdrawn on the legally questionable ground that they were to become ranger stations. Ballinger's action alarmed Chief Forester Gifford Pinchot, the darling of the conservationists. When Pinchot learned that Ballinger intended to validate the shaky claim of powerful mining interests to a large tract of coal-rich land in Alaska, he launched an intemperate attack on the secretary.

In the Ballinger-Pinchot controversy Taft felt obliged to support his own man. The coal lands dispute was complex, and Pinchot's charges were exaggerated and in poor taste. It was certainly unfair to call Ballinger "the most effective opponent the conservation policies have yet had." When Pinchot, whose own motives were partly political, persisted in criticizing Ballinger, Taft dismissed him, bringing down upon himself the wrath of the conservationists. He had no choice under the circumstances, but a more adept politician would have found some way of avoiding a showdown.

Breakup of the Republican Party

One ominous aspect of the Ballinger-Pinchot affair was that Pinchot was a close friend of Theodore Roosevelt. After Taft's inauguration, Roosevelt had gone off to hunt big game in Africa, bearing in his baggage an autographed photograph of his protégé and a touching letter of appreciation, in which the new president said: "I can never forget that the power I now exercise was a voluntary transfer from you to me." For months, as he trudged across Africa, guns blazing, Roosevelt was out of touch with affairs in the United States. As soon as he emerged from the wilderness in March 1910, bearing more than 3,000 trophies, including 9 lions, 5 elephants, and 13 rhinos, he was caught up in the squabble between the progressive members of his party and its titular head. Pinchot met him in Italy, laden with injured innocence and a packet of angry letters from various progressives. His intimate friend Senator Lodge, essentially a conservative, barraged him with messages, the gist of which was that Taft was lazy and inept and that Roosevelt should prepare to become the "Moses" who would guide the party "out of the wilderness of doubt and discontent" into which Taft had led it.

Roosevelt hoped to steer a middle course, but Pinchot's complaints impressed him. Taft had decided to strike out on his own, he concluded. "No man must render such a service as that I rendered Taft and expect the individual . . . not in the end to become uncomfortable and resentful," he wrote Lodge sadly. No immediate break took place, but Taft sensed the former president's coolness and was offended. He was egged on by his ambitious wife, who wanted him to stand clear of the Roosevelt shadow and establish his own reputation.

Perhaps the resulting rupture was inevitable. The Republican party was dividing into two factions, the progressives and the Old Guard. Forced to choose between them, Taft threw in his lot with the Old Guard. When House progressives revolted against the domination of Speaker Cannon, Taft deprived them of patronage, practically reading them out of the party.

Roosevelt backed the progressives. Speaking at Osawatomie, Kansas, in August 1910, he came out for a comprehensive program of social legislation, which he called the New Nationalism. Besides attacking "special privilege" and the "unfair money-getting" practices of "lawbreakers of great wealth," he called for a broad expansion of federal power. "The betterment we seek must be accomplished," he said, "mainly through the National Government."

The final break came in October 1911, when the president ordered an antitrust suit against U. S. Steel. Roosevelt, of course, opposed breaking up large corporations. "The effort at prohibiting all combination has substantially failed," he said in his New Nationalism speech. "The way out lies . . . in completely controlling them." Taft was prepared "to enforce [the Sherman] law or die in the attempt." What angered Roosevelt was Taft's emphasis in the steel suit on U. S. Steel's absorption of the Tennessee Coal and Iron Company, which Roosevelt had unofficially authorized during the panic of 1907. The government's antitrust brief made Roosevelt appear to have been either an abettor of monopoly or—far worse—a fool who had been duped by the steel corporation. He began to criticize Taft publicly, and early in 1912 he declared himself a candidate for the Republican presidential nomination.

The dramatic split between the nation's two leading Republicans intensified the conflict within the party. In January 1911 the liberal faction had organized a National Progressive Republican League, which was pushing Senator La Follette for the Republican nomination. Roosevelt's entry into the race encouraged the progressives to strike more boldly against the administration. Although some, particularly those from the Middle West, found Roosevelt's position on the Sherman Act

■ **Cartoonists had a field day with Roosevelt as a Bull Moose; in this cartoon from *Harper's* T. R. enters the political zoo.**

unpalatable, the fact that he stood a better chance than La Follette of being elected president led most of them to swing to his support.

Roosevelt plunged into the preconvention campaign with typical energy. He was almost uniformly victorious in states that held presidential primaries, carrying even Ohio, Taft's home state. However, the president controlled the party machinery and entered the national convention with a small majority of the delegates. Since some Taft delegates had been chosen under questionable circumstances, the Roosevelt forces challenged the right of 254 of them to their seats. The Taft-controlled credentials committee, paying little attention to the evidence, gave all but a few of the disputed seats to the president, who then won the nomination on the first ballot.

Had Roosevelt swallowed his resentment and bided his time, Taft would almost certainly have been defeated in the election and the 1916 Republican nomination would have been Roosevelt's for the asking. But he was understandably outraged by the ruthless manner in which the Taft "steamroller" had overridden his forces. When his leading supporters urged him to organize a third party, and when two of them, George W. Perkins, formerly a partner of the banker J. P. Morgan, and the publisher, Frank Munsey, offered to finance the campaign, he agreed to make the race. In August, amid scenes of hysterical enthusiasm, the first convention of the Progressive party met at Chicago and nominated him for president. Announcing that he felt "as strong as a bull moose," Roosevelt delivered a stirring "confession of faith," calling for strict regulation of corporations, a tariff commission, national presidential primaries, minimum-wage and workmen's compensation laws, the elimination of child labor, and many other reforms.

Election of 1912

The Democrats made the most of the opportunity offered by the Republican schism. Had they nominated a conservative or allowed Bryan a fourth chance, they would probably have insured Roosevelt's election. Instead, after battling through 46 ballots at their convention in Baltimore, they nominated Woodrow Wilson, who had achieved a remarkable liberal record as governor of New Jersey.

Although as a political scientist Wilson had sharply criticized the status quo and had taken a pragmatic approach to the idea of government regulation of the economy, he had objected strongly to the Bryan brand of politics. In 1896 he voted for the Gold Democratic party candidate for president. But by 1912, influenced partly by ambition and partly by the spirit of the times, he had been converted to progressivism. He called his brand of reform the New Freedom.

The federal government could best advance the cause of social justice, Wilson reasoned, by eradicating the special privileges that enabled the "interests" to flourish. Where Roosevelt had lost faith in competition as a way of protecting the public against monopolies, Wilson insisted that competition could be restored. The government must break up the great trusts and establish fair rules for doing business, subjecting violators to stiff punishments. Thereafter, the checks of the free enterprise system would protect the public from exploitation without destroying individual initia-

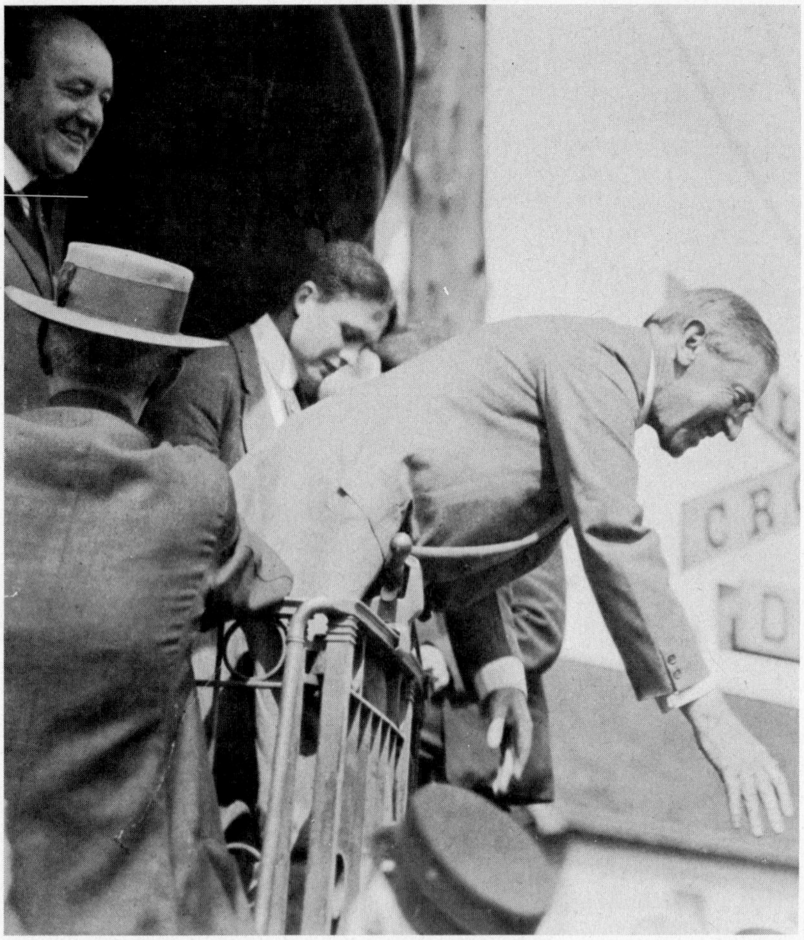

■ **Woodrow Wilson reaching out to his supporters from the rear car of his 1912 campaign train at a whistle stop in Marion, Indiana.**

tive and opportunity. "If America is not to have free enterprise, then she can have freedom of no sort whatever," he said. Although rather vague, this argument appealed to thousands of voters who found the growing power of large corporations frightening but who hesitated to make the thoroughgoing commitment to government control of business that Roosevelt was advocating.

Roosevelt's reasoning was perhaps theoretically sound. Fear of a powerful national government was an inheritance from the 18th century, when political power had been equated with monarchy and tyranny and when America had been sparsely settled and decentralized. In the early 20th century, with democratic institutions firmly established and with a closely integrated economy, citizens had less reason to fear political centralization and economic regulation. As Herbert Croly insisted in *The Promise of American Life* (1909), the time had come to employ Hamiltonian means to achieve Jeffersonian ends. Laissez faire made less sense than it had in earlier times. Philosophers and scientists had undermined the old view of an orderly society designed by a divine watchmaker and capable of running itself. The complexities of the modern world seemed to call for a positive approach, a plan, the close application of human intelligence to social and economic problems.

Yet Wilson's New Freedom, being less drastic and more in line with American experience, had much to recommend it. The danger that selfish individuals would use the power of the state for their own ends had certainly not disappeared, despite the efforts of progressives to make government more responsive to popular opinion. Any considerable expansion of national power would

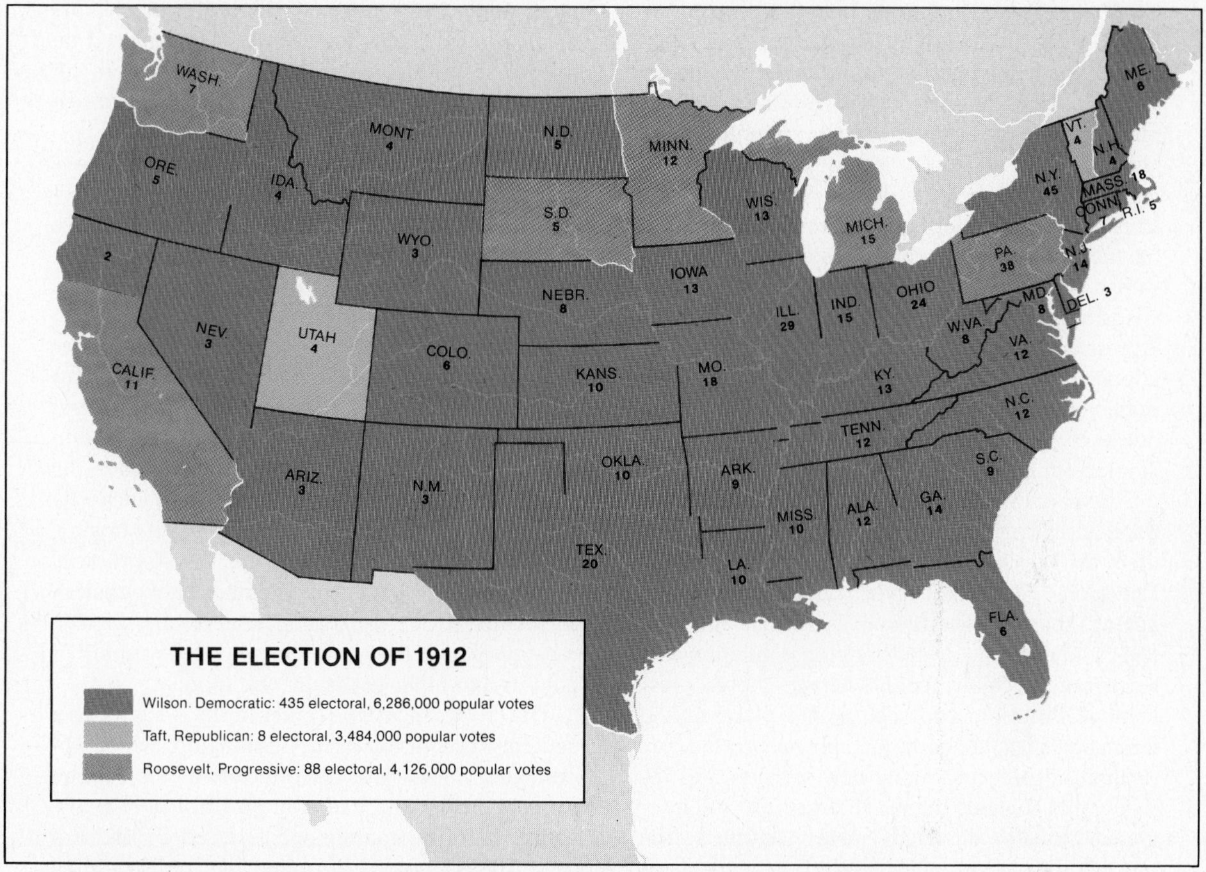

■ **The fourth largest vote getter in the election of 1912 was Eugene V. Debs of the Socialist party, who gained about 900,000 votes, or approximately 6 percent of the total popular vote.**

increase the danger and probably create new difficulties. Managing so complicated a thing as an industrialized nation was sure to be a formidable task. Furthermore, individual freedom of opportunity merited the toleration of a certain amount of inefficiency.

To choose between the New Nationalism and the New Freedom, between the dynamic Roosevelt and the idealistic Wilson, was indeed difficult. Thousands grappled with this problem before going to the polls, but partisan politics determined the outcome of the election. Taft got the hard-core Republican vote but lost the progressive wing of the GOP to Roosevelt. Wilson had the solid support of both conservative and liberal Democrats. As a result, Wilson won an easy victory in the electoral college, receiving 435 votes to Roosevelt's 88 and Taft's 8. The popular vote was Wilson, 6,286,000; Roosevelt, 4,126,000; and Taft, 3,484,000.

If partisan politics had determined the winner, the election was nonetheless an overwhelming endorsement of progressivism. The temper of the times was shown by the 897,000 votes given Eugene V. Debs, the Socialist candidate. Altogether, professed liberals amassed over 11 million of the 15 million ballots cast. Wilson was a minority president, but he took office with a clear mandate to press forward with further reforms.

Wilson: The New Freedom

No man ever rose more suddenly and spectacularly in American politics than Woodrow Wilson. In the spring of 1910 he was president of Princeton University; he had never held or even run for public office. In the fall of 1912 he was president-elect of the United States. Yet if his rise was meteoric, in a very real sense he had devoted his life to preparing for it. He was born in Staunton, Virginia, in 1856, the son of a Presbyterian minister. As a student he became deeply interested in political theory, developing a profound admiration for the British parliamentary system and for such British statesmen as Edmund Burke and William Gladstone. While still in college he dreamed of representing his state in the Senate. He studied law solely because he thought it the best avenue to public office, and when he discovered that he did not like legal work, he took a doctorate at Johns Hopkins in political science.

For years Wilson's political ambitions appeared doomed to frustration. He taught at Bryn Mawr, then at Wesleyan, finally at his alma mater, Princeton. He wrote several influential books, among them *Congressional Government* and *The State,* and achieved an outstanding reputation as a teacher and lecturer. In 1902 he was chosen president of Princeton and soon won a place among the nation's leading educators. He revised the curriculum, introducing many new subjects and insisting that students pursue an organized and integrated course of study. He instituted the preceptorial system, which placed the students in close intellectual and social contact with their teachers. He attracted many outstanding young scholars to the Princeton faculty.

In time, Wilson's advanced educational ideas and his overbearing manner of applying them got him in trouble with some of Princeton's alumni and trustees. Though his university career was wrecked, the controversies, in which he appeared to be championing democracy and progress in the face of reactionary opponents, brought him at last to the attention of the politicians. Then, in a great rush, came power and fame.

Wilson was an immediate success as president. Since Roosevelt's last year in office Congress had been almost continually at war with the executive branch and with itself. Legislative achievements had been relatively few. Now a small avalanche of important measures received the approval of the lawmakers. In October 1913 the Underwood Tariff brought the first significant reduction of duties since before the Civil War. Food products, wool, iron and steel, shoes, agricultural machinery, and other items that could be produced more cheaply in the United States than abroad were placed on the free list. Rates on most other goods were cut substantially, the object being to equalize foreign and domestic costs. To compensate for the expected loss of revenue, the act provided for a graduated tax on personal incomes.*

Two months later the Federal Reserve Act gave the country a central banking system for the first time since Jackson destroyed the Bank of the United States. The measure divided the nation into 12 banking districts, each under the supervision of a Federal Reserve Bank, a sort of bank for bankers. All national banks in each district and those state banks that wished to participate had to invest 6 percent of their capital and surplus in the Reserve Bank, which was empowered to exchange (the technical term is *rediscount*) paper money, called Federal Reserve notes, for the commercial and agricultural paper that member banks took in as security from borrowers. The volume of currency was no longer at the mercy of the supply of gold or any other particular commodity.

The crown and nerve center of the system was a Federal Reserve Board in Washington, which appointed a majority of the directors of the Federal Reserve Banks and had some control over rediscount *rates* (the commission charged by the Reserve Banks for performing the rediscounting function). The board provided a modicum of public control over the banks, but the effort to weaken the power of the great New York banks by decentralizing the system proved ineffective. Nevertheless a true central banking system was created. When inflation threatened, the Reserve Banks could raise the rediscount rate, discouraging borrowing and thus reducing the amount of money in circulation. In bad times it could lower the rate, making it easier to borrow and injecting new dollars into the economy. Much remained to be learned about the proper management of the money supply, but the nation finally had a flexible yet safe currency.

In 1914 Congress passed two important laws affecting corporations. One created a Federal Trade Commission to replace Roosevelt's Bureau of Corporations. In addition to investigating interstate corporations and publishing reports, this nonpar-

*The Sixteenth Amendment, ratified in February 1913, authorized the imposition of a federal income tax.

tisan board could issue "cease and desist" orders against "unfair" trade practices brought to light through its researches. The law did not define the term "unfair," and the commission's rulings could be taken on appeal to the federal courts, but the FTC was nonetheless a powerful instrument for protecting the public against the trusts.

The second measure, the Clayton Antitrust Act, made certain specific business practices illegal, including price discrimination that tended to foster monopoly, "tying" agreements—which forbade retailers from handling the products of a firm's competitors—and the creation of interlocking directorates as a means of controlling competing companies. The act exempted labor unions and agricultural organizations from the antitrust laws and curtailed the use of injunctions in labor disputes. The officers of corporations could be held individually responsible when their companies violated the antitrust laws.

While Wilson was not in sympathy with all the terms of these laws, the laws reflected his desires. The Democrats controlled both houses of Congress for the first time since 1890 and were eager to make a good record, but Wilson's imaginative and aggressive use of presidential power was decisive. He entered office determined, like a British prime minister, to play an active part in the formulation of legislation and the management of Congress.

Wilson called the legislators into special session in April 1913 and appeared before them to lay out his program, the first president to address Congress in person since John Adams. Then he followed the course of administration bills closely. He had a private telephone line installed between the Capitol and the White House. Administration representatives haunted the cloakrooms and lobbies of both houses. Cooperative congressmen began to receive notes of praise and encouragement, recalcitrant ones stern demands for support, often pecked out on the president's own portable typewriter. When lobbyists tried to frustrate his plans for tariff reform by bringing pressure to bear on key senators, he made a dramatic appeal to the people. "The public ought to know the extraordinary exertions being made by the lobby in Washington," he told reporters. "Only public opinion can check and destroy it." The voters responded so strongly that the Senate passed the tariff bill substantially as Wilson desired it.

Despite his lack of political experience, Wilson proved to be a masterful politician and an inspiring leader. He explained his success by saying, only half humorously, that running the government was child's play for anyone who had managed the faculty of a university. Responsible *party* government was his objective; he expected individual Democrats to support the decisions of the party majority, and his idealism never prevented him from awarding the spoils of office to city bosses and conservative congressmen, so long as they supported his program.

Nor did his career as a political theorist make him rigid and doctrinaire. In practice the differences between his New Freedom and Roosevelt's New Nationalism tended to disappear. The Underwood Tariff and the Clayton Antitrust Act fitted the philosophy Wilson had expounded during the campaign, but the Federal Trade Commission represented a step toward the kind of regulated economy that Roosevelt advocated. So did the Federal Reserve system.

There were limits to Wilson's progressivism, limits imposed partly by his temperament and partly by his philosophy. He disliked all forms of privilege, and objected as strenuously to laws granting special favors to farmers and workers as to those benefiting the tycoons. When a bill was introduced in 1914 making low-interest loans available to farmers, he refused to support it. "It is unwise and unjustifiable to extend the credit of the Government to a single class of the community," he said. He considered the provision exempting unions from the antitrust laws equally unsound. Nor would he push for a federal law prohibiting child labor; such a measure would be unconstitutional, he believed. Wilson refused to back the constitutional amendment giving the vote to women. Perhaps he thought it improper for women to mix in politics, but he argued publicly that it was wrong to deprive the states of their control of the suffrage.

Wilson proved far less unsympathetic to big business than some of his campaign pronouncements had led observers to expect. He appointed persons friendly to the corporations to the FTC and conducted no trustbusting crusade. When the business cycle took a turn downward in the fall of 1913, he adopted the Roosevelt policy of allowing corporation leaders to work out informal agreements with the Justice Department protecting them against antitrust actions. Delegations of businessmen and bankers were soon trooping through the White House, and the president went out of his way to insist that he had no quarrel with bigness per se.

By the end of 1914 the Wilsonian record, on balance, was positive but distinctly limited. The president believed that the major progressive goals had been achieved; he had no plans for further reform. Many other progressives thought that a great deal more remained to be done.

The Progressives and the Race Issue

On one important issue Wilson was distinctly reactionary. Black citizens had not, to put it mildly, fared well at the hands of the progressives. Populist efforts to unite white and black farmers in the southern states had led to the imposition of further repressive measures. Segregation became more rigid, white opposition to black voting more monolithic. In 1900 the body of a Mississippi black was dug up by order of the state legislature and reburied in a segregated cemetery; in Virginia in 1902 the daughter of Robert E. Lee was arrested for riding in the black section of a railroad car. "Insult is being added to injury continually," a black journalist in Alabama complained. "Have those in power forgotten that there is a God?"

Many progressive women, still smarting from the insult to their sex entailed in the Fourteenth and Fifteenth Amendments and eager to attract southern support for their campaign for the vote, adopted racist arguments. They contrasted the supposed corruption and incompetence of black voters with their own "purity" and intelligence. Southern so-called progressives of both sexes argued that disfranchising blacks would reduce corruption by removing from unscrupulous white politicians the temptation to purchase black votes! The typical southern attitude toward the education of blacks was summed up in the folk proverb, "When you educate a Negro, you spoil a good field hand." In 1910, only about 8,000 black children in the entire South were attending high schools. Yet despite the almost total suppression of black rights, lynchings continued to occur; between 1900 and 1914 more than 1,100 blacks were murdered by mobs, most (but not all) in the southern states. In the rare cases where local prosecutors brought the lynchers to trial, juries almost without exception brought in verdicts of not guilty.

Booker T. Washington was shaken by this trend, but he could find no way to combat it. The times were passing him by. He appealed to his white southern "friends" for help but got nowhere. Increasingly he talked about the virtues of rural life, the evils of big cities, and the uselessness of higher education for black people. By the turn of the century a number of young, well-educated blacks, most of them northerners, were breaking away from his leadership.

William E. B. Du Bois was the most prominent of the militants. Du Bois was born in Great Barrington, Massachusetts, in 1868. His father, a restless wanderer of Negro and French Huguenot stock, abandoned the family, and young William grew up on the edge of poverty. Neither accepted nor openly rejected by the overwhelmingly white community, he devoted himself to his studies, showing such brilliance that his future education was assured by scholarships: to Fisk University, then to Harvard, then to the University of Berlin. In 1895 Du Bois became the first American black to earn a Ph.D. from Harvard; his dissertation, *The Suppression of the African Slave Trade to the U.S.A., 1638–1870* (1896), is still a standard work on the subject.

Personal success and "acceptance" by whites did not make the proud and sensitive Du Bois complacent. Outraged by white racism and the willingness of many blacks to settle for second-class citizenship, he set out to make American blacks proud of their color—"beauty is black," he said—and of their African origins and culture. American blacks must organize themselves. They must establish their own businesses, run their own newspapers and colleges, write their own literature; they must preserve their identity rather than seek to amalgamate themselves into a society that offered them only crumbs and contempt.

Like Washington, Du Bois wanted blacks to lift themselves by their own bootstraps, and for a time he cooperated with the head of Tuskegee Institute. But in time he rejected Washington's limited goals and his accommodating approach to white prejudices. In 1903, in an essay "Of Mr. Booker T. Washington and Others," published in his book *Souls of Black Folk,* he subjected Washing-

■ Vigilante justice in Texas, 1893. A black man accused of killing a white child was captured and condemned to death without a trial after he was said to have confessed. Before a crowd estimated in the thousands he was burned at the stake—but only after the child's family took their revenge with branding irons.

ton's "attitude of adjustment and submission" to polite but searching criticism. Washington had asked blacks to give up political power, civil rights, and the hope of higher education, not realizing that "voting is necessary to modern manhood, that . . . discrimination is barbarism, and that black boys need education as well as white boys." Washington "apologizes for injustice," Du Bois charged. "He belittles the emasculating effects of caste distinctions, and opposes the higher training and ambitions of our brightest minds." This was totally wrong. "The way for a people to gain their reasonable rights is not by voluntarily throwing them away."

Du Bois was not an uncritical admirer of the ordinary American black. He believed that "immorality, crime, and laziness" were common vices. Quite properly he blamed the weaknesses

■ **John Henry Adams sketched William E.B. Du Bois in 1905, the year that Du Bois helped to initiate the Niagara Movement for racial equality.**

of blacks on the treatment afforded them by whites, but his approach to the solution of racial problems was frankly elitist. "The Negro race," he wrote, "is going to be saved by its exceptional men," what he called the "talented tenth" of the black population. As the historian Benjamin Quarles has said, Du Bois was "uncomfortable in the presence of the rank and file." After describing in vivid detail how white mistreatment had corrupted his people, Du Bois added loftily: "A saving remnant continually survives and persists, continually aspires, continually shows itself in thrift and ability and character."

Whatever his prejudices, Du Bois exposed both the weaknesses of Washington's strategy and the callousness of white American attitudes. "Accommodation" was not working. Washington was praised, even lionized by prominent southern whites, yet when Theodore Roosevelt invited him to a meal at the White House they exploded with indignation, and Roosevelt, although not personnally prejudiced, meekly backtracked, never repeating his "mistake."

Not mere impatience but despair led Du Bois and a few like-minded blacks to meet at Niagara Falls in July 1905 and to issue a stirring list of demands: the unrestricted right to vote; an end to every kind of segregation; equality of economic opportunity; higher education for the talented; equal justice in the courts; an end to trade union discrimination. This Niagara Movement did not attract mass support, but it did stir the consciences of some whites, many of them the descendants of abolitionists, who were also becoming disenchanted by the failure of accommodation to provide blacks with real opportunity.

In 1909, the centennial of the birth of Abraham Lincoln, a group of these liberals, including Oswald Garrison Villard (grandson of William Lloyd Garrison), the social worker Jane Addams, the philosopher John Dewey, and the novelist William Dean Howells, founded the National Association for the Advancement of Colored People (NAACP). The organization was dedicated to the eradication of racial discrimination. Its leadership was predominantly white in the early years, but Du Bois became a national officer and the editor of its journal, *The Crisis.*

A turning point had been reached: after 1909 virtually every important leader of the blacks, white and black alike, rejected the Washington approach. More and more, blacks turned to the study of their past in an effort to stimulate pride in their heritage. In 1915 Carter G. Woodson founded the Association for the Study of Negro Life and History; the following year he began editing the *Journal of Negro History,* which became the major organ for the publishing of scholarly studies of the subject.

This militancy produced few results in the Progressive Era. Theodore Roosevelt behaved no differently than earlier Republican presidents: he courted blacks when he thought it advantageous, turned his back when he did not. When he ran for president on the Progressive ticket in 1912, he pursued a "lily-white" policy, hoping to break the Democrats' monopoly in the South. By trusting in "[white] men of justice and of vision," Roosevelt argued in the face of decades of experience to the contrary, "the colored men of the South will ultimately get justice."

The southern-born Wilson was actively antipathetic to blacks. During the 1912 campaign he appealed to them for support and promised to "assist in advancing the interest of their race" in every possible way. Once elected, he refused even to appoint a privately financed commission to study the race problem. Southerners dominated his administration and the Congress; as a result, blacks were further degraded. No less than 35 blacks in the Atlanta Post Office lost their jobs. In Washington employees in many government offices were rigidly segregated, those who objected being summarily discharged.

These actions roused such a storm that Wilson backtracked a little, but he never abandoned his belief that segregation was in the best interests of both races. "Wilson . . . promised a 'new freedom,' " one newspaperman complained. "On the contrary we are given a stone instead of a loaf of bread." Even Booker T. Washington admitted that his people were more "discouraged and bitter" than at any time in his memory.

Du Bois, who had supported Wilson in 1912, attacked administration policy in *The Crisis.* In November 1914 the militant editor of the Boston *Guardian,* William Monroe Trotter, a classmate of Du Bois at Harvard and a far more caustic critic of the Washington approach, led a delegation to the White House to protest the segregation policy of the government. When Wilson accused him of blackmail, Trotter lost his temper and an ugly confrontation resulted. The mood of black leaders had changed completely.

By this time the Great War had broken out in Europe. Soon its effects would be felt by every American, by blacks perhaps more than by any other group. In November 1915, a year almost to the day after Trotter's clash with Wilson, Booker T. Washington died. One era had ended; a new one was beginning.

SUPPLEMENTARY READING

Titles marked with an asterisk have been published in paperback

Two excellent volumes trace the political history of the Progressive Era: G. E. Mowry, **The Era of Theodore Roosevelt*** (1958), and A. S. Link, **Woodrow Wilson and the Progressive Era*** (1954). A number of historians have offered new interpretations of progressivism in recent years. Richard Hofstadter, **The Age of Reform*** (1955), stresses the idea of the status revolution. Gabriel Kolko, **The Triumph of Conservatism*** (1963), sees the period as dominated by the efforts of big business to attain its objectives with the aid of the government. Other interesting studies include R. B. Nye, **Midwestern Progressive Politics** (1951), and R. H. Wiebe, **Businessmen and Reform*** (1962). D. P. Thelen, **The New Citizenship** (1972), is good on the origins of progressivism, though confined to the study of one state, Wisconsin.

The role of muckraking journalism is considered in C. C. Regier, **The Era of the Muckrakers** (1932), Louis Filler, **Crusaders for American Liberalism*** (1939), D. M. Chalmers, **The Social and Political Ideas of the Muckrakers*** (1964), and Peter Lyon, **Success Story: The Life and Times of S. S. McClure** (1963). Arthur and Lila Weinberg (eds.), **The Muckrakers*** (1961), is a convenient collection of writings by the muckrakers. Also useful are Lincoln Steffens, **Autobiography*** (1931), and I. M. Tarbell, **All in the Day's Work** (1939).

State and local progressivism are considered in G. E. Mowry, **The California Progressives*** (1951), R. S. Maxwell, **La Follette and the Rise of Progressivism in Wisconsin** (1956), R. E. Noble, **New Jersey Progressivism Before Wilson** (1946), R. M. Abrams, **Conservatism in a Progressive Era** (1964), H. L. Warner, **Progressivism in Ohio** (1964), Sheldon Hackney, **Populism to Progressivism in Alabama** (1969), Z. L. Miller, **Boss Cox's Cincinnati: Urban Politics in the Progressive Era*** (1968), J. D. Buenker, **Urban Liberalism and Progressive Reform** (1973), G. B. Tindall, **The Emergence of the New South** (1967), and C. V. Woodward, **Origins of the New South*** (1951). The story of the fight for reform in San Francisco is told in W. E. Bean, **Boss Ruef's San Francisco*** (1952).

The struggle for women's suffrage is described in A. S. Kraditor, **The Ideas of the Woman Suffrage Movement*** (1965), and in Eleanor Flexner, **Century of Struggle*** (1959). See also W. L. O'Neill, **Everyone Was Brave: The Rise and Fall of Feminism in America*** (1969). Books treating special aspects of progressivism include A. F. Davis, **Spearheads for Reform: The Social Settlements and the Progressive Movement*** (1967), Melvin Dubofsky, **When Workers Organize** (1968), Irwin Yellowitz, **Labor and the Progressive Movement in New York State** (1965), Samuel Haber, **Efficiency and Uplift** (1964), J. P. Felt, **Hostages of Fortune** (1965), J. H. Timberlake, **Prohibition and the Progressive Movement*** (1963), Albro Martin, **Enterprise Denied: Ori-**

gins of the Decline of American Railroads (1971), and W. L. O'Neill, **Divorce in the Progressive Era** (1967). On blacks in this period, see C. F. Kellogg, **NAACP: A History of the National Association for the Advancement of Colored People*** (1970), E. M. Rudwick, **W. E. B. Du Bois: Propagandist of the Negro Protest*** (1960), W. E. B. Du Bois, **The Souls of Black Folk*** (1903), J. T. Kirby, **Darkness at the Dawning: Race and Reform in the Progressive South** (1972), and August Meier, **Negro Thought in America: 1880–1915*** (1963).

Many progressives have written autobiographical accounts of their work. See especially Theodore Roosevelt, **Autobiography** (1913), R. M. La Follette, **Autobiography*** (1913), W. A. White, **Autobiography** (1946), and G. W. Norris, **Fighting Liberal*** (1945).

W. H. Harbaugh, **Power and Responsibility: The Life and Times of Theodore Roosevelt*** (1961), is the soundest scholarly treatment of Roosevelt's career. G. W. Chessman, **Theodore Roosevelt and the Politics of Power*** (1969), is a good brief account, while Chessman's **Governor Theodore Roosevelt: The Albany Apprenticeship** (1965), throws much light on the development of Roosevelt's ideas before 1901. J. M. Blum, **The Republican Roosevelt*** (1954), is a brilliant analysis of his political philosophy and his management of the presidency. The essays on Roosevelt—and on Wilson—in Richard Hofstadter, **The American Political Tradition*** (1948), merit close reading.

For specific events during Roosevelt's presidency, consult R. J. Cornell, **The Anthracite Coal Strike of 1902** (1957), the essay on the Northern Securities case in J. A. Garraty (ed.), **Quarrels That Have Shaped the Constitution*** (1964), S. P. Hays, **Conservation and the Gospel of Efficiency*** (1959), and J. R. Hollingsworth, **The Whirligig of Politics** (1963).

On Taft, see D. F. Anderson, **William Howard Taft: A Conservative's Conception of the Presidency** (1973), and P. E. Coletta, **The Presidency of William Howard Taft** (1973). On the Ballinger-Pinchot controversy, see M. N. McGeary, **Gifford Pinchot** (1960). The breakup of the Republican party and the history of the Progressive party are discussed in G. E. Mowry, **Theodore Roosevelt and the Progressive Movement*** (1946), and J. A. Garraty, **Right-Hand Man: The Life of George W. Perkins** (1960).

The standard biography of Wilson, still incomplete, is A. S. Link, **Wilson** (1947–). Two brief biographies are J. M. Blum, **Woodrow Wilson and the Politics of Morality*** (1956), and J. A. Garraty, **Woodrow Wilson*** (1956).

Among the many biographies of political leaders in the period are J. M. Blum, **Joe Tumulty and the Wilson Era** (1951), C. G. Bowers, **Beveridge and the Progressive Era** (1932), R. M. Lowitt, **George W. Norris** (1963), B. C. and Fola La Follette, **Robert M. La Follette** (1953), P. C. Jessup, **Elihu Root** (1938), J. A. Garraty, **Henry Cabot Lodge** (1953), A. T. Mason, **Brandeis** (1946), and M. J. Pusey, **Charles Evans Hughes** (1951).

The student should sample some of the political writings of the progressives themselves. See especially Theodore Roosevelt, **The New Nationalism*** (1910), Woodrow Wilson, **The New Freedom*** (1913), Herbert Croly, **The Promise of American Life*** (1909), Walter Weyl, **The New Democracy*** (1912), and Walter Lippmann, **Drift and Mastery*** (1914).

Portfolio Five

WOMEN'S LOT

The typical social unit in the late 19th century was the large family clustered in one home. And if traditionally the father was head of the family, the mother was traditionally its heart. As Grover Cleveland wrote, "The refining, elevating influence of woman, especially in her allotted sphere of home and in her character of wife and mother, supplements man's strenuous struggles in social and political warfare." It was woman's mission to make her home a sanctuary of love and moral purity. Her husband's duty was to protect his family from the fierce world outside, where men lived by the rule of root, hog, or die.

In reality, many women—and many children, too—had to work outside the home. By the 1870s more and more women were moving out of the home by choice rather than necessity. Some were inspired by a good education; others were simply impatient with the stereotype of female domesticity. Relatively they were a small group, but in time they modified people's ideas about women's place. Although most early 20th-century women were still preoccupied with bearing children and taking care of their families, Americans by then were growing accustomed to seeing women working outside the home and to hearing women demand rights and privileges previously held only by men.

The Family Circle

The lives of most Americans were far removed from the Park Avenue elegance of the family of Alfrederick S. Hatch, shown in the painting by Eastman Johnson on the previous page. People like the Hatches—he was later president of the New York Stock Exchange—enjoyed luxuries unknown to the vast majority of Americans. But whether families were affluent, moderately well-off, or poor, they were generally large and closely knit. Managing this busy social unit was supposed to be the task of the mother. Thus a young woman's first aim was to marry; then her life's work could begin.

Women's Work

Wives were expected to run their households on whatever income their husbands brought in, to bear children and to rear them properly, and to provide the family with harmonious surroundings. *"Housewives!"* an antisuffragist leaflet declared, "you do not need a ballot to clean out your sink spout. A handful of potash and some boiling water is quicker and cheaper. . . . Control of the temper makes a happier home than control of elections. . . . Clean houses and good homes, which cannot be provided by legislation, keep children healthier and happier than any number of laws."

■ The special relationship between women and their children was a major theme of the impressionist painter Mary Cassatt (left). She herself was one of the American women who decided to follow a profession rather than marry.

■ Many middle-class families had a servant to help with the work, but the majority of American households were run by the wife alone. These women sewed, washed, cooked, cleaned, and did many other chores, taking care of the children as they worked. With or without a maid to share the labor, the job required energy, patience, organizing ability, and plain physical stamina.

For families that could afford them, new household appliances were beginning to ease the domestic routine. Gas lighting, interior plumbing, and better stoves, washtubs, and furnaces were introduced in the late 19th century. One of the most useful appliances of the age was the sewing machine, which stitched stronger seams in less time than was possible with hand sewing.

During the 1870s and 1880s, sewing machines, invented in the 1840s, became a fixture not only in cozy middle-class parlors but also in slum apartments and sweatshops. The neighborhood around Jane Addams' settlement house in Chicago was filled with families like the one below, who did piecework for garment manufacturers. The entire family often worked all day and on into the night to earn a bare existence. Jane Addams saw one four-year-old "bunch of human misery" who sat hour after hour at her mother's feet, pulling out basting threads.

HOUSEHOLD
SEWING MACHINE CO.
PROVIDENCE, R.I.

NORTH
AMERICA
The Singer Seam
UNITES
TWO CONTINENTS.
SOUTH
AMERICA
"ALL OVER THE WORLD"
SINGER
THE
UNIVERSAL
SEWING MACHINE

■ Women tend yarn-spinning machines (above) in a textile mill in Brockton, Mass. Although this shot shows a relatively clean working environment, many such mills were full of lung-damaging dust and lint.

■ A hotel staff, at left, advertises the services it offers: cleaning, cooking, table waiting, and baby sitting. The jobs that were easiest for women to find were those based on housekeeping skills.

■ Office work multiplied as businesses grew, and secretarial schools began to train women in shorthand, typing, and other clerical skills (right). When customers bought typewriters, which were novelties in the 1880s, the manufacturer often sent typists along to operate them. Women were rapidly accepted in offices because their labor was a bargain: a skilled woman typist earned $15 a week while a less competent man could command $20.

Breadwinning

Though the domestic stereotype did not acknowledge it, there had always been large numbers of women who worked for a living. As the economy expanded during the 1880s, more and more women entered the work force, usually filling the lowest-paid jobs. In 1880 more than 2.5 million women were working outside the home; in 1890 more than 4 million; in 1910 more than 7 million. In addition, more than a million children were employed.

Almost one-third of working women were servants in other people's homes or held jobs in hotels, laundries, and similar service industries. Another large percentage were employed in factories, particularly in plants that manufactured textiles and clothing. The third largest group were farm laborers. And by 1900 a substantial number were finding jobs as stenographers, typists, secretaries, and clerks.

■ Cotton picking, shown in Winslow Homer's painting *Upland Cotton* (left), was a major occupation in the South, particularly for black labor. A skilled worker could pick 100 pounds of cotton a day; some could double that figure.

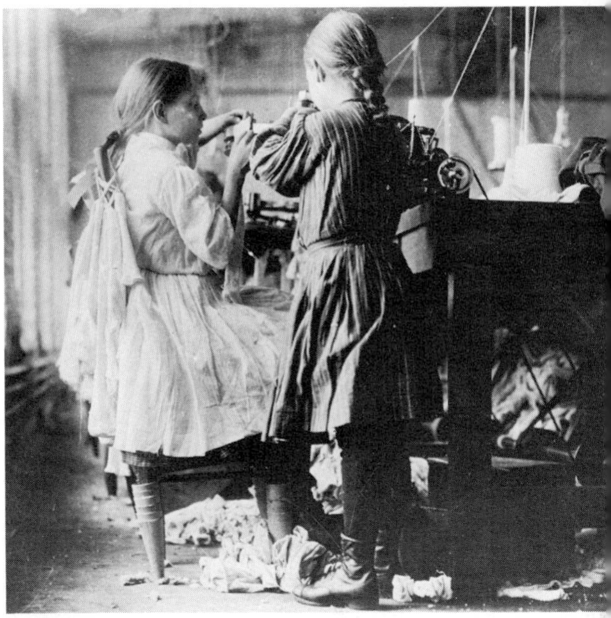

■ Children, at right, working in a textile mill. A muckraker wrote:

> The golf links lie so near the mill
> That almost every day
> The laboring children can look out
> And see the men at play.

Children who were hurt by the machinery they operated did not usually receive compensation. Most employers made parents sign waivers in the event of a child's injury through "carelessness."

■ A delivery boy in the garment district of New York's lower east side. The coats he carries have been basted together; they will go now to a sweatshop for machine stitching.

■ The actress Maude Adams in 1900. A few stars had glamorous careers and substantial incomes. After 50 years in the theater, where she is best remembered for her role as Peter Pan, Adams became teacher of dramatics at Stephens College in Missouri.

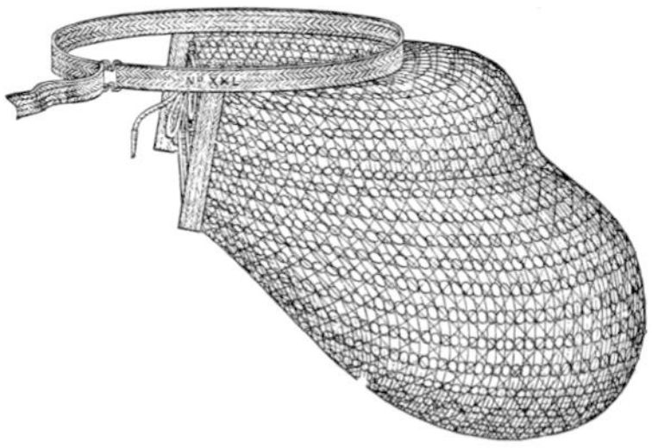

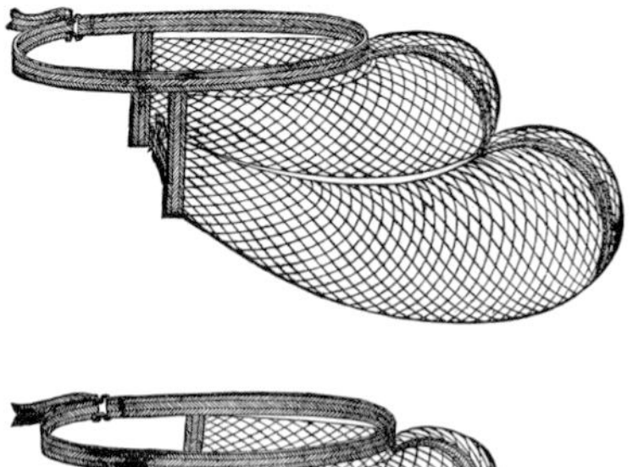

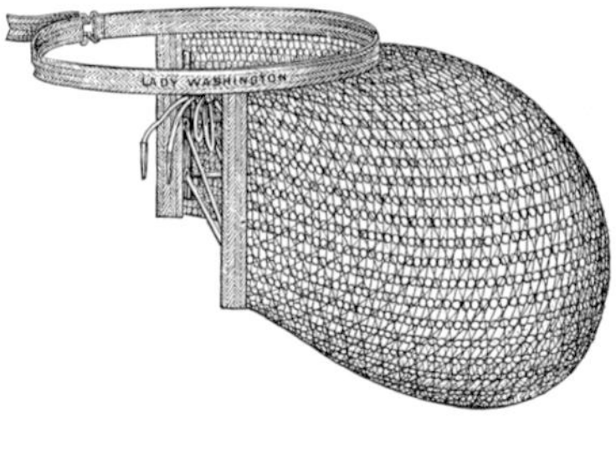
LADY WASHINGTON

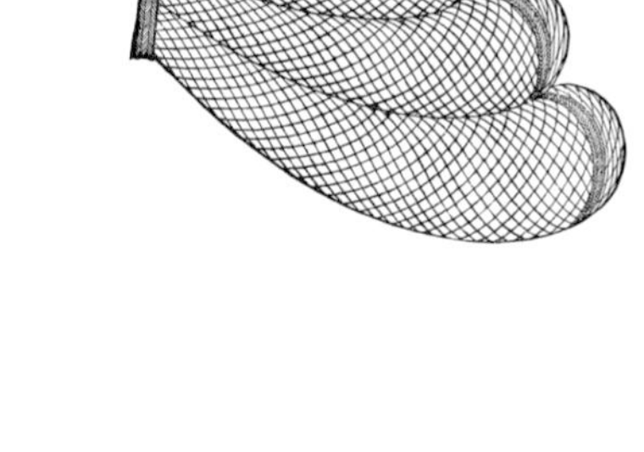

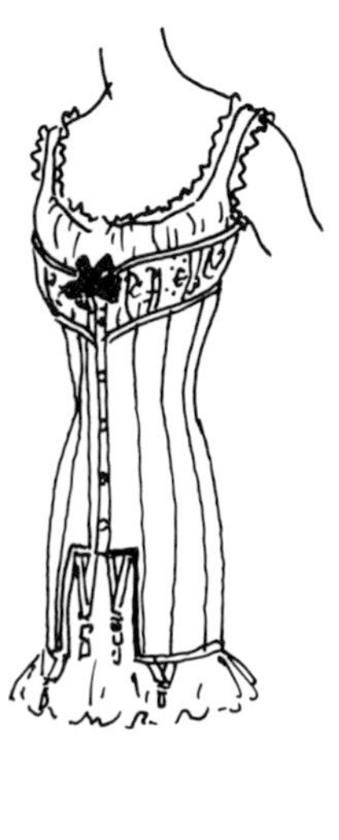

Fashionable Women

Stylish dresses of the 1870s, shown at left, were festooned with drapery and covered with buttons, bows, tucks, ruffles, lace, and fringe. A single gown could weigh as much as 50 pounds. The heavy padding in the back was created by bustles like those at lower left—made of one, two, or three rolls of braided wire and fastened around the waist. Although the everyday clothes of most women were less ornate, they were fashioned on the same lines.

Dresses of the 1880s, such as the wedding gown at right, had more elegant curves and slimmer contours. Indeed, they were so tight in the front that some had to be weighted down with fine chains sewn into the skirt. Women wearing the more extreme models could not sit down and could walk only with difficulty.

By 1910 the stylish silhouette had changed to the "natural" look shown at lower right. This look was created by a viselike corset that, as illustrated in the sketch at lower left, began above the waist and constricted the ribs, hips, and upper legs. The resulting figure had a broad, spreading bosom that appeared to rest on a column.

In *Theory of the Leisure Class* (1899), Thorstein Veblen spoke of "the high heel, the skirt, the impracticable bonnet, the corset, and the general disregard of the wearer's comfort which is an obvious feature of all civilized women's apparel." This "elaborate show of unnecessary expensiveness," he said, was designed to flaunt the husband's wealth and demonstrate that, in theory if no longer in practice, the woman was "the man's chattel."

Educated Women

Women's emotional nature, one minister wrote in the 1880s, "painfully disqualifies" them for the life of the mind. This was a commonly held view despite the fact that women had been going to college and doing as well at their studies as men for more than twenty years. As early as 1870 one-third of American colleges were coeducational, and most of the major women's colleges were founded between 1870 and 1900. Yet throughout this period the college woman was the exception.

M. Carey Thomas, who graduated from Cornell in 1877 and went on to become the first president of Bryn Mawr, said, "The passionate desire of the women of my generation for higher education was accompanied . . . by the awful doubt, felt by women themselves as well as men, as to whether women as a sex were physically and mentally fit for it." College women responded to this doubt by developing a sense of dedication and high purpose. According to Jane Addams, she and her classmates at Rockford Seminary in Illinois worked in "an atmosphere of intensity, a fever of preparation."

Most women college graduates married and settled into domestic life. Those who wanted a career went largely into teaching, for education was expanding as rapidly as business. And women had long been in demand as teachers because they would work for less money than men. In the 1850s there were already more women teachers than men; by 1890 two-thirds of American schoolteachers were women.

Nursing, a relatively new career, was the only other job with professional status that women entered in large numbers. The first American schools of nursing opened in the 1870s and offered a one-year course. Soon three-year programs were available, and the schools were preparing nurses to work in slums and schools as well as in hospitals.

■ The May 1908 issue of *Scribner's* magazine (left) contained an article about undergraduate life at Wellesley that contrasted the "extreme conscientiousness" of Wellesley students with the laziness of young men at Harvard and Yale. Wellesley, then a little more than 20 years old, had 700 students and a faculty of 80. According to the article, the college laid down few rules except for those "which would naturally govern the actions of any well-bred girl. While at college she is required to have a chaperone to any entertainment in Boston, or to a foot-ball game at Harvard, or to an afternoon tea, just as she would be if she were at home with her own people."

■ Vocational training (below center), introduced into public schools in the 1880s and 1890s, included homemaking classes for girls as well as shopwork for boys.

■ Student nurses, at right, watch a patient being made ready for an operation at St. Luke's Hospital, New York City, in 1899. Nursing had become an accepted occupation for women.

■ In many cities, night schools were established so that working children could continue their education. Classes like the one shown at right below were usually held four evenings a week.

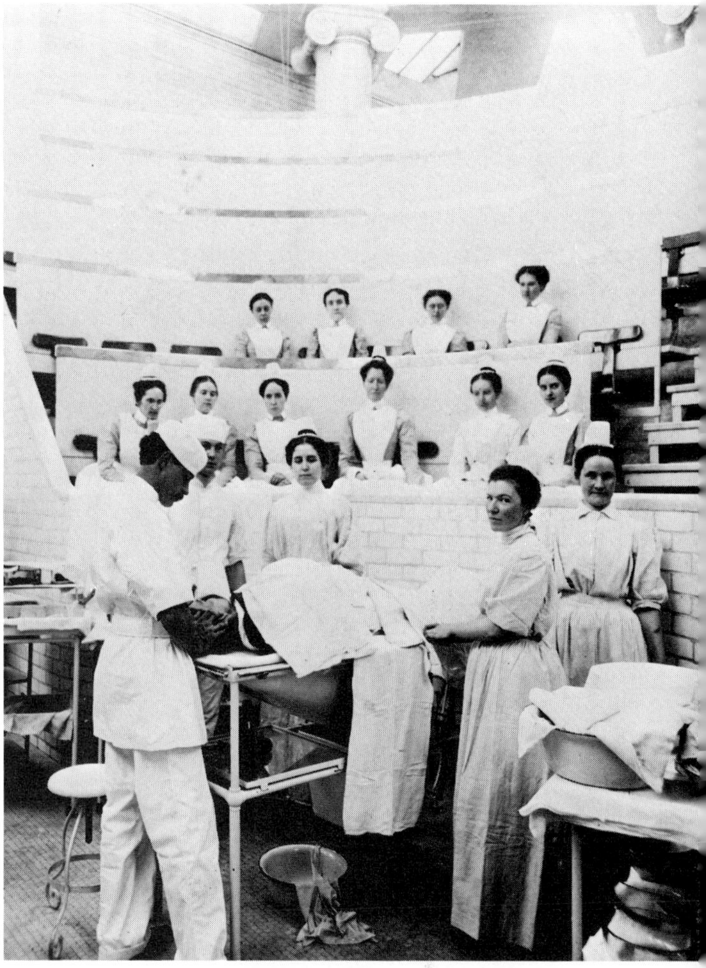

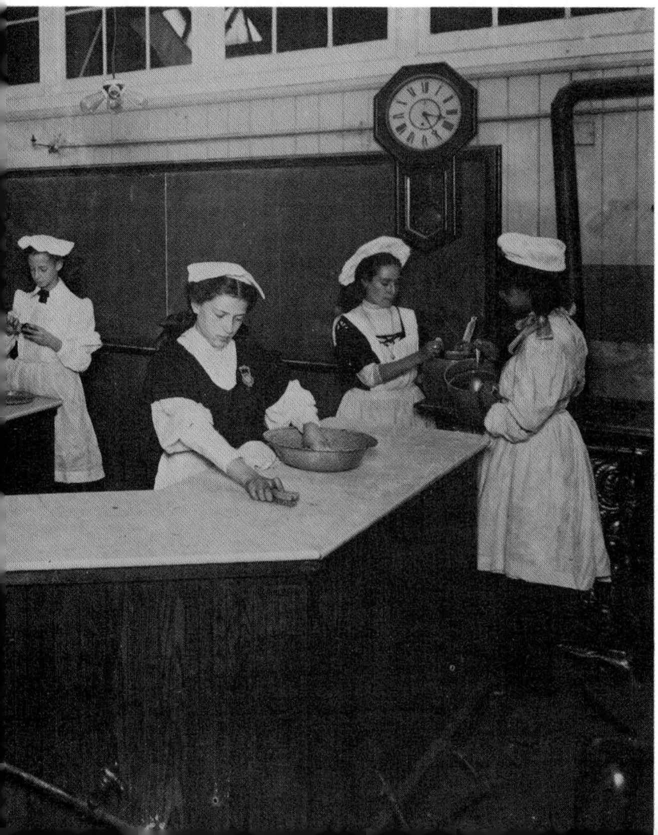

Fallen Women

In the 19th century most people believed so profoundly in the ideal of woman's purity that the subject of "fallen" women was a painful one. In general the public regarded prostitutes as depraved creatures who deserved whatever horrible fate befell them.

For most prostitutes life was indeed grim. Their minds were often clouded by liquor and drugs, their days shortened by venereal disease. Girls usually became prostitutes around the age of sixteen. In 1900 young women could earn only $5 to $7 a week in an unskilled job, while prostitutes averaged $30 to $40 a week. Often the bulk of these earnings was siphoned off by pimps, madams, and the police, but young women entering the life did not discover this until "too late."

■ At the Haymarket, a dance hall in New York City, men paid admission but women who passed the doorman's inspection were guests of the house. Many vice investigations found that dance halls were places where young women were recruited for prostitution. In this painting by John Sloan, a washerwoman reproves her child for showing interest in the dressy women.

At the turn of the century the so-called white slave traffic attracted nationwide attention. Newspapers were filled with stories about young women (black as well as white) who had been kidnaped and held prisoner in brothels. Hearings and grand jury investigations were organized. The Immigration Service conducted an inquiry.

Katharine M. Hepburn (the mother of the actress), a leader in the women's suffrage movement, spoke about the white slave problem: "Although for the first time in the history of the human race thousands of girls of tender age are working in factories and shops away from all restraint, a regular traffic in women had to be organized to supply the demand."

Most official investigators concluded that few women had actually been forced into prostitution against their will. Some reformers disagreed; according to their findings, the American city in the early 20th century was an extremely dangerous place for unchaperoned girls.

The formal investigations did establish that prostitutes, however recruited, were being imported from abroad and shipped from state to state as casually as if they were cattle. It was a profitable business: procurers received from $200 to $2,000 a girl. The public uproar led to the passage of the Mann act (officially the White Slave Traffic Act) of 1910, which put heavy penalties on the transport of women into the country or between states for immoral purposes. This law cut down considerably on the wide-open traffic in prostitutes, but of course it did not put an end to prostitution or to the social evils with which it was associated.

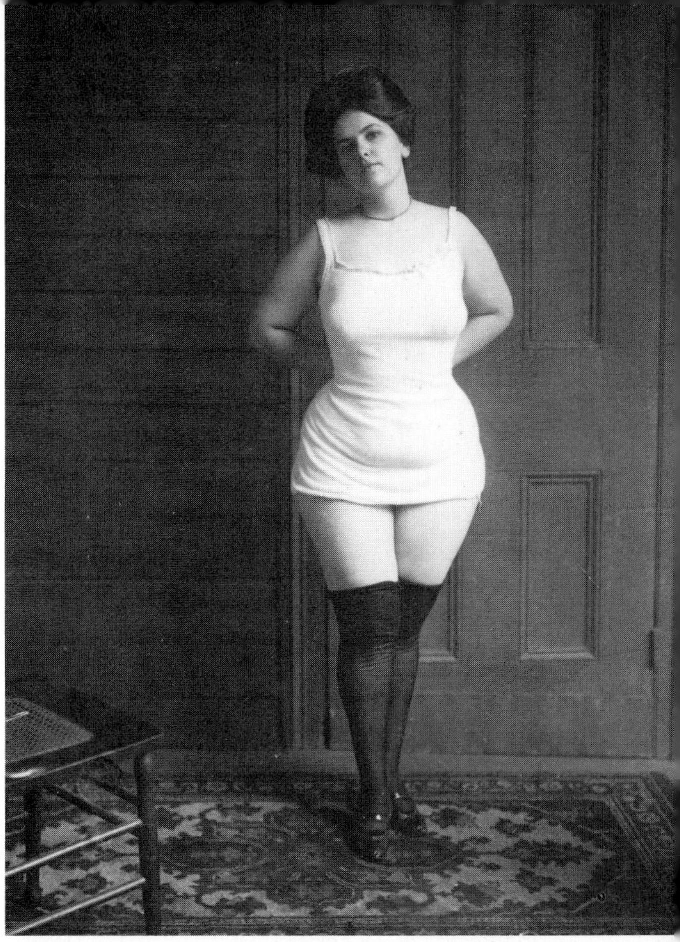

■ New Orleans prostitutes photographed by E. J. Bellocq in 1912.

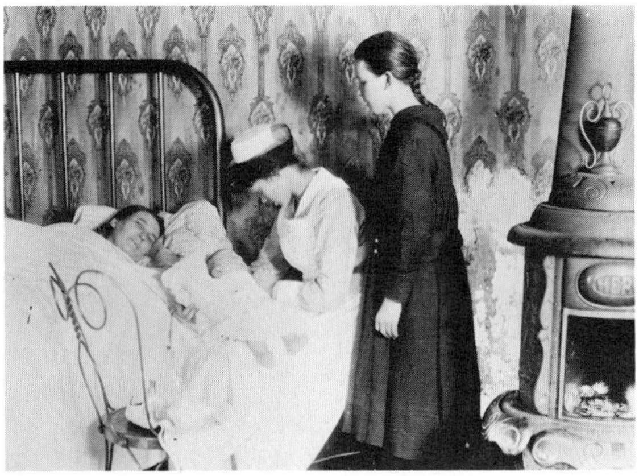

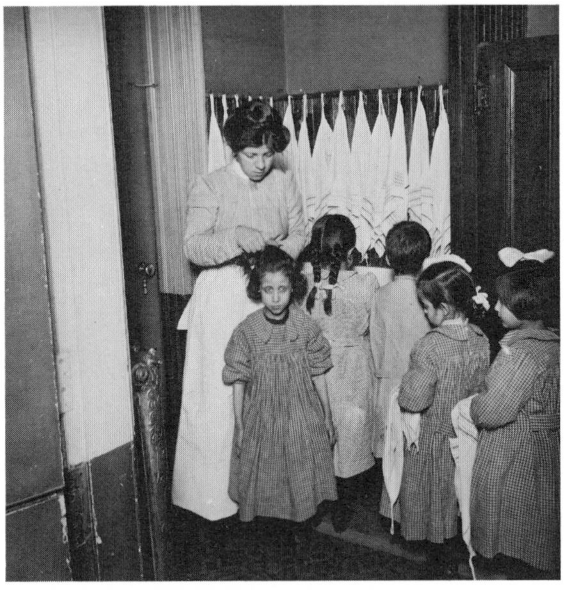

Careers in the Slums

"The streets were inexpressibly dirty, the number of schools inadequate, sanitary legislation unenforced." Jane Addams' description of her Chicago neighborhood could have been applied to the slums of any city in the nation. People like Addams established settlement houses because they wanted to help and learn from those who lived in the slums. As soon as Hull House opened in 1889, Addams wrote, "It seemed understood that we were ready to perform the humblest neighborhood services. We were asked to wash the newborn babies, and to prepare the dead for burial, to nurse the sick, and to 'mind the children.' "

Lillian Wald, a nurse, organized her Henry Street Settlement in New York City because she discovered that 90 percent of the sick in cities were sick at home, not in hospitals. In 1893 she and a colleague rented an apartment on the lower east side and began to go out with their bags every day to look for sick people. From this beginning, Wald built a city-wide visiting-nurse service. Visiting nurses had to have "enthusiasm, health, and uncommon good sense," she wrote; otherwise "they could not long endure the endless stair-climbing, the weight of the bag, and the pulls upon their emotions."

Wald's settlement house, like others, soon offered many services in addition to nursing. Jane Addams wrote: "We early found ourselves spending many hours in efforts to secure support for deserted women, insurance for bewildered widows, damages for injured [factory machine] operators, furniture from the clutches of the installment store."

Thus another profession, social work, emerged as a career for educated women. College graduates flocked to it, though most of the openings were volunteer jobs. Paid or unpaid, social workers were quickly recognized as useful people. The fact that many of their tasks were extensions of traditional woman's work hastened their acceptance.

■ At top, a nurse shows an older sister how to take care of the baby. Next, a visiting nurse making her rounds in the slums. Visiting-nurse services were established by settlement houses, hospitals, and charitable organizations. Bottom, day nurseries in the slums were critically needed; working women were known to have locked their children in their apartments and even to have tied children to a bed when they went off to work.

■ *Cliff Dwellers* was painted in 1913 by the New York artist George Bellows. (One of the preliminary drawings for this painting was titled, "Why Don't They All Go to the Country for Vacation?".) Lillian Wald, whose settlement house was in this neighborhood, described the scene at night: "Sleepless because of the heat, I leaned out of the window and looked down on Rivington Street. Life was in full course there. Some of the push-cart vendors still sold their wares. Sitting on the curb directly under my window, with her feet in the gutter, was a woman drooping from exhaustion, a baby at her breast. The fire-escapes, considered the most desirable sleeping-places, were crowded with the youngest and the oldest; children were asleep on the sidewalks, on the steps of the houses and in the empty push-carts; some of the more venturesome men and women with mattress or pillow staggered toward the riverfront or the parks."

■ In 1911 a fire in the Triangle Shirtwaist Company of New York City flashed through three top stories of the building, feeding on cotton scraps, paper patterns, and the wooden trim of the rooms (top and center). Scores of women were trapped and burned to death; fire escapes collapsed under the weight of the victims; desperate to escape, many plunged to their death from windows. More than 140 perished. Although the building had been a firetrap, the Triangle Company and the owners of the building were not legally responsible for the disaster. At a public meeting of protest, Rose Schneiderman, then an officer of the Shirtwaist Makers Union, said, "The life of men and women is so cheap and property is so sacred! There are so many of us for one job, it matters little if 140-odd are burned to death." The insurance company paid $65,000 for the property damage. Twenty-three suits by families of the dead were settled for $75 apiece.

■ The union organizer Rose Schneiderman speaks at an office workers' rally. As an executive of the Women's Trade Union League, it was her job to support unions that had women members. Schneiderman became a friend of Eleanor and Franklin Roosevelt.

Some Ladies Unite

Though women's work earned low wages, women did not readily join unions. Some of the reasons for this were given in a report in 1875 on workers in retail stores: "They are all women, and consequently unusually timid. . . . They are young, many being between the ages of fourteen and twenty. . . . Their trade . . . is mostly unskilled, and therefore there is an almost unlimited supply of applicants for their situation." The settlement worker Lillian Wald wrote that young women were unwilling to organize because they feared "it would be considered 'unladylike,' and might even militate against their marriage."

But trade unions did develop among women workers, and they began to win scattered victories early in the 20th century. Their main foothold was in the garment trades, their largest representative the International Ladies' Garment Workers Union. An unusual aspect of the movement was the support sometimes given by middle-class women and social leaders, particularly in New York City. In 1909, when the ILGWU struck the shirtwaist workers in New York and Philadelphia, society women raised bail for arrested pickets. After the Triangle fire in 1911 (left), women of all ranks worked together in a drive to improve factory conditions throughout the state.

Not only did wealthy women help factory women, but factory women began to join the middle-class women who were fighting for the vote. When a state senator claimed that the vote would destroy women's femininity, the labor leader Rose Schneiderman spoke out: "We have women in the foundries, stripped to the waist, if you please, because of the heat. Yet the Senator says nothing about these women losing their charm. They have got to retain their charm and delicacy, and work in the foundries. Of course you know the reason they are employed in foundries is that they are cheaper and work longer hours than men. . . . Surely these women won't lose any more of their beauty and charm by putting a ballot in a ballot box once a year than they are likely to lose standing in foundries."

■ A parade in New York City for the Women's Trade Union League. Parades, both for women's labor unions and for women's suffrage, became regular ceremonies in some cities during the early 1900s. Yet despite the efforts to organize women, in 1910 only about 5 percent of women factory workers belonged to unions.

Why Not Go the Limit?

■ Many people laughed at the idea that women might play the same roles in society as men. A few women were beginning to smoke in public, and this 1908 cartoon, "Why Not Go the Limit?" pictures a women's saloon. Among other details, the cigar-smoking women follow the stock market on ticker tape and refuse to go home when their children plead with them.

Women's Rights

By 1917, when the United States entered World War I, women's place was no longer exclusively in the home. Economic independence and better education had increased their social freedom. During World War I they went overseas with the YMCA, the Red Cross, and the Salvation Army. Some drove ambulances at the front and nursed in field hospitals. In this country the war temporarily opened new types of jobs to women, including skilled work in industry. The great majority of women were still engrossed in homemaking, but now they had other choices as well.

Once women were out in the world, their fathers or husbands could not protect them from exploitation. Women demanded some new laws, some political power, some new kinds of organizations—new social tools to ensure fair treatment. As a beginning they had to get the vote, but this elementary privilege had proved elusive for more than fifty years. It was plain in 1917, however, that suffrage was coming. M. Carey Thomas said at a suffrage meeting: "Women are one-half of the world, but until a century ago . . . women lived a twilight life, a half life apart, and looked out and saw men as shadows walking. It was a man's world. The laws were men's laws, the government a man's government, the country a man's country. Now women have won the right to higher education and economic independence. The right to become citizens of the state is the next and inevitable consequence of education and work outside the home. We have gone so far; we must go farther. We cannot go back."

Y.M.C.A.
ONE OF THE THOUSAND Y.M.C.A. GIRLS IN FRANCE
United War Work Campaign
Nov. 11th to 18th

■ A woman welding bombs in an American munitions factory in 1917.

■ The uniforms on these women trolley conductors lend an official, military air that suits the World War I period. These women were filling the jobs left vacant by men who were serving in the Army or in industry.

24/WOODROW WILSON AND THE GREAT WAR

Woodrow Wilson's approach to foreign relations was well intentioned and idealistic but somewhat confused. He knew that the United States had no wish to injure any foreign state and assumed that all nations would recognize this fact and cooperate. He wanted to help other countries, especially the republics of Latin America, achieve stable democratic governments and improve the living conditions of their people. Imperialism was in his eyes immoral. At the same time he felt obliged to sustain and protect American interests abroad. The maintenance of the Open Door in China and the completion of the Panama Canal were as important to him as they had been to Theodore Roosevelt.

Wilson's view of nations with traditions different from those of the United States was shortsighted and provincial. His attitude resembled that of 19th-century Christian missionaries: he wanted to spread the gospel of American democracy, to lift and enlighten the unfortunate and the ignorant—but in his own way. "I am going to teach the South American republics to elect good men!" he told one British diplomat.

Missionary Diplomacy

Wilson set out to raise the moral tone of American foreign policy by denouncing dollar diplomacy. Encouraging bankers to lend money to countries like China, he said, implied the possibility of "forcible interference" if the loans were not repaid, and that would be "obnoxious to the principles upon which the government of our people rests." To seek special economic concessions in Latin America was "unfair" and "degrading." The United States would deal with Latin American nations "upon terms of equality and honor."

In certain small matters Wilson succeeded in conducting American diplomacy on this idealistic basis. He withdrew the government's support of the international consortium that was arranging a loan to develop Chinese railroads, and American bankers pulled out. When the Japanese attempted, in the notorious Twenty-one Demands (1915), to reduce China almost to the status of a Japanese protectorate, he persuaded them to modify their conditions slightly. Congress had passed a law in 1912 exempting American coastal shipping from the payment of tolls on the Panama Canal in spite of a provision in the Hay-Pauncefote Treaty with Great Britain guaranteeing that the canal would be available to the vessels of all nations "on terms of entire equality." Wilson insisted that Congress repeal the law. He also permitted Secretary of State William Jennings Bryan to negotiate conciliation treaties with 21 nations. The distinctive feature of these agreements was the provision for a "cooling-off" period of one year, during which signatories agreed, in the event of a dispute, not to engage in hostilities.

Where more vital interests of the United States were concerned, Wilson sometimes failed to live up to his promises. Because of the strategic importance of the Panama Canal, he was unwilling to tolerate "unrest" anywhere in the Caribbean. Within months of his inauguration he was pursuing the same tactics that circumstances had forced on Roosevelt and Taft. The Bryan-Chamorro Treaty of 1914, which gave the United States an option to build a canal across Nicaragua, made that country virtually an American protectorate and served to maintain in power an unpopular dictator, Adolfo Díaz. When a revolution broke out in the Dominican Republic in 1916, United States marines occupied the country. American troops also took over in revolution-torn Haiti and installed a puppet president. By a treaty of September 1915, Haiti became a United States protectorate.

A much more serious example of missionary diplomacy occurred in Mexico. In 1911 a liberal coalition overthrew the dictator Porfirio Díaz, who had been exploiting the resources and people of Mexico for the benefit of a small class of wealthy landowners, clerics, and military men since the 1870s. Francisco Madero became president.

Madero, a wealthy landowner apparently influenced by the progressive movement in the United States, was committed to economic reform and the drafting of a democratic constitution. Unfortunately, he was both weak-willed and a terrible administrator. Conditions in Mexico deteriorated rapidly, and less than a month before Wilson's inauguration one of Madero's generals, Victoriano Huerta, treacherously seized power and had his former chief murdered. Huerta was an unabashed reactionary, but he was committed to maintaining the stability that foreign investors desired. Most of the powers promptly recognized his government.

The American ambassador in Mexico City, together with important American financial and business interests in Mexico and in the United States, urged Wilson to do so too, but he refused. His sympathies were all with the government of Madero, whose murder had horrified him. There were practical reasons for withholding recognition, for the followers of Madero remained in control of a large part of the country, but Wilson chose to act on moral grounds. "I will not recognize a government of butchers," he said firmly. This was unconventional; nations do not ordinarily consider the means by which a foreign regime has come to power before deciding to establish diplomatic relations.

Wilson brought enormous pressure to bear against Huerta. He dragooned the British into withdrawing recognition. He dickered with other Mexican factions. He demanded that Huerta hold

■ **Troopers of the 10th Cavalry, photographed in Mexico in 1916 during Pershing's pursuit of Villa. Pershing was an advocate of black troops; his nickname, "Black Jack," stemmed from his command of this crack regiment.**

free elections as the price of American mediation in the continuing civil war. Huerta would not yield an inch. Indeed, he drew strength from Wilson's effort to oust him, for even his enemies resented American interference in Mexican affairs. Frustration, added to his moral outrage, weakened Wilson's judgment. He subordinated his wish to let the Mexicans solve their own problems to his personal desire to destroy Huerta.

The tense situation exploded in April 1914, when a small party of American sailors was arrested in the port of Tampico, Mexico. Although a minor Mexican official had been responsible for the arrest and the men had been promptly released by higher authority, the Mexican government refused to supply the apology demanded by the sailors' commander. Wilson fastened on the affair as an excuse for sending troops into Mexico. Force would be used, he informed Congress, against "General Huerta and those who adhere to him," not against the Mexican people. His only object, he told a reporter, was "to help the [Mexican] people to secure [their] liberty."

The invasion took place at Veracruz, whence Winfield Scott had launched the assault on Mexico City in 1847. Instead of meekly surrendering the city, the Mexicans resisted tenaciously, suffering 400 casualties before falling back. This bloodshed caused dismay throughout Latin America and failed to unseat Huerta. The leader of the constitutionalist armies, General Venustiano Carranza, denounced the Americans vociferously.

At this point Argentina, Brazil, and Chile offered to mediate the dispute. Wilson accepted, Huerta also agreed, and the conferees met at Niagara Falls, Ontario, in May. Although no settlement was reached, Huerta, hard pressed by constitutionalist armies, abdicated. On August 20, 1914, General Carranza entered Mexico City in triumph.

Carranza's victory gave Wilson a chance to escape the consequences of his effort to impose good government on Mexico from the outside.* He failed to make the most of his good fortune. Carranza proved scarcely more successful than the tyrant Huerta in controlling his turbulent country. One of his own generals, Francisco "Pancho" Villa, rose against him and seized control of Mexico City.

Wilson now made a monumental blunder. Villa professed to be willing to cooperate with the United States, and Wilson, taking him at his word, gave him his support. However, Villa was little more than an ambitious bandit with no other objective than personal power. Carranza, while no radical, was committed to social reform and constitutional government. He had wide support among the middle class. Fighting back, he drove the Villistas into the northern provinces.

Wilson finally realized the extent of Carranza's influence in Mexico, and in October 1915 he recognized the Carranza government. Still his Mexican troubles were not over; Villa, seeking to undermine Carranza by forcing the United States to intervene, began a series of unprovoked attacks on Americans. Early in 1916 he stopped a train in

*During the occupation of Veracruz the American forces cleaned up the city, built roads and bridges, improved public services, and made the city, in the words of the historian Robert E. Quirk, "the most efficient, most honestly and justly governed city in all of Mexican history." Yet they succeeded only in arousing "the hatred and the scorn of the Mexicans," and when they withdrew in November 1914, Veracruz quickly reverted to its old ways.

northern Mexico and killed 16 American passengers in cold blood. Then he crossed into New Mexico and burned the town of Columbus, killing 19. Having learned his lesson, Wilson would have preferred to bear even this assault in silence, but public opinion forced him to send American troops under General John J. Pershing across the border in pursuit of Villa.

Villa proved impossible to catch. Cleverly he drew Pershing deeper and deeper into Mexico, and this alarmed Carranza, who insisted that the Americans withdraw. Several clashes occurred between Pershing's men and Mexican regulars, and for a brief period in June 1916 war seemed imminent. Wilson now acted bravely and wisely. He negotiated when it would have been far easier to fight, and in the end he was big enough to yield. The growing threat of involvement in the European war that was now raging made it easier to do so. Early in 1917 he recalled Pershing's force to American soil, and the Mexicans proceeded to work out their own destiny.

Missionary diplomacy in Mexico had produced mixed but in the long run beneficial results. By opposing Huerta, Wilson had surrendered to his prejudices, yet he had also helped the real revolutionaries even though they opposed his acts. His bungling bred anti-Americanism in Mexico, but by his later restraint in the face of stinging provocations, he permitted the constitutionalists to consolidate their power.

Outbreak of the Great War

On June 28, 1914, in the Austro-Hungarian provincial capital of Sarajevo, Gavrilo Princip, a young student, assassinated the Archduke Franz Ferdinand, heir to the imperial throne. Princip was a member of the Black Hand, a Serbian terrorist organization. He was seeking to further the cause of Serbian nationalism. Instead his rash act precipitated a general European war. Within little more than a month, following a complex series of diplomatic challenges and responses, two great coalitions, the Central Powers (chiefly Germany and Austria-Hungary) and the Allied Powers (chiefly Great Britain, France, and Russia), were locked in a brutal struggle that brought one era in world history to a close and inaugurated another.

The outbreak of what contemporaries were soon to call the Great War caught Americans psychologically unprepared; few understood the significance of what had happened. President Wilson promptly issued a proclamation of neutrality and asked the nation to be "impartial in thought." While no one, including the president, had the superhuman self-control that this request called for, the almost unanimous reaction of Americans, aside from dismay, was that the conflict did not concern them. They were wrong, for this was a world war and Americans were sure to be affected by its outcome.

There were good reasons, aside from a failure to understand the significance of the struggle, why the United States sought to remain neutral. Over a third of its 92 million inhabitants were either foreign-born or the children of immigrants. Sentimental ties bound former Europeans to the lands of their ancestors. American involvement would create new internal stresses in a society already strained by the task of assimilating so many diverse groups. War was also an affront to the prevailing progressive spirit, which assumed that human beings were reasonable, high-minded, and capable of settling disputes peaceably. Along with the traditional American fear of entanglement in European affairs, these were ample reasons for remaining aloof.

While most Americans hoped to keep out of the war, nearly everyone was partial to one side or the other. People of German or Austrian descent, about 8 million in number, and the nation's 4.5 million Irish-Americans, motivated chiefly by hatred of the British, sympathized with the Central Powers. The majority of the people, however, influenced by bonds of language and culture, preferred an Allied victory, and when the Germans launched a mighty assault across neutral Belgium in an effort to outflank the French armies, this unprovoked attack on a tiny nation whose neutrality the Germans had previously agreed to respect caused a great deal of anti-German feeling.

As the war progressed the Allies cleverly exploited American prejudices by such devices as publishing exaggerated tales of German atrocities against Belgian civilians. A supposedly impartial study of these charges by the widely respected James Bryce, author of *The American Commonwealth,* portrayed the Germans as ruthless and cruel barbarians. The Germans also conducted a shrewd and extensive propaganda campaign in the United States, but they labored under severe handicaps and won few converts.

Freedom of the Seas

Propaganda did not basically alter American attitudes; far more important were questions rising out of trade and commerce. All the warring nations wanted to draw on American resources. Under international law neutrals could trade freely with any belligerent. Americans were prepared to do so, but because the British fleet dominated the North Atlantic, they could not. While the specific issues differed somewhat, the situation was similar to that which had prevailed during the Napoleonic wars. The British declared nearly all commodities, even foodstuffs, to be contraband of war. They set limits on exports to neutral nations such as Denmark and the Netherlands so that those countries could not transship supplies to Germany. They forced neutral merchantmen into Allied ports in order to search them for goods headed for the enemy. Many cargoes were confiscated, often without payment. American firms that traded with the Central Powers were "blacklisted," which meant that no British subject could deal with them. When these policies caused protests in America, the British answered that in a battle for survival they dared not adhere to old-fashioned rules of international law.

Had the United States insisted that Great Britain abandon these "illegal" practices, as the Germans demanded, no doubt it could have had its way. The British foreign secretary, Sir Edward Grey, later admitted: "The ill-will of the United States meant certain defeat. The object of diplomacy, therefore, was to secure the maximum of blockade that could be enforced without a rupture with the United States." It is ironic that an embargo, which failed so ignominiously in Jefferson's day, would have been almost instantly effective if applied at any time after 1914, for American supplies were vital to the Allies.

While British tactics frequently exasperated Wilson, he never considered taking such a drastic step. He faced a dilemma. To allow the British to make the rules meant siding against the Central Powers. Yet to insist on the old rules (which had never been obeyed in wartime) meant siding against the Allies because that would have deprived them of much of the value of their naval superiority. *Nothing* the United States might do would be truly impartial.

Wilson's own sentiments made it doubly difficult for him to object strenuously to British practices. No American admired British institutions and culture more extravagantly. "Everything I love most in the world is at stake," he confessed privately to the British ambassador. A German victory "would be fatal to our form of Government and American ideals."

In any event, the immense expansion of American trade with the Allies made an embargo unthinkable. While commerce with the Central Powers fell to a trickle, that with the Allies soared from $825 million in 1914 to over $3.2 billion in 1916. An attempt to limit this commerce would have raised a storm; to have eliminated it would have caused a catastrophe. Munitions makers and other businessmen did not want the United States to enter the war. Neutrality suited their purposes admirably. Despite British harassments, they profited from the war and wished to continue to do so.

The Allies soon exhausted their ready cash and had to borrow in order to continue their purchases. Wilson first refused to let American bankers lend them money, then reversed himself. By early 1917 Britain and France had borrowed well over $2 billion. While these loans violated no principle of international law, they fastened the United States more closely to the Allies' cause.

During the first months of the Great War the Germans were not especially concerned about neutral trade or American goods because they expected to crush the Allied armies quickly. When their first swift thrust was blunted along the Marne and the war became a bloody stalemate, they began to challenge the Allies' control of the seas. Unwilling to risk their battleships and cruisers against the much larger British fleet, they resorted to a new weapon, the submarine, commonly known as the U-boat (*Unterseeboot*).

German submarines played a role in World War I not unlike that of American privateers in the Revolution and the War of 1812: they ranged the seas stealthily in search of merchantmen. However, submarines could not operate under the ordinary rules of war, which required that a raider

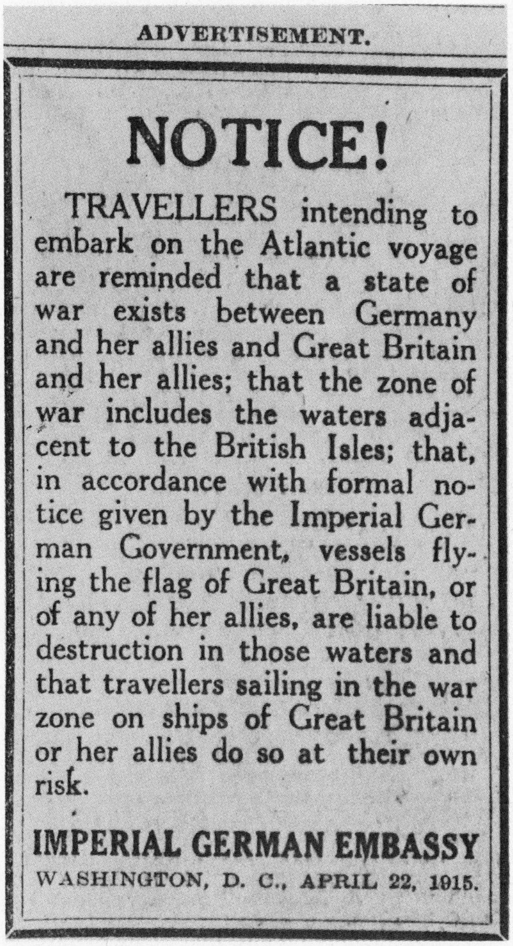

ADVERTISEMENT.

NOTICE!

TRAVELLERS intending to embark on the Atlantic voyage are reminded that a state of war exists between Germany and her allies and Great Britain and her allies; that the zone of war includes the waters adjacent to the British Isles; that, in accordance with formal notice given by the Imperial German Government, vessels flying the flag of Great Britain, or of any of her allies, are liable to destruction in those waters and that travellers sailing in the war zone on ships of Great Britain or her allies do so at their own risk.

IMPERIAL GERMAN EMBASSY
WASHINGTON, D. C., APRIL 22, 1915.

■ **Three weeks before the *Lusitania* was torpedoed this notice appeared in the classified sections of the Washington newspapers.**

stop its prey, examine its papers and cargo, and give the crew and passengers time to get off in lifeboats before sending it to the bottom. When surfaced, U-boats were vulnerable to the deck guns that many merchant ships carried; they could even be sunk by ramming, once they had stopped and put out a boarding party. Therefore they commonly launched their torpedoes from below the surface without warning. The result was often a heavy loss of life on the torpedoed ships.

In February 1915 the Germans declared the waters surrounding the British Isles a zone of war and announced that they would sink without warning all enemy merchant ships encountered in the area. Since Allied vessels sometimes flew neutral flags to disguise their identity, neutral ships entering the zone would do so at their own risk. This statement was largely bluff, for the Germans had only a handful of submarines at sea; but they were feverishly building more.

Wilson, perhaps too hurriedly considering the importance of the question, warned the Germans that he would hold them to "strict accountability" for any loss of American life or property resulting from violations of "acknowledged [neutral] rights on the high seas." He did not distinguish clearly between losses incurred through the destruction of *American* ships and those resulting from the sinking of other vessels. If he meant to hold the Germans responsible for injuries to Americans on *belligerent* vessels, he was changing international law as arbitrarily as the Germans were. Secretary of State Bryan, who opposed Wilson vigorously on this point, took sound legal ground when he said: "A ship carrying contraband should not rely upon passengers to protect her from attack—it would be like putting women and children in front of an army." "Strict accountability" ultimately meant war unless the Germans backed down. Yet Wilson was not prepared to fight; he refused even to ask Congress for increased military appropriations, saying that he did not want to "turn America into a military camp."

Wise or unwise, Wilson's position reflected the attitude of most Americans. It seemed barbaric to them that defenseless civilians should be killed without warning, and they refused to surrender their "rights" as neutrals to cross the North Atlantic on any ship they wished. The depth of their feeling was demonstrated when, on May 7, 1915, the submarine *U-20* sank the British liner *Lusitania* off the Irish coast. Nearly 1,200 persons, including 128 Americans, lost their lives in this catastrophe.

The torpedoing of the *Lusitania* caused as profound and emotional a reaction in the United States as that following the destruction of the *Maine* in Havana harbor. Wilson, like McKinley in 1898, was shocked, but he kept his head. He demanded that Germany disavow the sinking, indemnify the victims, and promise to stop attacking passenger vessels. When the Germans quibbled about these points, he responded with further diplomatic correspondence rather than with an ultimatum.

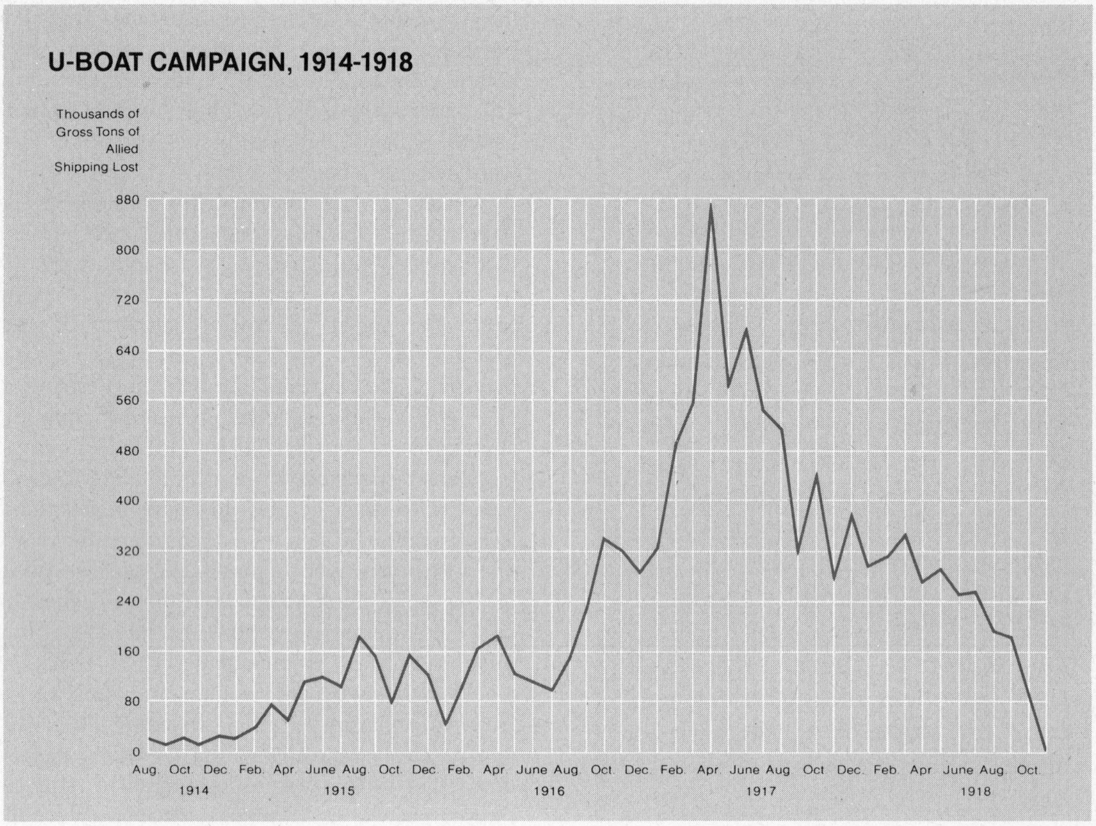

In one sense this was sound policy. The Germans pointed out that they had published warnings in American newspapers saying they considered the *Lusitania* subject to attack, that the liner was carrying munitions, and that on past voyages it had flown the American flag as a *ruse de guerre.* It would have been difficult politically for the German government to have backed down before an American ultimatum; however, after dragging the controversy out for nearly a year, it apologized and agreed to pay an indemnity. After the torpedoing of the French channel steamer *Sussex* in March 1916 had produced another stiff American protest, the Germans at last promised—the *Sussex* pledge—to stop sinking merchantmen without warning.

Had Wilson forced a showdown in 1915, he would have alienated a large segment of American opinion. Even his relatively mild notes resulted in the resignation of Secretary of State Bryan, who believed it unneutral to treat German violations of international law differently than Allied violations—and Bryan reflected the feelings of thousands.*

On the other hand, if Wilson had sought a declaration of war over the *Lusitania,* a majority of Congress and the country would probably have gone along, and in that event the dreadful carnage in Europe would have been ended much sooner. This is the reasoning of hindsight, yet such a policy would have been logical, given Wilson's assumptions about the justice of the Allied cause and America's stake in an Allied victory.

The president, and most Americans, were not clearheaded enough in 1915 to act entirely logically. In November 1915 Wilson at last began to press for increased military and naval expenditures. Nevertheless he continued to vacillate. He dispatched a sharp note protesting Allied blacklisting of American firms, and he told his confidante, Colonel Edward M. House, that the British

*Wilson appointed Robert Lansing, counselor of the State Department, to succeed Bryan.

■ **A Wilson campaign truck offered New York City voters a convenient summary of the 1916 Democratic platform. The 8-hour-day plank refers to the president's support of a federal law for railroad workers.**

were "poor boobs!" His position on preparedness remained so equivocal that his secretary of war, Lindley M. Garrison, resigned in protest.

Election of 1916

Part of Wilson's confusion in 1916 resulted from the political difficulties he faced in his fight for reelection. He had won the presidency in 1912 only because the Republican party had split in two. Now Theodore Roosevelt, the chief defector, had become so incensed by Wilson's refusal to commit the United States to the Allied cause that he was ready to support almost any Republican in order to guarantee the president's defeat. At the same time, many progressives were complaining about Wilson's unwillingness to work for further domestic reforms. Unless he could find additional support, he seemed likely to be defeated.

He attacked the problem by wooing the progressives. In January 1916 he appointed Louis D. Brandeis to the Supreme Court. In addition to being an advanced progressive, Brandeis was Jewish, the first American of that religion appointed to the Court. Wilson's action won him many friends among people who favored fair treatment for minority groups. In July he bid for the farm vote by signing the Farm Loan Act to provide low-cost loans based on agricultural credit. Shortly thereafter he approved the Keating-Owen Child Labor Act, barring goods manufactured by the labor of children under 16 from interstate commerce, and a workmen's compensation act for federal employees. He persuaded Congress to pass the Adamson Act, establishing an 8-hour day for railroad workers, and he modified his position on the tariff by approving the creation of a tariff commission and accepting "antidumping" legislation designed to protect American industry from cutthroat foreign competition after the war.

Each of these actions represented a sharp reversal. In 1913 Wilson had considered Brandeis too radical even for a Cabinet post. The new farm, labor, and tariff laws were all examples of the kind of "class legislation" he had refused to countenance in 1913 and 1914. As Arthur S. Link has pointed out, Wilson was putting into effect "almost every important plank of the Progressive platform of 1912." It would be uncharitable to conclude that he did so only to win votes, but his actions paid spectacular political dividends when Roosevelt refused to run as a Progressive and came out for the Republican nominee, Associate Justice Charles Evans Hughes. The Progressive convention then endorsed Hughes, who had compiled a fine liberal record as governor of New York, but many of Roosevelt's 1912 supporters felt he had betrayed them and voted for Wilson in 1916.

The key issue in the campaign was American policy toward the warring powers. Wilson intended to stress preparedness, which he was now wholeheartedly supporting. However, during the Democratic convention the delegates shook the hall with cheers whenever orators referred to the president's success in keeping the country out of the war. One spellbinder, referring to the *Sussex* pledge, announced that the president had "wrung from the most militant spirit that ever brooded above a battlefield an acknowledgement of American rights and an agreement to American demands," and the convention erupted in a demonstration that lasted more than 20 minutes. Thus "He Kept Us Out of War" became the Democratic slogan.

To his credit, Wilson made no promises. "I can't keep the country out of war," he told one member of his Cabinet. "Any little German lieutenant can put us into the war at any time by some calculated outrage." His attitude undoubtedly cost him the votes of extremists on both sides, but it won the backing of thousands of moderates.

The combination of progressivism and the peace issue placed the Democrats on substantially equal terms with the Republicans; thereafter personal factors probably tipped the balance. Hughes proved a poor campaigner. He was very stiff and an ineffective speaker; he offended a number of important politicians, especially in crucial California, where he inadvertently snubbed the popular progressive governor, Hiram Johnson; and he equivocated on a number of issues. Nevertheless, on election night he appeared to have won, having carried nearly all the East and Middle West. Late returns gave Wilson California, however, and with it victory by the narrow margin of 277 to 254 in the electoral college. He led Hughes in the popular vote, 9.1 million to 8.5 million.

The Road to War

Encouraged by his triumph, appalled by the continuing slaughter on the battlefields, fearful that the United States would be dragged into the holocaust, Wilson made one last effort to end the war by negotiation. In 1915 he had sent his friend Colonel House on a secret mission to London, Paris, and Berlin to try to mediate among the belligerents. House had been received cordially, but he made little progress and his negotiations were disrupted by the *Lusitania* crisis. A second House mission (January–February 1916) had proved equally fruitless. Now, after another long season of bloodshed, perhaps the powers would listen to reason.

Wilson's own feelings were more genuinely neutral than at any other time during the war, for the Germans had stopped sinking merchantmen without warning and the British had irritated him repeatedly by their arbitrary restrictions on neutral trade. He drafted a note to the belligerents asking them to state the terms on which they would agree to lay down their arms. Unless the fighting ended soon, he warned, neutrals and belligerents alike would be so ruined that peace would be meaningless. When neither side responded encouragingly, Wilson, on January 22, 1917, delivered a moving, prophetic speech aimed, as he admitted, at "the *people* of the countries now at war" more than at their governments. Any settlement imposed by a victor, he declared, would breed hatred and more wars. There must be a "peace without victory" based on the principles that all nations were equal and that every nationality group should determine its own form of government. He mentioned, albeit vaguely, disarmament and freedom of the seas, and he suggested the creation of some kind of international organization to preserve world peace. "There must be not a balance of power, but a community of power," he said, and he added, "I am speaking for the silent mass of mankind everywhere."

This noble appeal met a tragic fate. The Germans had already decided to renounce the *Sussex* pledge and unleash their submarines against *all* vessels headed for Allied ports. After February 1 any ship in the war zone would be attacked without warning. Possessed now of more than 100 U-boats, the German military leaders had convinced themselves that they could starve the British people into submission and reduce the Allied armies to impotence by cutting off the flow of American supplies. The United States would probably declare war, but the Germans believed they could overwhelm the Allies before the Americans could get to the battlefields in force. "The United States . . . can neither inflict material damage upon us, nor can it be of material benefit to our enemies," Admiral von Holtzendorff boasted. "I guarantee that for its part the U-boat war will lead to victory."

In *Tiger at the Gates* the French playwright Jean Giraudoux makes Ulysses say, while attempting to stave off what he considers an inevitable war with the Trojans: "The privilege of great men is to view catastrophe from a terrace." This is not always true, but in 1917, after the German military leaders had made their decision, events moved relentlessly, almost uninfluenced by the actors who presumably controlled the fate of the world:

In a 1916 drawing by the Dutch artist and Allied propagandist Louis Raemaekers, Kaiser Wilhelm is flanked by War and Hunger.

February 3: *S.S. Housatonic* torpedoed. Wilson announces to Congress that he has severed diplomatic relations with Germany. Secretary of State Lansing hands the German ambassador, Count von Bernstorff, his passport. *February 24:* Walter Hines Page, United States ambassador to Great Britain, transmits to the State Department an intercepted German dispatch (the "Zimmermann Telegram") revealing that Germany has proposed a secret alliance with Mexico, Mexico to receive, in the event of war with the United States, "the lost territory in Texas, New Mexico, and Arizona." *February 25:* Cunard liner *Laconia* torpedoed, two American women perish. *February 26:* Wilson asks Congress for authority to arm American merchant ships. *March 1:* Zimmermann Telegram released to the press. *March 4:* President Wilson takes oath of office, beginning his second term. Congress adjourns without passing the Armed Ship bill, the measure having been filibustered to death by antiwar senators. Wilson characterizes the filibusterers, led by Senator Robert M. La Follette, as "a little group of willful men, representing no opinion but their own." *March 9:* Wilson, acting under his executive powers, orders the arming of American merchantmen. *March 12:* Revolutionary provisional government established in Russia. *Algonquin* torpedoed. *March 15:* Czar Nicholas II of Russia abdicates. *March 16:* *City of Memphis, Illinois, Vigilancia* torpedoed. *March 21:* New York *World,* a leading Democratic newspaper, calls for declaration of war on Germany. Wilson summons Congress to convene in special session on April 2. *March 25:* Wilson calls up the National Guard. *April 2:* Wilson asks Congress to declare war. Germany is guilty of "throwing to the winds all scruples of humanity," he says. America must fight, not to conquer, but for "peace and justice. . . . The world must be made safe for democracy." *April 4, 6:* Congress declares war—the vote, 82–6 in the Senate, 373–50 in the House.

The bare record conceals Wilson's agonizing search for an honorable alternative to war. To admit that Germany posed a threat to the United States meant confessing that interventionists had been right all along. To go to war meant, besides sending innocent Americans to their death, unleashing the forces of hatred and intolerance in the United States and allowing "the spirit of ruthless brutality [to] enter into the very fibre of our national life." The president's Presbyterian conscience tortured him relentlessly. He lost sleep, appeared gray and drawn. When someone asked him which side he hoped would win, he answered petulantly, "Neither." "He was resisting," Secretary of State Lansing recorded, "the irresistible logic of events." In the end Wilson could satisfy himself only by giving intervention an idealistic purpose. The war had become a threat to humanity. Unless the United States threw its weight into the balance, western civilization itself might be destroyed. Out of the long bloodbath must come a new and better world. The war must be fought to end, for all time, war itself. Thus, in the name not of vengeance and victory but of justice and humanity, he sent his people into battle.

The Home Front

America's entry into the World War determined its outcome. The Allies were running out of money and supplies; their troops, decimated by nearly three years in the trenches, were disheartened and rebellious. In February and March 1917 U-boats sent over a million tons of Allied shipping to the bottom of the Atlantic. The outbreak of the Russian Revolution in March 1917, at first lifting the spirits of the western democracies, led to the Bolshevik takeover under Lenin. The Russian armies collapsed; by December 1917 Russia was out of the war and the Germans were moving masses of men and equipment from the eastern front to France. Without the aid of the United States, it is likely that the war would have ended in 1918 on terms dictated from Berlin. Instead American men and supplies helped contain the Germans' last drives and then push them back to final defeat.

It was a close thing, for the United States entered the war little better prepared to fight than it had been in 1898. For this Wilson was partly to blame. Because of his devotion to peace he had not tried hard enough to ready the country for war.

The conversion of American industry to war production had to be organized and carried out without prearrangement. What the historian Harvey A. DeWeerd has called "absurdly large" goals were set, far beyond what the army could use. Confusion and waste resulted. The hurriedly designed shipbuilding program was an almost total fiasco. The gigantic Hog Island yard, which cost $65 million and employed at its peak over 34,000 workers, completed its first vessel after the war ended. The nation's railroads, strained by immensely increased traffic, became progressively less efficient. A monumental tie-up in December and January 1917–1918 finally persuaded Wilson to appoint Secretary of the Treasury William G. McAdoo director-general of the railroads, with power to run the roads as a single system. Airplane, tank, and artillery construction programs, all too large to begin with, developed too slowly to affect the war. The big guns that backed up American troops in 1918 were made in France and Great Britain; of the 8.8 million rounds of artillery ammunition fired by American troops, only about 8,000 were manufactured in the United States. American pilots such as the great "ace" Captain Eddie Rickenbacker flew British Sopwiths and De Havillands or French Spads and Nieuports. Theodore Roosevelt's son Quentin was shot down while flying a Spad over Château-Thierry in July 1918.

The problem of mobilization was complicated. It took Congress six weeks of hot debate merely to decide on conscription. Only in September 1917, nearly six months after the declaration of war, did the first draftees reach the training camps, and it is hard to see how Wilson could have speeded this process appreciably. He wisely supported the professional soldiers, who insisted that he resist the appeals of politicians who wanted to raise volunteer units, even rejecting, at considerable political cost, Theodore Roosevelt's offer to raise an entire army division.

Wilson was a forceful and inspiring war leader once he grasped what needed to be done. Waste there was, and inefficiency, but no one in the country worked harder or displayed such unfailing patience in the face of frustration and criticism. Raising an army was only a small part of the job. The Allies had to be supplied with food and munitions, and immense amounts of money had to be collected.

Wilson placed the task in the hands of a Council of National Defense, consisting of six Cabinet officers and a seven-member advisory commission. The council attempted to coordinate the manufacture of munitions and other war goods, but it lacked the authority to do the job properly. After a series of experiments, it created (July 1917) the War Industries Board to oversee all aspects of industrial production and distribution. The head of the board, Bernard Baruch, a Wall Street speculator by trade, was given almost dictatorial power to allocate scarce materials, standardize production, fix prices, and coordinate American and Allied purchasing.

Evaluating the mobilization effort raises interesting historical questions. The antitrust laws were suspended and producers were encouraged, even compelled, to cooperate with one another. Government regulation went far beyond what the New Nationalists had envisaged in 1912. As for the New Freedom variety of laissez faire, it had no place in a wartime economy. McAdoo's Railroad Administration pooled all railroad equipment, centralized purchasing, standardized accounting practices, and raised wages and passenger rates. Under difficult conditions it ran the railroads effectively. Wilson accepted the kind of government-industry agreement developed under Theodore Roosevelt that he had denounced in 1912. Prices were set by the WIB at levels that allowed large profits—U. S. Steel, for example, despite high taxes, cleared over half a billion dollars in two years. Baruch justified these returns with what seemed to him irrefutable logic: "You could be forgiven if you paid too much to get the stuff, but you could never be forgiven if you did not get it, and lost the war." It is at least arguable that producers would have turned out just as much even though compelled to charge lower prices.

The system fostered a close relationship between business and the military. At the start of the war, army procurement was decentralized and inefficient—as many as eight bureaus were purchasing materiel independently. By 1918 the supply system was in a condition approaching chaos. Nevertheless the army resisted cooperating with civilian agencies, being, as the historian Paul Koistiner writes, "suspicious of, and hostile toward civilian institutions." Wilson finally compelled the War Department to place officers on WIB committees, and when the army discovered that its interests were not injured by the system, the foundation for what was later to be known as the "industrial-military complex" was laid, the alliance between business and military leaders that was to cause so much controversy after World War II.

The history of industrial mobilization was the history of the entire home-front effort in microcosm: prodigies were performed, but the task was so gigantic and unprecedented that a full year passed before an efficient system had been devised, and many unforeseen results occurred.

The problem of mobilizing agricultural resources was solved more quickly, and this was fortunate because in April 1917 the British had on hand only a six-weeks' supply of food. Wilson named Herbert Hoover, a mining engineer who had headed the Belgian Relief Commission earlier in the war, food administrator. Acting under powers granted by the Lever Act of August 1917, Hoover set the price of wheat at $2.20 a bushel in order to encourage production. He established a government corporation to purchase the entire American and Cuban sugar crop, which he then doled out to American and British refiners. To avoid rationing, he organized a campaign to persuade consumers to conserve food voluntarily. "Wheatless Mondays" and "Meatless Tuesdays" were the rule, and although no law compelled their observance, the public responded patriotically. Boy Scouts dug up back yards and vacant lots to plant vegetable gardens, chefs devised new recipes to save on scarce items, restaurants added horsemeat, rabbit, and whale steak to their menus. Chicago housewives were so successful in making use of leftovers that the volume of raw garbage in the city declined from 12,862 tons to 8,386 tons per month. Without subjecting its own citizens to serious inconvenience, the United States increased food exports from 12.3 million tons to 18.6 million tons. Farmers, of course, profited greatly: their real income went up nearly 30 percent between 1915 and 1918.

With the army siphoning so many men from the labor market and with immigration reduced to a trickle, unemployment disappeared and wages rose. Although the cost of living soared, imposing hardships on those with fixed incomes, the boom produced unprecedented opportunities for disadvantaged groups, especially blacks. The movement of blacks from the former slave states began with emancipation, but the mass exodus that many people had expected did not materialize. Between 1870 and 1890 only about 80,000 moved to the North, most of them settling in the cities. Compared with the urban influx from Europe and from northern farms, this was a trivial number; the percentage of blacks in New York City, for example, fell from over 10 percent in 1800 to under 2 percent in 1900.

Around the turn of the century, as the first post-slave generation reached maturity and as southern repression increased, the northward movement quickened—about 200,000 migrated between 1890 and 1910. Then, after 1914, the war boom drew blacks north in a flood, half a million in five years. The black population of New York rose from 92,000 to 152,000, that of Chicago from 44,000 to 109,000, that of Detroit from 5,700 to 41,000.

Early in the conflict the government began regulating the wages and hours of workers building army camps and manufacturing uniforms. In April 1918, Wilson created a National War Labor Board, headed by former president Taft and Frank P. Walsh, a prominent lawyer, to settle labor disputes. The board considered more than 1,200 cases and prevented many strikes. A War Labor Policies Board, chaired by Professor Felix Frankfurter of the Harvard Law School, set wages-and-hours standards for each major war industry. Since these were determined in consultation with employers and representatives of labor, the WLPB helped speed the unionization of workers by compelling management, even in antiunion industries like steel, to deal with labor leaders. Union membership rose by 2.3 million during the war; in 1920 the American Federation of Labor could boast a membership of more than 3.2 million.

On the other hand, the wartime emergency roused the public against strikers; some conservatives even demanded that war workers be conscripted just as soldiers were. While he opposed strikes that impeded the war effort, Wilson set great store in preserving the individual worker's freedom of action. It would be "most unfortunate . . . to relax the laws by which safeguards have been thrown about labor," he said. "We must accomplish the results we desire by organized effort rather than compulsion."

Trends in the steel industry reflect the improvement of the lot of labor in wartime. Wages of unskilled steelworkers more than doubled. Thousands of southern blacks flocked into the steel towns. Union organizers made inroads in many plants, especially after a War Labor Board decision forbade the companies to interfere with their activities. By the summer of 1918 they were preparing an all-out effort to unionize the industry. If the world was to be made safe for democracy, they argued, there must be "economic democracy [along] with political democracy."

■ **The nation's advertising and entertainment industries were mobilized to promote war-bond drives. This poster was aimed at recent immigrants from Europe.**

Wilson managed the task of financing the war effectively. The struggle cost the United States about $33.5 billion, not counting pensions and other postwar expenses. About $7 billion of this was lent to the Allies,* but since this money was largely spent in America, it contributed to the national prosperity.

Over two-thirds of the cost of the war was met by borrowing. Five Liberty and Victory Loan drives, spurred by advertising, parading, and appeals to patriotism, persuaded the people to open their purses. Industrialists, eager to inculcate in their employees a sense of personal involvement

*In 1914 Americans owed foreigners about $3.8 billion. By 1919 Americans *were owed* $12.5 billion by Europeans alone.

in the war effort, conducted campaigns in their plants. Some went so far as to threaten "A Bond or Your Job," but more typical was the appeal of the managers of the Gary, Indiana, plant of U. S. Steel, who published bond advertisements in six languages in order to reach their immigrant workers.

In addition to borrowing, the government collected about $10.5 billion in taxes during the war. A steeply graduated income tax took more than 75 percent of the incomes of the wealthiest citizens. A 65 percent excess-profits tax and a 25 percent inheritance tax were also enacted. Thus, while many individuals made fortunes out of the war, its cost was distributed far more equitably than was that of the Civil War. Americans also contributed generously to philanthropic agencies engaged in war work. Most notable, perhaps, was the great 1918 drive of the United War Work Council, an interfaith religious group, which raised over $200 million mainly to finance recreational programs for the troops overseas.

Propaganda and Civil Liberties

Wilson was preeminently a teacher and preacher, a specialist in the transmission of ideas and ideals. He excelled at mobilizing public opinion and inspiring Americans to work for the better world he hoped would emerge from the war. In April 1917 he created a Committee on Public Information, headed by the journalist George Creel. Soon hundreds of speakers and writers were blanketing the country with propaganda picturing the war as a crusade for freedom and democracy, the Germans as a bestial people bent on world domination.

Creel's committee served an important function. Thousands of persons—German-Americans and Irish-Americans, for example, and people of socialist and pacifist leanings—did not believe the war necessary or just. However, the committee, and a number of unofficial "patriotic" groups, allowed their enthusiasm for the conversion of the hesitant to become suppression of dissent. Persons who refused to buy war bonds were often exposed to public ridicule and even to assault. People with

■ In 1917 the Germania Life Insurance Building in St. Paul was renamed the Guardian Building; since Germania herself could not be disguised, down she came.

German names were persecuted without regard for their views; some school boards outlawed the teaching of the German language; sauerkraut was renamed "liberty cabbage." Opponents of the war of unquestionable patriotism were subjected to coarse abuse. The cartoonist Rollin Kirby pictured Senator Robert La Follette receiving an Iron Cross from the German militarists, and the faculty of his own University of Wisconsin voted to censure La Follette.*

Wilson, "a friend of free speech in theory," the historian David M. Kennedy has written, "was its foe in fact." He signed the Espionage Act of 1917, which imposed fines of up to $10,000 and jail sentences ranging to 20 years on persons convicted of aiding the enemy or obstructing recruiting, and authorized the postmaster general to ban from the mails any material which he considered treasonable or seditious.

In May 1918, again with Wilson's approval, Congress passed the Sedition Act, which made it a crime even to speak against the purchase of war bonds or to "utter, print, write, or publish any disloyal, profane, scurrilous, or abusive language" about the government, the Constitution, or the uniform of the army or navy. Socialist periodicals such as *The Masses* were suppressed, and Eugene V. Debs was sentenced to 10 years in prison for making an antiwar speech. Ricardo Flores Magon, an anarchist, was sentenced to 20 years in jail for publishing a statement criticizing Wilson's Mexican policy, an issue that had nothing to do with the war.

While legislation to prevent sabotage and control subversives was justifiable, these laws went far beyond what was necessary to protect the national interest. Some local officials used them to muzzle liberal opinion. Citizens were jailed for suggesting that the draft law was unconstitutional and for criticizing private organizations like the Red Cross and the YMCA. One woman was sent to prison for writing: "I am for the people, and the government is for the profiteers."

The Supreme Court upheld the constitutionality of the Espionage Act in *Schenck* v. *United States* (1919), a case involving a man who had mailed circulars to draftees urging them to refuse to report for induction into the army. Free speech has its limits, Justice Oliver Wendell Holmes, Jr., explained. No one has the right to cry *Fire!* in a crowded theater. When there is a "clear and present danger" that a particular statement would threaten the national interest, it can be repressed by law. In peacetime Schenck's circulars would be permissible, but not in time of war.

The "clear and present danger" doctrine did not prevent judges and juries from interpreting the Espionage and Sedition acts broadly, and while in many instances their decisions were overturned by higher courts, this usually did not occur until after the war. The wartime hysteria far exceeded anything that happened in Great Britain and France. In 1916 the French novelist Henri Barbusse published *Le Feu (Under Fire),* a graphic account of the horrors and purposelessness of trench warfare. In one chapter Barbusse described a pilot flying over the trenches on a Sunday, observing French and German soldiers at Mass in the open fields, each worshiping the same God. Yet *Le Feu* circulated freely in France and even won the coveted Prix Goncourt.

Wartime Reform

The American mobilization experience was part and product of the Progressive Era. The work of the progressives at the national and state levels in expanding government functions in order to deal with social and economic problems provided precedents and conditioned the people for the all-out effort of 1917–1918. This effort in turn had a great influence on national policy in later crises, notably during the New Deal period and in World War II. Social and economic planning and the management of huge business operations by public boards and committees got their first large-scale practical tests. College professors, technicians, and others with complex skills entered government service en masse. Congress imposed steeply graduated income taxes on the wealthy. The federal government for the first time entered actively such fields as housing and labor relations.

Many progressives, especially the social workers, believed that the war was creating the sense of common purpose that would stimulate the people to act unselfishly to benefit the poor and to eradi-

*Kirby later expressed deep regret for having defamed La Follette.

cate social evils. As one reformer said, "enthusiasm for social service is epidemic." Patriotism and public service seemed at last united. Secretary of War Newton D. Baker, a prewar urban reformer, expressed this attitude in supporting a federal child labor law: "We cannot afford, when we are losing boys in France to lose children in the United States." Men and women of this sort worked for a dozen causes only remotely related to the war effort. The women's suffrage movement was brought to fruition, as was the campaign against alcohol. Reformers began to talk about health insurance. A national campaign against prostitution and venereal disease was mounted.*

War-inspired cooperation brought social benefits to black Americans to supplement their new economic opportunities. Despite some terrible race riots in a number of cities, triggered by white resentment of the thousands of migrants who were crowding in to fill war jobs, significant forward steps were taken. The draft law applied to blacks and whites equally, and while it is possible to view this cynically, most blacks saw it as an important gain because it implicitly recognized their bravery and patriotism. Although most black soldiers served in labor battalions, some saw combat and a few were accepted for officer training. There were black Red Cross nurses, and some blacks held relatively high posts in government agencies.

W. E. B. Du Bois supported the war wholeheartedly. He praised Wilson for making, at last, a strong statement against lynching. He even went along with the fact that black officer candidates were trained in segregated camps. "Let us," he wrote in *The Crisis*, "while the war lasts, forget our special grievances and close ranks shoulder to shoulder with our fellow citizens and the allied nations that are fighting for democracy." Many blacks condemned Du Bois' accommodationism (which he promptly abandoned when the war ended), but for the moment the prevailing mood was one of optimism. "We may expect to see the walls of prejudice gradually crumble"—this was the common attitude of blacks in 1917–1918. If winning the war would make *the world* safe for democracy, surely blacks in the United States would be better off when it was won.

"Over There"

All activity on the home front had one ultimate objective: defeating the Central Powers on the battlefield. This was accomplished. The navy performed with special distinction. In April 1917 German submarines sank more than 870,000 tons of Allied shipping; after April 1918, monthly losses never reached 300,000 tons. American destroyers helped control the U-boats, but most important was the decision to send merchantmen across the Atlantic only in convoys screened by warships. Checking the U-boats was essential because of the need to transport American troops to Europe. The feat was carried out without the loss of a single soldier.

The first units of the American Expeditionary Force (AEF), elements of the regular army commanded by General John J. Pershing, reached Paris on Independence Day 1917. They took up positions on the front near Verdun in October. Not until the spring of 1918, however, did the "doughboys" play a significant role in the fighting—except insofar as their mere presence boosted French and British morale.

Pershing, as commander of the AEF, insisted on maintaining his troops as independent units; he would not allow them to be filtered into the Allied armies as reinforcements. This was part of a perhaps unfortunate general policy that reflected America's isolationism and suspicion of Europeans: its refusal to accept full membership in the Allied coalition. (Wilson always referred to the other nations fighting Germany as "associates," not as "allies.")

In March 1918 the Germans launched a great spring offensive, their armies strengthened by thousands of veterans from the Russian front. By late May they had reached a point on the Marne River near the town of Château-Thierry only 50 miles from Paris. Early in June the AEF fought its first major engagements, driving the Germans back from Château-Thierry and Belleau Wood.

*The effort to wipe out prostitution around military installations was a cause of some misunderstanding with the Allies, who provided licensed facilities for their troops as a matter of course. When the premier of France graciously offered to supply prostitutes for American units in his country, Secretary of War Baker is said to have remarked: "For God's sake . . . don't show this to the President or he'll stop the war."

■ **U. S. Second Division infantry troops crawling and fighting their way through the smoke of battle in the Argonne Forest.**

In this fighting only about 27,500 Americans saw action, but thereafter the number escalated rapidly. When the Germans advanced again in the direction of the Marne in mid July, 85,000 Americans were in the lines that withstood their charge. When the Allied armies counterattacked a few days later, 270,000 Americans participated, helping to flatten the German bulge between Reims and Soissons. By late August the American First Army, 500,000 strong, was poised before the Saint-Mihiel salient, a deep extension of the German lines southeast of Verdun. On September 12 this army, buttressed by French troops, struck and in two days wiped out the salient.

Then, late in September, began the greatest American engagement of the war. No fewer than 1.2 million doughboys drove forward west of Verdun into the Argonne Forest. For over a month of indescribable horror they inched ahead through the tangle of the Argonne and the formidable defenses of the Hindenburg Line, while to the west French and British armies staged similar drives. In this one offensive the AEF suffered 120,000 casualties. Finally, on November 1, they broke the German center and raced toward the vital Sedan-Mézières railroad. On November 11, with Allied armies advancing on all fronts, the Germans signed the Armistice, ending the fighting.*

Preparing for Peace

On November 11, 1918, western civilization stood at a turning point. The fighting had ended, but the shape of the postwar world remained to be deter-

*American losses in the war amounted to 112,432 dead and 230,074 wounded. More than half of the deaths, however, resulted from disease. While severe, these casualties were trivial compared with those of the other belligerents. British Commonwealth deaths amounted to 947,000, French to 1.38 million, Russian to 1.7 million, Italian to 460,000. Among the Central Powers, Germany lost 1.8 million men, Austria-Hungary 1.2 million, Turkey 325,000. In addition, about 20 million were wounded.

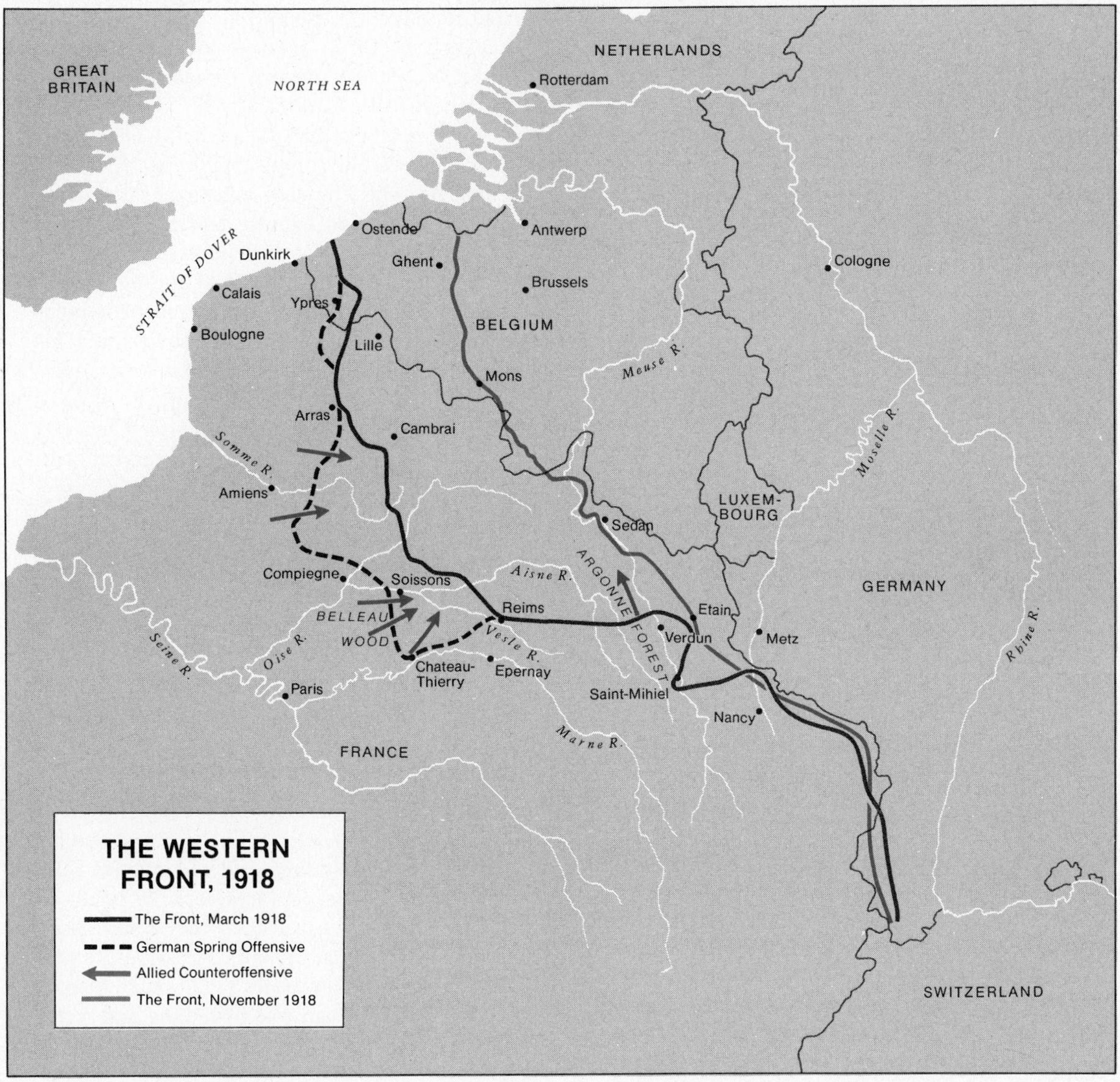

mined. European society had been shaken to its foundations. Confusion reigned. People wanted peace yet burned for revenge. Millions faced starvation. Other millions were disillusioned by the seemingly purposeless sacrifices of four years of horrible war. Communism—to some an idealistic promise of human betterment, to others a commitment to rational economic and social planning, to still others a danger to individual freedom, toleration, and democracy—having conquered Russia, threatened to envelop Germany and much of the defunct Austro-Hungarian empire, perhaps even the victorious Allies. How could stability be restored? How could victory be made worth its enormous cost?

Woodrow Wilson had grasped the significance of the war while most statesmen still thought that triumph on the battlefield would settle everything automatically. He faced the future on November 11 with determination and sober confidence. As early as January 1917 he had realized that victory would be wasted if the winners permitted themselves the luxury of vengeance. Such a policy would disrupt the balance of power and lead to economic and social chaos. American participation in the struggle had not blurred his vision. The victors must build a better society, not punish those they believed had destroyed the old.

Long before the war ended, in a speech to Congress on January 8, 1918, Wilson outlined a plan, known as the Fourteen Points, designed to make the world "fit and safe to live in." The peace treaty should be negotiated in full view of world opinion, not in secret. It should guarantee the freedom of the seas to all nations, in war as in peacetime. It should tear down barriers to international trade, provide for a drastic reduction of armaments, and establish a colonial system that would take proper account of the interests of the native peoples concerned. European boundaries should be redrawn so that no substantial group would have to live under a government not of its own choosing. More specifically, captured Russian territory should be restored, Belgium evacuated, Alsace-Lorraine returned to France, the heterogeneous nationalities of Austria-Hungary accorded autonomy. Italy's frontiers should be adjusted "along clearly recognizable lines of nationality," the Balkans made free, Turkey divested of its subject peoples, an independent Polish state (with access to the Baltic) created. To oversee the new system, Wilson insisted, "a general association of nations must be formed under specific covenants for the purpose of affording mutual guarantees of political independence and territorial integrity to great and small states alike."

Wilson's Fourteen Points for a fair peace lifted the hopes of people everywhere. After the guns fell silent, however, the vagueness and inconsistencies in the Points became apparent. Complete national self-determination was impossible in polyglot Europe; there were too many regions of mixed population for every group to be satisfied. Self-determination, like the war itself, fostered the spirit of nationalism that Wilson's dream of international organization, a league of nations, was designed to deemphasize. Furthermore, the Allies had made territorial commitments to one another in secret treaties that ran counter to the principle of self-determination, and they were not ready to give up all claim to Germany's sprawling colonial empire. Freedom of the seas in wartime posed another problem; the British flatly refused to accept the idea. In every Allied country millions rejected the idea of a peace without indemnities. They expected to make the enemy pay for the war, hoping, as David Lloyd George, the British prime minister, put it, to squeeze Germany "until the pips squeak."

Wilson assumed that the practical benefits of his program would compel opponents to fall in line. He had the immense advantage of seeking nothing for his own country and the additional strength of being leader of the one important nation to emerge from the war richer and more powerful than it had been in 1914. Yet this combination of altruism, idealism, and power was his undoing; it intensified his tendency to be overbearing and undermined his judgment. He had never found it easy to compromise. Once, at Princeton, he got into an argument over some abstract question with a professor while shooting a game of pool. To avoid acrimony, the professor finally said: "Well, Doctor Wilson, there are two sides to every question." "Yes," Wilson answered, "a right side and a wrong side." Now, believing that the fate of humanity hung on his actions, he was unyielding. Always a preacher, he became in his own mind a prophet—almost, one fears, a kind of god.

In the last weeks of the war Wilson proved to be a brilliant diplomat, first dangling the Fourteen Points before the German people to encourage them to overthrow Kaiser Wilhelm II and sue for an armistice, then sending Colonel House to Paris to persuade Allied leaders to accept the points as the basis for the peace. When the Allies raised objections, House made small concessions, but by hinting that the United States might make a separate peace with Germany, he forced them to agree. Under the Armistice, Germany had to withdraw behind the Rhine River and surrender its submarines, together with quantities of munitions and other materials. In return it received the assurance of the Allies that the Wilsonian principles would prevail at the peace conference.

Wilson then came to a daring decision: he would personally attend the conference, which convened on January 12, 1919, at Paris, as a member of the United States Peace Commission. This was a precedent-shattering step, for no previous president had left American territory while in office. (Taft, who had a summer home on the St. Lawrence River in Canada, never vacationed there during his term, believing that to do so would be unconstitutional.)

Wilson probably erred in going to Paris, but not because of the novelty or possible illegality of the act. In leaving the country he was turning his back on obvious domestic problems. Western farmers believed they had been discriminated against during the war, since wheat prices had been controlled while southern cotton had been allowed to rise unchecked from 7 cents a pound in 1914 to 35 cents in 1919. The administration's drastic tax program had angered many businessmen. Labor, despite its gains, was restive in the face of reconversion to peacetime conditions.

Wilson had increased his political difficulties by making a partisan appeal for the election of a Democratic Congress in 1918. Republicans, who had in many instances supported his war program more loyally than the Democrats, considered the action a gross affront. The appeal failed; the Republicans won majorities in both houses. Wilson appeared to have been repudiated at home at the very moment that he set forth to represent the nation abroad. Most important, Wilson intended to break with the isolationist tradition and bring the United States into a league of nations. Such a revolutionary change would require explanation; he should have undertaken a major campaign to convince the people of the wisdom of this step.

Wilson also erred in his choice of the other commissioners. He selected Colonel House, Secretary of State Lansing, General Tasker H. Bliss, and Henry White, a career diplomat. These men were thoroughly competent, but only White was a Republican, and he had no stature as a politician. Since the peace treaty would have to be ratified by the Senate, Wilson should have given that body some representation on the commission, and since the Republicans would have a majority in the new Senate, a Republican senator, or someone who had the full confidence of the Republican leadership, should have been appointed. (The wily McKinley named *three* senators to the American delegation to the peace conference after the Spanish-American War.)

The Paris Peace Conference

Wilson arrived in Europe a world hero. He toured England, France, and Italy briefly and was greeted ecstatically almost everywhere. The reception tended to increase his sense of mission and to convince him, in the fashion of a typical progressive, that whatever the European politicians might say about it, "the people" were behind his program.

When the conference settled down to its work, control quickly fell into the hands of the so-called Big Four: Wilson, Lloyd George, Premier Georges Clemenceau of France, and Prime Minister Vittorio Orlando of Italy. Wilson stood out in this group but did not dominate it. His principal advantage in the negotiations was his untiring industry. He alone of the leaders tried to master all the complex details of the task.

The 78-year-old Clemenceau cared only for one thing: French security. He viewed Wilson cynically, saying that since mankind had been unable to keep God's Ten Commandments, it was unlikely to do better with Wilson's Fourteen Points. Lloyd George's approach was pragmatic and almost cavalier. He sympathized with much that Wilson was trying to accomplish but found the president's frequent sermonettes about "right being more important than might, and justice being more eternal than force" incomprehensible. "If you want to succeed in politics," Lloyd George advised a British statesman, "you must keep your conscience well under control." Orlando, clever, cultured, a believer in international cooperation but inflexible where Italian national interests were concerned, was not the equal of his three colleagues in influence. He left the conference in a huff when they failed to meet all his demands.

The conference labored from January to May 1919 and finally brought forth the Versailles Treaty. American liberals whose hopes had soared at the thought of a peace based on the Fourteen Points found the document abysmally disappointing. The peace settlement failed to carry out the principle of self-determination completely. It gave Italy a large section of the Austrian Tyrol, though the area contained 200,000 people who considered themselves Austrians. Other German-speaking groups were incorporated into the new states of Poland and Czechoslovakia. Japan was allowed to take over the Chinese province of Shantung, and one or another of the Allies swallowed up all the German colonies in Africa and the Far East.

The victors forced Germany to accept responsibility for having caused the war—an act of senseless vindictiveness as well as a gross oversimplification—and to sign a "blank check," agreeing to

■ The Big Four at Versailles. From the left, Orlando of Italy, Lloyd George of Great Britain, Clemenceau of France, and Wilson of the United States.

pay for all damage to civilian properties and even future pensions and other indirect war costs. This reparations bill, as finally determined, amounted to $33 billion, a sum far beyond Germany's ability to pay. Instead of attacking imperialism, the treaty attacked *German* imperialism; instead of seeking a new international social order based on liberty and democracy, it created a great-power entente designed to crush Germany and to exclude Bolshevist Russia from the family of nations. It said nothing about freedom of the seas, the reduction of tariffs, or disarmament. To those who had taken Wilson's "peace without victory" speech and the Fourteen Points literally, the Versailles Treaty seemed an abomination.

The complaints of the critics were individually reasonable, yet their conclusions were not entirely fair. The new map of Europe left fewer people on "foreign" soil than in any earlier period of history. While the Allies seized the German colonies, they were required, under the mandate system, to render the League of Nations annual accounts of their stewardship and to prepare the inhabitants for eventual independence. Above all, Wilson persuaded the powers to incorporate the League of Nations in the treaty.

Wilson expected the League of Nations to make up for all the inadequacies of the Versailles Treaty. Once the League had begun to function, problems like freedom of the seas and disarmament would solve themselves, he argued, and the relaxation of trade barriers would surely follow. The League would arbitrate international disputes, act as a central body for registering treaties, and employ military and economic sanctions against aggressor nations. Each member promised (Article X) to protect the "territorial integrity" and "political independence" of all other members. No great power could be made to go to war against its will, but—and this Wilson emphasized—all were *morally* obligated to carry out League decisions. Liberal critics of the League were correct in saying that Wilson was seeking to prop up the existing social and economic system. He was gravely concerned lest communism or even democratic socialism gain the upper hand in central Europe. He hoped, unrealistically as it turned out, to see Europe develop a capitalist-laborer consensus like that which existed in the United States.

By any standard, Wilson had achieved a remarkably moderate peace, one full of hope for the future. Except for the war-guilt clause and the crushing reparations imposed on Germany, he could be justly proud of his work.

The Senate and the League of Nations

When Wilson returned from France, he finally directed his attention to the task of winning public approval of his handiwork. A large majority of the people probably favored the League of Nations in principle, though few understood all its implications or were entirely happy with every detail. Wilson had persuaded the Allies to accept certain changes in the original draft to mollify American opposition. One provided that no nation could be forced to accept a colonial mandate, another that "domestic questions" such as tariffs and the control of immigration did not fall within the competence of the League. The Monroe Doctrine was excluded from League control to satisfy American opinion, and a clause was added permitting members to withdraw from the organization on two years' notice.

Many senators found the modifications insufficient. Even before the peace conference ended 37 Republican senators signed a Round Robin, devised by Henry Cabot Lodge of Massachusetts, opposing Wilson's League and demanding that the question of an international organization be put off until "the urgent business of negotiating peace terms with Germany" had been completed. Wilson rejected this suggestion icily. The Allies had already exacted major concessions in return for the changes he had requested; further alterations were out of the question. "Anyone who opposes me . . . I'll crush!" he told one Democratic senator. "I shall consent to nothing. *The Senate must take its medicine.*" Thus the stage was set for a monumental test of strength between the president and the Republican majority in the Senate.

Partisanship, principle, and prejudice clashed mightily in this contest. A presidential election loomed. Should the League prove a success, the Republicans wanted to be able to claim a share of the credit, but Wilson had refused to allow them to participate in drafting the document. This predisposed all of them to favor changes. Politics aside, genuine alarm at the possible sacrifice of American sovereignty to an international authority led many Republicans to urge modification of the League Covenant, or constitution. Personal dislike of Wilson and his high-handed methods motivated others. Yet the noble purpose of the League made many reluctant to reject it entirely. The intense desire of the people to have an end to the long war made GOP leaders hesitate before voting down the Versailles Treaty, and they could not reject the League without rejecting the treaty.

Wilson could count on the Democratic senators almost to a man, but he had to win over many Republicans to obtain the two-thirds majority necessary for ratification. Republican opinion divided roughly into three segments. At one extreme were some dozen "irreconcilables," led by the shaggy-browed William E. Borah of Idaho, an able and kindly person of progressive leanings but an uncompromising isolationist. Borah claimed that he would vote against the League even if Jesus Christ returned to earth to argue in its behalf, and most of his followers were equally inflexible. At the other extreme stood another dozen "mild" reservationists who were in favor of the League but who hoped to alter it in minor ways, chiefly for political purposes. In the middle were the "strong" reservationists, senators willing to go along with the League only if American sovereignty were fully protected and it was made clear that their party had played a major role in fashioning the final document.

Senator Lodge, the leader of the Republican opposition, was a haughty, rather cynical, intensely partisan individual. He possessed a keen intelligence, a mastery of parliamentary procedure, and, as chairman of the Senate Foreign Relations Committee, a great deal of power. Although not an isolationist, he had little faith in the League. He also had a profound distrust of Democrats, especially Wilson, whom he considered a hypocrite and a coward. The president's pious idealism left him cold. While perfectly ready to see the country participate actively in world affairs, Lodge insisted that its right to determine its own best interests in every situation be preserved. He had been a senator since 1893 and an admirer of senatorial independence since early manhood. When a Democratic president tried to ram the Versailles Treaty down the Senate's throat, he fought him with every weapon he could muster.

Lodge belonged to the strong reservationist faction. His own proposals, known as the Lodge Reservations, 14 in number to match Wilson's Fourteen Points, limited the United States' obligations to the League and stated in unmistakable terms the right of Congress to decide when to honor these obligations. Some of the reservations were

mere quibbles. Others, such as the provision that the United States would not endorse Japan's seizure of Chinese territory, were included mainly to embarrass Wilson by pointing up compromises he had made at Versailles. The most important reservation applied to Article X of the League Covenant, which committed signatories to protect the political independence and territorial integrity of all member nations. Wilson had rightly called Article X "the heart of the Covenant." Lodge's reservation made it inoperable so far as the United States was concerned "unless in any particular case the Congress . . . shall by act or joint resolution so provide."

Lodge performed brilliantly if somewhat unscrupulously in uniting the three Republican factions behind the reservations. He got the irreconcilables to agree to them by conceding their right to vote against the final version in any event, and he held the mild reservationists in line by modifying some of his demands and stressing the importance of party unity. Reservations—as distinct from amendments—would not have to win the formal approval of other League members. In addition, the Lodge proposals dealt forthrightly with the problem of reconciling traditional concepts of national sovereignty with the new idea of world cooperation. Supporters of the League could accept them without sacrifice of principle. Wilson, however, refused to agree. "Accept the Treaty with the *Lodge* reservations," the president snorted when a friendly senator warned him that he must accept a compromise. "Never! Never!"

This foolish intransigence seems almost incomprehensible in a man of Wilson's intelligence and political experience. In part his hatred of Lodge accounts for it, in part his faith in his League. His physical condition in 1919 also played a role. At Paris he had suffered a violent attack of indigestion that was probably a symptom of a minor stroke. Thereafter many observers noted small changes in his personality, particularly an in-

■ Two views of the League of Nations: Above, in London's *Punch* the dove of peace looks askance at Wilson's hefty olive branch, asking "Isn't this a bit thick?" Right, a New York *World* cartoon by Rollin Kirby. The "gentlemen" who won't give up their seats to the lady are anti-League senators Borah, Lodge, and Hiram Johnson.

creased stubbornness and a loss of good judgment. Instead of making concessions, the president set out early in September on a nationwide speaking tour to rally support for the League. While some of his speeches were brilliant, they had little effect on senatorial opinion, and the effort drained his last physical reserves. On September 25, after an address in Pueblo, Colorado, he collapsed. The rest of the trip had to be canceled. A few days later, in Washington, he suffered a severe stroke that partially paralyzed his left side.

For nearly two months as he slowly recovered, the president was almost totally cut off from affairs of state, leaving supporters of the League leaderless while Lodge maneuvered the reservations through the Senate. Gradually, popular attitudes toward the League shifted. Organized groups of Italian-, Irish-, and German-Americans, angered by what they considered unfair treatment of their native lands in the Versailles Treaty, clamored for outright rejection. The arguments of the irreconcilables persuaded many citizens that Wilson had made too sharp a break with America's isolationist past and that the Lodge Reservations were therefore necessary. Other issues connected with the reconversion of society to a peacetime basis increasingly occupied the public mind.

A coalition of Democratic and moderate Republican senators could easily have carried the treaty. That no such coalition was organized was Wilson's fault. Lodge obtained the simple majority necessary to add his reservations to the treaty merely by keeping his own party united. When the time came for the final roll call on November 19, Wilson, bitter and emotionally distraught, urged the Democrats to vote for rejection. "Better a thousand times to go down fighting than to dip your colours to dishonourable compromise," he explained to his wife. Thus the amended treaty failed, 35 to 55, the irreconcilables and the Democrats voting against it. Lodge then allowed the original draft without his reservations to come to a vote. Again the result was defeat, 38 to 53. Only one Republican cast a ballot for ratification.

Dismayed but not yet crushed, friends of the League in both parties forced reconsideration of the treaty early in 1920. Neither Lodge nor Wilson would yield an inch. Lodge, who had little confidence in the effectiveness of any league of nations, was under no compulsion to compromise. That Wilson, whose entire being was tied up in the Covenant, would not do so is further evidence of his physical and mental decline. Probably he was incompetent to perform the duties of his office. Had he died or stepped down, the treaty, with reservations, would almost certainly have been ratified. When the Senate balloted again in March, half the Democrats violated Wilson's orders and voted for the treaty with the Lodge Reservations. The others, mostly southern party regulars, joined the irreconcilables. Together they mustered 35 votes, 7 more than the one-third that meant defeat.

Wilson still hoped for vindication at the polls in the presidential election, which he sought to make a "great and solemn referendum" on the League. The election was scarcely a referendum. While the Democrats, who nominated Governor James M. Cox of Ohio, took a stand for Wilson's Covenant, the Republicans, whose candidate was another Ohioan, Senator Warren G. Harding, equivocated shamelessly on the issue. The election turned on other matters, largely emotional. Disillusioned by the results of the war, many Americans had had their fill of idealism. They wanted, apparently, to end the long period of moral uplift and reform agitation that had begun under Theodore Roosevelt and return to what Harding called "normalcy."

To the extent that the voters were expressing opinions on Wilson's League, their response was overwhelmingly negative. Senator Harding had been a strong reservationist, yet he swept the country, winning over 16.1 million votes to Cox's 9.1 million. In July 1921 Congress formally ended the war with the Central Powers by passing a joint resolution.

The defeat of the League was a tragedy both for Wilson, whose crusade for a world order based on peace and justice ended in failure, and for the world, which was condemned by the result to endure another still more horrible and costly war. Perhaps this dreadful outcome could not have been avoided. The United States in 1919–1920 was not ready to assume the responsibility of preserving peace in other lands. Had Wilson compromised and Lodge behaved like a statesman instead of a politician, America would have joined the League, but it might well have failed to respond when called on to meet its obligations. As events soon demonstrated, the League powers acted pusillanimously and even dishonorably when challenged by aggressor nations.

Perhaps it would have been different had the Senate ratified the Versailles Treaty; America's retreat from international cooperation discouraged supporters of the League in other countries. The western democracies might have drawn closer together and become more firm of heart if *all* had been committed to the League. What was lost when the treaty failed in the Senate was not peace but the *possibility* of peace, a tragic loss indeed.

SUPPLEMENTARY READING

Titles marked with an asterisk have been published in paperback

Wilson's handling of foreign relations is discussed in several volumes by A. S. Link: **Wilson** (1947–), **Woodrow Wilson and the Progressive Era*** (1954), and **Wilson the Diplomatist*** (1957), as well as in the Wilson biographies listed in the preceding chapter. See also N. G. Levin, Jr., **Woodrow Wilson and World Politics: America's Response to War and Revolution*** (1968). Latin American affairs under Wilson are treated in S. F. Bemis, **The Latin American Policy of the United States*** (1943), H. F. Cline, **The United States and Mexico*** (1953), and D. G. Munro, **Intervention and Dollar Diplomacy in the Caribbean** (1964). R. E. Quirk, **An Affair of Honor: Woodrow Wilson and the Occupation of Veracruz*** (1962), is an admirable monograph, and C. C. Clendenen, **The United States and Pancho Villa** (1961), is also interesting.

For American entry into the Great War, see, in addition to the Link volumes mentioned above, E. R. May, **The World War and American Isolation*** (1959), E. H. Buehrig, **Woodrow Wilson and the Balance of Power** (1955), Charles Seymour, **American Diplomacy During the World War** (1934) and **American Neutrality** (1935), all essentially favorable to Wilson. For contrary views, see Walter Millis, **The Road to War** (1935), and C. C. Tansill, **America Goes to War** (1938).

The war on the home front is covered in D. M. Kennedy, **Over Here: The First World War and American Society** (1980), and more briefly in W. E. Leuchtenburg, **The Perils of Prosperity*** (1958). A good account of military preparation is H. A. DeWeerd, **President Wilson Fights His War** (1968). Other useful volumes include R. D. Cuff, **The War Industries Board** (1973), S. L. Vaughn, **Holding Fast the Inner Lines** (1980), which deals with the Committee on Public Information, M. I. Urofsky, **Big Steel and the Wilson Administration** (1969), Zechariah Chafee, **Free Speech in the United States*** (1941), Donald Johnson, **The Challenge to American Freedoms** (1963), David Brody, **Steelworkers in America*** (1960), Herbert Stein, **Government Price Policy During the World War** (1939), D. R. Beaver, **Newton D. Baker and the American War Effort** (1966), and S. W. Livermore, **Politics Is Adjourned: Woodrow Wilson and the War Congress*** (1966).

On American military participation, consult DeWeerd, **President Wilson Fights His War.** Laurence Stallings, **The Doughboys*** (1963), is a good popular account of the American army in France. See also F. E. Vandiver, **Black Jack: The Life and Times of John J. Pershing** (1977), J. J. Pershing, **My Experiences in the World War** (1931), E. E. Morison, **Admiral Sims and the Modern American Navy** (1942), and T. G. Frothingham, **The Naval History of the World War** (1924–1926). On blacks in the army, see A. E. Barbeau and F. Henri, **The Unknown Soldiers** (1974).

On the peace settlement, in addition to the biographies of Wilson, consult A. J. Mayer, **Politics and Diplomacy of Peacemaking** (1967), Paul Birdsall, **Versailles Twenty Years After** (1941), Harold Nicolson, **Peacemaking, 1919*** (1939), T. A. Bailey, **Woodrow Wilson and the Lost Peace*** (1944) and **Woodrow Wilson and the Great Betrayal*** (1945), J. A. Garraty, **Henry Cabot Lodge** (1953), H. C. Lodge, **The Senate and the League of Nations** (1925), Allan Nevins, **Henry White** (1930), Ralph Stone, **The Irreconcilables*** (1970), J. M. Keynes, **The Economic Consequences of the Peace** (1919), and Robert Lansing, **The Peace Negotiations: A Personal Narrative** (1921). On the election of 1920, see Wesley Bagby, **The Road to Normalcy*** (1962), and R. K. Murray, **The Harding Era** (1969).

25/THE TWENTIES: THE AFTERMATH OF THE GREAT WAR

The Armistice of 1918 ended the fighting, but the Great War had so shaken the world that for a whole generation most of the human race lived in its shadow. Americans sought desperately to escape from its influence, tried almost to deny that it had occurred. Yet every aspect of their lives in the postwar years reflected its baneful impact. Convinced that they had made a terrible mistake by going to war, a great many Americans rejected the values that had led them to do so. Idealism gave way to materialism, naiveté to cynicism, moral purposefulness to irresponsibility, faith to iconoclasm. This reaction, like so many defense mechanisms, was neurotic, based on unreal and conflicting assumptions.

Demobilization

To win the war the nation had accepted drastic regulation of the economy in order to increase production and improve social efficiency. When the war ended, the government, in Wilson's words, "took the harness off" at once, blithely assuming that the economy could readjust itself without direction. The army was hastily demobilized, pouring millions of veterans into the job market without plan. Nearly all controls established by the War Industries Board and other agencies were dropped overnight. Billions of dollars worth of war contracts were canceled. Despite the obvious benefits that government operation of the railroads had brought and the fact that the Plumb plan for government ownership had the support of the railroad unions, the roads were returned to private control.*

Business boomed in 1919 as consumers spent wartime savings on automobiles, homes, and other goods that had been in short supply during the conflict. But temporary shortages caused inflation; by 1920 the cost of living stood at more than twice the level of 1913.

Inflation in turn produced labor trouble. The unions, grown strong during the war, struck for wage increases in order to hold their gains. Over 4 million workers, one out of five in the labor force, were on strike at some time during 1919. Work stoppages aggravated shortages, triggering further inflation and more strikes. Then came one of the most precipitous economic declines in American history. Between July 1920 and March 1922 prices, especially agricultural prices, plummeted. Unemployment soared. Thus the unrealistic attitude of the Wilson government toward the complexities of economic readjustment caused considerable unnecessary strife.

*In 1920 the Esch-Cummins Transportation Act strengthened the Interstate Commerce Commission's power to set rates and oversee railroad financing and created a Railroad Labor Board to handle labor problems. Reversing previous efforts to encourage competition, the commission in the 1920s favored consolidation and authorized the pooling of traffic in the interest of efficiency.

Radicalism and Xenophobia

Far more serious than the economic losses were the social effects of these difficulties. Everyone wanted peace, but wartime tensions did not subside; apparently people continued to need some release for the aggressive drives they had formerly focused on the Germans. Most Americans recognized the services that industrial workers had contributed to the war effort and sympathized with their aspirations for a better way of life, but they found strikes frustrating and drew invidious comparisons between the lot of the unemployed soldier who had risked his life for a dollar a day and that of the striker who had drawn fat wages during the war in perfect safety.

The activities of radicals in the labor movement led millions of Americans to associate unionism and strikes with the new threat of communist world revolution. Although there were only a handful of communists in the United States—no more than 100,000—Russia's experience indicated to many that a tiny minority of ruthless revolutionaries could take over a nation of millions if conditions were right. Communists appointed themselves the champions of workers; labor unrest attracted them magnetically. When a wave of strikes broke out, some accompanied by violence, many people interpreted them as communist-inspired preludes to revolution. One businessman wrote the attorney general in 1919: "There is hardly a respectable citizen of my acquaintance who does not believe that we are on the verge of armed conflict in this country." Louis Wiley, an experienced New York *Times* reporter, told a friend at this time that anarchists, socialists, and radical labor leaders were "joining together with the object of overthrowing the American Government through a bloody revolution and establishing a Bolshevist republic."

Organized labor in America had seldom been truly radical. The Industrial Workers of the World (IWW), influential in western mining and among migratory workers in the Progressive Era, had advocated violence and the abolition of the wage system but had made little impression in most industries. Some labor leaders, among them Eugene V. Debs, had been attracted to socialism, and many Americans failed to distinguish between the common ends sought by communists and socialists and the entirely different methods by which they proposed to achieve those ends. When a general strike paralyzed Seattle in February 1919, the fact that a procommunist had helped organize it sent shivers down countless conservative spines. When the radical William Z. Foster began a drive to organize the steel industry at about this time, the fears became more intense. In September 1919, 343,000 steelworkers walked off their jobs, and in the same month the Boston police struck. Violence marked the steel strike, and the suspension of police protection in Boston led to looting and fighting that ended only when Governor Calvin Coolidge (who might have prevented the strike had he acted earlier) called out the National Guard.

During the same period a handful of terrorists caused widespread alarm by attempting to murder various prominent persons, including John D. Rockefeller, Justice Oliver Wendell Holmes, Jr., and Attorney General A. Mitchell Palmer. Although the terrorists were anarchists and anarchism had little in common with communism, many citizens lumped all extremists together and associated them with a monstrous assault on society.

What aroused the public even more was the fact that most radicals were not American citizens. Wartime fear of alien saboteurs easily transformed itself into peacetime terror of foreign radicals. In place of Germany, the enemy became the lowly immigrant, usually an Italian or a Jew or a Slav and usually an industrial worker. In this muddled way radicalism, unionism, and questions of racial and national origins combined to make many Americans believe that their way of life was in imminent danger. That few immigrants were radicals, that most workers had no interest in communism, that the extremists themselves were faction-ridden and irresolute did not affect conservative thinking. From all over the country came demands that radicals be ruthlessly suppressed. Thus the "Red Scare" was born.

Attorney General Palmer was the key figure in the resulting purge. He had been a typical progressive, a supporter of the League of Nations and such reforms as women's suffrage and child labor legislation. When the clamor against alien radicals began, he tried to resist it. Continued pressure from Congress and the press and his growing conviction that the communists really were a menace led him to change his mind. When he did, he joined the "red hunt" with the enthusiasm of the typical convert. Soon he was saying of the radicals: "Out of the sly and crafty eyes of many of them leap cupidity, cruelty, insanity, and crime; from their lopsided faces, sloping brows, and misshapen features may be recognized the unmistakable criminal type."

In August 1919 Palmer established a General Intelligence Division in the Department of Justice, headed by J. Edgar Hoover, to collect information about clandestine radical activities. In November Justice Department agents swooped down upon the meeting places in a dozen cities of an anarchist organization known as the Union of Russian Workers. More than 650 persons, many of them unconnected with the union, were arrested, but in only 43 cases could evidence be found to justify deportation. Nevertheless the public reacted so favorably that Palmer, thinking now of winning the 1920 Democratic presidential nomination, planned an immense roundup of communists. He obtained 3,000 warrants, and on January 2, 1920, his agents, reinforced by local police and self-appointed vigilantes, struck simultaneously in 33 cities.

Palmer's biographer, Stanley Coben, has described the "Palmer raids" vividly:

> There was a knock on the door, the rush of police. In meeting houses, all were lined up to be searched; those who resisted often suffered brutal treatment. . . . Prisoners were put in overcrowded jails or detention centers where they remained, frequently under the most abominable conditions. . . . Police searched the homes of many of those arrested; books and papers, as well as many people found in these residences, were carried off to headquarters. Policemen also sought those whose names appeared on seized membership lists; they captured many of these suspects in bed or at work, searching their homes, confiscating their possessions, almost always without warrants.

About 6,000 persons were taken into custody, many of them citizens and therefore not subject to the deportation laws, many others unconnected with any radical cause. Some were held incommunicado for weeks while the authorities searched for evidence against them. In a number of cases,

■ **During the Red Scare, radical cartoonist William Gropper sharply criticized the tactics of Attorney General Palmer. These drawings appeared in *The Liberator* early in 1920. At left, Palmer's agents warn, "Clear the road there, boys—we got a dangerous Red." At right, a suspect faces a loutish, unsympathetic audience.**

individuals who went to visit prisoners were themselves thrown behind bars on the theory that they too must be communists. Hundreds of suspects were jammed into filthy "bullpens," beaten, forced to sign "confessions."

The public tolerated these wholesale violations of civil liberties because of the supposed menace of communism. Gradually, however, protests began to be heard, first from lawyers and liberal magazines, then from a wider segment of the population. No revolutionary outbreak had taken place. Of 6,000 seized in the Palmer raids, only 556 proved liable to deportation. The widespread ransacking of communists' homes and meeting places produced mountains of inflammatory literature but only three pistols.

Palmer, attempting to maintain the crusade, announced that the radicals planned a gigantic terrorist demonstration for May Day 1920. In New York and other cities thousands of police were placed on round-the-clock duty; federal troops stood by anxiously. But the day passed without even a rowdy meeting. Suddenly Palmer appeared ridiculous. His presidential boom collapsed and the Red Scare swiftly subsided.

The ending of the Red Scare did not herald the disappearance of xenophobia. It was perhaps inevitable and possibly wise that some limitation be placed on the entry of immigrants into the United States after the war. An immense backlog of prospective migrants had piled up during the conflict, and the desperate postwar economic condition of Europe led hundreds of thousands to seek better circumstances in the United States. Immigration increased from 110,000 in 1919 to 430,000 in 1920 and 805,000 in 1921, with every prospect of continuing to rise.

In 1921 Congress, reflecting a widespread prejudice against eastern and southern Europeans, passed an emergency act establishing a quota system. Each year 3 percent of the number of foreign-born residents of the United States in 1910 (about 350,000 persons) might enter the country. Each country's quota was based on the number of its nationals in the United States in 1910. This meant that only a relative handful of the total would be from southern and eastern Europe. In 1924 the quota was reduced to 2 percent and the base year shifted to 1890, thereby lowering further the proportion of southern and eastern Europeans admitted.

In 1929 Congress established a system that allowed only 150,000 immigrants a year to enter the country. Each national quota was based on the supposed origins of the entire white population of the United States in 1920, not merely on the foreign-born. Here is an example of how the system worked:

$$\frac{\text{Italian quota}}{150{,}000} = \frac{\text{Italian-origin population, 1920}}{\text{White population, 1920}}$$

$$\frac{\text{Italian quota}}{150{,}000} = \frac{3{,}800{,}000}{95{,}500{,}000}$$

$$\text{Italian quota} = 6{,}000 \text{ (approximately)}$$

Presumably this method would preserve the status quo; in fact it heavily favored immigrants from Great Britain. The system was complicated and unscientific, for no one could determine with accuracy the "origins" of millions of citizens.

The law reduced actual immigration to far below 150,000 a year. British immigration between 1931 and 1939, for example, amounted to only 23,000 even though the *annual* British quota was over 65,000. Meanwhile, hundreds of thousands of southern and eastern Europeans waited for admission.

The United States had closed the gates. Instead of an open, cosmopolitan society eager to accept, in Emma Lazarus' stirring line, the "huddled masses yearning to breathe free," America now became committed to preserving a homogeneous, "Anglo-Saxon" population. Anglo-Saxon and homogeneous it did not become, but the foreign-born percentage of the population fell from about 13 percent in 1920 to 4.7 percent in 1970.

Urban-Rural Conflict

The war-born tensions and hostilities of the 1920s also found expression in ways related to an older rift in American society—the conflict between the urban and the rural ways of life. The census of 1920 revealed that for the first time a majority of Americans (54 million in a total population of 106 million) lived in "urban" rather than "rural" places. These figures are somewhat misleading when applied to the study of social attitudes because the census classified anyone in a community of 2,500 or more as urban. Of the 54 million "urban" residents in 1920, over 16 million lived in villages and towns of fewer than 25,000 persons, and the evidence suggests strongly that a large majority of them held ideas and values more like those of rural citizens than like those of city dwellers. But the truly urban Americans, the one person in four who lived in a city of 100,000 or more—and particularly the nearly 16.4 million who lived in metropolises of at least half a million—were increasing steadily in number and influence. More than 19 million persons moved from farms to cities in the 1920s, and the population living in centers of 100,000 or more increased by about a third.

To both the scattered millions who tilled the soil and the millions who lived in towns and small cities, the new city-oriented culture seemed sinful, overly materialistic, and unhealthy. Yet there was no denying its fascination. Made even more aware of the appeal of the city by such modern improvements as radio and the automobile, farmers and townspeople coveted the comfort and excitement of city life at the same time that they condemned its vices.

Out of this ambivalence developed strange social phenomena, all exacerbated by the backlash of wartime emotions. Rural society proclaimed the superiority of its ways, as much to protect itself from temptation as to denounce urban life. Change, omnipresent in the postwar world, must be resisted even at the cost of individualism and freedom. The fact that those who held such views were in the majority, yet were conscious that their majority was rapidly disappearing, explains their desperation and thus their intolerance.

One expression of this intolerance was the resurgence of religious fundamentalism. Although it was especially prevalent in certain Protestant sects, such as the Baptists and Presbyterians, fundamentalism was primarily an attitude of mind, profoundly conservative, rather than a religious idea. Fundamentalists rejected the theory of evolution, indeed all knowledge about the origins of the universe and the human race that had been discovered during the 19th century. Urban sophisticates tended to dismiss the fundamentalists as boors and hayseed fanatics, yet the persistence of old-fashioned ideas was understandable. In rural areas where educational standards were low and culture relatively static, old ideas remained unchallenged. The power of reason, so obvious in a technologically advanced society, seemed much less obvious to rural people. Farmers, living in close contact with the capricious, elemental power of nature, tended to have more respect for the force of divine providence than city folk. Beyond this, the majesty and beauty of the King James translation of the Bible, the only book in countless rural homes, made it extraordinarily difficult for many persons to abandon their belief in its literal truth.

What made crusaders of the fundamentalists, however, was their resentment of modern urban culture. While in some cases they harassed liberal ministers, their religious attitudes had little public significance; their efforts to impose their views on public education were another matter. The teaching of evolution must be prohibited, they insisted. Throughout the early twenties they campaigned

■ In *Baptism in Kansas* (1928) John Steuart Curry viewed sympathetically the sincerity and the depth of feeling that marked the revival of religious fundamentalism in much of rural America during the 1920s. Curry was a leader of the rural regionalist painters, seeking, he said, to show the "struggle of man against nature."

vigorously for laws banning discussion of Darwin's theory in textbooks and classrooms.

Their greatest asset in this unfortunate crusade was William Jennings Bryan. Age had not improved the "Peerless Leader." Never a profound thinker, after leaving Wilson's Cabinet in 1915 he devoted much time to religious and moral issues without applying himself conscientiously to the study of these difficult questions. He went about charging that "they"—meaning the mass of educated Americans—had "taken the Lord away from the schools" and denouncing the expenditure of public money to undermine Christian principles. Bryan toured the country offering $100 to anyone who would admit to being descended from an ape; his immense popularity in rural areas assured him a wide audience, and no one came forward to take his money.

The fundamentalists won a minor victory in 1925, when Tennessee passed a law forbidding instructors in the state's schools and colleges to teach "any theory that denies the story of the Divine Creation of man as taught in the Bible." Although the bill passed both houses by big majorities, few legislators really approved of it. They voted aye only because they dared not expose themselves to charges that they disbelieved the Bible. Educators in the state, hoping to obtain larger school appropriations from the legislature, hesitated to protest. Governor Austin Peay, an intelligent and liberal-minded man, feared to veto the bill lest he jeopardize other measures he was backing. "Probably the law will never be applied," he predicted when he signed it. Even Bryan, who used his influence to obtain passage of the measure, urged—unsuccessfully—that it include no penalties.

Upon learning of the passage of this act, the American Civil Liberties Union announced that it would finance a test case challenging its constitutionality if a Tennessee teacher would deliberately violate the statute. Urged on by friends, John T. Scopes, a young biology teacher in Dayton, reluctantly agreed to do so. He was arrested. A battery of nationally known lawyers came forward to defend him, while the state obtained the services of Bryan himself. The Dayton "Monkey Trial" became an overnight sensation.

Clarence Darrow, chief counsel for the defendant, stated the issue clearly. "Scopes isn't on trial," he said, "civilization is on trial. The prosecution is opening the doors for a reign of bigotry equal to anything in the Middle Ages. No man's belief will be safe if they win." The comic aspects of the trial obscured this issue. Big-city reporters like H. L. Mencken of the Baltimore *Evening Sun* flocked to Dayton to make sport of the fundamentalists. The judge, John Raulston, was strongly prejudiced against the defendant, refusing even to permit expert testimony on the validity of evolutionary theory. The conviction of Scopes was a foregone conclusion; after the jury rendered its verdict, Judge Raulston fined him $100.

Nevertheless the trial exposed both the stupidity and the danger of the fundamentalist position. The highpoint came when Bryan agreed to testify as an expert witness on the Bible. In a sweltering courtroom, both men in shirt sleeves, the lanky, roughhewn Darrow cross-examined the bland, aging champion of fundamentalism, mercilessly exposing his childlike faith and his abysmal ignorance. Bryan admitted to believing that the earth had been created in 4004 B.C., that Eve had been created from Adam's rib, and that a whale had swallowed Jonah. "I believe in a God that can make a whale and can make a man and make both do what He pleases," he explained.

The Monkey Trial ended in frustration for nearly everyone concerned. Scopes moved away from Dayton. Judge Raulston was defeated when he sought reelection to the bench. Bryan departed amid the cheers of his disciples only to die in his sleep a few days later. In retrospect the heroes of the Scopes trial—science, tolerance, freedom of thought—seem somewhat less stainless than they did to liberals at the time. The account of evolution in the textbook used by Scopes was far from satisfactory, yet it was advanced as unassailable fact. The book also contained statements that to the modern mind seem at least as bigoted as anything that Bryan said at Dayton. In a section on "the Races of Man," for example, it described Caucasians as "the highest type of all . . . represented by the civilized white inhabitants of Europe and America."

Prohibition: The Noble Experiment

The conflict between the countryside and the city was fought on many fronts, and in one sector the rural forces achieved a quick victory. This was the prohibition of the manufacture, transportation, and sale of alcoholic beverages by the Eighteenth Amendment, ratified in 1919. Although there were some big-city advocates of prohibition, on no issue did urban and rural views divide more clearly. The Eighteenth Amendment, in the words of the historian Andrew Sinclair, marked a triumph of the "Corn Belt over the conveyor belt."

The temperance movement had been important since the age of Jackson; by the time of the Progressive Era many reformers were eager to prohibit drinking entirely. Indeed, prohibition was a typical progressive reform, moralistic, backed by the middle class, aimed at frustrating "the interests"—in this case the distillers. The war aided the prohibitionists by increasing the nation's need for food. The Lever Act of 1917 outlawed the use of grain in the manufacture of alcoholic beverages, primarily as a conservation measure. The prevailing dislike of foreigners helped the dry cause still more: beer drinking was associated with Germans, wine consumption with Italians. State and local laws had made a large part of the country dry by 1917. National prohibition became official in January 1920.

This "experiment noble in purpose," as Herbert Hoover called it, achieved a number of socially desirable results. It reduced the national consumption of alcohol from 2.6 gallons per capita in the period just before the war to under one gallon in the early thirties. Arrests for drunkenness fell off sharply, as did deaths from alcoholism. Fewer workers squandered their wages on drink. If the drys had been more reasonable—if they had permitted, for example, the use of beer and wine—the experiment might have worked. Instead, by insisting on total abstinence, they drove moderates to violation of the law. In such circumstances

■ **Ben Shahn's *Prohibition Alley* is a richly symbolic summary of the seamier side of the "noble experiment." Under a diagram of the workings of a still, bootleggers stack whiskey smuggled in by ship, an operation eyed by Chicago gangster Al Capone. At lower left is a victim of gang warfare; at lower right, patrons outside a speakeasy.**

strict enforcement became impossible, especially in the cities.

The Prohibition Bureau had only between 1,500 and 3,000 agents to police the illicit liquor trade, and many of them were inefficient and corrupt. In areas where sentiment favored prohibition strongly, liquor remained difficult to find. Elsewhere, anyone with sufficient money could obtain it easily. Smuggling became a major business, "bootlegger" a household word. Private individuals busied themselves learning how to manufacture "bathtub gin." Fraudulent druggists' prescriptions for alcohol were issued freely. The manufacture of wine for religious ceremonies was legal—consumption of sacramental wine jumped by 800,000 gallons during the first two years of prohibition. The saloon disappeared, replaced by the speakeasy, a supposedly secret bar or club, operating under the benevolent eye of the local police.

That the law was often violated does not mean that it was ineffective any more than violations of laws against theft and murder mean that those laws are ineffective. While gangsters such as Alphonse "Scarface Al" Capone of Chicago were engaged in the liquor traffic, hijacking one another's shipments, gunning down their enemies in broad daylight, and bombing rival distilleries and warehouses without regard for passing innocents, they and their "organizations" existed before the passage of the Eighteenth Amendment.

In any case, prohibition widened already serious rifts in the social fabric of the country. Besides undermining public morality by encouraging hypocrisy, its repressive spirit pitted city against farm, native against immigrant, race against race. In the South, where the dominant whites had argued that prohibition would improve the morals of the blacks, it was the blacks who became the chief bootleggers. Prohibition almost destroyed the Democratic party as a national organization; Democratic immigrants in the cities hated it, but southern Democrats sang its praises (often while continuing to drink). The humorist Will Rogers quipped that Mississippi would vote dry "as long as the voters could stagger to the polls."

The hypocrisy of prohibition had a particularly deleterious effect on politicians, a class seldom fa-

■ **A Ku Klux Klan initiation ceremony, photographed in Kansas in the 1920s. During its peak influence at mid-decade, Klan endorsement was essential to political candidates in many areas of the West and Midwest. Campaigning for reelection in 1924, an Indiana congressman testified, "I was told to join the Klan, or else."**

mous for candor. Congressmen catered to the demands of the powerful lobby of the Anti-Saloon League yet failed to grant adequate funds to the Prohibition Bureau. Nearly all the prominent leaders, Democrat and Republican, from Wilson and La Follette to Hoover and Franklin D. Roosevelt, equivocated shamelessly on the liquor question. By the end of the decade almost every competent observer recognized that prohibition at least needed to be overhauled, but the well-organized and powerful dry forces rejected all proposals for modifying it.

The Ku Klux Klan

The most horrible manifestation of the social malaise of the 1920s was the revival of the Ku Klux Klan. Like its predecessor of Reconstruction days, the new Klan began as an instrument for oppressing southern blacks. In the reactionary postwar period lynchings increased in number. In the summer and fall of 1919 race riots broke out in a dozen cities. The new Klan, founded in 1915 by William J. Simmons, a former preacher, expanded rapidly in this atmosphere.

Simmons gave his society the kind of trappings and mystery calculated to attract gullible and bigoted persons who yearned to express their frustrations and hostilities without personal risk. Klansmen masked themselves in white robes and hoods and enjoyed a childish mumbo jumbo of magnificent-sounding titles and dogmas (kleagle, klaliff, kludd; kloxology, kloran). They burned crosses in the night, organized mass demonstrations to intimidate people they disliked, put pressure on businessmen to fire black workers from better-paying jobs. When its enemies resisted, the Klan frequently employed brutal means to achieve its ends.

The Klan admitted only native-born white Protestants. The distrust of foreigners, Catholics, and Jews implicit in this regulation explains why the Klan flourished in the social climate that spawned religious fundamentalism, immigration restriction, and prohibition. In 1920 two unscrupulous publicity agents, Edward Y. Clarke and Elizabeth Tyler, got control of the movement and organized a massive membership drive, diverting a major share of the initiation fees into their own pockets. In a little over a year they enrolled 100,000 recruits, and by 1923, they claimed the astonishing total of 5 million.

The Klan had relatively little appeal in the Northeast or in metropolitan centers in other parts of the country, but it found many members in middle-sized cities and in the small towns and villages of middle-western and western states like Indiana, Ohio, and Oregon. The scapegoats in such regions were immigrants, Jews, and especially Catholics. The rationale was an urge to return to an older, supposedly finer America and a desire to stamp out all varieties of nonconformity. Klansmen "watched everybody," themselves safe from observation behind their masks and robes. Posing as guardians of public and private morality, they persecuted gamblers, "loose" women, violators of the prohibition laws, and anyone who happened to differ from them on religious questions or who belonged to a "foreign race."

Klan leaders claimed that the pope intended to move his court from Rome to the United States, that American bishops were stockpiling guns in their cathedrals, that Catholic traitors had entrenched themselves in many branches of the government. Since a considerable percentage of Klan members were secret libertines and corruptionists, the dark, unconscious drives leading men to join the organization are not hard to imagine.

The very success of the Klan led to its undoing. Factionalism sprang up and rival leaders squabbled over the large sums that had been collected from the membership. The cruel and outrageous behavior of the organization roused both liberals and conservatives in every part of the country. And of course its victims joined forces against their tormentors. When the powerful leader of the Indiana Klan, a middle-aged reprobate named David C. Stephenson, was convicted of assaulting and causing the death of a young woman, the rank and file abandoned the organization in droves. It remained influential for a number of years, contributing to the defeat of the Catholic Alfred E. Smith in the 1928 presidential election, but it ceased to be a dynamic force after 1924. By 1930 it had only some 9,000 members.

The Disillusioned

The malaise of postwar society also produced dissatisfactions among urban sophisticates, and among others who looked to the future rather than to the past. To many young people the narrowness and prudery of the fundamentalists and the stuffy conservatism of the politicians seemed not merely old-fashioned but ludicrous. The repressiveness of redbaiters and Klansmen made them place an exaggerated importance on their right to express themselves in bizarre ways, and the casual attitude of drinkers toward the prohibition laws encouraged them to flout other institutions as well. The new psychology of Sigmund Freud, with its stress on the importance of sex, persuaded many who had never read Freud to adopt what they called "emancipated" standards of behavior that Freud, himself a staid, highly moral man, had neither advocated nor practiced.

This was the "Jazz Age," the era of "flaming youth." Young people danced to syncopated "African" rhythms, swilled bootleg liquor from pocket flasks, careened about the countryside in automobiles in search of pleasure and forgetfulness, made gods of movie stars and professional athletes. "Younger people," one shrewd observer noted as early as 1922, had only "contempt . . . for their elders." They were attempting "to create a way of life free from the bondage of an authority that has lost all meaning."

Conservatives bemoaned the breakdown of moral standards, the increasing popularity of divorce, the fragmentation of the family, and the decline of parental authority—all with some reason. Nevertheless, society was not collapsing. Much of the rebelliousness was faddish in nature, in a sense a kind of youthful conformity. It soon petered out.

The twenties proved disillusioning to feminists, who now paid a price for their single-minded pursuit of the right to vote in the Progressive Era. Superficially, sex-based restrictions and limitations seemed to be breaking down. Women discarded bulky, uncomfortable undergarments and put on short skirts; they could smoke and drink in public places without fear of being considered prostitutes or wantons. The birth control movement, led by Margaret Sanger, was making progress. The divorce laws had been modified in most states. Moreover, more women were finding jobs; over 10.6 million were working by the end of the decade, in contrast with 8.4 million in 1920.

Most of these gains were illusory. Relaxation of the strict standards of sexual morality did not eliminate the double standard. More women worked, but most of the jobs they held were menial or of a kind that few men wanted: domestic service, elementary school teaching, clerical work, selling behind a counter. Where they competed for jobs with men, women usually received much lower wages. Educational opportunities for women expanded, but the colleges placed more emphasis on subjects like home economics. As one Vassar College administrator (a woman!) said, colleges should provide "education for women along the lines of their chief interests and responsibilities, motherhood and the home."

The prosperity of the postwar years and the abandonment of taboos improved the position of women in an absolute sense, but the relative position of women remained virtually unchanged. This helps to explain their continuing dissatisfaction. So does the confusion resulting from the passage of the Nineteenth Amendment. After its ratification, Carrie Chapman Catt was exultant. "We are no longer petitioners," she announced, "but free and equal citizens." Many activists, assuming the battle won, lost interest in agitating for change and sat back smugly to enjoy the benefits of their new position.

Others believed that the suffrage amendment had given them the one weapon needed to achieve whatever women still lacked. In fact, being able to vote reduced rather than strengthened the influence of women, for it soon became apparent that women did not vote as a bloc. The Amendment increased the size of the electorate but did not add to the power of any particular party or interest group.

When radical women discovered that voting did not automatically bring true equality, they founded the Women's party and began campaigning for an Equal Rights Amendment. Their leader, Alice Paul, a dynamic if somewhat fanatical person, disdained specific goals such as disarmament, ending child labor, and liberalized birth control. Total equality for women was the one objective. The party considered protective legislation governing the hours and working conditions of women discriminatory.

The Women's party never attracted a wide following. Many more women joined the more moderate League of Women Voters, which attempted to mobilize support for a broad spectrum of reforms, some of which had no specific connection with the interests of women as such. Feminists also split on generational lines, the younger ones tending to adopt more liberal attitudes toward sexual relations, the older still bound by Victorian inhibitions. The entire women's movement lost momentum. The battle for the Equal Rights

■ Vanzetti (left) and Sacco were led into court handcuffed in April, 1927 to hear the death sentence pronounced. They were electrocuted in August of that year, six years after their conviction.

Amendment persisted through the 1930s, but it was lost. By the end of that decade the women's movement was almost dead.

The excesses of the fundamentalists, the xenophobes, the Klan, the redbaiters, and the prohibitionists disturbed American intellectuals profoundly. More and more they became alienated, bitter and contemptuous of those who appeared to control the country. Yet their alienation came at the very time that society was growing more dependent on brains and sophistication. This compounded the confusion and disillusionment characteristic of the period.

Nothing demonstrates this fact so clearly as the Sacco-Vanzetti case. In April 1920 two men in South Braintree, Massachusetts, killed a paymaster and a guard in a daring daylight robbery of a shoe factory. Shortly thereafter Nicola Sacco and Bartolomeo Vanzetti were charged with the crime, and in 1921 they were convicted of murder. Sacco and Vanzetti were anarchists and Italian immigrants. Their trial was a travesty of justice. The presiding judge, Webster Thayer, conducted the proceedings like a prosecuting attorney; privately he referred to the defendants as "those anarchist bastards."

The case became a *cause célèbre.* Prominent persons throughout the world protested, and for years Sacco and Vanzetti were kept alive by efforts to obtain a new trial. Vanzetti's quiet dignity and courage in the face of death wrung the hearts of millions. "You see me before you, not trembling," he told the court. "I never commit a crime in my life. . . . I am so convinced to be right that if you could execute me two times, and if I could be reborn two other times, I would live again and do what I have done already." When, in August 1927, the two were at last electrocuted, the disillusionment of American intellectuals with current values was profound. Some historians, impressed by modern ballistic studies of Sacco's gun, now suspect that he, at least, may have been guilty. Nevertheless, the truth and the shame remain: Sacco and Vanzetti paid with their lives for being radicals and aliens, not for any crime.

Literary Trends

The literature of the twenties reflects the disillusionment of the intellectuals. The prewar period had been an age of hopeful experimentation in the world of letters. Writers, applying the spirit of progressivism to the realism they had inherited from Howells and the naturalists, had been predominantly optimistic. Ezra Pound, for example, talked grandly of an American Renaissance and fashioned a new kind of poetry called Imagism, which, while not appearing to be realistic, abjured all abstract generalizations and concentrated on concrete word pictures to convey meaning. "Little" magazines and experimental theatrical companies sprang to life by the dozen, each convinced that it would revolutionize its art. New York's Greenwich Village teemed with youthful Bohemians contemptuous of middle-class values yet too fundamentally cheerful to reject the modern world. The poet Carl Sandburg, the best known representative of the "Chicago school," denounced the local plutocrats but sang the praises of the city they had made: "Hog Butcher for the World . . . City of the Big Shoulders." Most writers eagerly adopted Freudian psychology without understanding it. Freud's teachings seemed only to mean that they should cast off the senseless restrictions of Victorian prudery; they ignored his essentially dark view of human nature. Theirs was an "innocent rebellion," exuberant—and rather muddleheaded.

The historian Henry F. May has shown that writers, along with most other intellectuals, began to abandon this view about 1912. World War I and then the antics of the fundamentalists, the cruelty of the redbaiters, and the philistinism of the dull politicos of the 1920s turned them into critics of society. Ezra Pound dropped his talk of an American Renaissance and wrote instead of a "botched civilization." The soldiers, he said,

> walked eye-deep in hell
> believing in old men's lies, then unbelieving
> came home, home to a lie,
> home to deceits,
> home to old lies and new infamy. . .

Out of this negativism came a literary flowering of major importance. The herald of the new day was Henry Adams, whose autobiography, *The Education of Henry Adams,* was published posthumously in 1918. Adams' disillusionment long antedated the war, but his description of late 19th-century corruption and materialism and his warning that industrialism was crushing the human

■ The Fitzgerald family—F. Scott, Zelda, and daughter Scotty—do a sedate dance step for the photographer. They were celebrating Christmas in Paris that year.

spirit beneath the weight of its machines appealed powerfully to those whose pessimism was newborn. Soon hundreds of bright young men and women were referring to themselves with a self-pity almost maudlin as the "lost generation."

The symbol of the lost generation, in his own mind as well as to his contemporaries and to later critics, was F. Scott Fitzgerald. Born to modest wealth in St. Paul, Minnesota, in 1896, Fitzgerald rose to sudden fame in 1920 when he published *This Side of Paradise,* a somewhat sophomoric novel that captured the fears and confusions of the lost generation and the façade of frenetic gaiety that concealed them. In *The Great Gatsby* (1925), a more mature work, Fitzgerald dissected a modern millionaire—coarse, unscrupulous, jaded, in love with another man's wife. Gatsby's tragedy lay in his dedication to a woman who, Fitzgerald made clear, did not merit his passion. He lived in "the service of a vast, vulgar, meretricious beauty," and in the end he understood this himself.

The tragedy of *The Great Gatsby* was related to Fitzgerald's own. Pleasure-loving and extravagant, he squandered the money earned by *This Side of Paradise.* When *The Great Gatsby* failed to sell as well, he turned to writing potboilers. "I really worked hard as hell last winter," he told the critic Edmund Wilson, "but it was all trash and it nearly broke my heart." While some of his later work was first-class, he descended into the despair of alcoholism, and ended his days as a Hollywood scriptwriter.

Many young American writers and artists became expatriates in the twenties. They flocked to

■ **Ernest Hemingway at Key West, Florida, in 1929, the year that *A Farewell to Arms* was published.**

Rome, Berlin, and especially Paris, where they could live cheaply and escape what seemed to them the "conspiracy against the individual" prevalent in their own country. The *quartier latin* along the left bank of the Seine was a large-scale Greenwich Village in those days. Writers, artists, and eccentrics of every sort lived there. Some made meager livings as journalists, translators, and editors, perhaps turning an extra dollar from time to time by selling a story or a poem to an American magazine, a painting to a tourist. Others idled away the days, dreaming of fame and fortune rather than earning them.

Ernest Hemingway was the most talented of the expatriates. Born in 1898 in Illinois, Hemingway first worked as a reporter for the Kansas City *Star.* He served in the Italian army during the war, was grievously wounded (in spirit as well as in body), and then, after further newspaper experience, settled in Paris in 1922 to write. His first novel, *The Sun Also Rises* (1926), portrayed the café world of the expatriate and the rootless desperation, amorality, and sense of outrage at life's meaninglessness that obsessed so many in those years. In *A Farewell to Arms* (1929) he drew on his military experiences to describe the confusion and horror of war.

Hemingway's books were best sellers and he became a legend in his own time, but his style rather than his ideas explains his towering reputation. Few novelists have been such self-conscious craftsmen or capable of suggesting powerful emotions and action in so few words. Mark Twain and Stephen Crane were his models, Gertrude Stein, a queer, revolutionary genius, his teacher, but his style was his own, direct, simple, taut, sparse:

> I went out the door and down the hall to the room where Catherine was to be after the baby came. I sat in a chair there and looked at the room. I had the paper in my coat that I had bought when I went out for lunch and I read it. . . . After a while I stopped reading and turned off the light and watched it get dark outside. *(A Farewell to Arms)*

This kind of writing, evoking rather than describing emotion, fascinated readers and inspired hundreds of imitators; it has made a permanent mark on world literature. What Hemingway had to say was of less universal interest—he was an unabashed, rather muddled romantic, an adolescent emotionally. He wrote about bullfights, hunting and fishing, violence; while he did so with masterful penetration, these themes placed limits on his work that he never transcended. The critic Alfred Kazin summed Hemingway up in a sentence: "He brought a major art to a minor vision of life."

Although neither was the equal of Hemingway or Fitzgerald, two other writers of the twenties deserve mention: H. L. Mencken and Sinclair Lewis. Each reflected the distaste of intellectuals for the climate of the times. Mencken, a Baltimore newspaperman and founder of one of the great magazines of the era, the *American Mercury,* was a thoroughgoing cynic. He coined the word *booboisie* to define the complacent, middle-class majority and fired superbly witty broadsides at fundamentalists, prohibitionists, and "Puritans." "Doing Good," he once said, "is in bad taste."

But Mencken was never indifferent to the many aspects of American life that roused his contempt. Politics at once fascinated and repelled him, and he assailed the statesmen of his generation with magnificent impartiality:

> BRYAN: If the fellow was sincere, then so was P. T. Barnum. . . . He was, in fact, a charlatan, a mountebank, a zany without sense or dignity.
>
> WILSON: The bogus Liberal. . . . A pedagogue thrown up to 1000 diameters by a magic lantern.
>
> HARDING: The numskull, Gamaliel . . . the Marion stonehead. . . . The operations of his medulla oblongata . . . resemble the rattlings of a colossal linotype charged with rubber stamps.
>
> COOLIDGE: A cheap and trashy fellow, deficient in sense and almost devoid of any notion of honor—in brief, a dreadful little cad.
>
> HOOVER: Lord Hoover is no more than a pious old woman, a fat Coolidge. . . . He would have made a good bishop.

While amusing, Mencken's diatribes were not profound. In perspective he seems more a professional iconoclast than a constructive critic; like both Fitzgerald and Hemingway, he was something of a perennial adolescent. However, he consistently supported freedom of expression of every sort.

Sinclair Lewis was probably the most popular American novelist of the twenties. Like Fitzgerald, his first major work brought him instant fame and notoriety—and for the same reason. *Main Street* (1920) portrayed the smug ignorance and bigotry of the American small town so accurately that even Lewis' victims recognized themselves; his title became a symbol for provinciality and middle-class meanness of spirit. Next he created, in *Babbitt* (1922), an image of the businessman of the twenties. George Babbitt, gregarious, a "booster," was blindly orthodox in his political and social opinions, a slave to every cliché, and full of loud self-confidence. Underneath the surface he was a bumbling, rather timid fellow who would like to be better than he was but dared not try.

Lewis went on to dissect a variety of American attitudes and occupations: the medical profession in *Arrowsmith* (1925), religion in *Elmer Gantry* (1927), fascism in *It Can't Happen Here* (1935), and many others. Although his indictment of contemporary society rivaled Mencken's in savagery, Lewis was not a cynic. Superficially as objective as an anthropologist, he remained at heart committed to the way of life he was assaulting. His remarkable powers of observation depended on his identification with the society he described. He was frustrated by the fact that his victims, recognizing themselves in his pages, accepted his criticisms with remarkable good temper and, displaying the very absence of intellectual rigor that he decried, cheerfully sought to reform.

At the same time, lacking Mencken's ability to remain aloof, Lewis tended to value his own work in terms of its popular reception. He craved the good opinion and praise of his fellows. When he was awarded the Pulitzer prize for *Arrowsmith,* he petulantly refused it because it had not been offered earlier. He politicked shamelessly for a Nobel prize, which he received in 1930, the first American author to win this honor.

Lewis was preeminently a product of the twenties. When times changed, he could no longer portray society with such striking verisimilitude; none of his later novels approached the level of *Main Street* and *Babbitt.* When critics noticed this, Lewis became bewildered, almost disoriented. He died in 1951 a desperately unhappy man.

Popular Culture: Movies and Radio

The postwar decade saw immense changes in popular culture. Unlike the literary flowering of the era, these changes seemed in tune with the times, not a reaction against them. This was true in part because they were products as much of technology as of human imagination.

The first motion pictures were made around 1900 but the medium only came into its own after the Great War. The early films, such as the eight-minute epic *The Great Train Robbery* (1903), were brief, crude, and unpretentious, but their success was instantaneous. By 1908 the nation had between 8,000 and 10,000 nickelodeons, as the primitive exhibition halls were called. Thereafter the length and complexity of movies expanded rapidly, especially after David W. Griffith released his 12-reel *Birth of a Nation* in 1915.

By the mid twenties the industry, centered in Hollywood, California, was the fourth largest in

■ **Man against machine: Charlie Chaplin duels a folding Murphy bed in the film *One A.M.***

the nation in capital investment. Movie "palaces" seating several thousand people sprang up in the major cities, and they counted their yearly audiences in the tens of millions. With the introduction of talking movies, beginning with *The Jazz Singer* (1927), and color films a few years later, the motion picture reached technological maturity. Costs and profits mounted: by the thirties million-dollar productions were common.

Most movies were tasteless trash catering to the prejudices of the multitude. Sex, crime, war, romantic adventure, broad comedy, and luxurious living were the main themes, endlessly repeated in predictable patterns. Most popular actors and actresses were either handsome, talentless sticks or so-called character actors who were typecast over and over again as heroes, villains, comedians. The stars attracted armies of adoring fans and received thousands of dollars a week for their services. Critics charged that the movies were destroying the legitimate stage (which underwent a sharp decline), corrupting the morals of youth, and glorifying the materialistic aspects of life.

Nevertheless the motion picture made positive contributions to American culture. Beginning with the work of Griffith, filmmakers created an entirely new theatrical art, using close-ups to portray character and heighten tension, broad panoramic shots to transcend the limits of the stage. They employed with remarkable results special lighting effects, the fade-out, and other techniques impossible in the live theater. Movies enabled dozens of established actors to reach wider audiences and developed many first-rate new ones. In Charlie Chaplin, whose characterization of the sad little tramp with his cane, tight frock coat, and baggy trousers became famous throughout the world, the new form found perhaps the supreme comic artist of all time. The animated cartoon, perfected by Walt Disney, was a lesser but significant achievement that gave endless delight to millions of children. And as the medium matured, it produced many dramatic works of high quality. At its best the motion picture offered a breadth and power of impact superior to anything on the traditional stage.

Even more pervasive in its effects on the America people was radio. Wireless transmission of sound was developed in the late 19th century by many scientists in Europe and the United States. An American, Lee De Forest, working in the decade before the Great War, devised the key improvements that made long-distance broadcasting possible. During the war radio was put to important military uses and was strictly controlled; immediately thereafter the air waves were thrown open to everyone.

Radio was briefly the domain of hobbyists, thousands of "hams" chatting in indiscriminate fashion. Even under these conditions, the manufacture of radio equipment became a big business. In 1920 the first commercial station (KDKA in Pittsburgh) began broadcasting, and by the end of 1922 over 500 stations were in operation.

It took little time for broadcasters to discover the power of the new medium. When one pioneer interrupted a music program to ask listeners to phone in requests, the station received 3,000 calls in an hour. The immediacy of radio explained its tremendous impact. As a means of communicating the latest news, it had no peer; beginning with the broadcast of the 1924 presidential nominating conventions, all major public events were covered "live."

Advertisers seized on radio too; it proved to be as useful for selling soap as for transmitting news. Advertising had mixed effects on broadcasting. The sums paid by business for air time made possible elaborate entertainments performed by the finest actors and musicians, all without cost to listeners. However, advertisers hungered for mass markets. They preferred to sponsor programs of little intellectual content, aimed at the lowest tastes and utterly uncontroversial. And good and bad alike, programs were constantly interrupted by irritating pronouncements extolling the supposed virtues of one commercial product or another.

In 1927 Congress limited the number of stations and parceled out wavelengths to prevent interference. Further legislation in 1934 established the Federal Communications Commission with power to revoke the licenses of stations that failed to operate in the public interest. But the FCC placed no effective controls on programming or on advertising practices. The general level remained lamentably inferior to that of government-owned European systems.

The "New Negro"

Even more than for white liberals, the postwar reaction had brought despair for many blacks. Aside from the barbarities of the Klan, they suffered from the postwar middle-class hostility to labor (and from the persistent reluctance of organized labor to admit black workers to its ranks). The increasing presence of southern blacks in northern cities also caused conflict. Some 393,000 settled in New York, Pennsylvania, and Illinois in the twenties, most of them in New York City, Philadelphia, and Chicago. The black population of New York City more than doubled between 1920 and 1930.

In earlier periods blacks in northern cities had tended to live together but in small neighborhoods scattered over large areas. Now the tendency was toward concentration in what came to be called ghettos. Harlem, a white, middle-class residential section of New York City as late as 1910, had 50,000 blacks in 1914, 73,000 in 1920, and nearly 165,000 in 1930.

The restrictions of ghetto life produced a vicious circle of degradation. Population growth and segregation caused a desperate housing shortage; rents in Harlem doubled between 1919 and 1927. Since the average black worker was unskilled and ill paid, tenants were forced to take in boarders. Landlords converted private homes into rooming houses and allowed their properties to fall into disrepair. The process of decay was speeded by the influx of what the sociologist E. Franklin Frazier called "ignorant and unsophisticated peasant people" from the rural South, who were inexperienced in city living. These conditions caused disease and crime rates to rise sharply.

Even in small northern cities where they made up only a tiny proportion of the population, blacks were badly treated. When Robert S. and Helen M. Lynd made their classic sociological analysis of *Middletown* (Muncie, Indiana), they discovered that although black and white children attended the same schools, the churches, the larger movie houses, and other places of public accommodation were segregated. The local YMCA had a gymnasium where high school basketball was played, but the secretary refused to allow any team with a black player to use it. Even the news in Muncie was segregated. Local papers chronicled the affairs of the black community—roughly 5 percent of the population—under the heading "In Colored Circles."

Coming after the hopes inspired by wartime gains, the disappointments of the 1920s produced a new militancy among many blacks. In 1919 W. E. B. Du Bois wrote in *The Crisis:* "We are

■ **King Oliver's Creole Jazz Band, Chicago, 1923. Fourth from the left is Louis Armstrong; the pianist is Lil Hardin, his wife.**

cowards and jackasses if . . . we do not marshal every ounce of our brain and brawn to fight . . . against the forces of hell in our own land." He increased his commitment to black nationalism, organizing a series of Pan African Conferences in an effort—futile as it turned out—to create an international black movement.

Du Bois never made up his mind whether to work for integration or black separatism. Such ambivalence never troubled Marcus Garvey, a West Indian whose Universal Negro Improvement Association attracted hundreds of thousands of followers in the early twenties. Garvey had nothing but contempt for whites, for light-skinned Negroes like Du Bois, and for organizations such as the NAACP that sought to bring whites and blacks together to fight segregation and other forms of prejudice. "Back to Africa" was his slogan; the black man must "work out his salvation in his motherland." (Paradoxically, Garvey's ideas won the enthusiastic support of the Ku Klux Klan and other white racist groups.)

Garvey's message was naive, but it served to build racial pride among the masses of poor and unschooled blacks. He dressed in elaborate braided uniforms, wore a plumed hat, drove about in a limousine. Both God and Christ were black, he insisted. He organized black businesses of many sorts, including a company that manufactured black dolls. He established a corps of Black Cross nurses and a Black Star Line Steamship Company to transport blacks back to Africa. More sophisticated black leaders like Du Bois detested Garvey, whom they thought something of a charlatan. His motives are at this distance unclear, and part of his troubles resulted only from his being a terrible businessman. In 1923 his steamship line went into bankruptcy. He was convicted of defrauding the thousands of his supporters who had invested in its stock and was sent to prison. Nevertheless, his message, if not his methods, helped to create the "New Negro," proud of his color and his heritage and prepared to resist both white mistreatment and white ideas: "Up, you mighty race, you can accomplish what you will!"

The ghettos produced compensating advantages for blacks. One effect, not fully utilized until later, was to increase their political power by enabling them to elect representatives to state legislatures and to Congress, and to exert considerable influence in closely contested elections. More immediately, city life stimulated self-confidence; despite their horrors, the ghettos offered economic opportunity, political rights, and freedom from the everyday debasements of life in the South. The ghetto was a black world where black men and women could be themselves.

Black writers, musicians, and artists found in the ghettos both an audience and the "spiritual emancipation" that unleashed their capacities. Jazz, the great popular music of the age, was largely the creation of black musicians working in New Orleans before the turn of the century. By the 1920s it had spread throughout the country and to most of the rest of the world. White musicians and white audiences took it up—in a way, it became a force for racial tolerance and understanding. Jazz meant improvisation, and both players and audiences experienced in it a kind of liberation. Jazz was the music of the 1920s in part because it expressed the desire of so many people to break with tradition and throw off conventional restraints. Surely this explains why it was so important to blacks.

Harlem, the largest black city in the world, became in the 1920s a cultural capital, center of the "Harlem Renaissance." Black newspapers and magazines flourished along with theatrical companies and libraries. Du Bois opened *The Crisis* to young writers and artists, and a dozen "little" magazines sprang up. Langston Hughes, one of the best poets of the era, described the exhilaration of his first arrival in this city within a city, a "magnet" for every black intellectual and artist. "Harlem! I . . . dropped my bags, took a deep breath, and felt happy again."

With some exceptions, black writers like Hughes did not share in the disillusionment that afflicted so many white intellectuals. The persistence of prejudice angered them and made them militant. But to be militant, one must be at some level hopeful, and this they were. Sociologists and psychologists (for whom the ghettos were indispensable social laboratories) were demonstrating that environment rather than heredity was preventing black economic progress. Together with the achievements of creative blacks, which for the first time were being appreciated by large numbers of white intellectuals, these discoveries seemed to herald the eventual disappearance of race prejudice. The black, Alain Locke wrote in *The New Negro* (1925), "lays aside the status of beneficiary and ward for that of a collaborator and participant in American civilization." Alas, as Locke and other black intellectuals were soon to discover, this prediction, like so many made in the 1920s, did not come to pass.

The Era of "Normalcy"

The men who presided over the government of the United States during this era were Warren G. Harding of Ohio and Calvin Coolidge of Massachusetts. Harding was a newspaperman by trade, publisher of the Marion *Star*, with previous political experience as a legislator and lieutenant governor in his home state and as a United States senator. No president, before or since, looked more like a statesman; few were less suited for running the country. Coolidge, a taciturn New England type with a long record in Massachusetts politics climaxed by his inept but much-admired suppression of the Boston police strike while governor, made a less impressive appearance than Harding and did not much excel him as a leader. "Don't hurry to legislate" was a Coolidge slogan. He preferred to follow public opinion and hope for the best. "Mr. Coolidge's genius for inactivity is developed to a very high point," the correspondent Walter Lippmann wrote. "It is a grim, determined, alert inactivity, which keeps Mr. Coolidge occupied constantly."*

Harding won the 1920 Republican nomination because the party convention could not decide between General Leonard Wood, who represented the Roosevelt faction, and Frank Lowden, governor of Illinois. His genial nature and lack of strong convictions made him attractive to many of the politicos after eight years of the headstrong Wilson. During the campaign he exasperated sophisticates by his ignorance and imprecision. He coined the famous vulgarism "normalcy" as a substitute for the word "normality," referred, during a speech before a group of actors, to Shakespeare's play "Charles the Fifth," and committed numerous other blunders. "Why does he not get a

*Coolidge was physically delicate, being plagued by chronic stomach trouble. He required 10 or 11 hours of sleep a day.

private secretary who can clothe . . . his 'ideas' in the language customarily used by educated men?" one Boston gentleman demanded of Senator Lodge, who was strongly supporting Harding. Lodge, ordinarily a stickler for linguistic exactitude, replied acidly that he found Harding a paragon by comparison with Wilson, "a man who wrote English very well without ever saying anything." A large majority of the voters, untroubled by the candidate's lack of erudition, shared Lodge's confidence that he would be a vast improvement over Wilson.

Harding has often been characterized as lazy and incompetent. In fact he was hardworking and politically shrewd; his major weaknesses were indecisiveness and an unwillingness to offend. He turned the most important government departments over to efficient administrators of impeccable reputation: Charles Evans Hughes the secretary of state, Herbert Hoover in the Commerce Department, Andrew Mellon in the Treasury, and Henry C. Wallace in Agriculture. Harding kept track of what these men did but seldom initiated policy in their areas. However, many lesser offices, and a few of major importance, Harding gave to the unsavory "Ohio Gang" headed by Harry M. Daugherty, whom he made attorney general.

The president was too kindly, too well-intentioned, and too unambitious to be dishonest. He appointed corruptionists like Daugherty, Secretary of the Interior Albert B. Fall, Director of the Mint "Ed" Scobey, and Charles R. Forbes, head of the new Veterans Bureau, out of a sense of personal obligation or because they were old friends who shared his taste for poker and liquor. Before 1921 he had enjoyed officeholding; he was adept at mouthing platitudes, a loyal party man who seldom questioned the decisions of his superiors. In the lonely eminence of the White House, whence, as President Harry Truman later said, the buck cannot be passed, he found only misery. "The White House is a prison," he complained. "I can't get away from the men who dog my footsteps. I am in jail."

In domestic affairs Secretary of the Treasury Mellon, multimillionaire banker and master of the aluminum industry, dominated the Harding administration. Mellon set out to lower the taxes of the rich, reverse the low-tariff policies of the Wilson period, return to the laissez faire philosophy of McKinley, and reduce the national debt by cutting expenses and administrating the government more efficiently. In principle his program had considerable merit. Tax rates designed to check consumer spending in time of war and to raise the huge sums needed to defeat the Central Powers were undoubtedly hampering economic expansion in the early twenties. Certain industries that had sprung up in the United States during the Great War were suffering from German and Japanese competition now that the fighting had ended. Rigid regulations necessary during a national crisis could well be dispensed with in peacetime. And efficiency and economy in government are always desirable.

Yet Mellon carried his policies to unreasonable extremes. He proposed eliminating inheritance taxes and reducing the tax on high incomes by two-thirds in order to stimulate investment, but he opposed lower rates for taxpayers earning less than $66,000 a year, apparently not realizing that economic expansion required greater mass consumption as well. Freeing the rich from "oppressive" taxation, he argued, would enable them to invest more in potentially productive enterprises, the success of which would create jobs for ordinary people. Little wonder that Mellon's admirers called him the greatest secretary of the treasury since Alexander Hamilton.

Although the Republicans had large majorities in both houses of Congress, Mellon's proposals were too reactionary to win unqualified approval. Congress passed a Budget and Accounting Act (1921), creating a director of the budget to assist the president in preparing a unified budget for the government and a comptroller general to audit all government accounts. A general budget had long been needed; previously Congress had dealt with the requirements of each department separately, trusting largely to luck that income and expenditures would balance at year's end. The appointment of a comptroller general enabled Congress to check up on how the departments used the sums granted them.

Mellon's tax and tariff program ran into stiff opposition from middle-western Republicans and southern Democrats, who combined to form the so-called Farm Bloc. The revival of European agriculture cut the demand for American farm produce just when the increased use of fertilizers and machinery was boosting output. As in the era after the Civil War, farmers found themselves bur-

In September the market wavered. Amid volatile fluctuations, stock averages eased downward. Most analysts contended that the Exchange was "digesting" previous gains. A prominent Harvard economist expressed the prevailing view when he said that stock prices had reached a "permanently high plateau" and would soon resume their advance.

On October 24 a wave of selling sent prices spinning. Nearly 13 million shares changed hands—a record. Bankers and politicians rallied to check the decline, as they had during the Panic of 1907 (see page 580). J. P. Morgan, Jr., rivaled the efforts of his father in that earlier crisis. President Hoover assured the people that "the business of the country . . . is on a sound and prosperous basis." But on October 29, the bottom seemed to drop out. More than 16 million shares were sold, prices plummeting. The boom was over.

Hoover and the Depression

The collapse of the stock market did not cause the depression; stocks rallied late in the year, and business activity did not begin to decline significantly until the spring of 1930. The Great Depression was a worldwide phenomenon caused chiefly by economic imbalances resulting from industrialization and the chaos of the Great War. In the United States too much wealth had fallen into too few hands, with the result that consumers were unable to buy all the goods produced. The trouble came to a head mainly because of the easy-credit policies of the Federal Reserve Board and the Mellon tax structure, which favored the rich. Its effects were so profound and prolonged because the politicians (and for that matter the professional economists) did not fully understand what was happening or what to do about it.

The chronic problem of underconsumption operated to speed the downward spiral. Unable to rid themselves of mounting inventories, manufacturers closed plants and laid off workers, thereby causing demand to shrink further. Automobile output fell from 4.5 million units in 1929 to 1.1 million in 1932. When Ford closed his Detroit plants in 1931, some 75,000 workers lost their jobs, and the decline in auto production affected a host of suppliers and middlemen as well.

The financial system cracked under the strain. More than 1,300 banks closed their doors in 1930, 3,700 more during the next two years. Each failure deprived thousands of persons of funds that might have been used to buy goods; when the Bank of the United States in New York City became insolvent in December 1930, 400,000 depositors found their savings immobilized. And of course the industrial depression worsened the depression in agriculture by further reducing the demand for American foodstuffs. Every economic indicator reflected the collapse. New investments declined from $10 billion in 1929 to $1 billion in 1932, and the national income fell from over $80 billion to under $50 billion in the same brief period. Unemployment rose to at least 13 million.

President Hoover was an intelligent man, experienced in business matters and with a good layman's grasp of economics. Secretary of the Treasury Mellon insisted that the economy be allowed to slide unchecked until the cycle had found its bottom. "Let the slump liquidate itself," Mellon urged. "Liquidate labor, liquidate stocks, liquidate the farmers. . . . People will work harder, live a more moral life. Values will be adjusted, and enterprising people will pick up the wrecks from less competent people." Hoover realized that such a policy would cause unbearable hardship for millions. He rejected Mellon's advice to do nothing.

Hoover's program for ending the depression evolved gradually between 1929 and 1932. It called for cooperative action by businessmen, free from fear of antitrust prosecution, to maintain prices and wages; for tax cuts to increase consumers' spendable income; for public works programs to stimulate production and create jobs for the unemployed; for lower interest rates to make it easier for businesses to borrow in order to expand; for federal loans to banks and industrial corporations threatened with collapse; and for aid to homeowners unable to meet mortgage payments. The president proposed measures making it easier for farmers to borrow money, and he suggested that cooperative farm marketing schemes designed to solve the problem of overproduction be supported by the government. He called for an expansion of state and local relief programs and urged all who could afford it to give more to charity. Above all he tried to restore public confidence. The economy was basically healthy; the depression was only a minor downturn; prosperity was "just around the corner."

■ **James Rosenberg, an attorney and amateur artist sketched this grim view of the Wall Street financial district, Oct. 29, 1929 ("Black Tuesday"), as a Day of Judgment.**

In other words, Hoover rejected classical economics. Indeed, many laissez faire theorists attacked his handling of the depression. The English economist Lionel Robbins, writing in 1934, criticized Hoover's "grandiose buying organizations" and his efforts to maintain consumer income "at all costs." Numbers of "liberal" economists, on the other hand, praised the Hoover program.

While Hoover's plans were theoretically sound, they failed to check the economic slide, in part because of curious limitations in his conception of how they should be implemented. He placed far too much reliance on his powers of persuasion and the willingness of citizens to act in the public interest without legal compulsion. He urged manufacturers to maintain wages and keep their factories in operation, but the manufacturers, under the harsh pressure of economic realities, soon slashed wages and curtailed output sharply. He permitted the Federal Farm Board (created under the Agricultural Marketing Act of 1929) to establish semipublic stabilization corporations with authority to buy up surplus wheat and cotton, but he refused to countenance crop or acreage controls. These corporations poured out hundreds of millions of dollars without checking falling agricultural prices because farmers increased production faster than the corporations could buy up the excess for disposal abroad.

Hoover resisted proposals to shift responsibility from state and local agencies to the federal government, despite the fact—soon obvious—that the lesser government bodies lacked the resources to cope with the emergency. By 1932 the federal government, with Hoover's approval, was spending $500 million a year on public works projects, but because of the decline in state and municipal construction, the total public outlay fell nearly $1 billion below what it had been in 1930. More serious was his refusal, on constitutional grounds, to allow federal funds to be used for the relief of individuals. State and municipal agencies and private charities must take care of the needy.

Unfortunately the depression was drying up the sources of private charities just as the demands on these organizations were expanding. State and municipal agencies were swamped at a time when their capacities to tax and borrow were shrinking. By 1932 more than 40,600 Boston families were on relief (compared with 7,400 families in 1929); in Chicago 700,000 persons—40 percent of the work force—were unemployed. Only the national government possessed the power and the credit to deal adequately with the crisis. Yet Hoover would not act. He set up a committee to coordinate local relief activities but insisted on preserving what he called "the principles of individual and local responsibility." For the federal government to take over relief would "lead to the super-state where every man becomes the servant of the state and real liberty is lost."

Federal loans to businessmen were constitutional, he believed, because the money could be put to productive use and eventually repaid. When drought destroyed the crops of farmers in the South and Southwest in 1930, the government lent them money to buy seed and even food for their livestock, but Hoover would permit no direct relief for the farmers themselves. In 1932 he approved the creation of the Reconstruction Finance Corporation to lend money to banks, railroads, and insurance companies. The RFC represented an important extension of national authority, yet it was thoroughly in line with Hoover's philosophy.

Its loans, secured by solid collateral, were commercial transactions, not gifts; the agency did almost nothing for individuals in need of relief. The same could be said of the Glass-Steagall Banking Act of 1932, which eased the tight credit situation by permitting Federal Reserve banks to accept a wider variety of commercial paper as security for loans. The public grew increasingly resentful of the president's doctrinaire adherence to principle while breadlines lengthened and millions of willing workers searched fruitlessly for jobs.

Hoover stressed the importance of balancing the federal budget, reasoning that since citizens had to live within their limited means in hard times, the government should set a good example. This policy was impossible to carry out. Since the government's income fell precipitously, there was a good deal of what the economist Herbert Stein has called "fiscal stimulation by inadvertence"—by June 1931 the budget was nearly $500 million in the red. Efforts to balance the budget were also counterproductive; by reducing its expenditures the government made the depression worse.

Hoover understood the value of pumping money into a stagnant economy. He might have made a virtue of necessity. The difficulty lay in the fact that nearly all "informed" opinion believed that a balanced budget was essential to recovery. The most prestigious economists insisted on it; so did business leaders, labor leaders, and even most socialists. In 1932, when the House of Representatives refused to vote a tax increase, the Democratic Speaker compelled reconsideration of the bill by asking those "who do not want to balance the budget to rise." Not a single member did so. As late as 1939 a public opinion poll revealed that over 60 percent of the people (even 57.5 percent of the unemployed) favored reducing government expenditures in order to balance the budget. When Hoover said, "Prosperity cannot be restored by raids on the public Treasury," he was wrong, but it is also wrong to criticize him for failing to understand what almost no one understood in the 1930s.

Hoover can, however, be faulted for allowing his anti-European prejudices to interfere with the implementation of his program. In 1930 Congress passed the Hawley-Smoot Tariff Act, which raised duties on most manufactured products to prohibitive levels. While more than a thousand economists joined in urging Hoover to veto this measure on the grounds that it would encourage inefficiency and stifle world trade, he signed it cheerfully. The new tariff made it impossible for European nations to earn the dollars they needed to continue making payments on their World War I debts to the United States, and it helped bring on a financial collapse in Europe in 1931. In that year Hoover wisely proposed a one-year "moratorium" on all international obligations. But the efforts of Great Britain and many other countries to save their own skins by devaluing their currencies in order to encourage foreigners to buy their goods led him to blame them for the depression itself. He seemed unable to grasp what should have been obvious to a person of his intelligence: that high American tariffs made currency devaluation almost inevitable in Europe and that the curtailment of American investment on the Continent as a result of the depression had dealt a staggering blow to the economies of all the European nations.

Much of the contemporary criticism of Hoover and a good deal of that heaped upon him by later historians was unfair. Yet his record as president shows that he was too rigid and doctrinaire, too wedded to a particular theory of government to cope effectively with the problems of the day. Since these problems were in a sense insoluble—no one possessed enough knowledge and intelligence to understand entirely what was wrong or enough authority to enforce the proper corrective measures—flexibility and a willingness to experiment were essential to any program aimed at restoring prosperity. Hoover lacked these qualities. He was his own worst enemy, being too uncompromising to get on well with the politicians and too aloof to win the confidence and affection of ordinary people. As his biographer Joan Hoff Wilson has noted, he refused "to backslap, fraternize with local supporters, kiss babies." He had too much faith in himself and his plans. When he failed to achieve the results he anticipated, he attracted, despite his devotion to duty and his concern for the welfare of the country, not sympathy but scorn.

The Economy Sounds the Depths

During the spring of 1932, as the economy sounded the depths, thousands of Americans

■ **A breadline in New York in 1933. The Great Depression, an English observer said, "outraged and baffled" the nation that took it as "an article of faith . . . that America somehow, was different from the rest of the world."**

faced starvation. In Philadelphia during an 11-day period when no relief funds were available, hundreds of families existed on stale bread, thin soup, and garbage. In the nation as a whole, only about one-quarter of the unemployed were receiving any public aid. In Birmingham, Alabama, landlords in poor districts gave up trying to collect rents, preferring, one Alabama congressman told a Senate committee, "to have somebody living there free of charge rather than to have the house . . . burned up for fuel [by scavengers]." Many people were evicted, and they often gathered in ramshackle communities constructed of packing boxes, rusty sheet metal, and similar refuse on swamps, garbage dumps, and other wasteland. People began to call these places "Hoovervilles."

Thousands of tramps roamed the countryside begging for food. At the same time, food prices fell so low that farmers burned corn for fuel. In Iowa and Nebraska farmers organized Farm Holiday movements, refusing to ship their crops to market in protest against 31-cent-a-bushel corn and 38-cent wheat. They blocked roads and rail lines, dumped milk, overturned trucks, and established picket lines to enforce their boycott. The world seemed to have been turned upside down. Professor Felix Frankfurter of the Harvard Law School remarked only half humorously that henceforth the terms BC and AD would mean "Before Crash" and "After Depression."

The national mood ranged from apathy to resentment. In 1931 federal immigration agents and local groups in the Southwest began rounding up Mexican-Americans and deporting them. Some of those returned to Mexico had entered the United States illegally, others had come in properly. Unemployed Mexicans were ejected because they might become public charges, those with jobs because they were presumably taking bread from the mouths of citizens.

In June and July 1932, 20,000 veterans marched on Washington to demand immediate payment of their "adjusted compensation" bonuses. When Congress rejected their appeal, some 2,000 refused to leave, settling with their families in a jerry-built camp of shacks and tents at Anacostia Flats, a swamp bordering the Potomac. President

Hoover, alarmed, charged incorrectly that the "Bonus Army" was largely composed of criminals and radicals and sent troops into the Flats to disperse it with bayonets, tear gas, and tanks. The task was accomplished amid much confusion; fortunately no one was killed. The protest had been aimless and not entirely justified, yet the spectacle of the United States government chasing unarmed veterans with tanks appalled the nation.

The unprecedented severity of the depression led some persons to favor radical economic and political changes. The disparity between the lots of the rich and the poor, always a challenge to democracy, became more striking and engendered considerable bitterness. "Unless something is done to provide employment," two labor leaders warned Hoover, "disorder . . . is sure to arise. . . . There is a growing demand that the entire business and social structure be changed because of the general dissatisfaction with the present system."

The Communist party gained few converts among farmers and industrial workers, but a considerable number of intellectuals, alienated by the trends of the twenties, responded positively to the communists' emphasis on economic planning and the total mobilization of the state to achieve social goals. Even the popular cracker-barrel humorist Will Rogers was impressed by reports of the absence of serious unemployment in Russia. "All roads lead to Moscow," the former muckraker Lincoln Steffens wrote.

Literature in the Depression

Some American novelists found Soviet communism attractive and wrote "proletarian" novels, most of which were of little artistic merit and none of which achieved great commercial success. The best of the depression writers avoided the party line, though they were critical of many aspects of American life. One was John Dos Passos, author of the trilogy *U.S.A.* (1930–1936).

Dos Passos came from a well-to-do family of Portuguese descent. He was educated at Harvard and drove an ambulance in France during the Great War. *U.S.A.* was a massive work, rich in detail and intricately constructed, that advanced a fundamentally anticapitalist and deeply pessimistic point of view. It portrayed American society between 1900 and 1930 in broad perspective, interweaving the stories of five major characters and a galaxy of lesser figures. Throughout the narrative Dos Passos scattered capsule sketches of famous people, ranging from Andrew Carnegie and William Jennings Bryan to the movie idol Rudolph Valentino and the architect Frank Lloyd Wright. He included "newsreel" sections recounting events of the period and "camera eye" sections in which he revealed his personal reactions to the passing parade.

Dos Passos' method was relentless, cold, methodical—utterly realistic. He displayed immense craftsmanship but no sympathy for his characters or their world. *U.S.A.* was a monument to the despair and anger of liberals confronted with the Great Depression. However, it seemed to exhaust his creativity. After the depression he rapidly abandoned his radical views.

James T. Farrell, a clumsy novelist in the naturalist tradition established by Theodore Dreiser around the turn of the century, also wrote a trilogy in the thirties, the saga of *Studs Lonigan* (1932–1935). It described the squalid life of Chicago's Irish slums. Farrell's overly literal realism was full of anger and conviction and was therefore powerful. Unlike Dos Passos, he remained a radical in later, more prosperous times.

The novel that best portrayed the desperate plight of the millions impoverished by the depression was John Steinbeck's *The Grapes of Wrath* (1939), which described the fate of the Joads, an Oklahoma farm family driven by drought and bad times to abandon their land and become migratory laborers in California. Steinbeck captured the patient bewilderment of the downtrodden, the brutality bred of fear that characterized their exploiters, and the furious resentments of the radicals of the thirties. He depicted the parching blackness of the Oklahoma dust bowl, the grandeur of California, the backbreaking toil of the migrant fruit pickers, and the ultimate indignation of a people repeatedly degraded. "In the eyes of the hungry there is a growing wrath. In the souls of the people the grapes of wrath are filling and growing heavy, growing heavy for the vintage."

Like so many other writers of the thirties, Steinbeck was an angry man. "There is a crime here that goes beyond denunciation," he wrote. He had the compassion that Dos Passos and Farrell lacked, and this quality raised *The Grapes of Wrath* to the level of great tragedy. In other works, such as *Tortilla Flat* (1935) and *The Long Valley* (1938), Steinbeck described the life of California cannery workers and ranchers with moving warmth without becoming overly sentimental.

Although his work was less political than that of Dos Passos or Farrell or Steinbeck, Thomas Wolfe was another major interpreter of his times. Wolfe was born in Asheville, North Carolina, in 1900 and educated at the state university and at Harvard. A passionate, intensely troubled young man of vast but undisciplined talents, he sought to describe the kaleidoscopic character of American life, the limitless variety of the nation. "I will know this country when I am through as I know the palm of my hand, and I will put it on paper and make it true and beautiful," he boasted.

During the last 10 years of his short life (he died in 1938) Wolfe wrote four novels: *Look Homeward, Angel* (1929), *Of Time and the River* (1935), and two published posthumously, *The Web and the Rock* (1939) and *You Can't Go Home Again* (1940). All were autobiographical and to some extent repetitious, for he was an unabashed egoist. Nevertheless he was a superb interpreter of contemporary society. He crammed his pages with unforgettable vignettes—a train hurtling across the Jersey meadows in the dark, a young woman clutching her skirts on a windswept corner, a group of derelicts huddled for shelter in a public toilet on a frigid night. And no writer caught more clearly the frantic pace and confusion of the great cities, the despair of the depression, the divided nature of human beings, their fears and hopes, their undirected, uncontrollable energy.

William Faulkner, probably the finest of modern American novelists, responded to the era in still another way. Born in 1897, within a year of Fitzgerald and Hemingway, like Wolfe he attained literary maturity only in the thirties. After service in the Canadian air force in World War I, he returned to his native Mississippi, working at a series of odd jobs and publishing relatively inconsequential poetry and fiction. Suddenly, between 1929 and 1932, he burst into prominence with four major novels: *The Sound and the Fury, As I Lay Dying, Sanctuary,* and *Light in August.*

Faulkner created a local world, Yoknapatawpha County, and peopled it with some of the most remarkable characters in American fiction—the Sartoris family, typical of the old southern aristocracy worn down at the heels, the Snopes clan, shrewd, unscrupulous, boorish representatives of the new day, and many others. He pictured vividly the South's poverty and its pride, its dreadful racial problem, the guilt and obscure passions plaguing white and black alike. He also dealt effectively with the clash of urban and rural values. Yet Faulkner was far more than a local colorist. No contemporary excelled him as a commentator on

■ "I am completely partisan," Steinbeck (far left) wrote. "Every effort I can bring to bear is . . . at the call of the common working-people." Accepting the Nobel literature prize, Faulkner (near left) spoke of a lifelong attempt "to create out of the materials of the human spirit something which did not exist before."

the multiple dilemmas of modern life. His characters are possessed, driven to pursue high ideals yet weighted down with their awareness of their inadequacies and their sinfulness. They are imprisoned in their surroundings however they may strive to escape them.

Although capable of humor and full of the joy of life, Faulkner was essentially a pessimist. His weakness as a writer, aside from a sometimes exasperating obscurity and verbosity, resulted from his somewhat confused view of himself and the world he described. Much of his work was passion imprisoned in words without discernible meaning; his characters continually experienced emotions too intense to be bearable, often too profound and too subtle for the natures he had given them. Nevertheless his stature was beyond question, and unlike so many other novelists of the period he maintained a high level in his later years with *The Hamlet* (1940), *Intruder in the Dust* (1948), *A Fable* (1954), and *The Reivers* (1962). He was awarded the 1949 Nobel prize for literature and two Pulitzer prizes.

Election of 1932

As the end of his term approached, President Hoover seemed to grow daily more petulant and pessimistic. The depression, coming after 12 years of Republican rule, probably insured a Democratic victory in any case, but his attitude as the election neared alienated many voters and turned defeat into rout.

Confident of victory, the Democrats chose Governor Franklin Delano Roosevelt of New York as their presidential candidate. Roosevelt owed his nomination chiefly to his success as governor. Under his administration, New York had led the nation in providing relief for the needy and had enacted an impressive program of old-age pensions, unemployment insurance, conservation and public power projects. In 1928, while Hoover was carrying New York against Smith by a wide margin, Roosevelt won election by 25,000 votes. In 1930 he swept the state by a 700,000-vote majority, double the previous record. He also had the advantage of the Roosevelt name (he was a distant cousin of the inimitable T.R.), and his sunny, magnetic personality contrasted favorably with that of the glum and colorless Hoover.

Roosevelt was far from being a radical. Although he had supported the League of Nations while campaigning for the vice-presidency in 1920, during the twenties he had not seriously challenged the basic tenets of Coolidge prosperity. He never had much difficulty adjusting his views to prevailing attitudes. For a time he even served as head of the American Construction Council, a trade association. Indeed, his life before the depression gave little indication that he understood the aspirations of ordinary people or had any deep commitment to social reform.

Roosevelt was born to wealth and social status in Dutchess County, New York, in 1882. Pampered in childhood by a doting yet domineering mother, he was educated at the exclusive Groton School and then at Harvard, where he proceeded, as his biographer Frank Freidel has written, "from one extracurricular triumph to another." Ambition as much as the desire to render public service motivated his career in politics; even after an attack of polio in 1921 left him badly crippled in both legs, he refused to abandon his hopes for high office. During the 1920s he was a hardworking member of the liberal wing of his party. He supported Smith for president in 1924 and 1928.

To some observers Roosevelt seemed rather a lightweight intellectually. When he ran for the vice-presidency, the Chicago *Tribune* commented: "If he is Theodore Roosevelt, Elihu Root is Gene Debs, and Bryan is a brewer." Twelve years later many critics judged him too irresolute, too amiable, too eager to please all factions to be a forceful leader. Herbert Hoover thought he was "ignorant but well-meaning," and the political analyst Walter Lippmann, in a now-famous observation, called him "a pleasant man who, without any important qualifications for the job, would very much like to be President."

Despite his physical handicap—he could walk only a few steps, and then only with the aid of steel braces and two canes—Roosevelt was a brilliant campaigner. He traveled back and forth across the country, radiating confidence and good humor even when directing his sharpest barbs at the Republicans. Like every great political leader, he took as much from the people as he gave them, understanding the causes of their confusion, sensing their needs. "I have looked into the faces of thousands of Americans," he told a friend. "They have the frightened look of lost children. . . . They

■ Well-wishers greet the president at Warm Springs, Georgia, in 1933. The Roosevelt "magic," unfeigned and inexhaustible, amazed his associates. "I have never had contact with a man who was loved as he is," reported Secretary of the Interior Harold L. Ickes.

are saying: 'We're caught in something we don't understand; perhaps this fellow can help us out.'"

Voters responded in a similar manner. "The people," one member of the Hoover administration noted, "seem to be lifting eager faces to Franklin Roosevelt, having the impression that he is talking intimately to them." But this man then added: "I am glad of his enthusiasm and buoyance but I cannot escape the sense that he really does not understand the full meaning of his own recitations."

Roosevelt soaked up information and ideas from a thousand sources—from professors like Raymond Moley, from politicians like John N. Garner, the vice-presidential candidate, from social workers, businessmen, and lawyers. To those seeking specific answers to the questions of the day, he was seldom satisfying. On such vital matters as farm policy, the tariff, and government spending, he equivocated, contradicted himself, or remained silent.

Aided by hindsight, historians have discovered portents of much of his later program in his campaign speeches. These pronouncements, buried among dozens of conflicting generalities, often passed unnoticed at the time. He said, for example, "If starvation and dire need on the part of any of our citizens make necessary the appropriation of additional funds which would keep the budget out of balance, I shall not hesitate to . . . ask the people to authorize the expenditure of that additional amount." In the same speech he called for sharp cuts in federal spending and a balanced budget, and he castigated Hoover for presiding over "the greatest spending administration in peace time in our history."

Nevertheless Roosevelt's basic position was unmistakable. There must be a "re-appraisal of values," a "New Deal." Instead of adhering to conventional limits on the extent of federal power, the government should do whatever was necessary to protect the unfortunate and advance the public good. Lacking concrete answers, Roosevelt advocated a point of view rather than a plan: "The country needs bold, persistent experimentation. It is common sense to take a method and try it. If it fails, admit it frankly and try another. But above all, try something."

The popularity of this approach was demonstrated in November. Hoover, who had lost only eight states in 1928, won only six, all in the Northeast, in 1932. Roosevelt amassed 22.8 million votes to Hoover's 15.8 million and carried the electoral college, 472 to 59.

During the interval between the election and Roosevelt's inauguration in March 1933, the Great Depression reached its nadir. The holdover "lame duck" Congress, last of its kind, proved incapable of effective action.* President Hoover, perhaps understandably, hesitated to institute changes without the cooperation of his successor. Roosevelt, for equally plausible reasons, refused to accept responsibility before assuming power officially. The nation, curiously apathetic in the face of so much suffering, drifted aimlessly, like a sailboat in a flat calm.

Then the banking system disintegrated—no word less strong portrays the extent of the collapse. Starting in the rural West and spreading to major cities like Detroit and Baltimore, a financial panic swept the land. Depositors lined up before the doors of even the soundest institutions, desperate to withdraw their savings. Hundreds of banks were forced to close. In February, to check the panic, the governor of Michigan declared a "bank holiday," shutting every bank in the state for eight days. Maryland, Kentucky, California, and a number of other states followed suit; by inauguration day four-fifths of the states had suspended all banking operations. So great was the fear and confusion that the New York Stock Exchange was closed on March 4.

The Hundred Days

Something drastic had to be done. The most conservative business leaders were as ready for government intervention as the most advanced radicals. Partisanship, while not disappearing, was for once subordinated to broad national needs.

Roosevelt provided the spark that reenergized the American people. His inaugural address, delivered in a raw mist beneath dark March skies, reassured the country and at the same time stirred it to action: "The only thing we have to fear is fear itself. . . . Our true destiny is not to be ministered unto but to minister to ourselves and to our fellow men. . . . This Nation asks for action, and action now. . . . I assume unhesitatingly the leadership of this great army of our people. . . ." Many such lines punctuated the brief address, which concluded with a stern pledge: "In the event that Congress shall fail . . . I shall not evade the clear course of duty that will then confront me. I shall ask the Congress for the one remaining instrument to meet the crisis—broad Executive power to wage a war against the emergency."

The inaugural captured the heart of the country; almost half a million letters of congratulation poured into the White House. When Roosevelt summoned Congress into special session on March 9, the legislators outdid one another to enact his proposals into law. "I had as soon start a mutiny in the face of a foreign foe as . . . against the program of the President," one representative declared. In the following "Hundred Days" (Congress adjourned on June 16), an impressive body of legislation was placed on the statute books. Opposition, in the sense of an organized group committed to resisting the administration, simply did not exist.

Roosevelt had the power and the will to act but no comprehensive plan of action. He and his eager congressional collaborators proceeded in a dozen directions at once, sometimes wisely, sometimes not, often at cross-purposes with themselves and one another. Untangling the national financial mess was the most immediate task. On March 5 Roosevelt declared a nationwide bank holiday and placed an embargo on the exportation of gold. Within hours after it convened, Congress passed an emergency banking bill confirming these measures, outlawing the hoarding of gold, and giving the president broad power over the operations of the Federal Reserve system.

To explain the complexities of the banking problem to the public, Roosevelt delivered the first of his "fireside chats" over a national radio network. "I want to talk for a few minutes with the people of the United States about banking," he explained. His warmth and steadiness reassured millions of listeners. A plan for reopening the banks under Treasury Department licenses was devised, and soon most of them were func-

*The Twentieth Amendment (1933) provided for convening new Congresses in January instead of the following December. It also advanced the date of the president's inauguration from March 4 to January 20.

tioning again, public confidence in their solvency restored. In April Roosevelt took the country off the gold standard, hoping thereby to cause prices to rise. Before the session ended, Congress established the Federal Deposit Insurance Corporation to guarantee bank deposits. It also forced the separation of investment banking and commercial banking concerns while extending the power of the Federal Reserve Board over both types of institutions, and it created the Home Owners Loan Corporation to refinance mortgages and prevent foreclosures. It passed a Federal Securities Act requiring promoters to make public full financial information about new stock issues and giving the Federal Trade Commission the right to regulate such transactions.*

After the adjournment of Congress, the government began buying gold on the open market. When this policy failed to push up the price of gold, Congress, in January 1934, passed the Gold Reserve Act, which gave the president the power to fix the price of gold by proclamation. Roosevelt promptly set the price at $35 an ounce, an increase of about 40 percent.

Problems of unemployment and industrial stagnation had high priority during the Hundred Days. Congress appropriated $500 million for relief of the needy, and it created the Civilian Conservation Corps to provide jobs for men between the ages of 18 and 25 in reforestation and other conservation projects. To stimulate industry, Congress passed one of its most controversial measures, the National Industrial Recovery Act (NIRA). Besides establishing the Public Works Administration, with authority to spend $3.3 billion, this law permitted manufacturers to draw up industrywide codes of "fair business practices." Under the law producers could agree to raise prices and limit production without violating the antitrust laws. The law gave workers the protection of minimum-wage and maximum-hours regulations and guaranteed them the right "to organize and bargain collectively through representatives of their own choosing," an immense stimulus to the union movement.

The NIRA was a variant on the idea of the corporate state. This concept envisaged a system of industrywide organizations of capitalists and workers (supervised by the government) that would resolve conflicts internally, thereby avoiding wasteful economic competition and dangerous social clashes. It was an outgrowth of the trade association idea, although Hoover, who had supported *voluntary* associations, denounced it because of its compulsory aspects. It was also similar to experiments being carried out by the fascist dictator Benito Mussolini in Italy and by the Nazis in Adolf Hitler's Germany. It did not, of course, turn America into a fascist state, but it did herald an increasing concentration of economic power in the hands of interest groups, both industrialists' organizations and labor unions.

The act created a government agency, the National Recovery Administration (NRA), to supervise the drafting and operation of the business codes. Drafting posed difficult problems, first because each industry insisted on tailoring the agreements to its special needs and second because most manufacturers were unwilling to accept all the provisions of Section 7a of the law dealing with the rights of labor. While thousands of employers agreed to the pledge "We Do Our Part" in order to receive the Blue Eagle symbol of NRA, many were more interested in the monopolistic aspects of the act than in boosting wages and encouraging unionization. In practice, the codes were drawn up by the largest manufacturers in each industry. General Hugh Johnson, the head of NRA, was soon fulminating against "chiselers." His impetuosity and his violent tongue did much to destroy whatever spirit of cooperation the manufacturers possessed. After Johnson had been a year in office, President Roosevelt forced his resignation.

The effects of NIRA were both more and less than the designers of the system had intended. It did not end the depression. There was a brief upturn in the spring of 1933, but the expected revival of industry did not take place; in nearly every case the dominant producers in each industry used their power to raise prices and limit production rather than to hire more workers and increase output.

Beginning with the cotton textile code, however, the agreements succeeded in doing away with the centuries-old problem of child labor in industry.

*In 1934 this task was transferred to the new Securities and Exchange Commission, which was given broad authority over the activities of stock exchanges.

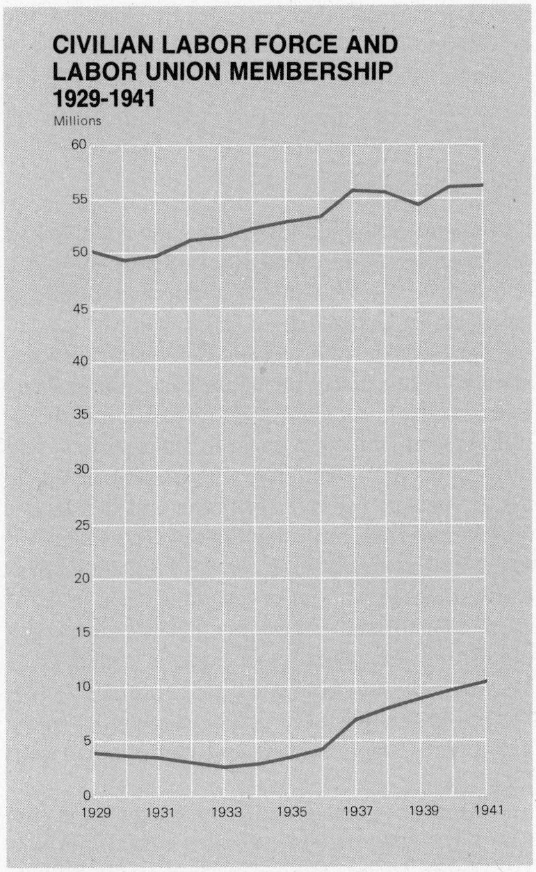

■ **The upper curve shows the total civilian labor force; the lower curve shows the number of those in labor unions. Note that the percentage of union members increased sharply after 1936, and kept on growing throughout the following years.**

They established the principle of federal regulation of wages and hours and led to the organization of thousands of workers, even in industries where unions had seldom been significant. Within a year John L. Lewis' United Mine Workers expanded from 150,000 members to half a million. About 100,000 automobile workers joined unions, as did a comparable number of steelworkers.

Labor leaders cleverly used the NIRA to persuade workers that the popular President Roosevelt *wanted* them to join unions—which was something of an overstatement. In 1935, because the conservative and craft-oriented AFL had displayed little enthusiasm for enrolling unskilled workers on an industrywide basis, John L. Lewis, together with officials of the garment trade unions, formed the Committee for Industrial Organization (CIO) and set out to rally workers in each of the mass-production industries into one union without regard for craft lines, a far more effective method of organization. The AFL expelled these unions, however, and in 1938 the CIO became the Congress of Industrial Organizations. Soon it rivaled the AFL in size and importance.

Roosevelt was more concerned about the plight of the farmers than that of any other group in the country because he believed that the nation was becoming overcommitted to industry. The New Deal farm program, incorporated in the Agricultural Adjustment Act of May 1933, combined compulsory restrictions on production with government subsidies to growers of wheat, cotton, tobacco, pork, and a few other staple crops. The money for these payments was raised by levying processing taxes on middlemen such as flour millers. The object was to lift agricultural prices to "parity" with industrial prices, the ratio in most cases being based on the levels of 1909–1914, when farmers had been reasonably prosperous. In return for withdrawing part of their land from cultivation, farmers received "rental" payments from the Agricultural Adjustment Administration (AAA).

Since the 1933 crops were growing when the law was passed, Secretary of Agriculture Henry A. Wallace, son of Harding's secretary of agriculture and himself an experienced farmer and plant geneticist, decided to pay farmers to destroy the crops in the field. Cotton planters plowed up 10 million acres, receiving $100 million in return. Six million baby pigs and 200,000 pregnant sows were slaughtered. Such ruthlessness appalled observers, particularly when they thought of the millions of hungry Americans who could have eaten all that pork.

Thereafter, limitation of acreage proved sufficient to raise agricultural prices considerably. Many farmers insisted, however, that NRA was raising the cost of manufactured goods more than AAA was raising the prices they received for their crops. "While the farmer is losing his pants to his creditors," one Iowan complained, "NRA is rolling up his shirt. [Soon] we'll have a nudist colony." A far more serious weakness of the program was its failure to assist tenant farmers and sharecroppers, many of whom lost their livelihoods completely when owners took land out of production to obtain AAA payments. Yet acreage restrictions and mortgage relief helped thousands. In addition, the farm program was a remarkable attempt to bring order to the chaotic agricultural economy. As one New Deal official described it, AAA was "the greatest single experiment in economic planning under capitalist conditions ever attempted by a democracy in times of peace."

Another striking achievement of the Hundred Days was the creation of the Tennessee Valley Authority (TVA). During World War I the government had constructed a hydroelectric plant at Muscle Shoals, Alabama, where the Tennessee River plunges 130 feet in a 40-mile stretch, to provide power for factories manufacturing synthetic nitrate explosives. After 1920 farm groups and public power enthusiasts, led by Senator George W. Norris of Nebraska, had blocked administration plans to turn these facilities over to private capitalists. Their efforts to have the site operated by the government had been defeated by presidential vetoes.

Roosevelt wanted to have the entire Tennessee Valley area incorporated into a broad experiment in social planning. Besides expanding the hydroelectric plants at Muscle Shoals and developing nitrate manufacturing in order to produce cheap fertilizers, he envisioned a coordinated program of soil conservation, reforestation, and industrialization. Since the Tennessee River flowed through seven states, national control of the project was essential.

Over the objections of private power companies, led by Wendell L. Willkie of the Commonwealth and Southern Corporation, Congress passed the TVA Act in May 1933. This law created a board authorized to build dams, power plants, and transmission lines and sell fertilizers and electricity to individuals and local communities. The board could undertake flood control, soil conservation, and reforestation projects and improve the navigation of the river. While TVA never became the comprehensive regional planning organization some of its sponsors had anticipated, it improved the standard of living of millions of inhabitants of the valley. In addition to producing electricity and fertilizers and providing a "yardstick" whereby the efficiency—and thus the rates—of private power companies could be tested, it took on other functions ranging from the eradication of malaria to the development of recreational facilities.

The New Deal Spirit

By the end of the Hundred Days the country had made up its mind about Roosevelt's New Deal, and despite the vicissitudes of the next decade, it never really changed it. A large majority labeled the New Deal a solid success. Considerable recovery had taken place, but more basic was the fact that Roosevelt, recruiting an army of forceful officials to staff the new government agencies, had infused his administration with a spirit of bustle and optimism. The director of the presidential Secret Service unit, returning to the White House on inauguration day after escorting Herbert Hoover to the railroad station, found the executive mansion "transformed during my absence into a gay place, full of people who oozed confidence." Washington was changed, one observer noted, "from a placid leisurely Southern town . . . into a gay, breezy, sophisticated and metropolitan center."

Dozens of people who lived through those stirring times have left records that reveal the New Deal spirit. "Come at once to Washington," Senator Robert La Follette, Jr., son of "Fighting Bob," telegraphed Donald Richberg, an old Theodore Roosevelt progressive. "Great things are under way." When Richberg arrived, he found his friends "seething with excitement and anticipation." "I have been in a constant spin of activity," another New Dealer wrote a friend. "I feel as if I were alive all over, and that this cockeyed world is taking us somewhere." Justice Harlan Fiske Stone of the Supreme Court recorded: "Never was there such a change in the transfer of government."

Although Roosevelt was not much of an intellectual, his openness to suggestion made him eager to draw on the ideas and energies of experts of all sorts. New Deal agencies soon teemed with college professors and young lawyers without political experience. Largely because of the influence of Eleanor Roosevelt and Molly Dewson, head of the Women's Division of the Democratic National Committee, the administration employed a number of women in positions of importance. Secretary of Labor Frances Perkins was the first woman

■ Workers at the Carnegie Steel Co. plant in Pittsburgh give a warm welcome to Frances Perkins, FDR's secretary of labor. She had been a prominent social worker and reformer in the Progressive Era.

appointed to a Cabinet post, and there were dozens of others; Dewson and Eleanor Roosevelt headed an informal but effective "network"—women in key posts who kept in touch constantly, always seeking to place reform-minded women in government jobs. (According to the historian William H. Chafe, "Washington seemed like a perpetual convention of social workers as women . . . [took] on government assignments.") Molly Dewson, a close friend of the Roosevelts, became a major force in the Democratic party. She won a larger influence for women in conventions and campaigns and a larger share of the "spoils" that came with victory. Between 1932 and 1938 the number of women postmasters increased 50 percent.

Roosevelt himself seemed to have been "transfigured," one reporter said, "from a man of charm and buoyancy to one of dynamic aggressiveness." During the first days of the New Deal the financial expert Norman H. Davis, who had known Roosevelt since the time of their joint service under Woodrow Wilson, encountered a mutual friend on the White House steps. "That fellow in there is not the fellow we used to know," he said. "There's been a miracle here."

The New Deal lacked any consistent ideological base. While the so-called Brains Trust (a group of college professors headed by Raymond Moley, a Columbia political scientist, that included Columbia economists Rexford G. Tugwell and Adolf A. Berle, Jr., and a number of others) attracted a great deal of attention, theorists never impressed Roosevelt much. His New Deal drew on the old populist tradition, as seen in its antipathy to bankers and its willingness to adopt schemes for inflating the currency; on the New Nationalism of Theodore Roosevelt in its dislike of competition and its deemphasis of the antitrust laws; and on the ideas of social workers trained in the Progressive Era. Techniques developed by the Wilsonians also found a place in the system: Louis D. Brandeis had considerable influence on Roosevelt's financial reforms, and New Deal labor policy grew directly out of the experience of the War Labor Board of 1917–1918.

Within the administrative maze that Roosevelt created, rival bureaucrats battled to enforce their views. The "spenders," led by Tugwell, clashed with those favoring strict economy, who gathered around Lewis Douglas, director of the budget. Blithely disregarding logically irreconcilable differences, Roosevelt mediated between the factions, deciding this time in favor of one, next in favor of the other. Washington became a battleground for dozens of special-interest groups: the Farm Bureau Federation, the unions, the trade associations, the silver miners. William E. Leuchtenburg has described New Deal policy as "interest-group democracy," another historian, Ellis W. Hawley, as "counterorganization" policy aimed at creating "monopoly power" among groups previously unorganized, such as farmers and industrial workers. While, as Leuchtenburg says, the system was superior to that of Roosevelt's predecessors—who had allowed one interest, big business, to predominate—it slighted the unorganized majority. NRA aimed frankly at raising the prices paid by consumers of manufactured goods; the AAA processing tax came ultimately from the pocketbooks of ordinary citizens. Yet the public assumed that Roosevelt's objective was to improve the lot of all classes of society and that he was laboring imaginatively in pursuit of this goal.

The Unemployed

At least 9 million persons were still without work in 1934, yet the Democrats confounded the political experts, including their own, by increasing their already large majorities in both houses of Congress in the 1934 elections. All the evidence indicates that most of the jobless continued to support the administration. Their loyalty can best be explained by Roosevelt's unemployment policies.

In May 1933 Congress had established the Federal Emergency Relief Administration and given it $500 million to be dispensed through state relief organizations. Roosevelt appointed Harry L. Hopkins, an eccentric but brilliant and dedicated social worker, to direct FERA. Hopkins insisted that the unemployed needed jobs, not handouts. In November he persuaded Roosevelt to create a Civil Works Administration, and within a month he put more than 4 million persons to work building and repairing roads and public buildings, teaching, decorating the walls of post offices with murals, and utilizing their special skills in dozens of other ways.

The cost of this program frightened Roosevelt—Hopkins spent about $1 billion in less than five months—and he soon abolished the CWA. But an extensive public works program was continued throughout 1934 under FERA. Despite charges that many of the projects were "boondoggles," thousands of roads, bridges, schools, and other valuable structures were built or refurbished, and the morale of several million otherwise jobless workers was immeasurably raised. Even those who did not benefit directly took the program as an indication of Roosevelt's determination to attack the unemployment problem on a broad front.

After the 1934 elections, Roosevelt committed himself wholeheartedly to the Hopkins approach. Returning "unemployables" to the care of state and local agencies (where their fate was often miserable), the federal government assumed the task of making work for many of the rest. In May 1935 Roosevelt put Hopkins in charge of a new agency, the Works Progress Administration (WPA). By the time this agency was disbanded in 1943 it had spent $11 billion and found employment for 8.5 million persons. Besides building public works, WPA developed the Federal Theatre Project, which put thousands of actors, directors, and stagehands to work; the Federal Writers' Project, which turned out valuable guidebooks, collected local lore, and published about a thousand books and pamphlets; and the Federal Art Project, which employed needy painters and sculptors. In addition, the National Youth Administration created part-time jobs for more than 2 million high school and college students and a larger number of other youths who could not technically be classified as unemployed but who needed financial help.

WPA did not reach all the unemployed. At no time during the New Deal years did unemployment fall below 10 percent of the work force, and in some places it was much higher. Unemployment in Boston, for instance, ranged between 20 and 30 percent throughout the 1930s. Like so many New Deal programs, WPA did not go far enough, chiefly because Roosevelt could not es-

■ Ben Shahn did this 1937 lithograph for the government's Resettlement Administration, an agency established to aid victims of "Dust Bowl" conditions.

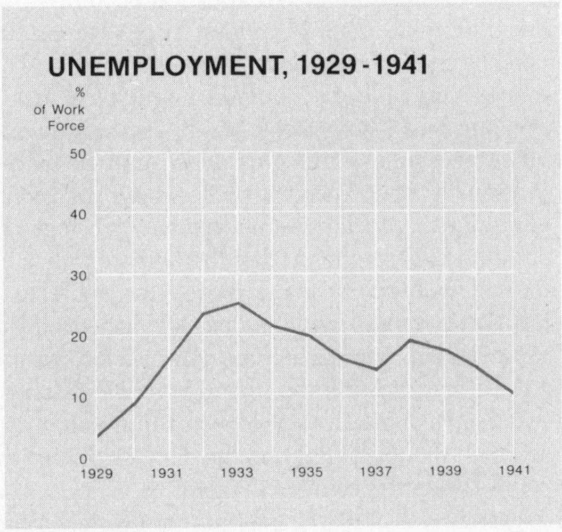

cape his fear of unbalancing the budget drastically. Halfway measures did not provide the massive stimulus the economy needed. The president also hesitated to pay adequate wages to WPA workers and to undertake projects that might compete with private enterprises for fear of offending business. Yet his caution did him no good politically; the business interests he sought to placate were becoming increasingly hostile to the New Deal.

The Extremists

Roosevelt's moderation roused extremists both on the left and on the right. The most formidable was Louisiana's Senator Huey Long, the "Kingfish." Raised on a farm in northern Louisiana, Long was successively a traveling salesman, a lawyer, state railroad commissioner, governor, and, after 1930, United States senator. By 1933 he ruled Louisiana with the absolutism of an oriental monarch.

Long was a controversial figure in his day and so he has remained. In many ways he was a typical southern conservative and he was certainly a demagogue. Yet the plight of all poor people concerned him deeply. More important, he tried to do something about it. His record in Louisiana is a mixture of egotism, sordid politicking, and genuine efforts to improve the lot of the poor, black as well as white.

Long did not question segregation or white supremacy, nor did he suggest that Louisiana blacks should be allowed to vote. He used the word *nigger* with total unself-consciousness, even when addressing northern black leaders. But he treated black-baiters with scathing contempt. When Hiram W. Evans, imperial wizard of the Ku Klux Klan, announced his intention to campaign against him in Louisiana, Long told reporters: "Quote me as saying that that Imperial bastard will never set foot in Louisiana, and that when I call him a sonofabitch I am not using profanity, but am referring to the circumstances of his birth."

As a reformer, Long stood in the populist tradition; he hated bankers and "the interests." He believed that poor people, regardless of color, should have a chance to earn a decent living and get an education. His arguments were simplistic, patronizing, possibly insincere, but effective.

■ **Senator Huey Long (left) explains his Share-Our-Wealth plan to an Iowa audience in April 1935. That same month, Father Charles Coughlin (right), the "Radio Priest," was photographed in Detroit as he promoted his National Union for Social Justice.**

"Don't say I'm working for niggers," he told one northern journalist. "I'm for the poor man—all poor men. Black and white, they all gotta have a chance. . . . 'Every Man a King'—that's my slogan."

Raffish, totally unrestrained, yet shrewd—a fellow southern politician called him "the smartest lunatic I ever saw"—Long had supported the New Deal at the start, but partly because he thought Roosevelt too conservative and partly because of his own ambition, he soon broke with the administration. While Roosevelt was probably more hostile to the big financiers than to any other interest, Long denounced him as a stooge of Wall Street.

By 1935 Long's "Share-Our-Wealth" movement had a membership of over 4.6 million. His program called for the confiscation of family fortunes of more than $5 million and a tax of 100 percent on incomes of over $1 million a year. The money thus collected would be enough to buy every family a "homestead" (a house, a car, and other necessities) and provide an annual family income of $2,000–$3,000 plus old-age pensions, educational benefits, and veterans' pensions. In addition Long proposed that the hours of labor be limited in order to make more jobs and that a farm price-support program be established. As the 1936 election approached, he planned to organize a third party to split the liberal vote. He assumed that the Republicans would win the election and so botch the job of fighting the depression that he could sweep the country in 1940.

Less powerful than Long but more widely influential was Father Charles E. Coughlin, the "Radio Priest." A big, genial Irishman of Canadian birth, Coughlin in 1926 began broadcasting a weekly religious message over station WJR in Detroit. His mellifluous voice and orotund rhetoric won him a huge national audience, and the depression gave him a secular cause. In 1933 he had been an eager New Dealer, but his dislike of New Deal financial policies—he believed that inflating the currency drastically would end the depression—and his need for ever more sensational ideas to hold his radio audience from week to week led him to turn against the New Deal. By 1935 he was calling Roosevelt a "great betrayer and liar."

Although Coughlin's National Union for Social Justice was especially appealing to Catholics, it attracted people of every faith, particularly in the lower-middle-class districts of the big cities. Some of his sensational radio talks caused more than a million people to send him messages of congratulation; contributions amounting to perhaps $500,000 a year flooded his headquarters. Coughlin attacked bankers, New Deal planners, Roosevelt's farm program, and the alleged sympathy of the administration for communism. His program resembled fascism more than any leftist philosophy, but he posed a threat, especially in combination with Long, to the continuation of Democratic rule.

Another rapidly growing movement alarmed the Democrats in 1934–1935: Dr. Francis E. Townsend's campaign for "Old-Age Revolving Pensions." Townsend, a retired California physician, who was colorless and low-keyed, had an oversimplified and therefore appealing "solution" to the nation's troubles. The pitiful state of thousands of elderly persons, whose job prospects were even dimmer than those of the mass of the unemployed, he found shocking. "We owe a decent living to the older people," he insisted. He advocated paying every person 60 and over a pension of $200 a month, the only conditions being that the pensioners not hold jobs and that they spend the entire sum within 30 days. Their purchases, he argued, would stimulate production, thereby creating new jobs and revitalizing the economy. A stiff transactions tax, collected whenever any commodity changed hands, would pay for the program.

Economists quickly pointed out that with about 10 million persons eligible for the Townsend pensions, the cost would amount to $24 billion a year, roughly half the national income. But among the elderly the scheme proved extremely popular. Townsend Clubs, their proceedings conducted in the spirit of revivalist camp meetings, flourished everywhere, and the *Townsend National Weekly* reached a circulation of over 200,000. Although most Townsendites were anything but radical in point of view, their plan, like Long's Share-Our-Wealth scheme, would have revolutionized the distribution of wealth in the country. On the one hand, the movement reflected a reactionary spirit like that of religious fundamentalists, on the other, the emergence of a new force in American society. With medical advances lengthening the average life span, the percentage of old people in the population was rising. The breakdown of close family ties in an increasingly mobile society now caused many of these citizens to be cast adrift to live out their last years poor, sick, idle, and alone. Dr. Townsend's program focused the attention of the country on a new problem—one it has not yet resolved.

With the possible exception of Long, the extremists had little understanding of practical affairs. (It might almost be said that Townsend knew what to do with money but not how to get it and Coughlin knew how to get money but not what to do with it.) Collectively they represented a threat to Roosevelt; their success helped to make the president see that he must move boldly to restore good times or face serious political trouble in 1936.

Political imperatives had much to do with his decision, and the influence of Justice Brandeis and his disciples, notably Felix Frankfurter, was great. They urged Roosevelt to abandon his pro-business programs, especially NRA, and stress restoring competition and taxing corporations more heavily. The fact that most businessmen were turning away from him encouraged the president to accept this advice; so did the Supreme Court's decision in *Schechter* v. *United States* (May 1935), which declared the National Industrial Recovery Act unconstitutional. (The case involved the provisions of the NRA Live Poultry Code; the Court voided the act on the grounds that Congress had delegated too much legislative power to the code authorities and that the defendants, four brothers engaged in slaughtering chickens in New York City, were not engaged in interstate commerce.)

The Second New Deal

Existing laws had failed to end the depression; extremists were luring away some of Roosevelt's supporters; conservatives had failed to appreciate his moderation; the Supreme Court was undermining his achievements. For these many reasons, Roosevelt, in June, launched the "Second New Deal."

The Second Hundred Days was one of the most productive periods in the history of American legislation. The National Labor Relations Act—commonly known as the Wagner Act—restored the labor guarantees wiped out by the Schechter decision. It gave workers the right to bargain collectively and prohibited employers from interfering with union organizational activities in their factories. A National Labor Relations Board (NLRB) was established to supervise plant elections and designate successful unions as official bargaining agents when a majority of the workers approved. It was difficult to force some big corporations to bargain "in good faith," as the law required, but the NLRB could conduct investigations of employer practices and issue cease-and-desist orders when "unfair" activities came to light. Repeatedly the NLRB forced corporations to rehire workers discharged for union activities. The law gave union leaders great control over the rank and file, and while in the long run this produced serious problems, its immediate effect was to make labor more powerful.

The Social Security Act of August 1935 set up a system of old-age insurance, financed partly by a tax on wages (paid by workers) and partly by a tax on payrolls (paid by employers). It created a state-federal system of unemployment insurance, similarly financed. Liberal critics considered this social security system inadequate because it did not cover agricultural workers, domestics, self-employed persons, and some other groups particularly in need of its benefits. Health insurance was not included, and because the size of pensions depended on the amount earned, the lowest-paid workers could not count on much support after reaching 65. Yet the law was of major significance. Over the years the pension payments were increased and the classes of workers covered expanded.

Among other important laws enacted at this time were a new banking act and a Public Utility Holding Company Act. The former strengthened the control of the Federal Reserve Board (renamed the Board of Governors) over member banks and over commercial credit and interest rates. The latter outlawed the pyramiding of control of gas and electricity companies through the use of holding companies and gave federal commissions the power to regulate the rates and financial practices of these companies. The hotly debated "death sentence" clause of the holding company law provided for the dismemberment of all utility complexes more than twice removed from the actual operating companies and authorized the Securities and Exchange Commission to break up smaller ones that could not demonstrate that their existence served some socially useful purpose.

The Rural Electrification Administration (REA), created by executive order, also began to function during this remarkable period. REA lent money at low interest rates to utility companies and to farmer cooperatives interested in bringing electricity to rural areas. When REA went into operation, only one farm in ten had electricity; by 1950 only one in ten did not.

Another important measure was the Wealth Tax Act of August 1935, which, while not the "soak the rich" measure both its supporters and its opponents claimed, raised taxes on large incomes considerably. Estate and gift taxes were increased. Stiffer taxes on corporate profits reflected the Brandeis group's desire to penalize corporate giantism. Much of the opposition to other New Deal legislation rose from the fact that after these changes in the tax laws were made, the well-to-do had to bear a larger share of the cost of *all* government activities.

Whether the Second New Deal was more radical than the First depends largely on the vantage point from which it is considered. Measures like the Social Security Act had greater long-range effect on American life than the legislation of the first Hundred Days but were fundamentally less revolutionary than laws like the National Industrial Recovery Act and the Agricultural Adjustment Act, which attempted to establish a planned economy. "Where the First New Deal contemplated government, business, and labor marching hand in hand toward a brave new society," Arthur M. Schlesinger, Jr., has written, "the Second New

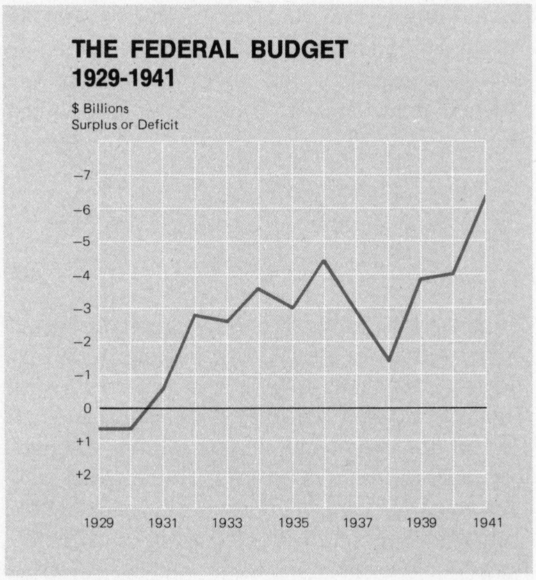

■ **A large drop in the deficit, such as in 1929 and 1930 (when there was an actual surplus), causes recession; an increase in the deficit, such as in 1936, eases recession.**

Deal proposed to revitalize the tired old society. . . . The First New Deal characteristically told business what it must do. The Second New Deal characteristically told business what it must *not* do."

This distinction escaped most of Roosevelt's critics, particularly the businessmen, who felt the impact of his assault on existing conditions most directly. If in theory NIRA threatened the free enterprise system, it was less objectionable to manufacturers than laws that increased their taxes and forced them to contribute to old-age pensions for their workers.

Herbert Hoover epitomized the attitude of conservatives when he called the New Deal "the most stupendous invasion of the whole spirit of Liberty that the nation has witnessed." Undoubtedly many opponents of the New Deal sincerely believed that it was undermining the foundations of American freedom. The cost of the New Deal also alarmed them. By 1936 some members of the administration had fallen under the influence of the British economist John Maynard Keynes, who argued that the world depression could be conquered if governments would deliberately unbalance their budgets by reducing interest rates and taxes and increasing expenditures in order to stimulate consumption and investment. Roosevelt never accepted Keynes' theories; he conferred with the economist in 1934 but could not grasp the "rigmarole of figures" with which Keynes deluged him.

Nevertheless the imperatives of the depression forced Roosevelt to spend more than the government was collecting in taxes; thus he adopted in part the Keynesian approach. Conservative businessmen considered him financially irresponsible, and the fact that deficit spending seemed to be good politics—one cynical New Dealer reputedly said that the administration would "spend, spend, spend" and "elect, elect, elect" until doomsday—made them seethe with rage.

Election of 1936

The election of 1936 loomed as a showdown. "America is in peril," the Republican platform declared. The GOP candidate, Governor Alfred M. Landon of Kansas, was reasonably liberal, a former follower of Theodore Roosevelt, a foe of the Ku Klux Klan in the twenties, and a believer in government regulation of business. But he was a poor speaker, colorless, and handicapped by the reactionary views of many of his backers. Against the charm and political astuteness of Roosevelt, Landon's arguments—chiefly that he could administer the government more efficiently than the president—made little impression. He won the support of some anti-New Deal Democrats, among them two former presidential candidates, Al Smith and John W. Davis, but this was not enough.

The radical fringe put a third candidate in the field, Congressman William Lemke of North Dakota, who ran on the Union party ticket. Father Coughlin, denouncing Roosevelt as the "dumbest man ever to occupy the White House," rallied his National Union for Social Justice behind Lemke; Dr. Townsend also supported him. However, the extremists were losing ground by 1936. Huey Long had fallen victim of an assassin in September 1935, and his organization was taken over by a blatantly demagogic rightist, Gerald L. K. Smith. The New Deal, Smith said in 1936, was led by "a slimy group of men culled from the pink campuses of America." The Townsendites fell under a cloud because of rumors that some of their leaders had their fingers in the organization's treasury. Father Coughlin's slanderous assaults on Roosevelt caused a backlash; a number of American Catholic prelates denounced him, and the Vatican issued an unofficial but influential rebuke. Lemke made little impression on the country, polling only 892,000 votes.

Roosevelt did not win in 1936 because of the inadequacies of his foes. Having abandoned his efforts to hold the businessmen, whom he now denounced as "economic royalists," he appealed for the votes of workers and the underprivileged. The new labor unions gratefully poured thousands of dollars into the campaign to reelect him. Black voters switched to the Democrats in large numbers. In 1932, despite the fact that blacks were harder hit by the depression than any other group, they had maintained their traditional loyalty to the Republican party. "Who but Hoover?" had been their slogan. In 1936 more than three-quarters of northern black voters supported Roosevelt.

Farmers liked Roosevelt because of his evident concern for their welfare: when the Supreme Court declared the Agricultural Adjustment Act unconstitutional (*United States* v. *Butler*, 1936), he immediately rushed through a new law, the Soil Conservation and Domestic Allotment Act, which accomplished the same objective by paying farmers to divert land from commercial crops to soil-building plants like clover and soybeans. Countless elderly persons backed Roosevelt out of gratitude for the Social Security Act. Homeowners were grateful for his program guaranteeing mortgages—eventually about 20 percent of all urban private dwellings were refinanced by the Home Owners Loan Corporation—and for the Federal Housing Administration, which, beginning in 1934, made available low-cost, long-term loans for modernizing old buildings and constructing new ones. A modest upturn, which raised industrial output to the levels of 1930, played into Roosevelt's hands. For the first time since 1931 U. S. Steel was showing a profit.

On election day the country gave the president a tremendous vote of confidence. He carried every state but Maine and Vermont. The Republicans elected only 89 members of the House of Representatives, and their strength in the Senate fell to 16, an all-time low. Both Roosevelt's personality and his program had captivated the land. He seemed irresistible, the most powerfully entrenched president in the history of the United States.

Roosevelt and the Supreme Court

On January 20, in his second inaugural, Roosevelt spoke feelingly of the plight of millions of citizens "denied the greater part of what the very lowest standards of today call the necessities of life." A third of the nation, he added without exaggeration, was "ill-housed, ill-clad, ill-nourished." He interpreted his landslide victory as a mandate for further reforms, and with his prestige and his immense congressional majorities, nothing appeared to stand in his way. Nothing, that is, except the Supreme Court.

Throughout Roosevelt's first term the Court had stood almost immovable against increasing the scope of federal authority and broadening the general power of government, state as well as national, to cope with the exigencies of the depression. Of the nine justices, only Louis Brandeis, Benjamin N. Cardozo, and Harlan Fiske Stone viewed the New Deal sympathetically. Four others, James C. McReynolds, Willis Van Devanter, Pierce Butler, and George Sutherland, were intransigent reactionaries. Chief Justice Charles Evans Hughes and Justice Owen J. Roberts, while more open-minded, tended to side with the reactionaries on many questions.

Much of the early New Deal legislation, pushed through Congress at top speed during the Hundred Days, had been drafted without proper regard for the Constitution. Even the liberal justices considered the National Industrial Recovery Act unconstitutional (the Schechter decision was a unanimous one). The Court had also voided the federal Guffey-Snyder Act, establishing minimum wages in the coal industry, and a New York minimum-wage law, thereby creating, as Roosevelt remarked, a "no man's land" where neither national nor state government could act. The conservative majority had adopted what Roosevelt called a "horse-and-buggy" interpretation of the commerce clause of the Constitution, closing off one of the most important avenues for expanding federal power. Worse, the reactionaries on the Court seemed governed by no consistent constitutional philosophy; they tended to limit the police power of the states when wages-and-hours laws came before them and to interpret it broadly when state laws restricting civil liberties were under consideration. In 1937 all the major measures of the Second Hundred Days appeared doomed. The Wagner Act had little chance of winning approval, experts predicted. Lawyers were advising employers to ignore the Social Security Act, so confident were they that the Court would declare it unconstitutional.

Faced with this situation, Roosevelt decided to ask Congress to shift the balance on the Court by increasing the number of justices, thinly disguising the purpose of his plan by making it part of a general reorganization of the judiciary. A member of the Court reaching the age of 70 would have the option of retiring at full pay. Should such a justice choose not to retire, the president was to appoint an additional justice, up to a maximum of six, in order to ease the burden of work for the aged jurists who remained on the bench.

Roosevelt knew that this measure would run into strenuous resistance, but he expected that the huge Democratic majorities in Congress could override any opposition and that the public would back him solidly. No astute politician had erred so badly in estimating the effects of an action since Stephen A. Douglas introduced the Kansas-Nebraska bill in 1854.

Although polls showed the public fairly evenly divided on the "court-packing" bill, the opposition was vocal and influential. To the expected denunciations of conservatives were added the complaints of liberals fearful that the principle of court packing might in the future be used to subvert civil liberties. What, Senator Norris asked, would have been the reaction if a man like Harding had proposed such a measure? Opposition in Congress was immediate and intense; many who had cheerfully supported every New Deal bill came out against the plan. The press denounced it, and so did most local bar associations. Chief Justice Hughes released a devastating critique; even the liberal Brandeis—the oldest judge on the court—rejected the bill out of hand. And many voters felt that Roosevelt had tried to trick them. The 1936 Democratic platform had spoken only of

■ Al Hirschfield titled his mid 1930s caricature of the Supreme Court, "Nine Old Men." In 1937 the justices and their ages were (from left to right) Owen J. Roberts (62), Pierce Butler (71), Louis D. Brandeis (81), Willis Van Devanter (78), Charles Evans Hughes (the chief justice) (75), James C. McReynolds (75), George Sutherland (75), Harlan Fiske Stone (65), and Benjamin N. Cardozo (67). Their average age was a bit over 72 years.

a possible amendment "clarifying" the Court's power, and Roosevelt had studiously avoided the issue during the campaign.

For months Roosevelt stubbornly refused to concede defeat, thus tying up the rest of his legislative program while Congress wrangled over the court reform bill. Finally, in July 1937, he had to yield. Minor administrative reforms of the judiciary were enacted, but the size of the Court remained unchanged.

The struggle did result in saving the legislation of the Second New Deal. Alarmed by the threat to the Court, Justices Hughes and Roberts, never entirely committed to the conservative position, beat a strategic retreat on a series of specific issues. While the debate was raging in Congress, they sided with the liberals in upholding first a minimum-wage law of the state of Washington that was little different from the New York act the Court had recently rejected, then the Wagner Act, then the Social Security Act. In May Justice Van Devanter retired, and Roosevelt replaced him with Senator Hugo Black of Alabama, an advanced New Dealer. The conservative justices thereupon gave up the fight, and soon Roosevelt was able to appoint enough new judges to give the Court a large pro-New Deal majority. No further measure of significance was declared unconstitutional during his presidency.

The Court fight hurt Roosevelt severely. His prestige never fully recovered. Conservative Democrats who had feared to oppose him because of his supposedly invulnerable popularity took heart and began to join with the Republicans on key issues. When the president summoned a special session of Congress in November 1937 and submitted a program of "must" legislation, not one of his bills was passed.

The End of the New Deal

The Court fight marked the beginning of the end of the New Deal. Social and economic developments contributed to its decline, and the final blow originated in the area of foreign affairs. With unemployment high, wages low, and workers relatively powerless against their employers, most Americans had liked New Deal labor legislation and sympathized with the industrial unions whose growth it stimulated. Strength made the unions ambitious and aggressive; their organizational drives in industries like steel and automobiles changed the power structure within the economy. This gave many members of the middle class second thoughts concerning labor's demands.

In 1937 a series of "sit-down strikes" broke out, beginning at General Motors' Flint, Michigan, plant. Striking workers barricaded themselves *inside* the factories; when police and strikebreakers tried to dislodge them, they drove them off with barrages of soda bottles, tools, spare parts, and crockery. The tolerant attitude of the Roosevelt administration insured the strikers against government intervention. "It is illegal," Roosevelt said of the General Motors strike, "but shooting it out . . . [is not] the answer. . . . Why can't those fellows in General Motors meet with the committee of workers?" Fearful that all-out efforts to clear their plants would result in the destruction of expensive machinery, most employers capitulated to the workers' demands. All the automobile manufacturers but Henry Ford quickly came to terms with the United Automobile Workers.

The major steel companies, led by U. S. Steel, recognized the CIO and granted higher wages and a 40-hour week. The auto and steel unions alone boasted more than 725,000 members by late 1937; other CIO units conquered the rubber industry, the electrical industry, the textile industry, and many more. Together with the seizures of property in sit-down strikes, the disregard of unions for the "rights" of nonunion workers, and the violence that accompanied some strikes, the rapid growth alarmed many moderates. The enthusiasm of such people for all reform cooled rapidly.

While the sit-down strikes and the Court fight were going on, the New Deal suffered another heavy blow. Business conditions had been gradually improving since 1933. Heartened by the trend, Roosevelt, who had never fully grasped the importance of government spending in stimulating recovery, cut back sharply on the relief program in June 1937—with disastrous results. Between August and October the economy slipped downward like sand through a chute. Stock prices plummeted, unemployment rose by 2 million, industrial production slumped. This "Roosevelt recession" further damaged the president's reputation, and for many months he aggravated the

■ A group of sit-down strikers inside the Chevrolet plant in Flint, looking out. They are hanging a "G-M stool" in effigy. The sign directly above the dummy reminds fellow workers: "Don't Scab."

situation by adopting an almost Hoover-like attitude. "Everything will work out all right if we just sit tight and keep quiet," he actually said.

While the president hesitated, rival theorists within his administration warred. The Keynesians, led by WPA head Harry Hopkins, Marriner Eccles of the Federal Reserve, and Secretary of the Interior Harold Ickes, clamored for stepped-up government spending. The conservatives, led by Treasury Secretary Henry Morgenthau, Jr., advocated retrenchment. Perhaps confused by the conflict, Roosevelt seemed incapable of decisive action. When Keynes offered him "some bird's eye impressions" of the recession in February 1938, urging "large scale recourse to . . . public works and other investments aided by Government funds," Roosevelt sent him only a routine acknowledgment drafted by Morgenthau.

In April 1938 Roosevelt finally committed himself to heavy deficit spending. At his urging Congress passed a $3.75 billion public works bill. Two major pieces of legislation were also enacted at about this time. A new AAA program (February 1938) set marketing quotas and acreage limitations for growers of staples like wheat, cotton, and tobacco and authorized the Commodity Credit Corporation to lend money to farmers on their surplus crops. The surpluses were to be stored by the government; when prices rose, farmers could repay the loans, reclaim their produce, and sell it on the open market, thereby maintaining an "ever-normal granary."

The second measure, the Fair Labor Standards Act, abolished child labor and established a national minimum wage of 40 cents an hour and a maximum work week of 40 hours, with time-and-a-half for overtime. Although the law failed to cover many of the poorest-paid types of labor, its passage meant wage increases for 750,000 workers. In later years many more classes of workers were brought within its protection and the minimum wage was repeatedly increased.

These measures further alienated conservatives without dramatically improving economic conditions. The resistance of many Democratic congressmen to additional economic and social "experiments" hardened. As the 1938 elections approached, Roosevelt decided to go to the voters in an effort to strengthen party discipline and reenergize the New Deal. He singled out a number of conservative Democratic senators, notably Walter F. George of Georgia, Millard F. Tydings of Maryland, and "Cotton Ed" Smith of South Carolina, and tried to "purge" them by backing other Democrats in the primaries.

The purge failed. Southern voters liked Roosevelt but resented his interference in local politics. Smith dodged the issue of liberalism by stressing the question of white supremacy in South Carolina; Tydings emphasized Roosevelt's "invasion" of Maryland; in Georgia the president's enemies compared his campaign against George to General Sherman's march across the state during the Civil War. All three senators were easily renominated and then reelected in November. In the nation at large the Republicans made important gains for the first time since Roosevelt had taken office. The Democrats maintained nominal control of both houses of Congress, but the conservative coalition, while unable to muster the votes to do away with accomplished reforms, succeeded in blocking additional legislation.*

Significance of the New Deal

By 1939 Roosevelt was ready to abandon further efforts at reform. The mounting danger of war in Europe as a result of the aggressions of the German dictator, Adolf Hitler, dominated his thinking. After war broke out in 1939, the Great Depression was swept away on a wave of orders from the beleaguered European democracies. For this prosperity, Roosevelt received much undeserved credit. His New Deal had not returned the country to full employment. It is a truth still ominous for the future that no convincing reply has been devised to the argument that modern capitalism cannot flourish without the stimulus of massive military expenditures.

The perspective of time reveals other inadequacies of the New Deal. Despite the aid given the jobless, the generation of workers born between 1900 and 1910 who entered the 1930s as unskilled laborers had their careers permanently stunted by the depression. Far fewer rose to middle-class status than at any time since the 1830s and 1840s. Roosevelt's willingness to experiment with different means of combating the depression made sense because no one really knew what to do; however, his uncertainty about the ultimate objectives of the New Deal was counterproductive. He vacillated between seeking to stimulate the economy by deficit spending and trying to balance the budget; between a narrow "America First" economic nationalism and a broad-gauged international approach; between regulating monopolies and trustbusting; between helping the underprivileged and bolstering those already strong. At times he acted on the assumptions that the United States had a "mature" economy and that the major problem was overproduction. At other times he appeared to think that the answer to the depression was more production. He could never make up his mind whether to try to rally liberals to his cause without regard for party or to run the government as a partisan leader, conciliating the conservative Democrats.

Roosevelt's fondness for establishing new agencies to deal with specific problems vastly increased the federal bureaucracy, indirectly added to the influence of lobbyists, and made it more difficult to monitor government activities. His cavalier attitude toward constitutional limitations on executive power, which he justified as being necessary in a national emergency, set in motion trends that so increased the prestige and authority of the presidency that the balance between the executive, legislative, and judicial branches was threatened.

Yet these are criticisms after the fact; they ignore what one historian has called the "sense of urgency and haste" that made the New Deal "a mixture of accomplishment, frustration, and mis-

*The so-called conservative coalition was never a well-organized group. Its membership shifted from issue to issue; it had no real leaders and certainly no long-range plans. If any common policy united its adherents, it was opposition to the New Deal's "overconcern" for the interests of unions, the unemployed, and underprivileged urban minorities.

■ Black sharecroppers evicted from their tenant farms were photographed by Arthur Rothstein along a Missouri road in 1939. Rothstein was one of a group of outstanding photographers who created a unique "sociological and economic survey" of the nation under the aegis of the Farm Security Administration between 1936 and 1942.

directed effort." On balance, the New Deal had an immense constructive impact. By 1939 the country was committed to the idea that the federal government should accept responsibility for the national welfare and act to meet specific problems in every necessary way. What was most significant was not the proliferation of new agencies or the expansion of federal power. These were continuations of trends already a century old when the New Deal began. The importance of the "Roosevelt revolution" was that it removed the issue from politics. "Never again," the Republican presidential candidate was to say in 1952, "shall we *allow* a depression in the United States."

Because of New Deal decisions, many formerly unregulated areas of American life became subject to federal authority: the stock exchange, agricultural prices and production, labor relations, old-age pensions, relief of the needy. After the New Deal the federal government accepted its obligation to try to provide all the people with a decent standard of living and to pay some attention to achieving the Jeffersonian goal of happiness for all. If the New Deal failed to end the depression, it effected changes that have—so far, at least—prevented later economic declines from becoming catastrophes. By encouraging the growth of unions the New Deal probably helped workers obtain a larger share of the profits of industry. By putting a floor under the income of many farmers it checked the decline of agricultural living standards, though not that of the agricultural population. The social security program, with all its inadequacies, lessened the impact of bad times on an increasingly large proportion of the population and provided immense psychological benefits to all.

The New Deal hastened other major changes in

the United States. One of the most dramatic was the movement of black voters from the Republican to the Democratic party. Blacks supported the New Deal for the same reasons that whites did, but how the New Deal affected blacks in general and racial attitudes specifically are more complicated questions. Claiming that he dared not antagonize southern congressmen, whose votes he needed for his recovery programs, Roosevelt did nothing about civil rights before 1941 and little thereafter. Many of the early New Deal programs treated blacks as second-class citizens. They were often paid at lower rates than whites under NRA codes (and so joked sardonically that NRA stood for "Negroes Ruined Again"). The early farm programs shortchanged black tenants and sharecroppers. Blacks got far fewer appointments in the Civilian Conservation Corps than their numbers warranted, and those who were accepted were assigned to all-black camps. TVA developments were rigidly segregated, and almost no blacks got jobs in TVA offices. New Deal urban housing projects inadvertently but nonetheless effectively increased the concentration of blacks in particular neighborhoods. The Social Security Act, by excluding agricultural laborers and domestic servants, did nothing for hundreds of thousands of poor black workers or for Mexican-American farmhands in the Southwest. In 1939 unemployment was twice as high among blacks as among whites, and whites' wages were double the level of blacks' wages.

The fact that members of racial minorities got less than they deserved did not keep most of them from becoming New Dealers: half a loaf was more than any American government had given them before. Moreover, aside from the direct benefits, blacks profited in other ways. Some New Deal officials—Secretary of the Interior Harold L. Ickes was a shining example—gave important places to black executives. Eleanor Roosevelt, truly the first lady of the land in this respect, as in so many others, worked steadily for the cause. Her influence on the president in these matters was subtle but significant. Her championing of racial justice encouraged some New Deal administrators to hire more blacks in professional posts, not merely as laborers and clerks.

In the labor movement the new CIO unions accepted black members, and this was particularly significant because these unions were organizing industries—steel, automobiles, and mining among others—that employed large numbers of blacks. Thus, while black Americans suffered horribly during the depression, New Deal efforts to counteract its effects brought them some relief and a measure of hope. And this was increasingly true as time passed. During Roosevelt's second term, blacks found far less to criticize than had been the case earlier.

Among other important social changes, the TVA and the New Deal rural electrification program made farm life literally more civilized. Urban public housing, while never undertaken on a massive scale, helped rehabilitate some of the nation's worst slums. Government public power projects, such as the giant Bonneville and Grand Coulee dams in the Pacific Northwest, were only the most spectacular part of a comprehensive New Deal program to develop the natural resources of the country. The NIRA and later labor legislation forced businessmen to reexamine their role in American life and to become more socially conscious. The WPA art and theater programs widened the horizons of millions. All in all, the spirit of the New Deal heightened the people's sense of community, revitalized national energies, and stimulated the imagination and creative instincts of countless citizens.

An important example of this was the Indian policy of the New Deal. Roosevelt's commissioner of Indian affairs, John Collier, admired the community spirit and stress on nonmaterial values of the Indians of the Southwest, and he was determined to help all Indian groups preserve their ancient cultures. In part at his urging Congress passed the Indian Reorganization Act of 1934, which enabled Indians to establish tribal governments with powers like those of cities and encouraged Indians to return individually owned lands to tribal control.

How much of the credit for these achievements belongs personally to Franklin D. Roosevelt is debatable. He had little to do with many of the details and some of the broad principles behind the New Deal. His knowledge of economics was skimpy, his understanding of many social problems superficial, his political philosophy distressingly vague. The British leader Anthony Eden described him as "a conjuror, skillfully juggling with balls of dynamite, whose nature he failed to understand," and the historian David Brody writes shrewdly of Roosevelt's "unreflective acceptance" of the basic structure of American society.

Nevertheless, every aspect of the New Deal bears the brand of his remarkable personality. His political genius constructed the coalition that made the program possible, his humanitarianism made it a reform movement of major significance. Although considered by many a terrible administrator because he encouraged rivalry among his subordinates, assigned different agencies overlapping responsibilities, failed to discharge many incompetents, and frequently put off making difficult decisions, he was in fact one of the most effective chief executives in the nation's history. His seemingly haphazard practice of dividing authority among competing administrators unleashed the energies and sparked the imaginations of his aides, which gave the ponderous federal bureaucracy a remarkable flexibility and *élan*.

Like Wilson, Roosevelt was almost a prime minister, taking charge of the administration forces in Congress, drafting bills, buttonholing legislators, deluging the lawmakers with special messages. Like Jackson, he maximized his role as leader of all the people. His informal, biweekly press conferences proved a matchless means of keeping the public in touch with developments and himself in tune with popular thinking. He made the radio an instrument for communicating with the masses in the most direct way imaginable: his "fireside chats" convinced millions that he was personally interested in each citizen's life and welfare, as in a way he was. At a time when the size and complexity of the government made it impossible for any one person to direct the nation's destiny, Roosevelt managed the minor miracle of personifying that government to 130 million people. "There was a real dialogue between Franklin and the people," Eleanor Roosevelt said after the president's death, and she did not exaggerate. Under Hoover, a single clerk was able to handle the routine mail that flowed into the office of the president from ordinary citizens. Under Roosevelt, the task required a staff of 50.

While the New Deal was still evolving, contemporaries recognized Roosevelt's right to a place beside Washington, Jefferson, and Lincoln among the great presidents. The years have not altered their judgment. Yet as his second term drew toward its close, some of his most important work still lay in the future.

SUPPLEMENTARY READING

Titles marked with an asterisk have been published in paperback

The Great Depression and the New Deal are covered briefly in J. D. Hicks, **Republican Ascendancy*** (1960), and W. E. Leuchtenburg, **Franklin Roosevelt and the New Deal*** (1963). The first three volumes of A. M. Schlesinger, Jr.'s still incomplete **The Age of Roosevelt*** (1957–1960) treat the period to 1936 in vivid fashion. L. V. Chandler, **America's Greatest Depression*** (1970), is also important. Broadus Mitchell, **Depression Decade*** (1947), is a good economic history. O. L. Graham, Jr., **An Encore for Reform*** (1967), compares the New Deal and Progressive ideologies, and R. H. Pells, **Radical Visions and American Dreams*** (1973), is an excellent study of intellectual currents.

For the stock market crash, consult Robert Sobel, **The Great Bull Market: Wall Street in the 1920's*** (1968), which is highly analytical; John Brooks, **Once in Golconda: A True Drama of Wall Street** (1969), a more lively account; and J. K. Galbraith, **The Great Crash*** (1955). The Hoover administration is discussed in A. U. Romasco, **The Poverty of Abundance*** (1965), David Burner, **Herbert Hoover** (1980), J. H. Wilson, **Herbert Hoover: Forgotten Progressive*** (1975), and in Herbert Hoover's **Memoirs: The Great Depression** (1951–1952). Roger Daniels, **The Bonus March: An Episode of the Great Depression** (1971), is fascinating and insightful. Robert Bendiner, **Just Around the Corner*** (1968), is full of interesting details. Irving Bernstein, **The Lean Years*** (1960), contains an excellent account of the early years of the depression but is too critical of Hoover. Abraham Hoffman, **Unwanted Mexican Americans in the Great Depression*** (1974), is useful for the entire decade.

On literature in the 1930s, see Alfred Kazin, **On Native Grounds*** (1942) and **Contemporaries*** (1962), Daniel Hoffman (ed.), **Harvard Guide to Contemporary American Writing** (1979), Townsend Ludington, **John Dos Passos** (1981), and Joseph Blotner, **Faulkner** (1974).

Franklin D. Roosevelt's early career is treated exhaustively in Frank Freidel, **Franklin D. Roosevelt*** (1952–1973), but see also Bernard Bellush, **Franklin D. Roosevelt as Governor of New York** (1955). Of the many biographies of Roosevelt, see especially J. M.

Burns, **Roosevelt: The Lion and the Fox*** (1956). Daniel Fusfeld, **The Economic Thought of Franklin D. Roosevelt and the Origins of the New Deal** (1958), is important. Richard Hofstadter has interesting essays on Hoover and Roosevelt in **The American Political Tradition*** (1948). On Eleanor Roosevelt, see J. P. Lash, **Eleanor and Franklin*** (1971) and **Eleanor: The Years Alone** (1972). J. T. Patterson, **Congressional Conservatism and the New Deal*** (1967), is a solid study of congressional politics. On the Brains Trust, see E. A. Rosen, **Hoover, Roosevelt, and the Brains Trust** (1977).

Useful special studies of the New Deal include J. M. Blum, **From the Diaries of Henry Morgenthau, Jr.** (1959–1964), Gilbert Fite, **George N. Peek and the Fight for Farm Parity** (1954), V. L. Perkins, **Crisis in Agriculture: The AAA and the New Deal** (1969), Donald Wooster, **Dust Bowl** (1979), D. E. Conrad, **The Forgotten Farmers: The Story of Sharecroppers in the New Deal** (1965), S. F. Charles, **Minister of Relief: Harry Hopkins and the Depression** (1963), Bernard Bellush, **The Failure of NRA*** (1975), Roy Lubove, **The Struggle for Social Security** (1968), E. W. Hawley, **The New Deal and the Problem of Monopoly*** (1966), J. D. Matthews, **The Federal Theatre** (1967), M. N. Penkower, **The Federal Writers' Project** (1977), C. H. Trout, **Boston, the Great Depression, and the New Deal** (1977), Barbara Blumberg, **The New Deal and the Unemployed** (1979), Irving Bernstein, **Turbulent Years** (1970), and two books by Sidney Fine, **The Automobile Under the Blue Eagle** (1963) and **Sit Down: The General Motors Strike of 1936–1937** (1969). On constitutional questions, see P. L. Murphy, **The Constitution in Crisis Times*** (1972).

For the activities of the "radical fringe," consult D. R. McCoy, **Angry Voices: Left-of-Center Politics in the New Deal Era** (1958), and D. H. Bennett, **Demagogues in the Depression: American Radicalism and the Union Party** (1969). On Huey Long, see T. H. Williams, **Huey Long: A Biography** (1969). On blacks during the 1930s, see Raymond Wolters, **Negroes and the Great Depression*** (1970), and Harvard Sitkoff, **A New Deal for Blacks*** (1978); on women, W. H. Chafe, **The American Woman*** (1972), and Susan Ware, **Beyond Suffrage: Women in the New Deal** (1981).

Of the many published memoirs and diaries of New Deal figures, the following are outstanding: Raymond Moley, **After Seven Years*** (1939), Frances Perkins, **The Roosevelt I Knew*** (1946), Eleanor Roosevelt, **This I Remember*** (1949), H. L. Ickes, **The Secret Diary of Harold L. Ickes** (1953–1954), Marriner Eccles, **Beckoning Frontiers** (1951), and D. E. Lilienthal, **Journals: The TVA Years: 1939–1945** (1964).

27/ISOLATIONISM AND WAR 1921–1945

Presidents Harding, Coolidge, and Hoover handled foreign relations in much the same way they managed domestic affairs. Harding deferred to senatorial prejudice against executive domination in the area and let his secretary of state, Charles Evans Hughes, make policy. Coolidge adopted a similar course. Hoover understood his diplomatic problems clearly and devised intelligent plans for dealing with them but was perhaps excessively cautious. In directing foreign relations, all three faced the obstacle of a resurgent isolationism. The same forces of war-bred hatred, postwar disillusion, and fear of communist subversion that produced the Red Scare at home led Americans to turn their backs on the rest of the world. The bloodiness and apparent senselessness of the Great War, combined with an awareness that war was the ultimate method of settling international controversies, convinced millions that the only way to be sure it would not happen again was to "steer clear" of "entanglements." That these famous words had been used by Washington and Jefferson in vastly different contexts did not deter the isolationists of the 1920s from attributing to them the same authority they gave to Scripture.

Americans were so suspicious of internationalism that the Harding administration treated the League of Nations with what the historian Richard W. Leopold calls "studied hostility." In 1922 the career diplomat Joseph C. Grew was stationed in Switzerland. One day, while waiting for a friend outside the League of Nations headquarters in Geneva, he ran into a reporter from the Chicago *Tribune.* Poor Grew felt obliged to explain at length why he was standing in so incriminating a place and to plead with the reporter not to publicize his "indiscretion." For a time the State Department refused even to answer letters from the League Secretariat in Geneva.

Peace Without a Sword

The presidents of the twenties were not uninterested in foreign affairs, but they backed away from disabusing the public of its naive belief that foreign affairs did not affect American interests. Too often they allowed domestic questions to control American relations with other countries. Their interest in disarmament flowed chiefly from their desire to cut taxes; tariffs were adjusted to satisfy American manufacturers without regard for how they affected the world political situation.

The first important diplomatic event of the period revealed a great deal about American foreign policy after World War I. In November 1921 delegates representing the United States, Great Britain, Japan, France, Italy, China, and three other nations gathered at Washington to discuss disarmament and the problems of the Far East. By the following February the Washington Armament Conference had drafted three major treaties and a number of lesser agreements.

The Four-Power Treaty, signed by the United States, Great Britain, Japan, and France, committed these nations to respect one another's interests in the islands of the Pacific and to confer in the event that any other country launched an attack in the area. The Five-Power Treaty, in which Italy joined the four, committed the signatories to stop building battleships for 10 years and to reduce their fleets of capital ships to a fixed ratio, with Great Britain and the United States limited to 525,000 tons, Japan to 315,000 tons, and France and Italy to 175,000 tons. All conferees signed the Nine-Power Treaty, agreeing to respect China's independence and to maintain the Open Door. In a separate pact they permitted China to raise its tariffs on imports.

For the first time in history, the major powers accepted limitations on their right to arm themselves. The Open Door, never before more than a pious expression of American hopes, received the formal endorsement of all nations with far eastern interests except Russia. Japan agreed to restrict its ambitions in the Pacific area. By taking the lead in drafting the agreements, the United States regained some of the moral influence it had lost by not joining the League of Nations.

These gains masked grave weaknesses. The treaties were uniformly toothless. The signers of the Four-Power pact agreed only to consult in case of aggression in the Pacific; they made no promises to help one another or to restrict their freedom of action. As President Harding assured the Senate, "There [was] no commitment to armed force, no alliance, no written or moral obligation to join in defense." The naval disarmament treaty said nothing about the number of other warships that the powers might build, about the far more important question of land and air forces, or about the underlying industrial and financial structures that controlled the ability of the nations to make war.* Nor did the signers of the Nine-Power Treaty intend to surrender their special privileges in China.

The United States entered into these agreements without accepting real responsibilities in the Far East. Congress failed to provide enough money to maintain the navy even at the limit set by the Five-Power pact. While stressing the fact that they had won overall naval equality with Great Britain, American diplomats failed to make clear that the 5:5:3 ratio permitted the Japanese to dominate the western Pacific. This ratio left the

*A second disarmament conference, held at London in 1930, attempted to place limits on smaller warships, but no agreement could be reached.

Philippine Islands undefendable and exposed Hawaii to possible attack. In a sense these American bases became hostages of Japan. Yet Congress was so unconcerned about Japanese sensibilities that it refused to grant *any* immigration quota to Japan under the National Origins Act of 1924, even though the formula applied to other nations would have allowed only 100 Japanese a year to enter the country. The Harding administration boasted of having been able to "force" the powers to "recognize" the Open Door principle in China, but it was unprepared to keep the door open if a more determined nation slammed it shut.

The Americans of the twenties wanted peace but would neither surrender their prejudices and dislikes nor build the defenses necessary to make it safe to indulge these passions. "The people have had all the war, all the taxation, and all the military service that they want," President Coolidge announced in 1925. But neither would they contribute significantly to the building of stable institutions and prosperous economic conditions in other parts of the world.

Peace societies flourished, among them the Carnegie Endowment for International Peace, designed "to hasten the abolition of war, the foulest blot upon our civilization," and the Woodrow Wilson Foundation, aimed at helping "the liberal forces of mankind throughout the world . . . who intend to promote peace by the means of justice." In 1923 Edward W. Bok, retired editor of the *Ladies' Home Journal,* offered a prize of $100,000 for the best workable plan for preserving international peace, and he was flooded with suggestions. Franklin D. Roosevelt drafted one while recovering from his attack of infantile paralysis.* Such was the temper of the times that he felt constrained to include in the preamble this statement:

> We seek not to become involved as a nation in the purely regional affairs of groups of other nations, nor to give to the representatives of other peoples the right to compel us to enter upon undertakings calling for a leading up to the use of armed force without our full and free consent, given through our constitutional procedure.

So great was the opposition to international cooperation that the United States refused to accept membership on the World Court, although this tribunal could settle disputes only when the nations involved agreed. Probably a majority of the American people favored joining the Court, but its advocates were never able to bring enough pressure on Senate isolationists to prevent them from blocking ratification of the necessary treaty. Too many peace lovers believed that their goal could be attained simply by pointing out the moral and practical disadvantages of war.

The culmination of this illusory faith in preventing war by criticizing it came with the signing of the Kellogg-Briand Pact in 1928. The treaty was born in the fertile brain of French Foreign Minister Aristide Briand, who was eager to collect allies against possible attack by a resurgent Germany. In 1927 Briand proposed to Secretary of State Frank B. Kellogg that their countries agree never to go to war with each other. Kellogg found the idea as repugnant as any conventional alliance, but American isolationists and pacifists found the suggestion fascinating. They plagued Kellogg with demands that he negotiate such a treaty.

To extricate himself from this situation, Kellogg

■ The Women's International League for Peace and Freedom issued this cartoon broadside as part of their 1920s drive against the arms race.

*Roosevelt did not submit the plan because Eleanor Roosevelt was named one of the judges.

cleverly suggested that the pact be broadened to include *all* nations. Now Briand was angry. Like Kellogg, he saw how meaningless such a treaty would be, especially when Kellogg insisted that it be hedged with a proviso that "every nation is free at all times . . . to defend its territory from attack and it alone is competent to decide when circumstances require war in self-defense." Nevertheless, Briand too found public pressures irresistible. In August 1928, at Paris, diplomats from 15 nations bestowed upon one another an "international kiss," condemning "recourse to war for the solution of international controversies" and renouncing war "as an instrument of national policy." Seldom has so unrealistic a promise been made by so many intelligent people. Yet most Americans considered the Kellogg-Briand Pact a milestone in the history of civilization: the Senate, habitually so suspicious of international commitments, ratified it 85 to 1.

The Good Neighbor Policy

Isolationism did not deter the government from seeking to advance American economic interests abroad. The Open Door concept remained predominant; the State Department worked to obtain opportunities in underdeveloped countries for exporters and investors, hoping both to stimulate the American economy and to bring stability to "backward" nations in the interests of world peace.

While this policy sometimes roused local resentments because of the tendency of the United States to cooperate with conservative forces abroad, it resulted in a further retreat from active interventionism. The pattern is well illustrated by events in Latin America. "Yankeephobia" had long been a chronic condition south of the Rio Grande. The continued presence of marines in Central America fed this ill feeling, as did the failure of the United States to enter the League of Nations (which all but four Latin American nations had joined). Basic, of course, was the immense wealth and power of the "Colossus of the North" and the feeling of Latin Americans that the wielders of this strength had little respect for the needs and values of their southern neighbors. However, the evident desire of the United States to limit its international involvements had a gradually mollifying effect on Latin American opinion.

In dealing with this part of the world, Harding and Coolidge performed neither better nor worse than Wilson. In the face of continued radicalism and instability in Mexico, which caused Americans with interests in land and oil rights to suffer heavy losses, President Coolidge acted with forbearance. His appointment of Dwight W. Morrow, a patient, sympathetic ambassador, resulted in an improvement in Mexican-American relations. The Mexicans were able to complete their social and economic revolution in the twenties without significant interference by the United States.

Under Herbert Hoover the United States began at last to treat Latin American nations as equals. Hoover reversed Wilson's policy of trying to teach them "to elect good men." The Clark Memorandum (1930), written by Undersecretary of State J. Reuben Clark, disassociated the right of intervention in Latin America from the Roosevelt Corollary. The corollary had been an improper extension of the Monroe Doctrine, Clark declared. The right of the United States to intervene depended rather on "the doctrine of self-preservation."

The distinction seemed slight to Latin Americans, but the underlying reasoning was important. Obviously any nation capable of doing so will intervene in the affairs of another when its own existence is at stake. But the long-established "right" of the United States under the Monroe Doctrine to keep *other* nations out of Latin America as a matter of principle did not give it a similarly broad authority to intervene there itself.

Hoover's policies were taken over and advanced by Franklin Roosevelt. At the Montevideo Pan-American Conference (December 1933) his secretary of state, Cordell Hull, voted in the affirmative on a resolution that "no state has the right to intervene in the internal or external affairs of another," a statement scarcely more meaningful than the Kellogg-Briand denunciation of war yet gratifying to sensitive Latin Americans. By 1934 the marines had been withdrawn from Nicaragua, the Dominican Republic, and Haiti. In 1934 the United States renounced the right to intervene in Cuban affairs, thereby abrogating the Platt Amendment to the Cuban constitution.

Beyond doubt the "Good Neighbor Policy" of Hoover and Roosevelt* persuaded many Latin Americans that the United States had no aggressive intentions south of the Rio Grande. Unfortunately, the United States did little to try to improve social and economic conditions in the region, so the underlying envy and resentment of "rich Uncle Sam" did not disappear. While isolationism paid some unearned dividends when applied to a part of the world that posed no threat to the United States, the inherent blindness of the policy meant the loss of opportunities to advance the national interest by *helping* other countries.

The Fascist Challenge

The futility and danger of isolationism were exposed in September 1931 when the Japanese invaded Chinese Manchuria. China had been torn by revolution since 1911. By the twenties the nationalists, led by Chiang Kai-shek, had adopted a policy of driving all "foreign devils" from their country. The Japanese, however, were not satisfied merely to protect rights already held. They overran Manchuria and converted it into a puppet state called Manchukuo. This action violated both the Kellogg-Briand and the Nine-Power pacts.

China appealed to the League of Nations and to the United States for help. Neither would intervene. When League officials asked about the possibility of American cooperation in some kind of police action, President Hoover refused to consider either economic or military reprisals. The United States was not a world policeman, he said. The Nine-Power and Kellogg-Briand treaties were "solely moral instruments."

The League sent a commission to Manchuria to investigate. Henry L. Stimson, Hoover's secretary of state, announced (the Stimson Doctrine) that the United States would never recognize the legality of seizures made in violation of American treaty rights. This served only to irritate the Japanese.

In January 1932 Japan attacked Shanghai, the bloody battle marked by the indiscriminate bombing of residential districts. When the League at last officially condemned their aggressions, the Japanese withdrew from the organization and extended their control of northern China. The lesson of Manchuria was not lost on Adolf Hitler, who became chancellor of Germany on January 30, 1933.

It is easy, in surveying the diplomatic events of 1920–1939, to condemn the western democracies for their unwillingness to stand up for principles, their refusal to resist when Germany, Italy, and Japan embarked on the aggressions that led to World War II and cost the world millions of lives and billions of dollars. The democracies failed, until it was almost too late, to realize that a new ideology, totalitarianism, had arisen in Europe and that unless they resisted it forcefully, it would destroy them. It is also proper to place some of the blame for the troubles of that era on the same powers: they controlled much of the world's resources and were far more interested in holding on to what they had than in righting past wrongs or helping other nations to improve the lives of their citizens.

Nevertheless the totalitarian states were the aggressors. Their system, which involved subordination of the individual to the state and the concentration of political power in the hands of a dictator, was made possible by the industrial revolution, which had produced tightly integrated national economies and the instruments of power and communication needed to control masses of people. The social and economic dislocations that followed World War I created the desperate conditions that led millions of Europeans to adopt totalitarian ideas.

The doctrine first assumed importance in 1922 in Italy, when Benito Mussolini seized power. Over the next few years Mussolini abolished universal suffrage, crushed everyone who dared speak out against him, and established a kind of dictatorial socialism which he called fascism *(fascismo),* the term referring to the Roman *fasces,* a symbol of governmental authority consisting of a bundle of rods bound around an ax. Mussolini blamed all the ills plaguing the Italian people on foreign sources, a convenient way to avoid the responsibilities that should have accompanied power.

Mussolini was an absurd poseur and mounte-

*Hoover coined this term, but it was typical of the relative political effectiveness of the two presidents that Roosevelt got most of the credit.

bank whose power in world affairs remained relatively slight. Western leaders could perhaps be excused for failing to take him seriously. But the German dictator Hitler presented a threat that the democracies ignored at their peril. Besides ruthlessly persecuting innocent Jews, whom he blamed for all Germany's troubles, Hitler established a monolithic police state that crushed every form of dissent, every humane value. He announced plainly that he intended to extend his control over all German-speaking peoples. He dismissed the international agreements made by his predecessors with contempt. Germany possessed a potential for war far greater than Italy's, yet to Hitler's cruelest and most flagrantly aggressive actions, the western nations responded only by making concession after concession in the vain hope of "appeasing" him.

In a way the democracies failed to resist totalitarianism because of their very virtues: their faith in humanity, their willingness to see the other side of complicated questions, their horror of war. Any history of the period that treats the leading figures as fools or cowards grossly distorts the truth. Nevertheless, an unbiased account must conclude that western diplomats should have acted more courageously than they did. This statement applies as fully to the Americans as to the Europeans.

■ A German magazine's bitter 1922 comment on the issue of war reparations. American loans (Uncle Sam in the tall hat holds a horn of plenty) intended to restore the German economy go instead, in the form of reparations, to fatten a militaristic Frenchman.

They did not stand together firmly against the aggressors in part because they disagreed among themselves. Particularly divisive was the controversy over war debts—those of Germany to the Allies and those of the Allies to the United States. The United States had lent more than $10 billion to its comrades in arms. Since most of this money had been spent on weapons and other supplies in the United States, it might well have been considered part of America's contribution to the war effort. The public, however, demanded full repayment—with interest. "These were loans, not contributions," Andrew Mellon, the "greatest Secretary of the Treasury since Alexander Hamilton," firmly declared. Even when the Foreign Debt Commission scaled down the interest rate from 5 percent to about 2 percent, the total, to be repaid over a period of 62 years, amounted to more than $22 billion.

Repayment of such a colossal sum was virtually impossible. In the first place, the money had not been put to productive use. Dollars lent to build factories or roads might be expected to earn profits for the borrower, but those devoted to the purchase of shells only destroyed wealth. Furthermore, the American protective tariff reduced the ability of the Allies to earn the dollars needed to pay the debts.

The Allies tried to load their obligations to the United States, along with the other costs of the war, on the backs of the Germans. They demanded reparations amounting to $33 billion. If this sum were collected, they declared, they could rebuild their economies and obtain the international exchange needed to pay their debts to the United States. But as John Maynard Keynes had predicted in his *Economic Consequences of the Peace* (1919), Germany could not pay such huge reparations. When Germany defaulted, so did the Allies.

Everyone was bitterly resentful: the Germans because they felt they were being bled white; the Americans, as Senator Hiram Johnson of California would have it, because the wily Europeans were treating the United States as "an international sucker"; the Allies because (as the French said) *"l'oncle Shylock"* was demanding his pound of flesh with interest. "If nations were only business firms," Clemenceau wrote Calvin Coolidge in 1926, "bank notes would determine the fate of the world. . . . Come see the endless lists of dead in our villages."

Everyone shared the blame: the Germans because they resorted to a runaway inflation that reduced the mark to less than one *trillionth* of its prewar value, at least in part in hopes of avoiding their international obligations; the Americans because they refused to recognize the connection between the tariff and the debt question; the Allies because they made little effort to pay even a reasonable proportion of their obligations.

In 1924 an international agreement, the Dawes Plan, provided Germany with a $200 million loan designed to stabilize its currency. Germany agreed to pay about $250 million a year in reparations. In 1929 the Young Plan further scaled down the reparations bill. In practice, the Allies paid the United States about what they collected from Germany. Since Germany got the money largely from private American loans, the United States would have served itself and the rest of the world far better had it written off the war debts at the start. In any case, in the late 1920s Americans stopped lending money to Germany, the Great Depression struck, Germany defaulted on its reparations payments, and the Allies then gave up all pretense of meeting their obligations to the United States.

In 1931 President Hoover arranged a one-year moratorium on all international obligations. When the period of grace expired, the question of reparations and debts expired with it—the last token payments were made in 1933. All that remained was a heritage of mistrust and hostility. In 1934 Congress passed the Johnson Debt Default Act, banning loans to nations that had not paid their war debts.

Franklin Roosevelt was at heart an internationalist. He believed that for the United States to recover from the depression, the rest of the world must also recover and that world prosperity was the best insurance against fascism and the threat of another world war. However, he was unwilling to buck the isolationist trend or to rely on international cooperation alone to end the depression. In April 1933 he took the United States off the gold standard, hoping that devaluing the dollar would make it easier to sell American goods abroad.

The following month a World Economic Conference met in London. Delegates from 64 nations sought ways to increase world trade, perhaps by a general reduction of tariffs and the stabilization of currencies. After flirting with the idea of currency stabilization, Roosevelt threw a bombshell into the conference by announcing that the United States would not return to the gold standard. Like most world leaders, he now placed revival of his own nation's limping economy ahead of general world recovery. His decision increased international ill feeling, and the conference collapsed amid anti-American recrimination. In every country, narrow-minded nationalists increased their strength. The German financier Hjalmar Schacht announced smugly that Roosevelt was adopting the maxim of the great *Führer,* Adolf Hitler: "Take your economic fate in your own hands."

American Isolationism

Against this background of depression and international tension, vital changes in American foreign policy took place. Unable to persuade the country to take positive action against aggressors, internationalists like Secretary of State Stimson had begun in 1931 to work for a *discretionary* arms embargo law, to be applied by the president in time of war against whichever side had broken the peace. By early 1933 Stimson had obtained Hoover's backing for an embargo bill, as well as the support of president-elect Roosevelt. First the munitions manufacturers and then the isolationists pounced on it, and in the resulting debate it was amended to make the embargo apply impartially to *all* belligerents.

The amendment would have reversed the impact of any embargo. Instead of providing an effective if essentially negative weapon for influencing international affairs, a blanket embargo would intensify America's ostrichlike isolationism. Stimson's original idea would have permitted arms shipments to China but not to Japan, which might have discouraged the Japanese from attacking. As amended, the embargo would have automatically applied to both sides, thus removing the United States as an influence in the conflict. While Roosevelt accepted the change, the internationalists in Congress did not, and when they withdrew their support the measure died.

The attitude of the munitions makers, who opposed both forms of the embargo, led to a series of studies of the industry. The most important was a Senate investigation (1934–1936) headed by Gerald P. Nye of North Dakota. Nye was convinced that "the interests" had conspired to drag America into World War I; his investigation was more an inquisition than an honest effort to discover what American bankers and munitions makers had been doing between 1914 and 1918. The committee's staff, ferreting into subpoenaed records, uncovered sensational facts about the lobbying activities and profits of various concerns. The Du Pont company's earnings, for example, had soared from $5 million in 1914 to $82 million in 1916. When one senator suggested to Irénée Du Pont that he was displaying a somewhat different attitude toward war than most citizens, Du Pont replied coolly: "Yes; perhaps. You were not in the game, or you might have a different viewpoint."

Munitions makers had profited far more from neutrality than from American participation in the war, but Nye, abetted by the press, exaggerated the significance of his findings. Millions of citizens became convinced that the bankers who had lent the Allies money and the "merchants of death" who had sold them arms had tricked the country into war and that the "mistake" of 1917 must never be repeated.

■ **Popular 1930s cartoonist Fitzpatrick did many daily drawings on the theme of the munitions industry. The caption reads: "Fellow diplomats—."**

While the Nye committee labored, Walter Millis published *The Road to War: America, 1914–1917* (1935). In this best seller Millis advanced the thesis that British propaganda, the heavy purchases of American supplies by the Allies, and Wilson's differing reactions to violations of neutral rights by Germany and Great Britain had drawn the United States into a war it could and should have steered clear of. Thousands found Millis' logic convincing. International lawyers, notably Charles Warren, a former assistant attorney general, argued that modern warfare had made the idea of freedom of the seas for neutrals meaningless. The United States could stay out of wars, Warren claimed, only by abandoning the seas, clamping an embargo on arms shipments, closing American ports to belligerent vessels, and placing quotas based on prewar sales on the exportation of all contraband. "Under modern conditions there is no reason why the United States Government should run the risk of becoming involved in a war simply to preserve and protect . . . [the] excessive profits to be made out of war trading by some of its citizens," Warren wrote.

These developments led in 1935 to what the historian Robert A. Divine has called "the triumph of isolation." The danger of another world war mounted steadily as Germany, Italy, and Japan repeatedly resorted to force to achieve their expansionist aims. In March 1935 Hitler instituted universal military training and began to raise an army of half a million. In May Mussolini massed troops in Italian Somaliland, using a trivial border clash as pretext for threatening the ancient kingdom of Ethiopia.

Each aggression drove the United States deeper into its shell. Congress responded by passing the Neutrality Act of 1935, which forbade the sale of munitions to *all* belligerents whenever the president should proclaim that a state of war existed. Americans who took passage on belligerent ships after such a proclamation had been issued would do so at their own risk. Roosevelt would have preferred a discretionary embargo or no new legislation at all, but he dared not rouse the ire of the isolationists by vetoing the bill.

In October 1935 Italy invaded Ethiopia and

■ **University of Chicago undergraduates prepare to march in support of a nationwide antiwar demonstration in April 1937. During the spring of that year American isolationism reached its height.**

Roosevelt invoked the new neutrality law. Secretary of State Hull asked American exporters to support a "moral embargo" on the sale of oil and other products not covered by the act. His plea was ignored; oil shipments to Italy tripled between October and January. Italy quickly overran and annexed Ethiopia. In February 1936 Congress passed a second neutrality act forbidding all loans to belligerents.

Then, in the summer of 1936, civil war broke out in Spain. The rebels, led by the reactionary General Francisco Franco and strongly backed by Italy and Germany, sought to overthrow the somewhat leftist Spanish Republic. Here, clearly, was a clash between democracy and fascism, and the neutrality laws did not apply to civil wars. However, Roosevelt now became more fearful of involvement than some isolationists. (Senator Nye, for example, favored selling arms to the legitimate Spanish government.) The president believed that American interference might cause the conflict in Spain to become a global war, and he was wary of antagonizing the substantial number of American Catholics who were sympathetic to the Franco regime. He warned the Glenn L. Martin aircraft company that selling warplanes to the Spanish Republic "would not be in line with the policy of this government," and at his urging Congress passed another neutrality act broadening the arms embargo to cover civil wars.

Isolationism now reached its peak. A public opinion poll revealed in March 1937 that 94 percent of the people thought American policy should be directed at keeping out of all foreign wars rather than trying to prevent wars from breaking out. In April Congress passed still another neutrality law. It continued the embargo on munitions and loans, *forbade* Americans to travel on belligerent ships, and gave the president discretionary authority to place the sale of other goods to belligerents on a cash-and-carry basis. In theory this would preserve the nation's profitable foreign trade without the risk of war; in fact it played into the hands of the aggressors. While German planes and cannon were turning the tide in Spain, the United States was denying the hard-pressed Spanish loyalists even a case of cartridges.

"With every surrender the prospects of a European war grow darker," Claude G. Bowers, the American ambassador to Spain, warned. The New York *Herald Tribune* pointed out that the neutrality legislation was literally reactionary—designed to keep the United States out of the war of 1914–1918, not the new conflict looming on the horizon. President Roosevelt, in part because of domestic problems such as the Supreme Court packing struggle and the wave of sit-down strikes, and in part because of his own vacillation, seemed to have lost control over the formulation of American foreign policy. The American people, like wild creatures before a forest fire, were rushing in blind panic from the conflagration.

The Road to Pearl Harbor

There were limits beyond which Americans would not go. In July 1937 the Japanese again attacked China. Peiping fell and the invaders pressed ahead on a broad front. Roosevelt believed that invoking the neutrality law would only help the well-armed Japanese. Taking advantage of the fact that neither side had formally declared war, he allowed the shipment of arms and supplies to both sides.

Then the president went further. Speaking at Chicago in October, he condemned the nations—he mentioned none by name—who were "creating a state of international anarchy and instability *from which there is no escape through mere isolation or neutrality.*" He proposed that "peace-loving nations" have nothing to do with the aggressors. The way to deal with "the epidemic of world lawlessness" was to "quarantine" it. Evidently Roosevelt had no specific plan in mind; nevertheless the "quarantine speech" produced a windy burst of isolationist rhetoric that forced him to back down. "It's a terrible thing," he said, "to look over your shoulder when you are trying to lead—and to find no one there."

Roosevelt came only gradually to the conclusion that resisting aggression was more important than keeping out of war; when he did, the need to keep the country united led him at times to be less than candid in his public statements. Hitler's annexation of Austria in March 1938 caused him deep concern. The Nazis' vicious anti-Semitism had caused many of Germany's 500,000 Jewish citizens to seek refuge abroad. Now 190,000 Austrian Jews were under Nazi control. When Roosevelt learned that the Germans were burning synagogues, expelling Jewish children from schools, and otherwise mistreating innocent people, he said that he "could scarcely believe that such things could occur." But public opinion opposed changing the immigration law so that more refugees could be admitted, and the president did nothing.

In September 1938 Hitler demanded that Czechoslovakia cede the German-speaking Sudetenland region to the Reich. British Prime Minister Neville Chamberlain and French Premier Edouard Daladier, in a conference with Hitler at Munich, yielded to Hitler's threats and promises and persuaded the Czechs to surrender the Sudetenland. Roosevelt, though he found this example of appeasement disturbing, did not speak out. Then, when the Nazis seized the rest of Czechoslovakia in March 1939, no one could any longer doubt their aggressive purposes. In a memorable address to Congress, Roosevelt said: "Acts of aggression against sister nations . . . automatically undermine all of us." He called for "methods short of war" to demonstrate America's determination to defend its institutions.

When Hitler threatened Poland in the spring of 1939, demanding the free city of Danzig and the Polish Corridor separating East Prussia from the rest of Germany, and when Mussolini invaded Albania, Roosevelt sent both dictators urgent appeals to keep the peace, but he also urged Congress to repeal the 1937 neutrality act so that the United States could sell arms to Britain and France in the event of war.

Congress refused. "Captain," Vice-President Garner told Roosevelt after counting noses in the Senate, "you haven't got the votes," and the president, perhaps unwisely, accepted this judgment and did not press the issue.

In August 1939 Germany and Russia signed a nonaggression pact, prelude to their joint assault on Poland. On September 1 Hitler's troops invaded Poland, at last provoking Great Britain and France to declare war. Roosevelt immediately summoned Congress into special session and again asked for repeal of the arms embargo. In November, in a vote that followed party lines closely, the Democratic majority pushed through a law permitting the sale of arms and other contraband on a cash-and-carry basis. Short-term loans were authorized, but American vessels were forbidden to carry any products to the belligerents. Since the Allies controlled the seas, cash-and-carry gave them a tremendous advantage.

The German attack on Poland effected a basic

■ **Mussolini and Hitler at one of their periodic joint appearances to present a united Fascist front; in September 1941 they were convinced that nothing could stop them.**

change in American thinking. Keeping out of the war remained an almost universal hope, but preventing a Nazi victory became the ultimate, if not always conscious objective of many citizens. In Roosevelt's case it was perfectly conscious, though he dared not express his feelings candidly because of isolationist strength in Congress and the country. He moved slowly, responding to rather than directing the course of events.

Cash-and-carry did not stop the Nazis. Poland fell in less than a month; then, after a winter lull that cynics called the "phony war," Hitler loosed his armored divisions against the western powers. Between April 9 and June 22 he taught the world the awful meaning of *Blitzkrieg*—lightning war. Denmark, Norway, the Netherlands, Belgium, and France were successively overwhelmed. The British army, pinned against the sea at Dunkirk, saved itself from annihilation only by fleeing across the English Channel. After the French submitted to his harsh terms on June 22, Hitler controlled nearly all of western Europe.

Roosevelt responded to these disasters in a number of ways. In the fall of 1939, reacting to warnings from Albert Einstein and other scientists that the Germans were trying to develop an atomic bomb, he committed federal funds to a top-secret atomic energy program. Even as the British and French were falling back, he sold them, without legal authority, surplus government arms. When Italy entered the war against France while that nation was reeling before Hitler's divisions, the president called the invasion a stab in the back. He froze the American assets of the conquered nations to keep them out of German hands. During the first five months of 1940 he asked Congress to appropriate over $4 billion for national defense. To strengthen national unity he named Henry L. Stimson secretary of war* and another Republican, Frank Knox, secretary of the navy. The United States had abandoned neutrality for nonbelligerency.

After the fall of France, Hitler attempted to bomb and starve the British into submission. The epic air battles over England during the summer of 1940 ended in a decisive defeat for the Nazis, but the Royal Navy, which had only about 100 destroyers, could not control German submarine attacks on shipping. Far more destroyers were needed. In this desperate hour, Prime Minister Winston Churchill, who had replaced Chamberlain in May 1940, asked Roosevelt for 50 old American destroyers to fill the gap.

The navy had 240 destroyers in commission and more than 50 under construction. But direct loan or sale of the vessels would have violated both international and American laws. Any attempt to obtain new legislation would have roused fears that the United States was going down the path that had led it into World War I. Long delay if not outright defeat would have resulted. Roosevelt therefore arranged to "trade" the destroyers for six British naval bases in the Caribbean. In addition, Great Britain leased bases in Bermuda and Newfoundland to the United States.

The destroyers-for-bases deal was one of Roosevelt's masterful achievements as a statesman and as a politician. It helped save Great Britain, and at the same time it circumvented isolationist prejudices, since the president could present it as a shrewd bargain that bolstered America's defenses. A string of island bastions in the Atlantic was more valuable than 50 old destroyers.

Lines were hardening throughout the world. In September 1940, despite last-ditch isolationist resistance, Congress enacted the first peacetime draft in American history. Some 1.2 million draftees were summoned for one year of service, and 800,000 reservists were called to active duty. That same month Japan signed a mutual-assistance pact with Germany and Italy. This Rome-Berlin-Tokyo axis fused the conflicts in Europe and Asia, turning the struggle into a global war.

In the midst of these events the 1940 presidential election took place. Why Roosevelt decided to run for a third term is a much-debated question. Partisanship had something to do with it, for no other Democrat seemed so likely to carry the country. Nor would the president have been human had he not been tempted to hold on to power, especially in such critical times. His conviction that no one else could keep a rein on the isolationists was probably decisive. In any case, he used his authority as party chief to control the Democratic convention and was easily renominated. Vice-President Garner, who had become disenchanted with Roosevelt and the New Deal, did not seek a third term; at Roosevelt's dictation, the party chose Secretary of Agriculture Henry A. Wallace for the second spot on the ticket.

The leading Republican candidates were Senator Robert A. Taft of Ohio, son of the former president, and District Attorney Thomas E. Dewey of New York, who had won fame as a "racket buster" and political reformer. Taft was considered conservative and lacking in political glamour; Dewey, barely 38, seemed too young and inexperienced. Instead the Republicans nominated the darkest of dark horses, Wendell L. Willkie of Indiana, the utility magnate who had led the fight against TVA in 1933.

Despite his political inexperience and Wall Street connections, Willkie made an appealing candidate. He was an energetic, charming, openhearted man capable of inspiring deep loyalties. His roughhewn, rural manner (one Democrat called him "a simple, barefoot Wall Street lawyer") won him wide support in farm districts. Willkie had difficulty, however, finding issues on which to oppose Roosevelt. Good times were at last returning. The New Deal reforms were too popular and too much in line with his own thinking to invite attack. He believed as strongly as the president that America could no longer ignore the Nazi threat.

In the end Willkie focused his campaign on Roosevelt's conduct of foreign relations. A preponderance of the Democrats favored all-out aid to Britain, while most Republicans still wished to avoid foreign "entanglements." But the crisis was causing many persons to shift sides. Among interventionists, organizations like the Committee to Defend America by Aiding the Allies, headed by Republican William Allen White, and the small but influential Century Group contained members

*Stimson had held this post from 1911 to 1913 in the Taft Cabinet!

of both parties. So did the isolationist America First Committee, led by Robert E. Wood of Sears Roebuck.

While rejecting the isolationist position, Willkie charged that Roosevelt intended to make the United States a participant in the war. "If you reelect him," he told one audience, "you may expect war in April 1941," to which Roosevelt retorted, disingenuously since he knew he was not a free agent in the situation, "I have said this before, but I shall say it again and again and again: Your boys are not going to be sent into any foreign wars." In November Roosevelt carried the country handily, though by a smaller majority than in 1932 or 1936. The popular vote was 27 million to 22 million, the electoral count 449 to 82.

The election indicated the direction in which public opinion was moving and encouraged Roosevelt to act more boldly. When Churchill informed him that the cash-and-carry system would no longer suffice because Great Britain was rapidly exhausting its financial resources, he decided at once to provide the British with whatever they needed. Instead of proposing to lend them money, a step certain to rouse memories of the vexatious war debt controversies, he devised the "lend-lease" program, one of his most ingenious and imaginative creations.

First he spoke directly to the people in a "fireside chat" that stressed the evil intentions of the Nazis and the dangers that a German victory would create for America. Aiding Britain should be looked at simply as a form of self-defense. "As planes and ships and guns and shells are produced," he said, American defense experts would decide "how much shall be sent abroad and how much shall remain at home." When the radio talk provoked a favorable public response, Roosevelt went to Congress in January 1941 with a plan calling for the expenditure of $7 billion for war materials that the president could sell, lend, lease, exchange, or transfer to any country whose defense he deemed vital to that of the United States. After two months of debate, Congress gave him what he had asked for.

Although the wording of the Lend-Lease Act obscured its immediate purpose, the saving of Great Britain, the president was frank in explaining his plan. He did not minimize the dangers involved. "If we are to be completely honest with ourselves," he said in his radio speech, "we must admit that there is risk in any course we may take." Yet his mastery of practical politics was never more in evidence. To counter Irish-American prejudices against the English, he pointed out that the Irish Republic would surely fall under Nazi domination if Hitler won the war. He coupled his demand for heavy military expenditures with his enunciation of the idealistic "Four Freedoms"—freedom of speech, freedom of religion, freedom from want, and freedom from fear—for which, he said, the war was being fought.

After the enactment of lend-lease, aid short of war was no longer seriously debated. The American navy began to patrol the North Atlantic, shadowing German submarines and radioing their locations to British warships and planes. In April 1941 United States forces occupied Greenland; in May the president declared a state of unlimited national emergency. After Hitler invaded the Soviet Union in June, Roosevelt moved slowly, for anti-Soviet feeling in the United States was intense.* But it was obviously to the nation's advantage to help any country that was resisting Hitler's armies. In November $1 billion in lend-lease aid was put at the disposal of the Russians.

Meanwhile, Iceland was occupied in July 1941, and the draft law was extended in August—by the margin of a single vote in the House of Representatives. In September the German submarine *U-652* fired a torpedo at the destroyer *Greer* in the North Atlantic. The *Greer*, which had provoked the attack by tracking *U-652* and flashing its position to a British plane, avoided the torpedo and dropped 19 depth charges in an effort to sink the submarine.

Roosevelt (nothing he ever did provided more ammunition for his critics) announced that the *Greer* had been innocently "carrying mail to Iceland." He called the U-boats "the rattlesnakes of the Atlantic" and ordered the navy to "shoot on sight" any German craft in the waters south and west of Iceland and to convoy merchant vessels as far as that island. After the sinking of the de-

*During the 1930s Russia took a far firmer stand against the fascists than any other power, but after joining Hitler in swallowing up Poland, it attacked and defeated Finland during the winter of 1939–1940 and annexed the Baltic states. These acts practically destroyed the small communist movement in the United States.

stroyer *Reuben James* on October 30, Congress voted to allow the arming of American merchantmen and to permit them to carry cargoes to Allied ports.

By December 1941 the United States was in fact at war, but it is hard to see how a formal declaration could have come about or how American soldiers could have been committed to the fray had it not been for Japan. Japanese-American relations had worsened steadily after Japan resumed its war on China in 1937. As they extended their control, the invaders systematically froze out American and other foreign business interests. They declared that the Open Door policy was obsolete. Roosevelt retaliated by lending money to China and asking American manufacturers not to sell airplanes to Japan. In July 1940, with Japanese troops threatening French Indochina, Congress placed exports of aviation gasoline and certain types of scrap iron to Japan under a licensing system; in September all sales of scrap were banned and loans to China increased. After the creation of the Rome-Berlin-Tokyo axis, Roosevelt extended the embargo to include machine tools and other items. The Japanese, determined to create what they euphemistically called a Greater East Asia Co-Prosperity Sphere, pushed ahead relentlessly despite the economic pressures.

Neither the United States nor Japan wanted war. In the spring of 1941 Secretary of State Cordell Hull conferred in Washington with the Japanese ambassador, Kichisaburo Nomura, in an effort to resolve their differences. Hull's approach, while morally irreproachable, showed little appreciation of the political and military situation in the Far East. He demanded that Japan withdraw from China and promise not to attack the Dutch and French colonies in southeast Asia, which were ripe for the plucking after Hitler's victories in Europe. How Hull expected to get Japan to give up its conquests without either making concessions or going to war is not clear. He refused to recognize that the old balance of power that had enabled the United States to attain its modest objectives in the Far East without the use of force had ceased to exist.

Japan might well have accepted limited annexations in the area in return for the removal of American trade restrictions, but Hull seemed bent on converting the Japanese to pacifism by exhortation. He insisted on total withdrawal, to which even the moderates in Japan would not agree. When Hitler invaded the Soviet Union, thereby removing the threat of Russian intervention in the Far East, Japan decided to occupy Indochina even at the risk of war with the United States. Roosevelt retaliated (July 1941) by freezing Japanese assets in the United States and clamping an embargo on oil.

Now the war party in Japan assumed control. Nomura was instructed to tell Hull that his country would refrain from further expansion if the United States and Great Britain would cut off all aid to China and lift the economic blockade. Japan promised to pull out of Indochina once "a just peace" had been established with China. When the United States rejected these demands and repeated (November 26) its insistence that Japan "withdraw all military, naval, air, and police forces" from China and Indochina, the Japanese prepared to assault the Dutch East Indies, British Malaya, and the Philippines. To immobilize the United States Pacific Fleet, they planned a surprise aerial raid on the Hawaiian naval base at Pearl Harbor.

An American cryptanalyst, Colonel William F. Friedman, had "cracked" the Japanese diplomatic code; the government therefore knew that war was imminent. On November 27 Hull warned an American general, "Those fellows mean to fight and you will have to watch out." The code breakers had also made it possible to keep close tabs on the movements of Japanese navy units. But in the hectic rush of events both military and civilian authorities failed to make effective use of the information collected. They expected the blow to fall somewhere in southeast Asia, possibly in the Philippines.

The garrison at Pearl Harbor was alerted against "a surprise aggressive move in any direction." The commanders there, Admiral Husband E. Kimmel and General Walter C. Short, believing an attack impossible, took precautions only against Japanese sabotage. Thus when planes from Japanese aircraft carriers swooped down upon Pearl Harbor on the morning of December 7, they found easy targets. In less than two hours they reduced the Pacific Fleet to a smoking ruin: two battleships destroyed, six others heavily battered, nearly a dozen lesser vessels put out of action. More than 150 planes were wrecked, over 2,300 servicemen killed and 1,100 wounded.

■ **A general view of just part of the havoc wreaked by the Japanese planes at Pearl Harbor. Starting from the bottom of the photo and moving clockwise: the capsized minelayer *Oglala*, the bomb-damaged 10,000-ton cruiser *Helena*, the battleship *Pennsylvania* (whose superstructure shows in back of the *Helena*), the destroyer *Shaw* on fire in drydock (right center), and the battleship *Maryland* burning at far right.**

Never had American arms suffered a more devastating or shameful defeat, and seldom has an event roused so much controversy or produced such intensive historical study. The official blame was placed chiefly on Admiral Kimmel and General Short. They might well have been more alert, but responsibility for the disaster was widespread. Military and civilian officials in Washington had failed to pass on all that they knew to Hawaii or even to one another. On the other hand, the crucial intelligence about the coming attack that the code breakers provided was mixed with masses of other information and was extremely difficult to evaluate. Perhaps, instead of seeking to find a scapegoat, we should admit that the Japanese attack, while dastardly, was both daring and brilliantly executed.

On December 8 Congress declared war on Japan. Formal war with Germany and Italy was still not inevitable—isolationists were far more ready to resist the "yellow peril" in the Orient than to fight in Europe. The Axis powers, however, honored their treaty obligations to Japan and on December 11 declared war on the United States. America was now fully engaged in the great world conflict.

Mobilizing the Home Front

War placed immense strains on the American economy and produced immense results. About 15 million men and women entered the armed services; they, and in part the millions more in Allied uniforms, had to be fed, clothed, housed, and supplied with equipment ranging from typewriters and paper clips to rifles and grenades, tanks and airplanes. Congress granted wide emergency powers to the president. It refrained from excessive meddling in administrative problems and in military strategy. However, while the Democrats retained control of both houses throughout the war, their margins were relatively narrow. A coalition of conservatives in both parties frequently prevented the president from having his way and exercised close control over expenditures.

Roosevelt was an inspiring war leader but not a very good administrator. Any honest account of the war on the home front must reveal glaring examples of confusion, inefficiency, and pointless bickering. The squabbling and waste characteristic of the early New Deal period made relatively little difference—what mattered then was raising the nation's spirits and keeping people occupied; efficiency was less than essential, however desirable. In wartime the nation's fate, perhaps that of the entire free world, depended on delivering weapons and supplies to the battlefronts.

The confusion attending economic mobilization can easily be overstressed. Nearly all Roosevelt's basic decisions were sensible and humane: to pay a large part of the cost of the war by collecting taxes rather than by borrowing and to base taxation on ability to pay; to ration scarce raw materials and consumer goods; to regulate prices and wages. If these decisions were not always translated into action with perfect effectiveness, they always operated in the direction of efficiency and the public good.

Roosevelt's greatest accomplishment was his inspiring of businessmen, workers, and farmers with a sense of national purpose. In this respect his function duplicated his earlier role in fighting the depression, and he performed it with even greater success.

A sense of the tremendous economic expansion caused by the demands of war can most easily be captured by reference to official statistics of production. The gross national product of the United States in 1939 was valued at $91.3 billion. In 1945, after allowing for changes in the price level, it was $166.6 billion. More specifically, manufacturing output nearly doubled and agricultural output rose 22 percent. In 1939 the United States turned out fewer than 6,000 airplanes, in 1944 more than 96,000. Shipyards produced 237,000 tons of vessels in 1939, 10 million tons in 1943. The index of iron and steel production leaped from 87 in 1938 to 258 in 1944, that of rubber goods from 113 to 238 in the same years. Petroleum output rose from 1.2 billion barrels in 1939 to 1.7 billion in 1945, iron ore from 28 million tons in 1938 to 105 million in 1942, copper from 562,000 tons in 1938 to over 1 million in 1942, aluminum from 286 million pounds in 1938 to 1.8 billion in 1943.

Wartime experience proved that the Keynesian economists were correct in saying that government spending would spark economic growth. About 8 million people were unemployed in June 1940. After Pearl Harbor, unemployment declined swiftly and by 1945 the *civilian* work force had increased by nearly 7 million. Millions of women flocked into defense industries, a trend memorialized in the popular song, "Rosie the Riveter."

Mobilization had begun well before December 1941, when 1.6 million men were already under arms. Economic mobilization got under way in August 1939, when the president created a War Resources Board to plan for possible conversion of industry to war production. This board became the Office of Production Management (January 1941) under William S. Knudsen, president of General Motors. In April 1941 Roosevelt set up an Office of Price Administration (OPA), headed by the economist Leon Henderson, in an attempt to check profiteering and control consumer prices, and in August a Supplies Priorities and Allocation Board, directed by Donald M. Nelson, to coordinate the requests of military purchasers for scarce materials with those of industry.

These prewar efforts worked poorly, mainly because the president refused to centralize authority. The separation of the responsibility for dispensing materials from the control of the prices paid for materials practically hamstrung both Nelson's and Henderson's organizations. For months after Pearl Harbor the civilian boards squabbled with the military over everything from the allocation of scarce raw materials to the technical specifications of weapons. Roosevelt refused to settle these conflicts as only he could have.

Yet by early 1943 the nation's economic machinery had been converted to a wartime footing and was functioning smoothly. Supreme Court Justice James F. Byrnes, a former senator from South Carolina, resigned from the Court to become a sort of "economic czar." His Office of War Mobilization had complete control over the issuance of priorities and over prices. Rents, food prices, and wages were strictly regulated, and items in short supply were rationed to consumers. While wages and prices had soared during 1942, after April 1943 they leveled off. Thereafter the cost of living scarcely changed until controls were lifted after the war (see graph, page 789).

Expanded industrial production together with conscription caused a labor shortage that increased the bargaining power of workers. At the same time, the national emergency required some limitation on the workers' right to take advantage of this power. In March 1941 Roosevelt appointed a National Defense Mediation Board to assist labor and management in avoiding work stoppages. After Pearl Harbor he created a National War Labor Board to arbitrate disputes and "stabilize"

■ **Women welders at work on an aircraft carrier, photographed in 1943 by Margaret Bourke-White of *Life*.**

wage rates, and he banned all changes in wages without NWLB approval. In the "Little Steel" case (July 1942), NWLB laid down the rule that wage increases should not normally exceed 15 percent of the rates of January 1941, a figure roughly in line with the increase in the cost of living since that date.

Prosperity and stiffer government controls added significantly to the strength of organized labor; indeed, the war had more to do with institutionalizing industrywide collective bargaining than the New Deal period. As workers recognized the benefits of union membership, they flocked into the organizations. Strikes declined sharply at first: 23 million hours of labor had been lost in 1941 because of strikes; only 4.18 million were lost in 1942.

Some crippling work stoppages did occur. In May 1943 the government seized the coal mines after John L. Lewis' United Mine Workers walked out of the pits. This strike led Congress to pass, over Roosevelt's veto, the Smith-Connally War Labor Disputes Act (June 1943), which gave the president the power to take over any war plant threatened by a strike. The act declared strikes against seized plants illegal and imposed stiff penalties on violators. Although strikes continued to occur—the loss in hours of labor zoomed to 38 million in 1945—when Roosevelt asked for a labor draft law, Congress refused to go along.

Wages and prices remained in fair balance. Overtime work fattened paychecks, and a new stress in labor contracts on fringe benefits such as paid vacations, premium pay for night work, and various forms of employer-subsidized health insurance added to the prosperity of labor. The war effort had almost no adverse effect on the standard of living of the average citizen, a vivid demonstration of the productivity of the American economy. The manufacture of automobiles ceased and pleasure driving became next to impossible because of gasoline rationing, but most civilian activities went on much as they had before Pearl Harbor. Because of the need to conserve cloth, skirts were shortened, cuffs disappeared from men's trousers, and the vest passed out of style. Plastics replaced metals in toys, containers, and other products. While items such as meat, sugar, and shoes were rationed, they were doled out in amounts adequate for the needs of most persons. Americans had both guns *and* butter; belt-tightening of the type experienced by the other belligerents was unheard of.

The federal government spent twice as much money between 1941 and 1945 as in its entire previous history. This made heavy borrowing necessary. The national debt, which stood at less than $49 billion in 1941, increased by more than that amount *each year* between 1942 and 1945 and totaled nearly $260 billion when the war ended. However, Roosevelt insisted that as much of the cost of the war as possible be paid for at the time: over 40 percent of the total was met by taxation, a far larger proportion than in any earlier war.

This policy helped to check inflation by siphoning off money that would otherwise have competed for scarce consumer goods. Heavy excise taxes on amusements and luxuries further discouraged spending, as did the government's war bond campaigns, which persuaded patriotic citizens to lend part of their income to Uncle Sam. The tax program also helped to maintain public morale. High taxes on incomes (up to 94 percent) and on excess profits (95 percent), together with a limit of $25,000 a year after taxes on salaries, convinced the people that no one was profiting inordinately from the war effort.

The income tax, which had never before touched the mass of white-collar and industrial workers, was extended downward until nearly everyone had to pay it. To collect efficiently the relatively small sums paid by most persons, Congress adopted the payroll-deduction system proposed by Beardsley Ruml, chairman of the Federal Reserve Bank of New York. Employers withheld the taxes owed by workers from their paychecks and turned the money over to the government.

The steeply graduated tax rates combined with a general increase in the income of workers and farmers effected a substantial shift in the distribution of wealth in the United States. The poor became richer, while the rich, if not actually poorer, collected a smaller proportion of the national income. The wealthiest 1 percent of the population had received 13.4 percent of the national income in 1935 and 11.5 percent in 1941. In 1944 this group received 6.7 percent.

Enormous social effects stemmed from this shift, but World War II altered the patterns of American life in so many ways that it would be wrong to ascribe the transformations to any single source. Never was the population more fluid. The millions who put on uniforms found themselves transported first to training camps in every section of the country and then to battlefields scattered from Europe and Africa to the far reaches of the Pacific. Burgeoning new defense plants drew other millions to places like Hanford, Washington, and Oak Ridge, Tennessee, where great atomic energy installations were constructed, and to the aircraft factories of California and other states. As in earlier periods the trend was from east to west, from south to north, and from countryside to the cities. The population of California increased by more than 50 percent in the forties, that of other far-western states almost as much.

The war affected blacks in many ways. Several factors operated to improve their lot. One was their growing tendency to demand fair treatment. Another was the reaction of Americans to Hitler's senseless murder of millions of Jews, an outgrowth of his doctrine of "Aryan" superiority. These barbarities compelled million of white citizens to reexamine their views about race. If the nation expected blacks to risk their lives for the common good, how could it continue to treat them as second-class citizens? Black leaders pointed out the inconsistency between fighting for democracy abroad and ignoring it at home. "We want democracy in Alabama," the NAACP announced, and this argument too had some effect on white thinking.

Blacks in the armed forces were treated somewhat better than they had been in World War I. Although segregation did not end, blacks were enlisted for the first time in the air force and the marines, and they were given more responsible positions in the army and navy. The army commissioned its first black general. Some 600 black pilots won their wings. Altogether about a million

■ **A group of interned Japanese in the process of being moved from one detention camp to another in Delta, Washington, in the fall of 1942.**

served, about half of them overseas. The extensive and honorable performance of many of these units could not be ignored by the white majority.

Economic realities operated significantly to the advantage of blacks. More of them had been unemployed in proportion to their numbers than any other group; now the labor shortage brought employment for all. The CIO industrial unions continued to enroll blacks by the thousands.

These gains failed to satisfy black leaders. The NAACP, which increased its membership from 50,000 in 1940 to almost 405,000 in 1946, adopted a more militant stance than in World War I. Discrimination in defense plants seemed far less tolerable than it had in 1917–1918. Even before Pearl Harbor, A. Philip Randolph, president of the Brotherhood of Sleeping Car Porters, organized a march of blacks on Washington to demand equal opportunity for black workers. To prevent this march from taking place at a time of national crisis, President Roosevelt agreed to issue an order prohibiting discrimination in plants with defense contracts, and he set up a Fair Employment Practices Committee to see that the order was carried out. Executive Order 8802 was not perfectly enforced, but it opened up better jobs to black workers and led many employers to change their hiring practices.

Prejudice and mistreatment did not cease. Race riots erupted in many cities; black soldiers were often provided with inferior recreational facilities and otherwise discriminated against in and around army camps. Negro blood plasma was kept separate from white, even though the two "varieties" were indistinguishable and the process of storing plasma had been devised by a black doctor, Charles Drew. Blacks, therefore, became increasingly embittered. Roy Wilkins, head of the NAACP, put it this way in 1942: "No Negro leader with a constituency can face his members today and ask full support for the war in the light of the atmosphere the government has created." Many black newspaper editors were so critical of the administration that conservatives demanded they be indicted for sedition.

Roosevelt would have none of this, but the militants annoyed him; he felt that they should hold their demands in abeyance until the war had been won. Apparently he failed to realize the depth of black anger, and in this he was no different from the majority of whites. A revolution was in the making, yet in 1942 a poll revealed that six out of ten whites still believed that black Americans were "satisfied" with their place in society.

While World War II affected the American people far more drastically than World War I had, it produced much less intolerance and fewer examples of the repression of individual freedom of opinion. The people seemed able to distinguish between the Nazis and Americans of German descent in a way that had escaped their parents. The fact that nearly all German-Americans were vigorously anti-Nazi helps explain this, but the underlying public attitude was more important. Americans went to war in 1941 without illusions and without enthusiasm, determined to win but expecting only to preserve what they had. They therefore found it easier to tolerate dissent, to view the dangers they faced realistically, and to concentrate on the real foreign enemy without venting their feelings on domestic scapegoats. The nation's 100,000 conscientious objectors met with little hostility.

The one flagrant example of intolerance was the relocation of the West Coast Japanese in internment camps in the interior of the country. About 110,000 Americans of Japanese ancestry were rounded up and sent off against their will. The excuse was fear that they might be disloyal, but frustration at not being able to strike a quick blow at Japan had much to do with this unjustified and callous act. The Supreme Court upheld the relocation order in *Korematsu* v. *United States* (1944), but in *Ex parte Endo* it forbade the internment of loyal Japanese-American citizens. Unfortunately the latter decision was not handed down until December 1944.

Other social changes that occurred during the war included a sharp increase in marriage and birth rates, a response both to prosperity and to the natural desire of young men going off to risk death in distant lands to establish roots before departing. The population of the United States had increased by only 3 million during the depression decade of the thirties; during the next five years it rose by 6.5 million. However, large numbers of hasty marriages followed by long periods of separation caused the divorce rate to rise from about 170 per thousand marriages in 1941 to 310 per thousand in 1945.

The War in Europe

Only days after Pearl Harbor, Prime Minister Churchill and his military chiefs were meeting in Washington with Roosevelt and his advisers. In every quarter of the globe, disaster threatened. The Japanese were gobbling up the Far East. Hitler's armies, checked outside Leningrad and Moscow, were preparing for a massive attack in the direction of Stalingrad, on the Volga River. German divisions under General Erwin Rommel were beginning a drive across North Africa toward the Suez Canal. U-boats were taking a heavy toll in the North Atlantic. British and American leaders believed that eventually they could muster enough force to smash their enemies, but whether or not the troops already in action could hold out until this force arrived was an open question.

The decision of the strategists was to concentrate first against the Germans. Japan's conquests were in remote and, from the Allied point of view, relatively unimportant regions. If Russia surrendered, Hitler might well be able to invade Great Britain, thus making his position in Europe impregnable by depriving the United States of a base for a counterattack.

But how to strike at Hitler? American leaders wanted a second front in France, and the harried Russians backed them up. The British, however, believed that this would require more power than the Allies could presently command. They advocated instead air bombardment of German industry combined with peripheral attacks by land forces to harass the enemy while armies and supplies were being massed. The British were probably right. When the invasion of France did come against a greatly weakened Germany in 1944, the difficulties were still enormous. A landing in 1942 would almost certainly have been repulsed.

During the summer of 1942 Allied planes began to bomb German cities. In a crescendo through 1943 and 1944, British and American bombers pulverized the centers of Nazi might. While air attacks did not destroy the German armies' capacity to fight, they hampered war production, tangled communications, and brought the war home to the German people in awesome fashion. Humanitarians deplored the heavy loss of life among the civilian population, but the response of the realists was that Hitler had begun indiscriminate bombing, and Allied survival depended on smashing the German war machine.

In November 1942 an Allied army commanded by General Dwight D. Eisenhower struck at French North Africa. After the fall of France, the Nazis had set up a puppet regime in those parts of

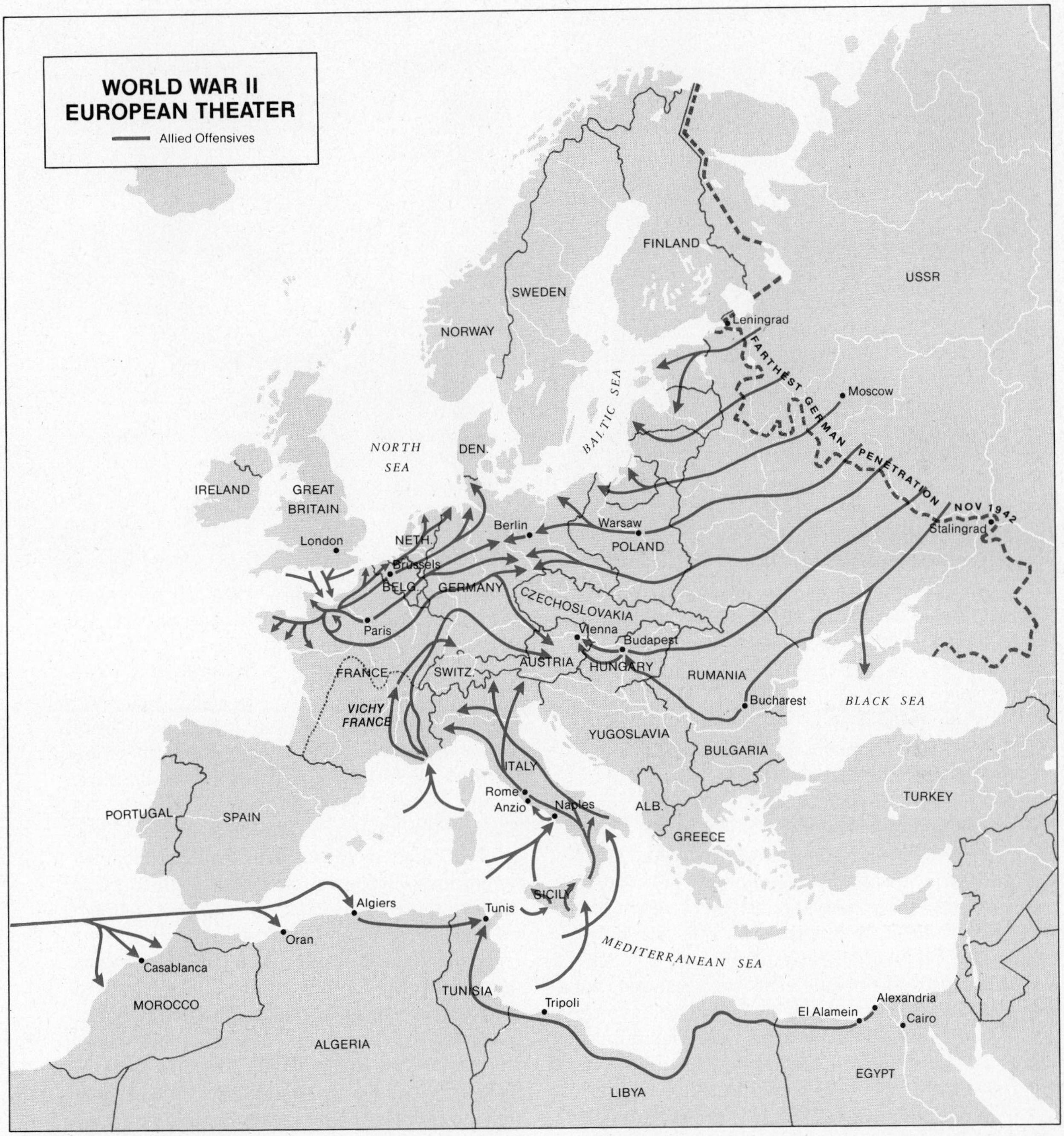

France not occupied by their troops, with headquarters at Vichy in central France. This collaborationist Vichy government controlled French North Africa. But the North African commandant, Admiral Jean Darlan, promptly switched sides when Eisenhower's forces landed. After a brief show of resistance, the French surrendered.

The Allies were willing to do business with Darlan despite his record as a collaborationist. This angered General Charles de Gaulle, who had organized a government-in-exile immediately after the collapse of France and who considered himself the true representative of the French people. Many liberals in the United States agreed

■ **Left, Bill Mauldin's long-suffering Willie and Joe discover their enemies will stop at nothing: "Them rats! Them dirty cold-blooded, sore-headed, stinkin' Huns! Them atrocity-committin' skunks!" Right, GI's counterattack during the Battle of the Bulge, Christmas, 1944.**

with de Gaulle. Darlan was assassinated in December, and eventually the Free French obtained control of North Africa, but the Allied attitude had much to do with de Gaulle's postwar suspicion of both Britain and the United States.

In 1942, however, the arrangement with Darlan paid large dividends. Eisenhower was able to press forward quickly against the Germans. In February 1943 at Kasserine Pass in the desert south of Tunis, American tanks met Rommel's *Afrika Korps.* The battle ended in a standoff, but with British troops closing in from their Egyptian bases to the east, the Germans were soon trapped and crushed. In May, after Rommel had been recalled to Germany, his army surrendered.

In July 1943, while air attacks on Germany continued and the Russians slowly pushed the Germans back from the gates of Stalingrad, the Allies invaded Sicily from Africa. In September they advanced to the Italian mainland. Mussolini had already fallen from power (eight months later he was caught and killed by Italian partisans), and his successor, Marshal Pietro Badoglio, surrendered. However, the German troops in Italy threw up an almost impregnable defense across the rugged Italian peninsula. The Anglo-American army inched forward, paying heavily for every advance. Monte Cassino, halfway between Naples and Rome, did not fall until May 1944, the capital itself until June; months of hard fighting remained before the country was cleared of Germans. The Italian campaign was an Allied disappointment even though it weakened the enemy.

By the time the Allies had taken Rome, the mighty army needed to invade France had been collected in England under Eisenhower's command. On D-Day, June 6, the assault forces stormed ashore at five points along the coast of Normandy, supported by a great armada and thousands of planes and paratroops. Against fierce but ill-coordinated German resistance, they established a beachhead: within a few weeks a million troops were on French soil.

Thereafter victory was assured, though nearly a year of hard fighting still lay ahead. In August the American Third Army under General George S. Patton, an eccentric but brilliant field commander, erupted southward into Brittany and then veered east toward Paris. Another Allied army invaded France from the Mediterranean in mid August and advanced rapidly north. Free French troops were given the honor of liberating Paris on August 25. Belgium was cleared by British and Canadian units a few days later. By mid September the Allies were fighting on the edge of Germany itself.

The front now stretched from the Netherlands along the borders of Belgium, Luxembourg, and France all the way to Switzerland. If the Allies had mounted a massive assault at any one point, as the British commander, Field Marshal Bernard Montgomery, urged, the struggle might have been brought to a quick conclusion. While the two armies were roughly equal in size, the Allies had complete control of the air and twenty times as many tanks as the foe. The pressure of the advancing Russians on the eastern front made it difficult for the Germans to reinforce their troops in the west. But General Eisenhower believed a concentrated attack too risky. His supply and communications problems were fantastically complex, and the defenses of Hitler's Siegfried Line, in some regions three miles deep, presented a formidable obstacle. He prepared instead for a general advance.

While he was regrouping, the Germans on December 16 launched a counterattack, planned by Hitler himself, against the Allied center in the Ardennes Forest. The Germans hoped to break through to the Belgian port of Antwerp, thereby splitting the Allied armies in two. The plan was foolhardy and therefore unexpected, and it almost succeeded. The Germans drove a salient ("the bulge") about 50 miles into Belgium, but once the element of surprise had been overcome, their chance of breaking through to the sea was lost. Eisenhower concentrated first on preventing them from broadening the break in his lines and then on blunting the point of their advance. By late January 1945 the old line had been reestablished. The "Battle of the Bulge" cost the United States 77,000 casualties and delayed Eisenhower's offensive, but it exhausted the Germans' last reserves.

The Allies pressed forward to the Rhine, winning a bridgehead on the far bank of the river on March 7. Thereafter, another German city fell almost daily. With the Russians racing westward against crumbling resistance, the end could not be long delayed. In April American and Russian forces made contact at the Elbe River. A few days later, with Russian shells reducing his capital to rubble, Hitler, by then insane, took his own life in his Berlin air raid shelter. On May 8 Germany surrendered.

The War in the Pacific

Defeating Germany first had not meant abandoning the Pacific region entirely to the Japanese. While armies were being trained and materiel accumulated for the European struggle, much of the available American strength was diverted to maintaining vital communications in the Far East and preventing further Japanese expansion. The navy's aircraft carriers had escaped destruction at Pearl Harbor, a stroke of immense good fortune. Without most tacticians realizing it, the airplane had revolutionized naval warfare. Commanders discovered that carrier-based planes were far more effective against warships than the heaviest naval artillery because of their greater range and more concentrated firepower. Battleships made excellent gun platforms from which to pound shore installations and support land operations, but against other vessels aircraft were of prime importance.

This truth was demonstrated in May 1942 in the Battle of the Coral Sea. Having captured an empire in a few months without the loss of any warship larger than a destroyer, the Japanese believed the war already won. They were suffering from what one of their admirals who knew better called the "victory disease." This led them to overextend themselves.

The Coral Sea lies northeast of Australia and south of New Guinea and the Solomon Islands. Mastery of these waters would cut Australia off from Hawaii and thus from American aid. Admiral Isoroku Yamamoto, believing that he could range freely over the waters west of Pearl Harbor, had dispatched a large fleet of troop ships screened by many warships to attack Port Moresby, on the southern New Guinea coast. On May 7–8 planes from the American carriers *Lexington* and *Yorktown* struck the convoy's screen, sinking a small carrier and damaging a large one. Superficially, the battle seemed a victory for the Japanese, for their planes mortally wounded the *Lexington* and sank two other ships, but the troop transports had been forced to turn back—Port

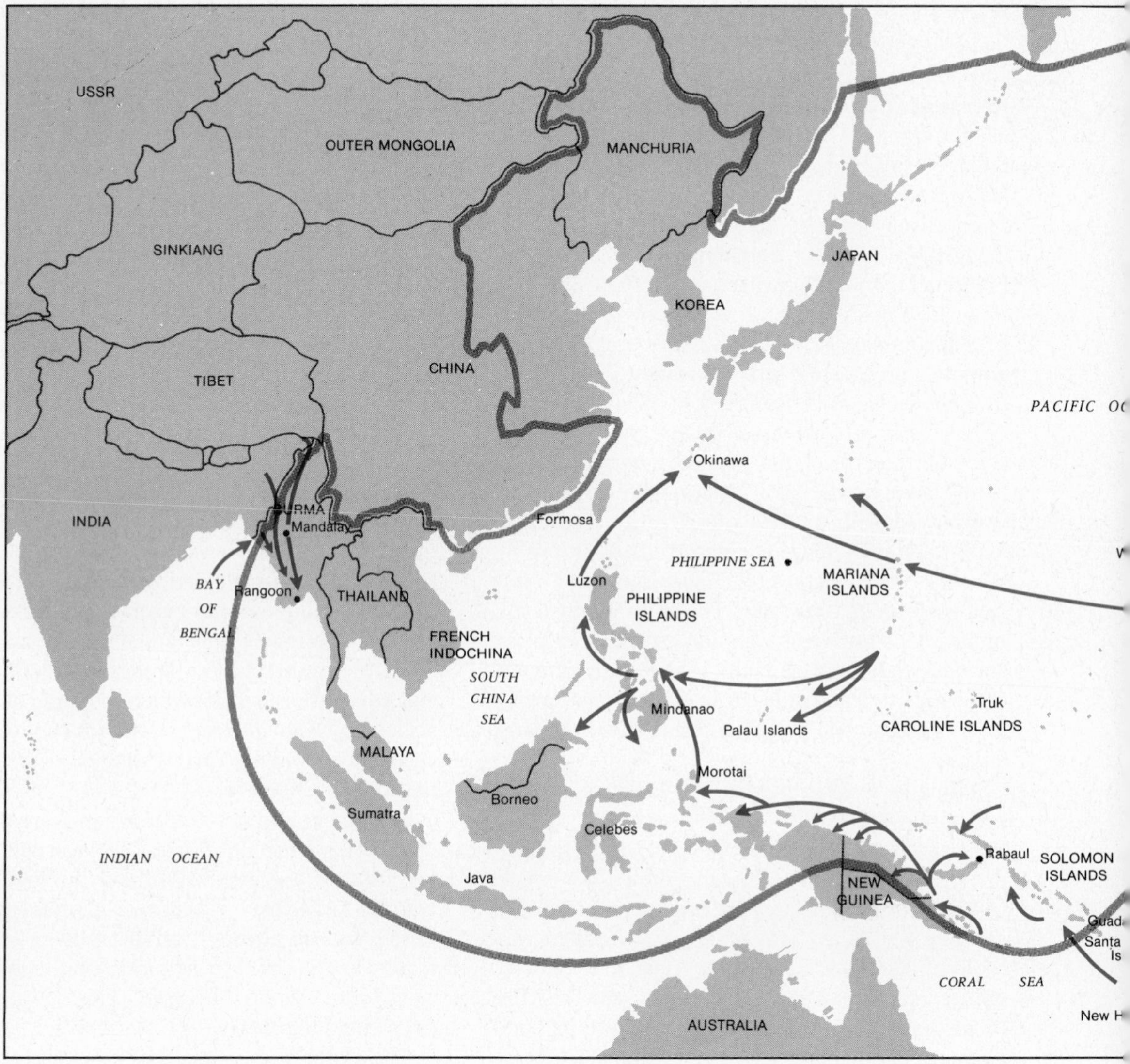

Moresby was saved. Although large numbers of cruisers and destroyers took part in the action, none came within sight or gun range of an enemy ship. All the destruction was wrought by carrier aircraft.

Encouraged by the Coral Sea "victory," Yamamoto decided to force the American fleet into a showdown battle by assaulting Midway Island, west of Hawaii. His armada never reached its destination. Between June 4 and 7 control of the Central Pacific was decided entirely by air power. American dive bombers sent four large carriers to the bottom. About 300 Japanese planes were destroyed. The United States lost only the *Yorktown* and a destroyer. The powerful Japanese battleships played no role in the action, and when deprived of air cover, they had to withdraw ignominiously. Thereafter the initiative in the Pacific war shifted to the Americans.

American successes in the Pacific were in part the result of the breaking of the Japanese codes. But even with advance knowledge of Japanese intentions, victory came slowly and at painful cost. American land forces were under the command of Douglas MacArthur, a brilliant but egocentric general whose judgment was sometimes distorted

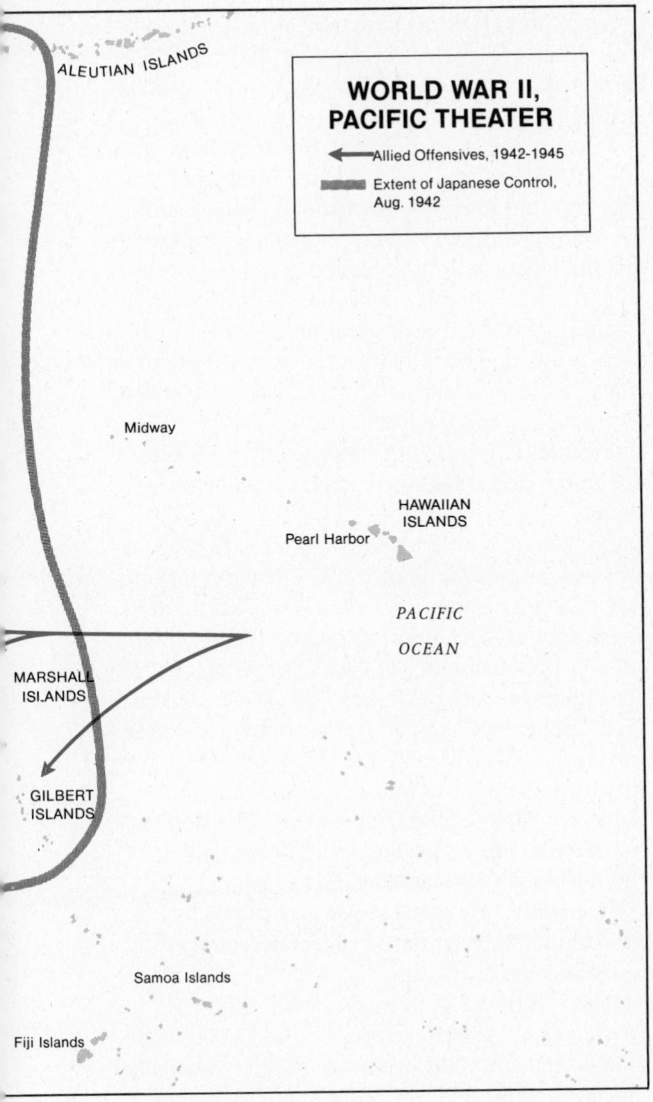

by his intense concern for his own reputation. Son of General Arthur MacArthur, who had played a major role in the original conquest of the Philippines, MacArthur was in command of American troops in the islands when the Japanese struck in December 1941. After his heroic but hopeless defense of Manila and the Bataan peninsula, President Roosevelt had him evacuated by P T boat to escape capture.

Thereafter MacArthur was obsessed with the idea of personally leading an American army back to the Philippines. Although many strategists believed that the islands should be bypassed in the drive on the Japanese homeland, in the end MacArthur convinced the Joint Chiefs of Staff, who determined strategy. Two separate drives were undertaken, one from New Guinea toward the Philippines under MacArthur, the other through the Central Pacific toward Tokyo, under Admiral Chester W. Nimitz.

Before commencing this two-pronged advance, the Americans had to eject the Japanese from the Solomon Islands in order to protect Australia from a flank attack. Beginning in August 1942, a series of land, sea, and air battles raged around Guadalcanal Island in this archipelago. Once again American air power was decisive, though the bravery and skill of the ground forces that actually won the island must not be underemphasized. American pilots, better trained and with tougher planes, had a relatively easier task. They inflicted losses five to six times heavier on the enemy than they sustained themselves. Japanese air power disintegrated progressively during the long battle, and this in turn helped the fleet to take a heavy toll of the Japanese navy. By February 1943 Guadalcanal had been secured.

In the autumn of 1943 the American drives toward Japan and the Philippines got under way at last. In the Central Pacific campaign the Guadalcanal action was repeated on a smaller but equally bloody scale from Tarawa in the Gilbert Islands to Kwajalein and Eniwetok in the Marshalls, islets theretofore unknown to history. The Japanese soldiers fought like the Spartans at Thermopylae for every foot of ground. They had to be blasted and burned from tunnels and concrete pillboxes with hand grenades, flamethrowers, and dynamite. They almost never surrendered. But Admiral Nimitz's forces were in every case victorious. By midsummer of 1944 this arm of the American advance had taken Saipan and Guam in the Marianas. Now land-based bombers were within range of Tokyo.

Meanwhile, MacArthur was leapfrogging along the New Guinea coast toward the Philippines. In October 1944 he made good his promise to return to the islands, landing on Leyte, south of Luzon. Two great naval clashes in Philippine waters, the Battle of the Philippine Sea (June 1944) and the Battle for Leyte Gulf (October 1944), completed the destruction of Japan's sea power and reduced its air force to a band of fanatical suicide pilots called *kamikazes,* who tried to crash bomb-laden planes against American warships and airstrips. The *kamikazes* caused much damage but could not turn the tide. In February 1945 MacArthur liberated Manila.

The end was now inevitable. B-29 Superfortress bombers from the Marianas rained high explosives and firebombs on Japan. The islands of Iwo Jima and Okinawa, only a few hundred miles from Tokyo, fell to the Americans in March and June 1945. But such was the courage of the Japanese soldiers that military experts were predicting another year of fighting and a million more American casualties before the main islands could be subdued.

At this point came the most controversial decision of the entire war, perhaps of all history, and it was made by a newcomer on the world scene. In November 1944 Roosevelt had been elected to a fourth term, easily defeating Thomas E. Dewey. Instead of renominating Henry A. Wallace for vice-president, the Democrats had picked Senator Harry S Truman of Missouri. The conservative Democratic politicos had considered Wallace too radical and too unstable; Truman was a reliable party man well liked by professional politicians. Then, in April 1945, Roosevelt died of a cerebral hemorrhage. Thus it was Truman, a man painfully conscious of his inferiority to his great predecessor yet equally aware of the power and responsibility of his office, who had to decide what to do when, in July 1945, American scientists placed in his hands a new and awful weapon, the atomic bomb.

After Roosevelt had responded to Albert Einstein's warning in 1939, government-sponsored atomic research had proceeded rapidly, especially after the establishment of the so-called Manhattan Project in May 1943. The manufacture of the artificial element plutonium at Hanford, Washington, and uranium 235 at Oak Ridge, Tennessee, continued along with the design and construction of a transportable atomic bomb at Los Alamos, New Mexico, under the direction of J. Robert Oppenheimer. Almost $2 billion was spent before a successful bomb was exploded at Alamogordo, in the New Mexican desert, on July 16, 1945.

Should a bomb with the destructive force of 20,000 tons of TNT be employed against Japan? By striking a major city, its dreadful power could be demonstrated convincingly, yet doing so would bring death to tens of thousands of Japanese civilians. Many of the scientists who had made the bomb now somewhat inconsistently argued against its use.

Truman was torn between his awareness that the bomb was "the most terrible thing ever discovered" and his hope that using it " would bring the war to an end." Every experience indicated that the Japanese army intended to fight to the last man, * but the bomb might cause a revolution in Japan, might lead the emperor to intervene, might even persuade the military to give up. Weighing American lives against Japanese, and influenced by a desire to end the Pacific war before the Soviet Union could intervene effectively and thus claim a role in the peacemaking, the president chose to go ahead.

On August 6 the Superfortress *Enola Gay* dropped an atomic bomb on Hiroshima, killing about 78,000 persons (including 20 American prisoners of war) and injuring nearly 100,000 more out of a population of 344,000. Over 96 percent of the buildings in the city were destroyed or damaged. Three days later, while the stunned Japanese still hesitated, a second atomic bomb, the only other one that had so far been assembled, blasted Nagasaki. This second drop was far less defensible morally, but it had the desired result. On August 15 Japan surrendered.

Thus ended the greatest war in history. Its cost was beyond calculation. No accurate count could be made even of the dead; we know only that the total was in the neighborhood of 20 million. As in World War I, American casualties—291,000 battle deaths and 671,000 wounded—were relatively smaller than those of the other major belligerents. About 7.5 million Russians died in battle, 3.5 million Germans, 1.2 million Japanese, and 2.2 million Chinese; Britain and France, despite much smaller populations, suffered losses almost as large as did the United States. And far more than in World War I, American resources, human and material, had made victory possible.

No one could account the war a benefit to mankind, but in the late summer of 1945 the future looked bright. Fascism was dead. Successful wartime diplomatic dealings between Roosevelt,

*In recapturing Guam, for example, the Americans killed 17,238 Japanese and took only 438 prisoners.

■ **Hiroshima. This photo was taken from the Red Cross Hospital about one mile from the spot where the bomb struck.**

Churchill, and Joseph Stalin, the Soviet dictator, encouraged many to hope that the communists were ready to cooperate in rebuilding Europe. In the United States isolationism had disappeared; the message of Wendell Willkie's best-selling *One World,* written after a globe-circling tour made by the 1940 Republican presidential candidate at the behest of President Roosevelt in 1942, appeared to have been absorbed by the majority of the people. Out of the death and destruction had come technological advances that seemed to herald a better world as well as a peaceful one.

Above all, there was the power of the atom. The force that seared Hiroshima and Nagasaki could be harnessed to serve peaceful needs, the scientists promised, with results that might free humanity forever from poverty and toil. Great strides in transportation and communication lay ahead, products of wartime research in electronics, airplane design, and rocketry. The development of penicillin and other antibiotics, which had greatly reduced the death rate among troops, would perhaps banish all infectious disease.

The period of reconstruction would be prolonged, but with all the great powers adhering to the new United Nations charter, drafted at San Francisco in June 1945, international cooperation could be counted on to ease the burdens of the victims of war and help the poor and underdeveloped parts of the world toward economic and political independence. And although in some respects a less powerful organization than the defunct League of Nations, the UN would stand guard over the peace of the world. Such at least was the hope of millions in the victorious summer of 1945.

SUPPLEMENTARY READING

Titles marked with an asterisk have been published in paperback

There are good summaries of diplomatic developments in Selig Adler, **The Uncertain Giant: American Foreign Policy Between the Wars*** (1965), and F. R. Dulles, **America's Rise to World Power*** (1955). J. C. Vinson, **The Parchment Peace** (1955), is the standard account of the Washington Armament Conference. R. H. Ferrell, **Peace in Their Time*** (1952), is excellent on the Kellogg-Briand Pact. Other important works on the diplomacy of the twenties include A. W. Griswold, **The Far Eastern Policy of the United States*** (1938), J. H. Wilson, **American Business and Foreign Policy*** (1971), E. E. Morison, **Turmoil and Tradition: A Study of the Life and Times of Henry L. Stimson*** (1960), and R. N. Current, **Secretary Stimson** (1954). R. H. Ferrell, **American Diplomacy and the Great Depression*** (1957), and Alexander De Conde, **Herbert Hoover's Latin American Policy** (1951), are also useful. Robert Dallek, **Franklin D. Roosevelt and American Foreign Policy*** (1979), is judicious and up-to-date.

On isolationism and the events leading to Pearl Harbor, see R. A. Divine, **The Reluctant Belligerent*** (1965), brief but comprehensive, and **The Illusion of Neutrality*** (1962), Manfred Jonas, **Isolationism in America*** (1966), Dorothy Borg, **The United States and the Far Eastern Crisis** (1964), T. R. Fehrenbach, **F.D.R.'s Undeclared War** (1967), W. S. Cole, **Senator Gerald P. Nye and American Foreign Relations** (1962) and **America First** (1953), W. F. Kimball, **The Most Unsordid Act** (1969), on lend-lease, Herbert Feis, **The Road to Pearl Harbor*** (1962), Roberta Wohlstetter, **Pearl Harbor: Warning and Decision*** (1962), and J. W. Pratt, **Cordell Hull** (1964). C. C. Tansill, **Back Door to War** (1952), C. A. Beard, **American Foreign Policy in the Making** (1946) and **President Roosevelt and the Coming of the War** (1948), are interesting interpretations by isolationists, while L. C. Gardner, **Economic Aspects of New Deal Diplomacy*** (1971), is a critical scholarly analysis. Akira Iriye, **Power and Culture: The Japanese-American War** (1981), contains a good account of Japanese actions and motives.

The home front is discussed in Richard Polenberg, **War and Society*** (1972). Special aspects of the subject are covered in Bruce Catton, **War Lords of Washington** (1948), Eliot Janeway, **The Struggle for Survival** (1951), David Novik et al., **Wartime Production Controls** (1949), David Brody, **Workers in Industrial America*** (1980), Joel Seidman, **American Labor from Defense to Reconversion** (1953), W. W. Wilcox, **The Farmer in the Second World War** (1947), Roland Young, **Congressional Politics in the Second World War** (1956), and J. P. Baxter, **Scientists Against Time*** (1946). Social trends are covered in Jack Goodman (ed.), **While You Were Gone** (1946). On the treatment of conscientious objectors, see P. E. Jacob and M. Q. Sibley, **Conscription of Conscience** (1952); on the relocation of the Japanese, see Roger Daniels, **Concentration Camps USA: Japanese Americans and World War II*** (1971). The effect of the war on blacks is discussed in Ulysses Lee, **The Employment of Negro Troops** (1966), and N. A. Wynn, **The Afro-American and the Second World War** (1976).

A. R. Buchanan, **The United States in World War II*** (1964), provides an excellent overall survey of the military side of the conflict. S. E. Morison, **The Two-Ocean War*** (1963), is exciting reading.

28/THE POSTWAR YEARS 1945–1960

On Christmas Eve 1943 Franklin D. Roosevelt reported to the nation on his first meeting with Soviet Premier Joseph Stalin at Teheran, Iran. "I 'got along fine' with Marshal Stalin," he said, "and I believe that we are going to get along very well with him and the Russian people—very well indeed." A little over a year later, describing to Congress his second meeting with Stalin, at Yalta in the Crimea, the president stressed again the good feeling that existed between the two nations and their leaders. "We argued freely and frankly across the table," he explained. "But at the end, on every point, unanimous agreement was reached. I may say we achieved a unity of thought and a way of getting along together." Privately Roosevelt characterized Stalin as "a very interesting man" whose rough exterior clothed an "old-fashioned elegant European manner." He referred to him almost affectionately as "that old buzzard" and on one occasion called him "Uncle Joe" to his face. At Yalta, Stalin gave Roosevelt a portrait photograph, with a long Cyrillic inscription in his small, tightly written hand.

Two months later Roosevelt was writing to Stalin of his "astonishment," "anxiety," and "bitter resentment" over the Soviet Union's "discouraging lack of application" of the agreements made at Yalta. A few days after dictating these words Roosevelt was dead. Before the end of the month his successor, Harry S Truman, was complaining that "our agreements with the Soviet Union had so far been a one-way street" and telling Foreign Minister Vyacheslav M. Molotov bluntly that Stalin must learn to keep his promises. "I have never been talked to like that in my life," Molotov said. "Carry out your agreements," Truman retorted, "and you won't get talked to like that!" Thus ended the brief period of Russo-American amity born of the struggle against Hitler.

Wartime Diplomacy

During the course of World War II every instrument of mass persuasion in the country was directed at convincing the people that the Russians were fighting America's battle as well as their own. Even before Pearl Harbor, former Ambassador Joseph E. Davies wrote in his best-selling *Mission to Moscow* (1941) that the communist leaders were "a group of able, strong men" with "honest convictions and integrity of purposes" who were "devoted to the cause of peace for both ideological and practical reasons." Communism was based "on the same principle of the 'brotherhood of man' which Jesus preached." Stalin possessed great dignity and charm, combined with much wisdom and strength of character, Davies said. "His brown eye is exceedingly kind and gentle. A child would like to sit in his lap and a dog would sidle up to him." In another book published in 1941 the journalist Walter Duranty described Stalin (who had ruthlessly executed hundreds of his former comrades) as "remarkably long-suffering in his treatment of various oppositions."

During the war Americans with as different points of view as General Douglas MacArthur and Vice-President Henry A. Wallace took strongly pro-Soviet positions, and American newspapers and magazines published many laudatory articles about Russia. *Life* reported that Russians "think like Americans." In 1943 *Time* named Stalin its Man of the Year. The film *Mission to Moscow*, a whitewash of the dreadful Moscow treason trials of the thirties based on Ambassador Davies' book, portrayed Stalin as a wise, grandfatherly type, puffing comfortably on an old pipe. In *One World* (1943) Wendell Willkie wrote glowingly of the Russian people, their "effective society," and their simple, warmhearted leader. When he suggested jokingly to Stalin that if he continued to make progress in improving the education of his people he might educate himself out of a job, the dictator "threw his head back and laughed and laughed," Willkie recorded. "Mr. Willkie, you know I grew up a Georgian peasant. I am unschooled in pretty talk. All I can say is I like you very much."

These views of the character of Joseph Stalin were naive, to say the least, but the identity of interest of the United States and the Soviet Union was very real during the war. Russian military leaders conferred regularly with their British and American counterparts and fulfilled their obligations scrupulously. In October 1943 Foreign Min-

■ **The close wartime cooperation between Roosevelt and Churchill is captured in this 1943 cartoon from a London magazine.**

■ **Oscar Berger made this sketch during the UN conference in San Francisco at a cocktail party given by Soviet Foreign Minister Molotov (right). Others, from the left, are Pearson of Canada, Senator Vandenberg of Michigan, Senator Connally of Texas, Velloso of Brazil, Prime Minister Soong of China, Spaak of Belgium, Representative Bloom of New York, Foreign Minister Masaryk of Czechoslovakia, General Romulo of the Philippines, Prime Minister King of Canada, U.S. Secretary of State Stettinius, and Prince Faisal of Saudi Arabia.**

ister Molotov committed his country to joining in the war against Japan as soon as the Germans were defeated, a promise confirmed the following month by Stalin at his meeting with Churchill and Roosevelt at Teheran.

The Soviets repeatedly expressed a willingness to cooperate with the Allies in dealing with postwar problems. Russia was one of the 26 signers of the Declaration of the United Nations (January 1942), in which the Allies promised to eschew territorial aggrandizement after the war, to respect the right of all peoples to determine their own form of government, to work for freer trade and international economic cooperation, and to force the disarmament of the aggressor nations.*

In May 1943 Russia dissolved the Comintern, its official agency for the promulgation of world revolution. The following October, during a conference in Moscow with Secretary of State Cordell Hull and British Foreign Minister Anthony Eden, Molotov joined in setting up a European Advisory Commission to divide Germany into occupation zones after the war. At the Teheran Conference Stalin willingly discussed plans for a new league of nations. When Roosevelt described the kind of world organization he envisaged, the Russian dictator offered a number of constructive suggestions.

Between August and October 1944, Allied representatives met at Dumbarton Oaks, outside Washington. The chief Russian delegate, Andrei A. Gromyko, opposed limiting the use of the veto by the great powers on the future UN Security Council, but he did not take a deliberately obstructionist position. At the Yalta Conference in February 1945 Stalin joined in the call for a conference to be held in April at San Francisco to draft a charter for the United Nations, incidentally modifying the Soviet position on the veto slightly by agreeing that no power might veto Security Council *discussion* of a controversy in which it had a stake.

While the powers argued at length over the form of that charter at the 50-nation San Francisco Conference, they conducted the debates in an atmosphere of optimism and international amity. Each UN member received a seat in the General Assembly, a body designed for discussion rather than action. The locus of authority in the new organization resided in the Security Council, "the castle of the great powers." This consisted of five permanent members (the United States, the Soviet Union, Great Britain, France, and China) and six others elected for two-year terms.

The Council was charged with responsibility for maintaining world peace. It could apply diplomatic, economic, or military sanctions against any nation threatening that peace, but any great power could block UN action whenever it wished to do

*These were the principles first laid down in the so-called Atlantic Charter, drafted by Roosevelt and Churchill at a dramatic meeting on the U.S.S. *Augusta* off Newfoundland in August 1941.

so. The United States insisted on this veto power as strongly as the Soviet Union did. In effect the charter paid lip service to the Wilsonian ideal of a powerful international police force, but to assure Senate ratification it incorporated the limitations that Henry Cabot Lodge had proposed in his 1919 reservations (see page 615). The big-power veto represented Lodge's reservation to Article X of the League Covenant, which would have relieved the United States from the obligation of enforcing collective security without the approval of Congress.

The UN charter also provided for a Secretariat to handle routine administration, headed by a secretary general who was in addition the chief executive officer of the entire organization; a Trusteeship Council to supervise dependent areas much in the fashion of the mandate system of the League; and an International Court of Justice. An Economic and Social Council was created to supervise such UN agencies as the International Labor Organization, the International Bank for Reconstruction and Development, the International Monetary Fund, the World Health Organization, and the United Nations Educational, Scientific, and Cultural Organization (UNESCO), which was assigned the task of "promoting collaboration among the nations through education, science, and culture."

Developing Conflicts

Long before the war in Europe ended the Allies had clashed over important policy matters. Since later world tensions developed from decisions made at this time, an understanding of the disagreements is essential for evaluating entire decades of history. Unfortunately, complete understanding is not yet possible, which explains why the subject remains controversial.

Much depends on one's view of the Soviet system. If the Soviet government under Stalin was bent on world domination, events of the so-called Cold War fall readily into one pattern of interpretation. If Russia, having bravely and at enormous cost endured an unprovoked assault by the Nazis, was seeking only to protect itself against the possibility of another invasion, these events are best explained differently. Because the United States has opened nearly all its diplomatic records to scholars, we know a great deal about how American foreign policy was formulated and about the mixed motives and mistaken judgments of American leaders. This helps explain why many students have been critical of American policy and the "cold warriors" who made and directed it. The Soviet Union on the other hand has excluded historians from its archives, and consequently we know little about the motivations and inner workings of Soviet policy. Was Russia "committed to overturning the international system and to endless expansion in pursuit of world dominance?" Daniel Yergin asks in *Shattered Peace.* Only access to Soviet records can make possible an answer to this vitally important question.

The Russians resented the British-American delay in opening up a second front. They were fighting for survival against the full power of the German armies; any invasion, even an unsuccessful one, would relieve some of the pressure. Roosevelt and Churchill would not move until they were ready, and the Russians had to accept their decision. At the same time, the Russians never concealed their determination to protect themselves against future attack by extending their western frontier after the war. Stalin warned the Allies repeatedly that he would not tolerate any anti-Soviet government along Russia's western boundary.

Most Allied leaders, including Roosevelt, admitted privately during the war that the Soviet Union would annex territory and possess preponderant power in eastern Europe after the defeat of Germany, but they never said this publicly. They believed that free governments could somehow be created in countries like Poland and Bulgaria that the Soviets would trust enough to leave to their own devices. "The Poles," Winston Churchill said early in 1945, "will have their future in their own hands, with the single limitation that they must honestly follow . . . a policy friendly to Russia. This is surely reasonable."

However reasonable, Churchill's statement was impractical. The Polish question was a terribly difficult one. The war, after all, had been triggered by the German attack on Poland; the British in particular felt a moral obligation to restore that nation to its prewar independence. During the war a Polish government-in-exile was set up in London, and its leaders were determined, especially after the murder of some 5,000 Polish officers in 1943 at Katyn, in Russia, presumably by the Soviet secret police, to make no concessions to So-

■ **Churchill, Roosevelt, and Stalin photographed at the week-long Yalta Conference in February 1945. By April 1945, Roosevelt was dead.**

viet territorial demands. Public opinion in Poland (and indeed in all the states along Russia's western frontier) was strongly anti-Soviet. Yet Russia's legitimate interests (to say nothing of its power in the area) could not be ignored.

Stalin apparently could not understand why his allies were so concerned about the fate of a small country so remote from their strategic spheres. That they professed to be concerned seemed to him an indication that they had some secret, devious purpose. He could see no difference (and "revisionist" American historians agree with him) between the Soviet Union's dominating Poland and maintaining a government there that did not reflect the wishes of a majority of the Polish people, and the United States' dominating many Latin American nations and supporting unpopular regimes within them. Roosevelt, however, was worried about the political effects that Russian control of Poland might have in the United States. Polish-Americans would be furious if the communists took over their homeland.

At the Yalta Conference, Roosevelt and Churchill agreed to Soviet annexation of large sections of eastern Poland. In return they demanded that free elections be held in Poland itself. "I want this election to be . . . beyond question," Roosevelt told Stalin. "It should be like Caesar's wife." In a feeble attempt at a joke he added: "I did not know her but they said she was pure." Stalin agreed, almost certainly without intending to keep his promise. The elections were never held; Poland was run by a pro-Russian puppet regime.

Thus the West "lost" Poland. How it might have "won" the country when it was already occupied by the Red Army has never been explained, but had Roosevelt described the difficulties to the American people more frankly, their reaction might have been less angry. Part of the problem was that Roosevelt believed he could charm Stalin into modifying his demands. "Stalin hates the guts of all your top people," he told Prime Minister Churchill in 1942. "I think I can personally handle Stalin better than either your Foreign Office or my State Department."

President Truman, being at first somewhat unsure of himself in foreign affairs, had no such illusion and perhaps for that reason took a much tougher stand. In July 1945, following the surrender of Germany, he, Stalin, and Churchill met at Potsdam, outside Berlin.* They agreed to try the Nazi leaders as war criminals, made plans for exacting reparations from Germany, and confirmed the division of the country into four zones to be occupied separately by American, Russian, British, and French troops. Berlin, deep in the Soviet zone, had itself been split into four sectors. Stalin rejected all arguments that he loosen his hold on eastern Europe, and Truman (who received news of the successful testing of the atom bomb while at Potsdam) made no concessions. On both sides suspicions were mounting, positions hardening.

At this point the United States stood, as Cassius said of Caesar, "bestride the narrow world like a Colossus." Besides its army, navy, and air force and its immense industrial potential, alone among the nations it possessed the atomic bomb. When Stalin's actions made it clear that he intended to control all eastern Europe and to exert an important influence elsewhere in the world, most Americans first reacted somewhat in the manner of a mastiff being worried by a yapping terrier: their resentment was tempered by amazement. They refused to believe that the Russians could honestly suspect their motives.

The war had caused a fundamental change in international politics. The United States might be the strongest country in the world, but the western European nations, victor and vanquished alike, were reduced to the status of second-class powers. The Soviet Union, on the other hand, had regained the influence it had held under the czars and lost as a result of World War I and the Communist Revolution.

The Postwar Economy

In late 1945 most Americans were probably more concerned with what was happening at home than with foreign developments, and no one was more aware of this than Harry Truman. When Roosevelt died in April 1945 Truman claimed that he felt as though "the moon, the stars, and all the planets" had suddenly fallen upon him. Although he could not have been quite as surprised as he indicated (Roosevelt was known to be in extremely poor health), he was acutely conscious of his own limitations.

Truman was born in Missouri in 1884. After service with a World War I artillery unit, he opened a men's clothing store in Kansas City. The store failed in the postwar depression. Truman then became a minor cog in the political machine of Democratic boss Tom Pendergast. In 1934 he was elected to the United States Senate, where he proved to be a loyal but obscure New Dealer. He first attracted national attention during World War II when his "watchdog" committee on defense spending, working with devotion and efficiency, had saved the government immense sums. This led to his nomination and election as vice-president.

As president, Truman sought to carry on in the Roosevelt tradition. Curiously, he was at the same time humble and cocky, idealistic and cold-bloodedly political. He had an immense fund of information about American history, but like most amateurs he lacked historical judgment and was prone to interpret past events in whatever manner best suited his current convenience. He read books but distrusted ideas, adopted liberal objectives only to pursue them sometimes by rash, even repressive means.

Truman was his own worst enemy. Too often he insulted opponents instead of convincing or conciliating them. Complications tended to confuse him, in which case he either dug in his heels or struck out blindly, usually with unfortunate results. On balance, however, he was a strong and in many ways a successful chief executive. Like Jackson, Wilson, and the two Roosevelts, he effectively epitomized the national will and projected a sense of dedication in his management of national affairs.

Nearly all the postwar leaders accepted the necessity of employing federal authority to stabilize the economy and speed national development. The Great Depression and the successful application of the theories of John Maynard Keynes during the war had convinced Democrats and Republicans alike that it was possible to prevent sharp swings in the business cycle and therefore to do away with serious unemployment. The new orthodoxy was written into law in the Employment

*Clement R. Attlee replaced Churchill during the conference after his Labour party won the British elections.

Act of 1946, which made it government policy "to promote maximum employment, production, and purchasing power" and created a Council of Economic Advisers to assist the president in working out the technical details. In its first report the council described how stabilization could be achieved by "control of the public purse," that is, by monetary and fiscal manipulation: "The agents of government must . . . put a brake at certain points where boom forces develop . . . and support purchasing power when it becomes unduly depressed."

Despite this commitment to Keynesian economics—a commitment shared by all industrial nations—regulating the economy remained a source of political controversy. The rejection of laissez faire did not mean that all citizens would always agree as to what should be done. When World War II ended, nearly everyone wanted to demobilize the armed forces, remove wartime controls, and reduce taxes. Yet everyone also hoped to prevent any sudden economic dislocation, check inflation, and make sure that goods in short supply were fairly distributed.

Neither the politicians nor the public were able to reconcile these conflicting objectives. No group seemed willing to limit its own demands in the general interest. Labor wanted price controls retained but wage controls lifted; industrialists wished to raise prices and to keep the lid on wages. Farmers wanted subsidies but opposed price controls and the extension of social security benefits to agricultural workers.

In this difficult situation President Truman failed to win either the confidence of the people or the support of Congress. He asked for too much and demanded it too vociferously—and this despite his obvious uncertainty as to what should be done. On the one hand he proposed a comprehensive program of new legislation that included a public housing scheme, aid to education, medical insurance, civil rights guarantees, a higher minimum wage, broader social security coverage, additional conservation and public power projects patterned after TVA, increased aid to agriculture, and the retention of anti-inflationary controls. The proposal of so many new ventures at a time when millions hoped to relax now that the war was over was sure to arouse strong resistance. On the other hand he ended rationing and other controls and in November 1945 signed a bill cutting taxes by some $6 billion. He speeded the sale of government war plants and surplus goods to private interests. Whenever opposition to his plans developed, he vacillated between compromise and inflexibility.

Yet the country weathered the reconversion period with remarkable ease. The pent-up demand for homes, automobiles, clothing, washing machines, and countless other products, backed by the war-enforced savings of millions, kept factories operating at capacity. The GI Bill of Rights, passed in 1944, provided demobilized veterans with loans to start new businesses and subsidies to continue their education or acquire new skills. However, the absence of uniform price and wage policies caused resentment and frustration, and late in 1946 all controls except those on rents were abandoned.

A period of rapid inflation followed. Food prices rose more than 25 percent between 1945 and 1947. Labor had already won large wage increases; these contributed to the rise of prices, which led to demands for still higher wages. As David Montgomery has written, "workers' determination to catch up with inflation" clashed with "management's determination to tighten up its control," which had been relaxed during the hectic prosperity of wartime. The result was a wave of strikes—nearly 5,000 in 1946 alone.

Inflation and labor unrest, together with concern about the activities of the Soviet Union, helped the Republicans to win control of Congress in 1946. High on the Republican agenda was the passage of a new labor relations act.

Labor leaders tended to support the Democrats, for they remembered gratefully the Wagner Act and other help given them by the Roosevelt administration during the labor-management struggles of the 1930s. In 1943 the CIO had created a Political Action Committee to mobilize the labor vote. Labor's political importance was highlighted at the democratic National Convention of 1944, when Roosevelt, debating the question of a replacement for Vice-President Henry Wallace, allegedly instructed his lieutenants to "clear it with Sidney," referring to Sidney Hillman of the Amalgamated Clothing Workers, a power in the PAC.

Yet the strikes of 1946 had alienated many citizens because they delayed the satisfaction of the demand for consumer goods. The strikes led Pres-

■ **Cartoonist Jim Berryman of the Washington *Evening Star* drew President Truman in a classic doomed pose as Don Quixote fighting the passage of the Taft-Hartley Labor Act.**

ident Truman, normally sympathetic to organized labor, to seize the coal mines, threaten to draft railroad workers, and ask Congress for other special powers to prevent national tie-ups.

This was the climate when in June 1947 the Republican-controlled Congress passed the Taft-Hartley Act over the veto of President Truman. The measure outlawed the closed shop (a provision written into many labor contracts requiring new workers to join the union before they could be employed) and declared illegal certain "unfair labor practices" such as secondary boycotts and strikes called as a result of disputes between unions over the right to represent workers. It compelled unions to register and file financial reports with the secretary of labor and, most important, it authorized the president to seek court injunctions to prevent strikes that in his opinion endangered the national interest. The injunctions would hold for 80 days—a "cooling off" period during which a presidential fact-finding board could investigate and make recommendations. If the dispute remained unresolved after 80 days, the president was to recommend "appropriate action" to Congress.

The Taft-Hartley Act, which they called a "slave labor law," alarmed labor leaders. They resented in particular a provision that made union officers state under oath that they were not communists, a gratuitously insulting and largely ineffective requirement. The law made the task of unionizing unorganized industries more difficult, but it did not seriously hamper existing unions. While it outlawed the closed shop, it permitted union shop contracts, which forced new workers to join the union *after* accepting employment. And the provision requiring unions to file financial statements, together with other regulations aimed at protecting individual members against union officials, had only salutary effects.

The Containment Policy

Foreign policy issues continued to vex the Truman presidency. American and Russian attitudes stood in sharp confrontation when the control of atomic energy came up for discussion in the UN. Everyone recognized the threat to human survival posed by the atomic bomb. In November 1945 the United States suggested allowing the UN to supervise all nuclear energy production, and the General Assembly promptly created an Atomic Energy Commission to study the question. In June 1946 Commissioner Bernard Baruch offered a plan for the eventual outlawing of atomic weapons. A system would be set up under which UN inspectors could operate without restriction anywhere in the world to make sure that no country was making bombs clandestinely. When, at an unspecified date, the system had been established, the United States would destroy its stockpile of bombs.

Most Americans thought the Baruch plan magnanimous and some considered it positively foolhardy, but the Soviets rejected it. That no timetable for destroying the American bombs had been established, and that the American atomic monopoly would continue until one was, made the Russians suspicious. They stated flatly that they would neither permit UN inspectors in the Soviet Union nor surrender their veto power over Security Council actions dealing with atomic energy. They demanded that the United States destroy its bombs at once. Unwilling to trust the Russians or to surrender what they considered their "winning weapon," the American leaders refused to agree. The resulting stalemate increased international tension.

Postwar cooperation had failed. At the end of 1945, besides dominating most of eastern Europe, the Soviet Union controlled Outer Mongolia, parts of Manchuria, and northern Korea. It had annexed the Kurile Islands, regained the southern half of Sakhalin Island from Japan, and was fomenting trouble in Iran. The United States reacted to Russia's moves first by direct diplomatic appeals and threats and then by strenuous objections in the UN, where American influence was great.

By early 1946 a new policy was emerging. Many minds contributed to its development, but the key ideas were provided by George F. Kennan, a scholarly Foreign Service officer. Kennan had been stationed for five years in Russia and had studied Soviet history carefully. He believed that the Soviet leaders were prisoners of their own ideology. They saw the world as divided into socialist and capitalist camps separated by irreconcilable differences. Nothing the United States might do, however conciliatory, would reduce Soviet hostility, Kennan claimed. Therefore the nation should accept this hostility as a fact of life and either resist Russian aggression firmly wherever it appeared or wait for time to bring about some change in Soviet policy.

Kennan's second alternative seemed both irresponsible and dangerous, whereas "getting tough with Russia" would find wide popular support; according to polls, a substantial majority considered American policy "too soft." At the same time the public was reluctant to maintain a powerful military force and to aid nations threatened by the Soviets. During 1946 the Truman administration gradually adopted a tougher stance.

The decisive shift came early in 1947 as a result of a crisis in Greece. Local Greek communists, waging a guerrilla war against the monarchy, were receiving aid from Russian-dominated Yugoslavia and Bulgaria. Great Britain was assisting the monarchists. For more than a year an inconclusive civil war had wracked the country. However, Britain, its economy shaken by World War II, could not long afford this drain on its resources. In February 1947 the British informed President Truman that they would have to cut off further aid to Greece.

To American policymakers, Russia's "Iron Curtain" (a phrase invented by Winston Churchill) seemed about to ring down on another nation. That the Greek government was reactionary appeared to them less important than that it was threatened by communist forces. On March 12 President Truman went before a joint session of Congress and enunciated what became known as the Truman Doctrine. If Greece or Turkey fell to the communists, he said, all the Middle East might be lost. This in turn might shake the morale of anti-communist elements throughout western Europe. To prevent this "unspeakable tragedy," he asked Congress to appropriate $400 million for military and economic aid for Greece and Turkey. "It must be the policy of the United States to support free peoples who are resisting attempted subjugation by armed minorities or by outside pressures," he said. By exaggerating the consequences of inaction and justifying his request on ideological grounds, Truman obtained his objective. Congress appropriated the funds by margins approaching three to one in both houses.

Once official sanction was given to the communism-versus-democracy approach to foreign relations, foreign policy began to dominate domestic policy and to become more rigid. Compromise became more difficult, even when Soviet attitudes began to change. The communist threat loomed

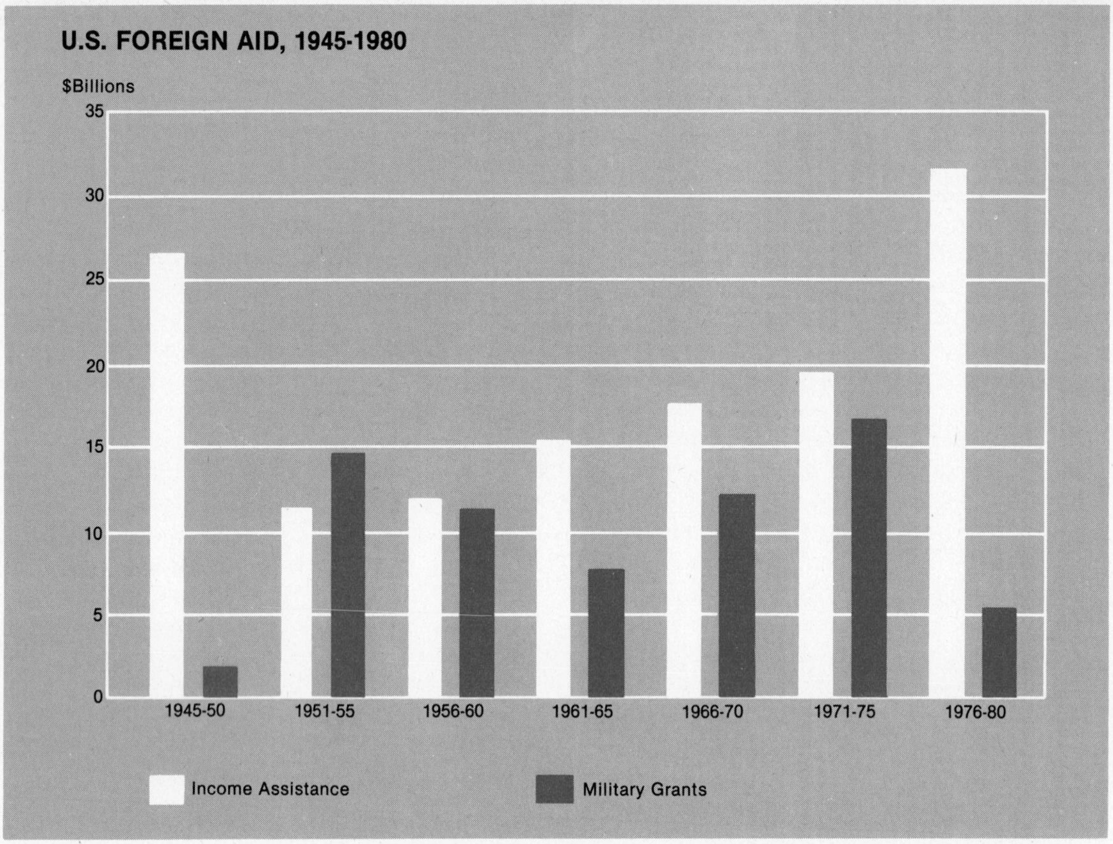

■ **In 1945 the dollar was worth over four times its value in 1980, so in uninflated dollars United States foreign aid has lessened over the years, especially during the decade 1971–1980. Even so, the total amount of U.S. foreign assistance from 1945 to 1980 was more than $200 billion. Data from Department of Commerce, Bureau of Economic Analysis.**

large. In May 1947 the American ambassador in Moscow reported confidentially: "There are no limits to the Soviet objectives. Statements . . . that a great struggle between Communism and capitalism will take place and that one or the other must go down are still being reiterated by Stalin. They have no inhibitions."

Meanwhile western Europe, in the words of Winston Churchill (the great phrasemaker of the era), was "a rubble-heap, a charnel house, a breeding-ground of pestilence and hate." There was a food shortage in France and something approaching a famine in occupied Germany. All of western Europe seemed in danger of falling into communist hands without the Soviet Union raising a finger to speed the process. For humane reasons as well as for political advantage the United States felt obliged to help these nations regain some measure of economic stability.

How might this be done without appearing to be as expansionist as the Russians? George Kennan provided an answer in an anonymous article in the July 1947 issue of *Foreign Affairs,* "The Sources of Soviet Conduct." The article gave public expression to the argument Kennan had advanced in his diplomatic reports. A policy of "long-term, patient but firm and vigilant containment" based on the "application of counter-force" was the best means of dealing with Soviet pressures. The Cold War might be "a duel of infinite duration," Kennan admitted. It could be won if, without bluster, America maintained its own strength and convinced the communists that it would resist aggression firmly in any quarter of the globe.

Although he approved its purpose, Kennan disagreed with the *psychology* of the Truman Doctrine, which seemed to him essentially defensive as well as vulnerable to criticism by anti-imperialists. He proposed a broad program to finance European recovery, the aid to be offered even to Russia if the Soviets would contribute some of their own resources to the cause. The Europeans themselves should work out the details, America providing the money, materials, and technical advice.

George C. Marshall, army chief of staff during World War II and now secretary of state, formally suggested this program, which became known as the Marshall Plan, on June 5, 1947. "Hunger, poverty, desperation, and chaos" were the real enemies of freedom and democracy, Marshall said. The need was to restore "the confidence of the European people in the economic future of their own countries." But it would be "neither fitting nor efficacious" to impose an aid plan on any country. "This is the business of the Europeans. . . . The program should be a joint one, agreed to by a number, if not all European nations."

The Marshall Plan succeeded brilliantly. Led by Great Britain and France, the European powers seized eagerly upon Marshall's suggestion. They set up a 16-nation Committee for European Economic Cooperation, which soon submitted plans calling for up to $22.4 billion in American aid. After protracted debate, much influenced by a communist coup in Czechoslovakia in February 1948, which drew still another country behind the Iron Curtain, Congress appropriated over $13 billion for the program. Results exceeded all expectations. By 1951 western Europe was booming.

Whether the policymakers realized it or not, containment and the Marshall Plan were America's response to the power vacuum created in Europe by the debilitating effects of the war. Just as

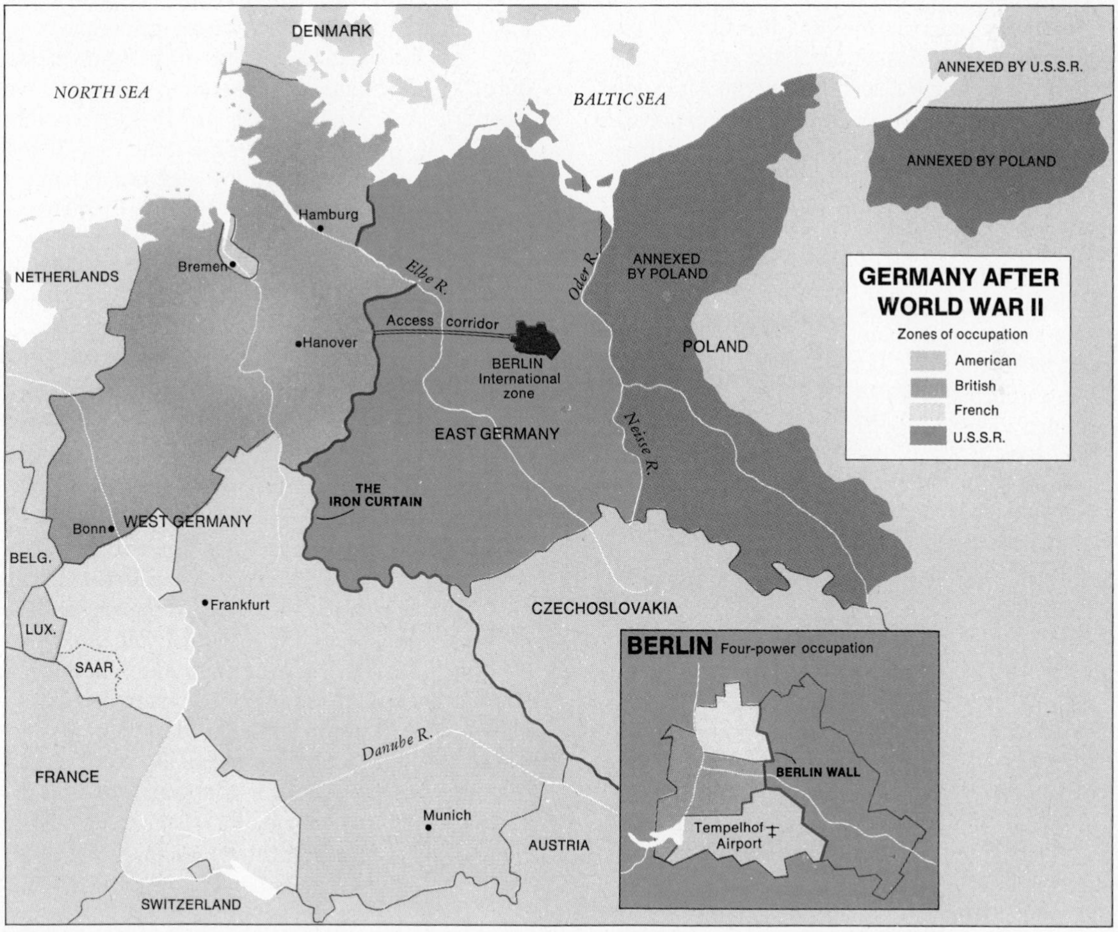

■ **West Germany was created out of the merged French, British, and U.S. zones in 1947, as was West Berlin. The Russian zone became East Germany. The Wall was built later, in 1961, to keep an estimated 700 people a day from fleeing from East to West Germany.**

the Soviet Union extended its influence over the eastern half of the Continent, The United States extended its influence in the west. Yet there was a vital difference: in the east "influence" meant domination; in the west it meant what the dictionaries say it means—"power independent of force or authority."

The Marshall Plan formed the basis for European political cooperation. In March 1948 Great Britain, France, Belgium, the Netherlands, and Luxembourg signed an alliance aimed at social, cultural, and economic collaboration. The western nations abandoned their understandable but counterproductive policy of crushing Germany economically. They instituted currency reforms in their zones and announced plans for creating a single West German Republic with a large degree of autonomy.

These decisions alarmed the Russians. In June they retaliated by closing off Allied surface access to Berlin. For a time it seemed that the Allies must either fight their way into the city or abandon it to the communists. Unwilling to adopt either alternative, Truman decided to fly supplies through the air corridors leading to the capital from Frankfurt, Hanover, and Hamburg. American C-47 and C-54 transports shuttled back and forth in weather fair and foul, carrying enough food, fuel, and other goods necessary to maintain more than 2 million West Berliners. The "Berlin Airlift" put the Soviets in an uncomfortable position; if they were determined to keep supplies from West Berlin, they would have to begin the fighting. They were not prepared to do so. In May 1949 they lifted the blockade.

Containment, some of its advocates argued, required the development of a powerful military force. In May 1948 Republican Senator Arthur H. Vandenberg of Michigan, a prewar leader of the isolationists who had been converted to internationalism largely by President Roosevelt's solicitous attention to his views, introduced a resolution stating the "determination" of the United States "to exercise the right of individual *or collective* self-defense . . . should any armed attack occur affecting its national security." The Senate approved this resolution by a vote of 64 to 4, proof that isolationism had ceased to be an important force in American politics.

Containment worked well in Europe, at least in the short run; in the Far East, where the United States lacked powerful and determined allies, it was both more expensive and less effective. V-J Day found the Far East a shambles. Much of Japan was a smoking ruin. In China social chaos was complicated by a disorganized political situation. The nationalists under Chiang Kai-shek dominated the south, the communists under Mao Tse-tung controlled the northern countryside, and Japanese troops still held most northern cities.

President Truman acted decisively and effectively with regard to Japan, unsurely and with unfortunate results where China was concerned. Even before the Japanese surrendered, he had decided not to allow the Soviet Union any significant role in the occupation of Japan. A four-power Allied Control Council was established, but American troops commanded by General MacArthur governed the country. MacArthur displayed exactly the proper combination of imperiousness, tact, and intelligence needed to accomplish his purposes. The Japanese, revealing the same remarkable adaptability that had made possible their swift westernization in the latter half of the 19th century, accepted political and social changes that involved universal suffrage and parliamentary government, the encouragement of labor unions, the breakup of large estates and big industrial combines, and the deemphasis of the importance of the emperor. Japan lost its far-flung island empire and all claim to Korea and the Chinese mainland. Efforts to restrict economic development were abandoned in order to build up the country as a Far Eastern bastion against communism. Japan emerged economically strong, politically stable, and firmly allied with the United States.

The difficulties in China were probably insurmountable. No one appreciated the latent power of the Chinese communists. When the war ended, the United States tried to install Chiang in control of all China. The Japanese were allowed to hold key north Chinese sectors until Chiang could take them over. At the same time Truman tried to bring Chiang's nationalists and Mao's communists together. He sent General Marshall to China to seek a settlement, but neither Chiang nor Mao would make significant concessions. Mao was convinced—correctly, as time soon proved—that he could win all China by force, while Chiang, presiding over a corrupt and incredibly incompetent regime, grossly exaggerated his popularity among the Chinese people. In January 1947 Truman recalled Marshall and named him secretary of state. Soon thereafter civil war erupted in China.

Election of 1948

In the spring of 1948 President Truman's fortunes were at low ebb. Public opinion polls suggested that a majority of the people considered him incompetent or worse. The Republicans were in control of Congress and had rejected his legislative proposals. They seemed sure to win the 1948 presidential election, especially if Truman was the Democratic candidate. The Republican candidate, Governor Thomas E. Dewey of New York, ran confidently, even complacently, certain that he would carry the country with ease.

Truman's position seemed hopeless because he had alienated both southern conservatives and northern liberals. The southerners were particularly distressed because in 1946 the president had established a Committee on Civil Rights, which had recommended antilynching and anti-poll-tax legislation and the creation of a permanent Fair Employment Practices Commission. They founded the States' Rights ("Dixiecrat") party and nominated J. Strom Thurmond of South Carolina for president.

As for the liberals, in 1947 a group of them had founded Americans for Democratic Action (ADA) and sought an alternative candidate for the 1948 election. A faction led by former vice-president Henry A. Wallace, which believed Truman's containment policy a threat to world peace, favored greater cooperation with the Soviet Union. This group organized a new Progressive party and nominated Wallace. Most members of ADA,

■ **In 1948 the strongly Republican Chicago *Daily Tribune* guessed disastrously wrong in headlining its post-election editions before all the returns were in. For Truman, it was the perfect climax to his hard-won victory.**

however, thought Wallace too pro-Soviet; in the end the organization supported Truman. Yet with two minor candidates sure to cut into the Democratic vote, the president's chances seemed minuscule.

Truman launched an aggressive "whistle-stop" campaign, making hundreds of informal but hard-hitting speeches. He excoriated the "do-nothing" Republican Congress, which had rejected his program and passed the Taft-Hartley Act, and he warned labor, farmers, and consumers that a Republican victory would undermine all the gains of the New Deal years.

Millions were moved by his arguments and by his courageous fight against great odds. The success of the Berlin Airlift during the presidential campaign helped him considerably. The Progressive party fell increasingly into the hands of communist sympathizers, driving away many liberals who might otherwise have supported Wallace. Dewey's smug, lackluster campaign failed to attract independents. The president, therefore, was able to reinvigorate the New Deal coalition, and he won an amazing upset victory on election day. He collected 24.1 million votes to Dewey's 21.9 million, the two minor candidates being held to about 2.3 million. In the electoral college his margin was a thumping 303 to 189.

Truman's victory gave the ADA considerable influence over what the president called his Fair Deal program. ADA leaders took a middle-of-the-road approach, well described in Arthur M. Schlesinger, Jr.'s *The Vital Center* (1949), which left room for both individualism and social welfare, government regulation of the economy and the encouragement of private enterprise. The approach fitted well with Cold War conditions, which favored both massive military output and continued expansion of the supply of civilian goods. Economic growth would solve all problems, social as well as material. Through growth the poor could be helped without taking from the rich. The way to check inflation, for example, was not by freezing prices, profits, or wages but by expanding production. However, relatively little of Truman's Fair Deal was enacted into law. Congress approved a federal housing program and measures increasing the minimum wage and social security benefits, but these were merely extensions of New Deal legislation.

Containing Communism Abroad

During Truman's second term the confrontation between the United States and the Soviet Union, and more broadly between what was seen as "democracy" and "communism," dominated the headlines and occupied a major part of the attention of the president and most other government officials. To strengthen ties with the European democracies, in April 1949 the North Atlantic Treaty was signed in Washington. The United States, Great Britain, France, Italy, Belgium, the Netherlands, Luxembourg, Denmark, Norway, Portugal, Iceland, and Canada* agreed "that an armed attack against one or more of them in Europe or North America shall be considered an attack against them all" that in the event of such an attack each would take "individually and in concert with the other Parties, such action as it deems necessary, including the use of armed force." No more entangling alliance could be imagined, yet the Senate ratified this treaty by a vote of 82 to 13. The pact established the North Atlantic Treaty Organization (NATO). Disturbed by the news, released in September 1949, that the Soviet Union had produced an atomic bomb, Congress appropriated $1.5 billion to arm NATO. In 1951 General Eisenhower was recalled to active duty and placed in command of NATO forces.

The success of containment was not without price; every move evoked a Russian response. The Marshall Plan led to the seizure of Czechoslovakia, the buildup of Germany to the Berlin blockade, the creation of NATO to the multilateral military alliance known as the Warsaw Pact. George Kennan, the "father" of containment, now downplayed the Soviet military threat. He thought the stress on rearming Europe a "regrettable diversion" from the task of economic reconstruction. In any case, both sides contributed by their actions and their continuing suspicions to the heightening of Cold War tensions.

In Asia the effort to contain communism exploded into war. By the end of 1949 Mao Tse-tung's communist armies had administered a crushing defeat to the nationalists. The remnants

*In 1952 Greece and Turkey joined the alliance, and in 1954 West Germany was admitted.

of Chiang Kai-shek's forces fled to the island of Formosa, now called Taiwan. The "loss" of China to communism divided the American people. It strengthened right-wing opponents of internationalism in the Republican party. They and other critics charged that Truman had not backed the nationalists strongly enough and that he had stupidly underestimated Mao's dedication to the cause of world revolution.

Despite a superficial plausibility, neither charge made much sense. Nothing short of massive American military aid, including the commitment of American troops, could have prevented the communist victory. American opinion would not have supported military intervention, and such intervention would unquestionably have alienated the Chinese people, who were fed up with foreign meddling in their affairs. That *any* American action could have changed the outcome in China is unlikely, given the unpopularity of Chiang's repressive government and the ruthless zeal of the communists. The United States probably gave the nationalists to much aid rather than too little.

The attacks of his critics roused Truman's combativeness and led him into serious miscalculations elsewhere in the Orient. After the war the province of Korea was taken from Japan and divided along the 38th parallel, the Russians controlling the northern half of the country, the Americans the southern. The occupying powers agreed to set up a unified and independent Korean republic at some future date, but in the highly charged atmosphere of the postwar years they could not agree on how this should be done. By September 1948 there were two "independent" governments in Korea, the Democratic People's Republic, backed by the Soviet Union, and the Republic of Korea, backed by the United States and the UN. Both powers withdrew their troops from the peninsula, the Russians leaving behind a well-armed local force while the Republic of Korea's army was small and ill trained.

American military strategists had decided that South Korea was not worth defending. In January 1950 Dean Acheson, who had succeeded Marshall as secretary of state, deliberately excluded Korea from the "defensive perimeter" of the United States in the Far East. It was up to the republic, backed by the UN, to protect itself from attack, he said. This the republic was unable to do; when North Korean armored divisions struck suddenly across the 38th parallel in June 1950, they quickly routed the defenders.

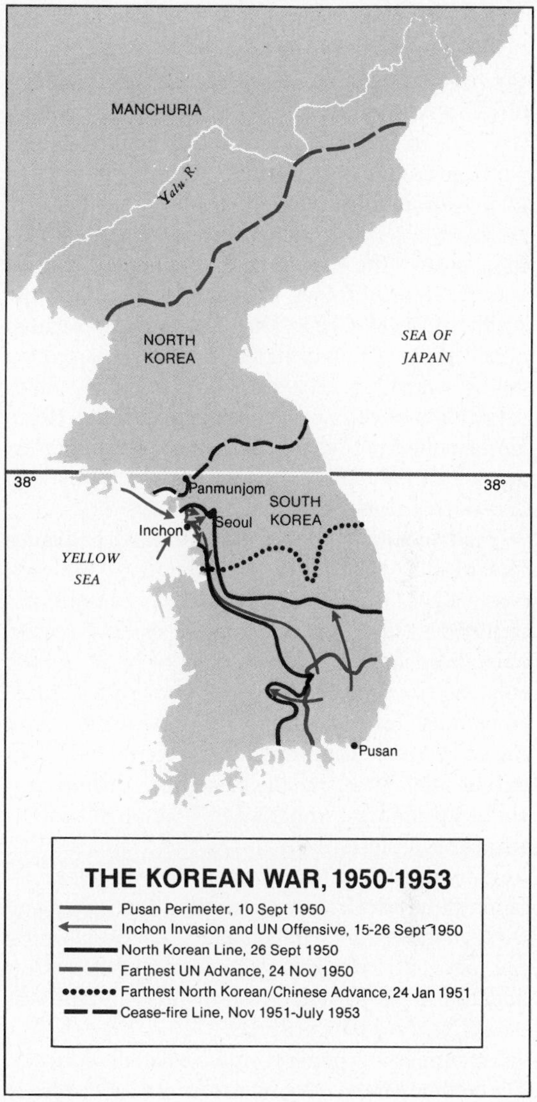

At this point Truman exhibited his finest qualities: decisiveness and courage. Recalling the dire results that had followed when earlier acts of aggression—beginning with the Japanese assault on Manchuria—had been allowed to pass unchecked, he decided to defend South Korea. With the backing of the UN Security Council (but without asking Congress to declare war), he sent American planes into battle.* Ground troops soon followed.

Nominally the Korean War was a struggle between the invaders and the United Nations. General MacArthur, placed in command, flew the blue UN flag over his headquarters, and 16 nations supplied troops for his army. However, more than 90 percent of the forces employed were American. At first the North Koreans pushed them back rapidly, but by the beginning of September a front was stabilized around the port of Pusan, at the southern tip of Korea. Then MacArthur executed a brilliant amphibious flanking maneuver, striking at the west coast city of Inchon, about 50 miles south of the 38th parallel. Outflanked, the North Koreans fled northward, losing thousands of men and much equipment. By October the battlefront had moved *north* of the old boundary.

Truman now permitted MacArthur to advance toward the Yalu River, the boundary between North Korea and China. It was a momentous and unfortunate decision, an example of how power, once unleashed, so often gets out of hand. As the advance progressed, ominous rumblings came from north of the Yalu. Foreign Minister Chou En-lai warned that the Chinese would not "supinely tolerate seeing their neighbors being savagely invaded by imperialists." Chinese "volunteers" began to turn up among the captives taken by UN units. Alarmed, Truman flew to Wake Island, in the Pacific, to confer with MacArthur, but the general assured him that the Chinese would not dare to intervene. If they did, MacArthur added, his army would crush them easily; the war would be over by Christmas.

Seldom has a general miscalculated so badly. On November 26, 33 Chinese divisions suddenly smashed through the center of MacArthur's line. Overnight a triumphant advance became a disorganized retreat. MacArthur now spoke of the "bottomless well of Chinese manpower" and justified his earlier confidence by claiming, not without reason, that he was fighting "an entirely new war."

The UN army rallied south of the 38th parallel and even managed to battle its way back across that line in the eastern sector. By the spring of 1951 the front had been stabilized. MacArthur then urged that he be permitted to bomb Chinese installations north of the Yalu. He also suggested a naval blockade of the coast of China and the use of Chinese nationalist troops in Korea. When Truman rejected these proposals on the ground that they would lead to a third world war, MacArthur, who tended to ignore the larger political aspects of the conflict, attempted to rouse Congress and the public against the president by criticizing administration policy openly. Truman ordered him to be silent, and when the general persisted, he removed him from command.

This unpopular but necessary step (a fundamental principle of democracy, civilian control over the military, was at stake) brought down a storm of abuse on the president. At first the Korean "police action" had been popular in the United States, but as the months passed and the casualties mounted many citizens became disillusioned and angry. The war had brought into the open a basic political (or better, psychological) disadvantage of the containment policy: its object was not victory but balance; it involved apparently unending tension without the satisfying release of an action completed. To Americans accustomed to triumph and fond of oversimplifying complex questions, containment seemed, as its costs in blood and dollars mounted, a monumentally frustrating policy. MacArthur's simple if dangerous strategy offered at least the hope of victory; all the president seemed to offer was a further loss of American lives and money. MacArthur returned home to launch what he called a "crusade" to rally opinion to his cause.

In time the fundamental correctness of both Truman's policy and his decision to remove MacArthur became apparent. As he reminded the country, an all-out war with Communist China, besides costing thousands of lives, would alarm America's allies and weaken the nation while the Soviet Union watched from the sidelines unscathed. Military men backed the president almost unanimously. General Omar N. Bradley, chairman of the Joint Chiefs of Staff, said that a showdown with the Chinese "would involve us in the wrong war, at the wrong place, at the wrong time and with the wrong enemy." In June 1951 the communists agreed to discuss an armistice in Ko-

*Russia, which could have vetoed this action, was at the moment boycotting the Security Council because the UN had refused to give the Mao Tse-tung regime China's seat on that body.

■ **Photographer David Douglas Duncan was with the 1st Marine Division in Korea when it was virtually isolated by the sudden Red Chinese offensive in November 1950. Conducting in frigid weather what the military historian S.L.A. Marshall called "the greatest fighting withdrawal of modern history," the marines broke out to safety.**

rea, and though the negotiations dragged on, with interruptions, for two years while thousands more died along the static battlefront, both MacArthur and talk of bombing China subsided.

The Communist Issue at Home: McCarthyism

The frustrating Korean War highlighted the paradox that at the pinnacle of its power, the influence of the United States in world affairs was declining. Its monopoly of nuclear weapons had been lost. China had passed into the communist orbit. Elsewhere in Asia and throughout Africa, new nations, formerly colonial possessions of the western powers, were adopting a "neutralist" position in the Cold War. Despite the billions poured into armaments and foreign aid, the safety and even the survival of the country seemed far from assured.

Internal as well as external dangers appeared to threaten the nation. Alarming examples of communist espionage in Canada, Great Britain, and in America itself convinced many citizens that clever conspirators were everywhere at work undermining American security. Republican critics of Truman's domestic policies were prominent among those charging that he was "soft" on communists. In 1947, responding to these pressures, Truman established a Loyalty Review Board to check up on government employees. He hoped to defuse the communists-in-government issue by being even more zealous in pursuit of spies than his critics, but the investigators found no significant trace of subversion.

In 1948 Whittaker Chambers, an editor of *Time* who had formerly been a communist, charged that Alger Hiss, president of the Carnegie Endowment for International Peace and a former State Department official, had been a communist in the thirties. Hiss denied the charge and sued Chambers for libel. Chambers then produced microfilms purporting to show that Hiss had copied classified documents for dispatch to Moscow. Hiss could not be indicted for espionage because of the statute of limitations; instead he was charged with perjury. His first trial resulted in a hung jury, his second, ending in January 1950, in conviction and a five-year jail term.

While many people considered Hiss the innocent victim of anticommunist hysteria, the case fed the fears of those who believed in the existence of a powerful communist underground in the United States. The disclosure in February 1950 that a respected British scientist, Klaus Fuchs, had betrayed atomic secrets to the Russians heightened these fears, as did the arrest and conviction of his American associate, Harry Gold, and two other American traitors, Julius and Ethel Rosenberg, on the same charge.

Although they were obviously not major spies and the information they revealed was not very important, the Rosenbergs were executed, to the consternation of many liberals in the United States and elsewhere. However, information gathered by other spies had speeded the Soviet development of nuclear weapons. This fact encouraged some Republicans to press hard the communists-in-government issue.

On February 9, 1950, an obscure senator, Joseph R. McCarthy of Wisconsin, casually introduced this theme in a speech before the Women's Republican Club of Wheeling, West Virginia. "The reason we find ourselves in a position of impotency," he stated, "is not because our only powerful potential enemy has sent men to invade our shores, but rather because of the traitorous actions of those who have been treated so well by this nation." The State Department, he added, was "infested" with communists. "I have here in my hand a list of 205—a list of names that were known to the Secretary of State as being members of the Communist Party and who nevertheless are *still working and shaping . . . policy.*"*

McCarthy had no shred of evidence to back up these statements, and a Senate committee headed by the conservative Democrat Millard Tydings of Maryland soon exposed his mendacity. But thousands of people were too eager to believe him to listen to reason. Within a few weeks he was the most talked-of man in Congress. Inhibited neither by scruples nor by logic, he lashed out in every direction, attacking international experts like Professor Owen Lattimore of Johns Hopkins and professional diplomats such as John S. Service and John Carter Vincent, who had pointed out the deficiencies of the Chiang Kai-shek regime during the Chinese civil war.

When McCarthy's victims indignantly denied his charges, he distracted the public by striking out with still more sensational accusations directed at other innocents. Even General Marshall, a man of the highest character and patriotism, was subject to McCarthy's abuse. The general, he said, was "steeped in falsehood," part of a "conspiracy

■ Senator Joseph McCarthy testifying before the Senate Foreign Relations Committee, March 13, 1951. McCarthy continued his attacks on alleged communists until he was "condemned" by the Senate by a vote of 67–22 in December 1954.

*McCarthy was speaking from rough notes, and no one made an accurate record of his words. The exact number mentioned has long been in dispute. On other occasions he said there were 57 and 81 "card-carrying communists" in the State Department.

so immense and an infamy so black as to dwarf any previous venture in the history of man."

McCarthy was a totally unscrupulous demagogue. The "big lie" was his most effective weapon: the enormity of his charges and the status of his targets convinced thousands that there must be *some* truth to what he was saying. Nevertheless, his crude tactics would have failed if the public had not been so worried about communism. The worries were caused by the reality of Soviet military power, the attack on Korea, the loss of the nuclear monopoly, and the stories about spies. The bitter disappointment of having been plunged again into the tensions of international conflicts so soon after World War II, when they had expected to relax and enjoy life, heightened the concern of many citizens and added an irrational element to their fears. By the fall of 1950 McCarthy had become a major force and the word "McCarthyism" had entered the lexicon of politics.

In the 1950 election campaign McCarthy "invaded" Maryland and contributed mightily to the defeat of Senator Tydings; two years later William Benton of Connecticut, who had introduced a resolution calling for McCarthy's expulsion from the Senate, failed of reelection when McCarthy campaigned against him. Thereafter many congressmen who detested him dared not incur his wrath, and large numbers of Republicans found the temptation to take advantage of his voter appeal irresistible.

The Farm Problem

Another of President Truman's many problems during his second term was what to do with surplus agricultural commodities. While the number of farms in the nation was declining, their output was increasing, mainly because a veritable technological revolution was taking place. Just as the Civil War had speeded the switch from human to animal power in agriculture, World War II speeded the switch from animals to the gasoline engine. Besides using more machines, farmers stepped up their consumption of fertilizers. New chemicals controlled weeds and reduced the ravages of insect pests and plant diseases. Geneticists developed more productive varieties of food plants. Better feeds made for meatier cattle and hogs; new antibiotics checked animal diseases.

Efficiency and expansion did not bring prosperity to most farmers. Conditions roughly resembled those after the Civil War and after World War I; overproduction and declining foreign markets caught agriculturalists in a price squeeze. Their relative share of the national income declined.

No significant group suggested abandoning the New Deal policy of subsidizing agriculture; the controversy concerned how much aid and what kind. The New Deal system of maintaining the price of staple crops like wheat and cotton at or near "parity" with the prices paid by farmers for manufactured goods left much to be desired in practice. First, declining farm income did not mean cheaper food for consumers; prices in groceries and butcher shops kept pace with those of other goods, since the cost of distributing and processing food rose steadily. By boosting food prices still higher, the support program aggravated the problem of the rising cost of living.

Second, acreage controls proved an ineffective way to curtail production. When farmers withdrew land from cultivation, they plowed more fertilizer into their remaining acres and continued to increase output. Potatoes were a glut on the market principally because per-acre yields rose from 155 to 215 bushels in three years. Third, Henry Wallace's "ever-normal granary" concept resulted in the piling up of huge reserves in government elevators and warehouses at great expense to the public. Finally, the system had never helped small farmers or those who raised perishable commodities. It was accelerating the trend toward large-scale agriculture, thus stimulating the movement of people from farm to city.

Despite these flaws, thousands of rural voters had supported Truman in 1948 largely because of his somewhat demagogic argument that a return to Republican rule would mean scrapping the price-support program. His own farm policy was developed by Secretary of Agriculture Charles F. Brannan, a former administrator of New Deal agricultural programs. In 1949 Brannan drafted a new approach to the problem. While continuing to support the prices of storable crops, the government, he suggested, should guarantee fixed minimum incomes to farmers raising perishable crops. The products could then seek their own price levels in the marketplace. Consumers would benefit, but not at the expense of farmers.

This scheme ran into a wall of resistance. Big farmers objected to its upper limit on guaranteed income, and even smaller operators disapproved of extending social security and minimum wage legislation to farm workers, which Brannan also advocated. Conservatives charged that the Brannan plan was both too costly and socialistic, "a controlled economy with a vengeance." Most economists thought the plan overly complicated. After much debate, Congress rejected it—along with most of President Truman's other suggestions.

The Korean War eased the situation for farmers temporarily; after it ended, surplus crops began to pile up alarmingly. Soon the government was storing grain in the holds of idle merchant ships. In June 1952 there was $1.4 billion worth of crops in storage; by June 1956 this figure had risen to $8.3 billion. Yet food prices continued to rise.

Dwight D. Eisenhower

As the 1952 presidential election approached, Truman's popularity was again at a low ebb. Senator McCarthy attacked him relentlessly for his handling of the Korean conflict and his "mistreatment" of General MacArthur. In choosing their candidate, the Republicans passed over the twice-defeated Dewey and their most prominent leader, Senator Robert A. Taft of Ohio, an outspoken conservative, and nominated General Dwight D. Eisenhower.

Eisenhower's popularity did not grow merely out of his achievements in World War II. Although a West Pointer (class of 1915), he struck most persons as anything but warlike. After the bristly, combative Truman, his genial tolerance and evident desire to avoid controversy proved widely appealing. His reluctance to seek political office reminded the country of Washington, while his seeming ignorance of current political issues was no more a handicap to his campaign than the similar ignorance of Jackson and Grant in their times. People "liked Ike" because of his personality—he radiated warmth and sincerity—and because his management of the allied armies promised that he would be equally competent as head of the complex federal government.

The Democrats nominated Governor Adlai E. Stevenson of Illinois, whose grandfather had been vice-president under Cleveland. Stevenson's lucid, witty, urbane speeches captivated intellectuals. His common sense and genuine humility led large numbers of young people to become active in the Democratic party at a time when it was much in need of new blood. In retrospect, however, it is clear that Stevenson had not the remotest chance of defeating the popular Eisenhower. Disillusionment with the Korean War and a widespread belief that the Democrats had been too long in power were added handicaps. His foes turned his strongest assets against him, denouncing his humor as frivolity, characterizing his appreciation of the complexities of life as self-doubt, and tagging his intellectual followers "eggheads," an appellation that effectively caricatured the balding, slope-shouldered, somewhat endomorphic candidate. "The eggheads are for Stevenson," one Republican pointed out, "but how many eggheads are there?" There were far too few to carry the country, as the election revealed.

McCarthy's attacks helped to defeat the Democrats, as did Eisenhower's promise to go to Korea himself if elected to try to bring the long conflict to an end. The result was a Republican landslide: Eisenhower received almost 34 million votes to Stevenson's 27 million, and in the electoral college his margin was 442 to 89.

In office, Eisenhower was the antithesis of Truman. The Republicans had charged the Democratic administration with being wasteful and extravagant. Eisenhower planned to run his administration on sound business principles and to eschew increases in the activities of the federal government. He spoke scornfully of "creeping socialism," called for more local control of government affairs, and promised to reduce federal spending in order to balance the budget and cut taxes. He believed that under Roosevelt and Truman the presidency had lost much of its essential dignity. By battling with congressmen and pressure groups over the details of legislation, his immediate predecessors had sacrificed part of their status as chief representative of the American people. His natural wish to preserve his great popularity reinforced his conviction in this regard. Like Washington, he tried to place himself above narrow partisan conflicts. Like Washington, he was not always able to do so.

■ **Flashing his famous grin, Eisenhower prepares to make his acceptance speech to the delegates at the 1952 Republican National Convention. He was nominated on the first ballot.**

Having successfully managed the complexities of military administration, Eisenhower used the same kind of staff system as president. He appointed Sherman Adams, a former governor of New Hampshire, as his personal assistant, a role similar to that of chief of staff in the army. Adams had a great deal of influence over whom the President saw and what reports he read. Eisenhower also gave his Cabinet officers more responsibility than many modern presidents. He did not like to waste time and energy on administrative routine. This did not mean that he was lazy or politically naive. He knew that if he left too many small decisions to others, they would soon be controlling, if not actually making, the large decisions as well.

Although conservative, Eisenhower was neither a reactionary nor a fool. He hoped to balance the federal budget and lower taxes, but he was unwilling to do away with existing social and economic legislation or to cut back on military expenditures. Some economists claimed that he reacted too slowly in dealing with business recessions and that he showed insufficient concern for speeding the rate of national economic growth. Yet he adopted a Rooseveltian, almost a Keynesian approach to economic problems; that is, he tried to check downturns in the business cycle by stimulating the economy. In his memoir *Mandate for Change* (1963) he wrote of resorting to "preventative action to arrest the downturn [of 1954] before it might become severe" and of being ready to use "any and all weapons in the federal arsenal, including changes in monetary and credit policy, modifications of the tax structure, and a speed-up in the construction of . . . public works" to accomplish this end.

Eisenhower approved the extension of social security to an additional 10 million persons, created a new Department of Health, Education, and Welfare, and in 1955 came out for federal support of school and highway construction. But his somewhat doctrinaire belief in decentralization and private enterprise reduced the effectiveness of his social welfare measures. When Dr. Jonas Salk's polio vaccine was introduced in 1955, Secretary of Health, Education, and Welfare Oveta Culp Hobby opposed its free distribution by the government. To do so, she said, would lead to socialized medicine "by the back door."

Just as Woodrow Wilson's exposure to faculty politics at Princeton had prepared him for running the federal government (see page 587), so Eisenhower's experience with military politics in World War II made him an excellent politician when he moved into the White House. He knew how to be flexible without compromising his basic values. His "conservatism" became first "dynamic conservatism" and then "progressive moderation." He summarized his attitude by saying that he was liberal in dealing with individuals but conservative "when talking about . . . the individual's pocketbook." But the main reason why so many Americans loved Eisenhower was because he epitomized what they wished the world was like. This helps to explain why he never succeeded in forging an effective political coalition.

■ **Dulles during a 1956 press conference at which he rejected suggestions by Russia and India that the United States suspend further hydrogen bomb tests. His stance and gesture project his "hard line" approach.**

The Eisenhower-Dulles Foreign Policy

After the 1952 election Eisenhower kept his pledge to go to Korea. His trip produced no immediate result, but the truce talks, suspended before the election, were resumed. In July 1953, perhaps influenced by a hint that the United States might use "tactical" atomic bombs in Korea, the communists agreed to an armistice. Korea remained divided. Containment had proved extremely expensive; the United States had suffered more than 135,000 casualties, including 33,000 dead. Yet aggression had been confronted and fought to a standstill.

The American people, troubled and uncertain, counted on Eisenhower to find a way to employ the nation's immense strength constructively. The new president shared the general feeling that a change of tactics in foreign affairs was needed. He counted on Congress and his secretary of state to solve the practical problems.

Given this attitude, his choice of John Foster Dulles as secretary of state seemed inspired. Dulles' experience in diplomacy dated to 1907, when he had served as secretary to the Chinese delegation at the Second Hague Conference.* Later he had a small place among the army of experts advising Wilson at the Versailles Conference. More recently he had been an adviser to the American delegation to the San Francisco Conference and a representative of the United States in the UN General Assembly. Since 1948 he had been recognized as one of the Republican party's chief foreign policy experts, by no one more unquestioningly than himself. "With my understanding of the intricate relationships between the peoples of the world and your sensitiveness to the political considerations involved, we will make the most successful team in history," he told Eisenhower.

*The delegation was headed by Dulles' grandfather John W. Foster, who had been secretary of state under Benjamin Harrison.

Like Eisenhower, Dulles believed in change within the framework of internationalism. "What we need to do," he said, "is to recapture the kind of crusading spirit of the early days of the Republic." Dulles combined amazing energy and strong moral convictions—"there is no way to solve the great perplexing international problems except by bringing to bear on them the force of Christianity," he insisted. His objectives were magnificent, his strategy grandiose. Instead of waiting for the communists to attack and then "containing" them, the United States should warn them that "massive retaliation" directed at Moscow or Peking would be the fate of all aggressors. With the communists immobilized by this threat, positive measures aimed at "liberating" eastern Europe and "unleashing" Chiang Kai-shek against the Chinese mainland would follow. Dulles professed great faith in NATO, but he believed that if America's allies lacked the courage to follow its lead, the nation would have to undertake an "agonizing reappraisal" of its commitments to them.

Thus Dulles envisioned a policy broader, more idealistic, and more aggressive than Truman's. Not the least of its virtues, he claimed, was that it would save money; by concentrating on nuclear deterrents and avoiding "brushfire" wars in remote regions, the cost of defense could be dramatically reduced.

Despite his determination, energy, and high ideals, Dulles failed to make the United States a more effective force in world affairs. Massive retaliation made little sense when the Soviet Union possessed nuclear weapons as powerful as those of the United States. In November 1952 America had won the race to make a hydrogen bomb, but the Russians duplicated this feat the following August. Thereafter the only threat behind massive retaliation was the threat of human extinction.

Most of Dulles' other schemes were equally unrealistic. "Unleashing" Chiang Kai-shek would have been like matching a Pekingese against a tiger. "Liberating" Russia's European satellites would of necessity have involved a third world war. "You can count on us," Dulles told the peoples of eastern Europe in a radio address in January 1953. But when East German workers rioted in June of that year and when the Hungarians revolted in 1956, no help was forthcoming from America. Dulles certainly did not err in refusing to prevent the Russians from crushing these rebellions, but his earlier statements had roused hopes behind the Iron Curtain that now were shattered.

Dulles' saber-rattling tactics were badly timed. While he was planning to avert future Koreas, the Soviet Union was shifting its approach. Stalin died in March 1953, and after a period of internal conflict within the Kremlin, Nikita Khrushchev emerged as the new master of Russia. Khrushchev set out to obtain communist objectives by indirection. He appealed to the antiwestern prejudices of the underdeveloped countries just emerging from the yoke of colonialism, offering them economic aid and pointing to Soviet achievements in science and technology, such as the launching of *Sputnik*, the first earth satellite (1957), as proof that communism would soon "bury" the capitalist system without troubling to destroy it by force. The Soviet Union was the friend of all peace-loving nations, he insisted.

Khrushchev was a master hypocrite, yet he was a realist too. While Dulles, product of a system that made a virtue of compromise and tolerance, insisted that the world must choose between American good and Russian evil, Khrushchev, trained to believe in the incompatibility of communism and capitalism, began to talk of "peaceful coexistence."

Dulles failed to win the confidence of America's allies or even that of his own department. Senator McCarthy moderated his attacks on the State Department not a jot when it came under the control of his own party. In 1953 its overseas information program received his special attention. He denounced Voice of America broadcasters for quoting the works of "controversial" authors and sent Roy M. Cohn, youthful special counsel of his Committee on Governmental Operations, on a mission to Europe to ferret out subversives in the United States Information Service.

Dulles did not come to the defense of his people. Instead he seemed determined to out-McCarthy McCarthy in his zeal to get rid of "undesirables" of all sorts. He sanctioned the discharge of nearly 500 State Department employees, not one of whom was proved to have engaged in subversive activities. People were let go merely because they were suspected of being homosexuals, the argument being that they might be blackmailed into giving state secrets to the communists. By making such "concessions" to McCarthy, Dulles hoped to end attacks on the administration's foreign policy.

■ **The Washington *Post's* Herblock was a sharp critic of the Eisenhower administration. In a comment on John Foster Dulles' "brinkmanship" diplomacy, Dulles in a Superman outfit assures Uncle Sam, "Don't be afraid—I can always pull you back."**

The tactic failed; its only result was to undermine the morale of career Foreign Service officers.

But McCarthy finally overreached himself. Early in 1954 he turned his guns on the army. After a series of charges and countercharges, he accused army officials of trying to blackmail his committee and announced a broad investigation. The resulting Army-McCarthy Hearings, televised before the country, proved the senator's undoing. For weeks his dark scowl, his blind combativeness and disregard for every human value stood exposed for millions to see. When the hearings ended in June 1954 after some million words of testimony, his spell had been broken. The Senate, with President Eisenhower quietly applying pressure behind the scene, at last moved to censure him in December 1954. This reproof completed the destruction of his influence. Although he continued to issue statements and wild charges, the country no longer listened. In 1957 he died, victim of cirrhosis of the liver.

While the final truce talks were taking place in Korea, new trouble was erupting far to the south in French Indochina. Since December 1946 nationalist rebels led by the communist Ho Chi Minh had been harassing the French in Vietnam, one of three puppet kingdoms (the others were Laos and Cambodia) fashioned by France in Indochina after the defeat of the Japanese. When Communist China began supplying arms to the rebels, who were known as the Vietminh, Truman, applying the containment policy, countered with economic and military assistance to the French. When Eisenhower succeeded to the presidency, he continued and expanded this assistance.

Early in 1954 Ho Chi Minh's troops trapped and besieged a French army in the remote stronghold of Dien Bien Phu. Faced with the loss of 20,000 soldiers, France asked the United States to commit its air force to the battle. Eisenhower, after long deliberation, decided against doing anything. Although the possibility of communist control of Vietnam worried him deeply, he did not seriously consider sending troops into the area. Any idea of air strikes, he believed, was "just silly." The communists were "secreted all around in the jungle. How are we, in a few air strikes, to defeat them?"

In May the French garrison at Dien Bien Phu surrendered, and in July, while Dulles watched from the sidelines, France, Great Britain, Russia, and China signed an agreement at Geneva dividing Vietnam along the 17th parallel. France withdrew from the area. The northern sector became the Democratic Republic of Vietnam, controlled by Ho Chi Minh; the southern remained in the hands of the emperor, Bao Dai. An election to settle the future of all Vietnam was scheduled for 1956.

When it seemed likely that the communists would win that election, Ngo Dinh Diem, a conservative anticommunist, overthrew Bao Dai and became president of South Vietnam. The United States supplied his government liberally with aid. The planned election was never held, and Vietnam remained divided into two nations.

Dulles responded to the diplomatic setback in Vietnam by establishing the Southeast Asia Treaty Organization (September 1954), but only three Asian nations—the Philippine Republic, Thailand, and Pakistan—joined this alliance.* At the same time, the unleashed Chiang Kai-shek was engaging in a meaningless artillery duel with

*The other signatories were Great Britain, France, the United States, Australia, and New Zealand.

the Chinese communists from the tiny, nationalist-held islands of Quemoy and Matsu, which lay in the shadow of the mainland. When it was suggested that the United States join in the fight, Eisenhower refused on the ground, sensible but inconsistent with Dulles' rhetoric, that intervention might set off an atomic war. The United States would not protect the offshore islands, Dulles announced, but it would defend Taiwan at all costs.

In Europe the Eisenhower and Dulles policies differed little from those of Truman. When Eisenhower announced his plan to rely more heavily on nuclear deterrents, the Europeans drew back in alarm, believing that in any atomic showdown they were sure to be destroyed. Khrushchev's talk of peaceful coexistence found many receptive ears, especially in France.

The president therefore yielded to European pressures for a diplomatic "summit" conference with the Russians. In July 1955 Eisenhower, Prime Minister Anthony Eden of Great Britain, and French Premier Edgar Faure met at Geneva with Khrushchev and his then coleader, Nikolai Bulganin, to discuss disarmament and the reunification of West and East Germany. The meeting produced no specific agreement, but with the Russians beaming cheerfully for the cameramen and talking of peaceful coexistence and with Eisenhower pouring martinis and projecting his famous charm, observers noted a softening of tensions that was dubbed "the spirit of Geneva."

In fact Geneva represented only a brief thaw in the Cold War; within a year the world teetered once again on the brink of conflict. This time trouble erupted in the Middle East. American policy in that region, aside from the ubiquitous question of restraining Russian expansion, was influenced by the huge oil resources of Iran, Iraq, Kuwait, and Saudi Arabia—about 60 percent of the world's known reserves—and by the conflict between the new Jewish state of Israel (formerly the British mandate of Palestine) and its Arab neighbors. Although he tried to woo the Arabs, President Truman had consistently placed support for Israel before other considerations in the Middle East. When Israel formally declared its independence in 1948, he recognized it even more quickly than Theodore Roosevelt had recognized Panama in 1903.

Angered by the creation of Israel, the surrounding Arab nations tried to smash the country by force. (The Israeli question had the same impact on Arab emotions that the "bloody shirt" had on Republicans after the Civil War.) While badly outnumbered, the Israelis were better organized and better armed than the Arabs and drove them off with relative ease. With them departed nearly a million Palestinian Arabs, thereby creating a desperate refugee problem in nearby countries. Truman's support of Israel and the millions of dollars contributed to the new state by American Jews produced much Arab resentment of the United States.

Dulles and Eisenhower, worried by the growing influence of the Soviet Union in the Arab world, tried to redress the balance by deemphasizing American support of Israel. In 1952 a revolution in Egypt had overthrown the dissolute King Farouk. Colonel Gamal Abdel Nasser emerged as the strong man of Egypt.

The United States was prepared to lend Nasser money to build a huge dam on the Nile at Aswan. The dam was to be the key to an Egyptian irrigation program to expand agricultural development, and it would be a source of electric power. However, the Eisenhower administration would not sell Egypt arms. The communists would. For this reason, while he accepted American economic assistance, Nasser drifted toward the communist orbit. In May 1956 he established diplomatic relations with Red China.

Eisenhower then decided not to finance the Aswan Dam. In July Dulles informed the Egyptian ambassador that the deal was off. Nasser responded a week later by nationalizing the Suez Canal. This move galvanized the British and French. Influenced by Dulles' argument that Egypt could be made an ally by cajolery, the British had acceded in 1954 to Nasser's demand that they evacuate their military base at Suez. Now their traditional "lifeline" to the Orient was at Egypt's mercy. In conjunction with the French, and without consulting the United States, the British decided to take back the canal by force. The Israelis, alarmed by repeated Arab hit-and-run raids along their borders, also attacked Egypt.

Events moved swiftly. Israeli armored columns crushed the Egyptian army in the Sinai Peninsula in a matter of days. France and Britain occupied Port Said, at the northern end of the canal. Nasser blocked the canal by sinking ships in the channel. In the UN the Soviet Union and the United States introduced resolutions calling for a cease-fire. Both were vetoed by Britain and France.

Then Khrushchev thundered a warning from Moscow that he might send "volunteers" to Egypt and launch atomic missiles against France and Great Britain if they did not withdraw. Eisenhower also demanded that the invaders pull out of Egypt. In London large crowds demonstrated against their own government. On November 6, only nine days after the first Israeli units invaded Egypt, Prime Minister Eden, haggard and shaken, announced a cease-fire. Israel withdrew its troops. The crisis subsided as rapidly as it had arisen.

The United States had adhered to its principles and thus won a measure of respect in the Arab countries. But at what cost! Its major allies had been humiliated. Their ill-timed attack had enabled Russia to recover much of the prestige lost as a result of its brutal suppression of a Hungarian revolt which had broken out a week before the Suez fiasco. Eden and French Premier Guy Mollet were claiming with considerable plausibility that Dulles' futile attempt to win Arab friendship without abandoning Israel had placed them in a dilemma and that the secretary had behaved dishonorably or at least disingenuously in handling the Egyptian problem. In fact Dulles was only carrying out Eisenhower's orders, though his self-righteous, moralizing criticisms of Egyptian dealings with Russia and of his allies' attack on Egypt made the situation worse. "Mr. Dulles kicked Nasser in the teeth, with a missionary twist," one observer noted.

The bad feeling within the western alliance soon passed. When Russia seemed likely to profit from its "defense" of Egypt in the crisis, the president announced the "Eisenhower Doctrine" (January 1957), which stated that the United States was "prepared to use armed force" anywhere in the Middle East against "aggression from any country controlled by international communism." The Eisenhower Doctrine amounted to little more than a restatement of the containment policy. No sudden shift in the Middle Eastern balance of power resulted.

Eisenhower and the Russians

In 1956 Eisenhower was reelected, defeating Adlai Stevenson even more decisively than he had in 1952. Despite their evident satisfaction with their leader, however, the mood of the American people was one of sober, restrained determination. Hopes of pushing back the Soviet Union with clever stratagems and moral fervor were fading. America's first successful earth satellite, launched in January 1958, brought cold comfort, for it was much smaller than the Russian *Sputniks.*

In 1957 Dulles underwent surgery for an abdominal cancer, and in April 1959 he had to resign. The next month he was dead. Although Christian A. Herter, a former congressman and governor of Massachusetts, became the new secretary of state, President Eisenhower personally took over much of the task of conducting foreign relations.

Eisenhower had never avoided making decisions in the foreign policy area. The key to his approach was restraint; he exercised commendable caution in every crisis. Like U. S. Grant, he was a soldier who hated war. From Korea through the crises over Indochina, Hungary, and Suez, he avoided risky new commitments. His behavior, like his temperament, contrasted sharply with that of the aggressive, oratorically perfervid Dulles. While Dulles ran the State Department, the difference between the rhetoric of American foreign policy and its underlying philosophy was confusing. This brought the administration much unnecessary criticism.

Amid the tension that followed the Suez crisis, the belief persisted in many quarters that the "spirit of Geneva" could be revived if only a new summit meeting could be arranged. World opinion was insistent that the great powers stop making and testing nuclear weapons, for every test explosion was contaminating the atmosphere with radioactive debris that threatened the future of all life. Unresolved controversies, especially the argument over divided Germany, might erupt at any moment into a globe-shattering war.

Neither the United States nor the Soviet Union dared ignore these dangers; each therefore adopted a more accommodating attitude. In the summer of 1959 Vice-President Richard M. Nixon visited the Soviet Union and his opposite number, Vice Premier Anastas I. Mikoyan, toured the United States. Although Nixon's visit was marred by a heated argument with Khrushchev, conducted before a gaping crowd in the kitchen of a model American home that had been set up at a

Moscow fair, the results of the exchanges raised hopes that a summit conference would prove profitable.

In September Khrushchev came to America. His cross-country tour had its full share of comic contretemps—when denied permission to visit Disneyland because authorities feared they could not protect him properly on the grounds, the heavy-handed Khrushchev accused the United States, only half humorously, of concealing rocket launching pads there. But the general effect of his visit seemed salutary. At the end of his stay, he and President Eisenhower agreed to convene a new four-power summit conference.

The meeting never took place. On May 1, 1960, high over Sverdlovsk, an industrial center deep in the Soviet Union, an American U-2 reconnaissance plane was shot down by antiaircraft fire. The pilot of the plane, Francis Gary Powers, survived the crash, and he confessed to being a spy. His cameras contained aerial photographs of Soviet military installations. When Eisenhower assumed full responsibility for the mission, Khrushchev accused the United States of "piratical" and "cowardly" acts of aggression. The summit conference collapsed.

Latin American Problems

Events in Latin America compounded Eisenhower's difficulties. During World War II the United States, needing Latin American raw materials, had supplied its southern neighbors liberally with economic aid. In the period following victory an era of amity and prosperity seemed assured. A hemispheric mutual defense pact was signed at Rio de Janeiro in September 1947, and the following year the Organization of American States (OAS) came into being. The United States appeared to have committed itself to a policy of true cooperation with Latin America. In the OAS decisions were reached by a two-thirds vote; the United States had neither a veto nor any special position.

The United States tended to neglect Latin America during the Cold War years. Economic problems plagued the region, and in most nations reactionary governments did little to improve the lot of their peoples. Radical Latin Americans accused the United States of supporting cliques of wealthy tyrants, while conservatives tended to use the United States as a scapegoat, blaming lack of sufficient American economic aid for the plight of the poor.

Eisenhower, eager to improve relations, sent his brother Dr. Milton Eisenhower on a South American tour, and when Dr. Eisenhower recommended stepped-up economic assistance, the president concurred. Resistance to communism nonetheless continued to receive first priority. In 1954 the government of Jacobo Arbenz Guzmán in Guatemala began to import Soviet weapons. The United States promptly dispatched arms to the neighboring state of Honduras. Within a month an army led by an exiled Guatemalan officer marched into the country from Honduras and overthrew Arbenz. Elsewhere in Latin America, Eisenhower, as Truman had before him, continued to support conservative regimes that were often kept in power by the bayonets of the local military. He did so because the alternative seemed to be communist revolution and social chaos.

The depth of Latin American resentment of the United States became clear in the spring of 1958, when Vice-President Nixon went to South America on an eight-nation goodwill tour. Everywhere he was met with hostility. In Lima, Peru, he was mobbed; in Caracas, Venezuela, students kicked his shiny Cadillac and pelted him with eggs and stones. He had to abandon the remainder of his trip. For the first time the American people gained some inkling of Latin American opinion and the social and economic troubles that lay behind this opinion.

That there was no easy solution to Latin American problems was made clear by the course of events in Cuba. In 1959 a revolutionary movement headed by Dr. Fidel Castro overthrew Fulgencio Batista, one of the most noxious of the Latin American dictators. Eisenhower recognized the Castro government at once, but the Cuban leader soon began to criticize the United States in highly colored speeches. He ordered American property in Cuba confiscated without providing adequate compensation. Castro suppressed civil liberties, entered into close relations with the Soviet Union, and drove many of his original supporters into exile. After he negotiated a trade agreement with the Soviet Union in February 1960, which enabled the Russians to obtain Cuban sugar at bargain rates, the United States retaliated by prohibiting the importation of Cuban sugar into America. Khrushchev then announced that if the United States intervened in Cuba, he would defend the country with atomic weapons. "The Monroe Doctrine has outlived its time," Khrushchev warned. With the Castro movement—called *Fidelismo*—making inroads in many Latin American countries, Eisenhower, shortly before the end of his second term, broke off diplomatic relations with Cuba.

The Politics of Civil Rights

During Eisenhower's presidency a major change occurred in the legal status of American blacks. Eisenhower had relatively little to do with the change himself; indeed, one might say that it occurred in spite of the president more than because of him. For the change was part of a broad shift in attitudes toward the civil rights of all individuals.

After 1945 the question of racial equality took on special importance because of the ideological competition with communism. Evidence of color prejudice in the United States damaged the nation's image, particularly in Asia and Africa, where the United States and Russia were competing for influence, trade, and strategic bases. An awareness of foreign criticism of American racial attitudes, along with resentment that almost a century after the Emancipation Proclamation they were still second-class citizens, produced a growing militancy among American blacks. At the same time, fears of communist subversion in the United States led to the repression of the rights of many whites, culminating in the excesses of McCarthyism. Both these aspects of the civil rights question divided Americans along liberal and conservative lines and shook the political structure of the country.

As we have seen, the World War II record of the federal government on civil rights was mixed. Except for the treatment of the Japanese in California there was no hysterical pursuit of imaginary spies and subversives. Yet as early as 1940, in the Smith Act, Congress made it illegal to advocate or teach the overthrow of the government by force or to belong to an organization with this objective. A dead letter during the era of Soviet-American cooperation, the law was used in the Truman era to jail the leaders of the American Communist party. The Supreme Court upheld its constitutionality in *Dennis et al.* v. *United States* (1951), in effect modifying the "clear and present danger" test established in the Schenck case of 1919 (see page 608).

In 1950 Congress passed the McCarran Internal Security Act, which made it unlawful "to combine, conspire or agree with any other person to perform any act that would substantially contribute to the establishment . . . of a totalitarian dictatorship." The law required every "Communist-front organization" to register with the attorney general. Members of "front" organizations were barred from defense work and from travel abroad. Aliens who had ever been members of any "totalitarian party" were denied admission to the United States, a foolish provision that prevented many anticommunists behind the Iron Curtain from fleeing to America; even a person who had belonged to a communist youth organization was kept out by its terms.

Although his own loyalty program was administered without sufficient regard for individual rights, Truman vetoed the McCarran Act, saying that it would "put the Government into the business of thought control." Congress overrode the veto by a voice vote. As for blacks, besides setting up the Committee on Civil Rights and pressing for the desegregation of the armed forces, Truman favored anti-poll-tax and antilynching legislation. These proposals were filibustered to death in the Senate, and Congress refused Truman's request for a permanent Fair Employment Practices Commission.

Under Eisenhower, while the McCarthy hysteria reached its peak and declined, the government compiled a spotty record on civil rights. The search for subversive federal employees continued. While only a handful were charged with disloyalty, nearly 7,000 were declared "security risks" and fired. The refusal to grant security clearance to J. Robert Oppenheimer, one of the fathers of the atomic bomb, on the ground that he had associated with communists and communist sympathizers, was the most glaring instance of the administration's catering to anticommunist extremists, for it was based on the supposition that Oppenheimer could be denied access to his own discoveries.

As for black Americans, Eisenhower completed the formal integration of the armed forces and ap-

■ **School desegregation comes to Arkansas, 1957. Acting on President Eisenhower's orders, 101st Airborne Division paratroopers escorted black students (there were nine in all) into Central High School in Little Rock.**

pointed a Civil Rights Commission, but he was temperamentally incapable of making a frontal assault on the racial problem. This was done by the Supreme Court, which interjected itself into the civil rights controversy in dramatic fashion in 1954.

Under pressure of litigation sponsored by the National Association for the Advancement of Colored People, the Court had been gradually undermining the "separate but equal" principle laid down in *Plessy* v. *Ferguson* (see page 426). First it ruled that in graduate education segregated facilities must be truly equal. In 1938 it ordered a black admitted to the University of Missouri law school because no law school for blacks existed in the state. This decision gradually forced some southern states to admit blacks to advanced programs. "You can't build a cyclotron for one student," the president of the University of Oklahoma confessed when the Court, in 1948, ordered Oklahoma to provide equal facilities. Two years later, when Texas actually attempted to fit out a separate law school for a single black applicant, the Court ruled that truly equal education could not be provided under such circumstances.

In 1953 President Eisenhower appointed California's Governor Earl Warren chief justice of the United States.* Convinced that the Court must take the offensive in the cause of civil rights, Warren succeeded in welding his associates into a unit on the question. In 1954 an NAACP-sponsored case, *Brown* v. *Board of Education of Topeka,* came up for decision. The NAACP lawyer, Thurgood Marshall, challenged the "separate but equal" doctrine even at the elementary school level. He submitted a mass of sociological evidence to show that the mere fact of segregation made equal education impossible and did serious psychological damage to both black children and white. Speaking for a unanimous Court, Warren reversed the Plessy decision. "In the field of public education, the doctrine of 'separate but equal' has no place," he declared. "Separate educational facilities are inherently unequal." The next year the Court ordered the states to proceed "with all deliberate speed" in integrating their schools.

*Eisenhower first offered the post to John Foster Dulles, but he declined on the ground that he was too old to start a new career.

Despite these decisions, few districts in the 17 southern and border states seriously tried to integrate their schools. Two months after the ruling, White Citizens Councils dedicated to all-out opposition had sprung up throughout the South. When the school board of Clinton, Tennessee, integrated the local high school in September 1956, a mob roused by a northern fanatic rioted in protest, shouting "Kill the niggers!" and destroying the property of blacks. The school was kept open with the help of the National Guard until segregationists blew up the building with dynamite. In Virginia the governor announced a plan for "massive resistance" to integration that denied state aid to local school systems that wished to desegregate. When the University of Alabama admitted a single black woman in 1956, riots broke out. University officials forced the student to withdraw and then expelled her when she complained more forcefully than they deemed proper.

President Eisenhower thought equality for blacks could not be obtained by government edict. "I am convinced that the Supreme Court decision *set back* progress in the South *at least fifteen years*," he remarked to one of his advisers. "The fellow who tries to tell me you can do these things by *force* is just plain *nuts*." In 1957 events compelled him to act. That September the school board of Little Rock, Arkansas, opened Central High School to a handful of black children. However, the governor of the state, Orval M. Faubus, called out the National Guard to prevent them from attending. Unruly crowds taunted the children and their parents.

Eisenhower could not ignore the direct flouting of federal authority. After the mayor of Little Rock sent him a telegram saying in part, "SITUATION IS OUT OF CONTROL AND POLICE CANNOT DISPERSE THE MOB," he dispatched 1,000 paratroopers to Little Rock and summoned 10,000 National Guardsmen to federal duty. The black children then began to attend classes. A token force of soldiers was stationed at Central High for the entire school year to protect them.

Extremist resistance strengthened the determination of blacks and many northern whites to make the South comply with the desegregation decision. Besides pressing cases in the federal courts, leaders of the movement organized a voter registration drive among southern blacks. In the Civil Rights Act of September 1957 Congress authorized the attorney general to obtain injunctions to stop southern registrars and election officials from interfering with blacks seeking to register and vote. The law also established a Civil Rights Commission with broad investigatory powers and a Civil Rights Division in the Department of Justice. Enforcing this Civil Rights Act was another matter. A later study of a typical county in Alabama revealed that between 1957 and 1960 more than 700 blacks with high school diplomas were rejected as unqualified by white election officials when they sought to register.

Election of 1960

As the end of his second term approached, Eisenhower somewhat reluctantly endorsed Vice-President Nixon as the Republican candidate to succeed him. Richard Nixon had skyrocketed to national prominence by exploiting the public fear of communist subversion. "Traitors in the high councils of our government," he charged in 1950, "have made sure that the deck is stacked on the Soviet side of the diplomatic tables." In 1947 he was an obscure young congressman from California; in 1950 he won a seat in the Senate; two years later Eisenhower chose him as his running mate.

Whether Nixon believed what he said at this period of his career is not easily discovered; with his "instinct for omnidirectional placation," he seemed wedded to the theory that politicians should slavishly represent their constituents' opinions rather than hold to their own views. Frequently he appeared to count noses before deciding what he thought. He projected an image of almost frantic earnestness, yet he pursued a flexible course more suggestive of calculation than sincerity.

Reporters generally had a low opinion of Nixon, and independent voters seldom found him attractive. He was always controversial, distrusted by liberals even when he supported liberal measures. But his defense of American values in his confrontation with Khrushchev at the Moscow Fair had won him much praise. In any case, no prominent Republican rose to oppose his nomination.

The Democrats nominated Senator John F. Kennedy of Massachusetts, with Lyndon B. Johnson, the Senate majority leader, as his running mate. Kennedy was the son of Joseph P. Kennedy, a wealthy businessman and promoter who had served as ambassador to Great Britain under Franklin Roosevelt. As a P T boat commander in World War II, he was severely injured in action. In 1946 he was elected to Congress. Besides wealth, intelligence, good looks, and charm, Kennedy had the advantage of his war record and his Irish-Catholic ancestry, the latter a particularly valuable asset in Massachusetts. After three terms in the House, he moved on to the Senate in 1952 by defeating Henry Cabot Lodge, Jr. (Lodge's grandfather, Wilson's inveterate foe, had beaten Kennedy's maternal grandfather and namesake for the Senate in 1916). After his landslide reelection in 1958, only Kennedy's religion seemed to limit his political future. No Catholic had ever been elected president, and the defeat of Alfred E. Smith in 1928 had convinced most students of politics that none ever would be elected. Nevertheless, influenced by his victories in the Wisconsin and West Virginia primaries—the latter establishing him as an effective campaigner in a predominantly Protestant region—the Democratic convention nominated him.

Early in his congressional career Kennedy had been quite conservative. He was friendly with Richard Nixon and privately delighted when Nixon defeated a liberal Democrat for a Senate seat in 1950. At that time Kennedy admitted frankly that he liked Senator Joseph McCarthy and thought that "he may have something" in his campaign against supposed communists in government. However, he had gradually become more liberal as his career developed.

In the presidential campaign Kennedy stressed his youth and "vigor" (a favorite word). He promised an imaginative, forward-looking administration that would open a "New Frontier" for the country. Nixon ran on the Eisenhower record, which he promised to extend in liberal directions. A series of television debates between the candidates, observed by some 70 million viewers, helped Kennedy by enabling him to demonstrate his warmth, maturity, and mastery of the issues. Where Nixon appeared to lecture the unseen audience like an ill-at-ease schoolmaster, Kennedy seemed relaxed, thoughtful, and confident of his powers. Although both candidates laudably avoided it, the religious issue was important. His Catholicism helped Kennedy in eastern urban areas but injured him in many farm districts and throughout the West. Kennedy's victory, 303 to 219 in the electoral college, was paper thin in the popular vote, 34,227,000 to 34,109,000.

SUPPLEMENTARY READING

Titles marked with an asterisk have been published in paperback

For well-balanced treatments of wartime diplomacy, see Robert Dallek, **Franklin D. Roosevelt and American Foreign Policy*** (1979), and J. L. Gaddis, **The United States and the Origins of the Cold War*** (1972). Other important books on the subject include W. H. McNeill, **America, Britain and Russia: Their Cooperation and Conflict** (1953), Gar Alperovitz, **Atomic Diplomacy*** (1965), Gaddis Smith, **American Diplomacy During the Second World War*** (1965), Herbert Feis, **Churchill, Roosevelt, Stalin*** (1957) and **Between War and Peace: The Potsdam Conference*** (1960), R. E. Sherwood, **Roosevelt and Hopkins*** (1948), and Winston Churchill, **The Second World War*** (1948–1953).

A good summary of the Cold War is T. G. Paterson, **On Every Front: The Making of the Cold War*** (1979), which makes an effort to explain Soviet motives and tactics objectively. See also L. J. Halle, **The Cold War as History*** (1967), and, more critical of American policy, Walter La Feber, **America, Russia and the Cold War*** (1968), Daniel Yergin, **Shattered Peace** (1977), and Carl Solberg, **Riding High: America in the Cold War** (1973). H. S. Truman's **Memoirs*** (1955–1956) contain much useful information.

Postwar domestic politics is treated in A. L. Hamby, **The Imperial Years** (1976), E. F. Goldman, **The Crucial Decade—And After*** (1961), and G. E. Mowry, **The Urban Nation*** (1965). Interpretive works useful for understanding the period include Samuel Lubell, **The Future of American Politics*** (1952) and **Revolt of the Moderates** (1956), A. M. Schlesinger, Jr., **The Vital Center*** (1949), R. E. Neustadt, **Presidential Power*** (1960), J. M. Burns, **The Deadlock of Democracy*** (1963), Daniel Bell, **The End of Ideology*** (1959), C. Wright Mills, **The Power Elite*** (1962), and R. H. Rovere, **The American Establishment*** (1962).

Biographical material on postwar political leaders is voluminous but seldom satisfactory from the scholarly point of view. On Truman, see Truman's **Memoirs,** R. J.

Donovan, **Conflict and Crisis** (1977), and A. L. Hamby, **Beyond the New Deal: Harry S Truman and American Liberalism*** (1973).

Among many analyses and evaluations of American foreign policy, the following are important: W. W. Rostow, **The United States in the World Arena*** (1960), Norman Graebner, **New Isolationism** (1956), and H. A. Kissinger, **Nuclear Weapons and Foreign Policy*** (1957). G. F. Kennan's writings on the subject are both primary sources and important secondary interpretations. See his **Memoirs*** (1969, 1972), **Realities of American Foreign Policy*** (1954), and **Russia and the West under Lenin and Stalin*** (1961).

On Truman's foreign policy, see Donovan's **Conflict and Crisis** and, on the Truman Doctrine, J. M. Jones, **The Fifteen Weeks*** (1955); on the Marshall Plan, H. B. Price, **The Marshall Plan and its Meaning** (1955). R. E. Osgood, **NATO: The Entangling Alliance** (1962), is excellent. See also W. P. Davison, **The Berlin Blockade** (1958).

American relations with China are covered in Herbert Feis, **The China Tangle*** (1953), Tang Tsou, **America's Failure in China*** (1963), and A. D. Barnett, **Communist China and Asia: Challenge to American Policy*** (1960); for Japan, see E. O. Reischauer, **The United States and Japan*** (1957). On the Korean War, consult David Rees, **Korea: The Limited War** (1964), and J. W. Spanier, **The Truman-MacArthur Controversy and the Korean War*** (1959).

McCarthyism and the Hiss case are covered in Earl Latham, **The Communist Conspiracy in Washington** (1966), Alistair Cooke, **A Generation on Trial: *USA* v. *Alger Hiss**** (1950), Whittaker Chambers, **Witness*** (1952), Robert Griffith, **The Politics of Fear*** (1970), and R. H. Rovere, **Senator Joe McCarthy*** (1959).

Economic trends are considered in A. A. Berle, **The 20th Century Capitalist Revolution*** (1954) and **Power Without Property*** (1959), Herbert Stein, **The Fiscal Revolution in America*** (1969), J. K. Galbraith, **American Capitalism*** (1952) and **The Affluent Society*** (1958), H. G. Vatter, **The U. S. Economy in the 1950s** (1963), and Walter Adams and H. M. Gray, **Monopoly in America** (1955). On the 1946 Employment Act, see S. K. Bailey, **Congress Makes a Law** (1950).

On labor, consult Philip Taft, **Organized Labor in American History** (1964), Joel Seidman, **American Labor from Defense to Reconversion** (1953), E. L. Dayton, **Walter Reuther** (1958), Melvin Dubofsky and Warren Van Tine, **John L. Lewis** (1977), W. M. Leiserson, **American Trade Union Democracy** (1959), and P. A. Brinker, **The Taft-Hartley Act After Ten Years** (1958). On agriculture, see A. J. Matusow, **Farm Policies & Politics in the Truman Years*** (1970), M. R. Benedict and O. C. Stine, **The Agricultural Commodity Programs** (1956), and Lauren Soth, **Farm Trouble in an Age of Plenty** (1957).

Eisenhower's own view of his two terms can be found in D. D. Eisenhower, **Mandate for Change*** (1963) and **Waging Peace** (1965). Herbert Parmet, **Eisenhower and the American Crusades** (1972), as a balanced account of his two administrations. See also C. C. Alexander, **Holding the Line: The Eisenhower Era** (1975), and J. L. Sundquist, **Politics and Policy** (1968). Of the biographies, R. J. Donovan, **Eisenhower: The Inside Story** (1956), and M. J. Pusey, **Eisenhower: The President** (1956), are favorable, while Marquis Childs, **Eisenhower: Captive Hero** (1958), is critical. See also Dean Albertson (ed.), **Eisenhower as President*** (1963). Sherman Adams, **Firsthand Report*** (1961), is a pro-Eisenhower memoir, E. J. Hughes, **The Ordeal of Power*** (1963), an anti-Eisenhower one.

John Foster Dulles' views are discussed in M. A. Guhin, **John Foster Dulles** (1972), and in Dulles' own **War or Peace** (1950). For developments in the Far East, see R. H. Fifield, **The Diplomacy of Southeast Asia** (1958); for the Middle East, see J. C. Campbell, **Defense of the Middle East*** (1960), and Herman Finer, **Dulles over Suez** (1964), which is extremely critical of the secretary. The diplomacy of the Eisenhower era is also discussed in R. A. Divine, **Eisenhower and the Cold War*** (1981), and R. F. Smith, **The Defense of Berlin** (1963) and **The United States and Cuba*** (1960).

For postwar constitutional issues, see P. L. Murphy, **The Constitution in Crisis Times*** (1972), and on racial issues in particular, B. M. Ziegler, **Desegregation and the Supreme Court*** (1958), W. C. Berman, **Politics of Civil Rights in the Truman Administration** (1970), and Anthony Lewis et al., **Portrait of a Decade*** (1964). Richard Kluger, **Simple Justice*** (1976), is an excellent account of the Brown case.

Portfolio Six

THE PAINTER'S EYE

When Charles Sheeler painted San Francisco's Golden Gate Bridge he was approaching the end of a career during which he had celebrated more completely than any other artist the monumental achievements of American industrial society—its bridges, highways, ships, and factories. He did not use the word "bridge" in the title he gave to his rendition of this superb structure; to him it was "an opening . . . a gateway, a beckoning into the new." The words are a reminder of the dream that sustained the country through its formative years—the belief that American ingenuity and technology would surely make "a better world." These ideas have come under severe scrutiny in the second half of the century. One wonders what subjects Sheeler would be painting if he were alive today.

A century ago the English writer John Ruskin put forward the idea that artistic style is an expression of the "spirit of the society" rather than a private exploration of forms. The truth probably lies somewhere in between. In some periods the connection between art and society is easy to trace; in others the fumbling of the artist for new forms may be read as a parallel to the fumbling of society in pursuit of its own confused goals.

■ CHARLES SHEELER, *Golden Gate*, 1955

■ WILLIAM GLACKENS, *The Green Car,* 1910

■ JOHN SLOAN, *The Lafayette,* 1928

■ GEORGE BELLOWS, *Brutal,* 1917
(Lithograph of his *Stag at Sharkey's,* 1909)

■ EVERETT SHINN, *The Laundress,* 1903

The Passing of the Genteel Tradition: The Ashcan School

At the turn of the century American painters already had a rich tradition behind them, and some great modern masters—like Homer, Ryder, and Eakins—had made their mark. In the general taste of the time, however, the young painter found the best hope of a livelihood in painting what wealthy patrons wanted: lovely ladies with parasols at summer picnics, charming children, and impressive gentlemen. Everett Shinn complained that art in America was "merely an adjunct of plush and cut glass."

This peaceful scene was rudely interrupted in 1908 with the first exhibition of a group called The Eight, who preferred to paint life as they found it, with its ashcans and its laundry lines. Even when they painted elegant settings, as Sloan did in *The Lafayette,* an elite Fifth Avenue hotel, it was with a new critical bite. Their guiding spirit was Robert Henri, a successful painter and teacher who realized that change was in the wind. In retrospect the paintings of the ashcan school seem almost as nostalgic and romantic as the style they replaced because they depict a world now lost to us. But in their day The Eight were shockers, berated as "Apostles of Ugliness." In challenging the niceties of the genteel tradition, they opened subject matter that involved future artists of many persuasions.

■ MORGAN RUSSELL
Synchromy in Orange: To Form
1913–1914

■ MAX WEBER, *Chinese Restaurant,* 1915

Pioneer American Modernists

Paris was a mecca for young American artists early in the century. Like the expatriate writers assembled there, the artists experimented with whatever ideas they encountered—cubism, expressionism, fauvism, futurism, dadaism—movements now familiar in art history but then little known in America. In *Chinese Restaurant* Weber borrowed the cubist technique of shattering and reassembling shapes to recreate "a maze and blaze of light" that seemed to him to "split into fragments the interior and its contents."

Russell, who went to Paris in 1908, structured completely nonrepresentational works solely with planes of color in an innovative style known as synchromism, the first American modernist style to be dignified with a name. Marin, chiefly a watercolorist, used simplified and scattered shapes to paint nature's "warring, pushing, pulling" forces in cityscapes and seascapes. Burchfield clung to his American small-town orientation but used the new freedom to explore "a completely personal mood." With a haunted, fairy-tale quality he painted ramshackle buildings, dingy back streets, and hallucinated plant forms.

A sympathetic showcase for early modernists, whose work was otherwise ignored or ridiculed, was the gallery of Alfred Steiglitz at 291 Fifth Avenue in New York, which determinedly promoted avant-garde art of Europe and America.

■ JOHN MARIN, *Sun Spots,* 1920

■ CHARLES BURCHFIELD
Church Bells Ringing, Rainy Winter Night
1917

■ ARTHUR DOVE, *Ferry Boat Wreck—Oyster Bay,* 1931

■ PETER BLUME, *South of Scranton,* 1931

Americanizing the French Connection

Early in 1913 the Armory Show, an international exhibition of modern art held in New York, was a turning point in American painting. For the first time the modern works of Europeans and Americans were shown extensively side by side. The exhibition aroused a furor on the part of conservative critics and viewers, who were nevertheless compelled thereafter to see art with different eyes.

American artists ruefully recognized their work as provincial in comparison with the brilliant avant-garde European art they saw, and the next two decades produced much innovative work. Dove painted his Long Island boat wreck in a dramatically symbolic vein, incorporating the sun like a Cyclopean eye. Blume created a surrealist fantasy by freely associating what he saw on a trip south from the mining area around Scranton to Charleston, where he portrayed sailors exercising on the deck of a ship "like birds soaring through space." Hopper, indifferent to foreign ideas, had as his aim "the most exact transcription" of his "most intimate impressions." With concentrated simplicity and a penetrating use of light, he painted an essence of the American setting with an eerie sense of loneliness.

■ EDWARD HOPPER, *Early Sunday Morning,* 1930

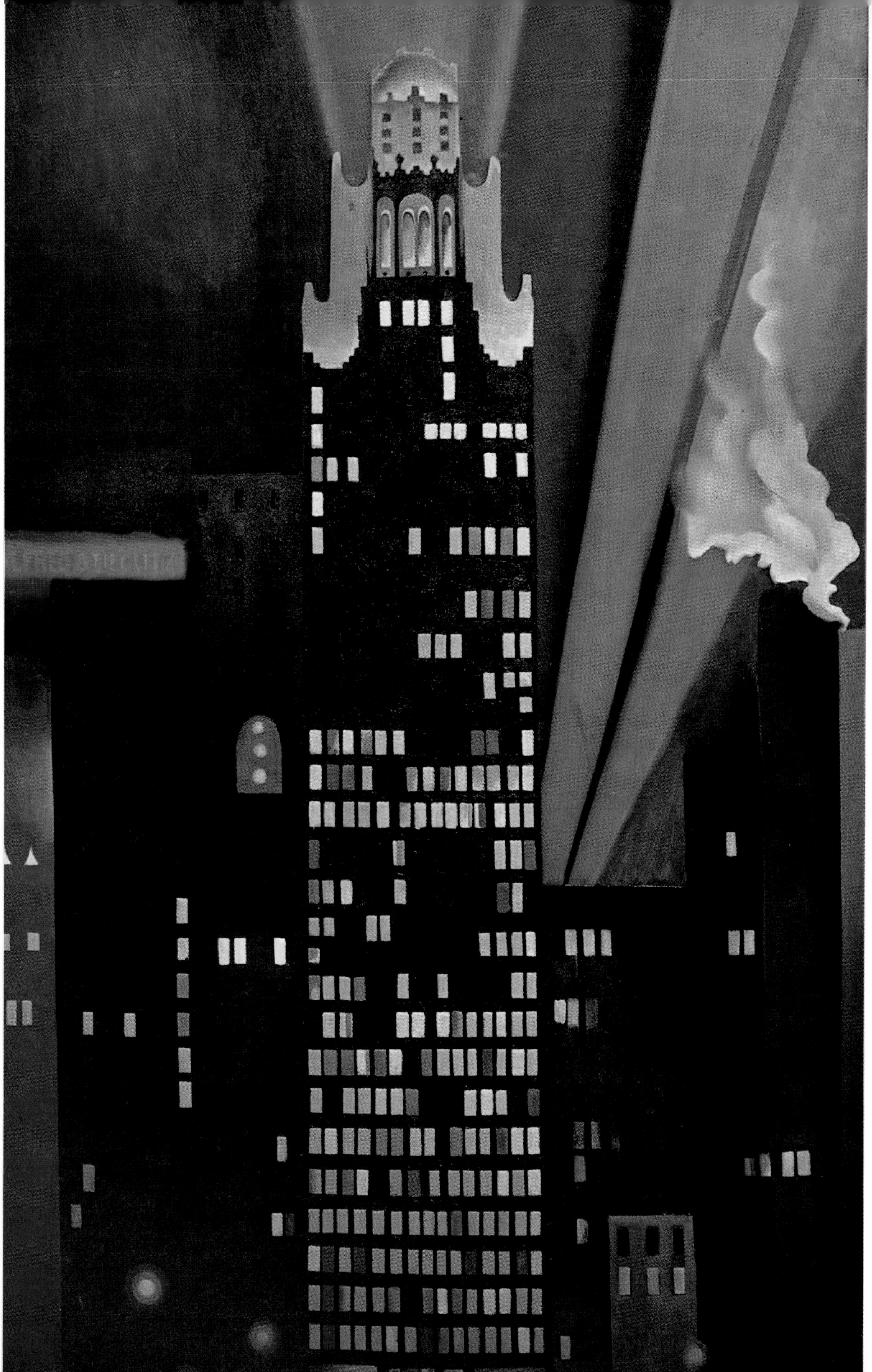

Art in a Technological Society: The Precisionists

The rapid scientific and technological advances of the 20th century provided painters with a new subject matter that seemed to some of them truly American: Sheeler's bridge, O'Keeffe's skyscraper, Davis' industrial street. Davis, fascinated with the gadgets of the new technology, painted a series of abstractions based on the eggbeater. A new approach to painting emerged that seemed to be allied more closely than before to a scientific point of view. The precisionists were a loosely knit group who found in the analytical methods of cubism a compatible source for the new style.

O'Keeffe, the doyenne of American women painters, celebrated her 90th birthday in 1977, still painting. In mid-career she moved to the Southwest where she applied her personal evolution of this style to the desert landscape.

Demuth's meditation on the Figure 5, an early example of a continuing interest in numeral and letter forms, was inspired by a poem by William Carlos Williams: "I saw the figure 5/in gold/on a red/firetruck/moving/tense/unheeded to gong clangs . . . through the dark city."

The precisionists used paint and canvas to interpret what they saw. Later artists looked to technology as a means for creating new forms of art, such as the "environments" produced in the sixties under EAT (Experiments in Art and Technology), a remarkable collaboration initiated by artists, technical institutions, and a labor union.

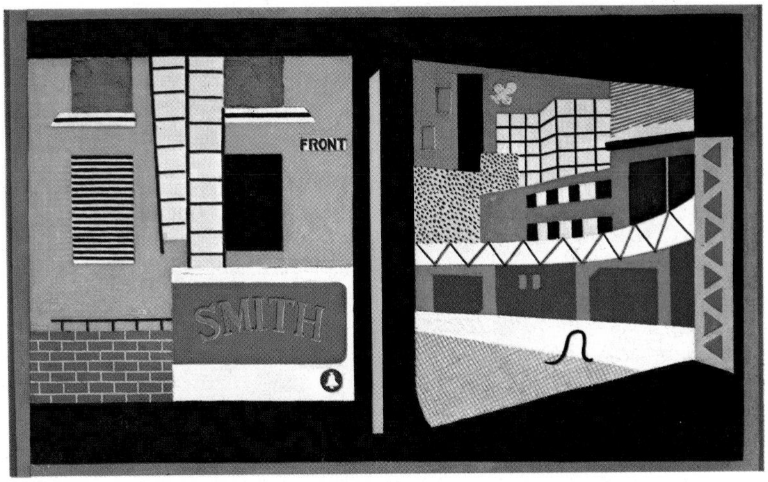

■ STUART DAVIS, *House and Street,* 1931

■ CHARLES DEMUTH
I Saw the Figure 5 in Gold, 1928

■ GEORGIA O'KEEFFE
Radiator Building—Night, New York, 1927

■ LOUIS BOUCHÉ, *Ten Cents a Ride*, 1942

■ REGINALD MARSH, *Subway, 14th Street*, 1930

■ THOMAS HART BENTON, *Romance*, 1931

■ GRANT WOOD, pencil sketches for *Dinner for Threshers,* 1933

"This Land Is My Land": The Regionalists

While some artists explored foreign styles, others concentrated on specific regions of America that they knew personally. Benton, the most controversial and perhaps the most influential of the regionalists, was politically active as a Populist and violently opinionated about art. He had flirted with modernism in Paris and turned his back on it, denouncing the entire modern movement as "dirt." He taught and painted for many years in New York, but his main subject was always his native Missouri, in both its contemporaneous and its historical aspects. Grant Wood, during his European studies, was most impressed by the meticulous attention to homely detail in Flemish painting; he returned home to apply the same loving care to his neighbors and their life in Iowa.

There were urban regionalists as well. Any New Jersey commuter who survives from the period will remember riding on Bouché's ferry boat and leaving behind an abandoned newspaper every weekday morning. Marsh haunted the seamy side of New York, documenting the Bowery bums, the women of the street, the Coney Island honkytonks, and the subways with a flamboyance that cameras could not rival.

■ BEN SHAHN, *Willis Avenue Bridge*, 1940

Art for a Cause: The Social Realists

The first Artists' Congress held in America opened on February 14, 1936, with a speech by the social historian Lewis Mumford. It was a grim era for the United States. "The time has come," Mumford said, ". . . to be ready to protect, and guard, and if necessary, fight for the human heritage which we, as artists, embody."

A number of American painters, now known as the social realists, were already using their work as just such a weapon. Ben Shahn grew up in an immigrant Lithuanian family in an atmosphere of strong radical protest. "I hate injustice," he said, "and I hope to go on hating it all my life." He lent his talents to many causes, but above all he painted, with power and sympathy, the abandoned, the homeless, the crippled, and the derelict. Evergood ranged through many strata of society, always with a sharp eye to which he added psychological subtleties and often a touch of fantasy; his *American Tragedy* commemorates a bloody labor clash in Chicago in 1937. Levine, who first studied art in a Boston settlement house, attacked the unscrupulous power of corrupt officials, greedy magnates, and vicious gangsters. Under its satiric title, his *Feast of Pure Reason* is a scene of collusion among such characters.

■ PHILIP EVERGOOD
American Tragedy
1937

■ JACK LEVINE, *The Feast of Pure Reason*, 1937

Public Support of the Arts: The WPA Breakthrough

The Roosevelt era inaugurated a New Deal in art as well as in politics when it was decided that artists, along with the other millions of unemployed, were a national resource deserving of federal assistance. Of four programs affecting the arts, the largest by far was the Federal Art Project (1935–1943), a division of the Works Progress Administration. At its peak the Art Project employed some 5,000 needy artists (at an average weekly salary of $23), and it produced an astonishing total of work: 108,099 easel paintings, 2,566 murals, and 17,744 sculptures. Many of these works are now unfortunately lost, but the Art Project helped to maintain a generation of artists who might otherwise have been forced to turn elsewhere for a living. The funds were allotted on the basis of need to both known and unknown artists, and the remarkable degree of freedom that was allowed led to the creation of works in many styles. Curry turned to regionalism, painting Kansas farm life; Lawrence, a pioneer black artist, tended toward social realism. Most of the abstract expressionists who achieved fame in the 1950s had received funds in their salad days from the WPA.

By the time the emergency had come to an end, there was a new awareness of art as a public concern. The National Endowment for the Arts, launched in 1966 with a budget of $2.5 million, was allocated $85 million in 1977. The General Services Administration now requires that one-half of 1 percent of construction costs for new or renovated federal buildings be allocated to art, which means that a building costing $12 million will have $60,000 worth of art. And there are state and municipal art councils with substantial budgets as well. While this is much less than some other governments allocate per capita for the arts, it is a far cry from the day when only an occasional commemorative statue was publicly commissioned.

To this support American corporate patronage has been added. In 1939 the New York World's Fair opened with many examples of modern American art commissioned or collected for the pavilions. Since then a number of corporations have assembled collections of contemporary art, and they, as well as various foundations, continue to make substantial grants to the arts.

What happens to the arts under these circumstances? In the Soviet Union government sponsorship resulted in the suppression of avant-garde art. Nothing like this has happened in America—so far quite the opposite has been true. It has been estimated that federal and other public support increased 13-fold between 1966 and 1975, and the wisdom with which these funds are allocated will no doubt affect the course of art in the United States.

■ JACOB LAWRENCE, *Blind Beggars*, 1938

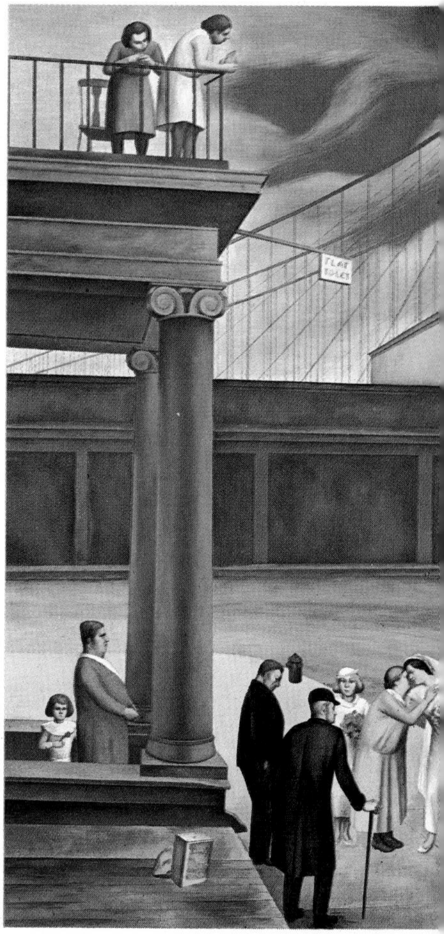

■ JOHN STEUART CURRY, *Comedy,* 1937

■ (Curry did two murals, *Comedy* and *Tragedy,* for a Westport, Connecticut, school. *Comedy* [above] has in its cast many of the comic-strip characters of the thirties, including Mutt and Jeff, Popeye and Olive Oyl, and Mickey Mouse. Below Charlie Chaplin [with roller skates and cane] are Amos and Andy of radio fame, dancers Vernon and Irene Castle, Will Rogers [in the cowboy hat] and, on either side of the curtain, Curry and his wife, Kathleen.)

■ L. GUGLIELMI, *Wedding in South Street,* 1936

After the War—A Golden Decade: The Abstract Expressionists

Abstract expressionism was an amalgam of modernist ideas, evolved among artists who had little in common other than the rejection of cubist geometry and a passion for personal expression. Hofmann, with his linear calligraphy imposed on amorphous areas of color, was an early inspiration of the movement and its chief theoretician. He explained that abstract expressionists sought to "present" their inner and often subconscious world rather than to "represent" the outer world of known objects. Pollock espoused "action" painting (related to the earlier "automatic" painting of the surrealists), which depended less on a preconceived plan than on his own body movements in the act of brushing, dripping, or throwing paint on the canvas. He painted his huge works on the floor, where he could walk around them and "literally be in the painting." Rothko, absorbed in the subtle interaction of areas of color, was a pioneer in "color-field abstraction."

The period was "golden" in a more literal sense as well. Widely exhibited in Europe, the more famous of these artists commanded prices previously paid only for old masters. Current art became a commodity subject to manipulation in the rich art market rather than by the patronage of a dedicated few, and New York replaced Paris as the art capital of the world.

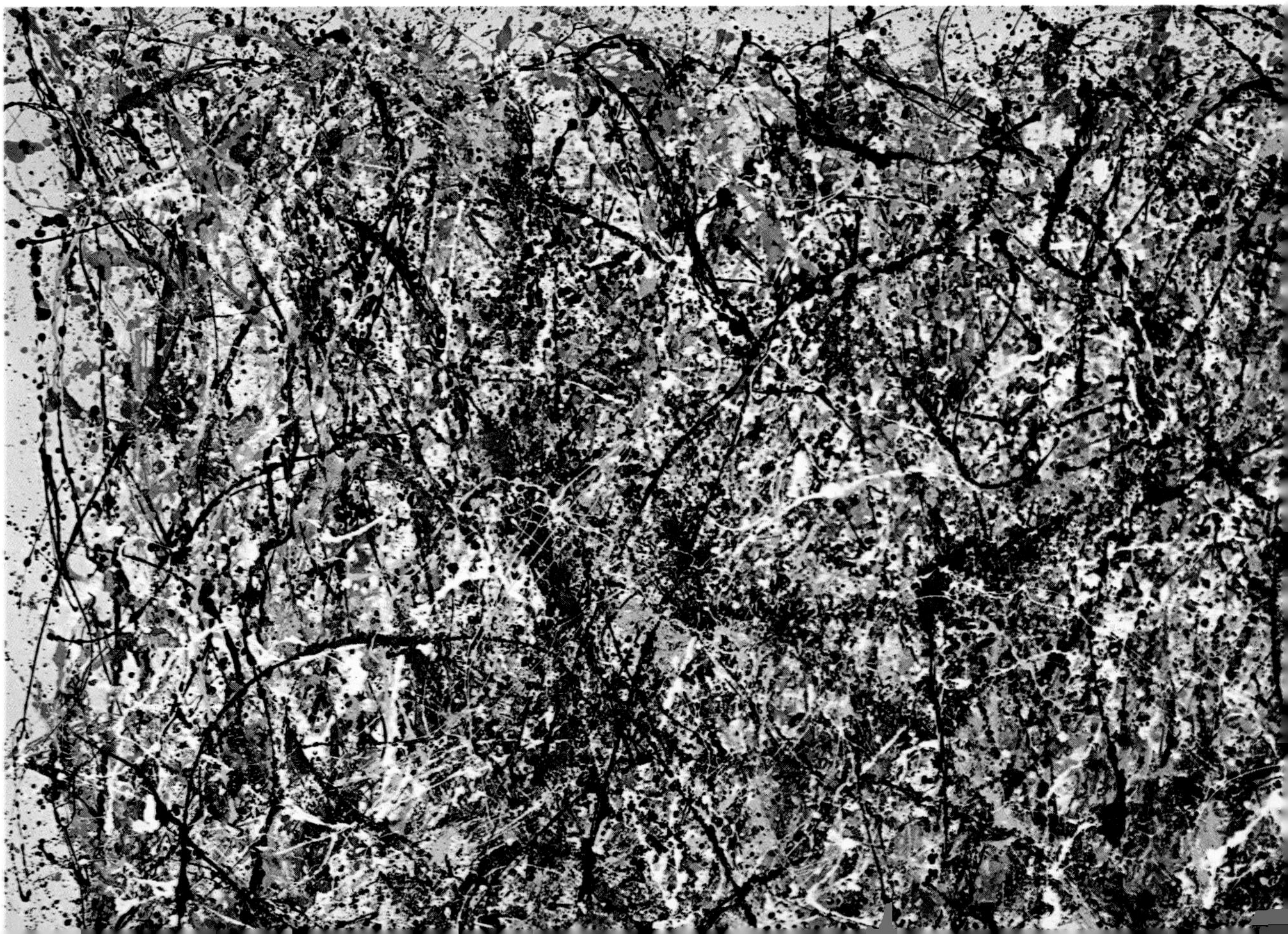

■ HANS HOFMANN, *Fantasia,* 1943

■ MARK ROTHKO, *Number 10,* 1950

■ JACKSON POLLOCK, *One,* 1950

■ ARSHILE GORKY, *Agony*, 1947

The abstract expressionists did not necessarily abandon subject matter. Gorky, early in the movement, retained figural elements, but his *Agony* represents not a person in pain but pain itself. De Kooning, an action painter, began a famous series of "women" in 1950. The work of Stamos, though even less specific, has mystical and often symbolic overtones. Both Motherwell and Kline, as their titles show, used actual places and events as a starting point for abstract comment. Motherwell's interest in the Spanish elegy theme was life-long, dating from 1949 to a version commissioned for the opening of the east wing of the National Gallery of Art in Washington, D.C., in June, 1978. The artists of the forties and fifties, commonly called the New York School, are misnamed, since many worked elsewhere and used New York only as a funnel to their public. Rothko (along with Clyfford Still, another painter in this group) was a seminal influence in West Coast art.

■ FRANZ KLINE, *New York*, 1953

■ ROBERT MOTHERWELL
Elegy to the Spanish Republic, 108
1965–1967

■ WILLEM DE KOONING
Woman VIII, 1961

■ THEODOROS STAMOS
High Snow—Low Sun II, 1957

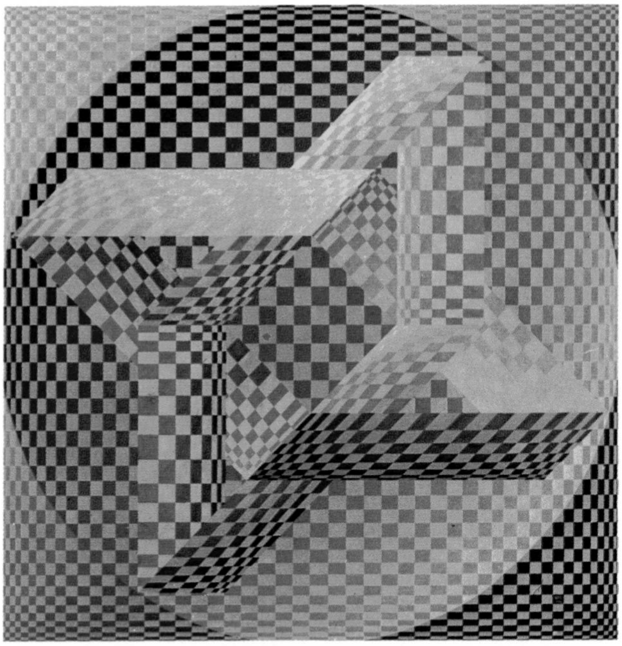

■ BEN CUNNINGHAM, *Equivocation*, 1964

■ HELEN FRANKENTHALER, *Good Luck Orange*, 1969

■ JOSEF ALBERS, *Homage to the Square: Apparition*, 1959

■ BARNETT NEWMAN, *Who's Afraid of Red, Yellow, and Blue III,* 1966–1967

Experiments in Perception and Design

In the diverse art of the sixties one important trend seems to have been away from the self-absorption, emotive content, and free forms of the preceding art toward a more cool, detached, and scientific approach. Minimalists bewildered the public with huge, seemingly monochrome canvases which required a sharp eye (or good glasses) to discern subtle variations; Newman sometimes limited himself to two simple color areas or the interruption of a single line in order to force attention on an elementary relationship of color or form. New applications of paint tended to eliminate the personal touch of the artist's brush: In the "color stain" paintings of Frankenthaler, thin pigment was allowed to spread over raw canvas in large areas; "hard edge" painters like Stella favored smooth flat surfaces, sharply defined, applied with heavy acrylic and sometimes fluorescent paints; Stella's *Sabra II* also used the new "shaped canvas," which, by escaping the conventional rectangle, opened fresh possibilities of design within a varied exterior frame.

The op artists applied the illusion of trompe l'oeil to abstract art and made new analyses of color in both its optical and its psychological effects. In their painstaking paintings, such as Cunningham's *Equivocation,* the forms seem to change and move in front of the eyes (the first comprehensive showing of op, at the Museum of Modern Art in 1964, was appropriately called The Responsive Eye). A major stimulus in these directions was the teaching and work of Albers, who, like Hofmann, was a refugee from Europe. His *Homage to the Square: Apparition* is one of a long series studying the variations of color and dimension possible within one simple design.

■ FRANK STELLA, *Sabra II,* 1967

■ JASPER JOHNS
Target with Four Faces
1955

■ ROBERT RAUSCHENBERG, *Retroactive I,* 1964

■ ROY LICHTENSTEIN, *Varoom,* 1963

■ ANDY WARHOL, *Marilyn Monroe,* 1967

Popular and Public Images

The highly abstract and theoretical art of the postwar decades was bound to arouse a countermovement, and the pop artists of the sixties provided it. They took delight in putting down elitist pretensions. They chose such popular subjects as a suicidal movie star and a murdered president, and they drew on mass-media techniques: the *Varoom* of the comic strip, silk-screened variations of the photo image, the dotted screen of commercial printing. Johns, while still working as an abstract expressionist, used repetitively such simple and easily identified symbols as the target and the flag.

The pop artists (and others), seeing that high prices were cutting off a potential audience, turned to the medium of the print in limited editions. They contributed to a renascence of this important medium, which had been more or less moribund since the 19th century when photography replaced its traditional uses.

Museums too had by now begun to alter their function, to become not merely repositories of art but to communicate art as a part of the total culture. As a result of the "new museology," museums sometimes had waiting lines as long as those at movie houses.

By the 1970s more avant-garde art was seen in public places than ever before. Anuszkiewicz, a subtle analyst of color, designed an exterior mural for a YWCA building that shows a dramatic accent in an urban setting.

■ RICHARD ANUSZKIEWICZ, mural, YWCA Building, New York, 1972

■ ANDREW WYETH, *Albert's Son,* 1959

■ RICHARD ESTES, *The Candy Store*, 1969

A Hold on Reality

Whatever the art fashion of the moment, representational art is consistently produced not only with the skills demanded by advertising and the media but in serious easel painting as well. The durable human appeal of the realist tradition is demonstrated by Andrew Wyeth, who painted in devoted and careful detail the people and places he knew best. Some painters, such as Philip Pearlstein and Alice Neel, while discarding traditional notions of beauty, stubbornly maintained the validity of figure and portrait painting in a new mode. Neel said, "I wouldn't know what flattery is."

The new realism that came to the fore in the seventies is quite different from anything in the past. Romanticism and special pleading gave way to an often brutal view of Americans and their culture—the chrome glitter of vehicles, storefronts, and supermarkets, a photo-realist record of every human blemish often enlarged to exaggerated size. These painters seem to be fixed upon a detached factual statement of life exactly as it looks.

For other artists the reality of the work exists in its germinal ideas or in the creative act of producing it rather than in a finished product crystallized on the walls of museums and collectors. They have produced ephemeral (even self-destroying) works and a "conceptual art," documented by photographic, verbal, or schematic description rather than a painted canvas. Art is no longer dictated either by a predominant style or by conventional categories; experimentation has no limit so long as there are sympathetic observers.

29/THE AFFLUENT SOCIETY

John F. Kennedy made a striking and popular president. He projected an image of originality and imaginativeness combined with moderation and good sense. He appointed two Republicans to his Cabinet. He further flouted convention by making his younger brother Robert F. Kennedy attorney general. (When critics objected to this appointment, the president responded with a quip, saying that he had "always thought it was a good thing for a young attorney to get some government experience before going out into private practice.")

Kennedy had a genuinely inquiring mind. Unlike Eisenhower, he waded eagerly through long, tedious reports. He kept up with dozens of magazines and newspapers and consumed books of all sorts voraciously. He invited leading scientists, artists, writers, and musicians to the White House. As Jefferson had sought to teach Americans to value the individual regardless of status, Kennedy seemed intent on teaching the country to respect and understand its most talented minds. He recruited a record number of intellectuals for government service.

Kennedy seemed bent on being a strong president; he was determined to change the direction in which the nation was moving. He hoped to revitalize the economy and extend the influence of the United States abroad. His inaugural address was a call for commitment: "Ask not what your country can do for you," he said. "Ask what you can do for your country." In 1962 he brought the weight of his entire administration, even that of the FBI, to bear on the steel corporations when they attempted to raise prices after having made what he considered a tacit promise not to do so in return for government help in persuading the steelworkers to forgo substantial wage increases. Faced with such a potent display of presidential disapproval, including the threat of an antitrust suit, the steelmen backed down. Kennedy lavished much energy on Congress, showering the legislators with special messages and keeping himself closely informed about their doings, even to the extent of assigning to one of his aides the unenviable task of wading through the *Congressional Record* every day.

Kennedy's New Frontier

But the president was no Wilson or Franklin Roosevelt when it came to bending Congress to his will. Perhaps he was too reasonable, too amiable, too diffident and conciliatory in his approach. A coalition of Republicans and conservative southern Democrats resisted his plans for federal aid to education, for urban renewal, for a higher minimum wage, for medical care for the aged.

The president reacted mildly, almost ruefully, when his opponents in Congress blocked proposals that in his view were reasonable and moderate. He seemed to doubt at times that the cumbersome machinery of the federal government could be made to work. Even to some of his warmest supporters he sometimes appeared strangely paralyzed, unwilling either to exert strong pressure on Congress or to appeal to public opinion. Pundits talked of a "deadlock of democracy" in which party discipline had crumbled and positive legislative action had become next to impossible.

During the presidential campaign Kennedy had promised "to get the country moving again." The slow growth of the economy in the Eisenhower years had troubled liberal economists. American output was increasing year by year, but at a much slower rate than the economies of other industrial nations. Three recessions occurred between 1953 and 1961, each marked by increases in unemployment. During the declines of 1958 and 1961, almost 7 percent of the work force was unemployed. Morever, in the latter years of Eisenhower's presidency the rate of inflation began to rise. This inflation encouraged workers to press for higher wages. It also added to the cost of government, which kept the budget out of balance and thereby worsened the inflation.

Despite Eisenhower's concern for balancing the budget, during the recessions his administration reacted in the orthodox Keynesian manner, cutting taxes, easing credit, and expanding public works programs. However, liberal economists argued that he was not employing the Keynesian medicine in large enough doses. Kennedy had fewer inhibitions about federal spending and was much influenced by the liberals' ideas. The lagging growth rate and the persistence of unemployment alarmed him. But because he was worried about the continuing inflation, he rejected proposals for cutting taxes in order to stimulate consumer spending. He was afraid that tax cuts would throw the federal budget further out of balance.

Economic growth remained sluggish. In January 1963 the economist Walter Heller persuaded Kennedy to try a different (but still Keynesian) approach. Any considerable increase in federal spending, Heller argued, would either require higher taxes that would drain money from the private sector of the economy and thus tend to be self-defeating or spark a new inflationary explosion. On the other hand, if personal and corporate income taxes were lowered, the public would have more money to spend on consumer goods and corporations could invest in new facilities for producing these goods. Federal expenditures need not be cut because the increase in economic activity would raise private and corporate incomes so much that tax revenues would rise even as the tax rate was falling.

Although the prospect of lower taxes was

■ John F. Kennedy was among the most photogenic of modern chief executives. Cornell Capa snapped him in a thoughtful mood behind the presidential desk.

tempting, Kennedy's call for reductions of $13.5 billion ran into strong opposition. Republicans and conservative Democrats thought the reasoning behind the scheme too complex and theoretical to be practicable. It went nowhere.

Race Relations

Kennedy's original approach to the race question was a cautious one. He did not integrate the National Guard, for example, because he was afraid that if he did, southern Guard units would withdraw. His lack of full commitment dismayed many who were concerned about the persistence of racial discrimination in the country. Seemingly without plan, a grass roots drive for equal treatment sprang up among southern blacks.

It began in the tightly segregated city of Montgomery, Alabama. On the evening of December 1, 1955, Rosa Parks boarded a bus on her way home from work. She dutifully took a seat toward the rear as law and custom required. After white workers and shoppers had filled the forward section the driver ordered her to give up her place. She refused. She had suddenly made up her mind, she later recalled, "never to move again."

Rosa Parks was arrested. The blacks of Montgomery, led by a young Baptist clergyman, Martin Luther King, Jr., promptly organized a boycott of the buses. For a full year they refused to ride until finally, after a Supreme Court ruling in their favor, Montgomery desegregated its public transportation system.

This success encouraged blacks elsewhere in the South to band together against the caste system. It made King, who preached civil (nonviolent) disobedience as the best way to destroy segregation, a national figure. His organization, the Southern Christian Leadership Conference, moved to the forefront of the civil rights movement, and in 1964 his work won him the Nobel Peace Prize. Other organizations joined the struggle, notably the Congress of Racial Equality (CORE), which had been founded in 1942.

In February 1960 four black students in Greensboro, North Carolina, sat down at a lunch counter in a Woolworth five-and-ten and refused to leave when they were denied service. Their "sit-in" sparked a national movement; students in dozens of other southern towns and cities copied the

Greensboro blacks' example. By the end of 1961 over 70,000 persons had participated in sit-ins. A new organization, the Student Nonviolent Coordinating Committee (SNCC), was founded to provide a focus for the sit-in movement.

In May 1961 black and white foes of segregation organized a "freedom ride" to test the effectiveness of federal regulations prohibiting discrimination in interstate transportation. Boarding buses in Washington, they traveled across the South, heading for New Orleans. In Alabama they ran into bad trouble: at Anniston racists set fire to their bus, in Birmingham they were assaulted by a mob. But violence could not stop the freedom riders. Other groups descended on the South, many deliberately seeking arrest in order to test local segregation ordinances in the courts. Repeatedly these actions resulted in the breaking down of racial barriers.

Integrationists like King attracted an enormous following, but some blacks, proud of their race and contemptuous of white prejudices, urged their fellows to reject "American" society and all it stood for. Black nationalism became a potent force. The followers of Elijah Muhammad, leader of the Black Muslim movement, disliked whites so intensely that they advocated racial separation. They demanded that a part of the United States be set aside for the exclusive use of blacks. The Muslims called Christianity "a white man's religion." They urged their followers to be industrious, thrifty, and abstemious—and to view all whites with suspicion and hatred. "This white government has ruled us and given us plenty hell, but the time has arrived that you taste a little of your own hell," Elijah Muhammad said. "There are many of my poor black ignorant brothers . . . preaching the ignorant and lying stuff that you should love your enemy. What fool can love his enemy?"

Out of the Black Muslim movement came one of the most remarkable Americans of the 20th century, Malcolm X. Born Malcolm Little in 1925, son of a Baptist minister who was an organizer for Marcus Garvey's Universal Negro Improvement Association, he grew up in poverty in Michigan. When he was 15 he moved to Boston, then to New York's Harlem. For several years he lived on the edge of the underworld, using and selling narcotics, working in the numbers racket, acting as a procurer for prostitutes. Soon he was carrying a gun. He became, he later explained, "a true hustler—uneducated, unskilled at anything honorable . . . exploiting any prey that presented itself." At the age of 21 he was convicted of stealing a watch and sentenced to 10 years in jail.

■ In Selma, Alabama, in 1965 Dr. Martin Luther King, Jr., knelt with his followers to offer a prayer. They had been arrested and were on their way to jail after committing an act of civil disobedience.

While in prison Malcolm was converted to the Black Muslim faith. He cast off his dissolute ways, and after being paroled in 1952, he rose rapidly in the Muslim hierarchy. A brilliant speaker and organizer, he preached the standard Muslim combination of idealism and hatred. "Let us rid ourselves of immoral habits and God will be with us to protect and guide us," he told a Harlem audience in 1960. Then he added: "For the white man to ask the black man if he hates him is just like the rapist asking the *raped,* or the wolf asking the *sheep,* 'Do you hate me?' "

Pushed by all these developments, President

■ Calling for black separatism, Malcolm X told an interviewer in 1964, "The Negro (must) develop his character and his culture in accord with his own nature."

Kennedy gradually changed his policy. Under the direction of his brother Robert, the Justice Department acted to force the desegregation of interstate transportation facilities in the South, to compel southern election officials to obey the civil rights laws, and to override resistance to school integration. In 1962, when Mississippi authorities led by Governor Ross Barnett blocked the admission of a black to the University of Mississippi, the president called the Mississippi National Guard to federal duty and, despite bloody riots, made the university accept the student.

In 1963 Kennedy came out for a comprehensive new civil rights bill. It made racial discrimination in hotels, restaurants, and other places of public accommodation illegal, and it gave the attorney general the power to bring suits on behalf of individuals in order to speed up the lagging school desegregation movement. The measure also authorized agencies of the federal government to withhold federal funds from state-administered programs that failed to treat people of all races equally. This bill ran into stiff opposition in Congress.

Blacks organized a demonstration in Washington, attended by 200,000 people, to rally support for the measure. At this gathering Martin Luther King, Jr., delivered his "I have a dream" address, looking forward to a time when racial prejudice no longer existed and people of all religions and colors could join hands and say, "Free at last! Free at last!" Kennedy sympathized with the purpose of the Washington gathering, but he feared it would make passage of the civil rights bill more difficult rather than easier. As in other areas, he was not a forceful advocate of his own proposals.

The Two Cuban Crises

His curious lack of determined leadership also marred Kennedy's management of foreign affairs, particularly during his first year in office. He hoped to reverse the Truman-Eisenhower policy of backing reactionary regimes merely because they were anticommunist. Recognizing that American economic aid could accomplish little in Latin America unless accompanied by internal reforms, he organized the Alliance for Progress, which committed the Latin Americans to land reform and economic development projects with the assistance of the United States. At the first sign of pro-Soviet activity in any Latin American country, however, he tended to overreact. Critics have described his behavior toward Latin America as a mixture of "overambitious idealism" and "pointless obsessiveness" about security.

His most serious blunder involved Cuba. Anti-Castro exiles were eager to organize an invasion of their homeland, reasoning that the Cuban masses would rise up against Castro as soon as "democratic" forces provided a standard they could rally to. Under Eisenhower the Central Intelligence Agency had begun training some 2,000 of these men in Central America. Kennedy, after much soul-searching, authorized the attack. The exiles were given American weapons, but no planes or warships were committed to the operation. The invaders struck on April 17, 1961, landing at the Bay of Pigs, on Cuba's southern coast.

■ **Wheeling his protégé Castro to safety, nursemaid Khrushchev snarls "Bully!" at President Kennedy. A comment from the Toronto *Star* on the Bay of Pigs affair.**

The Cuban people failed to flock to their lines, and they were soon pinned down and forced to surrender. Since America's involvement could not be disguised, the affair exposed the country to all the criticisms that a straightforward assault would have produced without accomplishing the overthrow of Castro. Worse, it made Kennedy appear impulsive as well as unprincipled. Castro soon admitted that he was a Marxist and tightened his connections with the Soviet Union.

In June Kennedy met with Premier Khrushchev in Vienna. During their discussions he evidently failed to convince the Russian that he would resist pressure with determination. In August Khrushchev abruptly closed the border between East and West Berlin and erected an ugly wall of concrete blocks and barbed wire across the city to check the exodus of dissident East Germans. When Kennedy did not order American forces in Berlin to tear down the wall, the Soviet leader found further reason to believe he could pursue aggressive tactics with impunity. Resuming the testing of nuclear weapons, he exploded a series of gigantic hydrogen bombs, one with a power three thousand times that of the bomb which had devastated Hiroshima.

When the Russians resumed nuclear testing, Kennedy followed suit. He expanded the American space program,* vowing that an American

*Russian superiority in space was gradually reduced. In April 1961 the "cosmonaut" Yuri Gagarin orbited the earth; in August another Russian circled the globe 17 times. The first American to orbit the earth, John Glenn, made his voyage in February 1962. In 1965 the United States kept a two-man Gemini craft in orbit two weeks, effecting a rendezvous between it and a second Gemini.

would land on the moon within 10 years, and called on Congress for a large increase in military spending. At the same time, he pressed forward along more constructive lines. He visited Latin America in an effort to counteract the bad impression resulting from the Bay of Pigs incident. He established the Agency for International Development to administer American economic aid throughout the world and the Peace Corps, an organization that attempted to mobilize American idealism and technical skills to help developing nations.

These actions had no effect on the Russians. In 1962 Khrushchev devised the boldest and most reckless challenge of the Cold War, one that brought the world to the verge of nuclear disaster. During the summer months he moved military equipment and thousands of Soviet technicians into Cuba. American intelligence reports revealed that, in addition to planes and conventional weapons, guided missiles were being imported and launching pads constructed on Cuban soil. Kennedy ordered U–2 reconnaissance planes to photograph these sites, and by mid October he had proof that intermediate-range missile sites capable of delivering hydrogen warheads to points as widely dispersed as Quebec, Minneapolis, Denver, and Lima, Peru, were rapidly being completed.

The president faced a dreadful decision. To blast these sites before they became operational might result in a third world war. To delay would be to expose the United States to great danger and increase the Russians' ability to obtain their objectives elsewhere in the world by threat. At a meeting with Soviet Foreign Minister Andrei Gromyko, Kennedy, without revealing what he knew, asked for an explanation of Soviet activity in Cuba. Gromyko told him that only "defensive" (antiaircraft) missiles were being installed.

Gromyko's duplicity strengthened Kennedy's conviction that he must take strong action at once. On October 22 he went before the nation on television. The Soviet buildup was "a deliberately provocative and unjustified change in the status quo," he said. The navy would stop and search all vessels headed for Cuba and turn back any containing "offensive" weapons. Kennedy called on Khrushchev to dismantle the missile bases and remove from the island all weapons capable of striking the United States. Any Cuban-based nuclear attack would result, he warned, in "a full retaliatory response upon the Soviet Union."

For several days, while the world held its breath, work on the missile bases continued. Then Khrushchev backed down. He withdrew the missiles and cut back his military establishment in Cuba to modest proportions. Kennedy then lifted the blockade.

Critics have argued that Kennedy overreacted to the Soviet missiles. There was no evidence that the Russians were planning an attack; the missiles might be seen as a deterrent against a possible attack on the Soviet Union by United States missiles in Europe. By demanding their withdrawal Kennedy risked triggering a nuclear holocaust. Yet he probably had no choice once the existence of the sites was known to the public. (In some respects this is the most frightening aspect of the crisis.)

For better or worse, Kennedy's firmness in the missile crisis repaired the damage done his reputation by the Bay of Pigs affair. It also led to a lessening of Soviet-American tensions. At last, it seemed, the Russians were beginning to realize what all-out nuclear war would mean. Khrushchev agreed to the installation of a "hot line" telephone between the White House and the Kremlin so that in any future crisis leaders of the two nations could be in instant communication. In July 1963 all the powers except France and China signed a treaty banning the testing of nuclear weapons in the atmosphere. Peaceful coexistence seemed more and more inevitable. The Soviet Union, the United States, and all the major nations appeared to be realizing that no power could shape the earth in its own exclusive image, that the planet's teeming, diverse billions must live together in mutual tolerance if they would live at all.

Lyndon Johnson and the Great Society

Although his domestic policies were making little progress in Congress and the economy remained in rather poor shape, Kennedy retained his hold on public opinion. In the fall of 1963 most observers believed he would easily win a second term.

Then, while visiting Dallas, Texas, on November 22, he was shot in the head by an assassin, Lee Harvey Oswald, and died almost instantly.

This senseless murder shocked the world and precipitated an extraordinary series of events. Oswald had fired on the president with a rifle from an upper story of a warehouse. No one saw him pull the trigger. He was apprehended largely because, in his demented state, he killed a policeman later in the day in another part of the city. He denied his guilt, but a mass of evidence connected him with the crime. Before he could be brought to trial, he was himself murdered by one Jack Ruby, the owner of a Dallas nightclub, while being transferred, in the full view of television cameras, from one place of detention to another.

This amazing incident, together with the fact that Oswald had defected to Russia in 1959 and then returned to the United States, convinced many people that some nefarious conspiracy lay at the root of the tragedy. Oswald, the argument ran, was a pawn, his murder designed to keep him from exposing the masterminds who had engineered the assassination. An investigation by a special commission headed by Chief Justice Earl Warren came to the conclusion that Oswald acted alone, yet doubts persisted in many minds.

Kennedy's death made Lyndon B. Johnson president. A 55-year-old Texan, the first southerner to reach the White House since Woodrow Wilson, Johnson could draw on a bottomless supply of political experience, having served in Congress almost continuously since 1937. From 1949 until his election as vice-president he had been a senator and, for most of that time, Senate Democratic leader. As a lawmaker he preferred to move with contemporary currents rather than flail fruitlessly against them in search of perfection; as a legislative leader he employed "the Johnson Treatment" to influence his colleagues. He could be heavy-handed, domineering, persistent, and at the same time obliging, infinitely patient, a master psychologist. Essentially he overwhelmed people by the sheer force of his personality. "The Treatment was an almost hypnotic experience and rendered the target stunned and helpless," the journalists Rowland Evans and Robert Novak explained.

Early in his career Johnson had voted against a bill making lynching a federal crime and had opposed bills outlawing state poll taxes and establishing a federal Fair Employment Practices Commission, but after he became important in national affairs he consistently championed racial equality. During the Eisenhower years he cooperated with the administration better than many Republicans, placing political responsibility above partisan ambition.

On taking office as president, Johnson benefited from the sympathy of the world and from the shame felt by many who had opposed Kennedy's proposals for political or selfish reasons. Bills that had long been buried in committee now sailed through Congress. Early in 1964 Kennedy's tax cut was passed, and the resulting economic stimulus caused a boom of major dimensions. A few months later the Civil Rights Act of 1964 became law. This measure broke down the last barriers to black voting in the southern states and outlawed formal racial segregation of all sorts. Racial discrimination by employers and unions was declared illegal, and an Equal Employment Opportunity Commission was created to enforce this provision.

Johnson could claim most of the credit for these accomplishments. He lobbied members of Congress relentlessly. He was on the telephone day and night, taking about a hundred calls a day. His energy, his earthy humor, and his almost poetic appeals for social and racial justice carried everything before him. Congressmen whom Kennedy had failed to budge succumbed to Johnson's combination of bullying and pleading and political back-scratching. One member of his Cabinet called him "a combination of Boccaccio and Machiavelli and John Keats." In the end he achieved what he called a "national consensus" without slipping into a series of meaningless compromises.

Johnson saw himself as a reformer in the tradition of Franklin Roosevelt. He declared war on poverty and set out to create a "Great Society" in which poverty no longer existed. During the New Deal, Franklin Roosevelt was accused of exaggeration when he said that one-third of the nation was "ill-housed, ill-clad, ill-nourished." In fact Roosevelt had underestimated the extent of poverty when he made that statement in 1937. Wartime economic growth reduced the percentage of poor people in the country substantially, but in 1960 between 20 and 25 percent of all American families—about 40 million persons—were living below the poverty line.

That so many millions could be poor in an "affluent" society was deplorable but not difficult to explain. In any community a certain number of persons cannot support themselves because of physical incapacity, low intelligence, or psychological difficulties. There were also in the United States entire regions, the best known being the Appalachian area, that had been by-passed by economic development and no longer provided their inhabitants with adequate economic opportunities.

More specific to the postwar situation was the increasing need for technical skills and the shift in the kinds of jobs available from the production of goods to distribution and communication. The shifts meant that educated workers with good verbal abilities could easily find well-paid jobs. Persons who had no special skills or were poorly educated could often find nothing.

Certain less obvious influences were at work too. Poverty tends to be more prevalent among the old and the young than among those in the prime of life; in the postwar decades these two groups were growing more rapidly than any other. Social security payments amounted to less than the elderly needed to maintain themselves decently, and some of the poorest workers, such as agricultural laborers, were not covered by the system at all. Unemployment was twice as high among youths in their late teens as in the nation as a whole and far higher among young blacks than young whites.

With the movement of the middle class to the suburbs, poverty became, in the words of Michael Harrington, whose book *The Other America* (1962) did much to call attention to the problem, "less visible" to those well-meaning citizens whose energies had to be mobilized if it was to be eradicated. Many poor people were becoming alienated from society. In earlier times most of the poor were recent immigrants, believers in the American dream of rags to riches, strivers who accepted their low status as temporary. The modern poor, many studies indicated, tended to lack motivation; they felt trapped by their condition and gave up.

Poverty exacted a heavy price, both from its victims and from society. Statistics reflected the relationship between low income and bad health. Only about 4 percent of people from middle-income families were chronically ill, whereas more than 16 percent of those with less than $2,000 were so afflicted. Mental illness varied inversely with income, as did alcoholism, drug addiction, and crime.

Johnson won a majority victory in his war on poverty when Congress passed the Economic Opportunity Act of 1964. This law created a mélange of programs, among them a Job Corps similar to the New Deal Civilian Conservation Corps, a community action program to finance local efforts; an educational program for small children (Project Head Start); a work-study program for college students; and a system for training the unskilled unemployed and for lending money to small businessmen in poor areas. The Economic Opportunity Act perfectly reflected Johnson's social philosophy. It combined the progressive concept of the welfare state with the conservative idea of individual responsibility. The government would support the weak and disadvantaged by giving them a fair chance to make it on their own.

Buttressed by his numerous legislative triumphs, Johnson sought election as president in his own right in 1964. He achieved this ambition in unparalleled fashion. His championing of civil rights won him the almost unanimous support of blacks; his economy drive attracted the well-to-do and the business interests; his war on poverty held the allegiance of labor and other elements traditionally Democratic. His southern antecedents counterbalanced his liberalism on the race question in the eyes of many white southerners.

The Republicans played into his hands by nominating a conservative, Senator Barry M. Goldwater of Arizona. A large majority of the voters found Goldwater out of date on economic questions and dangerously aggressive on foreign affairs. During the campaign Democrats told a joke that went something like this:

> Goldwater is president. An aide rushes into his office.
>
> AIDE: Mr. President, the Russians have just launched an all-out nuclear attack on us. Their missiles will strike in 15 minutes. What shall we do?
>
> GOLDWATER: Have all the wagons form a circle.

In November Johnson won a sweeping victory, collecting over 61 percent of the popular vote and carrying all the country except Goldwater's Ari-

■ **President Johnson and Vice-President-Elect Hubert Humphrey celebrate their 1964 election victory Texas style, complete with hunting outfits and a barbeque.**

zona and five states in the Deep South. Quickly he pressed ahead with his Great Society program. Working closely with Congressional leaders, he got a comprehensive medical insurance system established. The Medicare Act of 1965 combined hospital insurance for retired people (funded by social security taxes) with a voluntary plan to cover doctors' bills (paid for in part by the government). The law also provided for grants to the states to help pay the medical expenses of poor people below the retirement age of 65. This part of the system was called Medicaid.

Next Congress passed the Elementary and Secondary Education Act. This measure gave federal funds to schools based on the number of students from poor families that they enrolled. It concentrated large sums on upgrading education in urban slums and impoverished rural areas. Another major achievement was the Immigration Act of 1965, which did away with the national-origin system of admitting newcomers. Instead, 290,000 persons a year were to be admitted, priorities being based on such grounds as skill and the need for political asylum.* Other laws passed at Johnson's urging in 1965 and 1966 provided support for scientific research, highway safety, crime control, slum clearance, clean air, and the preservation of historic sites. It was one of the most remarkable outpourings of important legislation in American history.

Society in Flux

Despite his great victory and his ambitious plans, Johnson delivered a sober inaugural address when he took the oath of office on January 20, 1965. The nation was "prosperous, great, and mighty," he said, but "we have no promise from God that our greatness will endure." The president was obviously thinking of the enormous changes that were occurring in the country. He spoke of "this fragile existence," and he warned the people that they lived "in a world where change and growth seem to tower beyond the control, and even the judgment of men."

The population was expanding rapidly. During the depressed thirties it had increased by 9 million; in the fifties it rose by more than 28 million, and the trend was continuing. Population experts observed startling shifts within this expanding mass. The westward movement had by no means ended with the closing of the frontier in the 1890s. One indication of this was the admission of Hawaii and Alaska to the Union in 1959. More significant was the growth of the "sun belt"—Florida and the states of the Southwest. California added more than 5 million to its numbers between 1950 and 1960, and in 1963 it passed New York to become the most populous state in the Union. Nevada and Arizona were expanding at an even more rapid rate.

*The new law placed a limit of 120,000 persons a year on immigration from countries in the Western Hemisphere. Immigration from these countries had been unrestricted.

The climate of the Southwest was particularly attractive to older people, especially after the perfection of mass-produced room air conditioners, and the population growth reflected the prosperity that enabled pensioners and other retired persons to settle there. At the same time the area attracted millions of young workers, for it became the center of the aircraft and electronics industries and the government's atomic energy and space programs. These industries displayed the best side of modern capitalism: high wages, comfortable working conditions, complex and efficient machinery, and the marriage of scientific technology and commercial utility.

The same industries employed increasing numbers of women because much of the work demanded dexterity rather than brute strength. Yet being gainfully employed did not seem to discourage women from marrying and having children: in 1940 about 15 percent of American women in their early thirties were unmarried, in 1965 only 5 percent.

Advances in transportation and communication added to geographical mobility. In the postwar decades the automobile appeared to enter its golden age. In the booming 1920s, when the car became an instrument of mass transportation, about 31 million autos were produced by American factories. During the 1950s, 58 million rolled off the assembly lines; during the 1960s, 77 million.

Gasoline use rose sharply. The more mobile population drove further in more reliable and more comfortable vehicles over smoother and less congested highways. And the new cars were heavier and more powerful than their predecessors. Gasoline consumption first touched 15 billion gallons in 1931; it soared to 35 billion gallons in 1950 and to 92 billion in 1970. A new business, the motel industry (the word, typically

■ **A graphic example of one effect of modern highway construction: Interstate 80 slashes its way through an older neighborhood in Paterson, New Jersey.**

American, was a combination of *motor* and *hotel*), developed to service the millions of tourists and businessmen who burned all this fuel on their travels.

The development of the Interstate Highway System, begun under Eisenhower in 1956, was a major cause of increased mobility. The new roads did far more than facilitate long-distance travel; they accelerated the shift of population to the suburbs and the consequent decline of inner-city districts.

Despite the speeds that cars maintained on them, the new highways were much safer than the old roads. The traffic death rate per mile driven fell steadily, almost entirely because of the interstates. On the other hand, the environmental impact of the system was frequently severe. Elevated roads cut ugly swaths through cities, and the cars they carried released tons of noxious exhaust fumes into urban air. Hillsides were gashed, marshes filled in, forests felled—all in the name of speed and efficiency.

Although commercial air travel had existed in the thirties and had profited from wartime technical advances in military aircraft, it truly came of age when the first jetliner—the Boeing 707, built in Seattle, Washington—went into service in 1958. Almost immediately jets came to dominate long-distance travel, while railroad passenger service and transatlantic liners declined in importance.

Another important postwar change was the advent of television as a means of mass communication. Throughout the 1950s the public bought sets at a rate of 6 or 7 million annually; by 1961 there were 55 million in operation, receiving the transmissions of 530 stations. During the sixties the National Aeronautics and Space Agency (NASA) began launching satellites capable of transmitting television pictures to earth, and the American Telephone and Telegraph Company orbited private commercial satellites that could relay television programs from one continent to another.

Television combined the immediacy of radio with the visual impact of films, and it displayed most of the strengths and weaknesses of both in exaggerated form. It swiftly became indispensable to the political system, both for its coverage of public events and as a vehicle for political advertising. Its handling of the events following President Kennedy's assassination, of national conventions and inaugurations, and other news developments made history come alive for tens of millions. It brought sports events before the viewer vividly, attracting enormous audiences and producing so much money in advertising revenue that the economics of professional sports was revolutionized. Team franchises were bought and sold for millions, and star players commanded salaries in the hundreds of thousands.

Some excellent drama was presented, especially on the National Educational Television network, along with many filmed documentaries. *Sesame Street,* a children's program presented on the educational network, won international recognition for its entertainment value and for its success in motivating underprivileged children. Commercial television indirectly improved the level of radio broadcasting by siphoning off much of the mass audience; more radio time was devoted to serious discussion programs and to classical music, especially after the introduction of frequency modulation (FM) transmissions.

The entertainment offered by most television stations was generally abominable; Newton Minow of the FCC called it a "vast wasteland." The lion's share of television time was devoted to uninspired and vulgar serials, routine variety shows, giveaway and quiz programs designed to reveal and revel in the ignorance of the average citizen, and reruns of old movies cut to fit rigid time periods and repeatedly interrupted at climactic points by "commercials." Most sets had poor acoustical qualities, which made them inferior instruments for listening to music. Serious discussion programs were too often relegated to inconvenient times, and there were not enough of them. Yet children found television fascinating, remaining transfixed before the screen when—their elders said—they should have been out of doors or curled up with a book.

Another defect of television's virtues was its capacity for influencing the opinions and feelings of viewers. The insistent and strident claims of advertisers punctuated every program with monotonous regularity. Politicians discovered that no other device or method approached television as a means of reaching large numbers of voters with an illusion of intimacy. Since television time was expensive, only candidates who possessed or had access to huge sums could afford to use the me-

■ **Astronaut Edwin Aldrin on the moon, July 1969. Reflected in his helmet visor are flight commander Neil Armstrong, who took this picture, and part of their spacecraft. Television enabled some 600 million people to see the historic event.**

dium—a dangerous state of affairs in a democracy. In time Congress clamped a lid on campaign expenditures, but this action did not necessarily reduce the amounts spent on television, with its capacity to reach so many people.*

Another postwar change was the marked broadening of the middle class. In 1947 only 5.7 million American families had what might be considered middle-class incomes—enough to provide something for leisure, entertainment, and cultural activities as well as for life's necessities. By the early 1960s more than 12 million families, about a third of the population, had such incomes. As they prospered, middle-class Americans became more culturally homogeneous and broader-gauged in their interests.

The percentage of immigrants in the population declined steadily; by the mid sixties over 95 percent of all Americans were native-born. This trend made for social and cultural uniformity. So did the rising incomes of industrial workers and the changing character of their labor. By 1962 about 90 percent of all industrial workers enjoyed such "fringe benefits" as paid vacations and medical insurance at least partially financed by their employers, and nearly 70 percent participated in pension plans. The growth of pension funds made the union officials who managed them powers in the financial world. The merger in 1955 of the two great labor federations, the AFL and the CIO, added to the prestige of all union labor as well as to the power of the new organization.

As blue-collar workers invaded the middle class by the tens of thousands, they moved to suburbs previously reserved for junior executives, shopkeepers, and the like. They shed their work clothes for business suits. They took up golf. In sum, they adopted values and attitudes commensurate with their new status—which helps explain the growing conservatism of labor unions. During the Great Depression, when they were underdogs of sorts, the unions fought for social justice. In the

*The government now provides substantial public funds to major candidates in presidential elections.

1960s many union workers seemed more interested in preserving their gains against the ravages of inflation and taxation than they were in social reform.

Many social scientists found in the expansion of the middle class another explanation of the tendency of the country to glorify the conformist. They attributed to it the blurring of party lines in politics, the national obsession with "moderation" and "consensus," the complacency of so many Americans, their tendency, for example, to be at once more interested in churchgoing and less concerned with the philosophic aspects of religion than their forebears were. One prominent divine complained of "the drive toward a shallow and implicitly compulsory common creed," a "religion-in-general, superficial and syncretistic, destructive of the profounder elements of faith." Yet no one could deny that the new middle class had more creature comforts (automobiles, household appliances, even swimming pools).

More debatable was the impact of the expansion of the middle class on national standards of taste. For a time after World War II the nation seemed on the verge of a literary outburst comparable to that which followed World War I. A number of excellent novels based on the military experiences of young writers appeared, the most notable being Norman Mailer's *The Naked and the Dead* (1948) and James Jones' *From Here to Eternity* (1951). Unfortunately, a new renaissance did not develop. The most talented younger writers rejected materialist values but preferred to bewail their fate rather than rebel against it. Jack Kerouac, founder of the "beat" (for beatific) school, reveled in the chaotic description of violence, perversion, and madness. At the other extreme, J. D. Salinger, perhaps the most popular writer of the 1950s and the particular favorite of college students—*The Catcher in the Rye* (1951) sold nearly 2 million copies in hardcover and paperback editions—was an impeccable stylist, witty, contemptuous of all pretense; but he too wrote about people entirely wrapped up in themselves.

In *Catch-22* (1955), the book that replaced *Catcher in the Rye* in the hearts of college students, Joseph Heller produced a war novel at once farcical and an indignant denunciation of the stupidity and waste of warfare. In *The Victim* (1947), *The Adventures of Augie March* (1953), *Herzog* (1964), and many other novels, Saul Bellow described characters possessed of their full share of eccentricities and weaknesses without losing sight of the positive side of modern life. Bellow won many literary awards, including a Nobel prize.

All these novelists and a number of others whose books were of lesser quality were widely read. Year after year sales of books increased, despite much talk about how television and other diversions were undermining the public's interest in reading. Sales of paperbacks, first introduced in the United States in 1939 by Pocket Books, reached enormous proportions: by 1965 about 25,000 titles were in print and sales were approaching 1 million copies *a day*.

Cheapness and portability only partly accounted for the popularity of paperbacks. Readers could purchase them in drugstores, bus terminals, and supermarkets as well as in bookstores. Teachers, delighted to find out-of-print volumes easily available, assigned hundreds of them in their classes. And there was a psychological factor at work: the paperback became fashionable. People who rarely bought hardcover books purchased weighty volumes of literary criticism, translations of the works of obscure foreign novelists, specialized historical monographs, and difficult philosophical treatises now that they were available in paper covers.

The expansion of the book market, like so many other changes, was not an unalloyed benefit even for writers. It remained difficult for unknown authors to earn a decent living. Publishers tended to concentrate their interest and their money on authors already popular and on books aimed at a mass audience. Even among successful writers of unquestioned ability, the temptations involved in large advances and in book club contracts and movie rights diverted many from making the best use of their talents.

American painters were affected by the same forces that influenced writers. In the past the greatest American artists had been shaped by European influences. This situation changed dramatically after World War II with the emergence of abstract expressionism, or action painting. This "New York school" was led by Jackson Pollock (1912–1956), who composed huge abstract designs by laying his canvas on the floor of his studio and squeezing paint on it directly from tube or pot in a wild tangle of color. The abstract expressionists were utterly subjective in their approach to art.

"The source of my painting is the Unconscious," Pollock explained. "I am not much aware of what is taking place; it is only after that I see what I have done." Pollock tried to produce not the representation of a landscape but, as the critic Harold Rosenberg put it, "an inner landscape that is part of himself."

Untutored observers found the abstract expressionists crude, chaotic, devoid of interest. The swirling, dripping chaos of the followers of Pollock, the vaguely defined planes of color favored by Mark Rothko and his disciples, and the sharp spatial confrontations composed by the painters Franz Kline, Robert Motherwell, and Adolph Gottlieb required too much verbal explanation to communicate their meaning to the average observer. On the other hand, viewed in its social context, abstract expressionism reflected, like so much of modern literature, the estrangement of the artist from the world of the atomic bomb and the computer, a revolt against contemporary mass culture with its unthinking acceptance of novelty for its own sake.

The experimental spirit released by the abstract expressionists led to "op" art, which employed the physical impact of pure complementary colors to produce dynamic optical effects. Even within the rigid limitations of severely formal designs composed of concentric circles, stripes, squares, and rectangles, such paintings appeared to be constantly in motion, almost alive.

"Op" was devoid of social connotations; another variant, "pop" art, playfully yet often with acid incisiveness satirized many aspects of American culture: its vapidity, its crudeness, its violence. The painters Jasper Johns, Roy Lichtenstein, and Andy Warhol created portraits of mundane objects such as flags, comic strips, soup cans, and packing cases. "Op" and "pop" art reflected the mechanized aspects of life; the painters made use of technology in their work—for example, they enhanced the shock of vibrating complementary colors by using fluorescent paints. Some artists imitated newspaper-photograph techniques by fashioning their images of sharply defined dots of color. Others borrowed from contemporary commercial art, employing spray guns, stencils, and masking tape to produce flat, "hard-edge" effects. The line between "op" and "pop" was frequently crossed, as in Robert Indiana's *Love,* which was reproduced and imitated on posters, Christmas cards, book jackets, buttons, rings, and a postage stamp.

■ **Robert Indiana's many versions of *Love* (this is a 1966 oil) include an aluminum sculpture.**

Color and shape as ends in themselves, stark and often on a heroic scale, typified the new styles. Color-field painters covered vast planes with flat, sometimes subtly shaded hues. Frank Stella, one of the most universally admired of the younger artists, composed complicated bands and curves of color on enormous, eccentrically shaped canvases. To an unprecedented degree, the artist's hand—the combination of patience and skill that had characterized traditional art—was removed from painting.

The pace of change in artistic fashion was dizzying—far more rapid than changes in literature. Aware that their generation was leading European artists instead of following them gave both artists and art lovers a sense of participating in events of historic importance.

As with literature, the effects of such success were not all healthy. Successful artists became national personalities, a few of them enormously rich. For these, each new work was exposed to the glare of publicity, sometimes with unfortunate results. Too much attention, like too much money, could be distracting, even corrupting, especially for young artists who needed time and obscurity to develop their talents. "Schools" rose and fell in rapid order, often, it seemed, at the whim of one or another influential critic or dealer. Being different was more highly valued than aesthetic quality or technical skill. No matter how outlandish, "the newest thing" attracted respectful attention. The idea of the avant-garde as a revolt of creative minds against the philistinism of the middle class no longer had meaning, despite the fact that the existence of an expanding middle class made the commercial success of modern art possible.

Two Dilemmas

The many changes of the era help to explain why President Johnson expressed so much uncertainty in his inaugural address. Looking at American society more broadly, two dilemmas seem to have confronted people in the 1960s. One dilemma was that progress was often self-defeating. Reforms and innovations instituted with the best of motives often made things worse rather than better. Instances of this dilemma, large and small, are so numerous as to defy summary. DDT, a powerful chemical developed to kill insects that were spreading disease and destroying valuable food crops, proved to have lethal effects on birds and fish—and perhaps indirectly on human beings. Goods manufactured to make life fuller and happier (automobiles, detergents, electric power) produced waste products that disfigured the land and polluted air and water. Cities built in order to bring culture and comfort to millions became pestholes of crime, poverty, and depravity.

Change occurred so fast that experience (the recollection of how things had been) tended to become less useful and sometimes even counterproductive as a guide for dealing with current problems. Foreign policies designed to prevent wars, devised on the basis of knowledge of the causes of past wars, led, because the circumstances were different, to new wars. Parents who sought to transmit to their children the accumulated wisdom of their years found their advice rejected, often with good reason, because that "wisdom" had little application to the problems their children had to face.

The second dilemma was that modern industrial society placed an enormous premium on social cooperation, at the same time undermining the individual citizen's sense of being essential to the proper functioning of society. The economy was as complicated as a fine watch; a breakdown in any one sector had ramifications that spread swiftly to other sectors. Yet specialization had progressed so far that individual workers had little sense of the importance of their personal contributions and thus felt little responsibility for the smooth functioning of the whole. Effective democratic government required that all voters be knowledgeable and concerned, but few could feel that their individual voices had any effect on elections or public policies. The exhaust fumes of millions of automobiles poisoned the air, but it was difficult to expect the single motorist to inconvenience himself by leaving his car in the garage when his restraint would have no measurable effect on total pollution.*

People tried to deal with this dilemma by joining groups; then the groups became so large that members felt as incapable of influencing them as they did of influencing the larger society. The groups were so numerous and had so many conflicting objectives that instead of making citizens more socially minded they often made them more self-centered. The organization—union, club, party, pressure group—was a potent force in society. Yet few organizations were really concerned with the common interest, though logic required that the common interest be regarded if individuals or groups were to achieve their special interests.

These dilemmas produced a paradox. The United States was the most powerful nation in the world, its people the best educated, richest, and probably the most energetic. American society was technologically advanced and dynamic, American traditional values idealistic, humane, democratic. Yet the nation seemed incapable of mobilizing its resources intelligently to confront the most obvious challenges, its citizens unable to achieve personal happiness or identification with their fellows, the society helpless in trying to live up to its most universally accepted ideals.

In part the paradox was a product of the strengths of the society and the individuals who made it up. The populace as a whole was more sophisticated. People were more aware of their immediate interests, less willing to suspend judgment and follow leaders or to look on others as

*Shortly after writing these lines, I received a letter from my teenage daughter: "It is frustrating because one person just can't feel that she's doing anything. I can use soap instead of detergents and no paper bags, but what good do I feel I'm doing when there are people next door having a party with plastic spoons and paper plates?"

better qualified to decide what they should do. They belonged to the "me generation"; they knew that they lived *in* a society and that their lives were profoundly affected *by* that society, but they had trouble feeling that they were part *of* a society.

President Johnson recognized the problem. He hoped to solve it by establishing a "consensus" and building his Great Society. No real consensus emerged; American society remained fragmented, its members divided against themselves and often within themselves. Awareness of the complexities and contradictions of life and human institutions was a mark of increasing maturity but also a source of uncertainty and insecurity.

Mixed Blessings

The vexing character of modern conditions could be seen in every aspect of life. The economy, after decades of hectic expansion, accelerated still more rapidly. The gross national product approached one trillion dollars, but inflation was becoming increasingly serious. Workers were under constant pressure to demand raises—which only served to drive prices still higher. Socially the effect was devastating; it became impossible to expect workers to see inflation as a social problem and to restrain their personal demands. Putting their individual interests before those of the whole, they were prepared to disrupt the economy whatever the social cost. Even public employees traditionally committed to a no-strike policy because they worked for the entire community—teachers, garbage collectors, fire fighters, the police—succumbed to this selfish, if understandable, way of looking at life.

Economic expansion resulted in large measure from technological advances, and these too proved to be mixed blessings. As we have seen, World War II needs stimulated the development of plastics like nylon, of synthetic rubber, and of radar, television, and other electronic devices. After the war these products came into their own. Plastics invaded field after field—automobile parts, building materials, adhesives, packaging materials.

In 1951 scientists began to manufacture electricity from nuclear fuels; in 1954 the first atomic-powered ship, the submarine *Nautilus,* was launched. Although the peaceful use of atomic energy remained small compared to other sources of power, its implications were immense. Equally significant was the perfection of the electronic computer, which revolutionized the collection and storage of records, solved mathematical problems beyond the scope of the most brilliant human minds, and speeded the work of bank tellers, librarians, billing clerks, statisticians—and income tax collectors.

Computers lay at the heart of industrial automation, for they could control the integration and adjustment of the most complex machines. In automobile factories they made it possible to produce entire engine blocks automatically. In steel mills molten metal could be poured into molds, cooled, rolled, and cut into slabs without the intervention of a human hand, the computers locating defects and adjusting the machinery to correct them far more accurately than the most skilled steelworker, and in a matter of seconds. Taken in conjunction with a new oxygen smelting process six or eight times faster than the open-hearth method, computer-controlled continuous casting promised to have an impact on steel making as great as that of the Bessemer process in the 1870s.

The material benefits of technology commonly had what the microbiologist René Dubos described as "disastrous secondary effects, many of which are probably unpredictable." The consumption of petroleum necessary to produce power soared and began to outstrip supplies, threatening shortages that would disrupt the entire economy. The burning of this fuel released unmeasurable tons of smoke and other polluting gases into the atmosphere, endangering the health of millions. "Life is enriched by one million automobiles," Dubos noted, "but can be made into a nightmare by one hundred million."

The vast outpouring of flimsy plastic products and the increased use of paper, metal foil, and other "disposable" packaging materials seemed about to bury the country beneath mountains of trash. The commercial use of nuclear energy also caused problems. Scientists insisted that the danger from radiation was nonexistent, but the possibility of accidents could not be eliminated entirely, and the safe disposal of radioactive wastes became increasingly difficult.

Even an apparently ideal form of scientific advance, the use of commercial fertilizers to boost food output, had unfortunate side effects: phosphates washed from farmlands into streams some-

■ **The Chrysler assembly line, Detroit, 1982. Faster than the camera eye can record, multiple robot arms weld auto bodies, with not a human worker in sight.**

times upset the ecological balance and turned the streams into malodorous death traps for aquatic life. Above all, technology increased the capacity of the earth to support people. As population increased, production and consumption increased, exhausting supplies of raw materials and speeding the pollution of air and water resources. And where would the process end? Viewed from a world perspective, it was obvious that the population explosion must be checked or it would check itself by pestilence, war, starvation, or some combination of these scourges. Yet how to check it?

New Racial Turmoil

President Johnson and most of those who supported his policies expected that the 1964 Civil Rights Act, the Economic Opportunity Act, Medicare and Medicaid, and the other elements in the war on poverty would produce an era of racial peace and genuine social harmony—the Great Society that everyone wanted. The change that occurred in the thinking of the black radical Malcolm X seemed a straw in the wind. In 1964 Malcolm left the Muslims and founded his own Organization of Afro-American Unity. While continuing to stress black self-help and the militant defense of black rights, he now saw the fight for racial equality as part of a larger struggle for all human rights. "What we do . . . helps all people everywhere who are fighting against oppression," he said. Yet as in so many other aspects of modern life, progress itself created new difficulties. Early in 1965 Black Muslim fanatics, furious at his defection, murdered Malcolm X in cold blood while he was making a speech in favor of racial harmony.

The assassination was an act of vengeance, not one of social protest. More significant was the fact that official white recognition of past injustices was making blacks more insistent that all discrimination be ended. The very process of righting past wrongs gave them the strength to fight more vigorously. Black militancy, building steadily during the war and the postwar years, had long been ignored by the white majority; in the mid sixties it burst forth so powerfully that the most smug and obtuse white citizens had to accept its existence.

Even Martin Luther King, Jr., the herald of passive resistance, became more demanding. A few weeks after Malcolm's death King led a march from Selma, Alabama, to Montgomery as part of a campaign to force Alabama authorities to allow blacks to register to vote. His marchers were brutally assaulted by state policemen who wielded clubs and tossed canisters of tear gas. Liberal opinion was shocked as never before. Thousands of people descended on Selma to demonstrate their support for the black cause.

Soon militants found a slogan: "Black Power." The expression was given national currency by Stokely Carmichael, chairman of SNCC, in 1966. "The time for white involvement in the fight for equality has ended," Carmichael announced. "If we are to proceed toward true liberation, we must set ourselves off from white people." Since whites "cannot relate to the black experience," the movement "should be black-staffed, black-controlled, and black-financed." Black Power caught on swiftly among militants. This troubled white liberals because people like Carmichael refused "to discriminate between degrees of inequity" among whites. Liberals feared that Black Power would antagonize white conservatives. Liberals argued that since blacks made up only about 11 percent of the population, any attempt to obtain racial justice through the use of naked power was sure to fail.

Meanwhile, black anger erupted in a series of destructive urban riots. The most important occurred in Watts, a ghetto of Los Angeles, in August 1965. A trivial incident—police officers halted a motorist who seemed to be drunk and attempted to give him a sobriety test—brought thousands into the streets. The neighborhood almost literally exploded: for six days Watts was swept by fire, looting, and bloody fighting between local residents and 15,000 National Guardsmen, called up to assist the police. Order was restored only after 34 persons had been killed, more than 850 wounded, 3,100 arrested. Property damage in Watts came to nearly $200 million.

The following summer saw similar outbursts in New York, Chicago, and other cities. In 1967 further riots broke out, the most serious in Newark, where 25 were killed, and Detroit, where the death toll came to 43 and where looting and arson assumed monstrous proportions. Then, in April 1968, the revered Martin Luther King was murdered in Memphis, Tennessee, by a white man, James Earl Ray.* Blacks in more than a hundred cities swiftly unleashed their anger in paroxysms of burning and looting. White opinion was shocked and profoundly depressed. The death of King appeared to destroy the hope that his doctrine of pacific appeal to reason and right could solve the racial problem.

Public fear and puzzlement led to many investigations of the causes of the riots, the most important being that of the commission headed by Governor Otto Kerner of Illinois, which President Johnson appointed following the murder of King. The conclusions of most of the studies were complex but fairly clear. Race riots had a long history in the United States, but the outbursts of the 1960s were different. Earlier troubles usually began with attacks by whites that led to black counterattacks. Riots of the Watts type were begun by blacks, and the fighting was mostly between blacks and law enforcement officers trying to control them. White citizens tended to avoid the centers of trouble, and blacks seldom ranged outside their own neighborhoods.

The rioters were expressing frustration and despair; their resentment was directed more at the social system than at individuals. As the Kerner commission put it, the basic cause was an attitude of mind, the "white racism" that deprived blacks of access to good jobs, crowded them into slums, and, for the young in particular, eroded all hope of escape from such misery. Ghettos bred crime and depravity—as slums always have—and the complacent refusal of whites adequately to invest money and energy in helping ghetto residents, or even to acknowledge that the black poor deserved help, made the modern slum unbearable. While the ghettos expanded, middle-class whites tended

*Ray fled to England but was apprehended, extradited, convicted, and sentenced to 99 years in prison.

more and more to "flee" to the suburbs or to call on the police "to maintain law and order," a euphemism for cracking down hard on deviant black behavior no matter how obvious the connection between that behavior and the slum environment.

The victims of racism employed violence not so much to force change as to obtain psychic release; it was a way of getting rid of what they could not stomach, a kind of vomiting. Thus the concentration of the riots in the ghettos themselves, the smashing, Samsonlike, of the source of degradation even when this meant self-destruction. When fires broke out in black districts, the firefighters who tried to extinguish them were often showered with bottles and bricks and sometimes shot at, while above the roar of the flames and the hiss of steam rose the apocalyptic chant, *"Burn, baby, burn!"*

The most frightening aspect of the riots was their tendency to polarize society on racial lines. Advocates of Black Power became more determined to separate themselves from white influence; they exasperated white supporters of school desegregation by demanding schools of their own. Extremists formed the Black Panther party and collected weapons to resist the police. "Shoot, don't loot," the radical H. Rap Brown advised all who would listen. The Panthers demanded public compensation for injustices done to blacks in the past, pointing out that following World War II, West Germany had made payments to Jews to make up for Hitler's persecutions. In 1968 they nominated Eldridge Cleaver, a convict on parole, for president. Although Cleaver was an articulate and intelligent man whose autobiographical *Soul on Ice,* written in prison, had attracted much praise, his nomination for the presidency widened the racial breach.

Middle-class city residents often resented what seemed the "favoritism" of the federal government and state and local administrations, which sought through "affirmative action" to provide blacks with new economic opportunities and social benefits. Efforts to desegregate ghetto schools by "busing" children out of their local neighborhoods was a particularly bitter cause of conflict. Persons already subjected to the pressures caused by inflation, specialization, and rapid change that were undermining social solidarity, and worried by the sharp rise in urban crime rates and welfare costs, found black radicalism infuriating. In the face of the greatest national effort in history to aid them, blacks (they said) were displaying not merely ingratitude but contempt.

Ethnic Pride

The struggles of blacks for equality went hand in hand with those of Mexican-Americans, principally in the Southwest. After World War I, thousands of Mexicans flocked into the region. They could do so legally because the restrictive immigration legislation of the 1920s did not apply to Western Hemisphere nations. When the Great Depression struck, Mexican-Americans were the first to suffer—about half a million were either deported or "persuaded" to return to Mexico during the 1930s. During World War II and again between 1948 and 1965 federal legislation encouraged the importation of *braceros* (temporary farm workers), and many other Mexicans entered the country illegally. The latter were known as *mojados,* or "wet-backs," because they often slipped across the border by swimming the Rio Grande. In general, Mexican-Americans were badly housed, underpaid, and subject to all sorts of discrimination.

Spanish-speaking residents of the Southwest were for a time largely apolitical; they tended to accept their fate with resignation, to mind their own business, not to "make trouble." But in the early 1960s a new spirit of resistance arose. Leaders of the new movement called themselves *Chicanos.* The Chicanos demanded better schools for their children and easier access to higher education. They urged their fellows to take pride in their traditions and culture, to demand their rights, to organize themselves politically. As with the blacks, the dominant middle-class majority adjusted itself to Chicano demands grudgingly and very slowly.

One Chicano nationalist group, the *Alianza* (alliance) led by Reies López Tijerina, tried to secede from New Mexico, an act that brought it into confrontation with the army and ended with Tijerina in prison. Another, the Crusade for Justice headed by Rodolfo "Corky" Gonzales, a professional boxer, poet, and politician, focused on achieving social reforms and setting up political action

■ **In 1973 César Chávez was determinedly walking a picket line outside the regional headquarters of a national grocery chain. His United Farm Workers Union affiliation with the AFL-CIO did not prevent the Teamster's Union from becoming a serious rival in organizing farm workers.**

groups. Its slogan, *Venceremos,* was Spanish for Martin Luther King's pledge: We shall overcome.

The Chicano leader with the widest influence was César Chávez, who concentrated on what superficially was a more limited goal—organizing migrant farm workers into unions. Chávez, who was born in 1927, grew up in migrant camps in California; he had no schooling beyond the seventh grade. After serving in the navy during World War II he went to work for the Community Service Organization, a group seeking to raise the political consciousness of the poor and to develop self-help programs among them. Chávez became general director of the CSO but resigned in 1962 because he felt it was not devoting enough attention to the plight of migrant workers. He then founded the National Farm Workers' Association, later known as the United Farm Workers' Organizing Committee.

In 1965 the grape pickers in his union in Delano, California, struck for higher wages and union recognition. Chávez, seeing in the strike an opportunity to attack the very structure of the migrant labor system, turned it into a countrywide crusade. Avoiding violence, he enlisted the support of church leaders; he organized sit-ins, a march on the state capital, and then a national consumer boycott of grapes. He demonstrated convincingly that migrant workers could be unionized and that the militant demands of minorities for equal treatment did not necessarily lead to separatism and class or racial antagonism.

Nevertheless, racial controversies continued. Militant Indians (they preferred to be called Native Americans) used the term "Red Power" as the blacks spoke of Black Power. The National Indian Youth Council and later the American Indian Movement (AIM) demanded the return of lands taken illegally from their ancestors. AIM leaders sought total separation from the United States; they envisaged setting up states within states such as the Cherokees had established in Georgia in Jacksonian days. In 1973 some of the radicals occupied the town of Wounded Knee, South Dakota (site of one of the most disgraceful massacres of Indians in the 19th century), and held it at gunpoint for weeks.

Militant ethnic pride characterized the behavior of many white Americans too. Italian-Americans, Polish-Americans, and descendants of other "new immigrant" groups eagerly studied their histories in order to preserve their culture and where necessary revive dying traditions. The American "melting pot," some historians now argued, had not amalgamated the immigrant strains as completely as had been thought. Ethnic diversity became for some an end to be desired, despite the possibility that differences might as easily inspire conflict as harmonious adjustment.

For white "ethnics," the concern for origins was in part nostalgic and romantic. As the number of, say, Greek-Americans who had ever seen Greece declined, the appeal of Greek culture and the sense that some Greek-Americans had of belonging to a distinct cultural group increased. For blacks, whose particular origins were obscured by the catastrophe of slavery, awareness of their distinctiveness was more important. Racial pride was a reflection of the new black militancy and the achievements that blacks had made in the postwar period. There was a black on the Supreme Court (Thurgood Marshall, tactician of the fight for school desegregation). President Johnson had named the first black to a Cabinet post (Robert Weaver, secretary of housing and urban development). The first black since reconstruction (Edward W. Brooke of Massachusetts) was elected to the United States Senate in 1966. A number of large cities, including Atlanta, Georgia, elected black mayors.

The color line was broken in major league baseball in 1947, and soon all professional sports were open to black athletes. Where the reign of black heavyweight boxing champion Jack Johnson (1908–1915) had inspired an open search for a "white hope" to depose him, and where the next black champion, Joe Louis (1937–1949), was accepted by whites because he "knew his place" and was "well behaved," it was possible for champion Muhammed Ali to be a hero to both white and black boxing fans despite his often bizarre behavior and his militant advocacy of racial equality.

Their achievements and advances aside, black Americans had found real self-awareness. The attitude of mind that ran from the lonely Denmark Vesey to Frederick Douglass and to W. E. B. Du Bois had become the black consensus.

Women's Liberation

Concern for improving the treatment of minorities encouraged American women—as it frequently had in earlier times—to speak out more forcefully for their own rights. During the immediate postwar period the women's movement had been relatively quiescent. However, pressures were mounting because social and economic conditions were changing. When the war ended, many women who had taken jobs because of the labor shortage did not meekly return to the home. Some worked to help pay for their veteran-husbands' war-interrupted educations, others to counterbalance the onslaughts of inflation, still others (some married, some not) simply because they enjoyed the money and the independence that jobs made possible. Between 1940 and 1960 the proportion of women workers doubled, and thereafter it increased still more rapidly. The rise was particularly swift among married women, and the difficulties faced by anyone trying to work while having to perform household duties both increased the resentment of these workers and encouraged their husbands to accept changes in male and female family responsibilities.

Married or single, more numerous or not, women workers faced job discrimination of many kinds. In nearly every occupation they were paid less than men who did the same work. Many interesting jobs that they were capable of holding were either closed to them entirely or doled out on the basis of some illogical and often unwritten quota system. In challenging occupations where they could find employment they were rarely given a chance to rise to positions of leadership. Many women objected to this state of affairs even in the 1950s; in the 1960s their protest erupted into an organized and vociferous demand for change.

One of the earliest leaders of the new women's movement was Betty Friedan, whose book *The Feminine Mystique* (1963) sold over a million copies. Friedan argued that advertisers, popular magazines, and other opinion-shaping forces were undermining the capacity of women to use their intelligence and their talents creatively. They were stifling women's potential by a pervasive and not very subtle form of brainwashing designed to convince women of the virtues of domesticity. "The only way for a woman . . . to know herself as a person is by creative work of her own," she wrote.

Friedan had assumed that if able women acted with determination, employers would recognize their abilities and stop discriminating against them. This did not happen. In 1966 she and other feminists founded the National Organization for Women (NOW). Copying the tactics of black ac-

■ **At their second national conference, Betty Friedan (right) and Dr. Kathryn F. Clarenbach of NOW announced a "Bill of Rights for Women in 1968" that was to be presented to all political parties and candidates in that presidential election year.**

tivists, NOW called for equal employment opportunities and equal pay as civil rights. "An active, self-respecting partnership with men" was the objective.

Soon the women's movement became more militant. As black radicals had moved from racial integration to Black Power, so radical women shifted from talk of a partnership with men to war between the sexes. In 1967 NOW came out for an Equal Rights Amendment to the Constitution, for changes in the divorce laws, and for the repeal of laws against abortion. Some radical feminists advocated raising children in communal centers and doing away with marriage as a legal institution. "The family unit is a decadent, energy-absorbing, destructive, wasteful institution," one prominent feminist declared.

Militants attacked all aspects of the standard image of the female sex. Avoiding the error of the Progressive Era reformers who had fought for the vote by stressing differences between the sexes (the supposed "purity" and high moral character of women), they insisted on total equality. Clichés such as "the fair sex" and "the weaker sex" made them see red. They insisted that the separation of "Help Wanted—Male" and "Help Wanted—Female" classified ads in newspapers violated the Civil Rights Act of 1964. They took courses in self-defense in order to be able to protect themselves from muggers, rapists, and casual mashers. They denounced the use of masculine words like "chairman" (favoring "chairperson") and of such terms as "mankind" and "men" to designate people in general.* They substituted "Ms." for both "Miss" and "Mrs." on the ground that the language drew no such distinction between unmarried and married men.

Many women rejected the position even of moderate feminists like Betty Friedan, but few escaped being affected by the women's movement. The presence of women in new roles—as television commentators, airline pilots, police officers—did not prove that a large-scale shift in employment patterns had taken place. Yet even the most unregenerate male seemed to recognize that the balance of power and influence between the sexes

*The difficulty here was that this form of discrimination was built into the structure of the language. Even the word *woman* derives from the Anglo-Saxon *wif-mann,* wife of a man. Efforts to avoid the use of masculine words in general references led to such awkwardnesses as "his/her" and "(s)he."

had been altered. The Civil Rights Act of 1964 had outlawed job discrimination based on sex, and government agencies and the courts were steadily increasing the pressure on employers to conform to its terms.

Education: Youth in Revolt

Young people were in the forefront in both the fight for the rights of blacks and the women's liberation movement. In a time of uncertainty and discontent, full of conflict and dilemma, youth was affected more strongly than the older generations, and it reacted more forcefully. No institution escaped its criticisms, not even the vaunted educational system, which, youth discovered, poorly suited its needs. This was still another paradox of modern life, for American education was probably the best (it was certainly the most comprehensive) in the world.

After World War I, under the impact of Freudian psychology, the emphasis in elementary education shifted from using the schools as instruments of social change, as John Dewey had recommended, to using them to promote the emotional development of the students. "Child-centered" educators played down academic achievement in favor of "adjustment." It probably stimulated the students' imaginations and may possibly have improved their psychological well-being, but observers soon noted that the system produced poor work habits and fuzzy thinking and fostered plain ignorance. Although "educationists" insisted that they were not abandoning traditional academic subjects, they surely deemphasized them. "We've built a sort of halo around reading, writing, and arithmetic," one school principal charged.

The demands of society for rigorous intellectual achievement made this distortion of progressive education increasingly less satisfactory. Following World War II, critics began a concerted assault on the system. The leader of the attack was James B. Conant, former president of Harvard. His book *The American High School Today* (1959) sold nearly half a million copies, and his later studies of teacher education and the special problems of urban schools also attracted wide attention. Conant flayed the schools for their failure to teach English grammar and composition effectively, for neglecting foreign languages, and for ignoring the needs of both the brightest and the slowest of their students. He insisted that teachers' colleges should place subject matter above educational methodology in their curricula.

The success of the Russians in launching their first *Sputnik* in 1957 increased the influence of critics like Conant. To match this achievement, the United States needed thousands of engineers and scientists, and the schools were not turning out enough graduates prepared to study science and engineering at the college level. Suddenly the schools were under enormous pressure, for with more and more young people desiring to go to college, the colleges were raising their admission standards. The "traditionalists" thus gained the initiative, academic subjects a revived prestige. The National Defense Education Act of 1958 supplied a powerful stimulus by allocating funds for upgrading work in the sciences, foreign languages, and other subjects and for expanding guidance services and experimenting with television and other new teaching devices.

Concern for improving the training of the children of disadvantaged minority groups (Mexican-Americans, Puerto Ricans, Indians, blacks) pulled the system in a different direction. Many of these children lived in horrible slums, often in broken homes. They lacked the incentives and training that middle-class children received in the family. Many did poorly in school, in part because they were poorly motivated, in part because the system was poorly adapted to their needs. But catering to the needs of such children threatened to undermine the standards being set for other children. In the cities, where blacks and other minorities were becoming steadily more numerous, many schools failed to serve adequately either the disadvantaged or those fairly well off. Added to the strains imposed by racial conflicts, the effect was to create the most serious crisis American public education had ever faced.

The post-*Sputnik* stress on academic achievement profoundly affected higher education too. "Prestige" institutions such as Harvard, Yale, Columbia, Stanford, Swarthmore, and a dozen other colleges, able to pick and choose among floods of applicants, became training centers for the intellectual elite. The federal and state governments, together with private philanthropic institutions such as the Carnegie Corporation and the Ford Foundation, poured millions of dollars into dormitory and classroom construction, teacher education, and scholarship funds. At the graduate level the federal government's research and development program, administered by the National Science Foundation, provided billions of dollars for laboratories, equipment, professors' salaries, and student scholarships.

At the same time, population growth and the demands of society for specialized intellectual skills caused American colleges to burst at the seams. To bridge the gap between high school and college, the two-year junior college proliferated. Almost unknown before 1920, there were 600-odd junior colleges by the late sixties, and they were the most rapidly growing educational institutions in the country.

For a time after the war, the expansion of higher education took place with remarkable smoothness. Thousands of veterans took advantage of the GI Bill to earn degrees, and thousands more young men and women whose parents had not gone to college seized the new opportunity eagerly. During the 1950s the mood among students was complacency.

In the 1960s the mood changed. The members of this college generation had grown up during the postwar prosperity and had been trained by teachers who were, by and large, New Deal liberals. Modern industrial society with its "soulless" corporations, its bloodless computers, and its equally unfeeling human bureaucracies made them feel insignificant and powerless, despite the material and social advantages it brought them. The "advantages" also made them feel guilty when they thought about the millions of Americans who did not have them. The existence of poverty in a country as rich as the United States seemed intolerable, race prejudice both stupid and evil. The response of their elders to McCarthyism appeared contemptible—craven cowardice of the worst sort—and dangerous. In the age of the atom, rabid anticommunism might end in nuclear war.

If these students had little tolerance for injustice, they seemed to have none at all for personal frustration. Their dissatisfaction often found expression in public protests, riots, and other troubles. The first great outburst convulsed the University of California at Berkeley in the fall of 1964. Angry students staged sit-down strikes in university buildings, organized a "filthy speech" campaign, and disrupted the institution over a period of weeks. Hundreds were arrested; the state legislature threatened reprisals; the faculty became involved in the controversy; and the crisis led to the resignation of the president of the University of California, Clark Kerr. The situation was exacerbated by American involvement in the war in Vietnam, which increased steadily during the late 1960s (see pages 768–773). Large numbers of students considered all wars immoral and objected to university involvement in war-related research projects.

Equally significant in altering the student mood was the frustration that so many of them felt with the colleges. Rapid change made many traditional aspects of college life outmoded, yet like all institutions the colleges adapted slowly to new conditions. The "now" generation lost patience with the glacial pace of campus adjustment. Regulations that students had formerly merely grumbled about evoked determined, even violent opposition. Dissidents denounced rules that restricted their personal lives, such as prohibitions on the use of alcohol and the banning of members of the opposite sex from dormitories. They complained that required courses inhibited their intellectual development. They demanded a share in the government of their institutions, long the private preserve of administrators and professors.

Beyond their specific dissatisfactions, radical students developed an almost total refusal to endure anything they considered wrong. The knotty social problems that made their elders gravitate toward moderation led these students to become intransigent absolutists. The line between right and wrong became for radicals as sharply defined as the edge of a ruler. Racial prejudice was evil: it must be eradicated. War in a nuclear age was insane: armies must be disbanded. Poverty amid plenty was an abomination: end poverty *now*. To the counsel that evil can be eliminated only gradually, that misguided persons must be persuaded to mend their ways, that compromise was the path to true progress, they responded with scorn. Extremists among them, observing the weaknesses of American civilization, adopted a nihilistic position—the only way to deal with a "rotten" society was to destroy it; reform was impossible, constructive compromise corrupting.

■ **A tense moment during the occupation of Low Memorial Library at Columbia University in the spring of 1968. The striking students on the ledge are trying to catch food that is being thrown to them by sympathizers in the foreground; between the two groups a counter demonstration group "The Majority Coalition" is attempting to keep the food from reaching those occupying the library.**

Other young people were so "turned off' by the modern world that they tried to retreat from it, finding refuge in communes, drugs, and mystical religions. Unwilling to confront the two dilemmas described above, they developed a "counterculture" so directly opposite to the way of life of their parents' generation as to suggest to critics that they were still dominated by the culture they rejected. Being part of the counterculture of the "hippie" world meant not caring about money, or material goods, or power over other people. Love was more important than wealth or power, feelings more significant than thought, natural things superior to anything artificial.

Charles Reich, a professor at Yale, praised this view of the world in *The Greening of America* (1970). Reich gave a course on "Individualism in America." One semester he had over 500 students, not one of whom failed. According to the *Yale Course Guide,* published by students, Professor Reich "thinks kids are neat and what can be bad about someone telling you how the system and the older generation have warped and destroyed things for us?"

Critics found the radical students infantile, old-fashioned, and authoritarian: infantile because they could not tolerate frustration or delay, old-fashioned because their absolutist ideas had been exploded by several generations of philosophers and scientists, authoritarian because they rejected majority rule and would not tolerate views in disagreement with their own. And critics pointed out that the hippies' rejection of material values put them unwittingly in conflict with poor people and disadvantaged minorities.

The radicals were seldom numerous in any college, but they were organized in groups such as the Students for a Democratic Society (SDS) and were totally committed. On campus after campus in the late sixties they roused large numbers of their less extreme fellows to take part in sit-ins and other disruptive tactics. Frequently professors and administrators played into their hands, being so offended by their methods and manners that they refused to recognize the legitimacy of some of their demands.

At Columbia in 1968, SDS and black students occupied university buildings and refused to leave unless a series of "non-negotiable" demands (concerning such matters as the university's involvement in secret military research and its relations with minority groups living in the Columbia neighborhood) were met. When, after long delays, President Grayson Kirk called in the police to clear the buildings, a riot broke out in which dozens of students, some of them innocent bystanders, were clubbed and beaten. General student revulsion at the use of the police led to the resignation of Kirk and to the enactment of many university reforms.

The turmoil seemed endless. Extremist groups were torn by factionalism but—it was the bane of modern society—the ability of small groups to disrupt did not diminish.

One heartening aspect of the situation was the increased number of black students attending college. Almost without exception the colleges tried to increase black enrollments even when it meant allocating large percentages of their scholarship funds and lowering academic requirements to compensate for the poor preparation many of these students had received in the schools.

Black college students tended to keep to themselves, and they demanded more control over all aspects of their education than did the typical white. They wanted Black Studies programs, taught and administered by blacks. Achievement of these goals was difficult because of the shortage of black teachers and because professors—including most black professors—considered student control of appointments and curricula unwise and in violation of the principles of academic freedom. Nevertheless the general academic response to black demands was accommodating; if "confrontations" occurred frequently, they were usually resolved by negotiation. Unlike white radical students, blacks tended to confine their demands to matters directly related to local conditions. Although generalization is difficult, probably the majority of academics drew a distinction between black radicals, whose actions they found understandable even when they could not in conscience approve of them, and white radicals, most of whom they thought self-indulgent or emotionally disturbed.

The Sexual Revolution

Young people made the most striking contribution to the revolution that took place in the late 1960s in public attitudes toward sexual relationships. Here change came with startling swiftness. Almost overnight (it seemed in retrospect) conventional ideas about premarital sex, contraception and abortion, homosexuality, pornography, and a host of related matters were openly challenged. Probably the behavior of the majority of Americans did not alter radically. But the majority's beliefs and practices were no longer automatically acknowledged to be the only valid ones. It became possible for individuals to espouse different values and to behave differently with at least relative impunity. Actions that in one decade would have led to social ostracism or even to imprisonment were in the next decade accepted almost as a matter of course.

The causes of this revolution were complex and interrelated; one change led to others. More efficient methods of birth control and antibiotics that cured venereal disease removed the two principal practical arguments against sex outside marriage; with these barriers down, many people found their moral attitudes changing. Almost concurrently, the studies of Alfred C. Kinsey, *Sexual Behavior in the Human Male* (1948) and *Sexual Behavior in the Human Female* (1953), which were based on thousands of confidential interviews with persons from nearly every walk of life, revealed that where sex was concerned, large numbers of Americans did not practice what they preached. Premarital sex, marital infidelity, homosexuality, and various forms of perversion were, Kinsey's figures showed, far more common than most persons had suspected, among women as well as among men.

Once it became possible to look at sex in primarily physical and emotional terms and to accept the idea that one's own urges might not be as uncommon as one had been led to believe, it became much more difficult to object to any sexual activity practiced in private by consenting adults. Homosexuals, for example, began openly to admit their feelings and to demand that the heterosexual society cease to harass and discriminate against them.

Sexual freedom also contributed to the revival of the women's rights movement of the 1960s. For one thing, freedom involved a more drastic revolution for women than for men. Effective methods of contraception obviously affected women more directly than men, and the new attitudes heightened women's consciousness of the way the old sexual standards and patterns of family living had restricted their entire existence. In fact the two revolutions interacted with each other in innumerable ways, some clear, others obscure. Concern for job equality and for sexual freedom fed the demand for day-care centers for children. But an advocate of legalized abortion could be motivated by the belief that women should be as free not to have children as to have them, or by concern for sexual rights as such. And was a militant who denounced "male chauvinist pigs" a feminist or a lesbian?

That the sexual revolution in its many aspects served useful functions was beyond dispute. Reducing irrational fears and inhibitions was liberating for many persons of both sexes, and it tended to help young people form permanent associations on the basis of deeper feelings than their sexual drives. Women surely profited from the new freedom, just as a greater sharing of family duties by husbands and fathers opened men's lives to many new satisfactions. The sexual revolution undoubtedly contributed to the steep decline of the birthrate that set in at the end of the 1960s.

Like other changes, the revolution produced new problems, and some of its results were at best ambiguous. Equality could mean the loss of special advantages for women as well as the shuffling off of restrictions. The equal rights amendment to the Constitution, critics claimed, would sweep away valuable laws protecting working women. For young people, sexual freedom could be very unsettling; sometimes it generated social pressures that propelled them into relationships they were not yet prepared to handle, with grave psychological results. Easy *cures* did not eliminate venereal disease; on the contrary the relaxation of sexual taboos produced what public health officials called a veritable epidemic of gonorrhea and a frightening increase in the incidence of syphilis. Equally perplexing was the rise in the number of illegitimate births.

Exercising the right to advocate and practice previously forbidden activities involved subjecting people who found those activities offensive—still a large proportion of the population—to embarrassment and even to acute emotional distress. Pornography seemed ethically wrong to some people. Abortion raised difficult legal and moral questions, whatever the rights of women to control their own bodies and of society to protect itself from having to care for unwanted children. Did a fetus have rights? Must the father also consent before a woman could be aborted? Such questions exacerbated already serious social conflicts. Clearly, however, the revolution was not about to end, the direction of change not to be reversed.

SUPPLEMENTARY READING

Titles marked with an asterisk have been published in paperback

J. F. Heath, **Decade of Disillusionment: The Kennedy-Johnson Years** (1980), is a good survey of the period, while W. M. O'Neill, **Coming Apart: An Informal History of the 1960s*** (1971), and Godfrey Hodgson, **America in Our Time** (1976), deal more broadly with the decade. On Kennedy, consult J. M. Burns, **John Kennedy: A Political Profile*** (1960), H. S. Parmet, **Jack: The Struggles of John F. Kennedy** (1980), A. M. Schlesinger, Jr., **A Thousand Days*** (1965), and Theodore Sorensen, **Kennedy*** (1965).

On Johnson, see Rowland Evans and Robert Novak, **Lyndon B. Johnson*** (1966), Tom Wicker, **JFK and LBJ*** (1968), E. F. Goldman, **The Tragedy of Lyndon Johnson*** (1969), and Doris Kearns, **Lyndon Johnson and the American Dream*** (1976). The political developments are covered in Congressional Quarterly Service, **Congress and the Nation** (1965, 1969), and J. L. Sundquist, **Politics and Policy** (1968). Economic policies are discussed in S. E. Harris, **Economics of the Kennedy Years*** (1964), the election of 1964 in T. H. White, **The**

Making of the President* (1965). Peter Wyden, **Bay of Pigs** (1979), and Elie Abel, **The Missile Crisis** (1966), describe the most important foreign policy crises of the era. On the changes of the period, see J. K. Galbraith, **The Affluent Society*** (1958) and **The New Industrial State*** (1967), dealing with the economy, and also Paul Goodman, **Growing Up Absurd*** (1960), Kenneth Kenniston, **The Uncommitted*** (1965), and C. A. Reich, **The Greening of America*** (1970).

Population trends are described in C. and I. B. Taeuber, **The Changing Population of the United States** (1958), the movement to the suburbs in R. C. Wood, **Suburbia*** (1959). For television, see G. A. Steiner, **The People Look at Television** (1963). Daniel Hoffman (ed.), **Harvard Guide to Contemporary American Writing** (1979), contains convenient discussions of postwar literature. Morris Dickstein, **Gates of Eden: American Culture in the Sixties** (1977), is part history, part literary criticism, part memoir. Modern art is discussed in J. I. Baur, **Revolution and Tradition in Modern American Art** (1951), Samuel Hunter, **Modern American Painting and Sculpture*** (1959), and Barbara Rose, **American Art Since 1900*** (1967).

For the causes and character of the poverty and urban problems that led Johnson to devise his Great Society program, see Michael Harrington, **The Other America*** (1962), J. C. Donovan, **The Politics of Poverty*** (1967), Oscar Lewis, **La Vida: A Puerto Rican Family in the Culture of Poverty*** (1966), Mitchell Gordon, **Sick Cities: Psychology and Pathology of American Urban Life*** (1963), R. C. Weaver, **The Urban Complex*** (1964), and Jane Jacobs, **The Death and Life of Great American Cities*** (1962).

Students of contemporary race relations should begin with a number of brilliant, highly personal books by black Americans. James Baldwin, **The Fire Next Time*** (1963), first called the new black anger to white attention, but see also M. L. King, Jr., **Stride Toward Freedom*** (1958), Malcolm X, **Autobiography*** (1966), Stokely Carmichael and C. V. Hamilton, **Black Power: The Politics of Liberation in America*** (1967), and Eldridge Cleaver, **Soul on Ice*** (1967). Other important books on race relations include C. E. Silberman, **Crisis in Black and White*** (1964), K. B. Clark, **Youth in the Ghetto** (1964), L. E. Lomax, **The Negro Revolt*** (1963), David Lewis, **King: A Critical Biography** (1970), Clayborne Carson, **In Struggle: SNCC and the Black Awakening of the 1960s** (1981), and August Meier and Elliott Rudwick, **CORE: A Study in the Civil Rights Movement*** (1973). The **Report*** of the National Advisory (Kerner) Commission on Civil Disorders (1968) is full of interesting material. M. S. Meier and Feliciano Rivera, **The Chicanos*** (1972), provides a sympathetic discussion of the problems and aspirations of Mexican-Americans, but see also Joan London and Henry Anderson, **So Shall Ye Reap: The Story of César Chávez & the Farm Workers' Movement*** (1970), A. F. Corwin, **Immigrants—and Immigrants** (1978), and J. R. Garcia, **Operation Wetback** (1980). The revived interest in ethnicity is discussed in Michael Novak, **The Rise of the Unmeltable Ethnics** (1972), and Thomas Sowell, **Ethnic America** (1981).

The literature on the women's movement is voluminous and difficult to evaluate. In addition to W. H. Chafe, **The American Woman*** (1972) and **Women and Equality*** (1977), see Betty Friedan, **The Feminine Mystique*** (1963), Jo Freeman, **The Politics of Women's Liberation** (1975), S. M. Rothman, **Woman's Proper Place** (1978), and C. N. Degler, **At Odds*** (1981).

Educational trends are discussed in Richard Hofstadter and C. D. Hardy, **The Development and Scope of Higher Education in the United States (1952), Jacques Barzun, The House of Intellect*** (1959), R. N. Sanford (ed.), **The American College** (1962), R. O. Bower (ed.), **The New Professors** (1960), Martin Mayer, **The Schools*** (1961), A. E. Bestor, **The Restoration of Learning** (1955), J. B. Conant, **The American High School Today*** (1959) and **Slums and Suburbs*** (1964), and Robert Coles, **Children of Crisis*** (1967). On militancy among college students, see Kenneth Kenniston, **Young Radicals** (1968), S. M. Lipset and P. G. Altbach (eds.), **Students in Revolt** (1969), Roger Kahn, **The Battle of Morningside Heights** (1970), and Kirkpatrick Sale, **SDS** (1973). See also Irwin Unger, **The Movement: A History of the American New Left** (1974), and Theodore Roszak, **The Making of a Counter-Culture** (1969).

30/VIETNAM AND ITS AFTERMATH

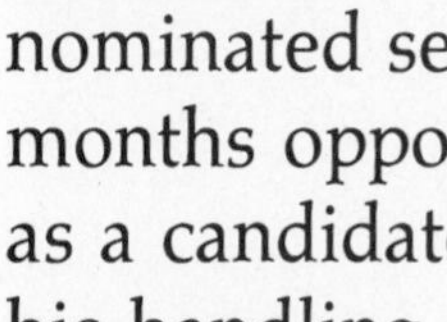

In the fall of 1967 President Lyndon Johnson seemed to have every intention of running for a second full term. Whether he would be reelected was not clear, but that any Democrat could prevent this shrewd and powerful politician from being nominated seemed out of the question. Nevertheless, within a few months opposition to him had become so bitter that he withdrew as a candidate for renomination. The cause of this opposition was his handling of a conflict on the other side of the world—the war in Vietnam.

The War in Vietnam

When Vietnam was divided following the defeat of the French in 1954, a handful of American military "advisers" were sent there to train a South Vietnamese army. As time passed, more American aid and "advice" were dispatched in a futile effort to establish a stable government. Procommunist forces, now called Vietcong, soon controlled large sections of the country, some almost within sight of the capital city of Saigon.

Gradually the Vietcong, drawing supplies from North Vietnam and indirectly from China and the Soviet Union, increased in strength. In response more American money and more military advisers were sent to bolster Ngo Dinh Diem's regime. By the end of 1961 there were 3,200 American military men in the country; by late 1963 the American military presence had risen to more than 16,000. However, no combat troops were involved and only 120 Americans had been killed.

The Diem government, despite the assistance, could not suppress the Vietcong rebels, and it steadily alienated more South Vietnamese interests. In November 1963, shortly before Kennedy was assassinated, a group of South Vietnamese generals overthrew Diem and killed him. (American officials encouraged the coup without realizing that the generals planned to execute Diem.)

In August 1964, after claiming that North Viet-

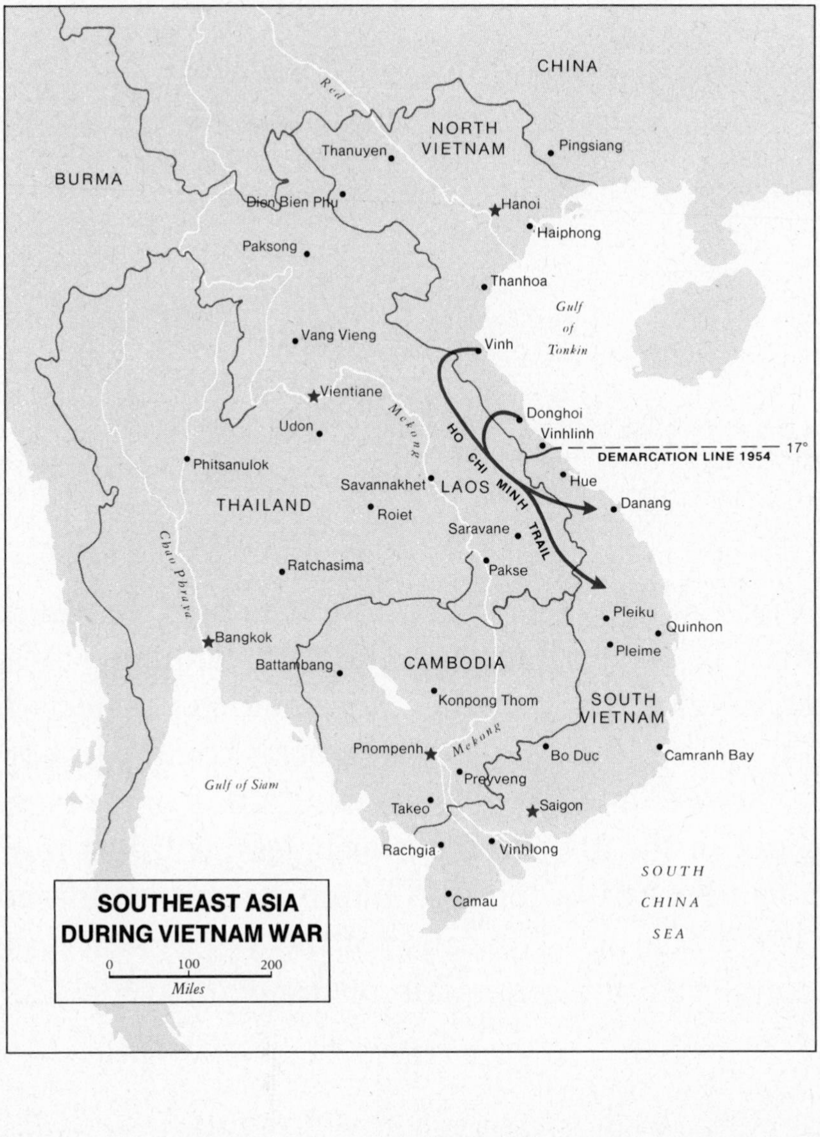

namese gunboats had fired on American destroyers in the Gulf of Tonkin, President Johnson demanded, and in an air of crisis obtained, an authorization from Congress to "repel any armed attack against the forces of the United States and to prevent further aggression."

With this blank check, and buttressed by his sweeping defeat of Goldwater in the 1964 presidential election, Johnson sent *combat* troops to South Vietnam and directed air attacks against targets in both South and North Vietnam. At first the American ground troops were supposed to be merely teachers and advisers of the South Vietnamese troops. Then they were said to be there to defend air bases, with the understanding that they would return fire if they were attacked. Next came word that the troops were being used to assist South Vietnamese units when they came under enemy fire. In fact the Americans were soon attacking the enemy directly, mounting "search and destroy missions" aimed at clearing the foe from villages and entire sections of the country.

Johnson's "escalation" of the American commitment occurred piecemeal and apparently without plan. At the end of 1965, 184,000 Americans were in the field; a year later, 385,000; after another year, 485,000. By the middle of 1968 the number exceeded 538,000. As the scope of the action broadened, the number of American casualties rose. Each increase in the number of troops was met by corresponding increases from the other side. Russia and China sent no combat troops but stepped up their aid, and thousands of North Vietnamese regulars filtered across the 17th parallel to join the Vietcong insurgents. The United States was engaged in a full-scale war, one that Congress never declared. Johnson based his actions on the controversial Gulf of Tonkin resolution.

From the beginning the war divided the American people sharply. Defenders of the president's policy, who were called hawks, emphasized the nation's moral responsibility to resist aggression and what President Eisenhower had called the "domino" theory (based on an analogy with the western powers' failure to resist Hitler before 1939), which predicted that if the communists were allowed to "take over" one country, they would soon take its neighbors, then *their* neighbors, and so on until the entire world had been conquered. The United States was not an aggressor in Vietnam, the hawks insisted, and they stressed Johnson's oft-expressed willingness to negotiate a general withdrawal of "foreign" forces from the country, which the communists repeatedly rejected.

American opponents of the war, called doves, argued that the struggle between the South Vietnamese government and the Vietcong was a civil war in which Americans should not meddle. They stressed the repressive, undemocratic character of the Diem regime and of those that followed as proof that the war was not a contest between democracy and communism. They objected to the massive aerial bombings (more explosives were dropped on Vietnam between 1964 and 1968 than on Germany and Japan combined in World War II), to the use of napalm and other chemical weapons such as the defoliants that were sprayed on forests and crops and which wreaked havoc among noncombatants, and to the killing of civilians by American troops. They discounted the domino theory, pointing both to the growing communist split into Chinese and Russian camps and to the traditional hostility of all Vietnamese to the Chinese, which they claimed made Chinese expansion into Southeast Asia unlikely. And they deplored the heavy loss of American life—over 40,000 dead by 1970—and the enormous cost in money, which came to exceed $20 billion a year. Besides being a major cause of the inflation of the 1960s, the war was diverting public funds from domestic programs aimed at solving the problems of poverty and race relations, reducing pollution, and improving education and urban life.

Although President Johnson sometimes acted deviously, he and his advisers believed they were defending freedom and democracy. What became increasingly clear as time passed and the costs mounted was that military victory was impossible. Yet American leaders were extraordinarily slow to grasp this fact. Repeatedly they advised the president that one more escalation (so many more soldiers, so many more air raids) would break the enemy's will to resist. The smug arrogance bred by America's brief postwar monopoly of nuclear weapons persisted in some quarters long after the monopoly had been lost. As late as 1965 McGeorge Bundy, President Johnson's special assistant for national security affairs, apparently told an interviewer (he later claimed to have been misunderstood) that "the United States was the

■ **Graphic proof of the effectiveness of defoliation: at top, an unsprayed mangrove forest; at bottom, a mangrove forest that had been sprayed with herbicides in 1965, as it looked in 1970.**

locomotive at the head of mankind, and the rest of the world the caboose." And like the proverbial donkey plodding after the carrot on the stick, Johnson repeatedly followed the advice of hawks like Bundy.

For a long time, as opinion polls demonstrated, a majority of the American people believed he was correct. Patriotism and pride, along with the costly "lessons" of 1931–1939 and a stubborn refusal to admit that a mistake had been made, held them to this course.

Election of 1968

Gradually the doves increased in number. Students, for idealistic reasons and because they resented being drafted to fight in Vietnam; businessmen, alarmed by the effects of the war on the economy; and others for different reasons became increasingly dissatisfied with the president's policy.

As late as the fall of 1967 opposition to the war, in Congress and elsewhere, remained disorganized. Then, in November 1967, Senator Eugene McCarthy of Minnesota, low-keyed, rather introspective, never a leading figure in the upper house, announced that he was a candidate for the 1968 Democratic presidential nomination. Opposition to the war was his issue.

Preventing Johnson from getting the Democratic nomination in 1968 seemed on the surface impossible. Aside from the difficulty of defeating a "reigning" president, there were the solid domestic achievements of Johnson's Great Society program: the Medicare Act of 1965, creating a health insurance program for retired people; greatly expanded federal funding of primary and secondary education and public housing; the Civil Rights Act of 1965, which provided for federal registration of black voters in districts where they had been systematically kept from the polls. McCarthy took his chances of being nominated so lightly that he did not trouble to set up a real organization. He entered the campaign only because he believed that someone must step forward to put the Vietnam question before the voters. He prepared to campaign in the primaries.

Suddenly, early in 1968, on the heels of the latest announcement by the American military that the communists were about to crack, North Vietnam and Vietcong forces launched a general offensive to correspond with their Lunar New Year (Tet). Striking 39 of the 44 provincial capitals, many other towns and cities, and every American base, they caused chaos throughout South Vietnam. They held Hue, the old capital of the country, for weeks. To root them out of Saigon the Americans had to level large sections of the city. Elsewhere the destruction was total, an irony highlighted by the remark of an American officer after the recapture of the village of Ben Tre: "It became necessary to destroy the town to save it."

The Tet offensive was essentially a series of raids; the communists did not expect to hold the cities indefinitely, and they did not. Their losses were enormous. Nevertheless the psychological impact in South Vietnam and in the United States made Tet a clear victory for the North. When General William C. Westmoreland described Tet as a communist defeat and when it came out that the administration was considering sending an additional 206,000 troops to South Vietnam, McCarthy, who was campaigning in New Hampshire, became a formidable figure. Thousands of students and other volunteers flocked to the state to ring doorbells in his behalf. On election day he polled 42 percent of the Democratic vote.

The political situation was monumentally confused. Many New Hampshire voters had supported McCarthy because they believed that Johnson was not prosecuting the war vigorously enough and saw voting for another person as a way to rebuke him. Before the primary, former attorney general Robert F. Kennedy, brother of the slain president, had refused either to seek the Democratic nomination or to support McCarthy, though he disliked Johnson intensely and was opposed to his policy in Vietnam. McCarthy's strong

■ **Hugh Haynie of the Louisville *Courier-Journal* drew this pointed 1968 cartoon comment about U.S. involvement in Vietnam.**

showing caused Kennedy to reverse himself. He entered the race. Had he done so earlier, McCarthy might have withdrawn in his favor, for Kennedy had powerful political and popular support. After New Hampshire, McCarthy understandably decided to remain in the contest.

Confronting this confusion, President Johnson withdrew from the race. Vice-President Hubert H. Humphrey then announced his candidacy, though not until it was too late for him to enter the primaries. Kennedy carried the primaries in Indiana and Nebraska. McCarthy won in Wisconsin and Oregon. In the climactic contest in California, Kennedy won by a small margin. However, immediately after his victory speech in a Los Angeles hotel, he was assassinated by Sirhan Sirhan, a young Arab nationalist who had been incensed by Kennedy's support of Israel. In effect, Kennedy's death assured the nomination of Humphrey; most professional politicians distrusted McCarthy, who was rather diffident and aloof for a politician.

The contest for the Republican nomination was far less dramatic, though its outcome, the nomination of Richard M. Nixon, would have been hard to predict a few years earlier. After his defeat in the California gubernatorial election of 1962, Nixon moved to New York City and joined a prominent law firm. He remained active in Republican affairs, making countless speeches and attending political meetings throughout the country. In 1967 Governor George Romney of Michigan seemed the likely Republican nominee, but he failed to develop extensive support. While Governor Nelson Rockefeller of New York was widely mentioned, conservative Republicans would not forgive his refusal to help Goldwater in 1964, and he decided not to enter the race. Nixon announced his candidacy in February 1968; after Romney withdrew in the midst of the New Hampshire contest, he swept the primaries and won an easy first-ballot victory at the Republican convention.

Nixon then astounded the country and dismayed liberals by choosing Governor Spiro T. Agnew of Maryland as his running mate. Aside from the fact that he had little national reputation ("Spiro who?" jokesters asked), Agnew had taken a tough, almost brutal stand on such matters as racial disturbances, urban crime, and other social problems. Nixon chose him primarily to attract southern votes.

Placating the South seemed necessary because Governor George C. Wallace of Alabama was making a determined bid to win enough electoral votes for his American Independent party to prevent any candidate's obtaining a majority. Wallace was flagrantly antiblack and sure to attract substantial southern and conservative support. He denounced federal "meddling," the "coddling" of criminals, and the forced desegregation of schools. He ridiculed intellectuals, planners, and any form of professional ability or mental distinction. Nixon's choice of Agnew appeared to be an effort to

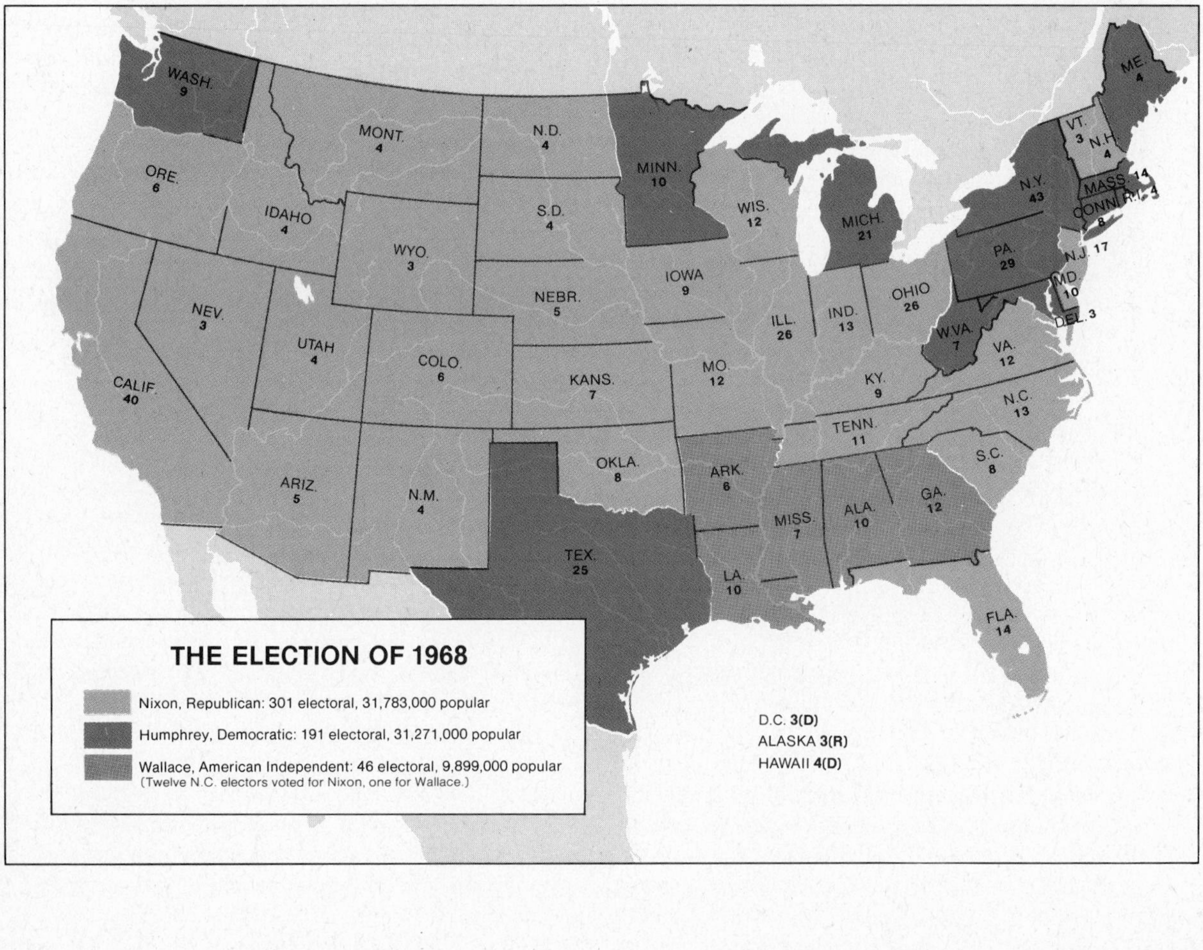

appeal to the groups that Wallace attracted: bigots, lower-middle-class whites, suburbanites, and the residents of small towns.

This Republican strategy disturbed liberals and heightened the tension surrounding the Democratic convention, which met in Chicago in late August. Humphrey delegates controlled the convention. The vice-president had a solid liberal record on domestic issues, but he had supported Johnson's Vietnam policy with equal solidity. Those who could not stomach the Nixon-Agnew ticket and who opposed the war faced a difficult choice. Hundreds of radicals and young activists descended on Chicago to put pressure on the delegates to repudiate the Johnson Vietnam policy.

In the tense atmosphere that resulted, the party hierarchy overreacted. Mayor Richard J. Daley, an old-fashioned political boss, ringed the convention with barricades and policemen to protect it from disruption. This was a reasonable precaution in itself. Inside the building the delegates nominated Humphrey and adopted a war plank satisfactory to Johnson. Outside, however, provoked by the abusive language and violent behavior of radical demonstrators, the police tore into the protesters, brutally beating dozens while millions watched on television in fascinated horror.

At first the mayhem at Chicago seemed to benefit Nixon by strengthening the convictions of many voters that the tougher treatment of criminals and dissenters that he and Agnew were calling for was necessary. Those who were critical of the Chicago police tended to blame Humphrey, whom Mayor Daley supported. Nixon campaigned at a deliberate, dignified pace. He made relatively few public appearances, relying instead on carefully arranged television interviews and taped commercials prepared by an advertising agency. He stressed firm enforcement of the law and his desire "to bring us together." Agnew, in a series of blunt, coarse speeches, assaulted Humphrey, the Democrats, and left-wing dissident groups. (Critics who remembered Nixon's own political style in the era of Joseph McCarthy called Agnew "Nixon's Nixon.")

The Democratic campaign was badly organized. Humphrey was subjected to merciless heckling from antiwar audiences. He seemed far behind in the early stages. Shortly before election day, President Johnson helped him greatly by suspending air attacks on North Vietnam, and in the long run the Republican strategy helped too. Black voters and the urban poor had no practical choice but to vote Democratic. Gradually Humphrey gained ground, and on election day the popular vote was close: Nixon slightly less than 31.8 million, Humphrey nearly 31.3 million. Nixon's electoral college margin, however, was substantial—301 to 191. The remaining 46 electoral votes went to Wallace, whose 9.9 million votes came to 13.5 percent of the total. Despite Nixon's triumph, the Democrats retained control of both houses of Congress.

Nixon as President

When he took office in January 1969, Richard Nixon projected an image of calm and deliberate statesmanship; he introduced no startling changes, proposed no important new legislation. The major economic problem facing him, inflation, was primarily a result of the heavy military expenditures and "easy money" policies of the Johnson administration. Nixon cut federal spending and balanced the 1969 budget, while the Federal Reserve Board forced up interest rates in order to slow the expansion of the money supply. The object was to reduce the rate of economic growth without causing heavy unemployment or precipitating a recession (the word *depression* had apparently passed out of the vocabulary of economists). Even its supporters admitted that this policy would check inflation only slowly, and when prices continued to rise, there was mounting uneasiness. Labor unions demanded large wage increases. The problem was complicated by mounting deficits in the United States' balance of trade with foreign nations, the product of an overvaluation of the dollar that encouraged Americans to buy foreign goods.

In 1970 Congress passed a law giving the president power to regulate prices and wages. Nixon had opposed this legislation, but in the summer of 1971 he decided to use it. First he announced a 90-day price and wage freeze (Phase I) and placed a 10 percent surcharge on imports. Then he set up a Pay Board and a Price Commission with authority to limit wage and price increases when the freeze ended (Phase II). These controls did not check inflation completely—and they angered union leaders, who felt that labor was being shortchanged—but they did slow the upward spiral. A 7.9 percent devaluation of the dollar in December 1971 helped the economy by making American products more competitive in foreign markets.

In handling other domestic issues, the president was less firm, sometimes even confused. He advocated a bold plan for shifting the burden of welfare payments to the federal government and equalizing such payments in all the states, and he came out for a "minimum income" for poor families, which alarmed his conservative supporters. These measures got nowhere in Congress. On the other hand, Nixon and his attorney general, John N. Mitchell, were so openly resistant to further federal efforts to force school desegregation on reluctant local districts as to dismay southern moderates and northern liberals. And in his eagerness to add what he called "strict constructionists" to the Supreme Court, which he believed had swung too far to the left in such areas as race relations and the rights of persons accused of committing crimes, Nixon allowed himself to be drawn into two foolish confrontations with the Senate.

When Chief Justice Earl Warren retired from the Court in June 1969, Nixon named a respected conservative, Warren E. Burger, the new chief justice. This caused no difficulties. But when Nixon sought to fill the seat of Justice Abe Fortas, who had resigned under fire after it came out that he had accepted fees from questionable sources while on the bench, he blundered. He first selected Judge Clement F. Haynesworth, Jr., of South Carolina, whom the Senate rejected because of his having failed to disqualify himself when cases involving corporations in which he had invested came before his court. Nixon's second nominee, Judge G. Harrold Carswell of Florida, was turned down because of his alleged racist attitudes and his generally mediocre record.

In the face of a mass of evidence, Nixon refused to believe that the nominations were rejected for the reasons stated; he declared that "no southern conservative" could run the "liberal" Senate gauntlet successfully, and to prevent the Senate from proving him wrong he nominated Harry A. Blackmun of Minnesota. Blackmun won the unanimous approval of the Senate. Since Nixon's analysis was as incorrect as his political tactics were ineffective, his prestige suffered accordingly. And while the Burger court was less liberal than the Warren court, it was far from being as conservative as Nixon apparently wanted. In 1970 it decided that 18-year-olds had the right to vote; in 1972 it declared that the death penalty, as currently used, was a cruel and unusual punishment and thus in violation of the Eighth Amendment; and in 1973 it struck down state antiabortion legislation.

Whatever his difficulties on the domestic front, Nixon considered the solution of the Vietnam problem his chief task. When the war in Southeast Asia first burst upon American consciousness in 1954, he had favored military intervention in keeping with the containment policy. As controversy over American policy developed, he had supported most of the actions of presidents Kennedy and Johnson. During the 1968 campaign he played down the Vietnam issue. Though he insisted he would end the war on "honorable" terms if elected, he suggested nothing very different from what Johnson was doing.

In office, Nixon proposed a phased withdrawal of all non-South Vietnamese troops, to be followed by an internationally supervised election in South Vietnam. The North Vietnamese rejected this scheme and insisted that the United States withdraw its forces unconditionally. Their intransigence left the president in a difficult position. Probably the majority of Americans considered his proposal eminently fair. With equal certainty a majority was unwilling to increase the scale of the fighting to compel the communists to accept it, and as the war dragged on, costs in lives and money rising, the desire to extricate American troops from the conflict became more intense. However, large numbers of Americans would not face up to the consequences of gratifying this desire: ending the war on the communists' terms. Nixon could not compel the foe to negotiate meaningfully, yet every passing day added to the strength of antiwar sentiment, which, as it expressed itself in ever more emphatic terms, in turn led to deeper divisions in the country.

The president responded to the dilemma by trying to build up the South Vietnamese armed forces so that American troops could pull out without the communists' overrunning South Vietnam. He shipped so many planes to the Vietnamese that they came to have the fourth largest air force in the world. The trouble with this strategy (called Vietnamization) was that for 15 years the United States had been trying without success to make the South Vietnamese capable of defending themselves. For complicated reasons—the incompetence, corruption, and reactionary character of the Saigon regime probably being the most important—South Vietnamese troops had seldom displayed much enthusiasm for the kind of tough jungle fighting at which the North Vietnamese and the Vietcong excelled. Nevertheless, efforts at Vietnamization were stepped up, and in June 1969 Nixon announced that he would soon reduce the number of American soldiers in Vietnam by 25,000. In September he promised that an additional 35,000 men would be withdrawn by mid December.

These steps did not quiet American protesters. On October 15 a nationwide antiwar demonstration, Vietnam Moratorium Day, organized by students, produced an unprecedented outpouring all over the country. This massive display produced one of Vice-President Agnew's most notorious blasts of adjectival invective: he said that the moratorium was an example of "national masochism" led by "an effete corps of impudent snobs who characterize themselves as intellectuals."*

A second Moratorium Day brought a crowd estimated at 250,000 to Washington to march past the White House. The president was unmoved. He could not be influenced by protests, he insisted, and during one of the Washington demonstrations he passed the time watching a football game on television. On November 3, he defended his policy in a televised speech. He stressed the sincerity of his peace efforts, the unreasonableness of the communists, the responsibility of the United States to protect the South Vietnamese people from communist reprisals and to honor its international commitments. He announced that he planned to remove all American ground forces from Vietnam. The next day, reporting a flood of telegrams and calls supporting his position, he declared that a "silent majority" of the American people approved his course.

For a season, events appeared to vindicate Nixon's position. A gradual reduction of military activity in Vietnam had reduced American casualties to what those who did not find the war morally unbearable considered "tolerable" levels. Troop withdrawals continued in an orderly fashion. A new lottery system for drafting men for military duty eliminated some of the inequities in the selective service law.

But the war continued. Early in 1970 reports that in 1968 an American unit had massacred civilians, including dozens of women and children, in a Vietnamese hamlet known as Mylai 4, revived the controversy over the purposes of the war and its corrosive effects on those who were fighting it. The American people, it seemed, were being torn apart by the war: one from another according to each one's interpretation of events, many within themselves as they tried to balance the war's horrors against their pride, their detestation of communism, and their unwillingness to turn their backs on their elected leader.

Nixon's most implacable enemy could find no reason to think he wished the war to go on. Its human, economic, and social costs could only vex his days and threaten his future reputation. When he reduced the level of the fighting, the communists merely waited for further reductions. When he raised it, many of his own people denounced him. If he pulled out of Vietnam entirely, other Americans would be outraged.

Perhaps his error lay in his unwillingness to admit his own uncertainty, something the greatest presidents—one thinks immediately of Lincoln and Franklin Roosevelt—were never afraid to do. Facing a dilemma, he tried to convince the world that he was firmly in control of events, with the result that at times he seemed more like a high school valedictorian declaiming sententiously about the meaning of life than the mature statesman he so desperately wished to be. Thus he heightened the tensions he sought to relax—in America, in Vietnam, and elsewhere.

Late in April 1970 Nixon announced that Vietnamization was proceeding more rapidly than he had hoped, that communist power was weakening, that within a year another 150,000 American soldiers would be extracted from Vietnam. A week later he announced that military intelligence had indicated that the enemy was consolidating its "sanctuaries" in neutral Cambodia and that he was therefore dispatching thousands of American

---

*A few days later he called on the country to "separate" radical students from society "with no more regret than we should feel over discarding rotten apples from a barrel," which at least had a quality of terseness that most of Agnew's pronouncements lacked.

■ **Prelude to violence: Behind a tear gas barrage, National Guardsmen march across the campus of Ohio's Kent State University in May 1970. Soon after this picture was taken, they opened fire, killing four students.**

troops to destroy these bases.* He was escalating (dread word) the war. He even resumed the bombing of targets in North Vietnam. "You've got to electrify people with bold decisions," he told the Joint Chiefs of Staff. "Let's go blow the hell out of them."

To foes of the war, Nixon's decision seemed so appallingly unwise that some of them began to fear that he had become mentally unbalanced. The contradictions between his confident statements about Vietnamization and his alarmist description of powerful enemy forces poised like a dagger 30-odd miles from Saigon did not seem the product of a reasoning mind. His failure to consult congressional leaders or many of his personal advisers before drastically altering his policy, the critics claimed, was unconstitutional and irresponsible. His insensitive response to the avalanche of criticism that descended on him from the universities, from Congress, and from other quarters further disturbed observers.

Students took the lead in opposing the invasion of Cambodia. Young people had been prominent in the opposition to the war from early in the conflict. Some objected to war in principle. Many more believed that this particular war was wrong because it was being fought against a small country on the other side of the globe where America's vital interests did not seem to be threatened. As the war dragged on and casualties mounted, student opposition to the draft became intense. For some the reason was obvious—they did not want to be drafted. Others (including many of the above) objected because the universal military service required was anything but universal. Thousands of students avoided the draft simply by remaining in college; poor and disadvantaged young men did most of the fighting.

*American planes had been bombing Cambodia for some time, but this fact was not known to the public (or to Congress) until 1973.

Nixon's shocking announcement triggered many campus demonstrations. One college where feeling ran high was Kent State University in Ohio. For several days students there clashed with local police; they broke windows and caused other damage to property. When the governor of Ohio called out the National Guard, angry students showered the soldiers with stones. During a noontime protest on May 4 the guardsmen, who were poorly trained in crowd control, suddenly opened fire. Four students were killed, two of them women who were merely passing by on their way to class.

While the nation reeled from this shock, two black students at Jackson State University were killed by Mississippi state policemen. A wave of student strikes followed, closing down hundreds of colleges, including many that had seen no previous unrest. Moderate students by the tens of thousands had joined with the radicals.

Nixon Triumphant

The almost universal condemnation of the invasion and of the way it had been planned and announced to the country shook Nixon hard. He backtracked, pulling American ground troops out of Cambodia quickly. But he did not change his Vietnam policy, and in fact Cambodia apparently stiffened his determination. As American ground troops were withdrawn, he stepped up air attacks. The balance of forces remained in uneasy equilibrium through 1971.

Late in March 1972 the North Vietnamese again mounted a series of assaults throughout South Vietnam. The president responded with heavier bombing, and he ordered the approaches to Haiphong and other northern ports sown with mines to cut off the communists' supplies. Meanwhile, he had devised a bold and (even his critics admitted it) ingenious diplomatic offensive. He sent his principal foreign policy adviser, Henry Kissinger, to China and the Soviet Union to arrange summit meetings with the communist leaders. In February 1972 Nixon flew to Peking to consult with Mao Tse-tung, Premier Chou En-lai, and other Chinese officials. The United States agreed to support the admission of China to the United Nations and to develop economic and cultural exchanges with the Chinese. Although these results appeared small, Nixon's visit, ending more than 20 years of adamantine American refusal to accept Mao's revolution, marked a dramatic reversal; as such it was hailed in the United States and elsewhere in the world.

Nixon's trip to Moscow in May 1972 produced equally striking results. A treaty limiting strategic missiles was the main concrete gain. But that the meetings took place at all after the mining of Haiphong harbor was of enormous significance. Both China and the Soviet Union had been willing to work for improved relations with the United States *before* America withdrew from Vietnam. This fact, plus the failure of their offensive to

■ **The famous meeting of February 1972 in Peking: from the left, Chinese Premier Chou En-lai; an interpreter; Communist Party Chairman Mao Tse-tung; President Nixon; and Henry A. Kissinger, then Nixon's foreign policy adviser and later secretary of state.**

overwhelm South Vietnam, led the North Vietnamese to make diplomatic concessions in the interest of getting the United States out of the war. Kissinger began negotiating seriously with their representatives in Paris in the summer of 1972. By October the draft of a settlement calling for a cease-fire in place, the return of American prisoners of war, and the withdrawal of United States forces from Vietnam had been hammered out. Shortly before the presidential election Kissinger announced that peace was "at hand."

A few days later President Nixon was reelected, defeating the Democratic candidate, Senator George McGovern of South Dakota, in a landslide—521 electoral votes to 17. McGovern carried only Massachusetts and the District of Columbia.

McGovern's campaign had been hampered by divisions within the Democratic party and by the discovery, shortly after the nominating convention, that the vice-presidential candidate, Senator Thomas Eagleton of Missouri, had in the past undergone electric shock treatments following serious psychological difficulties. After some hesitation, which left many voters with the impression that he was indecisive, McGovern forced Eagleton to withdraw. Sargent Shriver, former head of the Peace Corps, took Eagleton's place on the ticket. The affair hurt McGovern badly. Nevertheless, Nixon's triumph was so convincing that he interpreted it, understandably, as an indication that the people approved of everything for which he stood.

Suddenly Nixon loomed as one of the most powerful and successful presidents in American history. His bold attack on inflation, his tough-minded handling of the foreign trade question, even his harsh Vietnamese policy suggested decisiveness and self-confidence, qualities he had often seemed to lack. His willingness, despite his long history as a militant "cold warrior," to negotiate with the communist nations in order to arrive at a détente that would lessen world tensions indicated a new flexibility and reasonableness. His landslide victory appeared to demonstrate that a large majority of the people approved his way of tackling the major problems of the times.

His first reaction was to try to extract more favorable terms from the Vietnamese communists. Announcing that they were not bargaining in good faith over the remaining details of the peace treaty, he resumed the bombing of North Vietnam in December 1972, this time sending the mighty B-52s directly over Hanoi and other cities. The destructiveness of the attacks was large, but their effectiveness as a means of forcing concessions from the North Vietnamese was at best debatable, and they led for the first time to the loss of large numbers of the big strategic bombers.

Nevertheless, both sides had much to gain from ending the war. In January 1973 a settlement was finally reached. The North Vietnamese retained control of large sections of the South, and they agreed to release American prisoners of war within 60 days. When this was accomplished, the last American troops were pulled out of Vietnam. Nearly 46,000 Americans had died in the long war, and over 300,000 more had been wounded. The cost had reached a staggering $109 billion.

Whatever the price, the war was over for the United States, and Nixon took the credit for having ended it. He immediately turned to domestic issues, determined, he made clear, to change the direction in which the nation had been moving for decades. He sought on the one hand to strengthen the power of the presidency vis-à-vis Congress and on the other to decentralize administration by encouraging state and local management of government programs. He announced that he intended to reduce the interference of the federal government in the affairs of individuals. People should be more self-reliant, he said, and he denounced what he called "permissiveness." Overconcern for the interests of blacks and other minorities must end. Criminals should be punished "without pity." No person or group should be coddled by the state. These aims brought Nixon into conflict with liberal congressmen of both parties, with the leaders of minority groups, and with people concerned about the increasing power of the executive.

The conflict came to a head over the president's anti-inflation policy. After his second inauguration he ended Phase II price and wage controls and substituted Phase III, which depended on voluntary "restraints" (except in the areas of food, health care, and construction). This approach did not work. Prices soared; it was the most rapid inflation since the Korean War. In an effort to check the rise Nixon set a rigid limit on federal expenditures; to keep within the limit, he cut back or abolished a large number of social welfare programs, and he reduced federal grants in support of science and education. He even impounded (refused to spend) funds already appropriated by Congress for purposes of which he disapproved.

Impoundment created a furor on Capitol Hill, and when Congress, despite the fact that the Democrats had a majority in both houses, failed to override presidential vetoes of bills challenging his policy, it appeared that Nixon was in total command. The White House staff, headed by H. R. Haldeman ("the Prussian") and John Ehrlichman, dominated the Washington bureaucracy like princes of the blood or oriental viziers and dealt with congressmen as though they were dealing with lackeys or eunuchs. When asked to account for their actions they took refuge behind the shield of executive privilege, the doctrine, never before applied so broadly, that discussions and communications within the executive branch were confidential and therefore immune from congressional scrutiny. Critics began to grumble about a new "imperial presidency." No one seemed capable of checking Nixon at any point.

Nixon: Decline and Fall

On March 19, 1973, James McCord, a former FBI agent accused of burglary, wrote a letter to the judge presiding at his trial. His act precipitated a series of disclosures that disrupted and then destroyed the Nixon administration.

McCord had been employed during the 1972 presidential campaign as a security officer of the Committee to Re-elect the President (CREEP). At about 1 A.M. on June 17, 1972, he and four other men had broken into Democratic headquarters at the Watergate, an apartment house and office building complex in Washington. The burglars had been caught rifling files and installing electronic eavesdropping devices. Two other Republican campaign officials were soon implicated. Their arrest aroused suspicions that the Republican party was behind the break-in. Nixon denied this. "I can say categorically," he announced on June 22, "that no one on the White House staff, no one in this Administration presently employed, was involved in this very bizarre incident." Most people evidently took the president at his word, and the affair did not materially affect the election. When brought to trial early in 1973, most of the defendants pleaded guilty.

McCord, who did not, was convicted by the jury. Before Judge John J. Sirica imposed sentences on the culprits, however, McCord wrote his letter. High Republican officials had known about the burglary in advance and had persuaded most of the defendants to keep their connection secret, McCord claimed. Perjury had been committed during the trial.

The truth of McCord's charges swiftly became apparent. The head of CREEP, Jeb Stuart Magruder, and President Nixon's lawyer, John W. Dean III, admitted their involvement. Dean claimed in testimony before a special Senate Watergate investigation committee headed by Sam Ervin, Jr., of North Carolina, that Nixon had participated in efforts to cover up the affair. Among the disclosures that emerged over the following months were these:

That the acting director of the FBI, L. Patrick Gray, had destroyed documents related to the case.

That large sums of money had been paid the burglars at the instigation of the White House to insure their silence.

That agents of the Nixon administration had burglarized the office of a psychiatrist, seeking evidence against one of his patients, Daniel Ellsberg, who had been charged with leaking classified documents relating to the Vietnam War. (This disclosure led to the immediate dismissal of the charges against Ellsberg by the presiding judge.)

That the Central Intelligence Agency had (perhaps unwittingly) supplied equipment used in this burglary.

That CREEP officials had attempted to disrupt the campaigns of leading Democratic candidates during the 1972 primaries in a number of illegal ways.

That a number of corporations had made large contributions to the Nixon reelection campaign in violation of federal law.

That E. Howard Hunt, one of the Watergate criminals, had earlier forged State Department documents in an effort to make it appear that President Kennedy had been implicated in the assassination of President Ngo Dinh Diem of South Vietnam.

That the Nixon administration had placed wiretaps on the telephones of some of its own officials as well as on those of newspapermen critical of its policies without first obtaining authorization from the courts.

■ **Gary Trudeau and his politically biting cartoon strip *Doonesbury* enlivened the Vietnam and Watergate years. It became the first strip cartoon to win a Pulitzer prize. (Ron Ziegler was the presidential press secretary.)**

These revelations led to the resignations of most of Nixon's closest advisers, including Haldeman, Ehrlichman, Dean, and Attorney General Richard Kleindienst. They also raised the question of the president's personal connection with the scandals. This he steadfastly denied. He insisted that he would investigate the Watergate affair thoroughly and see that the guilty were punished. He refused, however, to allow investigators to examine White House documents, again on grounds of executive privilege, which he continued to assert in very broad terms.

In the face of Nixon's denials, John Dean, testifying under oath before the Ervin committee, stated flatly and in circumstantial detail that the president had been closely involved in the Watergate coverup. (Before testifying, Dean consulted with the conservative Senator Barry Goldwater, a Nixon supporter. When he explained what he was going to say, Goldwater replied: "Hell, I'm not surprised. That goddam Nixon has been lying all of his life.") Dean had been a persuasive witness, but—unlike Goldwater—many people were reluctant to believe that a president could lie so cold-bloodedly to the entire country. Therefore, when it came out during later hearings of the Ervin committee that the president had systematically made secret tape recordings of White House conversations and telephone calls, the disclosure caused a sensation. It seemed obvious that these tapes would settle the question of Nixon's involvement once and for all. Again he refused to allow access to the evidence.

One result of the scandals and of Nixon's attitude was a precipitous decline in his standing in public opinion polls. Calls for his resignation, even for impeachment, began to be heard. Yielding to pressure, he agreed to the appointment of an "independent" special prosecutor to investigate the Watergate affair, and he promised the appointee, Professor Archibald Cox of the Harvard Law School, full cooperation.

Cox swiftly aroused the president's ire by demanding White House records, including the tapes, and by digging into a number of other questions, such as the relationship between the administration and the International Telephone and Telegraph Company, which, it was charged, had offered to pay $400,000 toward the expenses of the 1972 Republican convention in return for favorable treatment of an antitrust case. When Nixon refused to turn over the tapes, Cox obtained a subpoena from Judge Sirica ordering him to do so. The administration appealed and lost in the appellate court. Then, while the case was headed for the Supreme Court, Nixon ordered the new attorney general, Elliot Richardson, to dismiss Cox. Both Richardson, who had promised the Senate during his confirmation hearings that the special prosecutor would have a free hand, and his chief assistant, William Ruckelshaus, resigned rather than do so. The solicitor general, third-ranking officer of the Justice Department, carried out Nixon's order.

These events, which occurred on Saturday, October 20, were promptly dubbed the Saturday Night Massacre. They caused an outburst of public indignation. Congress was bombarded by thousands of letters and telegrams demanding the president's impeachment. The House Judiciary Committee, headed by Peter W. Rodino, Jr., of New Jersey, began an investigation to see if enough evidence for impeachment existed.

Once again Nixon backed down. He agreed to turn over the tapes to Judge Sirica with the understanding that while relevant materials would be presented to the grand jury investigating the Watergate affair, nothing would be revealed to the public. He then named a new special prosecutor, Leon Jaworski, and promised him access to whatever White House documents he needed. However, it soon came out that some of the tapes were missing and that an important section of another had been deliberately erased.

The nation had never before experienced such a series of morale-shattering crises. While the seemingly unending complications of Watergate were unfolding during 1973, a number of unrelated disasters struck. First, pushed by a shortage of grains resulting from massive Russian purchases authorized by the administration as part of its "détente" with the Soviet Union, food prices shot up—wheat from $1.45 a bushel to over $5. Nixon imposed another price freeze, which led to shortages, and when the freeze was lifted, prices resumed their steep ascent. Then Vice-President Agnew (defender of law and order, foe of permissiveness) was accused of income tax fraud and of having accepted bribes while county executive of Baltimore and governor of Maryland. After vehemently denying all the charges for two months, Agnew (to escape a jail term) admitted in October that he had been guilty of tax evasion and resigned as vice-president. (He was fined $10,000 and placed on three years' probation, and the Justice Department published a 40,000-word description of his wrongdoings.)

Under the new Twenty-fifth Amendment, President Nixon nominated Gerald R. Ford of Michigan as vice-president, and he was confirmed by Congress. Ford, a graduate of the University of Michigan and the Yale Law School, had served continuously in Congress since 1949, as minority leader since 1964. His positions on public issues were close to Nixon's; he was an internationalist in foreign affairs and both conservative and a convinced Republican partisan on domestic issues.

Not long after the Agnew fiasco, Nixon, responding to charges that he had paid almost no income taxes during his presidency, published his 1969–1972 returns. They showed that he had paid only about $1,600 in two years during which his income had exceeded half a million dollars. Although Nixon claimed that his returns were perfectly legal—he had taken huge deductions for the gift of some of his vice-presidential papers to the National Archives—the legality and the propriety of his deductions were questionable. Combined with charges that millions of dollars of public funds had been spent on improvements for his private residences in California and Florida, the tax issue further eroded his reputation, so much so that he felt obliged, during a televised press conference, to assure the audience: "I am not a crook."

Still another disaster followed as a result of the new war that broke out in October 1973 between Israel and the Arab states. The fighting, while bloody, was brief and inconclusive; a truce was soon arranged under the auspices of the United

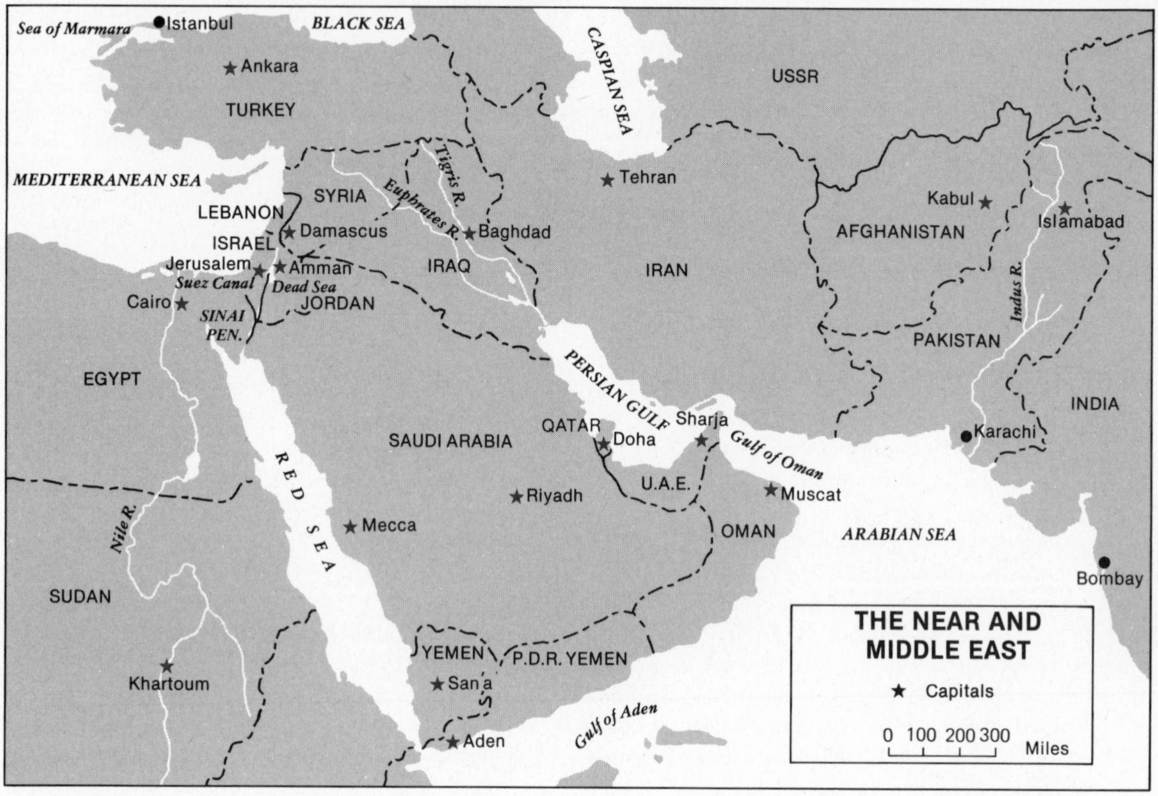

States and the Soviet Union. But in an effort to force western nations to compel Israel to withdraw from lands held since the "six-day" war of 1967, the Arabs cut off oil shipments to the United States, Japan, and most of western Europe. A worldwide energy crisis ensued.

The immediate shortage resulting from the Arab oil boycott was ended by the patient diplomacy of Henry Kissinger, whom Nixon had made secretary of state at the beginning of his second administration. After weeks of negotiating in the spring of 1974, first with Egypt and Israel, then with Syria and Israel, he obtained a tentative agreement which involved the withdrawal of Israel from some of the territory it had occupied in the 1967 war. The Arab nations then lifted the boycott.

A revolution had taken place. From the middle of the 19th century until after World War II the United States had produced far more oil than it could use. However, the phenomenal expansion of oil consumption that occurred after the war soon absorbed the surplus. By the late 1960s American car owners were driving more than a trillion miles a year. Petroleum was being used to manufacture nylon and other synthetic fibers as well as paints, insecticides, fertilizers, and many plastic products. Oil and natural gas became the principal fuels for home heating. Natural gas in particular was used increasingly in factories and electric utility plants, because it was less polluting than coal and most other fuels. The Clean Air Act of 1965 speeded the process of conversion from coal to gas by countless industrial consumers. Because of these developments, at the outbreak of the 1973 Arab-Israeli war the United States was importing one-third of its oil.

In 1960 the principal oil exporters, Venezuela, Saudi Arabia, Kuwait, Iraq, and Iran, had formed a cartel, the Organization of Petroleum Exporting Countries (OPEC). For many years OPEC had been unable to control the world price of oil, which, on the eve of the 1973 war, was about $3 a barrel. The success of the Arab oil boycott served to unite the members of OPEC, and when the boycott was lifted they boldly announced that the price was going up to $11.65 a barrel.

The announcement caused consternation

throughout the industrial world. Soaring prices for oil meant soaring prices for everything made from petroleum or with petroleum-powered machinery. In the United States gasoline prices doubled overnight and the trend of all prices rose at a rate of over 10 percent a year. This "double-digit" inflation, which afflicted nearly all the countries of the world, added considerably to President Nixon's woes.

Meanwhile, special prosecutor Jaworski continued his investigation of the Watergate scandals, and the House Judiciary Committee pursued its study of the impeachment question. In March 1974 a grand jury indicted Haldeman, Ehrlichman, former attorney general John Mitchell, who had been head of CREEP at the time of the break-in, and four other White House aides for conspiring to block the Watergate investigation. The jurors also named Nixon an "unindicted co-conspirator," Jaworski having informed them that their power to indict a president was constitutionally questionable. Judge Sirica thereupon turned over the jury's evidence against Nixon to the Judiciary Committee. Then both the Internal Revenue Service and a joint congressional committee, having separately audited the president's income tax returns, announced that most of his deductions had been unjustified. The IRS assessed him nearly half a million dollars in taxes and interest, which he agreed to pay.

In an effort to check the mounting criticism, Nixon late in April released edited transcripts of the tapes he had turned over to the court the previous November. If he had expected the material to convince the public that he had been ignorant of the attempt to cover up the administration's connection with Watergate, he was sadly mistaken. In addition to much incriminating evidence, the transcripts provided a fascinating and to most persons shocking view of how he conducted himself in private. His repeated use of foul language, so out of keeping with his public image, offended millions. The phrase "expletive deleted," inserted in place of words considered too vulgar for publication in family newspapers, became overnight a catchword. Nixon appeared to be ignorant of the simplest legal principles. In conversations he seemed confused and indecisive and lacking in any concern for the public interest. The publication of the transcripts led even some of his strongest supporters to demand that he resign. And once the Judiciary Committee obtained the actual tapes, it became clear that the White House transcripts were in crucial respects inaccurate. Much material prejudicial to the president's case had been suppressed.

Yet impeaching a president seemed so drastic a step that many people felt more direct proof of Nixon's involvement in the cover-up was necessary. Nixon insisted that all the relevant information was contained in these tapes; he adamantly refused to turn over others to the special prosecutor or the Judiciary Committee.

With the defendants in the Watergate case demanding access to tapes that they claimed would prove their innocence, Jaworski was compelled either to obtain them or to risk having the charges dismissed on the ground that the government was withholding evidence. He therefore subpoenaed 64 additional tapes. Nixon, through his lawyer James St. Clair, refused to obey the subpoena. Swiftly the case of *United States* v. *Richard M. Nixon* went to the Supreme Court.

In the summer of 1974—after so many months of alarms and crises—the Watergate drama reached its climax. The Judiciary Committee, following months of study of the evidence behind closed doors, decided to conduct its deliberations in open session. While millions watched on television, 38 members of the House of Representatives debated the charges. The discussions revealed both the thoroughness of the investigation and the soul-searching efforts of the representatives to render an impartial judgment. Three articles of impeachment were adopted. They charged the president with obstructing justice, misusing the powers of his office, and failing to obey the committee's subpoenas. Except in the case of the last article, many of the Republicans on the committee joined with the Democrats in voting aye, a clear indication that the full House would vote to impeach.

On the eve of the debates, the Supreme Court had ruled unanimously that the president must turn over the 64 subpoenaed tapes to the special prosecutor. Executive privilege had its place, the Court stated, but no person, not even a president, could "withhold evidence that is demonstrably relevant in a criminal trial." For reasons that soon became obvious, Nixon seriously considered defying the Court. Only when convinced that to do so would make his impeachment and conviction certain—and would compel his lawyer, St. Clair, to withdraw from the case—did he agree to comply.

He would not, however, resign. Even if the House impeached him, he was counting on his ability to hold the support of at least 34 senators (one-third plus one of the full Senate) to escape conviction. But events were passing beyond his control. The 64 subpoenaed tapes had to be transcribed and analyzed; following the Supreme Court decision, Judge Sirica pointedly ordered St. Clair to prepare this material promptly.

Incredibly, up to this time St. Clair had not listened to the tapes; Nixon had assured him that they contained no relevant evidence and had refused to allow him to judge the correctness of this statement for himself. Now St. Clair *had* to listen, and when he did, Nixon's fate was sealed. Three recorded conversations between the president and H. R. Haldeman on June 23, 1972 (less than a week after the break-in and only one day after Nixon had assured the nation that no one in the White House had been involved in the affair), proved conclusively that Nixon had tried to obstruct justice by engaging the CIA in an effort to persuade the FBI not to follow up leads in the case on the spurious ground that national security was involved.

The president's defenders had insisted not so much that he was innocent as that solid proof of his guilt had not been demonstrated. Where, in the metaphor of the moment, was the "smoking gun"? That weapon had now been found, and it bore unmistakably the fingerprints of President Richard M. Nixon.

Exactly what happened in the White House after St. Clair listened to the Nixon-Haldeman conversations is not yet known. The president's chief advisers pressed him to release the material at once and admit he had erred in holding it back. This he did on August 5; that in so doing he specifically admitted that he had withheld information from his lawyer suggests that St. Clair, whose professional reputation was at stake, had played a major role. When they read the new transcripts, all the Republican members of the Judiciary Committee who had voted against the impeachment articles reversed themselves. Understandably, they felt betrayed; they had accepted the president's assurances that all the evidence was in, and they had gone on record before millions of eyes in his defense. The last remnants of Nixon's congressional support crumbled. Republican leaders told him categorically that the House would impeach him and that no more than a handful of senators would vote to acquit him.

On August 8 Nixon announced his resignation. "Dear Mr. Secretary," his terse official letter to the secretary of state ran, "I hereby resign the Office of President of the United States. Sincerely, Richard Nixon." The resignation took effect at noon on August 9, when Gerald Ford was sworn in as president.

The meaning of "Watergate" became immediately the subject of much speculation and shall no doubt so remain for many years. Whether Nixon's crude efforts to dominate Congress, to crush or inhibit dissent, and to subvert the electoral process would have permanently altered the American political system had they succeeded is probably beyond knowing. However, the orderly way in which these efforts were checked suggests that the system would have survived in any case. Whether the long trend toward ever increasing presidential authority was reversed by Nixon's disgrace, the future will reveal.

Nixon's own drama is and must remain one of the most fascinating and enigmatic episodes in American history. Despite his fall from the heights because of personal flaws, his was not a tragedy in the Greek sense. Even when he finally yielded power he seemed without remorse or even awareness of his transgressions. Although he enjoyed the pomp and circumstance attendant on his high office and trumpeted his achievements to all the world, he was devoid of the classic hero's pride. Did he really intend to smash all opposition and rule like a tyrant, or was he driven by lack of confidence in himself? His stubborn aggressiveness and his overblown view of executive privilege may have reflected a need for constant reassurance that he *was* a mighty leader, that the nation accepted his right to exercise authority. One element in his downfall, preserved for posterity in videotapes of his television appearances, was that even while he was assuring the country of his innocence most vehemently he did not look like a victim of the machinations of overzealous supporters. Perhaps at some profound level he did not want to be believed.

This explanation of Richard Nixon, however

tentative, is at least comforting—it makes him appear less menacing. If it is correct, Americans can deplore the injuries he inflicted on society and still feel for him a certain compassion.

Ford as President

The country greeted the accession of Gerald Ford to the presidency with a collective sigh of relief. Most observers considered Ford unimaginative, certainly not brilliant. But he was hardworking and—most important under the circumstances—his record was untouched by scandal. Although he was an almost automaton-like Republican partisan, nearly all the Democrats in Congress liked and respected him. He was Nixon's opposite as a person, being gregarious and open, and he stated repeatedly that he took a dim view of Nixon's high-handed way of dealing with Congress. The president and Congress must work together in the nation's interest, he insisted. A most ordinary person, earnest but limited, Ford appeared unlikely to venture beyond conventional limits or to act rashly, and this was what nearly everyone wanted of the president in the wake of Nixon's resignation.

Ford obviously desired to live up to public expectations, yet he was soon embroiled in controversy and subject to considerable criticism, not all of it partisan. At the outset he roused widespread resentment by pardoning Nixon for whatever crimes, known or unknown, he had committed in office. Not many Americans wanted to see the ex-president lodged in jail; nevertheless, pardoning him seemed incomprehensible when he had admitted no guilt and had not yet been officially charged with any crime. (Nixon's instant acceptance of the pardon while claiming to have done no wrong was illogical but not incomprehensible.) Ugly rumors of a deal worked out before Nixon resigned were soon circulating, for the pardon seemed grossly unfair. Why should Nixon go scot-free when his chief underlings, Mitchell, Haldeman, and Erlichman, were being brought to trial for their part in the Watergate scandal? (All three were eventually convicted and jailed.)

Ford displayed inconsistency and apparent incompetence in managing the economy. He announced that inflation was the major problem and called on patriotic citizens to signify their willingness to fight it by wearing WIN buttons (Whip Inflation Now). Almost immediately the economy entered a precipitous slump. Production fell and the unemployment rate rose above 9 percent. The president was forced to ask for tax cuts and other measures aimed at stimulating business activity. While pressing for them, he continued to fulminate against spending money on social programs designed to help the urban poor.

That Ford would never act rashly proved to be an incorrect assumption. In the spring of 1975 North Vietnamese forces increased their attacks in South Vietnam. Dispirited, short of guns and ammunition, and incompetently led, the South Vietnamese armies fell back, then fled headlong, then simply dissolved. As the communists advanced, tens of thousands of South Vietnamese refugees asked for asylum in the United States, and about 140,000 were successfully evacuated. Many more were callously abandoned, though their earlier collaboration with the Americans made their situation in a communist-controlled Vietnam precarious. Ford had always taken a hawkish position on the Vietnam War. As the military situation deteriorated, he tried to persuade Congress to pour more arms into the South to stem the North Vietnamese advance. The legislators flatly refused to do so, and late in April Saigon fell. The long Vietnam War was finally over.

Two weeks earlier local communists of a particularly radical persuasion had overturned the pro-American regime in Cambodia. On May 12 Cambodian naval forces seized the American merchant ship *Mayaguez* in the Gulf of Siam. President Ford, apparently frustrated by his inability to prevent the communists from taking over South Vietnam and Cambodia, reacted to the seizure without fully investigating the situation or allowing the new regime time to respond to his perfectly proper demand that the *Mayaguez* and its crew be freed. He ordered marine units to attack Tang Island, where the captured vessel had been taken. The assault succeeded in that the Cambodians released the *Mayaguez* and its crew of 39, but 38 marines died in the operation. Since the Cambodians had released the ship before the marines struck, Ford's reflexive response was probably unnecessary, though it was popular with a majority of Americans.

After some hesitation Ford decided to seek the Republican presidential nomination in 1976. He was opposed by ex-governor Ronald Reagan of California, a movie actor turned politician who was the darling of the Republican right wing. Reagan's campaign was well organized and well financed. He was an excellent speaker, where Ford proved somewhat bumbling on the stump. The contest was close, both candidates winning important primaries and gathering substantial blocs of delegates in nonprimary states. At the convention in August, Ford obtained a slim majority. That he did not win easily, possessed as he was of the advantage of incumbency, made his chances of election in November appear slim.

In the meantime the Democrats had chosen James Earl Carter, a former governor of Georgia, as their candidate. Carter's rise from almost total obscurity was even more spectacular than that of George McGovern in the 1972 campaign and was made possible by the same forces: television, the democratization of the delegate-selection process, the absence of a dominant leader among the Democrats.

Carter had been a naval officer and a substantial peanut farmer and warehouse owner before entering politics. He was elected governor of Georgia in 1970. While governor he won something of a reputation as a southern public official who treated black citizens fairly. (He hung a portrait of Martin Luther King, Jr., in his office.) Carter's political style was informal—he preferred to be called Jimmy. During the campaign for delegates he turned his inexperience in national politics to advantage, emphasizing his lack of familiarity with the Washington establishment rather than apologizing for it, and trying to make a virtue of being an "outsider." He repeatedly called attention to his integrity and deep religious faith. "I'll never lie to you," he promised voters, a pledge that no candidate would have bothered to give before Nixon's disgrace. Carter entered nearly all the Democratic primaries and campaigned hard in nonprimary states. Running against many different candidates, he won few decisive victories. Nevertheless, he accumulated delegates steadily and went to the convention in New York City in July with a solid majority.

When the final contest began, Carter had a large lead. Most of it soon evaporated. Reagan supporters among the Republicans swung behind Ford, and the prestige of the presidency was another asset. Both candidates were vague with respect to issues. Ford made much of the need to control inflation, Carter of the distressingly high unemployment that the nation was enduring. Three televised debates between the candidates attracted huge audiences without enlightening the public or generating a trend toward either candidate.

As election day approached, pollsters predicted an extremely close contest, and they were right: Carter won, 297 electoral votes to 241, having carried most of the South, including Texas, and a few large industrial states. A key element in his victory was the fact that he got an overwhelming majority of the black vote (partly on his record in Georgia, partly because Ford had been unsympathetic toward the demands of the urban poor). He also ran well in districts dominated by labor union members and throughout the South. The public's wish to punish the party of Richard Nixon was probably a further reason for his victory.

The Carter Presidency

Carter shone brightly in comparison with Nixon, and he seemed more forward-looking and imaginative than Ford. He tried to give a tone of democratic simplicity and moral fervor to his administration. After delivering his inaugural address, instead of riding in a limousine he walked with his wife and small daughter, Amy, in the parade from the Capitol to the White House. He enrolled Amy, a fourth grader, in a largely black Washington public school. For his first talk on television he wore a sweater instead of a coat and tie, an advertisement for both his informality and the need to conserve energy by turning down thermostats. Soon after taking office he held a "call-in"; for two hours he answered questions phoned in by people from all over the country. From time to time thereafter he organized "town meetings" in small cities at which he fielded questions and chatted with ordinary citizens.

In foreign affairs Carter announced that he intended to deal with all nations in a fair and humane way. He would put defense of "basic human rights" before all other concerns. At home he would fight inflation by reducing government spending and balancing the budget, and he would

■ In the front row, from the left: Prime Minister Begin of Israel, President Carter, President Sadat of Egypt, and Moshe Dayan of Israel. The four were on a break from their negotiations at Camp David, and were touring the battlefield at Gettysburg.

stimulate the economy by cutting taxes and creating jobs for the unemployed. He advanced an admirable if complicated plan for conserving energy and reducing the dependence of the United States on OPEC oil.

Carter achieved several notable diplomatic successes. He negotiated treaties with Panama that provided for the gradual transfer of the isthmian canal to that nation and guaranteed its neutrality (see note, page 561). Critics denounced this "retreat," but in 1978, after long debate, the Senate ratified the treaties. The president also carried forward the Nixon-Ford policy of restoring relations with Communist China by ending official American recognition of Taiwan. In January 1979 the first exchange of ambassadors with the People's Republic of China took place. Six months later a Strategic Arms Limitation Treaty (SALT) was signed with the Soviet Union.

Carter's most striking diplomatic achievement was the so-called Camp David Agreement with Israel and Egypt. Avoiding war in the Middle East was crucial because war in that part of the world was likely to result in the cutting off of oil supplies from the Arab nations. In September 1978 the president of Egypt, Anwar Sadat, and Prime Minister Menachem Begin of Israel came to the United States at Carter's invitation to negotiate a peace treaty ending the state of war that had existed between their two countries for many years. For two weeks they conferred at Camp David, the presidential retreat outside the capital. Carter was in constant attendance, and his patient work as a mediator had much to do with their successful negotiations. In the treaty Israel promised to withdraw from territory captured from Egypt during the "six-day" war of 1967. Egypt in turn recognized Israel as a nation, the first Arab country to do so.

Carter's handling of domestic problems did not

go nearly so well. At the outset he appointed so many Georgians to important posts that his administration took on a most parochial character. Six of seven top White House aides came from his home state, as did his attorney general, the director of the Office of Management and Budget, the ambassador to the United Nations, and many lesser officials. Most of these people, like Carter, had little or no experience in national affairs. The administration developed a reputation for submitting complicated proposals to Congress with great fanfare and then failing to follow them up.

Sometimes Carter seemed to forget about supposedly vital measures that he had claimed required urgent action. In fact his memory was fine; the trouble was that he became too involved in the details of too many issues. Whatever matter he was considering at the moment seemed to absorb him totally—other urgent matters were allowed to drift. When he was working with Sadat and Begin at Camp David, he paid almost no attention to anything else for nearly two weeks.

This tendency frequently caused him to shift policies sharply when he returned to matters he had put aside. One journalist counted seven distinct changes of approach in Carter's economic policy in three years. While running for office he had emphasized the need to restrain inflation, but early in 1977 he came out for a $50 income tax rebate for individuals that would almost surely have caused prices to rise. When that idea ran into stiff congressional resistance, Carter turned to something else. And so it went. His energy policy was equally inconsistent. He advanced several plans for reducing consumption of OPEC oil but dropped each without a fight when it did not win quick congressional support.

In the face of so much frustration it was perhaps only human that Carter tended to blame others for his troubles. In a heralded television speech he described a national "malaise" that, he said, had sapped the people's energies and undermined civic pride. Although there was some truth in this observation, the effect was to make the president seem both ineffective and petulant.

A Time of Troubles

National self-confidence was indeed at a low ebb. The almost endless crises of the Cold War had subsided and the hot war in Vietnam was over, but the United States had lost a considerable portion of its international prestige. To a degree this was unavoidable. The very success of American policies after World War II had something to do with the decline of American influence in the world. The Marshall Plan, for example, enabled the nations of western Europe to rebuild their economies; thereafter they were less dependent on outside aid, and in the course of pursuing their own interests they sometimes adopted policies that did not seem to be in the best interests of the United States.

Similarly, to the extent that American aid to underdeveloped countries had improved their economies, they were more likely to act independently and not necessarily in ways that benefited the United States. On the other hand, when American aid was ineffective or used to bolster unpopular local regimes, American prestige also suffered. And the failure of the United States to achieve its objectives in the Vietnam War had a debilitating effect on its influence abroad long after the war ended.

At home the decay of the inner sections of the great cities was a continuing cause of concern. The older cities seemed almost beyond repair. Carter visited the South Bronx section of New York City in 1977. He was shocked to see block after block of rubble and rows of empty, fire-blackened buildings. He pledged that the federal government would clean up and rebuild this wasteland, but when his term ended that part of the South Bronx and similar parts of many cities remained barren ruins.

Crime rates were high in the inner cities, public transportation dilapidated and expensive, other city services undermanned and inefficient, the schools crowded, students' performances poor. Blacks, Hispanics, and other minorities made up a large percentage of the population in decaying urban areas. That they had to live in such surroundings made a mockery of the commitment made by the civil rights legislation of the 1960s and Lyndon Johnson's Great Society program to treat all people equally and improve the lives of the poor.

The most disturbing problem that vexed the nation in the Carter years was soaring inflation. Prices had been rising for an unprecedentedly long period and in recent years at an unprecedentedly rapid pace (see graph, page 789). In 1971 an

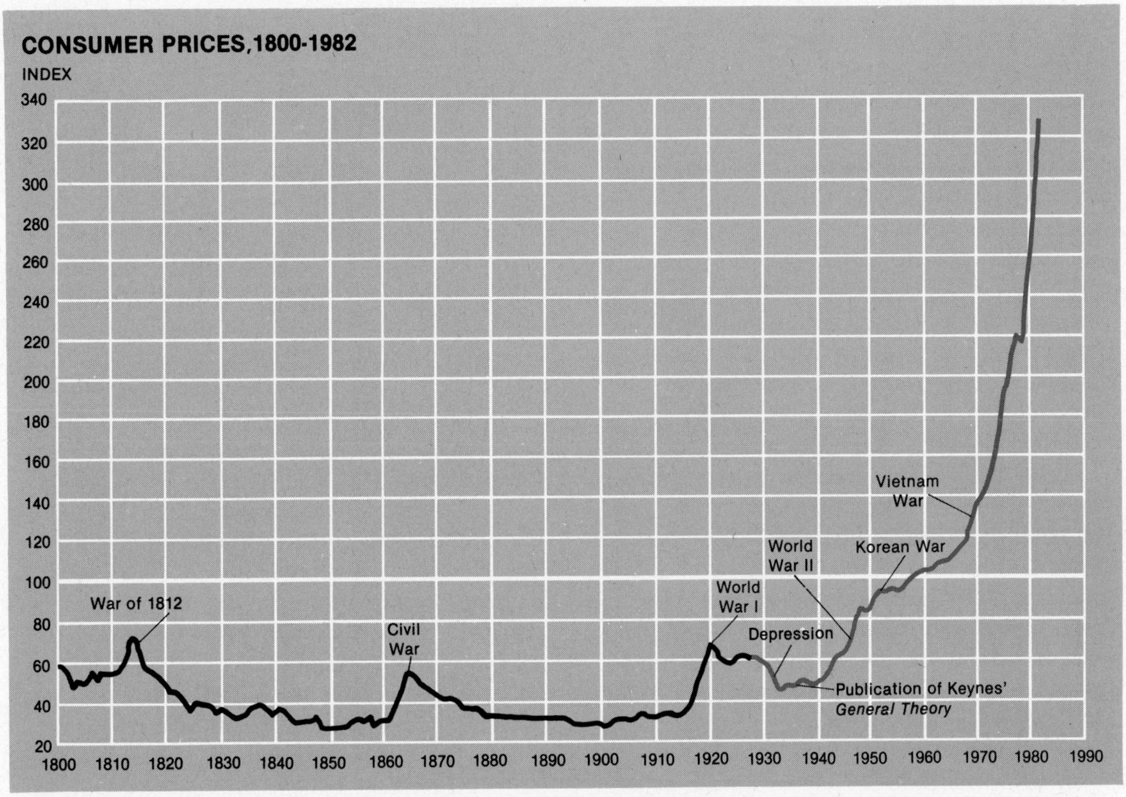

■ **The explanation of the basis of this chart appears on page 453. Recalling that the base line of 100 is the 1957–1959 average, and not the more commonly used average from the reference year 1967, the inflation that began right after World War II is shown in startling detail. For the first time in American history, a wartime inflation was *not* followed by a price deflation (as opposed to the usual sequence in previous postwar periods).**

inflation rate of 5 percent had so alarmed President Nixon that he had imposed a price freeze. In 1979 a 5 percent rate would have seemed almost deflationary—the actual rate was nearly 13 percent.

Double-digit inflation had a devastating effect on the poor, the retired, and others who were living on fixed incomes. However, the squeeze that price increases put on these unfortunates was only part of the damage done. People began to *anticipate* inflation. They bought goods they did not really need, and without much regard for cost, on the assumption that whatever today's price, tomorrow's would be much higher. This behavior increased demand and pushed prices up still more. Put differently, when the interest paid by savings banks was lower than the inflation rate, it seemed foolish to save money.

At another level, a kind of "flight from money" began. Well-to-do individuals transferred their assets from cash to durable goods such as land and houses, gold, works of art, jewelry, rare postage stamps, and other "collectables." Interest rates rose rapidly as lenders demanded higher returns to compensate for expected future inflation.

Congress raised the minimum wage to help low-paid workers cope with inflation. It pegged social security payments to the cost of living index in an effort to protect retirees. Thereafter, when prices rose social security payments went up automatically. The poor and the pensioners got some immediate relief because of these laws, but their increased spending power caused further upward pressure on prices. Inflation seemed to be feeding upon itself, and the price spiral seemed unstoppable.

The federal government made matters worse in several ways. People's wages and salaries rose in response to inflation, but their taxes went up more rapidly because higher dollar incomes put them in higher tax brackets. This "bracket creep" caused resentment and frustration among middle-class families. There were "taxpayer revolts" as many people turned against long-accepted but expensive government programs for aiding the poor. Inflation also increased the government's need for money. Year after year it spent more than it received in taxes. By thus unbalancing the budget it pumped billions of dollars into the economy, and by borrowing to meet the deficits it pushed up interest rates, increasing the costs of all businesses that had to borrow.

In 1978 President Carter laid down voluntary wage and price "guidelines" in another effort to apply the brakes. Unions and manufacturers responded fairly well, but the guidelines did not apply to the prices that were going up most rapidly. These were oil, houses, and food. Finally Carter named a conservative banker, Paul A. Volcker, as chairman of the Federal Reserve Board. Volcker belonged to the monetarist school of economics, which taught that the way to check inflation was to limit the growth of the money supply. Under his direction the Board adopted a tight-money policy, which caused already high interest rates to soar.

High interest rates hurt all borrowers, but they were especially damaging to the automobile and housing industries. American car manufacturers had been experiencing hard times because of the competition of Japanese and European automobiles, which gave better gasoline mileage and were seemingly better built than most American vehicles. High interest charges depressed sales still more by raising monthly payments on car purchases beyond the means of many prospective buyers. Automobile workers were among the highest paid in American industry, but tens of thousands of them were out of work. One of the "Big Three" manufacturers, Chrysler, teetered on the edge of bankruptcy, saved only by government-guaranteed loans. Soaring mortgage rates had a similar effect on the sale of homes. The housing slump meant unemployment for thousands of carpenters, bricklayers, and other construction workers and bankruptcy for many builders.

The Iranian Crisis

It was unfair to blame Carter for all the nation's troubles and particularly for the inflation. Blame him people did, however, and by the autumn of 1979 his standing in public opinion polls was extremely low. Blameless or not, he had failed to provide the fresh point of view and the firm leadership that he had promised in the 1976 campaign. His chances of being elected to a second term seemed dim.

At this point a dramatic upheaval in the Middle East revived his prospects. On November 4, 1979, about 400 university students broke into the huge American Embassy compound in Teheran, Iran, and took everyone within the walls captive.

Iran was a leading producer of petroleum and an enthusiastic member of OPEC. However, unlike the leaders of the Arab states, the shah of Iran, Mohammed Riza Pahlevi, had been a close ally of the United States. Over the years the shah had bought billions of dollars worth of American arms. Iran possessed the most powerful military force in the region; it seemed, as President Carter said in 1977, "an island of stability" in the troubled Middle East.

The appearance of stability was deceptive because the shah, who ruled with an iron hand, was extremely unpopular. His attempts to introduce western ideas and methods in Iran caused economic disruption and angered conservatives. Moslem religious leaders were particularly offended by such "radical" policies as the shah's tentative efforts to improve the position of women in Iranian society. Because his American-supplied army and his American-trained secret police kept the shah in power, his opponents hated the United States almost as much as they hated their autocratic ruler.

Throughout 1977 riots and demonstrations convulsed Iran. When the shah's soldiers fired on protesters, the bloodshed caused more unrest. Early in 1978 the whole nation seemed to rise against him, and the shah was forced to flee the country. A revolutionary government headed by a revered religious leader, the Ayatollah Ruhollah Khomeini, who had recently returned to Iran in triumph after a long exile in France, assumed power.

Khomeini denounced the United States, the "Great Satan" whose support of the shah, he claimed, had caused the Iranian people untold suffering. When President Carter allowed the shah, who had been living in Mexico, to come to the United States for medical treatment, the Iranian revolutionaries were convinced that an attempt would be made to restore him to his throne. The seizure of the Teheran embassy resulted.

The students announced that the captive Americans would be held as hostages until the United States returned the shah to Iran for trial as a traitor. They also demanded that the shah's vast wealth be confiscated and surrendered to the Iranian government. Of course President Carter rejected these demands. (He had no choice in the matter; deporting the shah, who had entered the United States legally, and confiscating his property were not possible under American law.) Instead he froze Iranian assets in the United States and banned trade with Iran until the hostages were freed.

Carter wanted to rescue the hostages, but there seemed to be no way to do this. Even going to war would surely result in their execution—and the deaths of others as well. He gave some consideration to blockading Iranian ports in order to force their release, but that could have no immediate effect and it might alarm the Arab states and lead to another cutoff of Middle Eastern oil. And there was always the danger of Soviet intervention.

The American public and most foreign observers approved of the president's restraint. If he made any mistake, it was a consequence of his habit of focusing so intently on one matter at a time. This exaggerated the importance of the hostage issue. Some critics believed that Carter was playing into the hands of the Iranians by calling attention to the fact that they could hold the mighty United States at bay.

A stalemate developed. The Iranians released the women and black captives, but the others, more than 50 in number, were subjected to countless indignities and in some cases were physically abused. Months passed. Even after the shah, who was terminally ill with cancer, left the United States for Panama, the Iranians remained adamant.

■ **The Iranian crisis produced many striking visual images that were seen worldwide. Here the students burn the American flag a few days after the embassy seizure.**

The crisis produced a remarkable emotional response in the United States. For once the entire country agreed on something. One result of this was a revival of Carter's political fortunes. Before the attack on the Teheran embassy, Senator Edward M. Kennedy of Massachusetts, youngest brother of John F. Kennedy, had decided to run against Carter in the Democratic presidential primaries. He seemed a likely winner until the seizure of the hostages, but that event caused the public to rally round the president.

Carter took clever political advantage of the national concern. He refused to campaign in the primaries, insisting (without good reason) that the crisis made his constant presence in Washington essential. Meanwhile, in December 1979, the Soviet Union had sent troops into Afghanistan in order to overthrow a government of which it disapproved. Since Afghanistan bordered Iran, some analysts believed that the invasion was prelude to Soviet intervention in that troubled country.

Carter denounced the invasion, stopped shipments of American grain to the Soviet Union, and withdrew the arms limitation treaty with the Soviets that the Senate had been considering. He refused to allow American athletes to compete in the Olympic games, which were held in the summer of 1980 in Moscow. Most people seemed to approve of Carter's handling of the Afghan situation; his ratings in opinion polls rose.

Nevertheless the hostages languished in Iran. In April 1980 Carter finally ordered a team of marine commandos flown into Iran by helicopter in a desperate attempt to rescue them. The raid was a fiasco. Several helicopters broke down. While the others were gathered at a desert rendezvous south of Teheran, Carter called off the attempt. In the confusion of a night departure there was a crash and eight commandos were killed. The Iranians made political capital of the incident, gleefully displaying on television the wrecked aircraft and captured American equipment. Unlike Carter's earlier actions, the raid was widely criticized. (Even before it began Secretary of State Cyrus Vance had quietly resigned on the ground that it was almost sure to result in many casualties and that if it succeeded the Iranians would only seize other Americans in the country.) And so, the stalemate continued. In July 1980 the shah, who had moved from Panama to Egypt, died. It made no difference to the Iranians.

Election of 1980

Despite the failure of the raid, Carter beat Kennedy decisively in the most important primaries without stirring from the White House. He had more than enough delegates at the Democratic convention to win nomination on the first ballot. His Republican opponent in the campaign that followed was Ronald Reagan, the former movie actor and governor of California who had almost defeated Gerald Ford for the nomination in 1976. At 69, Reagan was the oldest person ever nominated for president by a major party. However, his age was not a serious handicap in the campaign; he was physically trim and vigorous and seemed no older than most other prominent politicians.

Reagan had grown up a New Deal Democrat, but during and immediately after World War II he became disillusioned with liberalism. He denounced government inefficiency and high taxation. As president of the Screen Actors' Guild he attacked the supposed influence of communists in the movie industry. After his movie career ended (he always insisted that he had *not* been typed as "the nice guy who didn't get the girl"), Reagan did publicity for General Electric for a number of years. In 1960 he left GE to work for various conservative causes. He campaigned for Barry Goldwater during the 1964 presidential contest. Two years later, at the urging of a group of California conservatives, he ran for governor of that state and was elected. He was a controversial governor, in part because, despite his professed conservatism and his emphasis on economy, government spending in California increased dramatically during his term. Despite, or perhaps because of this shift, he was easily reelected in 1970.

The 1980 presidential campaign ranks among the most curious in American history. One of Reagan's opponents at the Republican convention, Congressman John Anderson of Illinois, refused to accept defeat and ran for president as an independent. He did so, he announced, because he thought both Carter and Reagan had little genuine popular support.

Indeed, many citizens were unable to decide whom to vote for. Of those who expressed a preference, many did so without enthusiasm. Anderson's problem was that he too inspired relatively little enthusiasm among voters. "None of the above" seemed the true desire of many citizens as they contemplated the list of candidates.

Both Carter and Reagan spent much time explaining why the other was unsuited to be president. Carter defended his record, though without much conviction. Reagan promised to install a "New Federalism": he would transfer some functions of the federal government to the states, on the theory that local governments reflected both the will and the wisdom of the citizenry better than the remote, bureaucracy-ridden government in Washington. He promised to reduce spending and cut taxes. At the same time, he insisted, the budget could be balanced and inflation sharply reduced.

Reagan's tendency to depend on popular magazine articles, half-remembered conversations, and other informal sources for his economic "facts" reflected a mental imprecision that alarmed his critics, but his sunny disposition and his "laid-back" style compared favorably with Carter's personality. The president seemed tight-lipped and tense even when flashing his habitual toothy smile. A television debate between Carter and Reagan pointed up their personal differences but apparently had little effect on public opinion.

Because so many people said they were undecided, the contest seemed close—"too close to call," most experts said on election eve. It did not turn out that way. The voting was light, but those who cast ballots gave Reagan over 43 million votes to Carter's 35 million and Anderson's 5.6 million. Reagan won a big electoral college majority, 489 to 49. Even more unexpected were the results of the congressional elections. The Republicans won control of the Senate and cut deeply into the Democratic majority in the House of Representatives. Clearly the country had turned in a conservative direction.

Carter devoted his last weeks in office to the continuing hostage crisis. War had broken out between Iran and Iraq. The additional strain on an Iranian economy already shattered by revolution raised hopes that Ayatollah Khomeini would release the captive Americans. Iran needed both the assets Carter had frozen and spare parts for its American-made planes and tanks. With Algeria acting as intermediary, American and Iranian diplomats worked out an agreement. Reagan avoided involvement in the negotiations, but to put pressure on the Iranians he announced that he opposed paying "ransom" for "people who have been kidnapped by barbarians." Perhaps in fear that the new president might take some drastic action, Iran at last agreed to release the hostages in return for its assets in the United States. After 444 days in captivity, the 52 hostages were set free on January 20, the day Reagan was inaugurated.

Reagan as President

Despite his amiable, unaggressive style, Reagan acted rapidly and with determination once in office. He hoped to change the direction in which the country was moving. He would replace inflation with price stability, an active, expanding federal government with more dependence on the states and still more dependence on individual initiative. The marketplace, not bureaucratic regulations, should govern most economic decisions. Yet he would greatly increase military spending and defend American interests more vigorously in order to check what he saw as a steadily increasing gap between the strength and influence of the United States and that of the Soviet Union.

Reagan made cutting taxes his first priority. He asked Congress to lower income taxes by 30 percent over three years. At the same time, he called for steep reductions in federal spending, focused chiefly on social services such as welfare payments and food stamps that went to poor people. He promised to maintain a "safety net" under the poor to protect them from real deprivation, and he insisted that in the long run they and everyone else would benefit from his program.

His reasoning was based on what was known as "supply-side economics." He claimed that people would have more money to invest because of the tax cut, that they would invest the money in productive ways rather than spend it on consumer goods (because they would be able to keep a larger share of their profits), and that the investments would lead to increased production, more jobs, prosperity, and therefore more income for the government despite the lower tax rates. There was a superficial similarity between this argument and the reasoning behind the successful tax cut engineered by President Johnson in 1964 (see pages 745–746). However, the danger of inflation was much greater in 1981. Many congressmen hesitated, but the "mandate" of Reagan's big election victory was hard to resist.

An unrelated event added to the president's popularity. On March 30, while leaving a Washington hotel, he was shot in the chest by one John W. Hinckley, Jr.* Although he was seriously wounded, Reagan reacted coolly and with his

*Two security officers and Reagan's press secretary, James Brady, were also wounded by the would-be assassin.

■ **Reagan has been tagged "The Great Communicator" for his effectiveness on television and in the media generally. In July of 1981 he went on the air to present his administration's arguments in favor of a phased-in three-year tax cut.**

usual self-deprecating style. When he was wheeled into the operating room for emergency surgery, he told the team of doctors before going under the anesthetic that he hoped they were all Republicans. Later he complained of his bad luck—he had been wearing a brand new suit and now it was ruined. It was hard to oppose such bravery and good humor. That he made a swift and total recovery despite his age further increased the admiration of the country.

Helped by the votes of conservative Democrats, Reagan won congressional approval of a budget that reduced government expenditures by $39 billion. In August 1981 Congress also gave him most of the tax cuts he had asked for. The law lowered individual income taxes by 25 percent over three years. Since the percentage was the same for everyone, high-income taxpayers would receive a very large proportion of the savings. Business taxes were liberalized, and capital gains, gift, and inheritance, levies were reduced. To further encourage investment, the law authorized the sale of special one-year savings certificates, the interest on which, up to $1,000 per person, was to be tax exempt. Anyone with earned income could now invest up to $2,000 a year in an Individual Retirement Account (IRA). This money, and the interest or dividends it earned, would not be taxed until the individual retired.

Reagan kept his campaign promise to eliminate many government regulations affecting businesses. Long and complicated antitrust suits against International Business Machines and American Telephone and Telegraph, two of the largest corporations in the country, were dropped.

"Reaganomics," as administration policy was called, was certainly not a new theory. Carter had also advocated tax cuts, reduced federal spending, and tight money. During his term the airlines were freed from control by the Civil Aeronautics Board. But Reagan's supply-side economics was old-fashioned to the point of being antique. It differed little from the policy Herbert Hoover had favored in the Great Depression, which his critics had derided as the "trickle-down" theory. As the economist James Tobin said in 1981, "old doctrines and policies, new forty years ago," were to be replaced by "new doctrines and policies, old forty years ago."

Tobin and most other economists did not think that Reaganomics would work. At the beginning of 1982 the economy was in a full-scale recession. More than 9 percent of the work force was unemployed. The gross national product was declining. The combination of lower tax rates and a slumping economy was further unbalancing the budget. Month after month the Treasury was forced to borrow billions; its needs and the continuing tight-money policy of the Federal Reserve Board kept interest rates high. Only the fact that inflation was slowing brightened the gloomy economic picture.

Most of Reagan's advisers urged him to reduce the military budget and seek some kind of tax increase in order to bring the government's income more nearly in line with its expenditures. However, the president remained firm in his commitment to the views of the supply-siders. Most ordinary citizens seemed to be skeptical of his policies but impressed by his personal qualities. His Democratic opponents (and some Republicans) were increasingly vocal in their criticisms but had few new ideas to suggest. This was the state of the nation as Reagan began his second year in the White House.

SUPPLEMENTARY READING

Titles marked with an asterisk have been published in paperback

On the election of 1968, T. H. White's **The Making of the President, 1968*** (1969), is lively and entertaining, while Joe McGinniss, **The Selling of the President, 1968*** (1969), is a fascinating account of the Republican advertising and television campaign. There is as yet no adequate biography of Nixon, but his own **Six Crises*** (1962) offers some insights into his character and view of political life, and Garry Wills, **Nixon Agonistes*** (1970), is a thoughtful though unfriendly analysis. See also Rowland Evans, Jr., and R. D. Novak, **Nixon in the White House*** (1971). White's **The Making of the President, 1972*** (1973) is less satisfactory than his earlier volumes.

The literature on the war in Vietnam is already enormous. The following are important studies: R. N. Goodwin, **Triumph or Tragedy: Reflections on Vietnam*** (1966), Frances Fitzgerald, **Fire in the Lake*** (1972), and David Halberstam, **The Best and the Brightest*** (1972), which contains a mass of detail on the evolution of American policy, based on extensive interviews. William Shawcross, **Side-Show: Kissinger, Nixon, and the Destruction of Cambodia*** (1979), is extremely critical. See also H. Y. Schandler, **The Unmaking of a President: Lyndon Johnson and Vietnam** (1977), Guenter Lewy, **America in Vietnam*** (1980), and Norman Mailer, **The Armies of the Night*** (1968), a vivid account of an antiwar demonstration in Washington. Henry Kissinger's memoir, **White House Years** (1979), is an important but self-serving account of American foreign relations during the Nixon years.

A convenient summary of the almost infinite complexities of the Watergate affair is New York Times (ed.), **The End of a Presidency*** (1974), but see also Carl Bernstein and Robert Woodward, **All the President's Men*** (1974) and **Final Days*** (1976), J. W. Dean, **Blind Ambition*** (1976), and Leon Jaworski, **The Right and the Power*** (1976).

Betty Glad, **Jimmy Carter: In Search of the Great White House** (1980), is a critical analysis of Carter's style and actions.

THE DECLARATION OF INDEPENDENCE

When in the Course of human events, it becomes necessary for one people to dissolve the political bands which have connected them with another, and to assume among the Powers of the earth, the separate and equal station to which the Laws of Nature and of Nature's God entitle them, a decent respect to the opinions of mankind requires that they should declare the causes which impel them to the separation.

We hold these truths to be self-evident, that all men are created equal, that they are endowed by their Creator with certain unalienable Rights, that among these are Life, Liberty and the pursuit of Happiness. That to secure these rights, Governments are instituted among Men, deriving their just powers from the consent of the governed, That whenever any Form of Government becomes destructive of these ends, it is the Right of the People to alter or to abolish it, and to institute new Government, laying its foundation on such principles and organizing its powers in such form, as to them shall seem most likely to effect their Safety and Happiness. Prudence, indeed, will dictate that Governments long established should not be changed for light and transient causes; and accordingly all experience hath shown, that mankind are more disposed to suffer, while evils are sufferable, than to right themselves by abolishing the forms to which they are accustomed. But when a long train of abuses and usurpations, pursuing invariably the same Object evinces a design to reduce them under absolute Despotism, it is their right, it is their duty, to throw off such Government, and to provide new Guards for their future security.—Such has been the patient sufferance of these Colonies; and such is now the necessity which constrains them to alter their former Systems of Government. The history of the present King of Great Britain is a history of repeated injuries and usurpations, all having in direct object the establishment of an absolute Tyranny over these States. To prove this, let Facts be submitted to a candid world.

He has refused his Assent to Laws, the most wholesome and necessary for the public good.

He has forbidden his Governors to pass Laws of immediate and pressing importance, unless suspended in their operation till his Assent should be obtained; and when so suspended, he has utterly neglected to attend to them.

He has refused to pass other Laws for the accommodation of large districts of people, unless those people would relinquish the right of Representation in the Legislature, a right inestimable to them and formidable to tyrants only.

He has called together legislative bodies at places unusual, uncomfortable, and distant from the depository of their Public Records, for the sole purpose of fatiguing them into compliance with his measures.

He has dissolved Representative Houses repeatedly, for opposing with manly firmness his invasions on the rights of the people.

He has refused for a long time, after such dissolutions, to cause others to be elected; whereby the Legislative Powers, incapable of Annihilation, have returned to the People at large for their exercise; the State remaining in the mean time exposed to all the dangers of invasion from without, and convulsions within.

He has endeavoured to prevent the population of these States; for that purpose obstructing the Laws of Naturalization of Foreigners; refusing to pass others to encourage their migration hither, and raising the conditions of new Appropriations of Lands.

He has obstructed the Administration of Justice, by refusing his Assent to Laws for establishing Judiciary Powers.

He has made Judges dependent on his Will alone, for the tenure of their offices, and the amount and payment of their salaries.

He has erected a multitude of New Offices, and sent hither swarms of Officers to harass our People, and eat out their substance.

He has kept among us, in times of peace, Standing Armies without the Consent of our legislature.

He has affected to render the Military independent of and superior to the Civil Power.

He has combined with others to subject us to a jurisdiction foreign to our constitution, and unacknowledged by our laws; giving his Assent to their acts of pretended legislation:

For quartering large bodies of armed troops among us:

For protecting them, by a mock Trial, from Punishment for any Murders which they should commit on the Inhabitants of these States:

For cutting off our Trade with all parts of the world:

For imposing taxes on us without our Consent:

For depriving us in many cases, of the benefits of Trial by Jury:

For transporting us beyond Seas to be tried for pretended offences:

For abolishing the free System of English Laws in a neighbouring Province, establishing therein an Arbitrary government, and enlarging its Boundaries so as to render it at once an example and fit instrument for introducing the same absolute rule into these Colonies:

For taking away our Charters, abolishing our most valuable Laws, and altering fundamentally the Forms of our Governments:

For suspending our own Legislature, and declaring themselves invested with Power to legislate for us in all cases whatsoever.

He has abdicated Government here, by declaring us out of his Protection and waging War against us.

He has plundered our seas, ravaged our Coasts, burnt our towns, and destroyed the lives of our people.

He is at this time transporting large armies of foreign mercenaries to compleat the works of death, desolation and tyranny, already begun with circumstances of Cruelty & perfidy scarcely paralleled in the most barbarous ages, and totally unworthy the Head of a civilized nation.

He has constrained our fellow Citizens taken Captive on the high Seas to bear Arms against their Country, to become the executioners of their friends and Brethren, or to fall themselves by their Hands.

He has excited domestic insurrections amongst us, and has endeavoured to bring on the inhabitants of our frontiers, the merciless Indian Savages, whose known rule of warfare, is an undistinguished destruction of all ages, sexes and conditions.

In every stage of these Oppressions We have Petitioned for Redress in the most humble terms: Our repeated Petitions have been answered only by repeated injury. A Prince, whose character is thus marked by every act which may define a Tyrant, is unfit to be the ruler of a free People.

Nor have We been wanting in attention to our British brethren. We have warned them from time to time of attempts by their legislature to extend an unwarrantable jurisdiction over us. We have reminded them of the circumstances of our emigration and settlement here. We have appealed to their native justice and magnanimity, and we have conjured them by the ties of our common kindred to disavow these usurpations, which, would inevitably interrupt our connections and correspondence. They too have been deaf to the voice of justice and of consanguinity. We must, therefore, acquiesce in the necessity, which denounces our Separation, and hold them, as we hold the rest of mankind, Enemies in War, in Peace Friends.

We, therefore, the Representatives of the united States of America, in General Congress, Assembled, appealing to the Supreme Judge of the world for the rectitude of our intentions, do, in the Name, and by Authority of the good People of these Colonies, solemnly publish and declare, That these United Colonies are, and of Right ought to be Free and Independent States; that they are Absolved from all Allegiance to the British Crown, and that all political connection between them and the State of Great Britain, is and ought to be totally dissolved; and that as Free and Independent States, they have full Power to levy War, conclude Peace, contract Alliances, establish Commerce, and to do all other Acts and Things which Independent States may of right do. And for the support of this Declaration, with a firm reliance on the Protection of Divine Providence, we mutually pledge to each other our Lives, our Fortunes and our sacred Honor.

THE CONSTITUTION OF THE UNITED STATES

We the people of the United States, in Order to form a more perfect Union, establish Justice, insure domestic Tranquility, provide for the common defence, promote the general Welfare, and secure the Blessings of Liberty to ourselves and our Posterity, do ordain and establish this CONSTITUTION for the United States of America.

ARTICLE I

Section 1. All legislative Powers herein granted shall be vested in a Congress of the United States, which shall consist of a Senate and House of Representatives.

Section 2. The House of Representatives shall be composed of Members chosen every second Year by the People of the several States, and the Electors in each State shall have the Qualifications requisite for Electors of the most numerous Branch of the State Legislature.

No Person shall be a Representative who shall not have attained to the Age of twenty-five Years, and been seven Years a Citizen of the United States, and who shall not, when elected, be an Inhabitant of that State in which he shall be chosen.

Representatives and direct Taxes shall be apportioned among the several States which may be included within this Union, according to their respective Numbers, which shall be determined by adding to the whole Number of free Persons, including those bound to Service for a Term of Years, and excluding Indians not taxed, three fifths of all other Persons. The actual Enumeration shall be made within three Years after the first Meeting of the Congress of the United States, and within every subsequent Term of ten Years, in such Manner as they shall by Law direct. The Number of Representatives shall not exceed one for every thirty Thousand, but each State shall have at Least one Representative; and until such enumeration shall be made, the State of New Hampshire shall be entitled to chuse three, Massachusetts eight, Rhode-Island and Providence Plantations one, Connecticut five, New-York six, New Jersey four, Pennsylvania eight, Delaware one, Maryland six, Virginia ten, North Carolina five, South Carolina five, and Georgia three.

When vacancies happen in the Representation from any State, the Executive Authority thereof shall issue Writs of Election to fill such Vacancies.

The House of Representatives shall chuse their Speaker and other Officers; and shall have the sole Power of Impeachment.

Section 3. The Senate of the United States shall be composed of two Senators from each State, chosen by the Legislature thereof, for six Years; and each Senator shall have one Vote.

Immediately after they shall be assembled in Consequence of the first Election, they shall be divided as equally as may be into three Classes. The Seats of the Senators of the first Class shall be vacated at the Expiration of the second Year, of the second Class at the Expiration of the fourth Year, and of the third Class at the Expiration of the sixth Year, so that one-third may be chosen every second Year; and if Vacancies happen by Resignation, or otherwise, during the Recess of the Legislature of any State, the Executive thereof may make temporary Appointments until the next Meeting of the Legislature, which shall then fill such Vacancies.

No Person shall be a Senator who shall not have attained to the Age of thirty Years, and been nine Years a Citizen of the United States, and who shall not, when elected, be an Inhabitant of that State in which he shall be chosen.

The Vice President of the United States shall be President of the Senate, but shall have no vote, unless they be equally divided.

The Senate shall chuse their other Officers, and also a President pro tempore, in the absence of the Vice President, or when he shall exercise the Office of the President of the United States.

The Senate shall have the sole Power to try all Impeachments. When sitting for that purpose, they shall be on Oath or Affirmation. When the President of the United States is tried, the Chief Justice shall preside: And no person shall be convicted without the Concurrence of two thirds of the Members present.

Judgment in Cases of Impeachment shall not extend further than to removal from Office, and disqualification to hold and enjoy any Office of honor, Trust, or Profit under the United States: but the Party convicted shall nevertheless be liable and subject to Indictment, Trial, Judgment, and Punishment, according to Law.

Section 4. The Times, Places and Manner of holding Elections for Senators and Representatives, shall be prescribed in each state by the Legislature thereof; but the Congress may at any time by Law make or alter such Regulations, except as to the Places of Chusing Senators.

The Congress shall assemble at least once in every Year, and such Meeting shall be on the first Monday in December, unless they shall by Law appoint a different Day.

Section 5. Each House shall be the Judge of the Elections, Returns and Qualifications of its own Members, and a Majority of each shall constitute a Quorum to do Business; but a smaller number may adjourn from day to day, and may be authorized to compel the Attendance of absent Members, in such Manner, and under such Penalties, as each House may provide.

Each House may determine the Rules of its Proceedings, punish its Members for disorderly Behavior, and, with the Concurrence of two thirds, expel a Member.

Each House shall keep a Journal of its Proceedings, and from time to time publish the same, excepting such Parts as may in their Judgment require Secrecy; and the Yeas and Nays of the Members of either House on any question shall, at the Desire of one fifth of those Present, be entered on the Journal.

Neither House, during the Session of Congress, shall, without the Consent of the other, adjourn for more than three days, nor to any other Place than that in which the two Houses shall be sitting.

Section 6. The Senators and Representatives shall receive a Compensation for their Services, to be ascertained by Law, and paid out of the Treasury of the United States. They shall in all Cases, except Treason, Felony, and Breach of the Peace, be privileged from Arrest during their Attendance at the Session of their respective Houses, and in going to and returning from the same; and for any Speech or Debate in either House, they shall not be questioned in any other Place.

No Senator or Representative shall, during the Time for which he was elected, be appointed to any civil Office under the Authority of the United States, which shall have been created, or the Emoluments whereof shall have been increased, during such time; and no Person holding any Office under the United States shall be a Member of either House during his continuance in Office.

Section 7. All Bills for raising Revenue shall originate in the House of Representatives; but the Senate may propose or concur with Amendments as on other bills.

Every Bill which shall have passed the House of Representatives and the Senate, shall, before it become a Law, be presented to the President of the United States; If he approve he shall sign it, but if not he shall return it, with his Objections, to that House in which it shall have originated, who shall enter the Objections at large on their Journal, and proceed to reconsider it. If after such Reconsideration two thirds of that House shall agree to pass the bill, it shall be sent, together with the objections, to the other House, by which it shall likewise be reconsidered, and if approved by two thirds of that House, it shall become a Law. But in all such Cases the Votes of both Houses shall be determined by Yeas and Nays, and the Names of the Persons voting for and against the Bill shall be entered on the Journal of each House respectively. If any Bill shall not be returned by the President within ten Days (Sundays excepted) after it shall have been presented to him, the Same shall be a Law, in like Manner as if he had signed it, unless the Congress by their Adjournment prevent its Return, in which Case it shall not be a Law.

Every Order, Resolution, or Vote to which the Concurrence of the Senate and House of Representatives may be necessary (except on a question of Adjournment) shall be presented to the President of the United States; and before the Same shall take Effect, shall be approved by him, or being disapproved by him, shall be repassed by two thirds of the Senate and House of Representatives, according to the Rules and Limitations prescribed in the Case of a Bill.

Section 8. The Congress shall have Power To lay and collect Taxes, Duties, Imposts and Excises, to pay the Debts and provide for the common Defence and general Welfare of the United States; but all Duties, Imposts and Excises shall be uniform throughout the United States;

To borrow money on the credit of the United States;

To regulate Commerce with foreign Nations, and among the several States, and with the Indian Tribes;

To establish an uniform Rule of Naturalization, and uniform Laws on the subject of Bankruptcies throughout the United States;

To coin Money, regulate the Value thereof, and of foreign Coin, and fix the Standard of Weights and Measures;

To provide for the Punishment of counterfeiting the Securities and current Coin of the United States;

To establish Post Offices and post Roads;

To promote the Progress of Science and useful Arts, by securing for limited Times to Authors and Inventors the exclusive Right to their respective Writings and Discoveries;

To constitute Tribunals inferior to the Supreme Court;

To define and punish Piracies and Felonies committed on the high Seas, and Offences against the Law of Nations;

To declare War, grant Letters of Marque and Reprisal, and make Rules concerning Captures on Land and Water;

To raise and support Armies, but no Appropriation of Money to that Use shall be for a longer Term than two Years;

To provide and maintain a Navy;

To make Rules for the Government and Regulation of the land and naval forces;

To provide for calling forth the Militia to execute the Laws of the Union, suppress Insurrections and repel Invasions;

To provide for organizing, arming, and disciplining the Militia, and for governing such Part of them as may be employed in the Service of the United States, reserving to the States respectively, the Appointment of the Officers, and the Authority of training the Militia according to the discipline prescribed by Congress;

To exercise exclusive Legislation in all Cases whatsoever, over such District (not exceeding ten Miles square) as may, by Cession of particular States, and the acceptance of Congress, become the Seat of Government of the United States, and to exercise like Authority over all Places purchased by the Consent of the Legislature of the State in which the Same shall be, for the Erection of Forts, Magazines, Arsenals, dock-Yards, and other needful Buildings;—And

To make all Laws which shall be necessary and proper for carrying into Execution the foregoing Powers, and all other Powers vested by this Constitution in the Government of the United States, or in any Department or Officer thereof.

Section 9. The Migration or Importation of such Persons as any of the States now existing shall think proper to admit, shall not be prohibited by the Congress prior to the Year one thousand eight hundred and eight, but a tax or duty may be imposed on such Importation, not exceeding ten dollars for each Person.

The privilege of the Writ of Habeas Corpus shall not be suspended, unless when in Cases of Rebellion or Invasion the public Safety may require it.

No Bill of Attainder or ex post facto Law shall be passed.

No capitation, or other direct, Tax shall be laid unless in Proportion to the Census or Enumeration herein before directed to be taken.

No Tax or Duty shall be laid on Articles exported from any State.

No Preference shall be given by any Regulation of Revenue to the Ports of one State over those of another: nor shall Vessels bound to, or from, one State, be obliged to enter, clear, or pay Duties in another.

No Money shall be drawn from the Treasury, but in Consequence of Appropriations made by Law; and a regular Statement and Account of the Receipts and Expenditures of all public Money shall be published from time to time.

No Title of Nobility shall be granted by the United States: And no Person holding any Office of Profit or Trust under them, shall, without the Consent of the Congress, accept of any present, Emolument, Office, or Title, of any kind whatever, from any King, Prince, or foreign State.

Section 10. No State shall enter into any Treaty, Alliance, or Confederation; grant Letters of Marque and Reprisal; coin Money; emit Bills of Credit; make any Thing but gold and silver Coin a Tender in Payment of Debts; pass any Bill of Attainder, ex post facto Law, or Law impairing the Obligation of Contracts, or grant any Title of Nobility.

No State shall, without the Consent of the Congress, lay any Imposts or Duties on Imports or Exports, except what may be absolutely necessary for executing its inspection Laws: and the net Produce of all Duties and Imposts, laid by any State on Imports or Exports, shall be for the Use of the Treasury of the United States; and all such Laws shall be subject to the Revision and Control of the Congress.

No State shall, without the Consent of Congress, lay any duty of Tonnage, keep Troops, or Ships of War in time of Peace, enter into any Agreement or Compact with another State, or with a foreign Power, or engage in War, unless actually invaded, or in such imminent Danger as will not admit of delay.

ARTICLE II

Section 1. The executive Power shall be vested in a President of the United States of America. He shall hold his Office during the Term of four years, and, together with the Vice-President, chosen for the same Term, be elected, as follows:

Each State shall appoint, in such Manner as the Legislature thereof may direct, a Number of Electors, equal to the whole Number of Senators and Representatives to which the State may be entitled in the Congress; but no Senator or Representative, or Person holding an Office of Trust or Profit under the United States, shall be appointed an Elector.

The Electors shall meet in their respective States, and vote by Ballot for two persons, of whom one at least shall not be an Inhabitant of the same State with themselves. And they shall make a List of all the Persons voted for, and of the Number of Votes for each; which List they shall sign and certify, and transmit sealed to the Seat of the Government of the United States, directed to the President of the Senate. The President of the Senate shall, in the Presence of the Senate and House of Representatives, open all the Certificates, and the Votes shall then be counted. The Person having the greatest Number of Votes shall be the President, if such Number be a Majority of the whole Number of Electors appointed; and if there be more than one who have such Majority, and have an equal Number of Votes, then the House of Representatives shall immediately chuse by Ballot one of them for President; and if no Person have a Majority, then from the five highest on the List the said House shall in like Manner chuse the President. But in chusing the President, the Votes shall be taken by States, the Representation from each State having one Vote; a quorum for this Purpose shall consist of a Member or Members from two-thirds of the States, and a Majority of all the States shall be necessary to a Choice. In every Case, after the Choice of the President, the Person having the greatest Number of Votes of the Electors shall be the Vice President. But if there should remain two or more who have equal votes, the Senate shall chuse from them by Ballot the Vice-President.

The Congress may determine the Time of chusing the Electors, and the Day on which they shall give their Votes; which Day shall be the same throughout the United States.

No person except a natural-born Citizen, or a Citizen of the United States, at the time of the Adoption of this Constitution, shall be eligible to the Office of President; neither shall any Person be eligible to that Office who shall not have attained to the Age of thirty-five years, and been fourteen Years a Resident within the United States.

In Case of the Removal of the President from Office, or of his Death, Resignation, or Inability to discharge the Powers and Duties of the said Office, the same shall devolve on the Vice President, and the Congress may by Law provide for the Case of Removal, Death, Resignation, or Inability, both of the President and Vice President, declaring what Officer shall then act as President, and such Officer shall act accordingly, until the disability be removed, or a President shall be elected.

The President shall, at stated Times, receive for his Services a Compensation, which shall neither be increased nor diminished during the Period for which he shall have been elected, and he shall not receive within that Period any other Emolument from the United States, or any of them.

Before he enter on the execution of his Office, he shall take the following Oath or Affirmation:—"I do solemnly swear (or affirm) that I will faithfully execute the Office of President of the United States, and will, to the best of my Ability, preserve, protect, and defend the Constitution of the United States."

Section 2. The President shall be Commander in Chief of the Army and Navy of the United States, and of the Militia of the several States, when called into the actual Service of the United States; he may require the Opinion, in writing, of the principal Officer in each of the executive Departments, upon any subject relating to the Duties of their respective Offices, and he shall have Power to Grant Reprieves and Pardons for Offences against the United States, except in Cases of Impeachment.

He shall have Power, by and with the Advice and Consent of the Senate, to make Treaties, provided two thirds of the Senators present concur; and he shall nominate, and by and with the Advice and Consent of the Senate, shall appoint Ambassadors, other public Ministers and Consuls, Judges of the supreme Court, and all other Officers of the United States, whose Appointments are not herein otherwise provided for, and which shall be established by Law: but the Congress may by Law vest the Appointment of such inferior Officers, as they think proper, in the President alone, in the Courts of Law, or in the Heads of Departments.

The President shall have Power to fill up all Vacancies that may happen during the Recess of the Senate, by granting Commissions which shall expire at the End of their next Session.

Section 3. He shall from time to time give to the Congress Information of the State of the Union, and recommend to their Consideration such Measures as he shall judge necessary and expedient; he may, on extraordinary occasions, convene both Houses, or either of them, and in Case of Disagreement between them, with respect to the Time of Adjournment, he may adjourn them to such Time as he shall think proper; he shall receive Ambassadors and other public Ministers; he shall take Care that the Laws be faithfully executed, and shall Commission all the Officers of the United States.

Section 4. The President, Vice President and all civil Officers of the United States, shall be removed from Office on Impeachment for, and Conviction of, Treason, Bribery, or other high Crimes and Misdemeanors.

ARTICLE III

Section 1. The judicial Power of the United States, shall be vested in one supreme Court, and in such inferior Courts as the Congress may from time to time ordain and establish. The Judges, both of the supreme and inferior Courts, shall hold their Offices during good Behaviour, and shall, at stated Times, receive for their Services, a Compensation, which shall not be diminished during their Continuance in Office.

Section 2. The judicial Power shall extend to all Cases, in Law and Equity, arising under this Constitution, the Laws of the United States, and treaties made, or which shall be made, under their Authority;—to all Cases affecting ambassadors, other public ministers and consuls;—to all cases of admiralty and maritime Jurisdiction;—to Controversies to which the United States shall be a Party;—to Controversies between two or more States;—between a State and Citizens of another State;—between Citizens of different States,—between Citizens of the same State claiming Lands under Grants of different States, and between a State, or the Citizens thereof, and foreign States, Citizens or Subjects.

In all Cases affecting Ambassadors, other public Ministers and Consuls, and those in which a State shall be Party, the supreme Court shall have original Jurisdiction. In all the other Cases before mentioned, the supreme Court shall have appellate Jurisdiction, both as to Law and Fact, with such Exceptions, and under such Regulations as the Congress shall make.

The trial of all Crimes, except in Cases of Impeachment, shall be by Jury; and such Trial shall be held in the State where the said Crimes shall have been committed; but when not committed within any State, the Trial shall be at such Place or Places as the Congress may by Law have directed.

Section 3. Treason against the United States, shall consist only in levying War against them, or in adhering to their Enemies, giving them Aid and Comfort. No Person shall be convicted of Treason unless on the Testimony of two Witnesses to the same overt Act, or on Confession in open Court.

The Congress shall have power to declare the Punishment of Treason, but no Attainder of Treason shall work Corruption of Blood, or Forfeiture except during the Life of the Person attainted.

ARTICLE IV

Section 1. Full Faith and Credit shall be given in each State to the public Acts, Records, and judicial Proceedings of every other State. And the Congress may by general Laws prescribe the Manner in which such Acts, Records and Proceedings shall be proved, and the Effect thereof.

Section 2. The Citizens of each State shall be entitled to all Privileges and Immunities of Citizens in the several States.

A Person charged in any State with Treason, Felony, or other Crime, who shall flee from Justice, and be found in another State, shall on demand of the executive Authority of the State from which he fled, be delivered up, to be removed to the State having Jurisdiction of the crime.

No Person held to Service or Labour in one State, under the Laws thereof, escaping into another, shall, in Consequence of any Law or Regulation therein, be discharged from such Service or Labour, but shall be delivered up on Claim of the Party to whom such Service or Labour may be due.

Section 3. New States may be admitted by the Congress into this Union; but no new State shall be formed or erected within the Jurisdiction of any other State; nor any State be formed by the Junction of two or more States, or parts of States, without the Consent of the Legislatures of the States concerned as well as of the Congress.

The Congress shall have Power to dispose of and make all needful Rules and Regulations respecting the Territory or other Property belonging to the United States; and nothing in this Constitution shall be so construed as to Prejudice any Claims of the United States, or of any particular State.

Section 4. The United States shall guarantee to every State in this Union a Republican Form of Government, and shall protect each of them against Invasion; and on Application of the Legislature, or the Executive (when the Legislature cannot be convened) against domestic Violence.

ARTICLE V

The Congress, whenever two-thirds of both Houses shall deem it necessary, shall propose Amendments to this Constitution, or, on the Application of the Legislatures of two-thirds of the several States, shall call a Convention for proposing Amendments, which, in either Case, shall be valid to all Intents and Purposes, as part of this Constitution, when ratified by the Legislatures of three-fourths of the several States, or by Conventions in three-fourths thereof, as the one or the other Mode of Ratification may be proposed by the Congress; Provided that no Amendment which may be made prior to the Year One thousand eight hundred and eight shall in any Manner affect the first and fourth Clauses in the Ninth Section of the first Article; and that no State, without its Consent, shall be deprived of its equal Suffrage in the Senate.

ARTICLE VI

All Debts contracted and Engagements entered into, before the Adoption of this Constitution, shall be as valid against the United States under this Constitution, as under the Confederation.

This Constitution, and the Laws of the United States which shall be made in Pursuance thereof; and all Treaties made, or which shall be made, under the Authority of the United States, shall be the supreme Law of the Land; and the Judges in every State shall be bound thereby, any Thing in the Constitution or Laws of any State to the Contrary notwithstanding.

The Senators and Representatives before mentioned, and the Members of the several State Legislatures, and all executive and judicial Officers, both of the United States and of the several States, shall be bound by Oath or Affirmation to support this Constitution; but no religious Test shall ever be required as a qualification to any Office or public Trust under the United States.

ARTICLE VII

The Ratification of the Conventions of nine States shall be sufficient for the Establishment of this Constitution between the States so ratifying the same.

Done in Convention by the Unanimous Consent of the States present the Seventeenth Day of September in the Year of our Lord one thousand seven hundred and Eighty seven, and of the Independence of the United States of America the Twelfth. In Witness whereof We have hereunto subscribed our Names.

Articles in Addition to, and Amendment of, the Constitution of the United States of America, Proposed by Congress, and Ratified by the Legislatures of the Several States, Pursuant to the Fifth Article of the Original Constitution.

AMENDMENT I [1791]

Congress shall make no law respecting an establishment of religion, or prohibiting the free exercise thereof; or abridging the freedom of speech, or of the press; or the right of the people peaceably to assemble, and to petition the Government for a redress of grievances.

AMENDMENT II [1791]

A well regulated Militia, being necessary to the security of a free State, the right of the people to keep and bear Arms shall not be infringed.

AMENDMENT III [1791]

No Soldier shall, in time of peace, be quartered in any house, without the consent of the Owner, nor in time of war, but in a manner to be prescribed by law.

AMENDMENT IV [1791]

The right of the people to be secure in their persons, houses, papers, and effects, against unreasonable searches and seizures, shall not be violated, and no Warrants shall issue, but upon probable cause, supported by Oath or affirmation, and particularly describing the place to be searched, and the persons or things to be seized.

AMENDMENT V [1791]

No person shall be held to answer for a capital or otherwise infamous crime, unless on a presentment or indictment of a Grand Jury, except in cases arising in the land or naval forces, or in the Militia, when in actual service in time of War or public danger; nor shall any person be subject for the same offence to be twice put in jeopardy of life or limb; nor shall be compelled in any criminal case to be a witness against himself, nor be deprived of life, liberty, or property, without due process of law; nor shall private property be taken for public use, without just compensation.

AMENDMENT VI [1791]

In all criminal prosecutions, the accused shall enjoy the right to a speedy and public trial, by an impartial jury of the State and district wherein the crime shall have been committed, which district shall have been previously ascertained by law, and to be informed of the nature and cause of the accusation; to be confronted with the witnesses against him; to have compulsory process for obtaining witnesses in his favor, and to have the Assistance of Counsel for his defence.

AMENDMENT VII [1791]

In suits at common law, where the value in controversy shall exceed twenty dollars, the right of trial by jury shall be preserved, and no fact tried by a jury, shall be otherwise reexamined in any Court of the United States, than according to the rules of the common law.

AMENDMENT VIII [1791]

Excessive bail shall not be required, nor excessive fines imposed, nor cruel and unusual punishments inflicted.

AMENDMENT IX [1791]

The enumeration in the Constitution, of certain rights, shall not be construed to deny or disparage others retained by the people.

AMENDMENT X [1791]

The powers not delegated to the United States by the Constitution, nor prohibited by it to the States, are reserved to the States respectively, or to the people.

AMENDMENT XI [1798]

The Judicial power of the United States shall not be construed to extend to any suit in law or equity, commenced or prosecuted against one of the United

States by Citizens of another State, or by Citizens or Subjects of any Foreign State.

AMENDMENT XII [1804]

The Electors shall meet in their respective States and vote by ballot for President and Vice-President, one of whom, at least, shall not be an inhabitant of the same State with themselves; they shall name in their ballots the person voted for as President, and in distinct ballots the person voted for as Vice-President, and they shall make distinct lists of all persons voted for as President, and of all persons voted for as Vice-President, and of the number of votes for each, which lists they shall sign and certify, and transmit sealed to the seat of the government of the United States, directed to the President of the Senate;—The President of the Senate shall, in the presence of the Senate and House of Representatives, open all the certificates and the votes shall then be counted;—The person having the greatest number of votes for President, shall be the President, if such number be a majority of the whole number of Electors appointed; and if no person have such majority, then from the persons having the highest numbers not exceeding three on the list of those voted for as President, the House of Representatives shall choose immediately, by ballot, the President. But in choosing the President, the votes shall be taken by states, the representation from each state having one vote; a quorum for this purpose shall consist of a member or members from two-thirds of the states, and a majority of all the states shall be necessary to a choice. And if the House of Representatives shall not choose a President whenever the right of choice shall devolve upon them, before the fourth day of March next following, then the Vice-President shall act as President, as in the case of the death or other constitutional disability of the President.—The person having the greatest number of votes as Vice-President, shall be the Vice-President, if such number be a majority of the whole number of Electors appointed, and if no person have a majority, then from the two highest numbers on the list, the Senate shall choose the Vice-President; a quorum for the purpose shall consist of two-thirds of the whole number of Senators, and a majority of the whole number shall be necessary to a choice. But no person constitutionally ineligible to the office of President shall be eligible to that of Vice-President of the United States.

AMENDMENT XIII [1865]

Section 1. Neither slavery nor involuntary servitude, except as a punishment for crime whereof the party shall have been duly convicted, shall exist within the United States, or any place subject to their jurisdiction.

Section 2. Congress shall have power to enforce this article by appropriate legislation.

AMENDMENT XIV [1868]

Section 1. All persons born or naturalized in the United States, and subject to the jurisdiction thereof, are citizens of the United States and of the State wherein they reside. No State shall make or enforce any law which shall abridge the privileges or immunities of citizens of the United States; nor shall any State deprive any person of life, liberty, or property, without due process of law; nor deny to any person within its jurisdiction the equal protection of the laws.

Section 2. Representatives shall be apportioned among the several States according to their respective numbers, counting the whole number of persons in each State, excluding Indians not taxed. But when the right to vote at any election for the choice of electors for President and Vice-President of the United States, Representatives in Congress, the Executive and Judicial officers of a State, or the members of the Legislature thereof, is denied to any of the male inhabitants of such State, being twenty-one years of age, and citizens of the United States, or in any way abridged, except for participation in rebellion, or other crime, the basis of representation therein shall be reduced in the proportion which the number of such male citizens shall bear to the whole number of male citizens twenty-one years of age in such State.

Section 3. No person shall be a Senator or Representative in Congress, or elector of President and Vice-President, or hold any office, civil or military, under the United States, or under any State, who, having previously taken an oath, as a member of Congress, or as an officer of the United States, or as a member of any State legislature, or as an executive or judicial officer of any State, to support the Constitution of the United States, shall have engaged in insurrection or rebellion against the same, or given aid or comfort to the enemies thereof. But Congress may by a vote of two-thirds of each House, remove such disability.

Section 4. The validity of the public debt of the United States, authorized by law, including debts incurred for payment of pensions and bounties for services in suppressing insurrection or rebellion, shall not be questioned. But neither the United States nor any State shall assume or pay any debt or obligation incurred in aid of insurrection or rebellion against the United States, or any claim for the loss or emancipation of any slave; but all such debts, obligations, and claims shall be held illegal and void.

Section 5. The Congress shall have the power to enforce, by appropriate legislation, the provisions of this article.

AMENDMENT XV [1870]

Section 1. The right of citizens of the United States to vote shall not be denied or abridged by the United States or by any State on account of race, color, or previous condition of servitude—

Section 2. The Congress shall have power to enforce this article by appropriate legislation.

AMENDMENT XVI [1913]

The Congress shall have power to lay and collect taxes on incomes, from whatever source derived, without apportionment among the several States, and without regard to any census or enumeration.

AMENDMENT XVII [1913]

The Senate of the United States shall be composed of two Senators from each State, elected by the people thereof, for six years; and each Senator shall have one vote. The electors in each State shall have the qualifications requisite for electors of the most numerous branch of the State legislatures.

When vacancies happen in the representation of any State in the Senate, the executive authority of such State shall issue writs of election to fill such vacancies: *Provided,* That the legislature of any State may empower the executive thereof to make temporary appointments until the people fill the vacancies by election as the legislature may direct.

This amendment shall not be so construed as to affect the election or term of any Senator chosen before it becomes valid as part of the Constitution.

AMENDMENT XVIII [1919]

Section 1. After one year from the ratification of this article the manufacture, sale, or transportation of intoxicating liquors within, the importation thereof into, or the exportation thereof from the United States and all territory subject to the jurisdiction thereof for beverage purposes is hereby prohibited.

Section 2. The Congress and the several States shall have concurrent power to enforce this article by appropriate legislation.

Section 3. This article shall be inoperative unless it shall have been ratified as an amendment to the Constitution by the legislatures of the several States, as provided in the Constitution, within seven years from the date of the submission hereof to the States by the Congress.

AMENDMENT XIX [1920]

The right of citizens of the United States to vote shall not be denied or abridged by the United States or by any State on account of sex.

Congress shall have power to enforce this article by appropriate legislation.

AMENDMENT XX [1933]

Section 1. The terms of the President and Vice-President shall end at noon on the 20th day of January, and the terms of Senators and Representatives at noon on the 3d day of January, of the years in which such terms would have ended if this article had not been ratified; and the terms of their successors shall then begin.

Section 2. The Congress shall assemble at least once in every year, and such meeting shall begin at noon on the 3d day of January, unless they shall by law appoint a different day.

Section 3. If, at the time fixed for the beginning of the term of the President, the President elect shall have died, the Vice-President elect shall become President. If a President shall not have been chosen before the time fixed for the beginning of his term, or if the President elect shall have failed to qualify, then the Vice-President elect shall act as President until a President shall have qualified; and the Congress may by law provide for the case wherein neither a President elect nor a Vice-President elect shall have qualified, declaring who shall then act as President, or the manner in which one who is to act shall be selected, and such person shall act accordingly until a President or Vice-President shall have qualified.

Section 4. The Congress may by law provide for the case of the death of any of the persons from whom the House of Representatives may choose a President whenever the right of choice shall have devolved upon them, and for the case of the death of any of the persons from whom the Senate may choose a Vice-President whenever the right of choice shall have devolved upon them.

Section 5. Sections 1 and 2 shall take effect on the 15th day of October following the ratification of this article.

Section 6. This article shall be inoperative unless it shall have been ratified as an amendment to the Constitution by the legislatures of three-fourths of the several States within seven years from the date of its submission.

AMENDMENT XXI [1933]

Section 1. The eighteenth article of amendment to the Constitution of the United States is hereby repealed.

Section 2. The transportation or importation into any State, Territory, or possession of the United States for delivery or use therein of intoxicating liquors, in violation of the laws thereof, is hereby prohibited.

Section 3. This article shall be inoperative unless it shall have been ratified as an amendment to the Constitution by conventions in the several States, as provided in the Constitution, within seven years from the date of the submission hereof to the States by the Congress.

AMENDMENT XXII [1951]

No person shall be elected to the office of the President more than twice, and no person who has held the office of President, or acted as President, for more than two years of a term to which some other person was elected President shall be elected to the office of the President more than once.

But this Article shall not apply to any person holding the office of President when this Article was proposed by the Congress, and shall not prevent any person who may be holding the office of President, or acting as President, during the term within which this Article becomes operative from holding the office of President or acting as President during the remainder of such term.

AMENDMENT XXIII [1961]

Section 1. The District constituting the seat of Government of the United States shall appoint in such manner as the Congress may direct:

A number of electors of President and Vice President equal to the whole number of Senators and Representatives in Congress to which the District would be entitled if it were a State, but in no event more than the least populous State; they shall be in addition to those appointed by the States, but they shall be considered, for the purposes of the election of President and Vice President, to be electors appointed by a State; and they shall meet in the District and perform such duties as provided by the twelfth article of amendment.

Section 2. The Congress shall have power to enforce this article by appropriate legislation.

AMENDMENT XXIV [1964]

Section 1. The right of citizens of the United States to vote in any primary or other election for President or Vice President, for electors for President or Vice President, or for Senator or Representative in Congress, shall not be denied or abridged by the United States or any State by reason of failure to pay any poll tax or other tax.

Section 2. The Congress shall have the power to enforce this article by appropriate legislation.

AMENDMENT XXV [1967]

Section 1. In case of the removal of the President from office or his death or resignation, the Vice President shall become President.

Section 2. Whenever there is a vacancy in the office of the Vice President, the President shall nominate a Vice President who shall take the office upon confirmation by a majority vote of both houses of Congress.

Section 3. Whenever the President transmits to the President pro tempore of the Senate and the Speaker of the House of Representatives his written declaration that he is unable to discharge the powers and duties of his office, and until he transmits to them a written declaration to the contrary, such powers and duties shall be discharged by the Vice President as Acting President.

Section 4. Whenever the Vice President and a majority of either the principal officers of the executive departments, or of such other body as Congress may by law provide, transmit to the President pro tempore of the Senate and the Speaker of the House of Representatives their written declaration that the President is unable to discharge the powers and duties of his office, the Vice President shall immediately assume the powers and duties of the office as Acting President.

Thereafter, when the President transmits to the President pro tempore of the Senate and the Speaker of the House of Representatives his written declaration that no inability exists, he shall resume the powers and duties of his office unless the Vice President and a majority of either the principal officers of the executive departments, or of such other body as Congress may by law provide, transmit within four days to the President pro tempore of the Senate and the Speaker of the House of Representatives their written declaration that the President is unable to discharge the powers and duties of his office. Thereupon Congress shall decide the issue, assembling within 48 hours for that purpose if not in session. If the Congress, within 21 days after receipt of the latter written declaration, or, if Congress is not in session, within 21 days after Congress is required to assemble, determines by two-thirds vote of both houses that the President is unable to discharge the powers and duties of his office, the Vice President shall continue to discharge the same as Acting President; otherwise, the President shall resume the powers and duties of his office.

AMENDMENT XXVI [1971]

Section 1. The right of citizens of the United States, who are 18 years of age or older, to vote shall not be denied or abridged by the United States or any state on account of age.

Section 2. The Congress shall have the power to enforce this article by appropriate legislation.

PRESIDENTIAL ELECTIONS, 1789–1980

Year	Candidates	Party	Popular Vote	Electoral Vote
1789	**George Washington**			69
	John Adams			34
	Others			35
1792	**George Washington**			132
	John Adams			77
	George Clinton			50
	Others			5
1796	**John Adams**	Federalist		71
	Thomas Jefferson	Democratic-Republican		68
	Thomas Pinckney	Federalist		59
	Aaron Burr	Democratic-Republican		30
	Others			48
1800	**Thomas Jefferson**	Democratic-Republican		73
	Aaron Burr	Democratic-Republican		73
	John Adams	Federalist		65
	Charles C. Pinckney	Federalist		64
1804	**Thomas Jefferson**	Democratic-Republican		162
	Charles C. Pinckney	Federalist		14
1808	**James Madison**	Democratic-Republican		122
	Charles C. Pinckney	Federalist		47
	George Clinton	Independent-Republican		6
1812	**James Madison**	Democratic-Republican		128
	DeWitt Clinton	Federalist		89
1816	**James Monroe**	Democratic-Republican		183
	Rufus King	Federalist		34
1820	**James Monroe**	Democratic-Republican		231
	John Quincy Adams	Independent-Republican		1
1824	**John Quincy Adams**	Democratic-Republican	108,740 (30.5%)	84
	Andrew Jackson	Democratic-Republican	153,544 (43.1%)	99
	Henry Clay	Democratic-Republican	47,136 (13.2%)	37
	William H. Crawford	Democratic-Republican	46,618 (13.1%)	41

Year	Candidates	Party	Popular Vote	Electoral Vote
1828	**Andrew Jackson**	Democratic	647,231 (56.0%)	178
	John Quincy Adams	National Republican	509,097 (44.0%)	83
1832	**Andrew Jackson**	Democratic	687,502 (55.0%)	219
	Henry Clay	National Republican	530,189 (42.4%)	49
	William Wirt	Anti-Masonic	33,108 (2.6%)	7
	John Floyd	National Republican		11
1836	**Martin Van Buren**	Democratic	761,549 (50.9%)	170
	William H. Harrison	Whig	549,567 (36.7%)	73
	Hugh L. White	Whig	145,396 (9.7%)	26
	Daniel Webster	Whig	41,287 (2.7%)	14
1840	**William H. Harrison**	Whig	1,275,017 (53.1%)	234
	(**John Tyler**, 1841)			
	Martin Van Buren	Democratic	1,128,702 (46.9%)	60
1844	**James K. Polk**	Democratic	1,337,243 (49.6%)	170
	Henry Clay	Whig	1,299,068 (48.1%)	105
	James G. Birney	Liberty	62,300 (2.3%)	
1848	**Zachary Taylor**	Whig	1,360,101 (47.4%)	163
	(**Millard Fillmore**, 1850)			
	Lewis Cass	Democratic	1,220,544 (42.5%)	127
	Martin Van Buren	Free Soil	291,263 (10.1%)	
1852	**Franklin Pierce**	Democratic	1,601,474 (50.9%)	254
	Winfield Scott	Whig	1,386,578 (44.1%)	42
1856	**James Buchanan**	Democratic	1,838,169 (45.4%)	174
	John C. Frémont	Republican	1,335,264 (33.0%)	114
	Millard Fillmore	American	874,534 (21.6%)	8
1860	**Abraham Lincoln**	Republican	1,865,593 (39.8%)	180
	Stephen A. Douglas	Democratic	1,382,713 (29.5%)	12
	John C. Breckinridge	Democratic	848,356 (18.1%)	72
	John Bell	Constitutional Union	592,906 (12.6%)	39
1864	**Abraham Lincoln**	Republican	2,206,938 (55.0%)	212
	(**Andrew Johnson**, 1865)			
	George B. McClellan	Democratic	1,803,787 (45.0%)	21
1868	**Ulysses S. Grant**	Republican	3,013,421 (52.7%)	214
	Horatio Seymour	Democratic	2,706,829 (47.3%)	80
1872	**Ulysses S. Grant**	Republican	3,596,745 (55.6%)	286
	Horace Greeley	Democratic	2,843,446 (43.9%)	66
1876	**Rutherford B. Hayes**	Republican	4,036,572 (48.0%)	185
	Samuel J. Tilden	Democratic	4,284,020 (51.0%)	184

Year	Candidates	Party	Popular Vote	Electoral Vote
1880	**James A. Garfield** (**Chester A. Arthur**, 1881)	Republican	4,449,053 (48.3%)	214
	Winfield S. Hancock	Democratic	4,442,035 (48.2%)	155
	James B. Weaver	Greenback-Labor	308,578 (3.4%)	
1884	**Grover Cleveland**	Democratic	4,874,986 (48.5%)	219
	James G. Blaine	Republican	4,851,981 (48.2%)	182
	Benjamin F. Butler	Greenback-Labor	175,370 (1.8%)	
1888	**Benjamin Harrison**	Republican	5,444,337 (47.8%)	233
	Grover Cleveland	Democratic	5,540,050 (48.6%)	168
1892	**Grover Cleveland**	Democratic	5,554,414 (46.0%)	277
	Benjamin Harrison	Republican	5,190,802 (43.0%)	145
	James B. Weaver	People's	1,027,329 (8.5%)	22
1896	**William McKinley**	Republican	7,035,638 (50.8%)	271
	William J. Bryan	Democratic; Populist	6,467,946 (46.7%)	176
1900	**William McKinley** (**Theodore Roosevelt**, 1901)	Republican	7,219,530 (51.7%)	292
	William J. Bryan	Democratic; Populist	6,356,734 (45.5%)	155
1904	**Theodore Roosevelt**	Republican	7,628,834 (56.4%)	336
	Alton B. Parker	Democratic	5,084,401 (37.6%)	140
	Eugene V. Debs	Socialist	402,460 (3.0%)	
1908	**William H. Taft**	Republican	7,679,006 (51.6%)	321
	William J. Bryan	Democratic	6,409,106 (43.1%)	162
	Eugene V. Debs	Socialist	420,820 (2.8%)	
1912	**Woodrow Wilson**	Democratic	6,286,820 (41.8%)	435
	Theodore Roosevelt	Progressive	4,126,020 (27.4%)	88
	William H. Taft	Republican	3,483,922 (23.2%)	8
	Eugene V. Debs	Socialist	897,011 (6.0%)	
1916	**Woodrow Wilson**	Democratic	9,129,606 (49.3%)	277
	Charles E. Hughes	Republican	8,538,221 (46.1%)	254
1920	**Warren G. Harding** (**Calvin Coolidge**, 1923)	Republican	16,152,200 (61.0%)	404
	James M. Cox	Democratic	9,147,353 (34.6%)	127
	Eugene V. Debs	Socialist	919,799 (3.5%)	
1924	**Calvin Coolidge**	Republican	15,725,016 (54.1%)	382
	John W. Davis	Democratic	8,385,586 (28.8%)	136
	Robert M. La Follette	Progressive	4,822,856 (16.6%)	13
1928	**Herbert C. Hoover**	Republican	21,392,190 (58.2%)	444
	Alfred E. Smith	Democratic	15,016,443 (40.8%)	87

Year	Candidates	Party	Popular Vote	Electoral Vote
1932	**Franklin D. Roosevelt**	Democratic	22,809,638 (57.3%)	472
	Herbert C. Hoover	Republican	15,758,901 (39.6%)	59
	Norman Thomas	Socialist	881,951 (2.2%)	
1936	**Franklin D. Roosevelt**	Democratic	27,751,612 (60.7%)	523
	Alfred M. Landon	Republican	16,681,913 (36.4%)	8
	William Lemke	Union	891,858 (1.9%)	
1940	**Franklin D. Roosevelt**	Democratic	27,243,466 (54.7%)	449
	Wendell L. Wilkie	Republican	22,304,755 (44.8%)	82
1944	**Franklin D. Roosevelt**	Democratic	25,602,505 (52.8%)	432
	(**Harry S Truman**, 1945)			
	Thomas E. Dewey	Republican	22,006,278 (44.5%)	99
1948	**Harry S Truman**	Democratic	24,105,812 (49.5%)	303
	Thomas E. Dewey	Republican	21,970,065 (45.1%)	189
	J. Strom Thurmond	States' Rights	1,169,063 (2.4%)	39
	Henry A. Wallace	Progressive	1,157,172 (2.4%)	
1952	**Dwight D. Eisenhower**	Republican	33,936,234 (55.2%)	442
	Adlai E. Stevenson	Democratic	27,314,992 (44.5%)	89
1956	**Dwight D. Eisenhower**	Republican	35,590,472 (57.4%)	457
	Adlai E. Stevenson	Democratic	26,022,752 (42.0%)	73
1960	**John F. Kennedy**	Democratic	34,227,096 (49.9%)	303
	(**Lyndon B. Johnson**, 1963)			
	Richard M. Nixon	Republican	34,108,546 (49.6%)	219
1964	**Lyndon B. Johnson**	Democratic	43,126,233 (61.1%)	486
	Barry M. Goldwater	Republican	27,174,989 (38.5%)	52
1968	**Richard M. Nixon**	Republican	31,783,783 (43.4%)	301
	Hubert H. Humphrey	Democratic	31,271,839 (42.7%)	191
	George C. Wallace	Amer. Independent	9,899,557 (13.5%)	46
1972	**Richard M. Nixon**	Republican	45,767,218 (60.6%)	520
	(**Gerald R. Ford**, 1974)			
	George S. McGovern	Democratic	28,357,668 (37.5%)	17
1976	**Jimmy Carter**	Democratic	40,828,657 (50.6%)	297
	Gerald R. Ford	Republican	39,145,520 (48.4%)	240
1980	**Ronald Reagan**	Republican	43,899,248 (51%)	489
	Jimmy Carter	Democrat	36,481,435 (41%)	49
	John B. Anderson	Independent	5,719,437 (6%)	

Because only the leading candidates are listed, popular vote percentages do not always total 100. The elections of 1800 and 1824, in which no candidate received an electoral-vote majority, were decided in the House of Representatives.

THE VICE-PRESIDENCY AND THE CABINET, 1789–1982

Vice-President

John Adams	1789–97
Thomas Jefferson	1797–1801
Aaron Burr	1801–05
George Clinton	1805–13
Elbridge Gerry	1813–17
Daniel D. Tompkins	1817–25
John C. Calhoun	1825–33
Martin Van Buren	1833–37
Richard M. Johnson	1837–41
John Tyler	1841
George M. Dallas	1845–49
Millard Fillmore	1849–50
William R. King	1853–57
John C. Breckinridge	1857–61
Hannibal Hamlin	1861–65
Andrew Johnson	1865
Schuyler Colfax	1869–73
Henry Wilson	1873–77
William A. Wheeler	1877–81
Chester A. Arthur	1881
Thomas A. Hendricks	1885–89
Levi P. Morton	1889–93
Adlai E. Stevenson	1893–97
Garret A. Hobart	1897–99
Theodore Roosevelt	1901
Charles W. Fairbanks	1905–09
James S. Sherman	1909–13
Thomas R. Marshall	1913–21
Calvin Coolidge	1921–23
Charles G. Dawes	1925–29
Charles Curtis	1929–33
John Nance Garner	1933–41
Henry A. Wallace	1941–45
Harry S Truman	1945
Alben W. Barkley	1949–53
Richard M. Nixon	1953–61
Lyndon B. Johnson	1961–63
Hubert H. Humphrey	1965–69
Spiro T. Agnew	1969–73
Gerald R. Ford	1973–74
Nelson Rockefeller	1974–77
Walter F. Mondale	1977–81
George Bush	1981–

Secretary of State (1789–)

Thomas Jefferson	1789
Edmund Randolph	1794
Timothy Pickering	1795
John Marshall	1800
James Madison	1801
Robert Smith	1809
James Monroe	1811
John Q. Adams	1817
Henry Clay	1825
Martin Van Buren	1829
Edward Livingston	1831
Louis McLane	1833
John Forsyth	1834
Daniel Webster	1841
Hugh S. Legaré	1843
Abel P. Upshur	1843
John C. Calhoun	1844
James Buchanan	1845
John M. Clayton	1849
Daniel Webster	1850
Edward Everett	1852
William L. Marcy	1853
Lewis Cass	1857
Jeremiah S. Black	1860
William H. Seward	1861
E.B. Washburne	1869
Hamilton Fish	1869
William M. Evarts	1877
James G. Blaine	1881
F.T. Frelinghuysen	1881
Thomas F. Bayard	1885
James G. Blaine	1889
John W. Foster	1892
Walter Q. Gresham	1893
Richard Olney	1895
John Sherman	1897
William R. Day	1897
John Hay	1898
Elihu Root	1905
Robert Bacon	1909
Philander C. Knox	1909
William J. Bryan	1913
Robert Lansing	1915
Bainbridge Colby	1920
Charles E. Hughes	1921
Frank B. Kellogg	1925
Henry L. Stimson	1929
Cordell Hull	1933
E.R. Stettinius, Jr.	1944
James F. Byrnes	1945
George C. Marshall	1947
Dean Acheson	1949
John Foster Dulles	1953
Christian A. Herter	1959
Dean Rusk	1961
William P. Rogers	1969
Henry A. Kissinger	1973
Cyrus R. Vance	1977
Alexander M. Haig, Jr.	1981

Secretary of the Treasury (1789–)

Alexander Hamilton	1789
Oliver Wolcott	1795
Samuel Dexter	1801
Albert Gallatin	1801
G.W. Campbell	1814
A.J. Dallas	1814
William H. Crawford	1816

Richard Rush 1825
Samuel D. Ingham 1829
Louis McLane 1831
William J. Duane 1833
Roger B. Taney 1833
Levi Woodbury 1834
Thomas Ewing 1841
Walter Forward 1841
John C. Spencer 1843
George M. Bibb 1844
Robert J. Walker 1845
William M. Meredith 1849
Thomas Corwin 1850
James Guthrie 1853
Howell Cobb 1857
Philip F. Thomas 1860
John A. Dix 1861
Salmon P. Chase 1861
Wm. P. Fessenden 1864
Hugh McCulloch 1865
George S. Boutwell 1869
William A. Richardson 1873
Benjamin H. Bristow 1874
Lot M. Morrill 1876
John Sherman 1877
William Windom 1881
Charles J. Folger 1881
Walter Q. Gresham 1884
Hugh McCulloch 1884
Daniel Manning 1885
Charles S. Fairchild 1887
William Windom 1889
Charles Foster 1891
John G. Carlisle 1893
Lyman J. Gage 1897
Leslie M. Shaw 1902
George B. Cortelyou 1907
Franklin MacVeagh 1909
William G. McAdoo 1913
Carter Glass 1919
David F. Houston 1919
Andrew W. Mellon 1921
Ogden L. Mills 1932
William H. Woodin 1933
Henry Morgenthau, Jr. 1934
Fred M. Vinson 1945
John W. Snyder 1946
George M. Humphrey 1953
Robert B. Anderson 1957
C. Douglas Dillon 1961
Henry H. Fowler 1965
David M. Kennedy 1969
John B. Connally 1970
George P. Shultz 1972
William E. Simon 1974
W. Michael Blumenthal 1977
G. William Miller 1979
Donald T. Regan 1981

Secretary of War (1789–1947)

Henry Knox 1789
Timothy Pickering 1795
James McHenry 1796
John Marshall 1800
Samuel Dexter 1800
Roger Griswold 1801
Henry Dearborn 1801
William Eustis 1809
John Armstrong 1813
James Monroe 1814
William H. Crawford 1815
Isaac Shelby 1817
George Graham 1817
John C. Calhoun 1817
James Barbour 1825
Peter B. Porter 1828
John H. Eaton 1829
Lewis Cass 1831
Benjamin F. Butler 1837
Joel R. Poinsett 1837
John Bell 1841
John McLean 1841
John C. Spencer 1841
James M. Porter 1843
William Wilkins 1844
William L. Marcy 1845
George W. Crawford 1849
Charles M. Conrad 1850
Jefferson Davis 1853
John B. Floyd 1857
Joseph Holt 1861
Simon Cameron 1861
Edwin M. Stanton 1862
Ulysses S. Grant 1867
Lorenzo Thomas 1868
John M. Schofield 1868
John A. Rawlins 1869
William T. Sherman 1869
William W. Belknap 1869
Alphonso Taft 1876
James D. Cameron 1876
George W. McCrary 1877
Alexander Ramsey 1879
Robert T. Lincoln 1881
William C. Endicott 1885
Redfield Proctor 1889
Stephen B. Elkins 1891
Daniel S. Lamont 1893
Russell A. Alger 1897
Elihu Root 1899
William H. Taft 1904
Luke E. Wright 1908
J.M. Dickinson 1909
Henry L. Stimson 1911
L.M. Garrison 1913
Newton D. Baker 1916
John W. Weeks 1921
Dwight F. Davis 1925
James W. Good 1929
Patrick J. Hurley 1929
George H. Dern 1933
H.A. Woodring 1936
Henry L. Stimson 1940
Robert P. Patterson 1945
Kenneth C. Royall 1947

Secretary of the Navy (1798–1947)

Benjamin Stoddert 1798
Robert Smith 1801
Paul Hamilton 1809
William Jones 1813
B.W. Crowninshield 1814
Smith Thompson 1818
S.L. Southard 1823
John Branch 1829
Levi Woodbury 1831
Mahlon Dickerson 1834
James K. Paulding 1838
George E. Badger 1841
Abel P. Upshur 1841
David Henshaw 1843
Thomas W. Gilmer 1844
John Y. Mason 1844
George Bancroft 1845
John Y. Mason 1846
William B. Preston 1849
William A. Graham 1850
John P. Kennedy 1852
James C. Dobbin 1853
Isaac Toucey 1857
Gideon Welles 1861
Adolph E. Borie 1869
George M. Robeson 1869
R.W. Thompson 1877
Nathan Goff, Jr. 1881
William H. Hunt 1881
William E. Chandler 1881
William C. Whitney 1885
Benjamin F. Tracy 1889
Hilary A. Herbert 1893
John D. Long 1897
William H. Moody 1902
Paul Morton 1904
Charles J. Bonaparte 1905
Victor H. Metcalf 1907
T.H. Newberry 1908
George von L. Meyer 1909
Josephus Daniels 1913
Edwin Denby 1921
Curtis D. Wilbur 1924
Charles F. Adams 1929
Claude A. Swanson 1933
Charles Edison 1940
Frank Knox 1940
James V. Forrestal 1945

Secretary of Defense (1947–)

James V. Forrestal 1947
Louis A. Johnson 1949
George C. Marshall 1950
Robert A. Lovett 1951
Charles E. Wilson 1953
Neil H. McElroy 1957
Thomas S. Gates, Jr. 1959
Robert S. McNamara 1961
Clark M. Clifford 1968
Melvin R. Laird 1969
Elliot L. Richardson 1973
James R. Schlesinger 1973
Harold Brown 1977
Caspar W. Weinberger 1981

Postmaster General (1789–1971)

Samuel Osgood 1789
Timothy Pickering 1791
Joseph Habersham 1795
Gideon Granger 1801
Return J. Meigs, Jr. 1814
John McLean 1823
William T. Barry 1829
Amos Kendall 1835
John M. Niles 1840
Francis Granger 1841
Charles A. Wickliffe 1841
Cave Johnson 1845
Jacob Collamer 1849
Nathan K. Hall 1850
Samuel D. Hubbard 1852
James Campbell 1853
Aaron V. Brown 1857
Joseph Holt 1859
Horatio King 1861
Montgomery Blair 1861
William Dennison 1864
Alexander W. Randall 1866
John A.J. Creswell 1869
James W. Marshall 1874
Marshall Jewell 1874
James N. Tyner 1876
David M. Key 1877
Horace Maynard 1880
Thomas L. James 1881
Timothy O. Howe 1881
Walter Q. Gresham 1883
Frank Hatton 1884
William F. Vilas 1885
Don M. Dickinson 1888
John Wanamaker 1889
Wilson S. Bissel 1893
William L. Wilson 1895
James A. Gary 1897
Charles E. Smith 1898
Henry C. Payne 1902
Robert J. Wynne 1904
George B. Cortelyou 1905
George von L. Meyer 1907
F.H. Hitchcock 1909
Albert S. Burleson 1913
Will H. Hays 1921
Hubert Work 1922
Harry S. New 1923
Walter F. Brown 1929
James A. Farley 1933
Frank C. Walker 1940
Robert E. Hannegan 1945
J.M. Donaldson 1947
A.E. Summerfield 1953
J. Edward Day 1961
John A. Gronouski 1963
Lawrence F. O'Brien 1965
W. Marvin Watson 1968
Winton M. Blount 1969

Attorney General (1789–)

Edmund Randolph 1789
William Bradford 1794
Charles Lee 1795
Theophilus Parsons 1801
Levi Lincoln 1801
Robert Smith 1805
John Breckinridge 1805
Caesar A. Rodney 1807
William Pinkney 1811
Richard Rush 1814
William Wirt 1817
John M. Berrien 1829
Roger B. Taney 1831
Benjamin F. Butler 1833
Felix Grundy 1838
Henry D. Gilpin 1840
John J. Crittenden 1841
Hugh S. Legaré 1841
John Nelson 1843
John Y. Mason 1845
Nathan Clifford 1846
Isaac Toucey 1848
Reverdy Johnson 1849
John J. Crittenden 1850
Caleb Cushing 1853
Jeremiah S. Black 1857
Edwin M. Stanton 1860
Edward Bates 1861
Titian J. Coffey 1863
James Speed 1864
Henry Stanbery 1866
William M. Evarts 1868
Ebenezer R. Hoar 1869
Amos T. Ackerman 1870
George H. Williams 1871
Edward Pierrepont 1875
Alphonso Taft 1876
Charles Devens 1877
Wayne MacVeagh 1881
Benjamin H. Brewster 1881
A.H. Garland 1885
William H.H. Miller 1889
Richard Olney 1893
Judson Harmon 1895
Joseph McKenna 1897
John W. Griggs 1897
Philander C. Knox 1901
William H. Moody 1904
Charles J. Bonaparte 1907
G.W. Wickersham 1909
J.C. McReynolds 1913
Thomas W. Gregory 1914
A. Mitchell Palmer 1919
H.M. Daugherty 1921
Harlan F. Stone 1924
John G. Sargent 1925
William D. Mitchell 1929
H.S. Cummings 1933
Frank Murphy 1939
Robert H. Jackson 1940
Francis Biddle 1941
Tom C. Clark 1945
J.H. McGrath 1949
J.P. McGranery 1952
H. Brownell, Jr. 1953
William P. Rogers 1957
Robert F. Kennedy 1961
Nicholas Katzenbach 1964
Ramsey Clark 1967
John N. Mitchell 1969
Richard G. Kleindienst 1972
Elliot L. Richardson 1973
William Saxbe 1974
Edward H. Levi 1975
Griffin B. Bell 1977
Benjamin R. Civiletti 1979
William French Smith 1981

Secretary of the Interior (1849–)

Thomas Ewing 1849
T.M.T. McKennan 1850
Alexander H.H. Stuart 1850
Robert McClelland 1853
Jacob Thompson 1857

Caleb B. Smith 1861
John P. Usher 1863
James Harlan 1865
O.H. Browning 1866
Jacob D. Cox 1869
Columbus Delano 1870
Zachariah Chandler 1875
Carl Schurz 1877
Samuel J. Kirkwood 1881
Henry M. Teller 1881
L.Q.C. Lamar 1885
William F. Vilas 1888
John W. Noble 1889
Hoke Smith 1893
David R. Francis 1896
Cornelius N. Bliss 1897
E.A. Hitchcock 1899
James R. Garfield 1907
R.A. Ballinger 1909
Walter L. Fisher 1911
Franklin K. Lane 1913
John B. Payne 1920
Albert B. Fall 1921
Hubert Work 1923
Roy O. West 1928
Ray L. Wilbur 1929
Harold L. Ickes 1933
Julius A. Krug 1946
Oscar L. Chapman 1949
Douglas McKay 1953
Fred A. Seaton 1956
Stewart L. Udall 1961
Walter J. Hickel 1969
Rogers C.B. Morton 1971
Stanley K. Hathaway 1975
Thomas S. Kleppe 1975
Cecil D. Andrus 1977
James G. Watt 1981

Secretary of Agriculture (1889–)

Norman J. Colman 1889
Jeremiah M. Rusk 1889
J. Sterling Morton 1893
James Wilson 1897
David F. Houston 1913
Edward T. Meredith 1920
Henry C. Wallace 1921
Howard M. Gore 1924
William M. Jardine 1925
Arthur M. Hyde 1929
Henry A. Wallace 1933
Claude R. Wickard 1940
Clinton P. Anderson 1945
Charles F. Brannan 1948
Ezra Taft Benson 1953
Orville L. Freeman 1961
Clifford M. Hardin 1969
Earl L. Butz 1971
Bob S. Bergland 1977
John R. Block 1981

Secretary of Commerce and Labor (1903–1913)

George B. Cortelyou 1903
Victor H. Metcalf 1904
Oscar S. Straus 1906
Charles Nagel 1909

Secretary of Commerce (1913–)

William C. Redfield 1913
Joshua W. Alexander 1919
Herbert Hoover 1921
William F. Whiting 1928
Robert P. Lamont 1929
Roy D. Chapin 1932
Daniel C. Roper 1933
Harry L. Hopkins 1939
Jesse Jones 1940
Henry A. Wallace 1945
W.A. Harriman 1946
Charles Sawyer 1948
Sinclair Weeks 1953
Lewis L. Strauss 1958
F.H. Mueller 1959
Luther Hodges 1961
John T. Connor 1965
A.B. Trowbridge 1967
C.R. Smith 1968
Maurice H. Stans 1969
Peter G. Peterson 1972
Frederick B. Dent 1973
Rogers C.B. Morton 1975
Elliot L. Richardson 1976
Juanita M. Kreps 1977
Philip M. Klutznick 1979
Malcolm Baldrige 1981

Secretary of Labor (1913–)

William B. Wilson 1913
James J. Davis 1921
William N. Doak 1930
Frances Perkins 1933
L.B. Schwellenbach 1945
Maurice J. Tobin 1948
Martin P. Durkin 1953
James P. Mitchell 1953
Arthur J. Goldberg 1961
W. Willard Wirtz 1962
George P. Shultz 1969
James D. Hodgson 1970
Peter J. Brennan 1973
John T. Dunlop 1975
William J. Usery, Jr. 1976
F. Ray Marshall 1977
Raymond J. Donovan 1981

Secretary of Health, Education, and Welfare (1953–1980)

Oveta Culp Hobby 1953
Marion B. Folsom 1955
Arthur S. Flemming 1958
Abraham A. Ribicoff 1961
Anthony J. Celebrezze 1962
John W. Gardner 1965
Wilbur J. Cohen 1968
Robert H. Finch 1969
Elliot L. Richardson 1970
Caspar W. Weinberger 1973
F. David Matthews 1975
Joseph A. Califano, Jr. 1977

Secretary of Housing and Urban Development (1966–)

Robert C. Weaver 1966
George W. Romney 1969
James T. Lynn 1973
Carla A. Hills 1975
Patricia Roberts Harris 1977
Moon Landrieu 1979
Samuel Pierce, Jr. 1981

Secretary of Transportation (1967–)

Alan S. Boyd 1967
John A. Volpe 1969
Claude S. Brinegar 1973
William T. Coleman, Jr. 1975
Brock Adams 1977
Neil E. Goldschmidt 1979
Andrew L. Lewis, Jr. 1981

Secretary of Energy (1977–)

James R. Schlesinger 1977
Charles W. Duncan, Jr. 1979
James B. Edwards 1981

Secretary of Housing and Human Services (1980–)

Patricia Roberts Harris	1979
Richard S. Schweiker	1981

Secretary of Education (1980–)

Shirley Mount Hufstedler	1979
T.H. Bell	1981

TERRITORIAL EXPANSION

Louisiana Purchase	1803
Florida	1819
Texas	1845
Oregon	1846
Mexican Cession	1848
Gadsden Purchase	1853
Alaska	1867
Hawaii	1898
The Philippines	1898–1946
Puerto Rico	1899
Guam	1899
Amer. Samoa	1900
Canal Zone	1904
U.S. Virgin Islands	1917
Pacific Islands Trust Terr.	1947

POPULATION, 1790–1980

1790	3,929,214
1800	5,308,483
1810	7,239,881
1820	9,638,453
1830	12,866,020
1840	17,069,453
1850	23,191,876
1860	31,443,321
1870	39,818,449
1880	50,155,783
1890	62,947,714
1900	75,994,575
1910	91,972,266
1920	105,710,620
1930	122,775,046
1940	131,669,275
1950	151,325,798
1960	179,323,175
1970	204,765,770
1980	226,504,825

PICTURE CREDITS

Main Text

395 Brady-Handy Collection, Library of Congress *396* BOTH: Brady-Handy Collection, Library of Congress *401* Library of Congress *403* *Frank Leslie's Illustrated Newspaper*, January 6, 1877 *404* Malcolm F. J. Burns Collection *405* Library of Congress *406* Nebraska State Historical Society *409* Alabama Department of Archives and History *411* *Harper's Weekly*, August 24, 1872 *422* Culver Pictures, Inc. *424* Bella C. Landauer Collection, The New-York Historical Society, N.Y. *425* Museum of the American Indian, Heye Foundation *427* Brown Brothers *429* The New-York Historical Society, N.Y. *433* Library of Congress *435* BOTTOM: National Archives *436* Oakland Museum *440* Nebraska State Historical Society *444* Museum of Art, Rhode Island School of Design *447* Chicago Historical Society *449* BOTTOM: Minnesota Historical Society *450* Drake Museum *451* Edison National Historic Site *452* United States Department of Labor *454* Museum of Modern Art *455* The Granger Collection *457* Brown Brothers *459* Marshall Field's *463* *Harper's Weekly*, 1886 *469* New York Public Library, Picture Collection *470* *Century Magazine*, April, 1893 *472* Brown Brothers *473* UPI *475* Library of Congress *478* Jacob A. Riis Collection, Museum of the City of New York *480* New York Public Library, Picture Collection *482* Brown Brothers *485* Brown Brothers *492* Library of Congress *494* LEFT: Joseph Pulitzer, Jr., Collection RIGHT: *The Bee*, 1898 *498* Smith College Archives *504* The Granger Collection *505* *Life* *508* Philadelphia Museum of Art *509* Fort Worth Art Association *510* The Bettmann Archive, Inc. *515* The New-York Historical Society, N.Y. *517* The Granger Collection *520* *Puck*, August 25, 1880 *522* Culver Pictures *524* The Granger Collection *528* Western History Collection, University of Oklahoma Library *530* Culver Pictures *532* *Harper's Weekly*, April 14, 1894 *534* BOTH: The Granger Collection *545* *Harper's Weekly*, January 30, 1892 *548* *The Bee*, May 16, 1898 *550* BOTTOM: Wadsworth Atheneum, Hartford *553* Library of Congress *557* Culver Pictures *558* Library of Congress *561* © 1914/1945 by The New York Times Company *567* New York *Telegram*, May 5, 1906 *570* State Historical Society of Wisconsin *572* Culver Pictures, Inc. *575* Brown Brothers *581* Culver Pictures *583* Culver Pictures *584* Culver Pictures *589* Library of Congress *590* L. Hughes & M. Meltzer, *A Pictorial History of the Negro in America*, 1956 *596* Library of Congress *599* Brown Brothers *601* UPI *603* L. Raemaekers, *The Great War*, 1916 *606* The New-York Historical Society, N.Y. *607* National Archives *610* Culver Pictures *614* Brown Brothers *616* TOP: *Punch*, March 26, 1919 BOTTOM: Library of Congress *622* *The Liberator*, February 1920 *624* Whitney Museum of American Art *625* Museum of the City of New York *627* Kansas State Historical Society *629* Brown Brothers *631* Brown Brothers *632* Charles Scribner's Sons *634* Museum of Modern Art *636* Culver Pictures *640* Memphis *Commercial Appeal* *643* Ford Motor Company *650* Philadelphia Museum of Art *651* UPI *653* LEFT: Erich Hartmann, Magnum RIGHT: Bern Keating, Black Star *656* UPI *660* Brown Brothers *662* Museum of Modern Art *664* BOTH: UPI *669* Butler Institute of American Art *670* Wide World Photos *673* FSA Collection, Library of Congress *678* New York Public Library, Picture Collection *682* *Simplicissimus*, June 28, 1922 *684* The Granger Collection *685* Wide World *687* Wide World *690* Wide World *692* *Life*, © 1943, Time, Inc. *695* UPI *699* LEFT: Bill Mauldin and Wil-Jo Associates, Inc. RIGHT: Signal Corps *703* Wide World Photos *706* Courier Magazine, 1943 *707* © 1914/1945 by The New York Times Company *709* UPI *712* Washington *Evening Star* *717* UPI *721* © David Douglas Duncan, *Life* *722* UPI *725* UPI *726* UPI *728* Herbert Block, *Herblock's Special for Today*, 1958 *733* Burt Glinn, Magnum *740* Cornell Capa © Magnum Photos, Inc. *741* UPI *742* Bert Shavita, Pix *743* The Toronto *Star* *747* UPI *748* Hugh Rogers, Monkmeyer *750* NASA *752* Dayton's Gallery 12 *755* Woodfin Camp & Associates © Dick Durrance, 1982 *758* UPI *760* United Press International, Inc. *763* United Press International, Inc. *770* Wide World *771* Hugh Haynie © Los Angeles Times Syndicate *776* UPI *777* UPI *780* Copyright 1973, G. B. Trudeau/Distributed by Universal Press Syndicate *787* Jim Moore, Gamma, Liaison *791* Alain Mingam, Gamma, Liaison *794* Owen Franken, Sygma

Portfolios

Portfolio Four: *P. Four/1*: Northern Natural Gas Company Collection, Joslyn Art Museum *P. Four/2*: Kennedy Galleries *P. Four/3*: TOP: Museum of the American Indian, Heye Foundation BOTTOM: Public Archives of Canada *P. Four/4–5*: Library of Congress *P. Four/6*: Smithsonian Institution *P. Four/7*: TOP: Coe Collection, Yale University Library BOTTOM: Northern Natural Gas Company Collection, Joslyn Art Museum *P. Four/8*: Royal Ontario Museum, University of Toronto *P. Four/9*: TOP: Walters Art Gallery (© 1951 University of Oklahoma Press) *P. Four/10*: Northern Natural Gas Company Collection, Joslyn Art Museum *P. Four/11*: BOTTOM: Royal Ontario Museum, University of Toronto TOP: Smithsonian Institution *P. Four/12–13*: Yale University Library *P. Four/14*: New York Public Library *P. Four/15*: TOP: Walters Art Gallery (© 1951 University of Oklahoma Press) BOTTOM: Royal Ontario Museum, University of Toronto DRAWINGS: Newberry Library *P. Four/16*: Library of Congress *P. Four/17*: BOTTOM: New York Public Library TOP: Library of Congress *P. Four/18*: Oklahoma Historical Society *P. Four/19*: TOP: Walters Art Gallery (© 1951

University of Oklahoma Press) LOWER RIGHT: Museum of the American Indian, Heye Foundation *P. Four/20*: Coe Collection, Yale University Library *P. Four/21*: TOP: Peabody Museum, Harvard University BOTTOM: Museum of the American Indian, Heye Foundation *P. Four/22–23*: Montana Historical Society *P. Four/24*: Coe Collection, Yale University Library *P. Four/25*: Ruth Huffman Scott Collection

Portfolio Five: *P. Five/1*: The Metropolitan Museum of Art, Gift of Frederic H. Hatch, 1926 *P. Five/2*: BOTH: Brown *P. Five/3*: TOP: Library of Congress BOTTOM: Brown *P. Five/4*: The Metropolitan Museum of Art, Bequest of Mrs. H. O. Havemeyer, 1929. The H. O. Havemeyer Collection *P. Five/5*: ALL THREE: Brown *P. Five/6*: Culver *P. Five/7*: TOP: Culver BOTTOM: The New-York Historical Society, New York *P. Five/8*: TOP: Culver Pictures, Inc. BOTTOM: State Historical Society of Wisconsin *P. Five/9*: Brown *P. Five/10*: Courtesy of Weil Brothers-Cotton, Inc. *P. Five/11*: TOP AND CENTER: Brown BOTTOM: Theatre and Music Collection, Museum of the City of New York *P. Five/12*: ALL: New York Public Library, Picture Collection *P. Five/13*: TOP: Culver BOTTOM: New York Public Library, Picture Collection *P. Five/14*: TOP: Geoffrey Clements, Courtesy Columbia University Rare Book and Manuscript Library *P. Five/14–15*: Brown *P. Five/15*: TOP: Library of Congress BOTTOM: Granger *P. Five/16*: John Sloan, *The Haymarket*, 1907. The Brooklyn Museum, Gift of Mrs. Harry Payne Whitney *P. Five/17*: BOTH: *Storyville Portraits*, E. J. Bellocq. Courtesy of Lee Friedlander *P. Five/18*: ALL THREE: Brown *P. Five/19*: Los Angeles County Museum of Art, Los Angeles County Funds *P. Five/20*: ALL THREE: Brown *P. Five/21*: Brown *P. Five/22–23*: The New-York Historical Society, New York *P. Five/24*: Granger *P. Five/25*: TOP: Granger BOTTOM: Bettmann

Portfolio Six: *P. Six/1*: Metropolitan Museum of Art, George A. Hearn Fund *P. Six/2*: TOP: Metropolitan Museum of Art, Arthur H. Hearn Fund BOTTOM: Metropolitan Museum of Art, Gift of friends of John Sloan *P. Six/3*: LEFT: H. V. Allison & Co. RIGHT: Mr. and Mrs. Arthur G. Altschul Collection *P. Six/4*: TOP: Albright-Knox Art Gallery, New York, Gift of Seymour H. Knox BOTTOM: Whitney Museum of American Art *P. Six/5*: TOP: Metropolitan Museum of Art, Alfred Stieglitz Collection BOTTOM: The Cleveland Museum of Art, Gift of Mrs. Louise M. Dunn in memory of Henry G. Keller *P. Six/6*: TOP: Whitney Museum of American Art, Gift of Mr. and Mrs. Roy R. Neuberger BOTTOM: Metropolitan Museum of Art, George A. Hearn Fund *P. Six/7*: Whitney Museum of American Art *P. Six/8*: Alfred Stieglitz Collection, Fisk University *P. Six/9*: LEFT: Metropolitan Museum of Art, Alfred Stieglitz Collection RIGHT: Whitney Museum of American Art *P. Six/10*: TOP: Metropolitan Museum of Art, George A. Hearn Fund BOTTOM: The James and Mari Michener Collection, The Archer M. Huntington Art Gallery, The University of Texas at Austin *P. Six/10–11*: BOTTOM: Frank Rehn Gallery, New York TOP: Whitney Museum of American Art *P. Six/12*: Museum of Modern Art, Lincoln Kirstein gift *P. Six/13*: TOP: Armand G. Erpf Collection BOTTOM: Museum of Modern Art, WPA Art Program Loan *P. Six/14*: TOP: Metropolitan Museum of Art, New York City WPA Gift BOTTOM: Museum of Modern Art, WPA Art Project Loan *P. Six/15*: King's Highway Elementary School, Westport, Conn. © Westport (Conn.) Public Schools *P. Six/16*: Mr. and Mrs. Ben Heller Collection *P. Six/17*: TOP: Sam Kootz Gallery, New York BOTTOM: Museum of Modern Art, Philip C. Johnson gift *P. Six/18*: TOP: Museum of Modern Art, A. Conger Goodyear Fund BOTTOM: Albright-Knox Art Gallery, Buffalo, New York; Gift of Seymour H. Knox *P. Six/19*: TOP LEFT: Collection, The Museum of Modern Art, New York. Purchase. TOP RIGHT: S. C. Johnson & Son, Inc. TOP LEFT: S. C. Johnson & Son, Inc. BOTTOM: Whitney Museum of American Art, Gift of the Friends of the Whitney Museum *P. Six/20*: TOP LEFT: East Hampton Gallery, New York RIGHT: Andre Emmerich Gallery, New York BOTTOM LEFT: Collection, The Solomon R. Guggenheim Museum, New York *P. Six/20–21*: David Whitney Collection *P. Six/21*: TOP: M. Knoedler & Co. Inc. *P. Six/22*: TOP LEFT: Collection, The Museum of Modern Art, New York. Gift of Mr. and Mrs. Robert C. Scull TOP RIGHT: Wadsworth Atheneum, Hartford, Conn. CENTER LEFT: Collection of Kimiko and John Powers BOTTOM: Leo Castelli Gallery, New York *P. Six/23*: Courtesy of the artist *P. Six/24*: National Gallery, Oslo *P. Six/25*: Collection of the Whitney Museum of American Art, New York

INDEX

Some multiple subentries are arranged in chronological order.

WASHINGTON
Nov. 11, 1889
Olympia
Salem
OREGON
Feb. 14, 1859
IDAHO
July 3, 1890
Boise
MONTANA
Nov. 8, 1889
Helena
NORTH DAKOTA
Nov. 2, 1889
Bismarck
SOUTH DAKOTA
Nov. 2, 1889
Pierre
WYOMING
July 10, 1890
Cheyenne
NEBRASKA
Mar. 1, 1867
Lincoln
NEVADA
Oct. 31, 1864
Carson City
Salt Lake City
UTAH
Jan. 4, 1896
Sacramento
CALIFORNIA
Sept. 9, 1850
Denver
COLORADO
Aug. 1, 1876
Topeka
KANSAS
Jan. 29, 1861
P A C I F I C   O C E A N
OKLAHOMA
Nov. 16, 1907
Oklahoma City
Santa Fe
ARIZONA
Feb. 14, 1912
Phoenix
NEW MEXICO
Jan. 6, 1912
TEXAS
Dec. 29, 1845
Austin
Honolulu
HAWAII
Aug. 21, 1959
0 100 200
MILES
ALASKA
Jan. 3, 1959
Juneau
0 200 400
MILES

NNESOTA
ay 11, 1858
LAKE SUPERIOR
LAKE MICHIGAN
LAKE HURON
LAKE ONTARIO
LAKE ERIE
St. Paul
WISCONSIN
May 29, 1848
Madison
MICHIGAN
Jan. 26, 1837
Lansing
IOWA
ec. 28, 1846
Des Moines
ILLINOIS
Dec. 3, 1818
Springfield
INDIANA
Dec. 11, 1816
Indianapolis
OHIO
Mar. 1, 1803
Columbus
MISSOURI
Aug. 10, 1821
Jefferson City
KENTUCKY
June 1, 1792
Frankfort
WEST VIRGINIA
June 20, 1863
Charleston
VIRGINIA
Richmond
June 25, 1788
PENNSYLVANIA
Dec. 12, 1787
Harrisburg
NEW YORK
July 26, 1788
Albany
VERMONT
Mar. 4, 1791
Montpelier
MAINE
Mar. 15, 1820
Augusta
NEW HAMPSHIRE
June 21, 1788
Concord
MASSACHUSETTS
Feb. 6, 1788
Boston
RHODE ISLAND
May 29, 1790
Providence
Hartford
CONNECTICUT
Jan. 9, 1788
Trenton
NEW JERSEY
Dec. 18, 1787
Dover
DELAWARE
Dec. 7, 1787
Annapolis
MARYLAND
Apr. 28, 1788
ARKANSAS
June 15, 1836
Little Rock
TENNESSEE
June 1, 1796
Nashville
NORTH CAROLINA
Nov. 21, 1789
Raleigh
SOUTH CAROLINA
Columbia
May 23, 1788
MISSISSIPPI
Dec. 10, 1817
Jackson
ALABAMA
Dec. 4, 1819
Montgomery
GEORGIA
Jan. 2, 1788
Atlanta
LOUISIANA
Apr. 30, 1812
Baton Rouge
Tallahassee
FLORIDA
Mar. 3, 1845
GULF OF MEXICO
ATLANTIC OCEAN
0 100 200 300 400
MILES
PUERTO RICO
Territory, 1899
San Juan
VIRGIN ISLANDS
Territory, 1917
Charlotte Amalie
0 40 80
MILES

POLITICAL MAP OF THE UNITED STATES

84 85 9 8 7 6 5 4 3 2